REVOLUTIONARY EUROPE

REVOLUTIONARY EUROPE

POLITICS, COMMUNITY AND CULTURE IN TRANSNATIONAL CONTEXT, 1775−1922

Gavin Murray-Miller

BLOOMSBURY ACADEMIC
LONDON • NEW YORK • OXFORD • NEW DELHI • SYDNEY

BLOOMSBURY ACADEMIC
Bloomsbury Publishing Plc
50 Bedford Square, London, WC1B 3DP, UK
1385 Broadway, New York, NY 10018, USA

BLOOMSBURY, BLOOMSBURY ACADEMIC and the Diana logo are trademarks
of Bloomsbury Publishing Plc

First published in Great Britain 2020

Copyright © Gavin Murray-Miller, 2020

Gavin Murray-Miller has asserted his right under the Copyright, Designs and Patents Act,
1988, to be identified as Author of this work.

For legal purposes the Acknowledgments on p. x constitute
an extension of this copyright page.

Cover design by Tjaša Krivec
Cover image: Keeping an armed vigil over Paris, February 24, during the 1848 Revolution,
engraving. France, 19th century. (© DEA/G. DAGLI ORTI/Getty Images)

All rights reserved. No part of this publication may be reproduced or transmitted
in any form or by any means, electronic or mechanical, including
photocopying, recording, or any information storage or retrieval system,
without prior permission in writing from the publishers.

Bloomsbury Publishing Plc does not have any control over, or responsibility
for, any third-party websites referred to or in this book. All internet addresses given
in this book were correct at the time of going to press. The author and publisher regret
any inconvenience caused if addresses have changed or sites have ceased
to exist, but can accept no responsibility for any such changes.

A catalogue record for this book is available from the British Library.

A catalog record for this book is available from the Library of Congress.

ISBN: HB: 978-1-3500-2000-9
        PB: 978-1-3500-1999-7
        ePDF: 978-1-3500-2001-6
        eBook: 978-1-3500-2002-3

Typeset by Integra Software Services Pvt. Ltd.
Printed and bound in Great Britain

To find out more about our authors and books visit www.bloomsbury.com
and sign up for our newsletters.

For Lara,
From beginning to end.

CONTENTS

List of Illustrations   viii
List of Maps   ix
Acknowledgments   x

Introduction   1

1. Patriots and Citizens: America and France (1763–1789)   13

2. Liberty, Equality, Fraternity or Death: Radicalizing the French Revolution   35

3. Artisans, *Citoyennes* and Slaves: The Meaning of Equality in a Revolutionary World   59

4. Taming the Furies of Revolution: Order, Disorder and Empire (1794–1815)   83

5. Transnational Revolutionaries: Post-Napoleonic Europe and the Mediterranean (1815–1835)   111

6. Socialism and Social Protest: From Reform to Radicalism (1815–1848)   135

7. The Indian Summer of Romantic Revolution: 1848 and the Reassessment of European Radicalism   161

8. The Revolutionary Tradition at a Crossroads: The Anarchists (1865–1905)   187

9. The Revival and Failure of Revolutionary Constitutionalism: The Russian and Ottoman Empires (1905–1914)   215

10. Forging the New Regime: War and Revolution in the Russian Empire (1914–1922)   241

Epilogue: Revolutionary Currents beyond Europe   269

Notes   287
Selected Bibliography   334
Index   344

ILLUSTRATIONS

1. Maximilien Robespierre — 43
2. Illustration of a Tricolor and Musket — 45
3. Jean-Paul Marat — 51
4. Louis-Antoine de Saint-Just — 62
5. Slaves Cutting Sugar Cane on British Antigua — 68
6. Napoleon Bonaparte — 93
7. Toussaint Louverture — 97
8. Klemens von Metternich — 115
9. Rafael del Riego — 123
10. Giuseppe Mazzini — 131
11. Louis Blanc — 148
12. Karl Marx — 154
13. Count Latour and the Vienna Uprising, 1848 — 164
14. Lajos Kossuth — 171
15. "Paris under the Commune," 1871 — 199
16. Pyotr Alexeyevich Kropotkin — 201
17. Tsar Nicholas II and the Tsarina — 226
18. Student Demonstration in Saint Petersburg, 1905 — 228
19. The Civil Guard in Petrograd, 1917 — 248
20. Vladimir Ilyich Lenin — 252
21. The Multiethnic Qing Court in the Final Years of Dynastic Rule — 276

MAPS

1.	France during the French Revolution	50
2.	Saint Domingue and the imperial Caribbean	67
3.	The Napoleonic Empire at its height	95
4.	Spain's New World Empire, c. 1815	104
5.	Spanish America in the wake of decolonization	107
6.	Europe in 1815	114
7.	Revolutionary disturbances in 1848 by region	165
8.	Cities with major political unrest in 1848	169
9.	Major acts of terrorism, 1856–1914	204
10.	The Ottoman Empire during the Balkan Wars, 1912–1913	238
11.	Europe in 1914	242
12.	Russian territory occupied by Germany during the First World War	243
13.	The Qing Empire in the nineteenth century	277

ACKNOWLEDGMENTS

I would like to thank Evgeniya Prusskaya, Alexandre Tchoudinov and Denis Fomin-Nilov at the State Academic University for the Humanities for their warm friendship and generosity during my visits to Moscow. I would also like to thank Alan Forrest, whom I first met in Moscow, for his engaging insights on the French Revolution and Napoleonic period. The conversations and meetings while working on the grant project there have been intellectually stimulating and have fed directly into many of the topics treated in this book.

I would also like to thank my colleagues at Cardiff University. In particular, I owe a debt of gratitude to James Ryan for his eagerness to answer any questions I had on Russia and the Russian Revolution. The round table he organized in Cardiff on comparative revolutions and revolutionary paradigms in 2017 provided an excellent opportunity to elaborate many of the broad ideas explored in this book as well as exchange ideas with other participants such as Colin Jones and Geoffrey Hosking. I am also indebted to Federica Ferlanti and Ian Rapley. Their reading recommendations and insights on China and Japan respectively were extremely helpful and greatly appreciated.

I am also grateful for the assistance of Abbie Rands at Cardiff University who compiled data used in certain maps featured in this book.

Research for this book was funded by Cardiff University and through the State Academic University for the Humanities (Russia) with the support of project N 14.Z50.31.0045 from the Ministry of Education and Science of the Russian Federation.

INTRODUCTION

"Revolution is a term with a precise meaning," the essayist Perry Anderson once remarked: "the political overthrow from below of one state order and its replacement by another."[1] In an objective sense, Anderson's definition might seem straightforward, although to this list might also be added such things as a fundamental change in values, the violent transformation of social structures and the reorganization of power relationships.[2] Yet to claim that there is a "precise meaning" when it comes to revolution is misleading. If scholars share a general idea of revolutions as moments of political disruption and change, there is less agreement when it comes to questions regarding what generates revolutions, what causal factors influence them or why certain revolutions take the particular paths they do. These questions are, however, fundamental to how we conceptualize revolutions and the changes they produce. Revolutions have elicited a great deal of fascination among historians and theorists over the years. That said, they are also subjects of intense debate and speculation.

Writing in the aftermath of the abortive Italian revolution of 1848, the Milanese republican Carlo Cattaneo was candid when addressing what he believed to be the cause of the failed uprising. "Revolution is the execution of an idea," he remarked. "If there is no idea there can be no revolution."[3] Over a century-and-a-half later, Cattaneo's statement continues to possess a certain validity for experts when it comes to revolution. According to one school of thought, ideas do indeed drive revolutions. This link between Enlightenment and Revolution has led scholars to scrutinize the activities of leading intellectuals and elites or to dissected canonical texts such as the *Rights of Man* and *Communist Manifesto* in order to understand their inspirational powers and emulative qualities. Ideas, so the argument goes, permit individuals and groups to imagine new social and political horizons, often against political systems that are perceived as moribund and unjust. They stimulate collective desires to create a new order built upon principles believed to be moral and universal.[4]

The enlightenment paradigm remains only one among many received "traditions" that have sought to explain revolution in the modern world. For much of the twentieth century, Marxists emphasized class struggle and material factors in explaining the causal mechanisms that drove revolutions. Instead of ideas and ideology, they focused their attention on the social and economic inequalities that generated conflicts and propelled change within societies.[5] Others less convinced by the class struggle explanation looked to broader "structural" factors, noting how political institutions, demographic fluctuations and economic forces create the conditions for outbreaks of revolutionary upheaval. Structural interpretations questioned the idea of social revolution "from below" and directed attention toward dynamics associated with breakdown and destabilization from above.[6] Despite their differing positions, however, Marxist and structural theorists were inspired by a similar goal: to outline a general causal model explaining how and under what circumstances revolution occurred.

In recent years, various social theorists have sought to move away from static explanatory models built upon fixed criteria and rigid definitions of what does and does not constitute a revolution. As Bjørn Thomassen has argued, there is no "perfect model" that political theorists can turn to as an archetype of modern revolution.[7] Revolutions are historically situated and unique; they encompass a variety of events, processes and social groups specific to time and place.[8] It might be added that revolutions are dependent upon contingent factors, even if they do share similar "patterns" and "forms" that can be compared to one another. This "configurational" or "relational" approach recognizes that revolutions are distinct and subject to a range of internal and external influences that determine their unique character.[9] Stated otherwise, the French Revolution of 1789 is not the same as the Arab Spring that erupted across North Africa and the Middle East in 2011, even if both are broadly understood to be revolutions. Abandoning "generalized models" of revolution favored by Marxists and structural theorists, experts have identified the need for a more flexible approach that takes account of the specific causal factors and developmental logics that condition revolutionary movements.[10]

In turn, greater appreciation for revolution as a historically situated phenomenon has also renewed interest in comparative models of examination. Drawing upon methods of discourse analysis derived from cultural history, Keith Michael Baker and Dan Edelstein have proposed approaching revolution as a "script" which draws upon historical models and adapts them to local circumstances. In their opinion, revolutionaries are constantly working within inherited frameworks that provide a blueprint for political action in the present. These scripts are copied and modified as needed, and in some cases rewritten altogether to create new revolutionary models of action.[11] For the first half of the nineteenth century, the French Revolution indisputably furnished a model to which other revolutionaries looked. At mid-century, Marx revised the revolutionary script to offer a reworked model that would inform subsequent movements in the years ahead. In interpreting revolutions as scripts that are constantly acted out and elaborated upon, Baker and Edelstein have attempted to outline a comparative framework that eschews broad sociological "structures" and takes account of historical context and specificity. At base, this theory sees revolutions as essentially imitative and mimetic. It explains why revolutions might follow similar patterns or display a familiar repertoire of behaviors and actions. It also explains why revolutionaries often appeal to a common stock of symbols, representations and collective memories when engaging in acts of resistance.

This rough historiographic sketch is by no means definitive. Yet it does serve to underscore the contentions and diverse range of opinions surrounding the topic of political and social revolution in the modern period. This book intends a broad examination of Europe's revolutionary history and political culture in the "long nineteenth century." It argues that Europe's revolutionary events possessed their own distinct contours but were not necessarily unconnected phenomena. Rather than assessing revolution as a purely ideational, socially driven force or a structural occurrence, however, it seeks to understand these connections in relation to a shared revolutionary tradition that was reinforced through processes of community building and transnational cultural exchange throughout the period. Community is an ambiguous category, but its wide scope and multiple connotations can offer a broad organizing principle to help contextualize the different forms revolutions and political movements took during the nineteenth century. Communities are built upon connections, whether these connections are based in common values, social bonds or shared emotional experiences.[12] They are also imaginative creations that foster a sense of unity and group solidarity.[13] Nineteenth-century radicals and political thinkers often partook in such acts of creative imagining as they worked toward far-reaching social transformations and sketched the outlines of future utopias.

Taking into account moments of political upheaval and consolidation during the nineteenth century, this book examines the ways in which political actors attempted to construct new definitions of sovereignty and social unity in a period characterized by vast social, economic and governmental change. In this respect, it examines both the dynamics of revolutionary situations and how broader ideas of community informed movements and invested them with political agency. This approach enables a view of revolution as a process while also remaining conscious of the role revolutionary aspirations and discourses played in sustaining radical movements. In certain cases, the "after lives" of revolutions were just as important as the revolutionary experiences themselves, suggesting a wider lens is necessary to appreciate the types of communities that revolutionary aspirations fostered.[14] Intellectuals and elites of varying stripes reinforced solidarities through appeals to common revolutionary traditions, memories and experiences, which in turn provided the impetus for new radical ventures. While it is accepted that revolutions drew their substance from new ideas of natural rights and popular sovereignty stemming from the Enlightenment, these abstract ideas were only one factor among many that catalyzed revolutionary movements.

The long nineteenth century stood at the crossroads of a volatile and changing world. Popular protests responded and reacted to growing state bureaucracies. Racial and ethnic tensions boiled to the surface in European and colonial peripheries as imperial metropoles democratized. Elites agonized over the perceived social and political divisions generated by modernization. These and other anxieties typically served to animate instability during the period and encouraged political writers and actors to imagine new models of authority believed capable of reuniting societies that appeared hopelessly fractured. One of the principal arguments of this book insists that revolutions should be understood as efforts to manufacture new social relations and forms of collective authority at critical moments when established powers proved unable or unwilling to do so. Desires for social unity manifested themselves in various ways, from the French idea of a political "community of citizens" announced in 1789 to declarations of national "brotherhood" and Marxist notions of social egalitarianism elaborated later in the century. Although these envisaged societies frequently embodied the most extreme paradoxes—at once supporting democracy and terror, emancipation and empire, equality and slavery, universal rights and ethnic particularism—they nonetheless reflected the persistent promise of a restored and "regenerated" community that lay at the heart of nineteenth-century revolutionary movements.

Nineteenth-century radicalism evolved in a period characterized by greater mobility (encouraged by the transportation revolution), more expansive geographic boundaries (due to imperial overreach and migration) and greater access to print. These factors contributed to the creation of "interpretive communities"—networks facilitated through print culture and correspondence that incorporated participants into both real and imagined communities built upon ideology, political affiliation and perceived common values.[15] The creation of interpretative communities was essential to modern politics, as it allowed for the broad mobilization of ideas and the imagining of collectivities such as the nation-state and political parties. During periods of chronic political unrest generated by social change, economic pressures and war, these communities often became vehicles for radicalization and political activism. This book seeks to examine how European radicalism attempted to imagine and implement new communitarian visions linked through print and ideological affiliations, political networks built upon real social relations, and identities rooted in specific social discourses such as gender, class and nationality. All of these played a key role in revolutionary politics during the nineteenth century and, in many cases, were not mutually exclusive. Moreover, it was through these ideological associations and networks that the most dramatic examples of community-building occurred as intellectuals and activists attempted to mobilize supporters and actualize their political programs, frequently imposing them on others in the name of universal principles and the general good. As the case studies in this book will demonstrate, the nature of these communities was varied and diverse, ranging from newly founded nations to class solidarity and declarations of common ideological values. In this respect, the book aims to cover an array of revolutionary communities and analyze them through a chronological narrative bookended by the revolutionary upheavals of the late eighteenth century and the outbreak of a second world revolution led from Moscow in the early twentieth century.

By emphasizing the concept of community in the revolutionary process, this book also proposes a more expansive geographic scope in which to assess Europe's revolutionary tradition. Communities could be bounded by geographic space (as in the case of nations) or they could be decentered and multilayered. This book intends to demonstrate that revolutionary communities were never stable entities and operated within varying degrees of local, national, imperial and transnational formations. While the French Revolution decreed the sovereignty of the nation, it also fueled a project of imperial expansions across Europe and into North Africa. Anarchists championed localized forms of autonomy while associating their movements with a stateless and universal cause. Revolutionary secret societies commonly mobilized supporters across national and imperial borders, at times providing a global backdrop against which revolutionary aspirations were conceptualized and articulated. Identities as well were instrumental in promoting transnational ideas of community, not least of all the international, class-based proletariat appealed to by Marxists. By examining democratic, national and social revolution through the comparative context of community, this book proposes a transnational study of nineteenth-century revolution in an age of high nationalism, noting how radical politics both shaped and were shaped by the transnational currents connecting nineteenth-century Europe to the world at large.

The Absolutist Tradition

One of the most basic myths of revolution is that of the *tabula rasa*. In validating the innovations of their radical programs, revolutionaries of the eighteenth and nineteenth centuries presented their movements as inherently modern and unprecedented in history. The supposed modernity that revolutions embodied was more a judgment on the regimes revolutionaries sought to supplant than an established fact. Nonetheless, it constructed a neat dichotomy between the promise of a new liberated society and the evils of the past. For radical revolutionaries, therefore, revolution possessed no past. Rather, it sought to destroy the past as it remade society anew. Such ideological outlooks, however, obscured the fact that the age of European revolution did not occur *ex nihilo* and in many ways grew out of broader trends and developments preceding it.

During the sixteenth and seventeenth centuries, European monarchs carried out various reforms in government that would create the architecture of the modern state. Early modern polities were primarily dynastic in nature with rulers holding multiple territories. The Spanish polity was a union of different kingdoms incorporated under the Castilian crown. The Habsburgs wore three crowns—those of the Holy Roman Empire, Bohemia and Hungary—in addition to ruling over a constellation of duchies and principalities scattered throughout Central Europe and the Low Countries. Given these arrangements, royal power was often limited in scope. In many cases, the nobility possessed greater power than monarchs in their respective regions. They controlled the local economy; they dictated the laws in their jurisdictions; they were the backbone of the military. Monarchs were customarily required to consult with the nobility through representative bodies, or estates which effectively constrained the power of the royal court. The Church as well was largely independent. Clerics took their orders from Rome, not the monarch. The Church had its own legal systems, its own property, and even levied its own taxes on the people. In addition to the nobility and Church—the two primary pillars of royal authority—cities usually had their own representative bodies and councils that operated independently of the king. Wealthy merchants often used these councils to promote their own interests and dictate trade policies without consulting the central authority. As a result, monarchs continually found themselves having to resort to bargaining with representative bodies in order to rule.

This situation began to change in the eighteenth century. Absolutism marked a broad effort by European monarchs to concentrate power and authority over these various corporate bodies. Monarchs from Spain to Prussia began assuming control over taxation and law. They created government offices to supervise taxation and revenue collection. Public officials responsible to the monarch were made judges in the provinces to ensure the crown's law was being enforced. Monarchs now claimed to be the sole public authority with the rights of enforcing law, controlling public revenue and directing the military. To enforce these measures, new state bureaucracies were established. In its broadest sense, absolutism sought to expunge the traditional checks placed on royal authority. It aimed to give the power of law making and revenue collection to the crown, creating centralized states that could effectively wield power.

In some cases, these reforms extended well beyond continental Europe. The predominant European powers were not only European kingdoms. They were global empires that stretched from the Atlantic to the Pacific Oceans. Much like continental Europe, the overseas territories were characterized by a great deal of legal and political diversity. Since the fifteenth century, merchant firms and charter companies had played a key role in Europe's imperial expansion. These companies funded explorations, transported settlers and underwrote the operations and plantation agriculture that sustained imperialism. It was, ultimately, profit (or the expectations of profit) that drove empire, and some of the merchant firms responsible for colonial trade were quite powerful. Up until the mid-nineteenth century, the British East India Company governed India as its own fiefdom, providing the administration and military force required to secure British power in the Asian subcontinent. In most empires, colonial and creole elites occupied influential positions connected with government and the imperial economy. This was especially true in the British and Spanish colonies of the New World. In Spanish America, the *consulados*—merchant guilds that oversaw a wide variety of activities from imperial commerce to trade regulations—were virtually an entrenched oligarchy. They enforced the law, oversaw the local chamber of commerce, set prices on goods and influenced decision making at all levels of the colonial administration. In short, colonies enjoyed a good deal of autonomous power and rarely did they think of consulting with royal officials 4,000 miles away.

Yet as European monarchs began subscribing to absolutist ideas, the relationship between the metropole and periphery was due to change. Just as in Europe, royal government began to extend its reach over the colonies, clamping down on trade and subordinating colonial bodies to royal authority. Beginning in the 1760s, the Spanish King Carlos III implemented a series of reforms designed to tap into Spain's Atlantic wealth and revive the declining empire. In the coming decades, the crown managed to establish monopolies over certain colonial industries, tighten controls on revenue collection and reassert royal prerogative over the appointment of colonial officials.[16] Parallel efforts occurred in the British Atlantic world, where new taxes and greater controls over local assemblies provided an impetus for sustained colonial resistance during the 1760s and 1770s against the London parliament.

In theory, absolutism intended to create a more robust royal authority on the continent just as much as it refashioned imperial bureaucracies abroad. Whereas power had once been diffused and decentralized, royal governments were now bent on centralizing their authority and wresting power from the hands of peripheral bodies. Naturally, elites protested against these encroachments, sometimes generating profound social and political convulsions that revealed the limitations of the central court. At the heart of these contentions was a common struggle between center and periphery that cut across early-modern empires.[17] Absolutism posed critical questions regarding the nature of state power and the relationship between state and individual as bureaucratic structures were retooled and remodeled to meet the fiscal and administrative challenges at hand. Early-modern structures encompassed a multiplicity of regional and local powers. They possessed a rich variety of constitutional and legal traditions that resisted administrative uniformity and centralized authority.[18] These arrangements were the foundations on which the early-modern state rested, with power distributed between various corporate entities and local allegiances to the center. The structural tensions inherent within such polities were a key factor in the contentions that would fuel the major revolutionary movements of the late eighteenth century.[19]

By the eighteenth century, it was evident that a period of change was occurring as experiments in government and royal authority upset older arrangements. Slower to change, however, was the social organization of European societies. Monarchs may have been eager to enact reforms in the realm of government and the economy, but they were less inclined to encourage changes in traditional social hierarchies. To do so might bring into question the base of a society built upon royal privileges and obedience to established authority. European societies remained sharply stratified. Nobles retained privileged positions. They were exempt from most forms of taxation. They had their own legal codes distinct from the common people. They even sat in assemblies and government bodies as a separate order that ensured aristocratic interests were represented and defended. They were, in short, a social group unto themselves, and traditionally the only means of entering this group was through birth. The clergy as well was treated as a separate group with its own laws and privileges. The Church abided by cannon law which was codified in Rome. Church properties were tax exempt and in many cases outside the jurisdiction of the crown. In return for these privileges, religious authorities were committed to supporting the crown. They provided theological and religious justifications for royal rule, insisting that monarchies ruled through divine right ordained by God, sealing an alliance between throne and altar. Ethnic and foreign groups residing in countries equally had their own arrangements with the royal government. They were subject to special laws and they too had certain privileges guaranteed by the crown. Jews were among one of the most conspicuous groups, with Jewish communities subject to traditional rabbinical law and possessing their own community leaders.

Early-modern society comprised a mosaic of different communities and social orders. No idea of a common legal code or equality under the law existed. Different groups abided by different laws and had different arrangements with the central authority. European societies were, in this respect, corporatist societies. They were composed of various corporate groups with rights and privileges unique to them. Inequality was also evident in the colonial world and was even more explicit in many cases. In carving out their empires, Europeans had conquered various native populations in the process, either pushing them off the land or enslaving them. The Atlantic plantations were dependent upon slave labor, much of it obtained through the African slave trade. Slaves were considered property, not individuals, and the law treated them as such. This was the most extreme form of inequality, but various other forms of subjugation existed, ranging from white indentured servitude to "conquered" nations. Local colonial assemblies typically had their own laws that differed from those of the mother country. Moreover, colonial populations were highly diverse. Colonies possessed European settlers and creoles born in the colony. There were native groups (typically referred to as Indians) and people of mixed Afro-European decent. Each of these groups had particular legal systems and rights attached to them.

Under the circumstance, there could exist no concept of a single law or equal rights. This idea was simply alien to most Europeans. Yet, as absolutist regimes enacted changes in government and state structures, it was evident that certain people began considering what these changes entailed for society as a whole. These questions, by and large, came from outside royal circles.

The Enlightenment

Prior to the "age of revolution" there was the "age of criticism," or more precisely "public opinion." During the eighteenth century, a burgeoning print culture and new forms of sociability evident in the salons and coffeehouses that grew up across the continent provided for an understanding of "the public" as a new forum for rational debate. Writers and critics presented a range of opinions on pressing matters of the day through debating societies, pamphlets and the press. "The public" was composed of literate and educated individuals judged fit to comment on political and social issues. It rejected the corporate idea of specific orders and "particular" interests, instead speaking for society and the "general interest." As the voice of the general interest, the public was believed to be autonomous. It existed outside of state institutions and royal courts and represented, therefore, a sovereign authority in its own right, a "tribunal" to which all matters should be submitted for judgment. Writers and critics opened their works with an "address to the public" while certain monarchs showed themselves receptive to the new cult of "public opinion" even though it implicitly challenged royal claims to represent all public authority. Within the new private social realm of the eighteenth century, an embryonic concept of "civil society" began to emerge that was not associated with any one group or order. Consequently, criticism and public opinion were invested with a new sense of authority believed to be transparent, heterogonous and representative of educated society.[20]

The recognition of a public sphere was part and parcel of a new type of intellectual and political culture emerging in the eighteenth century, one that has broadly been categorized as the Enlightenment. A Pan-European and even Trans-Atlantic project, the Enlightenment consisted of various *philosophes*, political thinkers, reformers and writers reflecting a diverse range of opinions. In spite of this diversity, however, there did remain common threads linking these various movements and ideas together. For one, enlightened thinkers rejected the conventional sources of knowledge and authority, namely Classical knowledge and the Bible. Instead, they put their faith in the empirical sciences, in secular ideas of "natural law" that stood outside the domain of religion and divine providence. They also emphasized that man was rational. In possessing reason, they argued, man could understand and shape the world that he lived in. Fascination with the new cult of reason was one of the primary reasons why enlightened thinkers prized debate and criticism. *Philosophes* did not just think of themselves as abstract philosophers, but rather incisive social critics motivated by desires to clarify public opinion and combat all forms of prejudice and ignorance.

In acquiring a greater sense of self, moreover, educated society came to think of itself as a new elite class, one which was not necessarily restricted by national boundaries. If the printed word and ideas possessed an international reach and scope, so too did the Enlightenment. In fact, many *philosophes* spoke of the "republic of letters" to which educated Europeans from Spain to Eastern Europe now belonged. Just like any political state, this republic of intellectuals possessed its own social conventions and norms, its own rules of conduct and values. And just like any political state, it claimed to speak on behalf of a community, albeit one that transcended political boundaries. If kings governed over the political affairs of man, the *philosophes* saw themselves as governing over the new public authority which the eighteenth century had brought into existence. This mentality extended from the capitals of Europe to colonial cities on the peripheries of empires. Educated, civic-minded individuals in Spanish America—the so-called *letrados*—set up scientific societies in the colonies and regularly communicated with metropolitan centers such as Madrid and Paris.[21] Scientific communities in French Saint-Domingue were equally present in Atlantic cultural exchange. In Cap François the small *cercle des philadelphes* took its name from its correspondence with the Philadelphia American Philosophical Society in North America.[22] Enlightenment, as it was understood, relied upon intellectual clubs, the transmission of ideas and networking across boundaries. These activities created and sustained a context for lively debates and mutual forms of sociability that were central to the Enlightenment.[23]

Because of its cosmopolitan character, the Enlightenment was instrumental in shaping a new understanding of man and the individual. In insisting that man was rational, *philosophes* argued that individuals were "all partakers of the same common nature," as one writer claimed.[24] And because they were all governed by a common human nature, they were endowed with "natural rights" by virtue of this common humanity.[25] Climate, geography and "custom" were the only criteria that created differences between people. As the French natural scientist Georges de Buffon explained, man was a migratory creature "subject to different changes through the influence of climate, difference in diet, [and] manner of life. …"[26] All people derived from a common stock; milieu alone determined one's specific character and development.[27] Espousing a universal idea of human nature, Enlightenment thinkers were sensitive to the influence of social and geographic factors on human development, contributing to an idea of man existing within society. Yet through the application of reason, man was capable of transforming and mastering the environment. It therefore stood to reason that environment could be changed, entailing that humanity itself could be altered, improved and allowed to realize its fullest potentialities and become virtuous. Implicit within Enlightenment thought was a firm rejection of the old model of immutable social orders and a conviction in man's ability to exercise his natural rights under the proper conditions. At root, the Enlightenment project was inherently social and political in nature.

Political rationalism dictated that the legitimacy of existing institutions must be examined in light of universally valid principles. Humans were capable of understanding the social world and thus able to shape and direct it. Such lofty declarations fed a variety of new thinking on the nature of politics. The English political philosopher John Locke famously argued that government was a contract between the sovereign and the governed. Its function was, therefore, to protect the natural liberties of life, liberty and estate, or property. The need for civil government arose out of the need to protect these fundamental rights. Men are free in nature, Locke claimed, "till, by *their own consent*, they make themselves members of some political society."[28] With consent forming the base of Locke's political theory, contractual government ultimately meant representative government. The exercise of liberty depended upon limiting restraints on personal freedom, making the role of law indispensable. Simply put, the contract constrained public authority, limiting it to the protection of basic fundamental rights and nothing more. Society comprised an assortment of freely associated individuals able to pursue their own interests as they saw fit. As long as authority maintained the contract, power was legitimate and government would work for the good of all. If the contract was, however, broken, consent could be revoked and the governed permitted to form a new contract.

One did not have to subscribe to Locke's theories on contractual government to have an understanding of the limitations incurred upon political authority. Diderot, for example, remained adamant in his belief of man's natural and individual freedoms, arguing, "No man has received from nature the right to command others." This premise suggested that all individuals were equal, and this egalitarian spirit found expression in a variety of utopian suggestions throughout the mid-eighteenth century. The Benedictine monk Léger Marie Deschamps criticized the private property which Locke steadfastly defended, believing it created unnatural and artificial divisions within society. In his suggestion, it would be best to eliminate all unnatural social and political constraints and abolish private property, the root of human inequality, altogether.[29] These and other ideas hinted at the radicalism implicit within the Enlightenment as political thinkers speculated on the nature of man's freedom and the proper place of government in society.

Jean-Jacques Rousseau was the most intriguing and influential of these theorists. For Rousseau, human nature was shaped by politics. "No people will ever be more than what the nature of their Government makes them to be," he wrote.[30] Such an admission was unsurprising given Rousseau's Genevan origins. He had long come to think of himself as a citizen of his native republic, and characteristically signed his works as "Citizen of Geneva" with pride. Like Locke, he agreed that people, in their natural state, were born free. Yet in forming a civil society we run "headlong to our chains." If Locke praised civil society, Rousseau denigrated it, for it was political society that created inequality, inspired self-love and corrupted the individual with frivolity and superficial desires. Individuals, born into a state of pure freedom, were enslaved and compelled to suffer the indignities of "civilized" life. Locke's protection of individual liberties saw the state as external to the moral life of the individual. The result was a society in which each acted on their own selfish inclinations and pursued their own interests at the expense of others. The principles of civil government even abetted these activities, protecting the rights to commerce and selfishness. Rousseau's romanticized "natural man" stood in stark contrast to the corrupted individual of modern civil society. What was needed was a different type of social contract, "a form of association … in which each, while uniting himself with all, may still obey himself alone and remains as free as before."[31]

Rousseau's communitarian impulses prompted a re-evaluation of society. Consent alone was not enough to legitimate government. It had to also be moral. Just as he valorized a mythic "natural" man in rhapsodizing on man's innate liberty, so too did he valorize a mythic classical past in which individual and society coexisted in moral unity. Looking back to the politics of the Greek polis or Roman forum, Rousseau believed that it was the unanimous voice of the community—the general will—that provided the moral unity lacking in modern civil society. This morality could only come through popular sovereignty, a community of citizens that would instill virtue within the individual through collective participation.[32] "The fatherland cannot exist without liberty, nor liberty without virtue, nor virtue without citizens."[33] The general will calls upon the individual to act as a citizen, and in doing so to set aside their personal interests for the good of all. We are "forced" to be free, yet not in a coercive fashion. The citizen, properly formed, freely chooses to abide by the general will. As a citizen, we are enjoined by a sense of duty to act, and in doing so act virtuously.[34] A community based upon the general will could only find expression in law, Rousseau believed, and by obeying the laws of the community we are, in essence, obeying the only legitimate power one can, the concrete expression of the general will. In his veneration for the general will and the ideal of citizenship, Rousseau laid out the ideological base for a republican society rooted in natural law.

Modern critics have accused Rousseau of paving the way for the totalitarian state. In his theories, they have criticized his problematic formulation of sovereignty based upon the general will and claimed his ideals of communitarian unanimity reflect a procrustean classicism that undermines individual liberty and compels the individual to submit wholly to the will of the community.[35] Conversely, however, his emphasis on politics would inspire republican ideas of reforming human nature through the political order while his relationship between the state and sovereignty remains a central tenet of modern republican ideology. Moreover, his emphasis on liberty and freedom was consistent with many of his Enlightenment contemporaries.[36] Rousseau's republicanism consistently endeavored to find a means of restoring the liberty that had been lost once man exited from the natural world and joined civil society. He suggested that in losing our natural liberty we may gain a distinctly different type of moral liberty, "which alone renders man truly master of himself."[37] His theories were controversial even among his cohorts. His correspondence is filled with recriminations and insults hurled at his fellow Enlightenment thinkers. "Pitiful," "depraved" and "false" were the words Voltaire used to describe the Citizen of Geneva: a "bastard of Diogenes' dog."[38] Enlightenment sociability with its salons and conventions of debate was a difficult pill for Rousseau to swallow. He persistently dreamed of an idealized freedom found only beyond the corrupt civilized world that he deplored.[39] Yet despite his hatred for that world, he never advocated violently overturning it. He envisioned a change in social relations and a new type of morality that would compensate for man's loss of true freedom. It was, ultimately, the best a civilized world could offer.

Enlightenment thought contained the seeds of revolutionary ideas, but it was not revolutionary in itself. For the most part, *philosophes* wrote erudite treaties that dealt in abstractions. They rhapsodized about natural law and reason, concepts that were not easily grasped by a general readership. However, these ideas did trickle down through a variety of popular media such as novels and the underground press, and in the process became radicalized. By the last third of the eighteenth century, people were familiar with the language and ideas of the Enlightenment even if they had not read the canonical texts of the "high" Enlightenment.[40] Yet this new language only provided a backdrop for the series of political and social convulsions that would occur beginning in the 1760s. It was in these new circumstances that ideas of sovereignty and natural rights found their actualization, not necessarily as declarative principles, but rather as alternatives to established models of sovereignty and authority that had ceased to function.

CHAPTER 1
PATRIOTS AND CITIZENS: AMERICA AND FRANCE (1763–1789)

"From what we now see, nothing of reform on the political world ought to be held improbable," the radical Thomas Paine wrote in 1791. "It is an age of Revolutions, in which everything must be looked for."[1] Having witnessed political strife and conflict across two continents, Paine certainly knew of what he spoke. During the late eighteenth century, popular protests and political unrest were symptomatic of a transformation occurring throughout the Atlantic world that contemporaries did not hesitate to identify as a "revolution." If the term possessed a certain novelty, it was by no means unfamiliar to European and colonial elites. Nearly three decades earlier, the Enlightenment philosopher Voltaire had remarked, "Everything I see is sowing the seeds of a revolution that is bound to occur. ... Our young people are very fortunate, they will see great things."[2] As to whether the "revolution" imagined by Paine and Voltaire were one and the same is questionable. Yet it was undeniable that each in their one way saw themselves as living in a moment of profound change in which "everything must be looked for."

Historians have been inclined to view the late eighteenth century as an "age of democratic revolution" that began in the British colonies before spreading through Europe and the Americas. At the heart of this revolutionary drama were pitched battles for freedom and the creation of new independent nations founded on the ruins of illiberal early modern empires.[3] In more romantic variations of this narrative, the period saw "the people" or "the nation" awaken from their slumber to become the authors of their own destiny. To label the period an age of "democratic revolution" is, however, to focus on the outcomes rather than the causes. While ideas regarding rights and liberty had been circulating throughout eighteenth-century society for some time, the catalysts for the violent convulsions that took place had far more systemic and diverse origins. During the mid-eighteenth century, states confronted a series of new problems stemming from imperial rivalries and growing expenses associated with state building projects. These factors aggravated a common struggle between center and periphery that cut across early modern empires.[4] At the same time, economic growth and a budding consumer culture were undermining traditional social hierarchies in favor of wealth and market-driven relationships.[5] Taken together, historians have argued that these broad changes engendered social and political tensions that would encourage new models of sovereignty and political belonging underpinning modern conceptions of citizenship.

It is, however, important to note that these dynamics provided the backdrop against which revolutions unfolded. They establish a context for assessing radical change, but they do not sufficiently explain the process of revolution itself. Closer examination reveals that moments of crisis presented new opportunities for re-imagining sovereign and social bonds. As state structures and polities broke down, political actors were increasingly compelled to step in and fill the vacuum left by traditional authority. It was in this respect that concepts like "the people" and "the nation" acquired their saliency. The American and French revolutions were not so much "democratic" revolutions as they were "citizenship" revolutions that profoundly altered the relationship between state and individual.[6] Ideas focused on civic participation and contractual government cut across the Atlantic world and played a key factor in shaping understandings of community that reconfigured existing models of sovereignty and political authority. As political elites came to speak in the name of "the people" against kings and royal governors, they were obliged to define this entity and, in the process, furnish the basis for a novel type of society anchored in notions of rights and popular sovereignty. The democratic limitations of these revolutions were clearly evident. Fears over disorder often encouraged elites to seek means of constraining political participation and advancing concepts of citizenship that were compatible with desires for social stability.

In a more direct way, the changing circumstances associated with the collapse of order were also significant in reshaping the very understanding of revolution itself. The concept of "revolution" had a long tradition among European thinkers. It typically connoted a period of civil disorder spurred by tyrannical and corrupting forces. The pamphleteer Marchamont Nedham writing during the English Civil War commended Cromwell's protectorate as "a Revolution in Government" against the "inconveniences of Tyranny, Distractions [and] Misery" perpetrated by the Stuart monarchy.[7] For Thomas Hobbes, revolution implied a conservative principle linked to the restoration of just authority following a cycle of political turmoil. In the restoration of the Stuart dynasty after years of civil war, Hobbes was inclined to see "in this revolution a circular motion of the sovereign power" and a return to legitimate authority.[8] As such, revolution connoted a return to first principles and a means of correcting the anarchy and civil discord that tyranny invited.

This interpretation began to change after 1688 in response to the Glorious Revolution that unfolded in England. What one historian has deemed "the first modern revolution" in history saw England engulfed in a sustained period of popular and political violence as battles between monarchist and parliamentarian factions tore the county apart. The upheavals of 1688 radically transformed English society, securing religious tolerance, new political institutions guaranteed by a constitution and a modernizing economic policy that would enrich Great Britain over the coming century.[9] Enlightenment thinkers like David Hume and Voltaire were correct to see the seminal events of 1688 as a transformative moment, but others persisted to use the more familiar tropes of restoration and return in comprehending the changes that had occurred. In expressing his admiration for the Glorious Revolution, the English political writer and bibliophile Thomas Hollis saw fit to describe himself as "a lover of liberty, his country and its excellent constitution so nobly restored at the happy Revolution."[10] For Hollis as for many others, revolution continued to be understood as an instrument of restoration, not insurgency or innovation.[11]

The crises of authority that broke out during the late eighteenth century effectively ingrained the modern meaning of revolution in European political discourse. Reacting against royal "tyranny," North American colonists would initially call for a return to a society vested in traditional notions of British liberty. However, in the wake of the American war and the debates that grew up in the French Estates General during 1789, it was evident the meaning of revolution was in a state of transition. Rather than a return to the past, the idea of restoration gave way to a break with tradition. Both American and French political actors came to see themselves as creating new communities of citizens that favored "the people" over monarchy and royal absolutism. Such assertions became the central motif of a modern revolutionary tradition that would unequivocally associate revolutionary action with social, political and cultural modernization.

A British Imperial Community

"We are here at the end of the world," wrote William Byrd I from his plantation on the James River in 1690.[12] Two months travel by ship from the English metropole and inhabiting a Virginian wilderness populated with "wild Indians," it was indeed easy to imagine that one was living at the ends of the earth, or at least what most educated people of the period might have considered the "civilized" world. Two generations later, however, these expressions of isolation and detachment would hardly have been shared among Britons. By the mid-eighteenth century, colonists no longer felt they were inhabiting a distant frontier. Colonial particularism was being eroded by adherence to common British values, collective trade policies and an Anglicized culture. Cities such as London and Manchester seemed less distant thanks in part to the wide availability of English goods and commodities that circulated through the Atlantic.[13] Patriotism expressed in anthems and robust declarations testified to an emotional tie felt by individuals coming to see themselves as members of an intercontinental society known as the British Empire.[14]

Colonists took an interest in the ideas of early English nationalists whose veneration for Anglo-Saxon heritage and the traditions of English constitutionalism reinforced a cultural and historic connection with the metropole.[15] Prominent English legal writers and political philosophers such as John Locke insisted upon the unique system of law and government that set England (and later Britain) apart from other societies. While European kingdoms on the continent succumbed to a despotic royal absolutism, Britain clung fast to its traditions of jurisprudence and parliamentarianism, a point settled during the Glorious Revolution of 1688. Common law affirmed the right of subjects to resist arbitrary authority and oppose legislation passed without consent. These were considered the "absolute rights of every Englishman" as the legal historian William Blackstone dubbed them, the "birthright and privilege" of Britons and the basis of its parliamentary government. British "privilege" did not mean "equality"—for deep social cleavages and hierarchies remained entrenched in British society, not least of all slavery. It signified rather what the statesman Edmund Burke would later describe as an "entailed inheritance."[16] This inheritance manifested itself in the laws and institutions that protected the liberties belonging to all subjects.[17] It was, in short, what made Englishman "English" or Britons "British."

In the minds of colonists, liberty was crucial to their understanding of English and British identity. "*British* Blood runs in our Veins, and the spirit of *Englishmen* in our Hearts," as one Jamaican author proclaimed, and by this he meant the spirit of liberty common to all free-born subjects of the crown.[18] Settlers inhabiting the distal Atlantic colonies insisted their allegiance to Britain and its empire rested upon loyalty to a common monarchy which was committed to upholding and protecting the rights of its subjects throughout the world. Rights, liberty and privilege: this was how those in the colonies interpreted empire. It constituted a single community united under a sovereign crown and associated through a set of commonly recognized rights. As the governor of Massachusetts, Thomas Pownall explained in 1752: "Tis through this system only that a people become [a] political body; tis the chain, the bonds of union by which very vague and independent particles cohere."[19]

The New World provided fertile soil on which to put these ideas of liberty and freedom into practice. For most of the seventeenth and eighteenth centuries, mercantile firms and joint-stock companies participated in overseas expansion and founding settlements abroad. In this respect, colonization was viewed as a private business venture requiring minimal state oversight. The assemblies set up were, for the most part, autonomous, with settlers attending to local administration, trade and day-to-day affairs.[20] These bodies provided an education in the practices of political autonomy and self-governance distinct from the abstract theories of liberty found in Enlightenment philosophy.[21] For this reason, it was not uncommon that colonial assemblies served as forums of heated debate on the application of common law and the meaning of rights.[22] Also for this reason, colonists tended to be among the most ardent defenders of their liberal inheritance. They were quick to remind authorities they could not be treated as one treated conquered people nor that their voluntary departure from home had in any way forfeited their natural liberties. "No Englishman in their Wits will ever Venture their Lives and Estates to Enlarge the Kings Dominion abroad, and Enrich the whole English Nation," asserted the puritanical minister and Massachusetts official Increase Mathers, "if their Reward after all must be to be deprived of their *English Liberties*."[23] Colonists looked askance on anything that might be construed as a curtailment of their rights, perennially safeguarding the traditions of law and self-governance to which they believed themselves entitled.[24]

The freedoms that many colonists extolled were as practical as they were principled. London did not possess the resources or capabilities to administer its vast empire directly. In a very real sense, metropolitan rule depended upon the consent of the colonies, many separated from the mother country by an ocean. In essence, British power did not flow outward from London. Authority was distributed between center and periphery, producing an imperial polity characterized by indirect governance and largely self-governing bodies.[25] The fragmentary nature of British authority did not, however, dampen the emotional attachment that many colonists felt toward their empire. Imperial patriotism, whether expressed through shared political ideals or colonial wars fought primarily against the French, reinforced a sense of collective mission and destiny. In 1763, when colonists and the British army succeeded in expelling France from North America, British flags hung in every major colonial city and statues of King George III were erected in town squares. Yet if a British Atlantic commonwealth did exist, the nature of its relationship was never clearly spelled out, and herein lay the problem.

Metropolitans too spoke of British liberty, but in a different context. For them, liberty meant the sovereign authority of Parliament. It was Parliament's sovereign right to govern and legislate that underwrote Britain's system of governance and guaranteed the rights and liberties of free-born Britons. As British subjects, colonists were expected to submit to the supreme authority of the kingdom. It was evident that metropolitans and colonists were speaking two different languages of liberty that possessed contrasting understandings of what it meant to be British, a point that became clearly evident in the 1760s as Britain began restructuring the empire.

By mid-century, London faced a ballooning public debt, higher state expenditure and a host of administrative problems associated with managing a vast, multiethnic empire. Catholic French Canadians needed to be assimilated and relations between white settlers and indigenous people effectively managed to avoid violence; trading vessels required naval protection while debt needed to be curbed.[26] A more proficient and streamlined imperial structure was envisaged as a solution to these problems, promising what the political economist Malachy Postlethwayt referred to as a greater "union in government and constitution." "If the English colonies in America were wisely consolidated into one body and happily united in one common interest," he asked, "… would not such political concord and harmony establish invincible strength and power?"[27] In short, a British system of colonial governance was beginning to emerge as officials and policy makers sought to maximize revenue. Rule from the center was becoming the new guiding philosophy, and colonists did not hesitate to label it monarchial "tyranny."

In the coming years, a series of issues ranging from land policies in the West to new taxes placed on sugar, paper and most notoriously tea provided occasions for conflict. Merchants resorted to boycotts, bootlegging and noncompliance to circumvent the detested taxes. They even obstructed the collection of duties and applied social pressure on cohorts to resist. Tax collectors were particularly unwelcome, in some instances being lynched by mobs and run out of town. Rowdy groups of "patriots" like the Boston-based Sons of Liberty organized craftsmen and laborers and took to the streets. Rioting had a long tradition in English political culture. It was a popular means of expressing social grievances and injustice for those without a political voice, and the language and symbols used by colonists would have hardly been considered unique in the eighteenth century.[28] Rioters burned effigies in the street, compared unpopular officials to the devil and made appeals to liberty in public declarations. In 1765, mobs replied to the detested Stamp Act by burning an effigy of Andrew Oliver, the Massachusetts stamp collector. The crowd then gathered outside Oliver's home, decapitated the effigy to loud cries and proceeded to loot the house. The following week, it was Lieutenant-Governor Thomas Hutchinson's turn when an angry mob stormed his palatial house and razed it to the ground. Threats of violence echoed throughout the other colonies, with tax collectors and public officials singled out for popular retribution. In these moments of disorder, mobs attained their own authority with some colonists exhibiting a brazen hostility to all forms of social status and authority in the defense of their "liberties."

No less quarrelsome, colonial elites defended their autonomy in a torrent of pamphlets and petitions. Writers argued that the London parliament did not possess the authority to levy new taxes or shape policies without the consent of the colonial assemblies. Government by consent was one of the founding principles of English liberty, they reminded. Since colonists were not represented in Parliament, it could not reflect their interests. To ignore this point was to violate one of the fundamental bases of Britain's liberal inheritance. After 1765, colonists exhibited a new concern with "constitutional rights." Most educated colonists possessed a rough understanding of Locke and social contract theory, and they were not timid when it came to employing it in their polemics. A more pronounced rights talk suffused political criticism as questions over the relationship between center and periphery animated debate. When Virginia planter Thomas Jefferson attacked the "wanton exercise" of power and insisted that British Americans were "a free people claiming their rights" in 1774, he was repeating a commonplace that could have been found in most colonial newspapers of the day.[29]

Rioting, protest and armed conflict progressively eroded British authority. In defending their liberties, colonists were challenging the very base of Parliament's power, setting a potentially dangerous precedent. Yet their challenge was not necessarily radical. It remained couched in the familiar idiom of British rights and privilege that had long been central to the political life of the empire. At the center of these contentions stood one fundamental question: what was the nature of the British Atlantic Commonwealth? Britain's efforts to integrate its imperial domain had ironically brought into question the very foundation of the empire. As Elizabeth Mancke has argued, the American conflict did not mark a moment of national assertion and independence so much as it did a battle over the "plural and plastic" meaning of liberty in the British world.[30] Only once no consensus on the meaning of liberty, and hence the British Atlantic Commonwealth *tout court*, was obtained did secession become conceivable. In the meantime, the idea of a British imperial community disintegrated, providing opportunities to imagine new types of authority and community.

Revolution and the Making of "the People"

The American crisis began with a defense of British liberty and patriotism. It would end with their complete rejection and a new type of rights talk distinct from British subjecthood. Protest and oppositional rhetoric revealed the authority that colonists invested in rights.[31] As British authority melted away, however, Americans were forced to re-conceptualize their understandings of rights and sovereignty. "If we are no longer to be allowed the rights of Britons, we MUST be Americans," as one newspaper avowed in 1769.[32] Herein lay the logic for a republican revolution that had been largely unimaginable at the start of the conflict.

During its first year, the American crisis was experienced as a revolution, but a revolution understood in traditional terms. In their defense of British rights, patriots invoked an idealized vision of subjecthood. They claimed to be defending the natural conditions of British society threatened by a tyrannical king. Writing in early 1776, one journalist heartened readers to take confidence that the current conflict would not be without its benefits: "The civil constitutions of countries, altho' long neglected through the indolence of the people and tottering on the verge of dissolution, have nevertheless been thus purged of their corruptions, brought back to their first principles, and made to flourish, with renewed vigour, through many succeeding ages."[33] It was this insistence on a return to "first principles" and the promise of a purified constitution that spurred colonists on their revolutionary course. Revolution implied a return to the past and the repair of a corrupted, and thus disorderly system. As the pseudonymous writer Camillus explained, the object of government was to promote the public good. "But to effect such great purposes," he added, "the principles of the government must undergo a priori, a vast revolution. The change must be no less than from complication to simplicity; from corruption to purity."[34]

Various observers saw the American conflict as a civil war between Britons. In the past, wars against the French had typically helped solidify a common British identity. The American conflict, however, threw notions of British identity into doubt.[35] American resistance was a fight for the cause of British liberty, claimed a writer identifying themselves only by the title "One of the Public." Appealing to fellow compatriots across the Atlantic, One of the Public chided those who denounced American patriots as treacherous and disloyal. "Ye execrate them as rebels whom ye should reverence for their virtuous fortitude; they are fighting for us, and on them depend the liberties of this country."[36] By the end of 1776, however, such arguments had lost their credibility as American rights talk and patriotic rhetoric acquired a more radical character.

The reasons for this growing radicalism were many, but it was hard to deny the impact of a pamphlet written by a bankrupt and by all accounts undistinguished Englishman recently arrived in Philadelphia. The author was Thomas Paine and the pamphlet was *Common Sense*. An English corset maker and shopkeeper by trade, Paine exemplified the new opportunities afforded to individuals as authority broke down. Upon landing in America, he established a reputation for himself as a political firebrand and soon a leading voice of the patriot cause. Reading *Common Sense*, colonists did not necessarily find new ideas within its pages. It restated old grievances and Lockean ideas that had been circulating throughout the colonies for a decade. However, Paine organized all of these ideas into a single pamphlet written in plain and moving language. He offered a scathing criticism of monarchial government, informing readers they had little need for such contrivances. "The nearer any government approaches to a Republic, the less business there is for a King," he advised. America's republican qualities, evident in its assemblies and self-governing institutions, were sufficient unto themselves, and it would be better to dispense with monarchy and British rule altogether. "Nothing but Continental authority can regulate Continental matters," Paine boldly charged.[37]

Upon publication, *Common Sense* sold over 100,000 copies. It was passed from hand to hand among eager colonists and read aloud in taverns and other public places. It is doubtful that Paine's writing had any direct influence on the delegates attending the Continental Congress meeting in Philadelphia where colonists were debating their course of action. Nevertheless, the work presented a clear example of the power of the pamphlet in uncertain times. *Common Sense* influenced a specific sense of American self-awareness in the minds of its audience. In counseling colonists "'tis time to part," Paine offered the image of a youthful continent in its "seed-time." As a nation maturing into adulthood, America was fast emerging from its self-incurred immaturity and tutelage. With such evocative language, Paine placed American independence squarely within the framework of Enlightenment emancipation, providing a coming-of-age narrative that rationalized America's liberation from the parental tyranny of monarchy.[38]

In July of 1776, Thomas Jefferson, a leading patriot statesman, gave credence to Paine's injunctions when, at the behest of the Continental Congress, he drafted a formal Declaration of Independence from Great Britain. The document contained basic Lockean principles of contractual government glossed with Enlightenment moral precepts. Jefferson alluded to the "inalienable rights" that all men possessed, the legitimate power of a people to "institute" government and a firm assertion that "just" rule derived from consent. While not necessarily innovative in its claims, the Declaration did underscore one evident claim. Americans were "one people" who, having suffered the injustices of royal tyranny, were now asserting their own sovereignty. In no uncertain terms, it established a new authority for America, one vested in republican ideas of a united "people" and popular sovereignty.

Rather than merely elucidating Enlightenment ideals of liberty and freedom—although these were in no short supply—writers like Paine and Jefferson were participating in the invention of American sovereignty. To invoke concepts of "America" and "the people" was to conjure them into existence and give them meaning. Colonists had thought of themselves as British subjects loyal to a sovereign monarch. They were now being asked to see themselves as a collective people and source of self-sovereignty. Revolution no longer implied a return to the past or the remodeling of a shared British community. With independence, British rights talk became republican rights talk, fundamentally reorienting the struggle. Assertions that "all men are created equal" and endowed with "inalienable rights" did not refer to the "entailed" rights of Englishmen, but rather the natural rights of the Enlightenment. Jefferson and his cohorts were not necessarily acting out of strong republican conviction. Rather, the situation compelled a republican response as colonial elites endeavored to create a new center of sovereign authority to fill the space vacated by British authority. "The people" became a powerful means of imagining this sovereignty, proposing a new type of social unity as imperial structures collapsed.

Yet "the people" was a concept that was as plastic as it was abstract. Who were the people? How were Americans to imagine this entity? Pamphlets and declarations may have invoked the people as a source of authority, but words alone could not make this concept a reality. On the day the Declaration of Independence was read aloud in New York City, patriots belonging to the local chapter of the Sons of Liberty gathered at Bowling Green Park around a statue of King George III. With crowbars and tethers, they proceeded to topple the imposing effigy, saw off the head and mount it on a pike. The Sons of Liberty visibly demonstrated what Jefferson's Declaration could only suggest, and similar acts of iconoclastic violence soon followed. Throughout the colonies, royal symbols were torn from buildings and statues defaced. These types of symbolic acts made "the people" real. Individuals could claim their own part in the remaking of society and, by doing so, enter into an unspoken compact with fellow citizens.[39]

Military conflict against Britain equally provided opportunities for imagining the American people as patriots enlisted in the Continental Army and took up arms in defense of what George Washington deemed "the glorious cause." Paradoxically, however, war also revealed the tenuous fiction that Americans were, in fact, "one people." Ideological division between patriots and loyalists tore communities apart and devolved into guerilla warfare. Local "committees of public safety" were organized to police localities and mete out punishment on suspected traitors. Free and enslaved African-Americans fought on both sides of the conflict. Those who joined the patriot cause did so with the intention of including themselves within the new body of "the people" and influencing a more inclusive definition of citizenship.[40] That many of these aspirations would be thwarted by the end of the conflict was indicative of the conservatism built into America's republican revolution. Revolutionaries had little inclination to alter existing governmental structures or social conditions. On the contrary, British modifications to imperial structures had been a prime cause of colonial discontent, and Americans would uphold the racial subjugation that empire supported after independence.[41] Patriotism and race came to shape specific conceptions of "the people" that hinted at the exclusionary nature of the modern citizenship regime, with loyalists, slaves and Native Americans among the "casualties" of republican nation-building.[42]

If the patriot revolution bore the marks of its reactionary character, independence did invest the "revolutionary" nature of patriot protest with new meaning. In 1779, the congressman Gouverneur Morris drafted a rebuttal to the British Commission on Conciliation entitled *Observations on the American Revolution*, one of the first official uses of the term. By the early 1780s, statesmen such as George Washington were inclined to make references to "our revolution" in public speeches and writing.[43] In 1782, Thomas Paine, always a zealous defender of the patriot cause, corroborated America's revolutionary credentials in a public exchange with the French political writer and cleric Guillaume Thomas Raynal. While the *abbé* expressed doubt as to whether a settler revolt over taxes constituted a significant "revolution," Paine took the liberty of correcting his "uniformed" opinion, claiming that America had, indeed, undergone a revolution. This revolution was, moreover, a world-changing event paving the way toward a worthier political order, in his opinion. "Our style and manner of thinking, have undergone a revolution, more extraordinary than the political revolution of the country," Paine argued. "We see with other eyes; we hear with other ears; and think with other thoughts than those we formerly used."[44]

As Paine's retort suggested, the meaning of revolution was shifting by the 1780s as a result of the American experience. Rather than a return to a golden age, "revolution" was becoming a communicable idiom for a process of political transformation and social improvement. Perhaps more significant, he noted, these revolutionary currents were not confined to North America. "Revolution … has engaged the attention, and affected the interest of Europe," Paine insisted, and in this he was certainly correct.[45]

"A Strong Leaven of Liberty"

Europeans widely discussed the American Revolution. It was a topic of conversation at salons and most newspapers of the day carried regular updates on the conflict. The French in particular took a keen interest in Atlantic affairs, if only out of a particular sense of Schadenfreude. During the French and Indian War, Britain had wrested Canada and the territories east of the Mississippi from French control. Its once formidable American empire lost, France consoled itself with the few small, lucrative islands in the West Indies left in its possession and licked its wounds. *Revanche* was never far from the minds of French policy makers as they watched Britain's North American empire implode. The foreign ministry provided colonial rebels with military aid and support in the hopes of striking a blow against France's erstwhile imperial rival. That an absolutist monarchy allying with a revolutionary republic might be a contradiction in principle was of minimal importance.

The call to arms found support among a generation of French aristocrats "tired of the *longueur* of peace," as the Comte de Ségur claimed. A young officer at the time, Ségur served in the French expeditionary force to America. Like many of his cohorts, he endeavored to satiate desires for military glory that could not otherwise be satisfied on the continent. Once abroad, these romantic fantasies surpassed expectation. The strong appeals of patriotism and republicanism that suffused the Continental Army were infectious. The American rebels were also enchanting. In the reserved yet paternal George Washington they found the embodiment of the classical citizen-soldier. The American representative to France throughout the war, Benjamin Franklin, was the paragon of rustic simplicity. With his plain dress and beaver pelt hat, he personified the humble American farmer amidst the frivolity of French aristocracy. Franklin's diplomatic propaganda aimed at garnering French support had its own allure. He touted the patriot cause as that of humanity in general and painted the virtuous and incorruptible nature of the American people in terms reminiscent of Rousseau's "natural" man. The dramatist and writer Louis-Sébastien Mercier was certainly taken by the new enthusiasm for America sweeping through France. "It is perhaps in America that the human race is to be recreated," he wrote in 1778; "that it is to adopt a new and sublime legislation, that it is to perfect the arts of sciences, that it is to recreate the nations of antiquity."[46] Fascination with the simplicity and egalitarianism of Americans stimulated popular support and spoke to a growing appreciation for values of patriotism and liberty evident among French elites and intellectuals raised in the milieu of the Enlightenment. As the Vicomtesse de Fars-Fausselandry candidly admitted, "The American cause seemed our own."[47]

With the conclusion of the American war, patriots sought out other noble causes worthy of their support. In 1782, an uprising in Geneva drew international attention as Swiss artisans seized control of the government and declared a republic over the entrench oligarchs who had traditionally dominated the city. A republican revolt in Rousseau's native city had its particular attraction. The young French journalist Jacques Pierre Brissot traveled to Geneva, finding there his own America to extol and celebrate. He lent his pen to the struggle for natural rights and liberty, insisting that Swiss republicans, like the Americans, were working to throw off the old world and recover their civil liberties. Brissot even adopted an American persona, signing his pamphlet as a "Philadelphian."[48] Yet a Genevan Republic in the center of monarchial Europe stood little chance of survival. With foreign aid, the oligarchs crushed the revolt, sending the republicans into exile. Passions were rekindled five years later when self-proclaimed patriots in the Netherlands revolted against the aristocratic Orangist faction in power. As in Geneva, pamphleteers lauded Enlightenment principles and drew comparisons with the American cause. And as in Geneva, the patriot revolt was suppressed with foreign intervention, this time supplied by Prussia. For the lawyer and patriot Charles Lambert d'Outrepont writing in the aftermath of the failed revolt, these uprisings signified more than localized rebellions. They spoke to a pervasive longing for liberty arising among the current generation. "Everywhere you look you see a continual struggle between a throne propped up by force and liberty supported by the voice of nature and law," he claimed.[49]

George Washington was no less observant. Writing to the Franco-American author Hector St. Jean Crèvecoeur in April of 1789, the aged statesman commented on the profound influence the American example appeared to exercise on hearts and minds throughout the world. "The American Revolution, or the peculiar light of the age, seems to have opened the eyes of almost every nation in Europe and a spirit of equal liberty appears fast to be gaining ground everywhere."[50] From its inception, the infant American Republic stood as a model of universal liberty radiating the "peculiar light of the age" for all to bear witness, or at least this was how American patriots had sold their cause to enlist international support against the British. This rationalization possessed, however, a powerful emotional resonance. "The name of liberty is so sweet, that all they who fight for it are sure to interest our secret wishes," claimed the Abbé Raynal. "Their cause is that of the whole human race; it becomes our own."[51] Patriots and political writers across Europe and the Atlantic world were coming to see themselves as participants in an international cosmopolitan community bound by shared ideals and values. Liberty was a battle cry that transcended geographic borders. Whether citizens of Geneva or the American Republic, patriots appealed to a higher allegiance above *patrie* or fatherland. To be a patriot was to be a "citizen of the world" and partake in the universal fraternity that liberation promised. The defense of common values for a common humanity: such was the message expounded by embattled republics in need of foreign aid and support.

Two weeks after Washington's remarks to Crèvecoeur, riots erupted in the Saint-Antoine quarter of Paris. Driven by low wages and high bread prices, workers lashed out at factory owners and clashed with armed guards in the streets. The outburst spoke more to the rowdy Boston and New York mobs of two decades past than the universal "light of the age" noted by Washington. Nonetheless, within the new context of revolution and popular protest, it appeared symptomatic of the times. As the English travel writer Arthur Young claimed, "a strong leaven of liberty" existed in France, one that had been "increasing every hour since the American Revolution."[52]

Monarchic Empire and Its Discontents

Like most early modern states, the French kingdom was an amalgam of provinces and feudal territories cobbled together over the centuries through marriage alliances, conquest and dynastic inheritance. Provinces far from the court in Versailles such as Dauphiné and Brittany possessed their own constitutions while other areas had independent assemblies and law courts. Rural districts, cities and even small towns had their exclusive jurisdictions and forms of government guaranteed by individual charter of royal patent.[53] The magistrates of Pau were not being facetious when considering themselves inhabitants of "a country foreign to France, although ruled by the same king."[54] Ancien Régime France was a patchwork of *petites patries* stitched together through allegiance to a common dynasty.[55] Maintaining this arrangement required a fair amount of negotiation and cooperation with a variety of local and regional power bases ranging from municipal councils to the French clergy to powerful aristocratic families of the countryside. The ruling Bourbon monarchs acknowledged the ancient "rights" and "liberties" claimed by provinces, but this acknowledgment was given grudgingly.

The Bourbons experimented with ways of correcting this situation beginning in the late seventeenth century as King Louis XIV brought a cluster of new territories along France's eastern border under his control. Seeking to avoid the power sharing agreements familiar in the older provinces and to promote "a closer union" with the crown, Louis curtailed the sovereign powers of the local dukes and counts and asserted direct control over the judicial and fiscal bodies in these areas.[56] As proponents of royal absolutism, the Bourbons intended to rule with a heavier hand. The Estates General, the principal representative institution of the kingdom, had been closed since 1614. Royal intendants increasingly monitored the magistrates and tax collectors to ensure the king's law was implemented and revenues flowed back to Versailles. Under Louis XIV, a more robust royalism was promoted through lavish court ceremonies and symbolic gestures that reinforced the monarch's image as a divinely appointed sovereign. In many ways, the royal court was the lynchpin of the absolutist system, providing a counterweight to the provincial magistrates and assemblies that constrained royal authority. Above all, the king sought to discipline his oldest rivals—the nobility—by making them dependent upon the court through official appointments and royal favor.[57]

Unfortunately, Louis' successors lacked his strong-willed approach to politics. By the mid-seventeenth century, it seemed to be the court which was dependent. Cash-strapped monarchs found the sale of offices an expedient means of raising money. Civil and judicial posts were sold to the highest bidders along with titles of nobility. The so-called *noblesse de robe* that purchased its way into the privileged ranks of society made up a quarter of the aristocracy by the 1780s with nearly all official posts through the kingdom occupied by aristocrats.[58] The case was similar for tax collection, which was farmed out for a price. These revenue-generating strategies relinquished control over local and regional tax bases as the wealthy *receveurs de taille* drew their incomes by extracting as much as possible from the inhabitants of their jurisdiction. Even the indirect taxes that the state did keep under their control were notoriously difficult to collect. It was not uncalled for when the finance minister Jacques Necker described the tax system as a "monster in the eyes of reason."[59]

Absolutist reforms may have promised a comprehensive legal and administrative system for the kingdom, but the reality often fell short. France remained a tangle of different legal regimes, unevenly applied regulations and customary power arrangements. A traveler making their way through the royal domain was apt to change laws as often as they did horses, as Voltaire quipped. He might have added that they were likely to hear a babel of regional dialects and patois as well. If the arm of the state failed to penetrate deep into the countryside, so too did elite culture. The *petites patries* were a world apart from Paris and Versailles and, indeed, often did seem like a "foreign" country when compared with the center. Rather than a modern centralized state, the Bourbons presided over a post-feudal empire composed of diverse people, cultures and political units.[60]

The social life of this empire was equally as byzantine. Although the old seigneurial system had been in decline for some time, French society bore the marks of its feudal traditions. Designations of *corps*, *communautés*, *états* and orders defined one's place in society. The lack of uniform legislative and political institutions meant no common law was applied to all the king's subjects. Different groups and orders enjoyed different rights and privileges, entailing that social distinctions, just as much as administrative ones, assumed a difference in quality and kind. The landed nobility was a distinct order unto itself with its own legal codes and institutions. Elites had separate law courts, received certain social dispensations guaranteed by the crown and represented themselves before the king as a distinct Estate. Clerical officials similarly had their own laws and institutions, just as did particular religious groups, foreigners and ethnic minorities residing in the kingdom.[61] Inequality and legal pluralism were accepted facets of early-modern society. More often than not, this system of orders was self-regulating and sustained through mutually observed notions of superiority and inferiority, inclusion and exclusion that governed social life and forms of sociability down to the local level.[62]

These concepts of hierarchy and deference were important to an absolutist system built upon personal loyalties and quasi-medieval concepts of monarchial leadership. This is not to suggest that the language of royalism remained static. In fact, it was quite the contrary. Notions of divine right and royal paternalism had sustained monarchy throughout the seventeenth century. Yet by the 1750s, ideologues were inclined to speak of "patriotism" and "the nation" when characterizing royal sovereignty. "The King and the *patrie* are two objects that are united, incorporated together," explained one commentator in 1762.[63] As broad cultural changes came to encourage a more secular worldview, the image of the scared king lost some of its ideological currency.[64] Consequently, the *roi sacré* was refashioned as a *roi patriot*, or "patriot king" with all the attachment to people and country this designation implied. Much as David Bell has argued, during the mid-eighteenth century the French kings became patriots of a specific type. Royal apologists proved ready and willing to adapt to the new cultural milieu of the seventeenth century in their efforts to reinvent the sacred bond between sovereign and people. What was true of absolutists, however, was also true of the nobility.

In the contentions between center and periphery, the Bourbons suffered a steady stream of complaints from outspoken aristocrats and provincial bodies that increasingly found new justification for their attacks. The appellate courts of the *parlements* proved particularly dynamic in this respect. Historically responsible for validating royal laws and edicts, these courts constituted one of the primary restraints on central authority. Anti-absolutist writers extolled the parlements as heirs of the medieval Frankish assemblies and, therefore, the legitimate defenders of the nation's immemorial rights over the king. While not all sitting on the court benches flaunted their mythic pedigree, they did remain vigilant when it came to guarding their traditional powers from royal overreach. When a religious controversy raised the subject of royal prerogative in 1753, the parlement of Paris did not fail to remind Louis XV that they were the guardians of "a kind on contract" between the sovereign and his people, and that the king was expected to abide by the customary laws of the kingdom. While parlementarians employed a language of traditional and historic rights in their defense, talk of government as a "contract" clearly owed more to the Enlightenment than ancient political traditions. References to contracts, rights and the nation were suggestive of the new tenor creeping into old power struggles. Parlementarians could be heard insisting that law ought to be subject to "the free consent of the nation" or that man was born free and equal, bold assertions evocative of Rousseau and Diderot.[65] By the late eighteenth century, it was evident that a stratum of the nobility was well-versed in Enlightenment ideas and, moreover, willing to deploy them in their battle against the court at Versailles.

Absolutists monarchs never enjoyed being reminded that they were, *in theory*, constitutional monarchs. For the newly ascendant Louis XVI, however, this incessant wrangling was especially displeasing. Years of spending and state-building projects had left the monarchy nearly bankrupt. Louis had inherited a precarious situation, and the military support given to the American cause pushed the government over the edge. Creditors had to be paid and state revenues increased if the monarchy wished to remain solvent. Finding new sources of income was, however, problematic. The nobility and clergy enjoyed numerous tax exemptions and the Third Estate making up the "common" people was financially overburdened as is. A series of bad harvests added to these woes, as the price of bread soared in 1788, generating waves of discontent and riots throughout the kingdom. Louis' finance ministers suggested tax reform as a potential remedy, but this plan possessed its own difficulties. New taxes required the approval of the obstinate parlement, and simply imposing them threatened to bring the simmering tensions between central and provincial authority to a boil. Faced with a financial crisis, the government could scarcely afford to have its authority challenged and invite a political crisis. In 1787, the ministry attempted to sidestep this scenario by calling an Assembly of Notables in Versailles at which the nobility and clergy were asked to consent to a new land tax. The notables refused to cooperate, and instead suggested summoning the Estates General to decide the matter. The ministry scoffed, seeing in this proposition yet another attempt to erode the foundations of the absolutist system. However, efforts to circumvent the parlements had thus far proven futile, leaving the Estates General a viable if undesirable option for working around the intractable parlementarians.

In the end, mounting financial pressures forced Louis's hand. In January of 1789 the Estates General was called by royal decree. The decision was unpopular among the king's ministers, none of whom were even certain of the procedures by which the Estates General should be called to order. The body had not met for over 150 years. Historically, the Estates General consisted of the three principal estates of the realm representing the clergy, the nobility and the commons, respectively. Custom dictated that each order meet separately and cast their vote by house, an arrangement that favored landed and clerical interests in the past. Seeing an opportunity to provide the frustrated nobility a chance to press their grievances, the parlement insisted on following the old system. Members of the Third Estate, however, challenged it outright, and in a series of pamphlets laid their case before the public.[66] Purporting to represent "the people," delegates of the Third Estate played upon their numerical majority when compared with the other estates, arguing against a system that would perpetuate the despotism of the privileged. "It is time a great people count for something," one writer adamantly declared, for it was "the people" whose labor cultivated the field, kept France fed and contributed to the general prosperity of the kingdom.[67] Rather than the customary vote *par ordre*, voting *par tête* was essential, giving the Third Estate an unprecedented yet justified influence over the assembly. Now that the Estates General had been called after so many years, delegates were determined to ensure that the commons had their grievances addressed. As the jurist Jean Joseph Mounier warned, "The coming Estates General will be useless if the orders are not joined together and votes counted by head."[68]

Mounier was among a growing number of non-noble elites critical of the institutions and conventions that had permitted the nobility to dominate French society for centuries. Indeed, as Mounier asserted, terms like "commoner" and "Third Estate" were "barbarous designations" that ought to be eliminated. The calling of the Estate General was opening a Pandora's Box, one which permitted men like Mounier to vent their anger at the privileges and ingrained hierarchies that persistently limited "the people." Emmanuel Joseph Sieyès, an embittered clergyman from Chartres, was especially vehement when it came to aristocratic privilege. The son of a tax collector, Sieyès had repeatedly experienced the indignity of France's deeply stratified social system firsthand over the course of his career. He had watched as noble sons with influential family connections were appointed to high religious office over those like him who were doomed to provincial obscurity. His loathing for privilege, not to mention his waning piety, found justification in the Enlightenment philosophies that "liberated" his mind from prejudice and superstition. Hardly a worthy priest, he did prove a skilled writer and orator, and in 1789 pressed his talents into the service of political reform. In his pamphlet "What Is the Third Estate?" he provided a succinct answer to the titular question, informing his readers that the Third Estate was "everything, but an everything shackled and oppressed." For Sieyès, the Third Estate constituted the productive forces and resources essential to society. Yet it nonetheless remained beholden to a parasitic aristocracy, prompting Sieyès to question how such a system could be considered just. "It is not sufficient to show that privileged persons, far from being useful to the nation, cannot but enfeeble and injure it; it is necessary to prove further that the noble order does not enter at all into the social organization; that it may indeed be a burden upon the nation, but that it cannot of itself constitute a nation?"[69]

By invoking the idiom of "the nation," Sieyès was not simply heaping scorn upon a defunct aristocracy. He was making a principled case for a distinctly different type of society, one with potentially radical implications. A "nation," as Sieyès understood it, constituted "a body of associates, living under a common law and represented by the same legislature." The system of order and estates was not a nation. On the contrary, the nobility, with its separate representative bodies and laws, stood apart from the national community forming an *imperium in imperia*. As a privileged order, the nobility defended "not the general, but the particular interest." They pursued their own selfish and self-serving policies without regard for their fellow compatriots, rendering them "an isolated people" and "a stranger to the nation." Underpinning this condemnation of aristocratic privilege was a conviction that a people was only a people by virtue of the unity they shared. This unity was achieved through adherence to laws and institutions common to all, a concept of citizenship without which there could be no society. "The Third Estate embraces then all that which belongs to the nation," argued Sieyès, "and all that which is not the Third Estate, cannot be regarded as being of the nation."[70]

In equating the Third Estate with the French "people" and "nation," pamphlet writers like Sieyès were appropriating the old oppositional language of the parlements and infusing it with a new anti-aristocratic and egalitarian element derived from Rousseau and the *philosophes*. Taken together, these claims presented an incisive criticism of the existing order. At base, absolutism reflected a dynastic principle emphasizing royal proprietorship over the state. If there was a nation or "body politic" of which to speak, the king alone was its visible representation. In his assertion of national unity, Sieyès had little to say of dynastic right or the royal body politic. His nation envisioned an organic link between the French people derived from adhesion to a common law independent of the king. It was a unified community of citizens rather than subjects isolated within *petites patries*. The challenge it posed to monarchial governance could hardly be missed by contemporaries. Within the cogent arguments laid out by Sieyès and others lay a powerful idea that threatened the very foundation of the reigning order.

The Changing Meaning of Revolution

The Estates General opened in May at Versailles among confusion. It remained unclear whether or not the orders would meet independently or whether voting would be carried out by head. In the absence of proper guidelines, each estate proceeded in accordance with their own desires. The nobility and clergy met separately and held their sessions behind closed doors, as was customary. The Third Estate, on the other hand, refused to accept the estate system and proceeded in anticipation of a general assembly in which all representatives of the nation would participate. To symbolize the implicit "national" character of their gatherings, the delegates decided to open their sessions to the public. Spectators were encouraged to come observe the proceedings and watch their representatives at work. Over the coming weeks, the galleries filled with onlookers. This measure of transparency served to give embodiment to the idea of a sovereign people à la Rousseau. It transformed a philosophical abstraction into a reality.[71]

The tone of debate was equally suggestive. The deputies couched their proposals in a nationalist rhetoric, referring to themselves as "an assembly of citizens." At first, the nobility and clergy scoffed at such declarations. During breaks, they would peer in on the chamber and amuse themselves with the grandiloquent speeches and gestures of the deputies. Yet by June, the deadlock had still not been broken and the speeches coming from the Third Estate had turned aggressive. Sieyès was goading his fellow deputies to take the initiative and seize power in the name of the nation. They would present the people with a new declaration of common rights. A representative body would be established to govern on the people's behalf, putting into practice the Rousseauvian idea of popular sovereignty.[72] By June 17, the Third Estate ceased to exist, instead taking the title of the National Assembly. These events, worrisome as they were, forced the question that had been lingering since January: where did sovereignty lie in French society? In the past, the king alone had granted the right and privilege of assembly. Louis XVI had not, however, authorized the creation of the new National Assembly. Was the body one that the king was to give to the nation? Or was the assembly constituted by the nation itself regardless of the king?

Various deputies attempted to soften the radicalism implicit in their actions. They claimed no intention of deposing the monarchy, but rather of "regenerating" French society. Under their care, the traditional basis of monarchy would be fortified and royal authority restored to its proper and legitimate place. "The National Assembly has been called upon to draft a constitution for the kingdom, effect the regeneration of public order and maintain the true principles of the monarchy," a declaration of principles proclaimed.[73] Many deputies stressed their revolutionary intentions, albeit not in the radical terms prescribed by men like Sieyès. "The French are not a new people that has just left the forest," Mounier bluntly reminded.[74] The existing government may have been in need of renovation, but it was nonetheless a political system suited to France. For these so-called *monarchiens*, constitutional monarchy blended with a healthy dose of enlightened statecraft remained the goal, presaging a restoration of the true principles and spirit of monarchial governance. France would recover its ancient rights corrupted by centuries of absolutism, constituting a "revolution" in the terms familiar to the period.

Yet as events took shape in Versailles, a different type of political ferment was becoming evident in Paris some thirteen miles away. Beset by rising food prices and stagnant wages, Parisian artisans and day laborers had periodically staged riots prior to the crisis of 1789. Sieyès's scathing criticism of the aristocracy had merely reiterated popular sentiments holding "aristocrats"—a generic term that masked difference among social elites—accountable for hoarding grain, driving up food prices and various other social ills. The declaration of the National Assembly was greeted enthusiastically in the city with Parisians donning tricolor cockades and setting up a municipal militia aptly named the National Guard. In the press, people followed the political debates taking place in Versailles, reading the stories and speeches aloud in the streets and at cafés. In early July, political effervescence transformed into panic as rumors of a royal coup d'état against the National Assembly circulated through the city. The regiments of foreign Swiss and German mercenary troops stationed in the city to maintain order did nothing to alleviate these fears.[75] As the young journalist Camille Desmoulins declared, these machinations signaled "the knell of a Saint Bartholomew for patriots!"[76]

Over the next few days, demonstrations erupted with participants sacking government stores and looting customs houses in search of food and valuables. Order rapidly deteriorated as protestors clashed with troops in the streets. On July 14, Parisians fearing a military reprisal marched to the Bastille, a medieval military garrison doubling as a prison on the right bank of the Seine River, in search of arms to defend themselves. When the governor of the fortress, Bernard-René de Launay, refused to arm the angry mob, a protracted siege ensued, ending with Launay and his men being hauled off to the nearby Hôtel de Ville where they were abused and executed before the crowd mutilated their corpses. The triumphant people of Paris proceeded to parade the heads of their victims around the city on pikes. Nine days later, the detested Controller-General Joseph Foullon de Doué was apprehended by the Paris mob. Accused of intentionally provoking famine, he was strung up and decapitated before a cheering crowd of onlookers. Desmoulins had warned of a Saint Bartholomew's massacre, only it was not the patriots who suffered.

News of bloodshed in Paris followed with reports of uprisings in the provinces that summer as peasants sacked manor houses, destroyed the old feudal registries and pelted royal officials with stones. In Caen, "patriots" even stormed an old castle built by William the Conqueror, staging their own Bastille. While these phenomena were not necessarily new for a country accustomed to periodic tax and grain riots, the ongoing political crisis in Versailles gave them an altogether novel dynamic. As authority broke down, revolution and popular violence were becoming forged into a single idea.[77] The country appeared on the verge of anarchy. In towns and cities, panic-stricken property owner and elites scrambled to establish general committees and militias to guard against looting and disorder. State sovereignty was rapidly eroding and self-described patriots were taking charge in the power vacuum. For the National Assembly, inaction could be fatal as authority slipped from the assembly to the crowd. The deputies needed to take back the initiative. That July, therefore, they organized a series of committees for the purposes of drafting a constitution and putting an end to the indecision. "The courageous and enlightened patriotism that animates all the national representatives will at last achieve the most beautiful revolution accomplished on earth," the journalist and delegate Bertrand de Barère proclaimed.[78]

This "beautiful revolution" marked the culmination of a series of events, none of which were explicitly revolutionary in and of themselves. Long-standing economic and political pressures, the reaction against the aristocracy, urban and rural social protest, and the influence of Enlightenment ideas on political discourse: these factors came together in the summer of 1789 as public order collapsed in France. As the country became ungovernable, a revolution appeared the only means of reconstructing sovereign authority in the kingdom and restoring unity to a fractured society. The question, however, was what form would this reconstituted society and government assume?

Rights and Citizens

Writing just after the fall of the Bastille, the Portuguese ambassador stationed in Paris remarked that "in all the world's annals there is no mention of a revolution like this one."[79] He was not alone in this assessment. Numerous contemporaries throughout Europe and the Atlantic world instantly accorded an immense importance to the event that had taken place in Paris. What might have been considered little more than an urban riot and mayhem in the past became a symbol of something more significant: an attack on a corrupt and oppressive system soon to be known as the "old regime." In towns and cities across the continent, patriots celebrated the event. "A visionary world seemed to open up," as the English poet Robert Southey claimed.[80] Monarchs and princes, however, greeted the news with trepidation, recognizing the threat this "revolution" posed to their own power and legitimacy. An attack on the most preeminent of Europe's absolutist monarchies was, observers keenly understood, an attack on the entire institution itself, setting a dangerous precedent for the future.

Amidst this mix of fanfare and anxiety, French delegates set to work determining the actual meaning and import of their revolution. The committees established in July raised a number of questions that were not immediately self-evident. Should a government be based upon the English or American models? Should it assume a wholly different form altogether? If a declaration of rights was to be promulgated, what was it to include? Would all existing social bonds be dissolved, and, if so, what would this imply for the society of orders and feudal hierarchies that had governed France for centuries? Various proposals were drafted, amended, debated and scrapped during the following weeks, revealing fundamental political differences within the National Assembly.

On August 4, however, liberal vanguards within the aristocracy and clergy took a preemptive step in resolving these issues. Before the assembly, they proposed that noble titles and feudal dues be abolished, effectively putting an end to the feudal system in France. The unrest roiling the countryside had to be quieted, and a clear demonstration of the National Assembly's commitment to social reform was imperative to do so. As the Duc d'Aiguillon declared, the time had arrived to end France's "feudal barbarism."[81]

Over the next hours, nobles and clerics came forward and renounced their former privileges, relinquishing their titles over territories, the provincial estates and special constitutions that had hitherto been stubbornly defended against absolutist reforms. Henceforth, all French would be equal citizens. These "patriotic" nobles were among the largest landholders of the kingdom. Ending feudalism did pose a devastating blow to their economic livelihood. Yet it would alleviate rising social tensions and commit the National Assembly to a definitive platform of social renovation. In the end, nobles were urged to sacrifice privilege for the sake of national unity and equality, allying the revolution with a program of sweeping social and economic change.

The official death knell of the absolutist corporate state came later that month when the National Assembly decreed the Declaration of the Rights of Man and Citizen. Both the wording and intent of the document had been an issue of sharp debate among committee members. It unequivocally declared that "men are born and remain free and equal in rights." It also identified "the nation" as the sovereign authority, insisting that "No body, no individual can exert authority which does not emanate expressly from it." These principles spoke to the Rousseauvianism of thinkers like Sieyès, who envisioned the nation as a political community of citizens invested with equal rights. Yet to appease conservative-minded deputies, this radicalism was tempered with certain provisions that aimed to constrain popular government and ensure social order. While all citizens were considered equal under the law, only certain tax-paying citizens—so-called "active citizens"—were given voting rights. Roughly 4 million men were empowered with the vote in a country of 28 million, circumscribing political power within an elite male group of property holders. As well, the declaration specifically tied these new rights to law and orderly legal precedent, dictating that "the exercise of natural rights … [is] determined only by the law." Law, and therefore the state, became the supreme authority in delimiting the scope of rights, preventing citizens from making any claims they pleased on the ground of possessing "natural" rights. In particular, it precluded against landless peasants and artisans seizing property under the pretext of equality. Property constituted "an inviolable and sacred right," according to the declaration. If the nobility had abandoned it rights to collect seigneurial dues, these dues were consequently transformed into rent incomes protected under the law.[82]

In many respects, the Rights of Man was a compromise that blended radical and conservative elements. Nonetheless, it did serve a critical function. It provided the National Assembly with a text they could stand behind and hold up as a collective declaration of principles. It also furnished the deputies with a much needed source of legitimacy. Up until this moment, the deputies had been working without a mandate. Necessity had compelled them to take matters into their own hands, making vague allusion to "the people" for which they were working. With a declaration of rights in hand, the relationship between the people and their representatives was made clear and explicit, furnishing the National Assembly with a source of legitimacy that had been previously lacking.

Despite its conflicting claims and intentions, one thing was certain: the Ancien Régime was finished. The *monarchiens* headed by Mounier had claimed they sought only to "regenerate" the monarchy and restore balance to the kingdom. They pushed back against Sieyès and his allies in the assembly, but their position appeared to be diminishing as events took their course. The Rights of Man issued by the National Assembly placed nation above king and recognized French citizens rather than royal subjects. The revolution imagined in the spring committed to maintaining "the true principles of the monarchy" was not the revolution that was playing out by the fall of 1789. Sieyès and his faction foresaw a government that would significantly restrain monarchial power and subject the king to the "great body of citizens." Hatred of the aristocracy and a resolute conviction that "France is, and must be, a single whole" eclipsed moderate hopes of a *modus vivendi* between monarch and people. For Sieyès, this hope had been illusory from the start. "What sort of agreement could one hope for between the energy of the oppressed and the rage of the oppressor?" he asked.[83]

In the polarizing terms prescribed by Sieyès, the *monarchiens* acquired the dreaded epithet of "aristocrats," a group outside "the people," and hence estranged from the nation. Fearful of the crowd and the excesses of popular politics, the *monarchiens* sought a constitution that would preserve royal powers and provide a check on the absolute sovereignty of the people. For those drawing inspiration from Rousseau, however, the notion that a strong king could coexist with a sovereign people was anathema. In early September, the *monarchiens* were defeated when the National Assembly agreed to a constitution that would diminish executive power and provide for a single-chamber legislature expressing the general will of the nation. Mounier threw in the towel, resigned his deputyship and retired to Dauphiné. The revolution was no longer the revolution he and the monarchists had envisioned. It had been coopted, precluding any hope of a return to first principles.

Mounier had the liberty of resigning himself to inconsequence. Louis XVI, however, did not. As the meaning and consequence of France's revolution shifted, it had yet to be seen how the principle of monarchy would accommodate and coexist with the new sovereignty of the nation. In a community of equal citizens, the persistence of monarchy appeared archaic, if not unnatural.

Conclusion

The French and American revolutions ushered in the age of the modern citizen. They equally marked a transformative moment in prevailing understandings of "revolution" as traditional concepts of sovereignty and the state were reconfigured and made anew. "The people" and "the nation" offered new idioms for imagining social unity across former imperial spaces. They furnished collective sources of authority that replaced faltering regimes no longer believed capable of commanding loyalties or maintaining order. As tensions between center and periphery destabilized societies, vital questions relevant to social inclusion and the community came to the forefront of political protest. Appeals to popular sovereignty were not so much articulations of an emergent national consciousness as they were a reaction to the changing conditions within imperial polities as fiscal crises and the imposition of centralized government spurred political opponents into action. "The people" and "the nation" spoke to desires for social unity in the midst of these crises, and acquired a saliency once the social, economic and political tensions dividing the community no longer held out hope of resolution.

Consolidating these new communities of citizens required powerful acts of imagining. Writers and political actors like Paine and Sieyès played a key role in this respect as they participated in the creation of new social imaginaries that could command emotional attachments and loyalties. In their pamphlets, they outlined the contours of "America" and "France" and proceeded to fill these abstractions with new connotations and meanings that galvanized people into action. Words proved to be a powerful medium. They did not simply transmit ideas or broadcast Enlightenment concepts to the public. They actively constructed new concepts of space and identity that provided a framework for revolutionary politics. There could be no American independence without first having a concept of a sovereign American people, just as there could be no French Revolution without a concept of "the great body of citizens" and "single whole" from which sovereignty must emanate. Rather than a return to first principles, modern revolution amounted to an exercise in community building.

The sense of a shared experience was not lost on contemporaries as they partook in their mutual revolutionary experiments. Arriving in Paris as part of an American commission to France in 1789, Gouverneur Morris found "a strong resemblance" to his native country: "The Reverence for ancient Establishments gone, existing Forms shaken to the very Foundation, and a New Order of Things about to take Place in which even the very names, all former Institutions will be disregarded." A New York republican with conservative views on democracy, Morris believed that America had valuable lessons to impart to France as it underwent its own revolution. In Paris, he corresponded with the *monarchiens* and encouraged their platform of moderate royal government. Yet over the coming months, Morris grew skeptical. The French had "romantic ideas of government," he observed, which, "happily for America, we were cured of before it was too late." He was appalled by the lynching and massacres that occurred in the capital that July, leaving him to speculate on the character of the French people. "The French have not those manners which are suited to a free constitution," he concluded sullenly.[84] Could America teach anything to a people long accustomed to despotism? He no longer believed so.

As Americans watched the violence of the French Revolution unfold, some like Morris became aware of the distinctiveness of their own revolution, of an *American* revolution. France appeared to be on a different course, casting doubts as to whether the two nations were bound by universal ties of liberty and enlightened fraternity. The increasingly radical tenor of French revolutionaries was unmistakable. "In the new hemisphere, the brave inhabitants of Philadelphia have given the example of a people seizing back its liberty," declared one French newspaper; "France will give it to the rest of the globe."[85]

CHAPTER 2
LIBERTY, EQUALITY, FRATERNITY OR DEATH: RADICALIZING THE FRENCH REVOLUTION

The National Assembly may have dispensed with the "feudal barbarism" of the past in 1789, but it had not dispensed with monarchy. Louis XVI remained on the throne, a king stripped of law-making powers and constricted by a powerful legislature, but King of the French nonetheless. For certain monarchists within the government and court, this outcome was palatable, although not desirable. For Louis and his wife, the Austrian Archduchess Marie Antoinette, it remained a humiliation. Deputies constantly assured the public that monarch and people stood united and that the revolution would soon be brought to its successful conclusion. In order to make this arrangement viable, however, the former aristocracy would have to be won over to the regime. From the very start, this hope proved elusory.

Three days after the Bastille fell, Louis XVI's brother, the Comte d'Artois, fled the country. Establishing an émigré court abroad, Artois began organizing a counter-revolutionary movement in exile. He negotiated with the European monarchs, massed forces along the Rhineland border and prepared for war against the National Assembly. Throughout the summer and autumn, French aristocrats followed his lead, taking up residence across the continent and in foreign courts. Some 150,000 people fled France over the next three years, motivated by ideological hostility to the revolution or simply fear for their lives. The exodus had a powerful psychological impact on revolutionaries at home. Aristocratic enemies abroad posed a clear threat, prompting both real and imagined suspicions of foreign conspiracies and counter-revolutionary cabals.[1] The Genevan pastor and patriot Étienne Dumont noticed a perceptible difference when taking stock of the mood in the capital. "Paris is strangely altered from what it was. Once the theater of luxury and pleasure, it is now perpetually harassed with supposed plots and real insurrections."[2]

Government policies did nothing to alleviate the situation. To pay off the crippling state debt, the state nationalized royal and Church lands. The estimated value of Church properties was used to back a new paper currency, the *assignat*, with which the government intended to pay back its creditors. The plan proved disastrous. The currency rapidly depreciated, exacerbating the country's economic downturn and generating a fresh round of uprisings and riots. Clerics also denounced the measure, and howls from religious officials intensified the following summer when on July 12, 1790, the National Assembly issued a Civil Constitution for the clergy. The measure claimed broad powers over clerical institutions and made religious officials salaried employees of the state.

Of deeper concern were the stipulations requiring clerics to take a compulsive oath of allegiance to the state and laws dictating priests be elected by the people. For a great number of Catholic officials who looked to Rome as a source of authority, the law was anathema. Spurred into action, Catholic and royalist deputies convoked a meeting at a Capuchin monastery in Paris, and there drew up a manifesto declaring religion imperiled. Moderate- and low-level clerical officials had been inclined to support the revolution and participate in the National Assembly. The Capuchin manifesto now declared the revolution a war on Catholicism.

The backlash was immediate. Bishops in the National Assembly vehemently challenged the state's right to alter Church structures. Riots erupted when the state attempted to impose the Civil Constitution on the church of Saint-Sulpice in Paris. Refractory priests stirred up unrest in the provinces while in areas with Catholic majorities officials obstructed the application of state laws. Catholic factions sided with royalists and encouraged armed resistance that divided entire communities along ideological lines. From 1791 onward, a religious war simmered throughout the country. Those who refused to take the detested oath of allegiance fled the country, joining the émigré movement abroad and furnishing it with a new ideological basis. The counter-revolution became both royalist and Catholic.

The threat of counter-revolution aside, the National Assembly remained uncertain whether it could command the revolutionary impulses it had unleashed. Political protests and street marches were on the rise. In spite of the Bastille and the public lynchings that followed, most demonstrations were peaceful. Demonstrators drew upon traditions of religious processions or familiar forms of protest such as effigy burning and petitioning. In the politicized atmosphere of 1789, these conventions were harnessed to new political ends, but violence remained exceptional and was usually provoked when police and state authorities attempted to suppress protesters. The growing presence of women in these marches often had a moderating influence as authorities were less inclined to intervene forcefully. That autumn, marches staged by women's religious groups and market women occurred without incident in the capital, and the participants made their patriotism and support for the new government known as they brandished revolutionary symbols and blessed public officials.[3] Yet the peaceful nature of most protests that year did not mean the government had nothing to fear. Political demonstrations were giving ordinary people a greater sense of themselves both as political actors and as a political force that officials would be ill-advised to ignore.

At certain moments, demands revealed this new sense of empowerment sharply. In early October 1789, a crowd of women appeared outside the palace of Versailles. Their protest concerned bread shortages in Paris but soon managed to draw in members of the Parisian National Guard who proceeded to raid the municipal armory and haul a large cannon on the trek to Versailles with the women in the lead. The crowd disrupted the legislative session, and the National Guardsmen exchanged fire with the royal bodyguards. Over the next twenty-four hours, the National Guard let it be known that the royal family would be returning with them to Paris. It was not a request. Louis XVI had little choice in the matter. If not for the intervention of the National Guard commander—Gilbert du Mortier, Marquis de Lafayette—the day may have ended in further bloodshed.

Lafayette was well acquainted with the fury of the mob. A veteran of the American war, he had assumed command of the National Guard in 1789, no easy task as royal authority crumbled. The violence of Parisian crowds needed to be curtailed, strict discipline in the National Guard enforced, order maintained and food supplies well stocked to stave off riots. He was equally determined to steer the political situation as the National Assembly debated the new form of government to be adopted. With the aid of Thomas Jefferson, an old American confrère then in Paris, Lafayette contributed drafts to the Rights of Man and forged alliances with moderates favorable to a constitutional monarchy. Yet the specter of "the people" perennially loomed over the National Assembly, a fact Lafayette never ignored.

Days after the Versailles fiasco and the recalling of the royal family back to Paris, the assembly passed a law on pain of death outlawing "unofficial" demonstrations. The law was symptomatic of a larger problem confronting revolutionaries. The revolution had declared the sovereignty of the nation, but how was the nation to be understood? Did sovereignty lie with the people who constituted the nation or with their representatives sitting in the National Assembly? Questions of how to square representative government with the sovereign collective body would remain a constant problem, one which would ultimately propel the French Revolution on a radical and self-destructive path.[4]

Making Sovereignty Real

With the breakdown of royal authority, a new era of French journalism was born. Censorship could no longer be enforced and the French had an insatiable hunger for news. Editors and writers filled this need. Newspapers like the Comte de Mirabeau's *États généraux* or the *Patriote Français* run by Jacques-Pierre Brissot printed accounts of the Estates General proceedings to keep the general public informed. Official permission to publish was rarely sought. As Brissot contended in no uncertain terms, liberty of the press was a "natural right" and required no authorization.[5] A score of *papiers-nouvelles* burst onto the scene. During the first year of the revolution alone, nearly 200 newspapers appeared, with a growing number catering to a provincial readership.[6] Conventional and international journals had previously existed in France, although they were typically expensive and written for elite audiences. Relatively cheap and written in plain language, the *papiers-nouvelles* were aimed at non-elites and actively engaged with the politics of the day. Sieyès's victory over the *monarchiens* certainly owed a debt to the new journalism and the editors who backed his camp. Their relentless barrage against "aristocrats" had helped turn opinion against the monarchists, demonstrating the potential of newspapers to mobilize and educate a broad base.

Given the expanding number of newspapers in France, competition for readers was fierce. To attract readers, editors claimed not only to keep the public informed, but also to serve as a veritable organ for the voice of the people.[7] Titles of papers were telling in this respect, with mastheads such as *l'Ami du Peuple, Oratuer du peuple* or *l'Ami des citoyens* emblazoned across their covers. Journalists claimed an authority to speak for the general interest and, through it, the people's revolution. More radical papers branded themselves guardians of the public good and sentinels on the watch for aristocratic plots. While deputies invoked "the people" in the chambers of the National Assembly to push their demands upon the royal court, journalists challenged their claims to be the true representatives of the people's interests, insisting that they, rather than the deputies, constituted the authentic voice of the populace. "I am the anger, the just anger of the people," explained Jean-Paul Marat, editor of the popular *l'Ami du Peuple*. "That is why they listen to me and believe in me."[8] Marat's posturing as a "friend of the people" and his journalistic audacity earned him a reputation as the "Rousseau of the gutter," a moniker indicative of the brand of populist radicalism that suffused revolutionary periodicals. In the pages of gazettes, "the people" acquired a presence in public and political life. Urban mobs and peasant uprisings were motivated by different social grievances and had distinct aims. Journalists brought these phenomena together within a common narrative that was broadcasted to readers and that represented "the people" as an agent of revolutionary politics and a collective source of sovereignty.

While deputies wrestled with questions of how to prevent the sporadic unrest that threatened to destabilize the country, radical journalists reveled in it. They pressed popular violence into service, transforming mobs and lynchings into demonstrations of political agency. "The people rise up only when it is pushed to despair by tyranny … and its vengeance is always just in its principle," implored Marat.[9] Elysée Loustalot, a young lawyer turned journalist, glorified the violence of the mob in his paper *Révolutions de Paris*, hailing it as the "terrible vengeance of a justly angered people." When the Parisian crowd massacred Foullon and paraded around the city with his head on a pike, Loustalot used the occasion to remind the people of their new empowerment, claiming, "Frenchmen, you exterminate tyrants!"[10] In their writings, radical journalists painted mob violence and peasant rebellions as manifestations of a new authority. The abstract "people" invoked by the deputies took on a frightening reality in the revolutionary press. Readers vicariously participated in these dramatic events, sharing in the triumphs and celebrations of freedom with their fellow patriots on a daily basis. If violence and street upheavals were suggestive of a chronic lack of sovereign authority, in the page of the *papiers-nouvelles* sovereignty was being reconstructed and made real for a wide segment of the population.

Newspapers provided the medium for collectively imagining new forms of sovereignty, but the environment in which newspapers were read was also significant. The blossoming of print culture after 1789 was matched with a rise in club meetings during the first year of the French Revolution. Clubs were one of the primary places where newspapers were read and discussed. Even the most popular papers had relatively limited print runs by contemporary standards. However, they reached broader audiences through the clubs which made papers available to members.[11] Clubs quickly became centers for news and political debates, replacing the elite reading salons and *chambres littéraires* that had grown up over the eighteenth century. After 1789, newly minted citizens took to gathering at cafés, in tennis courts, chapels and public buildings. The new preoccupation with politics lent itself to forms of sociability that were quite distinct from the Enlightenment era debating and reading societies, and clubs gave citizens a place to discuss current issues and participate in the revolution. As one historian has claimed, clubs provided an "alternative political sphere" suited to the immediacy and engagement that a revolutionary political culture demanded.[12]

The number of clubs established after 1789 spoke to the multiplicity of interests that the revolution encompassed. Political elites and moderates such as Lafayette, Sieyès and Brissot gravitated toward the Paris-based *Société de 1789*, which promised to "defend and propagate the principles of the constitution." British and American expatriates preferred the Society of the Rights of Man that met twice weekly at White's Hotel in the Passage des Petits Pères to celebrate the French Revolution, sing patriotic songs and discuss the latest international events. The Dutch feminist Etta Palm d'Aelders organized the first women's club in Paris, the Conféderation des Amies de la Vérité, which was followed by the more politically minded Société des Républicaines Révolutionnaires committed to obtaining political rights for women. Clubs reflected a diverse range of interests, and it was not uncommon that participants held multiple memberships. Be that as it may, the mania for clubs was initially an elite enterprise. Club dues, while varying, were often far beyond the means of average workers and many limited membership exclusively to active citizens.

It was not long, however, before the democratizing impulses of the revolution took hold. Over the coming year, locally based *sociétés populaires* proliferated and opened up politics to a broader section of French society. Passive citizens denied the vote enrolled in organizations that proudly branded themselves as "the people's clubs." With public meetings, elected memberships and relatively low monthly dues, they drew in a sufficient number of trade workers and day laborers—groups identified as the *sans-culottes*—in addition to the cadre of lawyers and professionals. The Cordelier Club in Paris became a bastion of *sans-culotte* radicalism and a bugbear of the Parisian municipal government alert to popular meetings that might descend into anarchy at any moment. Contrary to elite organizations, the *sociétés populaires* fashioned themselves as vehicles for public instruction and "schools of patriotism" working to integrate citizens into political life.[13] They organized public ceremonies and banquets in which members took solemn oaths before crowds, brandished revolutionary cockades and planted liberty trees in demonstrations of fraternal unity. Whether exclusive or popular, the club movement did nurture a new type of political sociability and culture in which people addressed one another as "citizen," exchanged news and partook in a mutual patriotic fervor. Association transformed "the people" from an imaginary construction into a social reality; and through the practices of debate, electing members and participation, the people were transformed into citizens.

The formation of clubs paralleled the changes wrought by the state. During its first year in power, the National Assembly ushered in a system of representative government that would establish a framework for the social "regeneration" promised by the revolution. In late 1789, new electoral laws stripped away the old statist and feudal institutions of the Ancien Régime, creating autonomous municipal institutions that formally put an end to the reign of the seigneurs and curés at the local level. Power was transferred to all citizens who could pay the six livres tax necessary to vote, a qualification that relegated most day laborers to "passive" citizens without a political voice. Despite its limitations, the legislation constituted a major conquest of the revolution, and the groundswell of patriotism that accompanied elections indicated as much. In towns and villages across the kingdom, patriots staged dozens of "festivals of federation," public ceremonies demonstrating the new unity between province and nation and between citizens and the national community. National Guardsmen and public officials gathered in town squares and spoke of the brotherly bonds uniting fellow citizens. Local clubs came out for the celebrations, singing patriotic songs and vowing to live free or die.[14]

The federation movement culminated in a large celebration staged in Paris to commemorate the anniversary of the Bastille. A massive crowd of 250,000 people gathered on the Champ de Mars to watch the parade of National Guardsmen, each unit representative of a different province marching in unison with their national brothers. Deputies from the National Assembly greeted Louis XVI as equals before the Altar of the Fatherland erected in the center of the park as *Fédérés* waved banners with revolutionary slogans and declared their allegiance to Nation, Law and King. The anthemic refrains of *Ça Ira*, already a popular *chant* sung among patriots, were intoned by citizens as an expression of revolutionary fraternity. On the Altar of the Fatherland, Louis XVI declared his loyalty to the nation and its laws, vowing to protect and uphold the constitution. The religious symbolism could not be mistaken by onlookers, nor could the sermonic language and religious rites being performed. Yet the carefully choreographed Fête de la Fédération was not celebrating the sovereignty of God. It symbolized the sovereignty of man and the nation announced by the revolution. The declarations of patriotism and loyalty that reverberated across the Champ de Mars embodied the "civic religion" envisaged by Rousseau, a cult of the nation befitting a free and sovereign people.[15]

From its inception, the French Revolution venerated the nation as "the sacred center of political life."[16] The success of the revolution was dependent upon the extent to which the new center of sovereign authority could be made real and meaningful following the collapse of the absolutist system. Celebrations like the Fête de la Fédération exhibited the regenerative force of the revolution as the French people reclaimed their liberties after centuries of monarchial despotism. Yet in the varied pronouncements of fraternal comradery, citizens were not reclaiming the "ancient" liberties of a feudal order. They were embarking on a wholly different project of regeneration: the creation of a new community and new state that aspired to invest a divided and fragmented society with a new life.[17]

For Sieyès, one of the leading architects of the early French Revolution, it was ultimately the creation of a rationally ordered society that would regenerate France, and in 1791 he would have the opportunity to put his conviction into practice.[18] That year, the National Assembly took aim at one of the remaining vestiges of the Ancien Régime: the provincial estates. Sovereignty, according to the constitution, was "single, indivisible, inalienable and imprescriptible." It belonged to the nation and to the nation alone. This concept of sovereignty was difficult to align with the old patchwork of medieval provinces. With their particular laws, customs and even dialects, the provinces appeared "foreign" enclaves. The French people lived in isolated tribes "like savages," the revolutionary Louis Antoine de Saint-Just criticized. They knew nothing of the common interests or affections that bound a community of citizens.[19] National sovereignty meant equality and an end to the corporatism tolerated under the old regime.[20] The collage of provincial estates had to be "sacrificed for the intimate union of all parts of the realm," as the decree claimed.[21] Executing this measure, Sieyès proposed a simplified administrative structure based upon reason and egalitarian principles. Eighty-three departments of approximately equal size were carved out of the thirty-four provincial estates. These departments were then subdivided into municipal communes to create a uniform administrative and legal structure governed by common law. In their feverish ambition to eradicate social divisions and the traces of the old regime, cultural difference was subordinated to political unity. With the provinces effaced, the French people now possessed a common unity as French nationals. Henceforth, all belonged to the national community.[22]

For Camille Desmoulins, this social remodeling of the kingdom was nothing short of monumental. "Having just been regenerated by the National Assembly, we are no longer from Chartres or from Monthléri, we are no longer from Picardy or Brittany, we are no longer from Aix or from Arras, we are all French, all brothers," he wrote.[23] The deputy Jean-Paul Rabaut de Saint-Etienne expressed similar admiration for the work of the National Assembly, insisting that with the elimination of the provinces "there is no longer a diversity of nations in the kingdom; there are only the French."[24] The reality, of course, was quite different. Regional identities persisted and the strict geometric precision acclaimed by Sieyès in mapping the new department did not materialize as planned.[25] Nonetheless, the implications of these measures were revealing. Efforts to remake people and society had now become the *raison d'être* of a revolutionary project that far exceeded ideas of reform or mere political restructuring. The French Revolution was, in essence, becoming revolutionary in action as well as speech.

The Rights of Man had declared the nation sovereign; yet the revolution brought this sovereign entity into existence. Herein lay the paradox. As the French Revolution played out, politics and political rhetoric were coming to play a crucial role in defining the new terms of revolutionary society. "The People" and "The Nation" were the vital center of the revolution. They were powerful ideas that lent authority to claims and actions. Yet their power extended only in so far as they were meaningful concepts that could mobilize individuals and command allegiances. The revolution was the crucible in which these new authoritative concepts were manufactured and made real.

The Rise of the Jacobins

Of the many clubs that grew up in France after 1789, one club in particular commanded special attention. Forming in the first days of the Estates General, it took the title of the *Société des Amis de la Constitution*. It was, however, to be known popularly as the Jacobin

Club, taking its name from the old convent where it met on the rue Saint Honoré in Paris. Despite its Parisian origins, the group quickly began affiliating with other like-minded organizations across the nation, forming a "holy coalition" that would protect the French constitution and the people's revolution. The Jacobin network soon cut across every part of the country, planting the roots of a "great tree," as Desmoulins claimed. In its organizational tactics and overtly political disposition, the Jacobin Club resembled the revolution's first political party, although members would have hardly described it as such. Yet with ties to other branches across the kingdom, the Jacobins proved able to mobilize its members unlike other organizations, ensuring that events occurring in the capital would have a ripple effect throughout the country. In all but name, the Jacobins constituted a national party, one capable of exercising an imposing influence on politics.[26]

In addition to reading newspapers and keeping citizens informed, Jacobin meetings were packed with energized debates and hyperbolic rhetoric that drew spectators. They brought this dynamism with them into the National Assembly where their deputies gave passionate speeches defending the values of the revolution as they understood them. Liberty, Equality and Fraternity: these were the core values of the revolution, the provincial barrister and Jacobin deputy Maximilien Robespierre informed his cohorts.[27] Taking this mantra to heart, he criticized the tax qualifications that barred citizens from political office and subverted true equality. "Each individual has the right to participate in making the law which governs him," declared Robespierre. "If not, it is not true that all men are equal in rights, that every man is a citizen."[28] In his adoration for nation and equality, Robespierre believed that revolutionaries had an obligation to actualize the principles announced in 1789. "Let us regenerate public mores, without which there is no freedom. ... Let us render all men equal under impartial laws dictated by justice and humanity. ... Let us love only the fatherland and virtue."[29] This pronounced Rousseauvian ideology was a hallmark of Jacobin discourse. One speaker at a meeting in Lyon professed: "We owe everything to Rousseau and the *Social Contract*. This immortal work prepared the Revolution and assures its success." Jacobins similarly appealed to the principle of equality when it came to the National Guard, insisting that every citizen should be able to participate in defending the revolution. As defenders of the revolution, they consistently warned of the nefarious threats that abounded, obsessing over clerical and émigré plots. In the Vendée where Catholic resistance was particularly prominent, clubs set up a *société ambulante* that went from town to town combatting clerical "fanaticism."[30]

Such zeal and patriotism built up fervent support at the local level. Outside of the assembly, the clubs exercised an influence that proved troublesome for the municipalities. Officials who did not agree with them were accused of harboring "counter-revolutionary" tendencies in Jacobin newspapers. The clubs put forward militant candidates in local elections and mobilized support behind them. They drafted petitions, used the press to browbeat opponents and exerted extra-parliamentary pressures where they could. The Jacobins became a political force that moderates and officials did not hesitate to deem a "faction," and an invidious, meddlesome one at that. Aware of the dangers the clubs posed, the government moved to defang them. In September of 1791, the Le Chapelier laws

Figure 1 Maximilien Robespierre © The British Library Board.

placed restrictions on club meetings and forbade them from participating collectively in public festivities or interfering with the legal administration of the kingdom in any way. Clubs ignored these proscriptions, indicating the mounting tensions between the sovereign "people" and the government.

For all the agitation generated by the clubs, however, it was the monarchy that ultimately proved the volatile factor. On the night of June 20, 1791, the royal family fled Paris. No longer able to uphold the pretense of being a constitutional monarch and fearful for the safety of his family, Louis XVI decided to escape across the Belgian border and establish contact with the royalist émigré leadership. The plan failed. The king was recognized, arrested at Varennes and hauled back to Paris as a political prisoner. In the wake of the abortive escape, anti-royalist sentiment surged. Since 1789, a core group of moderates congregating around Lafayette and the Eighty-Niners had been committed to realizing a constitutional monarchy that would restrain popular participation. They now found themselves in a perilous situation thrust between an unpredictable monarch and a small but vocal assemblage of republicans reviling the monarch as a traitor and threat to his people. Unwilling to placate the radicals, the assembly threw in its lot with the king. On July 16, they formally exonerated Louis XVI for his alleged treason. In response, radicals goaded by the leaders of the Cordeliers Club staged a massive demonstration on the Champ de Mars. Calls for a republic were heard, and signatures were collected on a petition demanding the abolition of the monarchy. Under pressure to silence the protestors, Lafayette sent in the National Guard, which dispersed the crowd with musket fire. In the wake of this bloodshed, the government proceeded to arrest the radical leadership and crack down on the clubs.

Over the next year, those supporting the monarchy found their situation increasingly precarious. The king's flight to Varennes had heightened counter-revolutionary suspicions. Radicals demanded punitive laws against émigrés and defiant priests. Louis steadfastly vetoed all such measures, reducing the government to inaction.[31] Incised by such obstinacy, a wing within the Jacobins intended to make the king show his true colors. Taking the lead was Brissot, recently elected to the Assembly on the strength of his fear-mongering rhetoric. An admirer of the American Revolution and a self-identified "patriot," Brissot loathed the radicalism emanating from Paris and the *sans-culottes*. He was no stranger to the barbed attacks of these *enragés* constantly riled up by slanderous journalists and splenetic politicians and then set loose like a pack of wild dogs. Within his own camp, Brissot agonized over what he perceived to be a waning commitment to the revolutionary cause. He was especially alarmed by recent overtures on the part of his more "moderate" colleagues to scale back their support for democratic rights and ally with the government. The revolutionary élan was in need of being reinvigorated, Brissot wagered. The revolution faced internal and external threats, and should patriotism diminish the forces of counter-revolution would prevail. In his opinion, war was the necessary corrective, a great national conflict capable of unleashing the nation's patriotic energies and rallying the people to a sacred cause.

In late 1791, Brissot and his allies, collectively known as the Girondins, began beating the war drum. There would be no security until the foreign threats were dispersed, they urged. The king needed to order a preemptive strike to save the revolution from its enemies, dispelling any suspicions of his counter-revolutionary leanings. Yet the calls of *la patrie en danger* ran deeper than national defense or rehabilitating the monarchy. According to Brissot, national defense would nurture and sustain a vibrant patriotism. Each individual would become a soldier and, in turn, learn the values of self-sacrifice and virtue essential to citizenship. Underpinning this classical ideal of the citizen-soldier was a novel brand of revolutionary militarism.[32] Revolution demanded war, a totalizing war that would engage the entire community and regenerate it through aggression. The patriotic defense of homeland went beyond the limits of a "defensive" war properly understood. In their speeches, the Girondins mixed nationalist zeal with messianic fervor, arguing France was called upon to spread its revolution across Europe and the world. In Brissot's opinion, the French Revolution was "the spark" that would "unite all nations" and destroy all tyrants.[33]

This revolutionary messianism echoed the patriotic cosmopolitanism growing since the American Revolution. However, it infused it with a militant revolutionary nationalism that ascribed a special place to the French Revolution and its values. The French Revolution was, the Girondins affirmed, a world revolution heralding universal emancipation. Robespierre, an unyielding rival of Brissot, scoffed at this revolutionary adventurism. "Nobody takes kindly to armed missionaries," he retorted, writing off the idea of a French-led European upheaval as hopelessly idealistic.[34] Ever fearful of counter-revolution, Robespierre admonished staying focused on the task at hand. It was the

Figure 2 Illustration of a Tricolor and Musket © The British Library Board.

people's war against their sovereign, not foreign war, that would safeguard the conquests of 1789. A continental war would pave the way for counter-revolutionary agitation and royal dictatorship. Jacobin hawks were no better than the counter-revolutionaries, in his view. "It is the war of the enemies of the French Revolution against the French Revolution," Robespierre declared.[35] These disagreements exposed the deep schisms running through the Jacobin camp just as much as it did the Manichean worldview of Jacobin ideologues.

Robespierre's analysis proved accurate. The royal court exploited the hawks to whip up enthusiasm for a war France could not win, practically inviting a counter-revolutionary invasion. Blind to these machinations, the Girondins began forming Foreign Legions and preparing for a French occupation of the Rhineland. On April 20, France declared war on Austria, and as expected the war effort floundered. Aristocratic emigration had thinned the ranks of the French officer corps and deprived the army of its top generals. Battalions were staffed with poorly trained volunteers prone to insubordination and mutiny. By August, Austrian troops had succeeded in routing French forces and were pushing across the French border. Only Verdun stood between the Austrian military and Paris, portending a full-scale invasion of the capital. A wave of panic seized Paris, and the king's persistent veto on measures believed essential to national defense only reinforced radical distrust of the monarchy.

With the government seemingly paralyzed in the midst of crisis, radical groups began enforcing their own policies in the name of defense and justice. For two years, the radical press had fed readers a steady diet of stories relating to aristocratic atrocities and sinister plots. With the country under attack, vigilante militias across the kingdom formed to root out these "enemies of the people," chiefly priests and unpopular local officials. The participation of National Guard units in the slaughter revealed the government's loss of control as the situation deteriorated. Catholics and royalists armed themselves against *enragé* hostility, fueling violence. Radicals killed hundreds of potential counter-revolutionaries, torched villages and called for the establishment of a republic. Paris in particular was a stronghold of republican radicalism. Jérôme Pétion, mayor of Pairs, was a left-wing Jacobin. Radicals had infiltrated the communal government and National Guard, while the local Sections (neighborhood councils) were firmly in the hands of the *sans-culottes*. As authority eroded, these bodies assumed control and led the calls for summary justice and a republic. By comparison, leading Jacobin figures like Robespierre were slow to take up the radical republican cause.

The government's refusal to consent to a republic marked the beginning of the end. On August 10, the Sections and National Guard launched an insurrection, massacring the king's guards outside the Tuileries Palace. For two years, monarchists had held out hope of reconciling royalty with national sovereignty. This fiction had run its course. With no other options available, the assembly declared the king's constitutional functions suspended and scheduled elections for a new National Convention. Since 1789, the assembly had failed to lay claim to the sovereignty engendered by the revolution. If "The Nation" and "The People" were a single community with a single will, who or what spoke for this community? This question was now being answered. In August, popular sovereignty was not being acted out in the assembly chambers but on the streets. A second French Revolution was underway, and in the momentary vacuum of power "the people" asserted themselves.

The Commune of Paris immediately began rounding up all suspected counter-revolutionaries. Makeshift jails quickly filled with priests, royal guards and social elites. In this frenetic atmosphere, the Sections functioned as instruments of *sans-culotte* fury, transforming themselves into death squads and revolutionary tribunals. Local public safety organizations doled out summary justice while impromptu committees demanded the execution of all counter-revolutionary prisoners. The Paris Commune debated possible courses of action, considering whether to hold individual trials or exonerate those accused of petty crimes. As they deliberated, however, others took action. On September 2, an armed group broke into the Carmelite monastery and killed over 100 priests detained on the premises. A general slaughter followed in all the jails during the next three days. In total, the September Massacres claimed 1,400 lives, a gruesome prelude to the political violence ahead.

The Universal Republic

On September 21, 1792, the newly elected National Convention unanimously voted for the abolition of the monarchy. France was declared a republic, "one and indivisible." The unity of the new-born republic was symbolically affirmed that January when Louis XVI was put on trial, found guilty of treason and sentenced to death. Traditionally, the call upon the monarch's death was "The king is dead. Long live the king." Yet on the January morning when Louis XVI was executed before a crowd of his former subjects, the call that rang out was "The king is dead. *Vive la nation!*" In a clear demonstration of republican sovereignty, Louis XVI was put to death by the national community.

Yet the bloodletting failed to unify the community. Factionalism beset the Convention as the Girondins and radicals sparred off against one another. By early 1793, France was at war with all the major European powers. Chronic food shortages and the wartime economy exacerbated social and regional tensions, thrusting the republic into a civil war that tore the country apart. The republican state was created in the midst of war and social conflict, and its revolutionary program would be shaped by struggles to combat counter-revolution from abroad and within.[36] The polarizing forces unleashed by social dissolution and conflict were the backdrop for the revolution, never the revolution itself. Nation and People—the two dominant idioms of the French Revolution— underscored the universal and syncretic aspirations of revolutionaries as they attempted to reconstruct a shattered society. The language and values of the revolution favored community, not conflict. Conflict existed, but it was the evil that had to be combatted.[37] These communitarian impulses radicalized ideologies as revolutionaries attempted to secure the republic "one and indivisible."

The Enlightenment had encouraged secular universalism, and revolutionaries built upon this intellectual inheritance. The patriot cause of the 1780s made frequent appeals to cosmopolitan internationalism and the common bond linking all those committed to liberty and natural rights. It reconfigured the former Republic of Letters into what George Washington described as "the great republic of humanity at large."[38] From the beginning, French revolutionaries identified with the international patriotic movement, and indeed imagined the French Revolution in these terms. In 1790, a deputation of foreigners composed of Europeans, Americans and subjects of the Ottoman Empire appeared before the National Assembly to eulogize the new era of man. Dressed in oriental robes, the Palestinian Al-Kahin Diyunysius Shawish, soon to be known as the "Arab Jacobin," was held up as an example of the revolution's international horizon.[39] Citizen Shawish was one of many "world citizens" who would bolster claims of universal solidarity and brotherhood. For all its nationalist pageantry, the Fête de la Fédération featured international delegations and American flags draped alongside the French

Tricolor. In the festivities, the British novelist Helen Maria Williams did not see a celebration of the French nation. "It was man reclaiming and establishing the most noble of rights," she wrote, "and all it required was a simple sentiment of humanity to become in that moment a citizen of the world."[40]

French politics were never divorced from the *fête cosmopolite*. Upon the declaration of the Rights of Man, the Prussian-born nobleman Anacharsis Cloots abandoned his titles and moved to Paris to take up the cause of cosmopolitan internationalism in the new "tribune of the world." Cloots identified with neither Prussia nor France, but instead professed allegiance to the "Great Nation" of humanity. "Emancipated humanity will one day imitate nature, which knows no strangers, and wisdom will reign on the two hemispheres within the Republic of United Individuals," he claimed.[41] An inveterate cosmopolitan, Cloots would assist in internationalizing the French Revolution through his speeches and persistent lobbying, and his efforts paid off. With the founding of the republic, French citizenship was extended to eighteen prominent patriots of foreign countries, including Cloots and Thomas Paine, both of whom took up positions as deputies in the National Convention.

Like Cloots, Paine placed himself in the service of the French Revolution. As the paladin of the American cause, Paine had performed a critical role in creating the intellectual conditions for independence and later locating the American experience within the framework of evolving currents of revolutionary internationalism. His strident defense of the French Revolution in his book *The Rights of Man* (1791) would be no different as he took on the critics of the revolution with a polemical ferocity. "[In] France we see a revolution generated in the rational contemplation of the rights of man …," Paine argued. "Natural rights are those which pertain to man in right of his existence."[42] Paine instructed readers to see the French Revolution as a national event with global consequences, lauding it as a testament to universal human reason prizing republican virtue over the "folly" of monarchy. "The characters of men are forming, as is always the case in Revolutions," he maintained, and within this revolutionary transformation was the germ of a new world extending beyond France or even Europe. The reign of universal reason was dawning, portending a revolution in men's minds that defied national boundaries. "Revolutions on the broad basis of national sovereignty and Government by representation are making their way in Europe. … It is an age of Revolutions in which everything may be looked for."[43]

Paine's *Rights of Man* resonated with European and Atlantic readers, becoming a veritable Bible of the patriot cause. In towns and cities across America, patriotic clubs and associations celebrated the French Revolution and sang revolutionary songs. "The Rights of Man shall become the supreme law of every land, and their separate fraternities be absorbed in one great Democratic society comprehending the human race," proclaimed one speaker at a Philadelphia civic dinner in 1794.[44] Through the cosmopolitan narrative of world revolution, Enlightenment rights talk was evolving from a language of natural right to one of universal and human rights.[45] By the early 1790s, France was imagined as the new center of the patriot community and the hearth of cosmopolitan fraternity. "She has addressed herself to the great principles of reason which are common to all men …"

the American poet and diplomat Joel Barlow wrote. "[Her revolution] teaches the people of all countries to regard each other as friends and fellow citizens of the world."[46] Cloots was no less commending: "People everywhere are shaken and a secret voice tells them to make common cause with France."[47]

Beneath the surface of the *fête cosmopolite*, however, lay the ugly realities of war and international conflict, and the two were not necessarily inseparable. Cloots had joined the Girondins in whipping up the war fever of 1791. Revolutionary universalism may have presented an irenic vision of a regenerated world, but it never fully rejected war and conquest in achieving this vision. In urging his cohorts to spread the French Revolution to Belgium and Germany, Cloots employed the language of conquest. "Twelve new squares will be added to the eighty-three squares of the French chessboard," he promised. He even nominated himself to head the German branch of the Foreign Legions created in 1792 to "revolutionize" the Rhineland.[48] The community envisaged by patriots like Cloots and Brissot imagined a universal republic open to all, but one nonetheless shaped in the image of France. *La patrie en danger* became the watchword of the war party just as *la république universelle* became the credo of cosmopolitans. These were two sides of the same coin. Through appeals to global fraternity and universal rights, revolutionaries sought to incite patriotic revolts abroad and attract defenders.[49] The patriot community was, ultimately, one shaped by universal values against its enemies.

Cosmopolitan universalism exercised a profound influence on revolutionary thinkers. It dictated that anyone committed to the cause of liberty could belong to the French republic. French citizenship was, in essence, world citizenship. However, this dictum inevitably raised questions regarding national sovereignty and allegiances that unsettled many Jacobins. Taking the floor in 1793, Robespierre dug into Cloots, accusing the Prussian of preferring to be a "citizen of the world" rather than a "French citizen." Vigilant against counter-revolution from abroad, radicals looked askance at the ominous "foreign party" that appeared to be hijacking the revolution.[50] Cloots was shut out of the Jacobin Club in late 1793 and accused of fomenting foreign plots. Radicals mocked Paine in the Convention for his poorly spoken French, eventually arresting and imprisoning him on suspicion of treason.

The heightened air of mistrust was reflective of the dire political situation by 1793. From the outset, the Convention faced challenges from the Paris Commune and Sections, strongholds of *sans-culotte* radicalism that continually pressed themselves on the national government. *Enragés* held meetings and mobilized workers, threatening revolt when the government did not heed their suggestions or petitions. Robespierre and his allies pandered to the Parisian radicals, seeing them as a potential base of support against their rivals. The Girondins, however, were tired of the undue influence enjoyed by the *sans-culottes* and had every intention of subordinating Paris to the will of the National Convention. "The people" would obey their government. In the summer of 1793, these tensions reached a head when the radicals demanded a purge of the Convention and the arrest of all "counter-revolutionary" Girondins. Brissot and others immediately fled the capital for the provinces. From there, they intended to organize resistance and wage war against Parisian radicalism.[51]

Revolutionary Europe

The Girondin rebellion occurred simultaneously with armed uprisings in the countryside that spring and summer. Anticlericalism divided rural France, where pockets of Catholic and royal support remained strong. The revolution had promised much, but for many peasants the changes appeared negligible. In some cases, the end of local tax codes led to higher taxes while in many regions landowners simply incorporated the abolished tithes and feudal dues into existing lease agreements.[52] With the end of local power structures, peasants were forced to consent to the new urban authorities that ruled them, and many were averse to do so. In March, the government issued demands for men and resources to fight the war. Communities in the south and west furthest from Paris and the warfront were reluctant to turn over animals, crops and their sons to the state. When the government moved to enforce the decree, the Vendée region erupted in armed resistance, soon to be followed by a royalist-led *chouannerie* in Brittany. Guerilla bands of peasants went from town to town killing republican officials and National Guardsmen. The Convention retaliated in kind, meting out death sentences to rebels and devastating whole regions.[53]

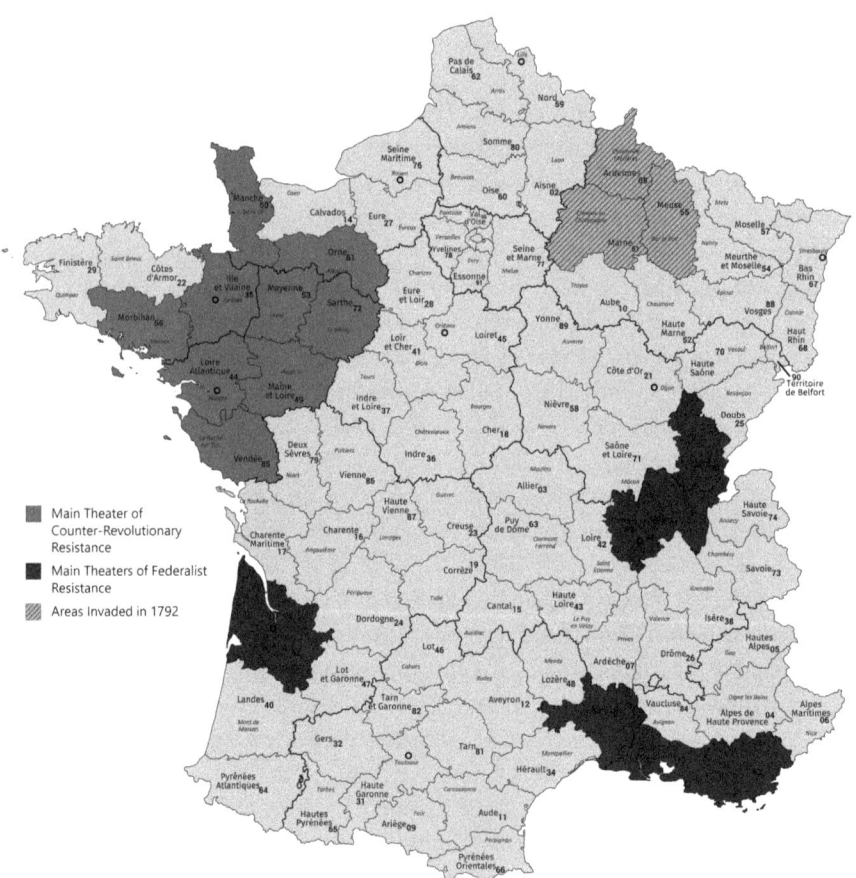

Map 1 France during the French Revolution.

Liberty, Equality, Fraternity or Death

Figure 3 Jean-Paul Marat © The British Library Board.

The republican government faced a grim situation in 1793 as the revolution disintegrating into civil war. Suspicions of internal counter-revolutionary plots appeared fully vindicated as the south-west rebelled. Nor was Paris necessarily insulated from the chaos. That July, the radical journalist and Jacobin spokesman Jean-Paul Marat was at home when a young woman appeared at his door claiming to possess intelligence on the Girondin rebels. Let into the apartment, she removed a dagger and plunged it into Marat's chest, killing him instantly. During the interrogation, it was learned that the young woman was a Girondin sympathizer, adding another layer to the counter-revolutionary plot that had now claimed one of the top Jacobin leaders. Marat was on his way to becoming a martyr of the revolutionary cause, and following the assassination the *sans-culottes* howled for blood. The counter-revolution had just struck in the heart of Paris, demanding a strong response.

As the specter of instability loomed, the government resorted to forceful measures. In April, a Committee of Public Safety was created to manage the republic and war effort. Revolutionaries-on-mission were dispatched to the departments to enforce the laws of the state and root out subversive elements. Section members set up local surveillance committees that proceeded to arrest suspect citizens and monitor the press for any deviant opinions. Robespierre and the Jacobins led the initiative as they clamped down on the institutions of government. The republic was fast becoming a radical dictatorship. To fight the counter-revolution, extreme measures were endorsed in the name of national security. That September, a Jacobin proclamation outlined the new direction republican politics was to take, calling for a campaign of terror against the enemies of the people.

"Legislators, place Terror on the order of the day!" it read. "Let us be in revolution, because everywhere counter-revolution is being woven by the enemies."[54]

Between September 1793 and July 1794, the revolutionary dictatorship authorized the execution of more than 16,000 political enemies, with an additional 25,000 put to death in summary executions throughout the country. First on the list was the Girondin leadership, who were eliminated in a mass execution. Government purges followed. In theory, France was a republic. A constitution was issued guaranteeing universal manhood suffrage and equality before the law. Yet these democratic principles were immediately suspended as Robespierre and the Committee of Public Safety set up a "revolutionary government" to fight the war and protect the republic. State-sponsored terrorism became the order of the day, resulting in military and political campaigns of extermination throughout the country. Radical groups were not spared in these massacres either. Leaders like the journalist Jacques Hébert who commanded authority among the *sans-culottes* ran afoul of the government when his efforts to mobilize workers and artisans challenged Jacobin control in the spring of 1794.[55] The execution of Hébert and his followers testified to the extensive nature of terror as well as the sheer malleability of categories like "enemy" and "counter-revolutionary" employed by the state.

Historians have long been divided on the causes of the political violence and state terror that burst forth in 1793. Those taking note of the war and ideological conflicts that split the republic have favored explanations arguing that invasion and fears of counter-revolution drove radicalization.[56] On the opposite side, historians have insisted that terror was inherent in revolutionary ideology and political culture from the start. Taking their cue from Rousseau, French revolutionaries emphasized themes of unanimity and unitary public authority, laying the groundwork for a totalitarian ideology that could only see descent and disagreement as a threat to republican unity and hence counter-revolutionary.[57] In 1789, Sieyès had criticized the aristocracy as "foreigners" within the nation. The leap from "foreigner" to "enemy" was seamless as foreign invasion and infighting tore the republic apart. The pathologies of French republican democracy sprang from Enlightenment principles of equality and reason. Yet in the context of war and civil strife, these principles translated into the fullest expression of a revolutionary ideology inclined toward extremism.

Robespierre never hid his admiration for Rousseau. He believed strongly that public authority must base itself on the general will of society and not the "personal interests" of elites or kings. As a political community composed of citizens, the republic was the expression of the general will and the embodiment of consensus, without which it could not exist. Like Rousseau, Robespierre vested authority in the unanimous voice of the community; and like Rousseau, he was a resolute egalitarian. Equality was "the immutable law of human society." Reason dictated that all men were equal. The customs of aristocracy and monarchy had subverted this fundamental truth. It was necessary to substitute "the empire of Reason for the tyranny of custom," as Robespierre saw it.[58] In his veneration for popular sovereignty and man's natural equality, Robespierre spoke the language of Enlightenment universalism. Yet it was not the cosmopolitan universalism of revolutionaries like Cloots. For Jacobin radicals, national sovereignty trumped internationalism. The republic was a community of equal and virtuous citizens united through the sovereign general will. As such, the Jacobin republic was imagined as a communitarian rather than a liberal state. Appeals to the "one and indivisible" republic rejected partisanship or dissenting voices that imperiled unity. The state was not called upon to arbitrate between competing interests, as Locke would have it. Rather, it was empowered to enforce a strong communitarian discipline against the forces of fragmentation and dissolution.[59]

This brand of radical universalism fed into the Manichean worldview engendered by counter-revolution and civil war, effectively transforming the course of the French Revolution. "We must smother the internal and external enemies of the Republic or perish with it …," Robespierre insisted. "Terror is nothing other than justice, prompt, severe, inflexible; it is an emanation of virtue."[60] Virtuous citizens were expected to protect the republic, employing terror against its enemies if necessary. This task now fell to the state, furnishing the basis for a truly "revolutionary government." In peacetime, republican government was expected to uphold the law and protect its citizens. Revolutionary government possessed a wholly different function. "Revolution is the war waged by liberty against its enemies," Robespierre explained; "a constitution is that which crowns the edifice of freedom once victory has been won and the nation is at peace." Revolutionary government was, therefore, "subject to less binding and less uniform regulations," releasing the state from constitutional and legal formalities that might endanger security.[61] According to Saint-Just, a leading Jacobin proponent and architect of the Reign of Terror, government was to be "revolutionary until peacetime." Peace, however, meant the elimination of all opposition, a logic that justified a permanent revolutionary regime. As the Jacobins abandoned constitutionalism, it was evident that they were espousing a new type of revolutionary ideology unimagined in 1789.[62] "The revolutionary system of government is liberty's despotism against tyranny," Robespierre contended.[63] In the crucible of revolution, liberty and dictatorial terror became one and the same.

Since 1789, moderates had unsuccessfully attempted to curtail popular violence and subordinate "the people" to the rule of law. The radical leadership was, however, embarking on a very different program. Rather than seeking to curb popular violence, the revolutionary regime incorporated it directly into the state. Spontaneous violence would be reined in and appropriated by the revolutionary tribunals. Mass terror implied a new measure of control in the struggle between "the people" and the government. Under the Jacobin dictatorship, violence was channeled through state institutions, establishing a template for a truly "revolutionary" style of government. "Liberty, Equality, Fraternity, or Death." Such became the motto of the Jacobin republic.

Cultural Revolution

Republican dictatorship brought into existence the creation of a self-identified "revolutionary" regime, the first of its kind in history. As such, the revolution became a source of authority in itself.[64] The Jacobins outlined a specific type of government actively committed to social and political "regeneration," brandishing their revolutionary *bone fides*. According to Robespierre, the "storms of the revolution" were to be transcended; revolutionary government was the guide that would navigate France through this tempest. If the object of constitutional government was "to preserve the Republic," the object of revolutionary government was "to establish it," he argued. Radicals were consciously engaged in a policy of community building, one that was both republican and revolutionary in its orientation. Moderates had previously expressed faith in the revolution's transformative power, but rarely did they formulate this conviction in terms of policy. Social transformation would simply occur through a "miraculous" act, they believed, as though the revolution possessed a transformative power in and of itself. The Jacobins adopted a more hardnosed approach. For them, revolution was a labor-intensive process requiring state resources and clear policy initiatives.[65] They aimed to construct a new society from raw human materials and saw the state as the instrument for pursuing this revolutionary program of modernization and regeneration.

To achieve this goal, however, the old regime had to first be destroyed. In an effort to wipe the slate clean, the government consciously targeted symbols and institutions reminiscent of France's Catholic, monarchial heritage. A de-Christianization campaign began in late 1793. Religious buildings were marked for demolition, statues pulled from pillars and royal iconography defaced. Any symbol "offensive to republican eyes" was ordered destroyed. That autumn, Bertrand Barère, chairman of the Committee of Public Safety, ordered the royal crypts housed in Saint-Denis to be exhumed, obliterating the "frightening memories of kings" forever.[66] In one of the more macabre examples of de-Christianization, the remains of the French kings from the Carolingians to the Bourbons were disinterred and deposited in pits of quicklime. Such dramatic acts often overshadowed the more widespread and varied forms that revolutionary iconoclasm assumed under the Jacobin dictatorship. Royal buildings were stripped of any metals that could be used in the manufacture of armaments. Church bells were removed, melted down and recast to make cannons. Streets and villages bearing the name of saints or kings were renamed, with toponyms like Place de la Révolution and Vallée-Rousseau replacing them. The revolution was imprinted onto the national geography.[67]

These policies did not simply stem from disdain for the past. They constituted part of a broad program to insert the revolution into the heart of national life. Festivals and public speeches continually recreated and commemorated the great moments of the revolution, transforming them into mythic events. Public oath taking reenacted the Tennis Coat Oath of 1789. The unearthing of royal bodies recalled the execution of Louis XVI and the empowerment of citizen over monarch. According to Lynn Hunt, these and other cultural practices repeatedly sought to conjure the "mythic present" of the revolution as ceremonies, codes of behavior and even vandalism enshrined the revolution as the founding myth of a regenerated France.[68] The fine arts were no exception. The painter Jacques-Louis David, friend of Robespierre and director of arts under the Jacobin dictatorship, treated national and revolutionary themes in his works. In place of history paintings focused on Classical subject matter, David treated the subject of the revolution itself, developing a new style of contemporary history painting.

"We will not be obliged any longer to go looking in the history of ancient peoples to use our brushes," he informed his cohorts.[69] His depiction of the Tennis Court Oath, which was never completed, visually conveyed the historic importance of the event, investing this foundational moment with mythic significance. David would do the same upon the death of Jean-Paul Marat, commemorating the Jacobin leader as a modern-day martyr immortalized by his dedication to *patrie* and revolution.[70]

Under David's hand, the familiar motifs of neoclassical history painting were redeployed to create a new national mythology. The revolution was presented as a cosmic drama worthy of celebration and veneration. Outside of contemporary history painting, David applied his talents to staging public ceremonies for the regime. In the Festival of Unity scheduled for 1793, David planned a revolutionary pilgrimage with a procession visiting the various monuments of the French Revolution starting at the Bastille and ending at the Champ de Mars. Within David's choreographed pageantry, places of resistance and celebration became sacred sites in the revolutionary mythos. De-Christianization bred its own forms of ritual and religiosity as Christian symbols and discourses were reinvented and adjusted to construct the civic religion of the nation. The revolutionary program of social and cultural regeneration instrumentalized public space. Festivals celebrating the sovereignty of the people served as vehicles for public re-education. Buildings and monuments were engraved with revolutionary slogans, giving the revolution a constant presence in the daily lives of individual.[71]

The extent to which radicals went to create a thoroughly revolutionary culture could sometimes defy the imagination. Following weeks of deliberation in September 1793, the government declared a new calendar for the country, replacing the Gregorian calendar with its religious and royal feast days. Every month was renamed and a ten-day week created complete with a host of revolutionary and national festival days. The founding of the French Republic corresponded to Year I marking the birth of a new era. This division of "old" and "new" time affirmed the French Revolution as a world-historical event, conveying both the regenerative promise and novelty of the revolutionary cause. "The revolution re-tempered the souls of the French; every day it educates them in republican virtue," stated Charles-Gilbert Romme, the director of the calendar commission. "Time is turning a new page of history."[72] As was evident, the Jacobins imagined the revolution as a rupture with the past. It was overthrowing the old to create the new.[73]

In the new terms prescribed by the radicals, the French Revolution represented the first modernizing agenda in world history committed to overturning all existing values.[74] Time was indeed "turning a new page of history" as Romme insisted. Revolution implied innovation and forward progress, claims which effectively radicalized the very idea of revolution. "Does there exist in ancient history a revolution such as ours?" Brissot had asked. "Can you show us a people that, after twelve centuries of slavery, has won back its liberty? We shall create what had never before existed."[75] His rival, Robespierre was no less confident in the modernizing potential of radical revolution. "The French people seem to be about two thousand years ahead of the rest of the human race," he boasted in 1794. "One is tempted to regard them as a separate species."[76]

Revolutionary Europe

Even for those who did not countenance Jacobin revolution, it was difficult to deny that French society had changed in the short interval between 1789 and 1794. Monarchy had been abolished. Alongside political terror, the Jacobin dictatorship waged a "cultural terror" that anticipated the transformation of society and the individual at the most basic levels.[77] Society became exceedingly militarized as war and rebellion wracked the country. In many cities, citizens were put to work under military discipline as part of the general conscription order. Churches were converted into storage depots for flour and grain destined for the front. As provisions grew scarce, breadlines and queues became a familiar sight. War and revolution impinged upon nearly every aspect of national life, reinforcing notions of change and discontinuity with the past. Looking back, one might be inclined to agree with the revolutionary cleric, Henri Grégoire. "France is truly a new world," he insisted, and he was not mistaken.[78]

Conclusion

In light of its political and cultural significance, the French Revolution has typically been regarded as "the basic script for the modern drama of revolution," to quote Keith Michael Baker.[79] Be this as it may, the development of this "basic script" emerged from more general questions over authority and sovereignty that were posed in the wake of 1789. As the Ancien Régime collapsed, elites struggled to define an authoritative framework capable of reconciling differing ideas of sovereignty and empowerment. People and Nation became the predominant idioms for imaging new forms of collective authority, yet disagreements persisted over who or what could claim to speak for these entities. In the flows and counter-flows that marked the revolution, these concepts were continually made and remade, generating conflicts that descended into violence. The success of the revolution depended on making sovereignty real and meaningful, a point which radicals would push to extreme limits in their quest to secure the "one and indivisible" republic.

The changing circumstances of revolution between 1789 and 1794 also furnished opportunities for imagining different types of communities which defined and shaped the revolutionary project in their own ways. The patriotic inheritance of the 1780s remained strong, generating support for a cosmopolitan order rooted in the idea of world revolution and citizenship. The deputy Jacques-Michel Coupé appealed to this patriotic sentiment when declaring before the Convention that the French people constituted an "enlarged family recognizing all children of the earth as brothers" possessing only "oppressors and kings" as enemies.[80] Although patriotic cosmopolitanism did not subside in the coming years, its overt universalism met with skepticism in the context of international and civil war.[81] Radicals increasingly came to inflect revolutionary universalism with a nationalist element, favoring ideas of Rousseauvian sovereignty and unity that resisted more expansive views of revolutionary fraternity. Patriots adhered to a conviction that "the people" made up the nation. Radical republicans inverted this relationship, contending it was the nation that made the people.

Under the republican dictatorship, the citizenship revolution became strongly nationalized as the Jacobins attempted to entrench the revolution and its values at the center of French national life. Jacobin cultural policies were animated by the fundamental goal of transforming the French people as a whole. In contrast to the localized and fragmented world of the Ancien Régime, a "regenerated" and republican France required unity *and* uniformity. Through radical initiatives, revolution became equated with purging old habits, combatting internal enemies and reshaping individuals in accordance with predetermined ideas of what a virtuous republican state ought to be.[82] The struggle to save the revolution from its enemies and ambitions of creating a "new man" came together within the context of revolutionary government, as outlined by Robespierre. In the hands of the Jacobins, revolution became both a method and program of radical social restructuring and community building, a "script" which others could, in fact, adopt and imitate.

CHAPTER 3
ARTISANS, *CITOYENNES* AND SLAVES: THE MEANING OF EQUALITY IN A REVOLUTIONARY WORLD

The age of revolution inspired acts of political revolt and social upheaval. As established models of authority collapsed, individuals and groups found opportunities to imagine and articulate new models of sovereignty and authority to replace them. This was particularly evident in the ways previously marginalized groups attempted to use revolution to fashion new identities and make a case for their social inclusion. For colonists, former slaves, "common" people and women alike, revolution would offer forms of empowerment.

The American and French revolutions sought to impart concrete legal meaning to abstract philosophical concepts of natural rights. In this respect, they marked the most pronounced phase in the eighteenth-century "citizenship revolution," proposing ideas of universal inclusion that theoretically transcended categories of class, race and gender.[1] It was unsurprising therefore that citizenship became one of the most contested concepts of revolutionary politics. Under the Ancien Régime, the term "citizen" conferred a limited and recognized set of rights on subjects. In the absence of a common legal code, systems of privilege and personal law were typically accorded based on membership in a certain social group.[2] The revolutionary period radically redefined the nature and significance of membership in the community. By making citizenship a hallmark of belonging, the revolutionaries of the late eighteenth century tied social inclusion directly to rights. Citizenship became the embodiment of an abstract equality that often proved difficult to reconcile with existing social realities. Ironically, revolutionary politics revealed the limits and contradictions of equality. Emancipation posed vital questions of who specifically constituted the community and in what capacity. As these debates progressed, they tended to harden particular group solidarities that foregrounded specific experiences of oppression and marginalization. Nonetheless, revolutionary actors maintained they spoke on behalf of the entire community even when making claims respective to certain social groups. Such tensions set the stage for a series of conflicts that probed the very meaning of equality and social unity across the Atlantic world.

Citizenship and Social Equality

From the beginning, the French Revolution possessed a noticeable social dimension. Political upheaval coincided with labor disturbances and widespread strike movements in cities as those traditionally excluded from politics directed resentment toward their superiors. Revolutionary politics spoke in the name of a new sovereign authority: "the people." Popular radicalism grew as the myriad worker clubs and societies that took shape after 1789 mobilized citizens on an unprecedented scale. Club meetings and local elections signaled a general revolt against social elitism as workers and artisans endeavored to claim the revolution as their own. These struggles inevitably raised debates over the nature of citizenship and popular sovereignty as ordinary people insisted that a revolution led in the name of "the people" must entail their empowerment. "Have the artisans and the day laborers and all the classes which have only their work to live by any lesser interest to uphold?" asked Claude-Charles Martin, a working-class organizer who took an active role in the Paris sections during the 1790s.[3] Martin's call for broad political rights was a direct affront to the "active" citizenship endorsed by revolutionary leaders after the fall of the Bastille. His message underscored the popular implication that many associated with the French Revolution and the firm belief that a people's revolution must realize equality for all.

Not everyone agreed with radicals like Martin, and the years immediately following 1789 revealed the limitations that elites attempted to impose on political power and participation. Nonetheless, the political ferment continued. The clubs and neighborhood militias served as organizational hubs for the working classes and offered them means of participating in "their" revolution. Through local assemblies and the sections, the "common people" (*menu peuple*) participated in government. Citizens would collect donations and oversee public charity for specific causes. They served in the militias, policing the streets of their neighborhoods and doling out justice based upon what they believed the revolution commanded.[4] For groups who had only known social exclusion, revolution was experienced as a moment of empowerment. As a statement issued by one Parisian district assembly explained: "A precious advantage that we owe to the Revolution … is that equality, that confusion of ranks, that sweet fraternity, whose first links have appeared so agreeable to us."[5] The local sections and assemblies served as schools of revolutionary citizenship, but they also made ideals of social and political equality real and meaningful to a larger section of urban society.

The ranks of artisans and professionals who claimed a role in public life identified with a particular social group, the *sans-culottes*. This label signified a repudiation of elite values and one's connection with the community of ordinary, productive citizens inhabiting the cities. It possessed connotations of ardent patriotism, an unwavering dedication to the revolutionary program and a commitment to "the people." While moderates invoked the term as a synonym for mob violence and anarchy, radical organizers bore the title with pride, affirming a link with their fellow citizens and using it to validate the righteousness of their demands.[6] In speaking for the *sans-culottes*, they defended equal political rights and called for social policies that would benefit the working classes. As wartime requisitioning and economic collapse resulted in scarcity and rising prices, radicals levied accusations of hording against their social betters and pressured the government to implement price controls, or a "maximum price" on necessities like milk, butter and bread. Clubs such as the Cordeliers proved especially effective at whipping up *sans-culotte* anger, calling for a war on hoarders and the installment of a radical republican regime receptive to the people's interests. Food scarcity infused domestic and household matters with new political meaning as well, provoking women to take a more active role in the politics of the day.[7] Like their male counterparts, they pressed for social welfare policies and demonstrated their commitment to republican values by harassing suspected hoarders. This style of female radicalism could and did incite violence in the streets. Women belonging to revolutionary clubs took it upon themselves to enforce fair prices, demonstratively attacked retailers in public and called upon the state to punish merchants who preyed on the people.[8]

Robespierre and the Jacobins tapped into this artisanal and working-class resentment as they built a popular base of support against their Girondin enemies. The Jacobins made vague promises for redistributing wealth and implementing a truly social revolution. According to Saint-Just, economic depravity and dependence reduced individuals to a state of corrupted "savagery." The republic had to ameliorate this position, and this meant combatting speculators, price gougers and merchants bent on profiting from misery. "We have founded a Republic on vice," he charged in 1792, taking aim at the profiteering and market excesses that were destabilizing the country. "We need to found one on virtue. It is not impossible to do."[9] Saint-Just went as far as to attack the base of social inequality itself: private property. "Man was not made for the workshop, the hospital or the poorhouse," he asserted. "We must have neither rich nor poor … Opulence is a crime."[10] Political revolution must proceed in tandem with social revolution. Not only was it moral. It was essential. To permit the people to wallow in misery was to invite another revolt, this time against the republic. Republicans could not allow the Rights of Man to be "written in the blood of the people on the tomb of liberty," Saint-Just warned.[11] As working-class agitation came to the surface of politics, the revolutionary ideal of *égalité* became suffused with connotations of social as well as political equality. "It is not enough to have declared that we are French republicans," explained a representative from the Paris sections to the National Assembly in 1793. "It is necessary that the people be happy, that they have bread, for without bread there is no longer any law, any freedom or any Republic."[12]

It was not that the Jacobins wholly endorsed the *sans-culotte* platform. Rather, they sought to harness the power of the urban crowds and retain control over Paris and the radical clubs.[13] With the establishment of the republic, the Jacobins consented to "the maximum" demanded by *enragés* in the hopes of diffusing rising social tensions and staving off another revolt. In early 1793, price controls were instituted forbidding retail vendors to sell specific goods for profit.[14] Anyone accused of flouting the law was labeled a counter-revolutionary enemy and subject to the people's wrath. The creation of the republic and the subsequent political terror were intended to instill confidence that the revolutionary state was acting on behalf of the *sans-culottes* and "common" people. The Jacobins catered to the sense of empowerment engendered by the revolution, and in doing so temporarily won over the working-classes and *sans-culotte* activists. Democratic political participation was effectively annulled under the Jacobin regime. However, it was replaced with a government ostensibly committed to the people's interests and ensuring *their* revolution.

Figure 4 Louis-Antoine de Saint-Just © The British Library Board.

Radical assertions of social equality were consistent with general perceptions held by eighteenth-century republicans. A republic could not survive amid stark economic disparities and social divisions, they argued. Economic independence and limiting wealth were important elements of a healthy republican polity. These claims resonated with republican egalitarians in France and certainly resonated with American republicans after 1776. As the Philadelphia newspaper the *National Gazette* informed its readers in 1793: "In every democratic government the laws ought to destroy and prevent too great an inequality of condition among the citizens."[15] While elites had hoped to restrict voting rights to property owners, more radical views contended that a broad electorate of free and independent men was essential to guarding against public corruption and tyranny. The "vision of '76" retained a strong influence among farmers and artisanal workers in the newly formed United States. This vision translated into a shared conviction that the American Revolution promised both political and economic empowerment for ordinary people. Much as in France, individuals and groups laid claim to a revolutionary inheritance, speaking in the name of *their* revolution against the power and authority of established elites. William Findley, a Pennsylvania weaver and representative in the state assembly, exemplified the populist tone of American revolutionary politics. He criticized the influence of the moneyed classes, claiming it was destructive to the equality that should prevail in a republic. The American Revolution had been fought to give "citizens their right of equal protection, power, privilege and influence," in his opinion.[16] Until the political participation and empowerment of ordinary people were assured, the American Revolution remained unfinished.

This populist rhetoric echoed throughout post-revolutionary America and was taken up by a host of war veterans, farmers and artisans. In 1786, the *Pittsburgh Gazette* gave an ominous warning stating, "the American war is over, but this is far from the case with the American revolution. On the contrary, nothing but the first act of the great drama is closed."[17] This pronouncement was in response to protests occurring in Massachusetts where crowds were disrupting court and government proceedings. That year, the veteran Daniel Shay led an armed uprising against the Massachusetts government, drawing together individuals and communities frustrated by heavy debt, controls on popular participation and land policies perceived to be favorable to speculators over common farmers.[18] Eight years later, groups in Western Pennsylvania and Kentucky took up arms under similar pretexts during the so-called "Whiskey Rebellion." The spark for the uprising had come with the levying of new taxes on distilled spirits, a blow to impoverished, cash-starved farmers in the region facing property foreclosure and repossession. However, protest transcended issues of taxation to encompass an array of social and political grievances. The insurrection marked a revolt against moneyed interests and elite leadership in favor of popular democracy. Leaders set up committees of correspondence throughout the region, organized local militias and raised liberty polls in town squares. Such symbolic gestures harkened back to the days of the American Revolution and underscored the defense of revolutionary ideals.[19] Their revolution was that of the common citizen seeking political empowerment and economic independence in the name of equality.

These uprisings brought into question state authority and the very nature of democratic republican government. American elites feared that "the people" might not submit to authority, and they only had to look to France to understand the possible repercussions. In both instances, the American government employed military force to subdue popular resistance, commanding that "the people" obey state authority. Yet this hardly settled the disputes over popular participation and social inequality that stimulated such unrest. Workers and farmers upheld the radicalism implicit in the American Revolution throughout the 1790s, and would continue to call for the empowerment of the "lower orders" and a more economically just society over social privilege and elite rule.

Britain was not immune to these democratic currents either. The Society for Constitutional Information set up in 1780 testified to a growing radicalism taking root in British society. John Horne Tooke, a London barrister and lead spokesperson for the society, was a staunch patriot committed to Thomas Paine's cosmopolitan republicanism. Under his leadership, the organization became a center of international radicalism that drew together a variety of participants sympathetic to "French ideas." A host of similar organizations followed suit during the 1790s, with societies growing up in Sheffield, Norwich, Manchester and Birmingham. Although these bodies reflected local interests, the commonality of grievances and demands frequently encouraged cooperation and mutual assistance across cities. It was not surprising that these urban centers were experiencing the incipient traumas of industrialization. Mechanics, book sellers, weavers and other artisans constituted the core members of the popular societies and clubs established in the country, integrating previously marginalized groups into politics who expressed their solidarity with "the people" of Great Britain.[20]

What has typically been considered an "age of reform" in Great Britain was not without its radical elements. Revolutionary agitation alarmed elites who worried whether the *sans-culotte* fury evident in France would spread across the Channel. Popular societies ran their own newspapers and published cheap editions of key works like Paine's *Rights of Man* while radical spokesmen praised the Jacobins in public speeches and organized events in support of the French revolutionary armies abroad. Above all, societies and clubs professed their desire to see a similar transformation take place in British society. In expressing support for the French Revolution, agitators pressed home a radical platform that called for universal suffrage and annual parliamentary meetings. Groups petitioned the government and staged public meetings to add force to their criticisms. For Henry Yorke, a prominent member of the Sheffield Constitutional Society, petitioning had to be accompanied with direct political action. "The people should lay aside leaders, discard factions and *act for themselves*," he urged. "*Revolution in sentiment* must precede revolution in government and manners."[21] The revolution in sentiment that Yorke had in mind was nothing less than transforming British subject into active citizens who would partake in national politics.

Yorke was among a new breed of activists in Britain condemned as English "Jacobins." In mobilizing laborers and radical manufacturers, they sought to engage the people in politics, bringing forth a democratic society distinct from the rigid social hierarchies and elite paternalism familiar to British society and politics. Radicals had few inhibitions regarding making their demands in the name of "the people." Society members took to addressing one another as "citizen," a mark of equality that rejected pretensions of social status. The American crisis of the late 1770s had raised pertinent questions over rights and representation that were debated on both side of the Atlantic. The French Revolution re-energized these debates, prompting British workers and laborers to draw inspiration from the egalitarianism coming from France and America. Workers and artisans adopted the language of Atlantic democracy to demand a voice in politics, representative institutions and a government based on the interests of the people. British authorities did not sit by idly as unrest unfolded. Beginning in 1793, the government undertook various measures to thwart radicalism at home. The fear of revolutionary subversion and French agents prompted a crackdown on the popular societies, beginning with the well-established London Correspondence Society run by the radical Thomas Hardy. Pro-French agitators were condemned as traitors, and by 1794 the Home Office was at war with the various societies and clubs fomenting instability in the country. It placed strict limitations on public meetings, curbed press freedoms and made every effort to suppress the political mobilization and activism encouraged by the popular societies.[22]

The language of revolutionary democracy had a powerful influence on social groups previously excluded from public and political life. Artisans and laborers on both sides of the Atlantic pressed governments for more participatory regimes that would allow ordinary people to fulfill and actualize the revolution as they understood it: a movement led and directed by equal citizens partaking in a common cause. States were often reluctant to concede these democratic ideas and instead opted to clamp down on popular protest. In 1794, "citizen" John Martin got before the London Corresponding Society and urged his fellow patriots not to be deterred. "We must choose now at once either liberty or slavery," he exclaimed.[23] The trope of slavery was a familiar metaphor in the revolutionary discourse of the period. As early as the 1770s, Jean-Paul Marat had published a book entitled *The Chains of Slavery*, alerting the people of England to the corruption and inequality that oppressed honest laborers. *Sans-culotte* spokesmen and radicals framed their situation in terms of enslavement and servitude, associating the struggle against aristocracy with the independence and emancipation that liberty promised. For some, however, such allusions were not merely metaphorical. The Atlantic world possessed populations who suffered the indignity and oppression of chattel slavery on a daily basis. If ideas of political participation and social equality motivated "common people" to revolt, what might it mean for those held in bondage?

Revolution in Two Hemispheres

Slavery was a common practice throughout Europe's Atlantic empires. As indentured servitude and coerced forms of labor declined over the course of the seventeenth century, colonial producers became dependent on the Atlantic slave trade. By the eighteenth century, some 6,000 Africans were being transported to Spanish America each year while the number in Portuguese Brazil was as high as 19,000.[24] In 1775, the inhabitants of British North America numbered around 2.5 million, with 20 percent of the population enslaved.[25] Under the circumstances, Atlantic society was defined by deep racial hierarchies that made distinctions based on physical difference, descent and skin color.[26] The revolutionary movements that would cut across the Atlantic world in the late eighteenth century would both politicize racial identities and call practices of human bondage into question.

Colonial struggles in British North America paralleled black freedom struggles and revealed the differing contexts that shaped ideas of revolutionary liberty.[27] Many white slaveholders had been hesitant to endorse independence or claims of natural rights fearing its consequences. For others, the assertion that "all men are created equal" enshrined in the Declaration of Independence bolstered hopes that the American cause would extend to the African-American population. Slaves and free blacks took an active role in drafting petitions and employed the language of radical emancipation for their own ends. Chattel slavery stood opposed to the ideals of liberty and equality for which colonists were fighting, fueling expectations that the American struggle would overturn all existing forms of bondage and servitude.[28] With the breakdown of civil order, many slaves took the initiative in declaring their own independence, whether by attempting to sue for their freedom in court or by running away and abandoning the farms and plantations of their masters.[29]

The conviction that the American Revolution could also be one of black independence inspired enslaved and free African-Americans to enlist in the Continental Army. By joining the war effort, those who fought as patriots hoped to attain liberty or at least expand black civil rights in post-independence society. While estimates of the African-Americans who served in the Continental Army and militias vary widely, it is undeniable that their service was grounded in ambitions of securing personal freedom and the promise of republican citizenship. Fighting as arms-bearing patriots, they endeavored to claim formal equality with their fellow white Americans and make the cause of revolution their own.[30] The British were aware of the delicate situation that slavery posed for American rebels and attempted to exploit it. When independence was declared, the British government let it be known that they would grant freedom to any slave who joined the British army. This declaration was aimed at destabilizing the southern plantation economy and bringing the patriots to heel, and slaves responded and took up arms against their masters.[31] After the war, the British relocated some 10,000 black loyalists to Nova Scotia or re-enslaved them in the Caribbean.[32]

Those who hoped the American crisis would be a crucible for black emancipation were left severely disappointed. With the conclusion of the war, the American republic preserved institutionalized slavery. The white independent yeomen and artisan became the embodiment of republican citizenship, relegating supporters of universal emancipation to the margins. The cause of black citizenship revealed the expectations that accompanied revolutionary democracy while simultaneously illuminating its many contradictions and hypocrisies. Yet it also encouraged a more concerted effort among critics to realize their vision of an inclusive and universal republicanism. If natural rights were inherent in man, they must be recognized without regard for race or skin color. Once the idea of natural rights had been introduced and translated into a reality, it raised vital questions pertinent to inclusion and citizenship that stabbed at the very heart of the racialized hierarchies and practices that structured Atlantic imperialism. As elites came to speak in the democratic and universal language of enlightened reform, the egregious disparity between principles and practice was difficult to ignore.

These ideas were vocalized through the anti-slavery movements that traversed the Atlantic world in the eighteenth century. Leading reformers set up civic organization with the goal of raising awareness of slavery and petitioning to end the international slave trade. The British abolitionist William Fox summed up the argument succinctly in 1791, accusing Britons of being complicit in one of the most immoral acts imaginable. "We, in an enlightened age, have greatly surpassed, in brutality and injustice, the most ignorant and barbarous ages: and while we are pretending to the finest feelings of humanity, are exercising unprecedented cruelty."[33] According to Fox, this modern barbarism was a global phenomenon because "the offices of humanity and functions of justice" were not "circumscribed by geographical boundaries."[34] Like Fox, others similarly attempted to increase awareness of the inequality and brutality perpetrated through the slave trade.

Thomas Clarkson traveled around England on horseback giving public lectures on the injustice of slavery. In his bag he always carried iron shackles and instruments of torture to show his audience.[35] The anti-slavery movement also found adherents beyond England. Jacques-Pierre Brissot corresponded with British abolitionists and in 1788 assisted in setting up a French corollary, the Société des Amis des Noirs which attracted other future revolutionaries such as Lafayette and Mirabeau. The following year, the society pressed its case before the National Assembly, hoping that the French government might endorse the cause of universal emancipation. Despite these efforts, their cause met with limited success due to poor organization and a lack of grass-roots activism. In the end, the society remained primarily a club attended by elites and nobles.[36]

The abolitionist movement in France never attained the widespread support that it found in Britain, although it did benefit from the leadership of dedicated social reformers.[37] The royal government refused to commit itself firmly to the cause of abolitionism, fearing it would alienate slaveholders in the French colonies. Even after the National Assembly passed the Rights of Man and Citizen that August, the government proceeded cautiously when it came to the status of slavery in the French empire. The philosopher Nicolas de Condorcet hit upon the dilemma now facing the country when he scoffed that perhaps the drafters of the Rights of Man should have thought to add "all *white* men are born free and equal in rights."[38] As Condorcet correctly perceived, the abstract principles of the French Revolution and the realities of imperialism were at loggerheads. Although a European kingdom, France was also a global imperial power. The relationship between the French metropole and its colonies had never been well-defined, nor did it necessarily need to be either. The Ancien Régime was a conglomeration of various provincial territories with their own particular laws and constitutions. It was not difficult to imagine the Atlantic colonies as an extension of this system. Paul-Ulric Dubisson, a former colonial postmaster and pamphleteer, made this point explicit when arguing that the Atlantic colonies were "provinces of the Kingdom of France, in the

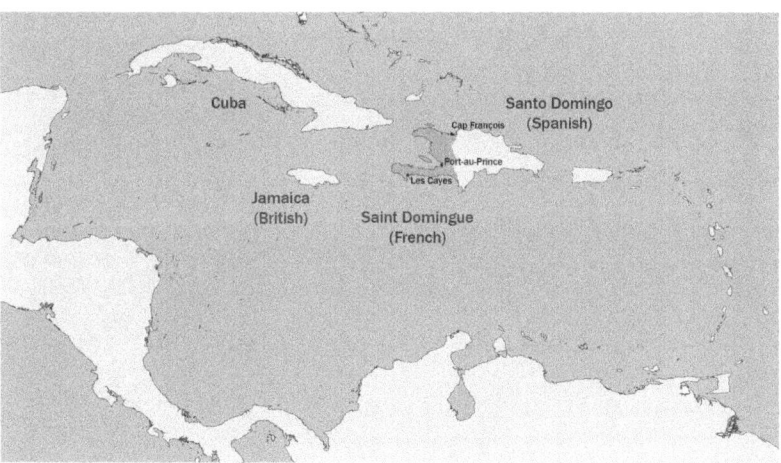

Map 2 Saint Domingue and the imperial Caribbean.

manner of Britany, Normandy and Guienne."[39] However, the abolition of provincial autonomies and the declaration of national unity placed the relationship between France and its overseas territories in a new context, a fact that many inhabitants of the French Atlantic recognized with a mix of anxiety and anticipation.

Saint-Domingue, the "pearl of the Antilles," was the most profitable of the French Caribbean colonies, producing sugar, coffee and indigo for world markets. Work was largely performed by an extensive labor force of African slaves which by 1789 numbered roughly 465,000. This compared with a white ruling class of 31,000 plantation owners and colonists.[40] For the respectively small white settler population, the dangers were evident. Slavery constituted one of the lynchpins of the colonial economy. To question slavery was to bring into question the economic livelihood of French colonial elites profiting from the plantation economy. More startling was the fact that colonists were isolated in the middle of the Caribbean, cut off from the French mainland and surrounded by a large enslaved population. Talk of liberty and freedom was a dangerous enterprise capable of inspiring violent slave revolts on a mass scale. Given these circumstances, it was the discipline of the whip that reigned in the French Atlantic world.

Dichotomies of black-white and slave-master concealed, however, the complex social arrangements that existed within the French Atlantic world. Wealthy planters were among the most influential group on the island, yet the majority of whites were not part of the ruling plantocracy. Colonists with fewer means had migrated to the Caribbean in search of new opportunities. Poor or middling colonists, so-called *petits blancs*, found employment on plantations or provided skilled labor in the cities. They harbored resentment against the wealthier colonists who stood accused of forming a veritable colonial "aristocracy" monopolizing politics and trade. Slavery as well had many

Figure 5 Slaves Cutting Sugar Cane on British Antigua © The British Library Board.

variations in practice. Some slaves possessed small garden plots that yielded minimal incomes and others in urban areas were free to contract their labor.[41] Slaves had certain "rights and privileges" under the Code Noir, a comprehensive set of laws that defined the conditions of slavery and theoretically protected slaves from excessive brutality and neglect.[42] Within the corporate system of the Ancien Régime, slaves were yet another group possessing their own legal statutes with specified privileges and prohibitions. The key difference, however, was that their legal status defined them as property, not as individuals.

These same laws also protected and spelled out the privileges of the *gens de couleur* (men of color) who inhabited the island. *Gens de couleur* possessed varying degrees of African ancestry and were roughly equal in number to the white population of Saint-Domingue on the eve of the Revolution. Some were among the wealthiest plantation owners on the island. They were unquestionably free men and in many cases owned slaves of their own. Yet because of their standing as "men of color" they did not possess the same status as whites and faced numerous discriminatory restrictions exclusive to their group, prohibition from colonial politics and certain professions among them. They were an ambiguous social group which by virtue of ancestry was neither wholly African nor European. The promise of revolutionary equality would have a strong appeal for the *gens de couleur* who remained conscious of their exclusion despite their wealth, education and respectability in colonial society.

Many plantation owners resided in France and recognized the danger the revolution posed to their economic livelihood as talk of rights and freedom circulated. Brissot and the Société des Amis des Noirs saw the opening of the Estates General as an ideal setting to promote their abolitionist platform. Slaveholders naturally intended to block them at all costs. Conservative planters and colonial merchants met regularly at the Club Massiac in Paris, forming a lobby that would work to further colonial interests. That summer, seventeen titular deputies from the colonies were admitted to the National Assembly, giving colonial elites a presence in the French government. Together, the Club Massiac and the deputies worked to ensure that any measures affecting the slave trade raised in the National Assembly were tabled indefinitely. Colonial elites took up an ambivalent stance on the French Revolution. Notwithstanding the abolitionist threat, revolution did present certain advantages. Planters were never warm to metropolitan authority and repeatedly resisted efforts at imperial consolidation. They had no qualms with being part of a French empire, but believed that the local assemblies rather than the royal governors were best suited to dictate laws and trade policies, thereby keeping power in the hands of colonial property owners. Autonomy remained a persistent goal, and the revolution afforded a new opportunity to revise the *Pacte colonial* and clarify the relationship between metropole and colony in their favor.[43]

The situation in the colonies was more complicated. From the start, elites confronted opposition from *petits blancs* who, although sympathetic to autonomist aspirations, harbored deep resentments when it came to the planter class. Spurning the Saint-Dominguan "aristocrats," *petit blanc* radicals in the cities organized patriotic clubs and rallied supporters to a patriotic platform. For them, the French Revolution promised political empowerment, a war of "the people" against the wealthy and privileged. Setting up revolutionary assemblies and local militias, self-proclaimed "Patriots" began passing decrees and issuing constitutions without the approval of colonial authorities. Like the planters, they feared the imposition of racial reform by the National Assembly. If fully applied, the Rights of Man augured the full enfranchisement of the *gens de couleur* and the emancipation of slaves under the pretext of natural rights. The question of what the French Revolution meant for the colonies was not altogether clear, but whites intended to ensure that it did not entail racial equality.[44] In their decrees and public statements, Patriots gave vent to a hardline racism that rejected any change in the status quo, often expressing more extreme opinions than those held by planters.

Heightened Patriot racism was a reaction to *gens de couleur* mobilization following the outbreak of revolution in the metropole. Free blacks and men of color set up their own local militias across Saint-Domingue and let it be known that they had every intention of participating in revolutionary politics on the island. Upon the calling of the Colonial Assembly, a petition was submitted by leading *gens de couleur* criticizing white despotism and expressing loyalty to the king and National Assembly. In no uncertain terms, the signatories anticipated acquiring "all the benefits precious to all French people," including the right to sit in the colonial assemblies.[45] More alarming was the fact that *gens de couleur* were gathering in Paris and courting supporters in the National Assembly and the Parisian clubs. Shut out of the colonial assemblies by the Patriots, *gens de couleur* could appeal directly to the metropole.

Julian Raimond, a Saint-Dominguan planter residing in Paris, was well-positioned to act on behalf of *gens de couleur* interests in the capital. Since the mid-1780s, he had been meeting privately with French officials to press for racial reform in the colonies. With the outbreak of the revolution, he took it upon himself to act as a "representative" for Saint-Domingue's mixed and free black community, pleading his case before the National Assembly and speaking with liberal-minded members of the Club Massiac and Brissot's abolitionist circle. He was joined by the planter Vincent Ogé and the Parisian barrister Etienne-Louis Hector de Joly at whose office the group met. Collectively, they formed their own lobby with influential backers that could defend their cause on the floor of the National Assembly when needed. The message conveyed in their appeals was straightforward. The *gens de couleur* were free and respectable property owners who fulfilled the requirements for active citizenship as laid out under the existing laws. Their demands were not radical. They merely sought to obtain the rights accorded to all French citizens and participate in the colonial assemblies currently dominated by whites. "The cry of liberty has been stifled in the other hemisphere," Joly informed the French deputies, prompting the question what value did the Rights of Man possess if only applied selectively.[46]

Underpinning these arguments was, however, a larger question: were the Caribbean colonies considered part of the nation? Under the Ancien Régime, the question was a trivial point. The National Assembly, however, had declared the nation sovereign, investing authority in a concept which was by no means fixed or determined. Colonial demands brought to light just how flexible this concept could be. Despite the conquests of the revolution, French citizens continued to "groan under the yoke of oppression" and suffer injustices just like "an obedient slave," a petition to the National Assembly reported. "You must return to these oppressed citizens the rights that have been unjustly stripped from them; you must gloriously complete your work, by ensuring the liberty of French citizens in both hemispheres."[47] The injunction to "complete" the work of the revolution made clear the outlook of the *gens de couleur* and their allies. The national soil extended from France proper to its most distal territories, making up a unified political community of equal French citizens. The laws of the nation were the laws of the colonies, without exception. On these grounds, mixed and free blacks were entitled to enjoy the same rights and privileges possessed by other colonists.[48]

Raimond, Joly and others pushed their case for a Trans-Atlantic French community, seeing it as the surest guarantee of creole enfranchisement based upon revolutionary principles. They equally sought out influential supporters in Paris to add force to their claims. Brissot and the Amis des Noirs were likely candidates who willingly lent their pens and voices to the cause of colonial freedom. In early 1790, Raimond also enlisted Henri-Baptiste Grégoire, a parish priest-turned deputy associated with Brissot's circle. Grégoire took up the cause with alacrity. He even proved more radical than anticipated as his line of argument developed over the next two years. In a series of pamphlets and speeches, he attacked the slave trade and condemned slavery as an immoral institution, a point not explicitly addressed by the *gens de couleur*, many of whom were slave owners.[49] His defense of universal principles and rights was more attuned to the tenor of reform and moderation desired by the lobby. "We do not believe that the difference in skin is capable of establishing different rights between the members of a political society," Grégoire claimed without reservation.[50] In framing the terms of this debate, Raimond and his allies were attempting to influence a distinct conception of sovereignty and citizenship deriving from the universal rights talk of the French Revolution.

Not all deputies were as enthusiastic as Grégoire. Nor did they necessarily agree that the French nation constituted a Trans-Atlantic political community. Most desired to settle the colonial question as quietly and expeditiously as possible. To this end, the National Assembly repeatedly sidestepped the thorny issues of race and slavery, offering only vague decrees that did little to clarify the position of the *gens de couleurs*. The government had no intention of alienating colonial elites and was not even certain whether officials would implement controversial policies on the ground. The acting governor in Saint-Domingue, the Comte de Blanchelande, and the military commander Thomas-Antoine de Mauduit had made known their royalist sympathies and refused to cooperate with the National Assembly. They were actively cracking down on Patriots and the *gens de couleur* alike to halt the contagion of revolution from spreading. Patriots reacted with hostility, asserting the authority of the colonial assemblies and barring all *gens de couleur* from participation. When Blanchelande moved to shut down the troublesome patriotic clubs, colonists hectored officials and denounced the "aristocratic plot" to subvert colonial liberty. Colonial Patriots were proving to be a destabilizing force, one that planters and moderates found difficult to control. In September of 1790, contentions between Martinican Patriots in Saint-Pierre and planters erupted into a full-scale civil war, while "Patriot" and "Aristocrat" factions agitated neighboring Guadeloupe.[51] On Saint-Domingue, armed bands of Patriot were threatening revolt should the government attempt to impose its will on the colonial assemblies and violent skirmishes were beginning to break out as racial tensions escalated.

Caught between these extremes and faced with royalist officials unwilling to take orders from Paris, the National Assembly appeared powerless as colonial authority disintegrated. In late 1790, the prominent *gens de couleur* spokesman Vincent Ogé returned to Saint-Domingue from Paris and led an uprising against the Patriot-dominated Colonial Assembly. The revolt failed and Ogé was sentenced to death, but violent suppression did little to temper *gens de couleur* outrage. Armed protests broke out in cities and authorities suppressed them mercilessly. Patriot radicalism was also ratcheting up the levels of violence. In March of 1791, Colonel Mauduit was lynched and murdered by local troops, revealing the temperament of anti-royalist sentiment. Local assemblies flouted government authorities and ordered militias to enforce public order as they saw fit. Alarmed by this recalcitrance, *gens de couler* and planters began arming their slaves in anticipation of war with the Patriots.[52]

In the gathering storm, the National Assembly took what measures it could to resolve tensions. In a series of decrees that May, the government attempted to clarify its position on the colonies and, by proxy, the relationship between the French Empire and the revolution. The key question at stake was whether natural rights were universal or limited in nature. The National Assembly ruled that all property owners had equal political and civil rights regardless of race, giving the *gens de couleur* a claim to political representation. Yet in a contradictory position, the Assembly also declared the colonies subject to local rather than national legislation as a sop to autonomists, meaning it would be the Colonial Assembly that would define the conditions of political participation. The issue of slavery was also broached, with the government unequivocally defining slaves as property without rights. A furious debate ensued when a Martinican deputy requested the word "slave" be inserted into the French constitution to avoid any confusion over the intent of the law. Robespierre sneered at this suggestion, retorting that slavery was contrary to the spirit and letter of the French Revolution. Slavery could not be constitutionally decreed without sacrificing the revolution's core values. "Abandon the colonies rather than the principle!" Robespierre declared, insisting that it would be better for France to relinquish its empire than flout its revolutionary ideals.[53]

Yet France did neither. The final verdict on slavery revealed the ambiguities that reconciling revolution and empire incurred. The "local circumstances" of the colonies had to be taken into consideration, the National Assembly argued.[54] Government, designed to work toward the public good, had to sustain public prosperity. The colonial economy was dependent upon slavery, therefore making it a necessary evil. More to the point, the Rights of Man had declared property sacred and inviolable. As private property, the government could not make any definitive rulings that might deprive citizens of property. Liberal principles had reached an impasse. Liberty and the right to property—both central to Enlightenment concepts of natural rights—were at odds when it came to chattel slavery. In a stark turn away from Enlightenment rights talk, slaves were denied claims to citizenship or national inclusion. As one deputy explained, slaves were not French national and should not be treated as such. Africa was their "true *patrie*."[55] The National Assembly formally concurred with this logic, claiming that slaves were "individuals of a foreign land who, by their profound ignorance [and] the misfortune of their exile" remained outside the domain of national sovereignty.[56] As ancestry came to replace arguments rooted in natural rights, French citizenship became not only a racial issue, but also a racialized concept.

The National Assembly attempted to mollify everyone. In doing so, it pleased nobody. Colonial Patriots refused to countenance racial reform and the *gens de couleur* maintained their opposition to the colonial assemblies. Radicals in the National Assembly felt that core revolutionary values were being betrayed while royalist governors continued to act on their own initiative. Amid this confusion, that August slave revolts began to erupt in the northern provinces of Saint-Domingue. The breakdown of Saint-Dominguan society was complete as slaves set fire to sugar plantations, pillaged plantation homes and formed localized guerilla bands. Slave rebellion significantly transformed the context of revolution in the colony as open conflict ensued. Leaders on both sides recruited slaves, promising freedom in return for military service. When the war between Patriots and the *gens de couleur* came to an end, armed slaves would fight their own war to ensure these promises were kept.[57]

Learning of these events from afar, Louis XVI lamented the current state of his empire. "Once the object of envy among all the nations of Europe … [Saint-Domingue] now offers the eye only a vast field of disorders, of pillage, fire, carnage, crime and revolutions," he remarked.[58] Yet the disorder only hinted at the more profound changes taking shape in the French Atlantic. Prior to 1790, colonial society had been diverse. Different degrees of African ancestry implied different levels of status and degrees of social inclusion. Slaves were not free blacks, just as *gens de couleur* were not labeled "*noir*" or "*nègre*." Revolution destroyed these social subtleties. Attempts to constrain the *gens de couleur* and stave of abolitionism had brought existing racial tensions to the surface just as the mass mobilization of slaves severely disrupted the institutions of slavery. A violent racial hostility now spilled over, polarizing identities. Politics divided along racial lines, centering conflict around stark terms of black or white.[59] Whereas in France, combatants gravitated around poles of revolutionaries and counter-revolutionaries, in Port-au-Prince, Le Cayes and Cap Français political struggles were re-oriented around race. Slaves and men of color took up the rhetoric of emancipation and racial equality, holding up the ideals of the French Revolution as a direct challenge to white colonial oligarchy.

As violence escalated, whites fled the island, many emigrating to the United States. In Philadelphia, Baltimore and New York, French refugees formed associations and pressed their case in local newspapers where they criticized the French government and decried their losses. Disgruntled colonial émigrés presented a sobering reminder of the casualties and dislocations that accompanied such revolutionary tumult on an international scale. With their grievances and politically charged diatribes, they proved to be disruptive guests for their American host, although they were by no means the most formidable challenge at hand. Slave rebellion off the coast of the United States did not bode well for a republic tolerant of slavery. In the summer of 1791, the US federal government sent thousands of dollars in aid to assist in putting down the Saint-Domingue revolt. As Thomas Jefferson reckoned, if the slave rebellion was not suppressed quickly, it would not be long before these "bloody scenes" were witnessed in the American republic.[60]

The violence and upheaval continued, however. Slaves were set against masters, whites against blacks and rebels against government officials. By 1792, the signs of revolution were evident everywhere. One encountered acres of scorched sugar fields, camps of armed slaves and militia commanders sporting revolutionary cockades. Food shortages became acute as unrest disrupted colonial trade. Once the "pearl" of the French Antilles, Saint-Domingue hardly resembled the prosperous colony it had been. Returning to his plantation in Le Clerc and observing the extent of devastation, one white colonist summed up the state of the colony succinctly: "We felt as though we were marching on the ruins of the world."[61]

Republican Emancipation and Its Limits

The breakdown of colonial society corresponded with the radicalization of the French Revolution in general. By 1792, the Jacobins were in the ascent, and many sympathized with the struggles for liberty taking place in the Caribbean. With the creation of the French Republic, a more direct policy vis-à-vis Saint-Domingue was outlined. The government would support the *gens de couleur* who were on the verge of driving the colonists into submission. Slaves would be disarmed and order restored. In September, republican commissioners were dispatched to the Atlantic colonies charged with the task of reigning in the colonial assemblies and reasserting French control. Yet no sooner did the civil commissioner Léger-Félicité Sonthonax arrive on Saint-Domingue than a new situation presented itself.

Since 1791, France had been at war with Europe. Britain and Spain, France's two principal imperial rivals, were eager to extend the conflict into the Caribbean and wrest colonial territories from France. Royalist planters welcomed invasion, confident Britain would retain slavery and silence republican talk of equality. Slave leaders, uncertain of republican intentions, secretly negotiated with Spain, offering military support in exchange for their freedom.[62] Sonthonax had few illusions when it came to France's ability to combat the powers and put down local revolts. Only by rallying the slave population to the republic could France wage a successful military campaign in the Atlantic. "It is with the natives of the country, that is the Africans, that we will save Saint-Domingue for France," Sonthonax informed the Convention.[63] To forge this alliance, the slave cause had to be made the cause of the republic. Thus, in August of 1793, Sonthonax took the necessary step and issued an emancipation proclamation upon his own authority. "Men are born free and equal in rights," it read. "There you have it, citizens: the Gospel of France."[64] The decree was nothing short of revolutionary in both its language and stated intent. It proposed the existence of a common body of French citizens engaged in revolutionary struggle. With equal rights for all citizens, the revolutionary republic was reconstituted as a French imperial nation-state. Much as the *gens de couleur* had argued as early as 1789, France was declared a trans-oceanic democracy, yet one molded in the egalitarian and universal principles championed by republican radicals.[65]

Beneath these lofty revolutionary principles, the necessities of war and order were apparent. Black citizenship was made conditional upon enlisting in the new Légions d'Égalité, with freedom dependent upon bearing arms for the republic. Republicans like Brissot had emphasized the ideal of the citizen-in-arms, insisting military service was a source of patriotism. Rebel leaders in the colonies adapted this outlook to the context of post-emancipation citizenship. In rallying his troops, the former slave Toussaint Louverture always appeared dressed in military attire, a rifle in hand. "Here is your freedom!" he would shout, holding out the firearm to his men. As colonial revolt became republican revolution, leaders accented the link between militarism and citizenship popularized in late eighteenth-century republican political culture.[66] Those who did not serve in the military were expected to make contributions as dutiful citizens through labor. "Liberated" slaves were ordered back to their plantations where they were subject to a work regiment under strict military discipline. Sonthonax's decree tied civilians to plantations, promising them a share in the agricultural yields as compensation for their work. The choice was not voluntary, however, and malingerers could expect to be arrested and forcibly returned to the fields. The realities of emancipation fell far short of the universal equality imagined by many. Outside of military service, post-emancipation citizenship was contingent upon belonging to a plantation, engendering a style of republican liberation that Caroline Fick has aptly described as "plantation citizenship."[67]

In the short term, the republican strategy proved successful. Rebel leaders allied with the republic, urging former slaves to fight for the cause of liberty and equality. A new republican army was pieced together in the colonies, taking the Jacobin moto of "Liberty, Equality, Fraternity or Death" to heart. Various *gens de couleur* resisted the motion, seeing abolition as far too radical for their tastes. Although supportive of Trans-Atlantic citizenship, *gens de couleur* found it difficult to endorse the egalitarian rhetoric of French republicanism. For the Jacobins, however, emancipation symbolized one more step in the destruction of the old regime and the full realization of the French Revolution. It also possessed a strong rhetorical value. As the Jacobin dictatorship consolidated its control at home and suspended democracy in the name of "revolutionary" government, the colonies provided an alternative theater in which to represent the universal and liberating values supported by revolutionaries in dramatic fashion. Dictatorship in France was counterbalanced by the creation of a black republican citizenry elsewhere, sustaining the image of the republic as an emancipatory and revolutionary force.

Jacobins were fast learning the ways in which empire could promote and symbolically convey revolutionary principles. Military engagements in Europe were no different in this regard. Brissot's injunction that "every French citizen is a soldier" fueled republican militarism as the war continued. The initial setbacks experienced in the summer of 1792 were overcome relatively quickly, with conscription and national mobilization reversing the course of the war effort. By November, French forces had pushed the Austro-Prussian armies out of French territory, leaving Belgium and Switzerland open to invasion. Over the next year, revolutionary armies occupied swaths of territory across the Low Countries and Rhineland, emancipating all people who "wished to recover their liberty."[68] The Jacobins presented the revolution as a process of recovering the rights of man vanquished by monarchy. This message was easily fungible with a new spirit of revolutionary expansion that saw French forces overturn governments in the name of universal liberation. Exporting revolution became the *modus operandi* of an invigorated revolutionary government, offering opportunities to demonstrate the values of liberty, equality and fraternity to the world.

Liberation and republican empire shared common boundaries, and the two were not always distinguishable. By 1794, colonial commissioners were already conceptualizing emancipation through the terms of imperialism. In the Atlantic colonies, republican officials retained the plantation system under the pretext of "regenerating" former slaves. Work and service previously tied to slavery were rebranded a "civilizing" force as nominally emancipated slaves undertook the laborious process of learning how to be dutiful and responsible citizens. Equality was never absolute. French administrators made distinction between citizens based upon supposed moral and intellectual capacities, insisting that ex-slaves did not possess a sufficient level of maturity to act as full citizens. Republican ideology never expunged the old criteria of "active" and "passive" citizenship; it merely reframed it through a logic of gradual emancipation. Martial law and compulsive work regiments constrained the supposed rights and freedom granted by the state, reflecting a brand of republican racism that persistently rested alongside the universal and liberating promises made by revolutionary thinkers.[69]

These elements had been present at the very beginning of the French Revolution and were, in many respects, products of rather than deviations from revolutionary principles. Republican citizenship celebrated the free individual invested with natural rights but consistently argued that citizens needed to be moral and educated so that they could make informed and disinterested decisions.[70] Robespierre spoke of universal rights but insisted that the citizen must also possess "virtue," an acquired rather than inherent quality.[71] In a similar fashion, Grégoire advocated on behalf of racial equality and reform, yet stopped short of advocating full enfranchisement for slaves. "The rights of citizenship granted too suddenly to those who are unaware of the duties that go with them might prove to be a fateful gift to them," he warned in 1791.[72] Slaves first needed to be morally "regenerated" before they could exercise the rights of citizenship, allowing the government to defer democracy.[73] Within the context of colonialism and black emancipation, such reasoning entailed that universal citizenship in theory translated into a racialized citizenship regime in practice.

The creation of a republican national-imperial community brought stark disagreements to light surrounding the nature of imperial sovereignty and, ultimately, the meaning of the French Revolution itself. Metropolitans grappled with the complexities of imperial revolution while confronting the changing circumstances in France, and in many ways the two mutually reinforced one another. Revolutionary rhetoric began to change as ideas traveled through and migrated across the empire. With collective emancipation and the creation of a French imperial nation-state in 1794, republicans gained a new sense of the universal values underpinning their revolution, even as war and domestic terror encouraged a more militant brand of republican nationalism focused on the cult of the *patrie*. "All the revolutions which till now had changed the face of empire had as their goal solely a change of dynasty or the transfer of power from one individual into the hands of many," Robespierre stated in 1794. "The French Revolution is the first which is based on the theory of the rights of humanity and on the principles of justice."[74]

Citizens and *Citoyennes*

As the debates over slavery and emancipation were beginning to take shape in 1789, the Estates General was presented with a list of grievances under the title *Cahier des doléances des femmes*. There was talk of freeing blacks, the author stated. "Why not free women also?"[75] Drafted in the moment of anticipation leading up to the meeting of the Estates General that summer, the document revealed the potentially radical implications that reform could unleash and the empowerment that many groups experienced as France headed toward revolution. As with issues of race and slavery, women's rights similarly illuminated the complexities that revolutionary ideas of equality presented. In fact, many advocates of female emancipation saw their cause in parallel terms, comparing their struggles for equality with the plight of the disenfranchised *gens de couleur* and slaves of the colonies.[76] Leading female activists participated in the abolition campaigns of the 1780s. In 1788, the playwright and feminists Olympe de Gouges argued against the rationale of inherent racial inferiority that many used to justify slavery. "Force and prejudices" alone explained enslavement, she contented; "Nature plays no role."[77] She would apply this principled defense of natural equality to her views on women as well, insisting that if equality entailed an end to racial subjugation it also entailed an end to gender hierarchies and exclusion based on sexual difference. Polemics against colonial bondage mirrored attacks on metropolitan social relations, demonstrating the power that the metaphor of "slavery" possessed in an age premised on liberation and universal emancipation.

The French Revolution brought the issue of women's rights to the forefront of politics. Yet as many historians have noted, women equally played an integral role in developing the ideology and politics of the French Revolution. It was women who led the march to Versailles in the autumn of 1789 that brought the royal family back to Paris; women were among the main protestors demanding bread and price controls on household goods; women participated in the revolutionary public festivals and played a key role in putting forward calls for social inclusion and universal citizenship as the revolution unfolded: in short, they played a vital role in the revolutionary events that shook France. Yet female participation was shaped by women's unique experiences in revolutionary politics. From the start, women's rights had a specific place in the general social restructuring that the revolution actualized. In taking up their newfound role as citizens, women appropriated revolutionary rhetoric to ensure that the revolution would also be their revolution.[78]

In pre-revolutionary France, women possessed very limited sets of rights. As the commodity of husbands and fathers, women were not permitted to hold independent wealth, could not serve in public office and had fewer opportunities to advance themselves through education. In most cases, women were relegated to the domestic sphere and denied a public role or identity. Some Enlightenment thinkers criticized the dependent role women endured and challenged prevailing notions that patriarchic rule was grounded in "nature," as various apologists maintained.[79] Moreover, the Enlightenment presented opportunities for elite women to fulfill certain public roles. During the eighteenth century, women served as organizers and arbiters of intellectual debate in the salons. *Salonnières* governed the rules of "polite conversation" that underpinned the Republic of Letters and in the process often exercised a marked influence on the rhetoric and texts of the Enlightenment. In the changing cultural and social attitudes of the eighteenth century, sociability came to embody an idea of gendered complementarity that held out the prospect of a greater public role for certain women.[80] Such ambitions would become radicalized after 1789. Yet paradoxically the French Revolution would also present new obstacles to female participation in the public sphere.

In dismantling the social and political conventions of the Ancien Régime, the revolution did draw into question the traditional relationship between man and wife. Attacks on the divine right of kings could easily be translated into an attack on the divine right of husbands. The possibilities for such a radical social revolution were, however, often held in check by the revolutionaries themselves and their reverence for Rousseau, the primary ideologue to which revolutionaries looked. Rousseau claimed that women had emerged from the state of nature as sensitive, passive and irrational creatures. They were nurturing beings that complemented the independent, rational male. In his famous novel *Émile*, the female protagonist Sophie was depicted as the iconic woman committed to counseling and serving men while instilling good republican values in their children. "These are the duties of woman at all times," Rousseau insisted, "and they ought to be taught from childhood."[81] Although revolutionaries did not deny women were citizens, the term "*citoyenne*" was never intended to connote female enfranchisement. Citizenship was a universal designator in the new revolutionary nation, with *citoyenne* constituting its female counterpart. Women were intended to be "passive" citizens. If men were rational and suited for public life, women were believed to lack the necessary qualities of self-governance and independence embodied by the virtuous citizen. Taking their cue from Rousseau, revolutionaries argued that women should fulfill their patriotic duty by serving as "moral guardians" of the revolution in the home. The public sphere was recast as an explicitly male space from which women were to be excluded. The revolution and the republic were never divorced from patriarchic attitudes that refused an active and civic identity for women; they merely reconfigured these traditional attitudes along new lines.[82]

If women persisted to find themselves confined to the "domestic sanctuary" and treated as second-class citizens, the revolution did nonetheless impress itself upon family life and break down many of the oppressive institutions of Ancien Régime society. In September 1792, the national legislature legalized divorce, making marriage a civil contract that offered women some legal control over their personal lives. This measure was accompanied by further rulings on inheritance laws and child custody. The practice of primogeniture intended to preserve aristocratic estates across generations was abandoned, mandating equal inheritance among children. Women were given the right to testify in court and promises were made to provide state-sponsored education for girls. These reforms effectively altered the legal status of women and the family in the French nation and provided new avenues for legal redress and advancement that had not existed in the pre-revolutionary period.[83] Despite evident shortcomings relating to equality of rights, the revolution did reshape gender and family relations in an effort to overturn the patriarchic institutions of the Ancien Régime and reinterpret the family as a compact of equal citizens. Moreover, the popular activism and radicalism of revolutionary politics did not preclude the hope of obtaining equal citizenship with men either.

The activist Olympe de Gouges in fact sought both social and political reform when it came to female emancipation. Transitioning from a literary into a political writer over the course of the 1780s, de Gouges was a leading advocate of women's rights during the revolution that allied with the Girondins. In 1791, she made her case for female equality in no uncertain terms, publishing her *Declaration of the Rights of Women and Citoyenne*, an obvious critique of the Declaration of Rights issued in 1789. "What gives you the sovereign right to oppress my sex?" de Gouges asked her imagined male readers in the preamble before enumerating a series of demands on behalf of women ranging from equal property rights to political participation. Her pointed retorts questioned why it was that women had been excluded from the universal claims made by the revolution and called upon women to seek their own liberation if men were unwilling to grant it. "Women awaken ... and acknowledge your rights!" she declared. "Whichever barriers may be encircling you, it is in your power to emancipate yourselves from them; you only have to wish to do so."[84]

De Gouges's appeal to female self-empowerment was consistent with events transpiring in the major French cities at this time. As clubs became centers of political activism in which citizens partook in the revolution, women sought to engage in the revolutionary sociability and fervor sweeping the country. The Société Fraternelle was the first club in France to allow women active membership and was rebuked by the Jacobins for its decision to do so. The radical Cordeliers Club permitted women to attend sessions but never allowed them to serve as active members, and this policy was typically shared among many other leading clubs of the day. The Cercle Club in Paris offered the outspoken Dutch feminist Etta Palm d'Aelders the opportunity to address her male counterparts and press upon them the necessity of pursuing a truly emancipatory policy as they carried out their work of social regeneration in 1790. "You have restored to men the dignity of his being in recognizing his rights ... [so why] allow women to groan beneath an arbitrary authority?" she asked pointedly.[85] Despite their presence in the clubs, women found it difficult to dispel attitudes held by many club members who refused to accept them as equal citizens.[86] These proscriptions did not, however, prevent women from trying to enter political life. Excluded from full participation in the existing clubs, they could set up their own clubs, adhering to de Gouges's injunction of self-empowerment.

Etta Palm was a pioneer in leading the movement, although her attempt to set up a network of women's clubs in Paris proved unsuccessful due to their high subscription rates. Nevertheless, women's clubs did sprout up in French cities over the next year. While advocates like de Gouges, Etta Palma and the more radical Théroigne de Méricourt, a singer-turned revolutionary patriot, continued to make demands for full women's rights in the name of equality, the clubs became the true embodiment of this principle. They presented a forum in which female revolutionary sociability advanced claims for natural rights and civic parity. "Before we were forgotten, reduced to housework and the education of our children; deprived of the benefits of law, we lived in abject obscurity, painfully enduring our degradation," Marie Dobre, member of a Bordelaise women's club, told her fellow *citoyennes* in 1792. "Now the blindfold which hid the truth from us has been lifted; in turn, we too have become free citizens."[87] Through these forms of popular participation, women projected themselves as revolutionary actors committed to the moral good of society. They challenged accepted gender roles and invested the term *citoyenne* with a civic connotation that surpassed the limited role imagined by legislators.[88] These changes proceeded apace with the general radicalization of the revolution, one often influencing the other.

Anne-Pauline Léon was emblematic of the new mood arising. The daughter of a chocolate manufacturer, she was twenty-two at the outbreak of the French Revolution and according to her own account assisted on the barricades in July 1789. In 1793, she married the *enragé* journalist Théophile Leclerc and began organizing women to foment riots and fuel the general *sans-culotte* protests erupting throughout Paris. Her republican feminism extended to the militant brand of citizenship endorsed by the Girondins. Gathering signatures on a petition that she presented to the government, Léon called for the arming of female citizens, creating a Garde Nationale soon rebranded as an "Amazon Legion" committed to defending the capital from invasion. The right to bear arms would turn women into active citizens and stand as a symbol of true equality in Léon's view. Female radicals aimed to ensure their part in the people's revolution, but the Jacobin leadership was hesitant to acknowledge this outburst of female patriotism. To push the matter, Léon helped create the Société des Citoyennes Républicaines Révolutionnaires, a club organized to recruit female volunteers and fight insurgents in the Vendée.[89] Over the next two years, the revolutionary wars provided opportunities for women to demonstrate their patriotism and challenge reigning images of female domesticity and republican motherhood. With the militarization of French society, women fought on the lines. In rare cases, they were awarded military honors and advanced to higher-ranking positions in the military.[90]

The Club de Citoyennes was indicative of the female *sans-culottism* growing up under the republic. Moreover, it signaled a split in the women's movement as radical *femmes patriotes* like Léon moved further to the left than the elite *clubistes* like Etta Palm and Méricourt. Whereas *clubistes* agitated for women's rights through pamphlets and lobbying, militants organized women workers and made them a political force in the streets. They embraced a range of social and political issues extending beyond specific questions of female participation and gender norms. Radicals joined and in many cases provoked the bread riots and protests demanding a war on hoarders. In pushing for price controls, they elicited fierce debates pertinent to the economy, the social contract and patriotism, indicating the varied registers that women used to articulate conceptions of citizenship and what it meant to be a good republican.[91] Occasionally these divisions resulted in outright violence. Market women refusing to abide by the maximum became targets of the self-styled Citoyennes Républicaines Révolutionnaires who gathered in central Paris flaunting red caps and vandalized market stalls. In May of 1793, Méricourt, a known Girondin supporter, was assaulted by a group of *femmes patriotes* in public. These divisions paralleled the growing divisions between *enragé* militants and the revolutionary leadership. The Robespierrists desired to maintain control of Paris and preserve order. *Sans-culotte* agitators were a persistent obstacle to this goal, raising the question of who really held power in the capital—the government or the radical organizers?

The Jacobins employed revolutionary justice and the maximum to pacify militants, but they had little intention of ceding control to the *enragés*. With the Terror, they proceeded to crack down on *sans-culotte* leaders while appeasing the *enragé* base. Their plan aimed to atomize the radical movements and reign in the popular clubs. Attacks on the female leadership were part and parcel of this strategy. In October 1793, women were formally banished from public life and forbidden from membership in political organizations.[92] Olympe de Gouges was among the female activists rounded up in the Jacobin witch hunt as the Terror commenced. Her refusal to sanction the execution of Louis XVI and her Girondist sympathies pegged her as a "monarchist" and threat to the nation. From jail, she condemned the Jacobins and the Terror in secret writing smuggled out by friends. This criticism hardly put her in good favor with her captors. Three days after the Girondin leadership was guillotined, de Gouges was sentenced to death and executed.

Despite this backlash, female political activities revealed how ideas of revolutionary empowerment spurred certain individuals and groups into action over the course of the early 1790s. Women writers and activists linked the cause of female emancipation to the broader ideals of the revolution. In adopting the universal rhetoric of revolution, they agitated on behalf of a particular group and argued that the French Revolution must also constitute a revolution in women's rights and social inclusion. Advocates like de Gouges called for a new sense of feminine solidarity in their declarations. Anne-Pauline Léon and other organizers transformed this imagined solidarity into a reality, and in doing so attempted to ensure that a nominally "women's revolution" and the people's revolution were one and the same. For a few hundred women, the clubs and popular societies represented the first recognition of their existence as citizens. Although part of the general mass politicization that clubs fomented, this experience was unique to women and highlighted the latent contradictions inherent within revolutionary concepts of equality and citizenship. In seeking inclusion in a community of equals, women were compelled to make a case for themselves and focus on the specific forms of oppressions and marginalization they faced. There was a certain irony evident. Attaining equality compelled female activists to rebel against the community and its ideology, at times pitting them against a revolution that rejected them.[93]

Conclusion

Revolution presented new opportunities to reshape the social body, and newly empowered spokespeople did not hesitate to do so as they vocalized their grievances and demands for inclusion. Leaders ranging from working-class activists to women to colonial populations endeavored to link their liberation to the general people's revolution. As they did, the articulation of specific social identities became intimately associated with acts of revolutionary community building in the late eighteenth century. The scenarios of empowerment that played out during the revolutionary period assumed various forms. Colonial elites employed revolutionary principles to secure their own autonomy; day-laborers in France challenged elite rule while female activists argued for gender equality and the recognition of women's rights. Such agitators endeavored to shape new conceptions of community based upon particular categories of race, class and gender that, nonetheless, expressed themselves through the universalist rhetoric of revolutionary equality and emancipation. In many cases, these groups referenced one another, with advocates of social equality tying their plight to the conditions of colonial slavery and demands for social leveling expressed through calls for gender equality. Yet if revolutionary situations provided a means of articulating particular forms of emancipation, they also met strong opposition as newly formed governments and states attempted to rein in destabilizing forces and enforce new definitions of sovereignty born from the revolutionary experience.

Revolutionary politics engendered new points of conflict that threatened to fragment the envisaged social unity that revolution promised. Upheaval brought into question existing social hierarchies and presented opportunities for empowerment. The question facing revolutionary governments was where did this process end? Desires for control and social order provoked efforts to fix identity regimes and social hierarchies, resulting in the disempowerment of certain revolutionary groups and actors. Attempts to impose order on revolutionary societies gave credence to ideas of limited citizenship and "civilization" as well as the discourse of separate gender spheres intended to deny women a public identity. As revolution threatened to spiral out of control, a general shift in attitudes was beginning to take shape as political elites contended with the consequences of radical empowerment and social upheaval.

CHAPTER 4
TAMING THE FURIES OF REVOLUTION: ORDER, DISORDER AND EMPIRE (1794–1815)

The Jacobin dictatorship marked the apogee of "revolutionary government" in France but the community it created relied upon forms of coercion and state discipline that were impossible to sustain indefinitely. Jacobin policies exacerbated rather than eliminated the political vendettas and divisions generated by the French Revolution. With war and violence straining the republic, the economy plummeted. Manufacturers, businessmen and educators fled the country. Goods and resources were requisitioned for the war effort while state powers were increasingly subject to revolutionary decree. The revolution became its own end as Robespierre, Saint-Just and those heading the Committee of Public Safety justified almost any action in its name. Yet by the summer of 1794, their arguments began to seem less convincing. Military victories in the Rhineland and Netherlands ensured that the revolution would not be suppressed by foreign counter-revolutionaries. Delegates in the Convention insisted there was no longer a need for the extreme terror tactics favored by the Robespierrists. The word "tyranny" began to be murmured by opponents who accused Robespierre and his allies of subverting the revolutionary principles of 1789. Robespierre was not oblivious to these allegations. In late June, he issued an ominous warning concerning the "conspiracy against public liberty" taking shape in the Convention.[1] Whether correctly or not, opponents interpreted these words to suggest a new wave of terror was about to be unleashed. "Moderate" republicans had little intention of leaving their fate in the hands of the revolutionary tribunals and secretly began conspiring to remove Robespierre and his men from power.

On 9 Thermidor of Year II (July 27, 1794), Convention deputies ordered the police to apprehend the radical leadership. Loyal Robespierrists immediately branded the motion a counter-revolutionary plot and attempted to rally supporters against the government. The effort, however, met with little success. Police stormed the Hôtel de Ville where Robespierre and his inner circle were hidden. Fire was exchanged with the outlaws. Some of the culprits already anticipating their fate committed suicide on the spot. Robespierre was found on the floor writhing in a pool of his own blood and carried out of the building by guards. Saint-Just, unharmed, was escorted out in shackles, his head held high in defiance. The following day, the group was sentenced without trial to death by guillotine. The guillotine had been the instrument of the Terror and the weapon used by Robespierre to silence his critics. Ironically, it now claimed him as well. Just before accepting his fate with his normal air of detachment, the young Saint-Just caught a glimpse of the Constitution of 1793 hanging on the wall. He pointed to it. "I'm the one who made that," he said, before his head was placed in the stock of the guillotine and the blade released.

The term "Thermidor" has become part of the general vocabulary of revolution. It is synonymous with counter-revolutionary "reaction" or an assault from above on the forces of radical popular revolution. According to this paradigm, radicalization leads to social and economic instability which, in turn, prompts elites to suppress revolutionary forces and restore elements of the traditional order. This process constituted a uniform stage in the classic "anatomy of revolution" outlined by Clarence Crane Brinton in the 1930s.[2] Recent scholarship has, however, questioned this neat schematic framework, noting the continuities that often cut across supposedly "revolutionary" and "post-revolutionary" periods.[3] The Thermidorian regime might best be understood as a period of transition rather than rupture. In the aftermath of the Terror, Thermidorians certainly sought a period of stability and national reconciliation. France needed to be rehabilitated, a stable government set up and radical republicanism curbed. Yet even if they criticized the excesses of the Robespierrists, the Thermidorians were republicans. Their views were "moderate" in comparison to the Jacobins, but they had ambitions of re-establishing a functioning republic nonetheless. Above all, they sought to place French government on a solid constitutional foundation and restore the rule of law. "Justice is the order of the day," as the government proclaimed following the coup. Thermidorians faced the task of providing an alternative to the "revolutionary government" of the Jacobins and creating the basis for a post-terror republic that would uphold the ideals of 1789 while purging the radicalism and excesses of the early 1790s.[4]

In this respect, certain statesmen interpreted the end of Jacobin rule as a "happy revolution" delivering the republic from tyranny.[5] To affect this revolution, the government took aim at the roots of the Jacobin movement. Former Girondins were permitted to seek redress and carry out a "revenge" terror that was almost as horrific as the September Massacres in some instances. Gangs hunted down former Jacobin officials and *sans-culotte* leaders. They raided Jacobin clubs, broke up meetings and purged the Paris sections.[6] The National Guard was reorganized to cleanse it of any radical elements. Many Jacobins quickly dissociated themselves from the Robespierrist camp to avoid retribution, and some, like the ex-terrorist Louis-Marie Stanislas Fréron, actively assisted in hunting down their former cohorts.[7] While the government proclaimed justice the "order of the day," this dictum rarely applied to combatting Jacobinism. As historians have argued, the terror and radicalism of the Jacobin regime did not necessarily come to an end after Thermidor. Ending the revolution was not an act but a process. As the state dismantled the machinery of revolutionary government, it reproduced and refined aspects of the terror regime. Political and administrative purges continued while dissenting and inflammatory opinions were suppressed.[8] Dictatorship gave way to a new type of state security designed to rein in political dissidents and ensure public order.[9]

In the summer of 1795 a new constitution was passed, officially dissolving the Convention. The Directory that replaced the Convention intended to anchor the republic in moderate political principles. The constitution provided for a balance of power between the branches of government. This careful system of checks and balances was to ensure that no single person or faction could monopolize the state as the Jacobins had. The Thermidorians were also conscious of the ways in which the Jacobins had deployed popular mobilization and fiery rhetoric to gain support for their illiberal policies. Post-terror republicans exhibited a patent distrust of popular democracy. The masses could be easily swayed and manipulated, it was argued, ultimately leading to tyranny. Under the new constitution, voting rights were scaled back to prevent the demagoguery that had fueled Robespierre's rise to power. "Active citizenship" was reinstated with voting rights dependent upon material and moral qualifications. As the official proclamation of the constitution declared: "The Revolution is established on the principles that began it: It is finished."[10]

This slogan was the mantra of the post-terror republic, a regime theoretically based on constitutional principles although not necessarily democratic. While these arrangements solved the immediate problem of political violence and radicalism, however, they did little to endear the vast majority of French citizens to the regime. The Directory's failure to stabilize the economy left the republic vulnerable to criticism. In "de-Jacobinizing" the state, the government repealed the maximum, abolishing the wage and price controls that had insulated workers from extreme economic hardship. As the value of the French currency continued to plummet and food became scarce, popular unrest followed. That spring, a new round of worker revolts broke out in Paris spurred by hunger and privation. For the first time since 1789, the military crushed these demonstrations, indicating that the Directory would not tolerate the *sans-culotte* populism to which the Jacobins had pandered.[11] The crackdown on working-class movements and popular protests drove radicals underground. Whereas once the clubs and local sections had furnished an organizational structure for political mobilization, after Thermidor these had collapsed. If the *sans-culottes* were to remain an active political force, the sections would have to be restored and given a new sense of unity.[12]

In this atmosphere, radical leaders formed secret clubs, the most prominent being the Society of Equals headed by the journalist François Noël Babeuf. During the early years of the revolution, Babeuf had made a name for himself agitating on behalf of small shopkeepers and artisans in the Somme. A proponent of social equality and democracy, he was among the first political thinkers to experiment with communal ownership schemes before moving to Paris to serve as a lower functionary for the Jacobin republic. His powerful denunciations of wealth and privilege landed him in jail on numerous occasions, transforming him into a self-identified "revolutionary" committed to the people. He even adopted the name "Gracchus" in tribute to the populist leader of the ancient Roman Republic. After Thermidor, Babeuf's attacks on the government and his radical ideas were received favorably by *sans-culotte* agitators and foreign patriots active in Paris.[13] Consisting of a small cadre of revolutionaries, the Society of Equals adopted a program calling for "true equality," and by this they meant the abolition of private ownership and all forms of social status. "The land belongs to no one … the fruit belongs to all," they declared. "The French Revolution was nothing but a precursor of another revolution, one that will be bigger, more solemn, and which will be the last." Legal and political equality were not enough, Babeuf and his followers argued. Real equality meant social equality, a claim attacking the very foundation of private property and individual wealth.[14]

For unemployed and starving workers, this brand of radical egalitarianism was certainly appealing. Songs carrying Babeuf's message were sung in the cafés where workers fraternized, with lyrics like "*mourant de faim, mourant de froid*" (dying of hunger, dying of cold) serving as rallying cries of a new working-class opposition. In his newspaper *Le Tribun du Peuple*, Gracchus Babeuf condemned governmental officials as "blood suckers" and thieves, inciting the *sans-culottes* against the new bourgeois aristocracy that had seized power. Only a year after Robespierre had been deposed, the specter of Jacobinism was rearing its head once again. This time, however, the government had no intentions of letting radicals get the upper hand. In 1796, it was discovered that Babeuf and The Equals were plotting an armed insurrection against the state. The authorities summarily rounded up Babeuf and his accomplices. The following February, they were tried for conspiracy against the government and later executed, putting an end to the threat.

The Directory could claim victory in having thwarted the conspiracy of The Equals, but the resurgence of Jacobinism remained indicative of a larger problem. The French Revolution had given rise to a host of new aspirations and expectations that sought to transform not only political institutions but the foundations of society. Revolution had politicized broad sections of the population and spread ideas of equality and freedom capable of provoking unrest. The Babeuvists had planned to channel these aspirations through an attack on the state, believing that popular rebellion would follow. Revolutionary ideas had suffused French society with a restless energy that needed to be pacified if order was to be preserved. How was a supposedly "moderate" regime like the Directory to manage this revolutionary fervor? The answer to this question was, ultimately, not to be found inside France but abroad.

Spreading Republican Revolution

The Directory inherited the Jacobin war. By 1795, France was pitted against the major European powers, all of whom saw the French Revolution as a threat to their very existence. The Jacobins had not only declared war on monarchy. They had transformed an ostensibly defensive war into a revolutionary crusade that pledged to assist all people "recover their liberty." This unquestionably meant spreading republican revolution abroad. Radicalism was looked upon as a "contagion." What the British statesman and inveterate Whig politician Edmund Burke called the "French malady" had to be combatted. "We are at war with a principle … which there is no shutting out by Fortresses or excluding by Territorial Limits," Burke warned. "No lines of demarcation can bound the Jacobin Empire."[15] His fears, if exaggerated, were not unwarranted.

French republicans actively encouraged revolt abroad and harbored radical conspirators. As Paris became a center of exile activity, the Jacobins willingly trained foreign revolutionaries on French soil to assist in their wars of liberation. Dutch patriots who had fled to France in 1787 following the Orangist repression allied with the Jacobins as early as 1792 to form a Batavian revolutionary committee inside France. These same patriots would be sent back to the Netherlands following French occupation in 1794 and help transform the various Netherlandish provinces into a unified republic based on the French model.[16] By 1793, the Society of United Irishmen formed in Belfast was in communication with Paris in the hopes of furthering its secessionist goals vis-à-vis Great Britain. The French government was happy to help. Fomenting an Irish revolution within the UK promised to bring the war across the English Channel. The militant Edward Fitzgerald lobbied for the Irish cause in Paris and joined the Jacobin club. Founding member of the United Irishmen, Theobald Wolfe Tone, also stayed in Paris during 1796 and was impressed by the model of the "armed nation" he observed in the country. In his opinion, the French were a free people committed to fighting for and defending their liberty, an ideal he hoped to replicate in a future Irish Republic.[17] French forces would assist in two military operations intended to secure Irish liberty during the 1790s, both of which failed.

Revolution was not always a subversive tactic employed by French hawks. Across the continent, self-styled patriots acted on their own initiative, emulating French radicals. When the Polish general and American War veteran Thaddeus Kościuszko staged an uprising in Kraków against Russian forces in the spring of 1794, patriots in neighboring Warsaw immediately set up their own Jacobin Club. Kościuszko's constitutional revolution quickly mutated into a militant republican movement. Polish Jacobins brandished familiar revolutionary symbols, organized crowds and lynched aristocrats in the streets. Although links between Paris and Warsaw were evident, Polish patriots were hardly the French provocateurs that the Russian government made them out to be. France was in no position to assist their fellow revolutionaries when Russia reinvaded the country in late 1794, suppressed the uprising and proceeded to partition Poland among the regional superpowers, effectively wiping Poland off the map.[18]

Radicals in Central Europe fared better in the short term. Along the Rhine River, France found German collaborators to work with once the Austro-Prussian armies were expelled from the region in 1792. When the Archbishop of Mainz fled in advance of the oncoming French army, a small group of patriots organized a Jacobin club, dubbing it the Society for the Friends of Liberty and Equality. Headed by the theologian Georg Wilhelm Böhmer and doctor Georg Wedekind, the club assisted in setting up a short-lived republican government that would support revolutionary reforms and serve as a pro-French party in the Rhineland, eventually voting for union with France a year later. Not all Germans were as enthusiastic as the Mainz Jacobins. Surrounding areas resisted the influence of new "French" ideas that threatened established cultural and political institutions.[19] As one pamphlet urged its readers, "Be German and remain German, and spit in the face of anyone who says a single word in favor of French liberty."[20] Those who "clung to old ways" were treated as enemies. The French military plundered whole regions of Germany and used the amassed loot to finance the costs of the occupation.

With their war cry of "*la patrie en danger*" the Jacobins had managed to secure territories in the Austrian Netherlands and Western Germany, dealing a significant blow to Habsburg authority in the center of the continent. France's borders were expanded to the Rhine, creating a *Grande Nation*. Upon taking power, the Directory had little choice than to deal with the realities of an enlarged French republic and ongoing military campaigns. As republicans, French statesmen were averse to outright imperial conquest. Moreover, the rationale of national defense that had fueled Jacobin expansion had not only inspired patriotism, but provided the justification for the Terror. This said, the war offered a much-needed source of revenue. Without the plunder accrued from occupied territories, the government would have been hard-pressed to meet its expenses. Immediate demobilization was also problematic. It was questionable whether the shaky national economy could shoulder an influx of French soldiers in need of employment. Under the circumstances, continuing the war seemed advantageous.

Over the coming year, a new system of republican expansion was outlined. The government maintained the *Grande Nation* extending to the Rhine. However, the occupied territories beyond France's "natural" frontiers were transformed into "sister republics."[21] Under the Directory, France actively created national democratic regimes along its borders with the goal of bringing into existence a republican federation based upon revolutionary principles of liberty and fraternity. Hesitant to encourage revolution at home, the Directory compensated for its lack of domestic zeal with state-building efforts abroad. This program redefined the ideology and rationale of the war. It also obscured the fact that these new republics were treated as tributary states by the French armies marching across the Low Countries, Germany and expanding into the Italian peninsula.[22]

Italy became a central focus of this new policy. In the early 1790s, self-identified Italian patriots had organized secret societies modeled on the Jacobins. These movements, however, possessed a unique character. Eighteenth-century Italy was an assemblage of regional dynastic kingdoms and small city-states. A branch of the Bourbon dynasty presided over the southern part of the peninsula while the Habsburgs claimed swaths of territories in the north. In the center lay the Papal states, which possessed their own jurisdictions. Italy was not a unified nation by any standard, and many were reluctant to recognize a common nationality among the people of the peninsula. For the most part, radicalism was locally oriented and channeled into regionalist movements. Sicilian conspirators agitated against the court in Naples while patriots in Bologna sought liberation from Roman tutelage. Given the insular nature of these groups, authorities were able to suppress and break them up with relative ease.[23]

Persecuted at home, patriots took up their cause in exile. The radical Filippo Buonarroti was a Tuscan patriot-turned Jacobin who arrived in Paris just as the Robespierrists were rising to power. Robespierre recognized Buonarroti's revolutionary fervor and put him in charge of organizing battalions of Italian expatriates. At Oneglia, he headed the local committee of public safety and prepared Italian refugees for an invasion of northern Italy. In serving the revolutionary cause abroad, Buonarroti espoused a more militant and republicanized brand of nationalism, placing his faith in a rejuvenated and unified Italian republic based upon the principles of Rousseau. The idea of a republic "one and indivisible" offered a new model for Italian patriots enamored by

Jacobin ideas and convinced them that with French support Italy too would enter onto the path of revolutionary nationhood. These aspirations were, however, cut short for the Tuscan radical. With the fall of Robespierre, Buonarroti was recalled from Oneglia and imprisoned as part of the Directory's general purge. Serving his sentence in Plessis, he became acquainted with Gracchus Babeuf, also a victim of the Directory's sweeping arrests. Upon release, he joined the Society of Equals and took up the struggle for the "egalitarian republic" with alacrity. A committed Babeuvist, he would be implicated in the conspiracy of 1796, jailed and deported. Buonarroti's years of French exile amounted to a valuable education in insurrectionary politics. By their conclusion, he was a steadfast republican revolutionary. If revolution was the spirit of the new age, Buonarroti was certainly indicative of its intoxicating influence.

With or without Buonarroti's participation, in 1796 Italy was on the cusp of revolution. That spring, French armies marched across the Italian frontier. In a string of victories against Austria, forces under the command of Napoleon Bonaparte seized control of Italy. With Italian power structures collapsing, French military field agents advocated republicanizing the peninsula and putting an end to the old regime forever. After some debate, the Directory concurred and authorized Bonaparte to "revolutionize" Italy. Patriots in the cities supported the French invasion, demonstrating the strength of local republicanism. Italian radicals believed their French "liberators" would assist in creating a democratic and egalitarian society based upon Rousseauvian principles. They were, however, to be disappointed. Patriotic nationalists favoring a unitary Italian state watched as Bonaparte brought into existence a series of small independent republics spanning the peninsula. In 1797, a Cisalpine Republic was created in the north, followed by the Ligurian Republic (1797), the Roman Republic (1798) and a Neapolitan Republic (1799) in the south. The Directory had little desire of creating a strong, united Italy on its eastern border and remained suspicious of existing links between Italian nationalists and French Jacobin groups like the Babeuvists. In "revolutionizing" Italy, the French government wanted to ensure that it was not sowing the seeds for a radical Jacobin republic abroad. The French administration attempted to dilute local democratic movements. It drew up constitutions for the new republics based upon the French model of 1795 and imparted republican institutions modeled on the Directory.[24] The elections guaranteed by the new constitutions were never held. The French military wielded authority to ensure that Italian republicanism was moderate in character and revolutionary agents were held in check.

Despite the reservations of the Directory, republican state-building transformed Western Europe and fueled revolutionary movements on the continent. French military intervention overturned existing regimes, and as established authorities either collapsed or fled self-styled patriots occupied the spaces vacated by traditional elites. Patriots founded newspapers, formed clubs and organized public festivals. They participated in a new culture that prized revolutionary nationhood over the old regime. Wherever revolution occurred the abolition of aristocratic privileges, reduced censorship and the end of feudalism followed. The Girondins had imagined the French Revolution as a universal cause. The Directory transformed this vision into a reality through war and military expansion.

Revolutionary Europe

Thermidor meant an end to the Terror, but it certainly did not entail an end to republican revolution. Between 1795 and 1799, the Directory continued and modified many of the tactics employed by the Jacobins. Whereas the Jacobins had trained and outfitted agents of radical revolution on French soil in the hopes of fomenting international revolution, Thermidorians exported the revolution in a more direct fashion through the creation of "sister republics" compatible with republican ideals of national liberation and freedom. Taming radical revolution at home corresponded to spreading revolution abroad, furnishing a centrist republican government with much-needed revolutionary credentials. This messianic foreign policy kindled patriotic fervor and placed France at the center of a cosmopolitan republican community.[25] As the diplomat François Cacault argued, the French had an obligation "to bluntly apply our principles and our law everywhere we go."[26] Contained within this agenda, however, were the seeds of a distinctly different type of revolutionary community, one that in the coming years would be translated into a vision of revolutionary empire.

Napoleon and Revolution from Above

The Italian campaign offered opportunities for notoriety and self-promotion, and the young Napoleon Bonaparte capitalized on both. A Corsican from a minor noble family, Napoleon had risen through the ranks of the revolutionary army to acquire a reputation as an effective and competent commander. He professed a deep commitment to the ideas of the Enlightenment and republicanism, although he made it known he was not a Jacobin. Nor did he encourage the political factionalism that consistently disrupted French politics. Napoleon was given a chance to prove his loyalty to the republic in autumn of 1795 when he was called to Paris to suppress a royalist rebellion against the Directory. The reward for his service was reappointment to Italy where he proceeded to lead French forces to victory. In managing the Italian republics, he used a mix of patriotism and military rule to constrain radicalism and implement French reforms. This experience made him an ideal candidate for France's next conquest: the Ottoman province of Egypt.

Since the loss of its American empire in the 1760s, France had kept an eye on the eastern Mediterranean as a potential new sphere of imperial expansion. Egypt in particular was given special consideration due to the French merchants already established in the area. Although nominally under the Ottoman sultan, Egypt had been ruled for centuries by a Mamluk elite who paid little more than lip service to Istanbul. It was believed that France could strike a quick blow against the Mamluk regime at minimal cost, and with Britain entering the war against France in 1793 the plan was revived. A French presence in the region would strangle British commerce and cut it off from the lucrative trading routes running from India through the Red Sea and Isthmus of Suez. Napoleon was up for the challenge. From Egypt he might even establish relations with rebel princes in India and expel the British East India Company from the subcontinent, completely routing British colonial interests.[27]

In July 1798, French troops besieged Alexandria and within weeks were moving down the Nile on their way to Cairo. The initial surge stalled, however, when Napoleon encountered strong local resistance. Sultan Selim III was not inclined to surrender his Egyptian territories without a fight and dispatched Ottoman military forces to expel the French. For added support, Selim mobilized religious leaders with calls to jihad. More devastating, British naval ships arrived in the bay of Alexandria and destroyed the French fleet sitting in the waters. Napoleon and his Armée d'Orient found themselves suddenly marooned in the Egyptian interior with British forces at their back and local resistance leaders attacking their flanks. The floundering situation compelled a new strategy, and Napoleon immediately shifted gears.

He muted talk of imperial conquest and took up the familiar rhetoric of national liberation and revolutionary universalism he had employed so effectively in Italy. Characterizing the Egyptian campaign as a liberation movement, Napoleon promoted a pro-Islamic and nationalist agenda aimed at drawing both the Arabs and Christian minorities to the French. As he spun it, France was liberating Egypt from foreign Mamluk oppression. In a series of proclamations, Napoleon made appeals to the "Egyptian nation" and declared a new government—the Diwan—centered in Cairo. His officers recruited Syrian Christians, Copts and Greeks into the government and army. To attract Muslims, Napoleon declared France a "friend" of Islam that was working to restore the Sultan. He proceeded to stage elaborate Islamic ceremonies and encouraged his top generals to convert to Islam in order to give the impression that the French were "sincere Muslims." These pro-Muslim sentiments were interspersed with a healthy dose of revolutionary pageantry. A Festival of the French Republic was held that September with revolutionary tricolors waving from the minarets of mosques. Through this blend of Islamic and revolutionary symbolism, Napoleon and his generals sought to create a national Egyptian republic that was cosmopolitan in character and founded upon revolutionary principles.[28]

Driven by necessity, the Egyptian campaign became an exercise in revolutionary community building. Yet the emancipatory promises made by the French proved more rhetoric than reality. The Diwan was an authoritarian military regime. Furthermore, for religious groups that had rarely thought of themselves in terms of nationality, the idea of an Egyptian nation was a hard sell. It was difficult to deny that the French were creating the very Egyptian nationality that they claimed to be liberating. A scientific committee was assembled to study and categorize Egypt, signifying France's "conquest of Egypt by reason." Teams of French savants compiled ethnographic statistics on the local populations, collected artifacts and drew up maps for trade and military use. This data furnished the regime with valuable information on the people and terrain of the newly conquered territory. By gaining a more informed idea of the local populations' customs and traditions, the French would create a republic reflecting the natural character and conditions of the Egyptian people, thereby "regenerating" them. These ambitions spoke to an implicit "civilizing mission" evident in French objectives.[29] Napoleonic Egypt was a laboratory for revolutionary community building. It provided a suitable environment for testing a new type of revolutionary project rooted in state authority and personal rule rather than democratic or civic principles.

The Egyptian republic was short-lived. Faced with resistance movements and British military intervention, Napoleon and his generals abandoned the eastern Mediterranean by 1802. Yet the experiments carried out by the Napoleonic administration were not to be ignored. In the coming years, revolutionary policies on the continent were set to undergo a transformation. In Egypt, Napoleon had established a militarized state committed to a revolutionary program, and he had recruited local support in sustaining it. Herein was a prototype of the future Napoleonic empire.[30] By the time he returned to Europe in 1799, Napoleon already possessed the broad outline of a new revolutionary program derived from his experiences in Italy and Egypt. As the eighteenth century came to a close, "revolution from above" was coming to replace the democratic and popular movements of the early 1790s. This shift was not a deviation from revolutionary principles so much as a logical extension of the revolutionary community building that had begun under the Jacobins.

Conditions for a change of policy were ripe in France. From its origins, the Directory had been beset by royalist plots and Jacobin conspirators. Its anemic economic policies and moderate brand of republicanism never endeared the majority of French citizens to the regime. Factionalism, always a problem, reduced the government to inefficiency and paralysis. Leading statesmen expressed skepticism as to whether the Directory could hold radical forces in check, and they were willing to put aside republican values for the promise of security. Sensitive to this growing unease, Napoleon presented himself as a plausible alternative. By his return to France, he enjoyed strong popular support as a proven leader and military hero. He was hailed as a man who had risen to greatness through his own merit, attaining glory for the revolution and republic on the battlefield. For many citizens, Napoleon was the embodiment of what the revolution symbolized: an accomplished individual who had not come from a privileged background, a true "child of the revolution," as the general liked to think of himself. Conscious of the Bonapartist movement growing up in the country, certain republican officials began conspiring with the general, believing this "child of the revolution" could provide a popular base of support for a strong and even authoritarian state dedicated to liberal policies and order.[31]

On 18 Brumaire year VIII (November 9, 1799) the Directory was unseated by a military coup. Like his co-conspirators, Napoleon was aware of the desire for stability following the Jacobin dictatorship and recognized that the shaky Directory was incapable of fulfilling this need. However, he was also aware of what the French Revolution meant to the country. It had become a source of pride for the nation. It had brought France glory and made it the focus of the world. Politicians and political thinkers continued to support its values of liberty and equality, even if they condemned the Jacobins. Napoleon understood that the revolution could not be suppressed or stamped out. Its appeal and mythology were too powerful. He himself had fought in the revolutionary army and made his name by it. Nonetheless, the revolution had to be tamed. To this end, Napoleon presented himself as a "man of order" who could restore confidence in government and rein in unruly forces. As he succinctly put it: "The Revolution ends with me." Yet to this pronouncement he also added the revolution ended with him because "I am the Revolution."[32] By harnessing the emotional and ideological power of the French

Figure 6 Napoleon Bonaparte © The British Library Board.

Revolution, Napoleon would inaugurate a new type of revolution within France and across Europe.

To deal with the problems besetting French society, Napoleon created an extensive bureaucracy that any absolutist monarch would have envied. State-appointed prefects were selected to govern each department of the country. These officials, responsible to the ministry in Paris, were charged with collecting taxes, enforcing law, devising new economic policies and carrying out all government policies flowing directly from the capital. Under the Napoleonic regime, tax collection became efficient and public revenues rose. The economic downturn that had accompanied the revolution was reversed as the mechanisms of state administration were vastly improved and perfected. Officials were ordered to make extensive reports of each region of the country regarding resources, land use and the population. From this information, detailed annual budgets were produced, adding a regularity to state finances that had been severely lacking over the past two decades. The state became a rational and well-organized machine capable of penetrating down to the most basic levels of society and mobilizing resources with efficiency.[33]

Revolutionary Europe

In showing his dedication to the French Revolution, Napoleon enforced a rigid legal equality, insisting that social status and privilege meant nothing before the law. Equality became the guiding maximum for the Code Napoléon issued in 1804. Formal legal procedures and the rights of every citizen were clearly spelled out under the code, dictating that the state would abide by specified legal formalities and powers guaranteed by contract. An assembly with advisory powers was also established, primarily to appease elites suspicious of Napoleon's authoritarian inclinations. Although the body had no formal power to initiate laws or state policies, it did ensure elite interests would be represented before the government. Lastly, a host of new schools were built in all major French cities to turn out competent officials and professionals. Unlike the old regime, these state institutions were declared opened to all individuals, promoting the idea of meritocracy. The objective behind these education reforms was to create a new generation of elites dedicated to the values of both the revolution and the Napoleonic state. A proponent of revolutionary ideals, Napoleon equally supported order and stability. By fulfilling the aspirations of the French Revolution on the one hand and resisting the anarchy of Jacobin-style republicanism on the other, the Napoleonic government set out to implement an orderly revolution that was neither reactionary nor radical.[34]

In the midst of these reforms, Napoleon declared France an empire in 1804. In his own words, to be named king would have meant to "inherit old ideas and an old genealogy."[35] In crowning himself Emperor of the French, Napoleon consciously referred to the novelty of the revolution and its repudiation of monarchy. This hardly changed the fact, however, that Napoleon intended to have the Bonaparte family recognized as a new national dynasty, albeit one ostensibly committed to the program of the revolution and not the old regime. Napoleon's popularity rested on his ability to appeal to a wide spectrum of public opinion. To republicans, he held out the promise of legal equality and administrative centralization. To liberals, he promised to uphold a constitutional regime bound by legal procedures. And now to royalists, he presented the possibility of a new French dynasty. The revolution had sharply divided French society along ideological lines, generating fissures between royalists and republicans, radicals and moderates, Catholics and secularists. Napoleon envisioned himself as a unifier. He was at once a child of the revolution and the most ambitious of the absolutist monarchs, and holding these seemingly contradictory elements together was a conviction in Napoleon's own greatness and abilities.[36]

Napoleon could proclaim France a new empire because under his rule it was, indeed, just that. With the war effort still underway, France controlled most of continental Europe. The west German principalities and Italian states had been reduced to nothing more than French puppet states. More startling, Austria and Prussia were on the verge of defeat and French occupation. The absolutist powers were being temporarily sustained through British loans, but this situation could not endure indefinitely. Britain reluctantly confronted the possibility of a French-dominated continent when in 1805 Napoleon routed Habsburg forces at Austerlitz. Within days, French troops were marching into Vienna. The Habsburgs had little choice other than to negotiate peace and recognize French supremacy throughout Germany and Italy. After Austerlitz, Napoleon was free to

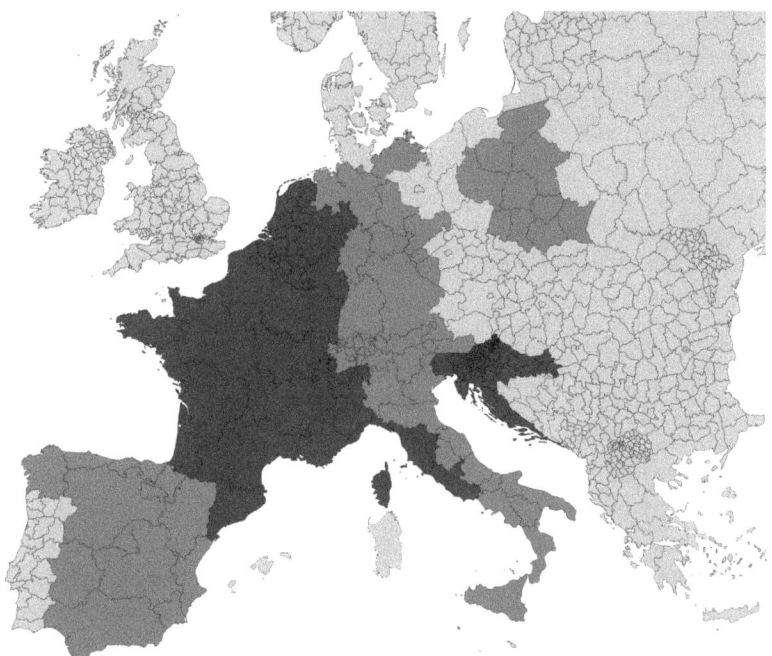

Map 3 The Napoleonic Empire at its height. The dark grey areas demarcated French national territories. The shaded areas comprise the satellite states and allied territories of the imperial periphery.

implement a series of reforms designed to transform the region and efface the traditional structure of absolutist rule in Central Europe.

Since the middle ages, Germany had been an assemblage of hundreds of autonomous principalities nominally under Habsburg control. As Napoleon moved into Germany, some princes welcomed him as a liberator, believing France would free them from Habsburg tutelage. These pro-French princes were rewarded with enlarged territories and kingships. In 1806, the German principalities were reorganized into thirty-six states bound in a federal union under the Confederation of the Rhine. Because Napoleon had appointed the kings of these German states, he could be assured of their loyalty, thereby bringing Germany directly into France's orbit. Much as in Germany, the assortment of Italian provinces and city-states was reorganized in accordance with the dictates of French imperialism, bringing into existence an Italian Kingdom headed by Napoleon's step-son, Eugène de Beauharnais. Napoleon even marched his troops eastward and took territory from Prussia and Austria in Poland. There he found support among the Polish nobles who had never acquiesced to foreign rule. In gaining their support, Napoleon empowered his Polish allies by re-establishing a Polish state, the Grand Duchy of Warsaw. This new Polish territory, while supposedly ruled independently by the Polish nobility, was in actuality a French client state. Just as in Germany and Italy, the Polish nobles were obliged to rally to Napoleon and comply with French demands if they wanted to remain independent.[37]

Revolutionary Europe

Through these new territorial arrangements, France was transformed into a European super-power. Moreover, in the areas under French control, Napoleon instituted the same types of reforms he had in France. Each new state was given a constitution, abolishing the traditional institutions that had propped up absolutism. Church properties were confiscated while each person was declared a national citizen. French administrators were dispatched from Paris to work with local rulers and supervise the tax collection and military conscription needed to sustain the Napoleonic war machine. By design, states were made dependent upon France for protection, ensuring compliance with French objectives. According to official ideology, these new countries were fighting with France to ensure their freedom from absolutist tyrants like Austria and Prussia. Yet such emancipatory rhetoric never concealed the realities of reliance on Paris or the power relations structuring France's revolutionary empire.[38]

Revolution "from above" unleashed an energetic program of state-building and centralization in the first decade of the nineteenth century. It also encouraged the same types of information gathering and ethnographic assessment elaborated during the Egyptian campaign. As administrators endeavored to impose French reforms on occupied territories, they came to think of their activities as a veritable "civilizing" mission.[39] In carrying ideas of rational government and "enlightened" values to the corners of Europe, Napoleonic officials asserted they were preparing local populations for modern, civilized existence. France was equated with the concept of "civilization" itself. At times, these attitudes scarcely concealed the underlying cultural imperialism they supported. In the Illyrian provinces (modern-day Croatia), administrators remarked on the "barbarous" people they encountered. Differences of "mores and customs," linguistic diversity and ethnic particularism ran counter to French ideas of national union and government. In Illyria, one administrator claimed there existed the vestiges of an archaic feudalism "such as existed in France in the fifteenth century."[40] French officials actively created new national governments, and in doing so modernized populations seen as hopelessly backward and even barbaric. "Civilization," a concept of recent invention despite its Classical connotations, provided the justification for administrative rule over these foreign populations. During the 1790s, French expansion had been guided by a rhetoric of emancipation and republicanization. Revolutionary imperialism, however, expressed itself through the less democratic idiom of "civilization."

Combatting Black Jacobinism

Napoleon's commitment to order provided a special point of contention when it came to the Atlantic colonies. Slaves had taken up arms in defense of the Jacobin republic, with Saint-Domingue remaining in a permanent state of war and revolution throughout the 1790s. Slave mobilization alarmed prominent *gens de couleur* on the island. Emancipation not only threatened to erode their social status as privileged "free men of color." It held the prospect of eliminating a key source of their wealth as slaveholders. It was not long before deep cleavages between former slaves and creole elites ignited a new race war on the island. André Rigaud, leader of the *gens de couleur* following Vincent Ogé's execution, was committed to preserving the plantation economy. While he was not averse to drafting slaves into the army, he had little intention of permitting them a leading role in colonial society. In France, colonial lobbyists had a similar outlook. They desired to restore slavery and re-establish order in France's most prosperous colonial possession. Slave liberation was only being tolerated in the short-term. It was not intended to last.

For Toussaint Louverture, this prospect was anathema. A former slave, Louverture had taken an active role in organizing slave resistance after 1791 and managed to consolidate a stronghold on the northern part of the island. His abilities as an effective general were evident as were his skills in diplomacy. During the war, he navigated between the Spanish, French and *gens de couleur*, siding with whichever power might further the cause of emancipation at the moment. He threw his support behind the French Republic once the abolition of slavery had been decreed, urging slaves to take up arms for the government. Nonetheless, Louverture was conscious of the pro-slavery factions that existed in France and on the island. As he saw it, the preservation of general emancipation would only persist as long as former slaves remained armed. Saint-Domingue could not depend upon the goodwill of France since its democratizing impulses could shift at a moment's

Figure 7 Toussaint Louverture © The British Library Board.

notice. True freedom meant securing colonial sovereignty under black governance, and this outcome was dependent upon restoring economic prosperity to Saint-Domingue. Without revenues to outfit and maintain the army, there could be no hope of self-governance.[41]

To this end, Louverture began restoring the island's plantation economy, the one true source of Saint-Dominguian wealth. Workers were subject to military supervision while a new *règlement de culture* (agricultural law) maintained the labor and property relations essential to large-scale agricultural production. These provisions were "the only means of furnishing sustenance for the military," without which emancipation would be a dead letter. "Liberty cannot exist without industry," the decree proclaimed.[42] While former slaves entertained hopes of becoming independent landowners, Louverture's plan foresaw a different type of freedom. Collective freedom and Saint-Dominguian independence took precedence over individual liberties, according to Louverture.[43] Sustaining independence required a militarized agricultural regime and institutionalized work system that would safeguard the island from predatory imperial powers bent on re-imposing slavery. In 1801, he went as far as promulgating a constitution for Saint-Domingue enshrining this system in law and formerly abolishing slavery forever. "All men are born, live and die free and French," the document declared. Louverture also took the liberty of appointing himself governor of the island for life, permitting him near-absolute power. Although the constitution did not openly declare Saint-Domingue independent, the authority it gave to Louverture and his administration amounted to a declaration of virtual autonomy.[44]

The fact that Louverture had not bothered to consult Napoleon on any of these measures only emphasized the move toward *de facto* independence. More galling, Louverture began launching military campaigns into neighboring Santo Domingo with the intention of liberating Spanish slaves and unifying the island. Louverture was showing himself to be both a "black Spartacus" and "black Jacobin" bent on spreading an emancipatory message and consolidating power. Napoleon had little patience for such recalcitrance and was eager for a new colonial policy. Reviving the once-profitable Caribbean sugar trade would offer a much-needed source of cash to fund his wars. Inevitably, this would require reinstalling slavery on the island. In 1799, Napoleon's new constitution had made provisions for just such a denouement, establishing "special laws" for the colonies that placed them beyond metropolitan legal precedent.[45] Louverture's bold gestures did nothing to deter these plans, although they did suggest military force would be needed to suppress the rebellious colony. Louverture and the threat of black Jacobinism needed to be suppressed and French control re-imposed.

In 1802, troops were sent across the Atlantic, with Napoleon's brother-in-law, General Charles Emmanuel Leclerc, selected to head the military expedition. On the orders of Leclerc, Louverture was arrested and deported to France to stand trial. While aboard the ship, Louverture used the moment to issue a firm warning to his captors, remarking that although they may have captured him, they could not suppress the desire for freedom held by the former slaves of the colony. "In overthrowing me you have cut down only the trunk of the tree of liberty of the blacks in Saint Domingue," he told them. "It will spring up again from the roots, for they are many and they are deep."[46] His rhetoric failed to move his captors. Louverture was found guilty of treason and imprisoned, eventually dying of pneumonia in jail a year later. Despite his death, however, his words proved to be prophetic.

When Leclerc attempted to disarm the thousands of former slaves who had served under Louverture, they resisted. French military force inspired another revolt as rebels formed guerilla bands in the mountains and carried on the war against the French. In their effort to suppress the uprising, French forces used increasingly brutal tactics, provoking a violent conflict that precipitated the complete disintegration of French rule in the colony. By late 1803, the French cause was completely lost. On January 1, 1804, one of Louverture's top generals who had carried on the resistance, Jean-Jacques Dessalines, announced the island's independence from France, declaring Saint-Domingue the independent and sovereign "Empire of Haiti." According to Dessalines, the new nation would serve as a bastion of unity against European racism and imperialism, offering refuge to any enslaved person who arrived on its shores. The same did not, however, apply to remaining white colonists on the island. As the French military troops pulled out, Dessalines and his men went from city to city massacring any whites who attempted to stay. Just as it had begun, the Haitian revolution ended in a wave of racial violence and brutality.

The establishment of an independent black state marked a radical turn of events in the revolutionary movements that had occurred since 1776. Haiti was the third nation born from these revolutionary struggles, but its character was unique. According to its founders, Haitian independence stood as a testament to principles of equality and human rights that other revolutionary societies had failed to implement. A nation of former slaves had fought for their liberty and overturned an oppressive colonial regime. Ideally, this achievement should have been celebrated as a victory for the revolutionary cause throughout the world, demonstrating the struggles of an oppressed and disenfranchised people against an imperial oppressor. Certainly the newly established American republic, having been a former colony itself which declared independence, could sympathize with the cause of Haitian liberty.

Such expectations were, however, greeted with a heavy dose of political realism. By the early nineteenth century, American leaders had begun to lose their taste for revolution and the Haitian Revolution in particular posed an especially frightening prospect. A nation of liberated slaves did not bode well for a country that tolerated the institution of slavery. Indeed, many American planters execrated the Haitian Revolution, fearing it might inspire slaves in the southern states to revolt against their masters. Shortly after declaring independence, Dessalines sent a letter to President Thomas Jefferson requesting closer ties between the two postcolonial nations. A Virginian slave holder sensitive to southern public opinion, Jefferson ignored the request, flatly refusing to recognize a nation of former slaves directly off the coast of North America. The contagion of black emancipation had to be kept at bay.[47] If ideals of revolutionary brotherhood and fraternity had once animated the Atlantic world, the limits of such promises were evident.

Revolutionary Europe

Resistance and Revolution

Challenges to French imperialism were not restricted to the Caribbean. Europeans as well bolstered claims of "liberty" and "freedom" against Napoleonic rule and in the process created conditions for revolutionary movements on the continent. Napoleon conscripted all abled-bodied Europeans into his military and deployed them across Europe. Italians fought in Iberia while Poles and German were sent into the Russian heartland and Ukraine. At its height, the Grande Armée was an impressive multi-national fighting force of over 600,000 men, the largest army Europe had ever seen. Local communities often bore the costs associated with these wars and were treated as little more than colonized peoples providing resources for the Napoleonic war machine. Persistent French demands for men and money took a toll on client states, which by the second decade of the nineteenth century were less willing to commit themselves to the French cause. French "liberation" at bayonet point provoked calls for national freedom and resistance.

Swiss intellectuals like Germaine de Staël and the political writer Benjamin Constant were vocal opponents of Napoleon and not afraid to expose his "civilizing mission" for the oppressive system of rule that it was. Rather than a liberator of nations, Napoleon was their captor, according to de Staël. Patriotism and the revival of "national sentiment" in her opinion would rid the continent of Napoleonic despotism. In contrast to an imperious and "foreign" French civilization thrust upon European populations, opponents promoted a form of cultural nationalism rooted in an organic national community.[48] Rather than national independence gifted by French military commanders, critics argued that true national independence would come only through resistance to French imperialism and the founding of properly national institutions.

Cultural nationalism marked the beginnings of nineteenth-century Romanticism, a movement that originated with Rousseau and the French Revolution but soon came to define itself in opposition to the abstract reasoning and generalization of Enlightenment thought. Romantics were interested in the ancient and primordial roots of national communities, often tracing them through complex ethnic genealogies corresponding with language and perceived traditions. Rousseau had envisaged the nation as a political community realized through the civic association of a people. Romantics, on the contrary, understood nations to be products of deeply rooted cultural traits and customs that had evolved over generations. Nations were not revolutionary constructs, as the French believed. They were pre-political communities defined by shared cultural ties and native affinities rather than constitutions and citizenship.

Many of these ideas dovetailed with Allied war aims, and Napoleon's enemies gave support to intellectuals who might stoke the flames of anti-French sentiment in occupied territories. Britain provided financial support for German intellectuals eager to mix cultural nationalism and politics. The philosopher Johan Gottlieb Fichte was encouraged to publish a series of addresses to the "German Nation" in which he tacitly compared the Napoleonic invasion to the Roman conquest of ancient Germania. In appealing to his fellow compatriots, Fichte urged Germans to look to their own national traditions and "spirit" as a source of liberation.⁴⁹ The German nation was a unity "already achieved, completed and existing," he claimed. Liberated from foreign despotism, it would be free to partake in a "new education" that would transform the Germans of Central Europe into a single people.⁵⁰ In reality, intellectuals like Fichte were actively inventing rather than rediscovering the historic German "nation" of which they wrote. Their works encourage Germans to reject the artificial assemblage of states created by Napoleon and look to a mythic German national past.

Certain Prussian officials were not above fueling German cultural nationalism if it aided the struggle against France, and some were forward-looking enough to believe Prussia might even press German nationalism into the service of the state, securing Prussian influence from the Rhine to Poland. In 1813, nationalism was channeled into the *Freiheitskrieg* (War of Liberation) led by Baron vom Stein who called upon all Germans to rise up and expel Napoleonic forces from Central Europe. The success of the effort startled many Prussian conservatives who remained wary of a mass movement preaching potentially revolutionary ideas.⁵¹ Conservatives endeavored to present this "liberation" as a movement led by the German princes rather than the people in order to discourage the war's popular and democratic connotations.⁵² No matter the interpretation given to the events, however, it was difficult to deny that in an age increasingly characterized by political nationalism, monarchs felt pressure to employ the rhetoric of "the nation" to achieve their ends.

The situation was no different for Spanish monarchists, although appeals to "national" liberation attained an altogether different dynamic in Iberia. Spain was placed in an uncertain position as revolution engulfed France. A revolutionary republic directly across the Pyrenees border posed a clear threat to the Spanish monarchy. However, Spain was also guarded when it came to Britain, its most formidable imperial rival. As the revolutionary wars unfolded, the Spanish government navigated between the two powers, often siding with one only to infuriate the other. In this complicated balancing act, Spain repeatedly faced invasion, naval bombardment and financial decline, all of which rattled an already shaky Spanish polity. Royal court politics in Madrid added an extra element of instability as resentment to the pro-French policies of the government drew indignation from officials and the populace alike. In March of 1808, the Spanish heir apparent orchestrated a coup against his unpopular father, taking the throne as Fernando VII. The coup was largely welcomed in Spain, with Fernando hailed as *el deseado*, "the desired one." This sudden shift in power unnerved Napoleon, however, who had reason to question the new king's loyalties. As a result, French forces were dispatched across the Pyrenees. Napoleon had been willing to tolerate the Bourbons in Spain, but only so far as they could be counted on to serve French interests. Given the instability at court, he found a puppet regime in Madrid preferable. Placing Fernando under arrest, Napoleon selected his brother Joseph to sit on the Spanish throne instead.⁵³

The Napoleonic invasion wrought havoc across the Iberian Peninsula. Royalists fled to the southern coast and in Cádiz set up a royal government in exile. Claiming to speak on behalf of the imprisoned king, royalists encouraged resistance to the French. To rally supporters, they espoused a strongly nationalist rhetoric centered on the trinity of God,

King and Patria. "Being thus united to all the other kingdoms of Spain," declared one proclamation, "we shall be invincible."[54] Royalists did not mince words. They invoked *la Nación Española*, an idea of Spanish unity tied to monarchy, faith and a single Spanish culture. This message was preached by officials and priests in villages and resonated with a broad spectrum of the population. As the war against Napoleon acquired a pronounced royalist character, a form of nationalism with monarchist roots developed in Spain. It unleashed a flood of patriotic nationalism that the exiled court was ill-equipped to control. As royal authority dissolved before the French onslaught, patriots set up independent *juntas* (councils) and banded together in local militias in defense of *la Nación Española*. Contrary to the conservative royalist program, some patriots among elite circles advocated for a new national government with greater liberties, acquiring the name "*libarales*." Liberals were willing to support the embattled monarch, but the price for their loyalty was a constitutional monarchy. As the Napoleonic government worked to shore up its control of Iberia, certain factions became evident. These divides highlighted tensions between local leaders, pro-monarchist liberals, conservatives bent on restoring the authority of the crown and Church, and pro-French collaborators—so-called *afrancesados*—coming chiefly from the Spanish bureaucracy and officer corps. As these rivalries came to the surface, Spain dissolved into civil war. Complicating this situation were the local *junta* militias that waged guerilla campaigns against the French but operated largely independent of the government.[55]

The breakdown of civil order across the Iberian Peninsula was driven in part by the local power structures and loyalties embedded within Spanish political life. Like all European monarchies, Spain was a composite of regional territories and jurisdiction. Yet its regional makeup was more pronounced than in other continental kingdoms. Each region constituted a veritable kingdom in its own right. Far more than other powers, the Spanish polity relied upon religious and dynastic associations rather than state structures as a source of unity. Territories retained their own legal codes, tax systems and political traditions. Areas such as Catalonia and Navarre possessed their own dialects and cultural identities. This system extended to the colonial domains stretching from the Atlantic to the Pacific. The Kingdoms of the Indies were never envisaged as a Spanish empire so much as parts of a composite monarchy attached to Madrid by particular dynastic arrangements and loyalties. Given the unique contours of Spain's Trans-Atlantic polity, any effort to bolster a "national" platform was bound to generate conflicts and raise vital questions regarding what constituted the Spanish national community. In many ways, these questions had already been anticipated in Spanish America for at least a decade before the Napoleonic invasions and royalist declarations in support of *la Nación Española* brought them to the center of Spanish politics.

Assuming the Spanish throne in the early eighteenth century, the Bourbon family adapted the practices of French absolutism to the Iberian Peninsula with the intention of transforming a sprawling medieval kingdom into a modern state with a centralized bureaucracy. To avoid conflict with the powerful nobility, the government focused most of its attention on the territories outside Iberia hoping to tap into the empire's Atlantic wealth and stave of Spanish decline.[56] These reforms drew the ire of colonial merchants and elites. They opposed the revenue collection schemes, arguing it would ruin the economy. They also bristled at the controls placed on American merchant guilds and the exclusion of creoles from government posts. Shared grievances brought together Spanish American elites as criticism of imperial centralization animated debates in newspapers, scientific societies and assembly halls. A nascent Trans-Atlantic public sphere was emerging as the so-called *letrados*—a mix of colonial merchants, priests, savants and educators—protested against Bourbon centralization.[57]

Creoles accused the Spanish monarchy of violating the natural constitution of the kingdom. Tradition dictated that Spaniards had "ancient rights" that must be respected by the crown. The New World territories were not colonies, they reminded. They were distinct communities, or *patrias* within the Spanish kingdom. The Peruvian creole writer Juan Pablo Viscardo went as far as to suggest that since Americans were distinct, they might even entertain the idea of independence if their rights were not taken seriously. "The New World is our Patria," he warned in 1792, "its history is our history and it is in light of that history that we must examine our present situation."[58] This brand of creole patriotism evoked the rhetoric of earlier colonial revolutionaries, echoing Paine's assertion of a sovereign American community with its own interests, history and culture. Viscardo reflected a radical position held among his compatriots. Most Spanish Americans did not reject Madrid, although they did remind the crown that their loyalty entailed respect for the traditional rights guaranteed to Spanish subjects.[59] It was not, however, too difficult to believe that creole patriotism might easily feed into outright independence if given the chance, and in the early nineteenth century the Spanish crown faced a political crisis that would offer this chance.

As order collapsed across Iberia, Spanish Americans had to decide what course the colonies would pursue. In the summer of 1808, Napoleon hastened to legitimate the French-backed regime and created a Spanish Cortes to approve a new constitution. Hoping to garner colonial support, he appointed six American delegates to the parliament and promised representative institutions for the Americas. Royalists responded that August by sending envoys to New Spain with similar terms and inviting Americans to participate in a rival Cortes based in Cádiz. They courted colonial elites with the promise of full integration, asserting, "the Spanish dominions in America are not colonies, but an essential and integral part of the Monarchy."[60] In no uncertain terms, *la Nación Española* was to be an imperial community with a common Spanish citizenry. Although couching their policies in claims of historic "Hispanic" sovereignty and tradition, royalists were in fact authorizing a radical transformation in Spanish government. To garner the loyalties of patriots and colonists, they were willing to re-imagine the kingdom as a liberal imperial nation-state spanning the Atlantic.

With the calling of the Cortes in 1810, liberals placed themselves at the head of a constitutional revolution in Spain carried out in the name of the absent king. Many conservative royalists were inclined to view this revolution as a matter of necessity and circumstance. However, it did generate a wave of patriotism that reinforced a common national resistance front against the French. In 1812, the Cádiz Cortes promulgated a constitution guaranteeing a representative parliament, freedom of expression and

Map 4 Spain's New World Empire, c. 1815.

citizenship with limited suffrage. Blending elements of French and American institutions with aspects of Spanish royal and Catholic tradition, the constitution was one of the most liberal of the period and a model for other anti-Napoleonic patriots across Europe. More importantly, the document provided *la Nación Española* with an institutional form and renewed sense of purpose that was immediately evident in the celebrations that took place across the kingdom. Town squares in every major Spanish city were renamed *plaza de la constitución* and cries of "*Viva Fernando!*" were heard followed by "*Viva la Constitución!*" In rejecting the French, Spanish liberals had ushered in an indigenous constitutional regime that promised to both liberalize and rejuvenate the Spanish nation.[61]

Across the Atlantic, however, the picture appeared quite different. The rhetoric of *la Nación Española* had initially resounded throughout the Americas. Many creole elites welcomed the new age of Spanish liberalism. With the calling of the Cortes, creoles foresaw the realization of longstanding aspirations for greater colonial autonomy and equality with metropolitans.[62] Cádiz had promised to reconstitute Spain as an imperial community, yet this eventuality raised a series of questions that were not explicitly clear at the outset. For starters, who exactly constituted the Spanish "nation" championed by the resistance? Colonial America possessed an exceedingly heterogonous population with specific hierarchies and a caste system. In the Americas, Spanish settlers lived alongside indigenous communities, people of African descent and varying mixed-castes categorized accordingly as *mestizo*, *mulatto* or *pardos*. Racial lineage often determined one's social position in American society and there existed very little sense of a common Spanish American identity. Iberian-born Spaniards (*peninsulares*) made up less than 1 percent of the colonial population while American-born Spaniards, called "creoles" (*criollos*), were little more than a quarter at most. These groups were typically at the forefront of colonial politics, but they could hardly claim to represent the entirety of the Americas.[63]

Even if racial and geographic differences could be overcome through the promotion of a common Trans-Atlantic nationality, the question of where authority would lie in this newly reconstituted Spanish empire was hardly self-evident. Colonial autonomists envisioned a federation of governments united through dynastic loyalty and a common citizenship. Under this model, colonial assemblies would have a fair amount of power exercised through the regional *juntas*. Certain colonial territories did not even wait for Madrid to authorize this conception of colonial sovereignty. In 1810, *juntas* began springing up across Central and South America, directly challenging established imperial authorities. As equal citizens, Americans anticipated a form of civic participation befitting a sovereign and liberated people. Although metropolitans were willing to endorse the creation of an imperial community, they were less inclined to permit self-governance in the overseas territories. Liberals in Madrid favored a centralized imperial model. They consented to colonial integration and representation in the Cortes, but they did not plan to diminish the authority of the Cortes. Power and laws would come from Madrid and flow outward with the metropole serving as the nerve center of a Spanish Trans-Atlantic nation.[64]

These two visions came into direct conflict as the Cortes gathered in Cádiz. American delegates invited to participate in drafting the constitution found their autonomist program repeatedly blocked. The promise of equal citizenship even became questionable as events proceeded. Liberals quickly realized that to enfranchise American colonists would inevitably subject the Cortes to American interests. With an American population of some 16 million compared with 10 million in Spain, universal democracy threatened to eclipse metropolitan primacy. To prevent this scenario, liberals created an artificial majority in the Cortes. Free colonists of African descent—the *castas pardas*—were deemed ineligible for full citizenship. By stripping this large group of voting rights, the American majority was diminished. Here was a familiar dilemma reminiscent of French Saint-Domingue. Colonial inclusion brought with it limited rights and a citizenship regime based on racial criteria. Although political crisis in Europe presented possibilities for greater inclusion and an end to illiberal colonial practices, revolutionary sovereignty rarely proved capable of reconciling claims of equality and citizenship across empires.[65]

Between 1808 and 1812, these crucial issues drove a wedge between the Iberian and American camps. Creole elites, frustrated with metropolitan efforts to curb colonial freedoms, increasingly reached out to the mixed-castes and Indian populations in order to counter the imperious rule of Spanish officials. Over the next decade, older ideas of American distinction were revived by creole leaders and, in some cases, given a new republican sheen as Spain attempted to impose its will through force on its colonies.

"I believe that the days of monarchies are past, and that they will not return until the corruption of men finally comes to drown their love of liberty," wrote the Venezuelan military commander Simón Bolivar in 1822. Rejecting Spanish rule, Bolivar believed that America could neither look to an oppressive Iberian past nor seek its roots in a largely mythic indigenous American heritage. The Americas were in a completely new state of affairs as colonists revolted. "Is not the entire New World stirred to action and armed for defense?" he asked. "If we look around, we observe a simultaneous struggle throughout this hemisphere."[66] This situation called for patriotic and virtuous men to step forward and create new societies on the ruins of the old world.[67]

Leading forces through Venezuela and New Grenada, Bolivar fashioned a revolutionary identity for himself as *El Libertador*, "the Great Liberator." At once modeling this persona on George Washington and Napoleon, he entertained ambitions of unifying South America and establishing a *Gran Columbia* in place of the Spanish empire. His revolutionary vision was strongly inspired by Rousseau and his republican ideals of a society composed of free and virtuous citizens. Yet forging this Greater Columbia ultimately proved impossible. Struggles between Spanish monarchists, patriots, ambitious military commanders and native Amerindian populations generated fierce and often bloody ethno-political struggles. To contain these centrifugal revolutionary forces, Bolivar, like many of his Latin American contemporaries, resigned himself to ruling through a strong authoritarian regime. Spanish Americans had little experience in self-government and were "not yet ready to take on the full and independent exercise of their rights," he reasoned gloomily.[68] Without sufficient restraints, republics would be torn apart by internal rivalries and factionalism. In order to preserve his idealized republican community, *El Libertador* paradoxically resorted to a heavy-handed and illiberal style of rule as Spanish authority deteriorated in the Americas. More a Napoleon than a Washington in the end, Bolivar would see through his own Thermidor, seeking to consolidate his revolution and preserve the independence of postcolonial Greater Columbia over the next fifteen years.

The revolutionary wave that swept across Latin America in the first three decades of the nineteenth century marked both a coda to the Spanish revolution of 1812 and a continuation of the independence struggles that had been destabilizing the Atlantic since the 1770s. As early as 1794, Baron Carondolet, the observant governor of Louisiana and Spanish Florida, was capable of seeing the threat revolutionary ideas circulating through the Atlantic posed for Spain's empire. "A general revolution … threatens Spain in America, unless it applies a powerful and speedy remedy," he warned in one of his many reports.[69] That this "remedy" was not sufficiently applied became evident by the late 1820s as Spain lost a significant part of its once impressive American empire to liberation movements led by charismatic generals like Bolivar and the Argentine nationalist José de San Martín.

This outcome was not, however, predetermined. Imperial restructuring, the collapse of Iberian authority and the ensuing political crises that emerged in the wake of the Napoleonic invasion provide conditions in which new social and political relations could be imagined. The royal government's efforts to fortify colonial allegiance were initially successful as Spanish Americans rallied to the idea of *la Nación Española* touted

Map 5 Spanish America in the wake of decolonization.

by *peninsulares*. Yet this nationalist rhetoric also generated conflicts surrounding issues of citizenship and sovereignty that highlighted tension inherent in the idea of a Trans-Atlantic Spanish community. Only once agreement with Spain proved impossible did creoles begin to consider alternatives. The diverse racial and ethnic composition of the Americas and the absence of a purely "native" constituency implied that a new identity had to be imagined through concepts of American sovereignty and a uniform citizenry. Revolutionaries reached out to a heterogeneous population and crafted polities that were at once republican and distinctly *americano*.[70] Diversity lay at the very heart of empire, and as imperial authority collapsed elites found themselves obliged to present new models of social unity that imperial sovereignty could no longer fulfill. Revolution did not imply a rejection of an overarching imperial system. It signified a process of community building as elites attempted to re-impose order in the midst of increasing anarchy and social dissolution.

Conclusion

Regimes seeking to temper radicalism were often revolutionary in their own right. They exported republican institutions, promoted Enlightenment notions of "civilization" or incited nationalist resistance against French hegemony in the hopes of realizing their own liberty. Rather than a Thermidorian "reaction," the late eighteenth and early nineteenth centuries witnessed a mutation in the revolutionary program as statesmen and officials reacted to the threat of Jacobinism and foreign occupation. After 1795, taming revolution inside France occurred in tandem with the spread of revolutionary ideals across the continent, and the two were not mutually exclusive. In quieting the revolutionary furies at home, the Directory and Napoleon redirected them outward. Generals and military officials could express their patriotism by fighting in Germany or Italy. They could engage in revolutions in Poland or the Balkans, playing out the struggle for freedom and national independence on the European periphery rather than within France. Harnessing the emotional and ideological power of the French Revolution, Napoleon created a revolutionary empire based on a model of revolution "from above" that checked popular movements.

Squaring revolutionary principles with imperial structures was a difficult balance to strike, but it was not necessarily impossible at the outset. Louverture in Saint-Domingue and elites in Spanish America both endorsed models of revolutionary nationhood that rested upon integrative ideas of equality and citizenship. Revolution inspired notions of imperial regeneration, heightening what one historian has called an "age of imperial revolutions."[71] This optimism was slowly diminished as tensions over race, equality and citizenship divided metropolitans and overseas territories and sparked waves of anti-colonial resistance that increasingly came to speak the revolutionary language of national independence. In both Haiti and Latin America, efforts to consolidate independence led to the creation of authoritarian and militarized regimes premised on similar ideas of order and revolution "from above" expressed by Napoleon. Founding revolutionary communities lent itself to acts of radical resistance, but sustaining these communities ultimately necessitated reining in unstable elements and imposing order through the new institutions of state. In its most aggressive form, it translated into new forms of empire, whether Napoleonic imperialism on the continent or Bolivar's vision of a Greater Columbia.

For some observers, revolution from above amounted to a betrayal of the emancipatory ideals first articulated in the late eighteenth century. Opponents of Napoleon criticized his authoritarian and illiberal practices, questioning how revolutionary values could be used to enslave nations. The American Joel Barlow had enthusiastically welcomed the French Revolution, believing it would fulfill man's aspirations for cosmopolitan and patriotic liberation throughout the world. By 1811, however, his optimism had waned. Serving as an American diplomat in France, Barlow had come to reject the pretense of Napoleonic liberation. Waiting in Eastern Europe to meet with the emperor and finalize a series of Franco-American trade negotiations, he used the opportunity to put his reservations into verse.

> Hurl from his blood-built throne this king of woes
> Dash him to dust and let the world repose.[72]

Barlow reflected the pessimism and disillusion expressed by many early nineteenth-century elites. They had placed their faith in the liberating potential of revolutionary emancipation and ended up with a tyrant who subverted republican freedoms through militarism and conquest.

Yet Barlow's pessimism could equally be applied to his own country. The American Revolution had served as the "spark from the altar" that had set the world ablaze. Following independence and war, however, elites revealed their inclination for order and remained skeptical of radical forms of emancipation. The founding fathers who had supported the revolutionary idea of equality proved reluctant to extend this new-found freedom to the thousands of slaves held in bondage on American soil. Jefferson suffered the criticism of his revolutionary cohorts like the Marquis de Lafayette, who levied accusations of hypocrisy and foot-dragging against him. His refusal to recognize Haitian independence confirmed the famed Virginian's perspectives on the limits of revolutionary emancipation.[73] For a post-revolutionary American republic, the dangers of continued radical liberation and social upheaval were a dangerous prospect.

In 1802, Thomas Paine returned to the United States. He had left America in 1787, first returning to England and then traveling on to France where he lent his pen and voice to the cause of liberty. Although a republican, Paine had found it difficult to support the Jacobins who employed violence and force to impose their revolutionary program. Arrested in 1793, he spent the period of the Terror in jail, perhaps more fortunate than most. After his release, Paine remained in France and wrote a series of articles praising the Enlightenment and denouncing the influence of religion and religious officials on society. A committed republican secularist to the end, Paine found a French audience receptive to his ideas. Having made the acquaintance of Jefferson while in France, he retained his ties to America over the tumultuous decade, never loosing affection for the country he had helped forge in his own way. In 1802, Paine wrote to his old comrade, who at the time was the acting president, and requested a travel visa and entrance into the country. Jefferson granted it, suggesting that the old Trans-Atlantic comradery persisted.

Returning to America, Paine expected to be hailed as a hero of the revolution, a man who had stood by his principles and supported the cause of liberty in both hemispheres. Yet Paine was in for a bitter surprise. News of his return sparked a public outcry. Journalists lambasted the former patriot for his anti-religious and radical views. Jefferson's political enemies used the presidential invitation extended to Paine as a means of attacking the presidential administration, adding further flames to the fire. The fact that

Jefferson would invite a radical atheist to the country revealed, opponents insisted, that Jefferson himself was an atheist who desired nothing less than to see religion abolished in America. These accusations were extreme and intended to discredit Jefferson. Yet the fact remained that Paine, a hero of the revolutionary cause some twenty years earlier, was now a vilified public figure. While Paine published a series of articles in his defense, accusing the American people of ingratitude and a short memory, this did little to amend his public image. Collapsing under the deluge of public criticism and excessive drinking, Paine retired to upstate New York and died there in 1809. Every church in the locality refused to accept his body for burial, claiming a man who had spoken so vilely against religion had no place in a Christian cemetery. His remains were buried under a walnut tree on his small farm in New Rochelle where a service was held that only six people attended, two of whom were African-American. His obituary in *The New York Citizen* was short and to the point: "He lived long, did some good and much harm."

Paine's sorrowful end was telling of the realities facing a post-revolutionary America. The America that Paine had left in the 1780s was no longer the same America that he returned to in 1802. In a post-revolutionary world desirous of stability, there was no place for a radical thinker like Thomas Paine anymore.[74] America's democratic revolution was finished. The *fête révolutionnaire* was over.

CHAPTER 5
TRANSNATIONAL REVOLUTIONARIES: POST-NAPOLEONIC EUROPE AND THE MEDITERRANEAN (1815–1835)

"After me, the Revolution, or rather the ideas that produced it, will resume their course," Napoleon once claimed. "It will be as though, opening a book at the marker, one were to begin again where one had left off."[1] As a revolutionary "liberator," Napoleon perceptively understood the emotional resonance that 1789 produced across Europe and the world. If he believed he could harness and channel its power, he nonetheless remained skeptical of the potential to contain these forces permanently. Events would bear out his warning.

Following Napoleon's defeat in 1815 at the hands of the major European powers, revolutionary sentiments continued to smolder across the continent. Elites had reacted to Napoleonic imperialism with strong declarations of nationalism and demands for self-determination against French hegemony. Conservatives rejected dangerous "French" ideas outright in combatting Napoleonic forces. These poles of opposition contributed to the toppling of Napoleon's continental empire. Yet defeat did not entail that broad aspirations for equality and fraternity were expunged. Years of political struggle and military conflict had bolstered hopes for a new and "regenerated" world, and such desires found expression in new revolutionary programs. It has typically been assumed that nationalist ideologies inspired by the French Revolution and wars of liberation became the basis for the revolutionary romanticism of the post-Napoleonic period. However, such assumptions require re-evaluation. The nationalist revolutions that would roil Europe in the wake of the Napoleonic Wars often bore the marks of revolutionary brotherhood and cosmopolitanism preached by eighteenth-century patriots. Romantic revolutionaries in the post-Napoleonic era certainly advanced ideas of national sovereignty and emancipation, but they also positioned themselves within broader revolutionary communities beyond the nation.

In the immediate post-Napoleonic period, revolutionary communities were articulated in both national and transnational terms, demonstrating the resilience of cosmopolitan ideas prevalent during the Age of Atlantic Revolutions. Secret societies, political networks and a shared commitment to liberal values provided the means of imagining novel types of communities that cut across national and imperial borders in the mid-nineteenth century. During the 1820s, revolutionaries took up arms in Spain, Italy, Greece and South America, often transforming localized nationalist revolts into broader European and even global movements that provoked concerted international responses from the leading powers of Europe. From the Old World to the New World, revolutionaries actively attempted to apply revolutionary ideas of liberty, equality and brotherhood within a transnational context, giving rise to a liberal international that would drive insurrection and political mobilization in the decades following the Napoleonic Wars.

Restoration and the International War on Terror

While writing his memories in the 1830s, the French romantic poet François-René de Chateaubriand claimed he had "witnessed the death not only of men but of ideas" during his lifetime. "Principles, customs, tastes, pleasures, sorrows, opinions: none of these resemble what [I] used to know."[2] Chateaubriand's sense of loss spoke to the disruptive force of the French Revolution and its impact on all aspects of European society. Moreover, it was a sentiment shared by many of his contemporaries. The new doctrine of popular sovereignty had overturned centuries of royal authority and tradition. Preaching war on Christianity and the Church, republicans had attacked the foundations of social and moral order. From Portugal to Poland, new institutions were created based on revolutionary principles and entire regions remapped according to the dictates of French imperialism. In the midst of these upheavals, aristocratic families fled their ancestral estates and sought refuge in European capitals outside French control. Some even traveled across the Atlantic and established themselves temporarily in the United States. As revolution spread to the Caribbean, white plantation owners joined this migration, oftentimes arriving on the shores of France or the United States destitute and with their remaining human property in tow. In European capitals from London to St. Petersburg, émigrés held meetings and strategized on how to restore the French monarchy and reclaim their estates. In cities like Charleston and New York, colonial plantation owners published petitions in American newspapers demanding that the French government restore their property. In total, some 140,000 people fled France after 1789 while perhaps 20,000 left Saint-Domingue. All lived lives of exile, some more comfortably than others.

These details reveal that the Age of Revolution was also an age of refugees. They equally suggest that the French Revolution was a European-wide and even global event. It overturned and challenged existing systems, but it also impacted the daily lives of people across the world. Newspapers carried daily stories of political events in France and writers printed horrific accounts of the wars waged by Napoleon. Wartime propaganda influenced social outlooks and politicized groups outside elite circles. Educated society was acquainted with revolutionary ideas and often debated them in coffee houses, libraries and at public meetings. Armies and French troops became a familiar sight in towns and villages across Europe. The wars of the French Revolution marked the first "total war" in European history.[3] Conflict fundamentally upset society at its most basic levels, and for this reason almost everybody had an opinion on the French Revolution, whether positive or negative.

Opponents abounded. As early as 1790—before the outbreak of the Terror—the British polemicist Edmund Burke reviled the French National Assembly, accusing it of destroying France's traditional structures of leadership and subjecting civil society to the demagoguery and vengeance of "the people."[4] Burke's *Reflections on the French Revolution* was among the best-known criticisms of the French Revolution, but there were many others ranging from political tirades to wild conspiracy theories and religious condemnation. These critics, whether justly or not, were branded "conservatives," a position dictated by one's opposition to the French Revolution and everything for which it stood. For religious thinkers, the Enlightenment was a particular point of disgust. With their secular and democratic ideas, Enlightenment philosophers had unleashed man's most excessive and violent impulses. They had sought nothing short of the complete destruction of society, producing the mayhem and anarchy that had led to the Jacobins. As the call went: "*C'est la faute à Rousseau! C'est la faute à Voltaire!*" Such criticism furnished the base of a counter-enlightenment movement across Europe committed to restoring throne and altar at the center of society. Religious conservatives like the French émigré Joseph de Maistre insisted that "legitimate" authority came from God alone, necessitating a return to royal authority and Catholic morality without which there could be no social order.[5] In the wake of the Napoleonic Wars, these views fueled claims for restoration and restitution from those who had been dispossessed by the revolution.[6]

Many of these ideas found supporters at the highest levels of European society. Kings and traditional leaders rallied behind the doctrine of "legitimism," calling for a return to solid royalist principles threatened by revolution. The continental Allies that defeated Napoleon gave these demands serious consideration as they met in Vienna during 1814–1815 and hashed out what a post-Napoleonic order would look like for the European continent. This was no easy task. Napoleon had fundamentally destroyed the old state system. On his march across Europe, he had created new states governed along national lines, radically changing the political geography of Europe. Over the course of nine months, the Allies disassembled the French empire, redrew the map of Europe and attempted to restore a balance of power on the continent to ensure a lasting peace. The so-called "northern courts" of Austria, Prussia and Russia enshrined legitimism at the center of the reconstituted European polities. Monarchs toppled by Napoleon were reinstated to their thrones. Prussia and Russia were permitted to retake territories in Germany and Poland while Austria secured its hold over Italy once again. For many critics, it appeared the old regime was being restored, undoing the French Revolution completely.[7]

Although popular, this perception was inaccurate. Kings and dynasts may have spoken the language of conservative royalism and even outwardly projected such an image through the use of elaborate royal and religious ceremonies, but these gestures were part of a general "reinvention" of monarchy in the post-revolutionary period.[8] The restoration period was hardly a return to a mythic Ancien Régime. Legitimism, with its baroque court ceremonies and rituals, was just as modern as republicanism. Moreover, monarchs who publicly identified with time-honored royal traditions proved hesitant to give up the new Napoleonic institutions they inherited. They maintained

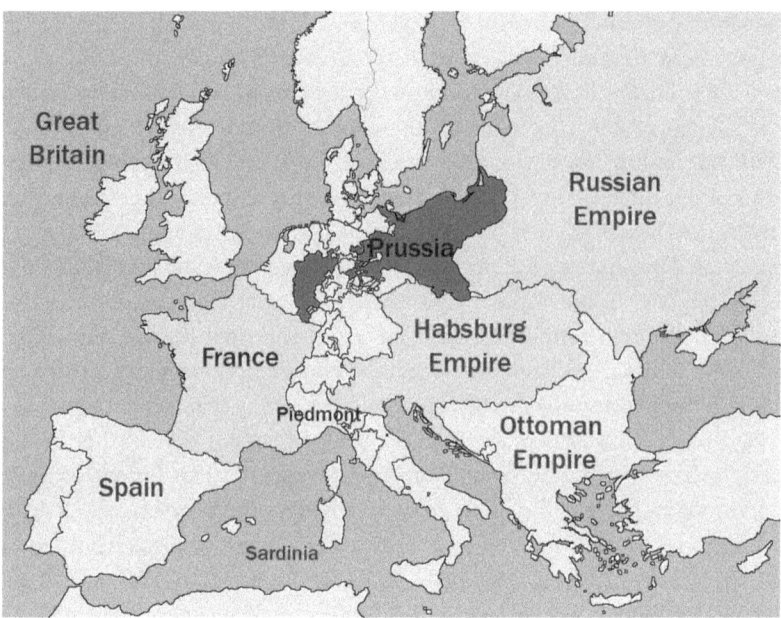

Map 6 Europe in 1815.

the centralized bureaucracies put into place by the French occupiers and welcomed the erosion of aristocratic prerogatives that had previously checked royal authority. Likewise, for all their lip service to religious revivalism, restoration regimes did not return the monasteries and Church lands confiscated by Napoleon. Some even accepted, albeit grudgingly, that they would have to rule through limited constitutions unless they wanted to court the furies of the revolution. The Allies proved disinclined to undo certain geo-political reforms brought into existence by Napoleon. In Germany, the new system of large and middle-sized states was preserved. The Napoleonic Confederation of the Rhine was altered slightly to ensure Austrian hegemony across Central Europe, but the new German Confederation was hardly a revival of the former Holy Roman Empire. Those calling for restoration often exhibited an appreciation for political realism and pragmatism at odds with popular perceptions of restoration. In a period of unrest, security and control was paramount. Many of the institutions created during the revolutionary wars could provide for these needs, even if Napoleon and the revolution itself were deemed detestable and heretical.[9]

The leading statesman at the Congress of Vienna, Prince Klemens von Metternich, exemplified the restoration spirit. Metternich had been a university student in Strasbourg in 1789 and recoiled at the demonstrations of popular support for the French Revolution that broke out across Germany. A committed absolutist from a young age, he was perceptive enough to understand the threat ideas of natural rights and popular sovereignty posed to the monarchial system. In 1809, he was appointed Foreign Minister and Chancellor of the Habsburg Empire as Napoleon's armies threatened to invade. One

Figure 8 Klemens von Metternich © The British Library Board.

of his key tasks was to stave off foreign occupation and organize a European coalition against the French. This he did with skill. By 1814, Allied forces led by Austria, Russia, Prussia and Britain had managed to push the French military out of Central Europe and drive France into submission. Metternich played a key role in the subsequent peace process at the Congress of Vienna, and by its conclusion was acting as the chief arbiter of the European peace and the primary advocate of legitimate government across the continent. A conservative monarchist and absolutist, Metternich symbolized the *bête noir* of revolutionaries and Bonapartists.

Yet it was not simply his conservatism that made Metternich the poster child of European reaction. Metternich was a committed enemy of revolution. Revolution unseated legitimate authority and invited anarchy. It promoted violence and political vengeance over good government and sound administration. At the Congress of Vienna, he was a leading advocate for a concerted European effort to stamp out revolutionary ideas and societies across the continent. The Russian Tsar Alexander had proposed a Holy Alliance to preserve throne and altar. For Metternich, this Holy Alliance was to serve as a guarantee of order and security. It was not simply a question of preserving the post-Napoleonic status quo, although this too was important. The European powers were obliged to thwart the spread of liberalism and revolutionary nationalism, ideologies that threatened the European peace and in particular the multiethnic empire presided over by the Habsburg dynasty. Under Metternich's system, the great powers would serve as Europe's policemen, and the statesman himself did not fail to boast that he was "the great minister of police of Europe."[10] The French Revolution was followed by a concerted diplomatic war on terror that sought to extirpate the roots of radical insurgency across the continent.

Metternich's boasting only stated the obvious. Since the 1790s, states had been busy creating internal policing regimes and weeding out possible revolutionary agents or foreigners suspected of being Jacobin agents. In Britain, a series of acts had been passed as early as 1794 permitting local authorities extralegal measures to combat domestic resistance and foreign subversion. The French Directory had set up its security state to uncover internal conspiracies and maintain order, policies which Napoleon perpetuated in the coming years with the *gendarmerie*. In a similar fashion, Austria created the *Polizeihofstelle* and *Fremdenpolizie* to monitor seditious groups within the kingdom while Metternich set up the *Beobachtung Anstalt* to gather information throughout the Italian Peninsula and report on Jacobin or Bonapartist groups conspiring underground. The model of the security state became the norm across Europe, continuing the "administrative terror" first implemented under Napoleon.[11] The Holy Alliance merely extended these new security apparatuses into the diplomatic sphere, committing the European powers to an international struggle against revolutionary groups operating across national boundaries. For the most part, these threats proved unfounded and were often concocted by police spies and sensationalist political writers cautioning against underground Jacobin clubs and secret revolutionary societies bent on fomenting chaos. That "terror" could be broadly construed to encompass worker protests, liberal constitutionalists and anyone suspected of disloyalty made the nineteenth-century war on terror an effective domestic and foreign policy tool.[12]

The Radical Underground

Restoration also meant demobilization as the European continent recovered from a quarter-century of war and upheaval. With the fall of Napoleon, the imperial army was dissolved. The liberation armies that had repelled the French were no longer needed. Restoration regimes purged political and military administrations to cleanse them of suspected Bonapartist and liberal sympathizers. Geriatric royalists, many of whom had fled the French and not seen military service in over a decade, were reinstated to their former positions, squeezing out junior officers who had served the Napoleonic governments or fought in the liberation wars. Officers who were not let go were put on half-pay to trim the bloated military budgets incurred during the war years.[13] The result was a sharp decrease in the financial and social status of former combatants and general resentment directed toward restored monarchies. For all their mayhem, the Napoleonic Wars had provided channels of upward mobility and career advancement for ambitious military officials. These were now blocked. The shift from war to peacetime was especially noticeable in the ranks of the military. According to Alfred de Vigny, an officer fortunate enough to obtain a post in the French army under the restored Bourbon monarchy, the effect was one of demoralization and disillusionment. The Napoleonic era had shaped the outlooks and expectations of his generation. "War was constantly in our midst; the roll of drums drowned the voices of my teachers. ... No subject of contemplation could hold our attention for any length of time when our minds were awhirl with the thunder of cannon-fire and the clamor of bells pealing out the *Te Deum*." Peace and demobilization amounted to a "universal shipwreck" for a generation weaned on dreams of military glory and militant patriotism.[14]

Demobilization not only posed psychological and social consequences that needed to be addressed. They also presented new political dangers. Disaffected military men eager to restore their former status were susceptible to revolutionary ideas circulating throughout post-Napoleonic Europe. There was no shortage of charismatic commanders with aspirations of being a second Bonaparte who might seek to capitalize on these feelings. Restored monarchs did not ease this situation, often permitting royalists to carry out "white terrors" of vengeance against liberals and former revolutionaries that served to harden ideological divides. In Spain, a series of small uprisings occurred between 1814 and 1820 led by former liberation fighters with the support of dissatisfied military men. The episodes were disorganized and easily crushed, but nonetheless revealed the extent of discontent toward the restored Bourbon crown in places like Pamplona, Catalonia and Valencia.[15] The French Bourbons faced a similar challenge across the Pyrenees. In 1816, the lawyer Jean-Paul Didier persuaded half-pay officers at Grenoble to mutiny while investigations conducted at other barracks throughout the country unveiled secret revolutionary plots and isolated movements to topple the restored monarchy. Authorities rarely took into account the post-revolutionary mood afflicting many junior officers and soldiers. For them, these supposed plots were the work of nefarious revolutionary organizations and Masonic networks bent on fomenting anarchy. The hand of the shadowy Paris-based *comité directeur*—a supposed secret revolutionary organization with branches extending across the continent—was implicated in every manifestation of discontent, prompting an energetic response by legitimate governments committed to waging the post-revolutionary war on terror.

The often-referenced *comité directeur* was pure fantasy concocted by police spies and authorities. However, secret societies did exist. In Italy, the years of French occupation witnessed a significant growth in secret societies, both pro- and anti-French in nature. They adopted various names, ranging from allusions to Classical antiquity such as the *Silencio dei Greci* to religious-based groups with names like *Cattolica* and *Apostolica Romana*. Many overlapped with existing Masonic societies driven underground during the war years. Radical leaders infused Masonic societies with a new political purpose that extended beyond sociability. The former Babeuvist Filippo Buonarroti actively participated in these groups as he moved between France, Switzerland, Belgium and Italy during the Napoleonic Wars. Having gained experience conducting subversive underground political activities through his work with Babeuf, he demonstrated a talent for creating insurrectionary cells, disseminating propaganda and organizing radical anti-Napoleonic groups. Through his organizational methods and diverse activities across national borders, Buonarroti was emblematic of a new type of political dissident coming of age in post-Napoleonic Europe: the "professional revolutionary" committed to insurrectionary politics.[16] In the early nineteenth century, he formed his own society, the Sublimi Maestri Perfetti which communicated with like-minded radicals across Europe. Buonarroti also popularized the Babeuvist legend by writing a history of Babeuf and the Conspiracy of the Equals that would romanticize the role of secret societies and his own revolutionary organizational tactics. The book, published in 1828, became a manual for political conspirators. Post-revolutionary figures from the French Neo-Jacobin Louis Auguste Blanqui to Karl Marx credited the tome as a valuable part of their political education, revealing its importance in nurturing a commitment to underground and subversive politics among a new generation of thinkers.[17]

The romantic image of the revolutionary conspirator popularized by individuals like Buonarroti contributed to the perpetuation of revolutionary politics in the period. Yet the revolutionary conspirator was only a symbol of a larger underground republican movement that remained active in restoration Europe and abroad. Republican organizations were entrenched in a web of political networks stretching across different European towns and cities. Many of them produced pamphlets, brochures and manifestos which traveled with members across borders and came to reinforce a commitment to a transnational republican movement. Although diverse in their origins, societies were driven by a core republican leadership which had not abandoned their ideals in the wake of the Napoleonic Wars. They preached popular uprising and indoctrination as the principal means of effecting revolutionary change. Secret societies sought to preserve the republican spirit of government in an age of reaction, fostering open debate among members that encouraged democratic practices of organization. These practices were intended to furnish the architecture of republican governance once the revolution commenced. Military men attracted to these groups put forward different ideas, often revealing tensions within the societies that were not easily resolved. Whereas republicans favored popular uprising and transparency, officers were inclined to advocate coups and infiltration as vehicles of revolutionary change. Secret command structures, centralized control and military-style discipline were, they believed, the only way of continuing the fight for liberty and constitutionalism.[18]

Many of these ideas blended together in societies, reflecting the diverse ideological outlooks of members. The most notorious and visible of these organizations was the Carbonari, a revolutionary society whose program stressed a mix of liberal internationalism and patriotic nationalism.[19] An offshoot of the Free Masons, the Carbonari set up its first lodge in Naples around 1810 and soon established branches, or *vèndita* in other parts of Southern Italy thereafter. Carbonaros were a mix of former Jacobins and liberal constitutionalists, all of whom had little in common other than their opposition to the Napoleonic government installed in Italy.[20] Membership estimates ranged from 3,000 to an implausible 600,000. Rumors of the society's initiation rituals were legendary at the time and served to shroud the organization in an aura of romantic mystique. Initiates were required to appear blindfolded in a secret location and proclaim sacred vows, recite revolutionary "catechisms" and participate in quasi-religious ceremonies in which one reenacted ancient rites of fidelity and, in some instances, the crucifixion of Christ. Secret handshakes and symbols ranging from daggers to skulls completed the conspiratorial aura that became a trademark of Carbonarism in the popular imagination.[21] This playacting of secret brotherhood aside, the Carbonari did exercise a prominent influence in the underground politics of the period. It counted high-ranking Italian officials among its members and in 1817 drew together the various Carbonari *vèndita* from different provinces for a secret meeting fittingly held at night among the ruins of Pompeii.[22] Its ability to attract influential activists and organize made it a force in Italian politics, allowing it to infiltrate the ranks of the military and local levels of government.

Its ties extended to France where Carbonari affiliates drew together and organized various individuals dissatisfied with the restored Bourbon monarchy. The lawyer and Free Mason Joseph Rey took an active role in setting up local associations that perpetuated the cult of Napoleon and in so doing provided a setting in which former military officers could meet and socialize.[23] These meetings soon formed the nucleus of a secret society, the *L'Union*, which forged connections to prominent liberal circles in Paris in the coming years. In time, members established contacts with Buonarroti and by the early 1820s create a veritable branch of the Carbonari (the *Charbonnerie*) in France uniting students, Free Masons, disaffected military commanders and liberal politicians such as the Marquis de Lafayette and the future socialist Amand Bazard. Buonarroti hoped to use the Carbonari networks much as he had previously used the Masonic societies to associate their branches and transform them into an international revolutionary network. Most French liberals, however, had more immediate goals at hand. Although they were conscious of being part of an underground liberal international with ties across Europe, their efforts were aimed at organizing liberal opposition in their own country and combatting the rise of ultra-royalist conservatism. While a constitution was in place in France, the restored monarchy had slowly been chipping away at its provisions and sidelining liberal opponents in the process. Authorities harassed newspapers and cracked down on political clubs, painting liberals as dangerous terrorists who posed an imminent danger to stability in the country. The French Carbonari drew together the vanguard of the liberal opposition, transforming the secret societies into bastions of revolutionary liberalism.[24]

Conservative statesmen and authorities hardly needed provocation in waging their war on terror. This is not to insist, however, that certain politicians were above exploiting events that might assist their cause. German authorities expressed alarm over the growth of young nationalist fraternities in the wake of the Napoleonic Wars. The war of liberation had unleashed a wave of patriotic and nationalist sentiment throughout the Confederation of the Rhine. Student organizers set up fraternal associations (*Burschenschaften*) that staged nationalist celebrations and mobilized support for the creation of a unified German fatherland. Although these demonstrations of young German nationalism were conducted peacefully and posed no overt threat to order,

Metternich and the German princes did not hesitate to peg them as variants of German Jacobinism. In 1819, this suspicion was given support when Karl Sand, a university student, stabbed the conservative dramatist August von Kotzebue to death at his home in Manheim. Sand had acted on his own initiative, believing that Kotzebue's attacks on German patriots in the press made him a "traitor to the nation." However, Sand had been a member of a Manheim *Burschenschaft*, and the association appeared to establish a clear link between this act of political terror and the German fraternities. Metternich wasted no time. He intended to "destroy the German revolution," as he put it, and imposed a series of harsh police laws and censorship on the German states that collectively became known as the Carlsbad Decrees. A Central Investigative Commission was set up in Mainz that transformed the German Confederation into a virtual police state under Austrian supervision. Authorities broke up student and democratic groups, silencing the incipient liberal-nationalist movements in the name of public order.[25]

An isolated act of terror similarly provided the impetus for conservative reaction in France. In February of 1820, the Duc de Berry, nephew of Louis XVIII and second in line for the French throne, was stabbed to death in the streets of Paris. The assassin was Louis-Pierre Louvel, an artisan and fervent Bonapartist who hoped to extinguish the Bourbon family line. Although Louvel freely admitted to acting on his own, royalists claimed he had been inspired by liberal doctrines. As one critic charged, it was not an "isolated fanatic" that had slain Berry, but "the pernicious doctrines that sap all thrones and all authorities, attack civilization in its entirety, and menace the world with new upheavals."[26] Following the assassination, the government clamped down on all forms of political opposition in the country. New electoral laws were enacted to marginalize the presence of liberal opponents in the chamber, effectively muzzling political opinion. These measures were aimed at subverting revolution, but they tended to have a contrary effect. Prohibited from organizing, liberals and moderates resorted to extra-parliamentary means like conspiracy and secret societies such as the Carbonari. A seasoned military veteran and revolutionary icon, the Marquis de Lafayette became the doyen of the Carbonarist circles that took root in France. "The ideas of liberty ferment everywhere ... [and] the revolution and the counter-revolution are now engaged," he confided in a letter. "This new generation is enlightened and generous, above the impressions of Jacobinism and Bonapartism. They support the rights of a pure liberty, of this I am sure."[27] Lafayette was no advocate of radical revolution. However, he did not intend to stand by idly and watch conservatives erode the base of liberal government in the country either. He publicly acknowledged that he had been wrong to assume the Bourbons would honor their commitment to liberal institutions. "Counter-revolution is in the government," he warned in 1820. Anyone sympathetic to freedom and liberty was compelled to resist, in his opinion.[28]

In hounding French liberals, the government accused opponents of all varieties of machinations, some valid but many trumped up. Investigations implicated Lafayette and his allies in plots involving conspiracies in Paris, the cavalry school at Saumur and at a military garrison in Belfort. By 1822, authorities were convinced that the revolutionary infection was spreading into the French army.[29] If these threats were real enough, they were not the well-orchestrated plot directed by some nebulous *comité directeur* repeatedly noted by investigators. A growing liberal international movement was becoming evident as restoration regimes cracked down and silenced opponents across Europe. Yet it remained a loose affiliation of professional revolutionaries, liberals and republicans who communicated with one another across the continent. Secret societies existed within a network of disaffect political elites and military officials reflecting a range of ideological positions. Nationalists, Bonapartists and Jacobins blended Napoleonic militarism with republican conspiracy and revolt, bringing into existence a Pan-European movement broadly committed to liberal constitutionalism. What gave these groups their coherence was the mutual experience of suppression and ostracization they faced. In the final analysis, the war on terror engendered the very revolutionary conspirators it sought to subvert and destroy, transforming moderates and liberals into revolutionary antagonists.[30]

As it became apparent that Metternich and the conservative powers were committed to preserving their Holy Alliance against the cause of national liberation, opponents came to identify their causes with the international currents of post-revolutionary liberalism. Secret societies and conspiratorial networks created a context for a new type of imagined community across Europe built upon common ideological beliefs and values. Persecuted at home and attentive to the political struggles occurring outside France, Lafayette increasingly came to see the struggle for liberty in international terms, insisting it was not simply the issue of French constitutionalism at stake in this new war. "The friends of liberty were never in such perfect sympathy as in this moment of European crisis," the aged revolutionary professed in 1821. "Ours is a holy alliance which is well worth the other one."[31] His declaration was apposite, for by 1821 it appeared that the entire continent was on the verge of a Pan-European revolution.

Madrid Sets Europe Aflame

King Fernando VII was restored to the Spanish throne at the behest of the Allies in 1814. He had spent the years of the Napoleonic Wars at the Château de Valençay where he was permitted to maintain a relatively luxurious, if isolated lifestyle. Privately, he had showed little compunction in deferring to his French captors. While his subjects fought a vicious war in his name to liberate the kingdom from Napoleonic rule, Fernando proved to be one of the foremost *afrancesados*. Moreover, in the six years since his departure, Spain had been transformed. Deep ideological rifts opened during the war years persisted to simmer, Spanish America was in revolt and the Cortes had instituted a constitution in his absence. Fernando had left an absolutist monarch and was now returning as a constitutional one. Loath to recognize the principle of national sovereignty, he allied with conservatives at court. The question was not whether the liberal regime would be preserved, but rather what form absolutism would take in a post-revolutionary Spain. Receiving council from trusted ministers, Fernando abolished the constitution of 1812, insisting that the Cortes had convened illegally in his absence. The liberal leadership that had taken charge during the war was jailed or exiled. In hindsight, these reactionary measures were imprudent. The liberals had led the patriotic war for king and nation and played a major role in protecting the Spanish Bourbon inheritance. They were repaid with ingratitude and hostility.[32]

Fernando alienated the liberals, but the absolutists who supported him were hardly a well-organized pillar of support. Catholic conservatives and powerful provincial nobles detested the enlightened absolutism of the previous century almost as much as they did liberalism. These ultra-conservatives banding together under the label of *serviles* harkened back to a mythic medieval Spain ruled by landed families and clerical authority. They desired a king who would govern in conjunction with Church and nobility, restoring the "natural" foundations of Spanish society. More forward-looking monarchists rejected this policy out of hand. They hoped for a return to the pre-war model of enlightened absolutism which promised above all a strong monarchy capable of imposing its will over a meddlesome aristocracy and clergy. If these political divisions were not enough, Fernando also had to contend with the military. During the Peninsular War, military leaders had gained prestige and new powers as they defended the kingdom. After the war, certain commanders remained guarded against any perceived attempt to limit their newfound status. Already in 1814, commanders were threatening to create a rival point of authority against an absolutist restoration. They had backed the Cortes as a check against royal power believing a constitutional monarchy would preserve the gains of the war years. The patriot militias complicated matters further. The guerilla bands that had fought the French on the ground were hesitant to disarm and cede authority to Madrid.

These were just some of the problems that beset Fernando as he retook his throne, and it did not help that the Spanish monarchy found itself pressed financially. The war effort, not to mention the military expeditions in America, had taken a toll on the treasury. Fernando had to navigate between these various interests and factions. An absolutist, he sought to continue with centralization and had little intention of catering to the *serviles*. Moreover, he knew that he had been returned to power by the military and did not necessarily need the support of the aristocratic grandees. Nonetheless, he felt it wise to make symbolic gestures toward conservatives to keep them close to the crown. To this end, the Catholic Church was superficially restored to power as the moral authority of society, although it was not compensated for its loss of property during the Napoleonic Wars. He even placed greater state controls on Church officials, making them an arm of the state. Likewise, Fernando brushed aside the demands of regional aristocrats and pursued a policy of centralization to generate state revenue. Lastly, the military and militias had to be dealt with. Financial pressures made cutting back the military essential, and so to cut costs the officer corps was reduced and many officers forced to retire. At the same time, Fernando began disarming the patriot militias, drawing the resentment of local patriots.[33]

Fernando's efforts to restore absolutism left the monarchy isolated on numerous fronts. Conservatives and regional powers objected to royal centralization, correctly perceiving it as an attempt to curb their powers. The attack on liberals encouraged the formation of secret societies and conspiratorial plots in the immediate years after the war. As well, the military persistently expressed discontent over cutbacks and demotions. The sense of betrayal was nearly complete on all sides, and in 1820 these frustrations boiled over into outward revolt.

That January, troops garrisoned outside Cádiz mutinied. Tensions had been growing within the military for some time, but one of the key sparks to ignite the mutinies was the orders to ship some 14,000 men to America and wage a violent military campaign to subdue the Spanish American rebels. Liberal-minded soldiers were averse to suppressing colonial freedom fighters and many soldiers had little inclination to go to the New World where the toll from yellow fever and malaria was just as deadly as combat.[34] Capitalizing on this discontent, the commander Rafael del Riego issued a *pronunciamiento* calling upon troops to defend the constitution of 1812. "Love and trust your officers and we will lead you to immortality," he implored his men.[35] Although the uprising was seemingly spontaneous, Riego had been in close contact with liberal conspirators within the military and Spanish political society for some years. His *pronunciamiento* aimed to rally the underground opposition and drew support from prominent officers and constitutionalists. Within the month, Riego's call had spread to other barracks and had a ripple effect in Madrid where liberals pressured the king for reforms. Having few options at his disposal, Fernando agreed that March, professing that he would follow "the will of the people" and swear an oath of loyalty to the Cortes and the constitution of 1812. This

Figure 9 Rafael del Riego © The British Library Board.

liberal victory occurred with little bloodshed, opening a period referred to as the Trienio Liberal in Spanish history.

The initial moment of exuberant celebration proved brief. Spanish liberals quickly found themselves in disagreement over the nature of this latest Spanish revolution. So-called *exaltados* supported a broad electorate, extensive local rights and recognition for the newly formed political clubs organizing the revolution at the municipal level. In contrast, *moderatos*, many of whom were members of the generation of 1812, looked askance at the growing radicalism evident in the patriotic clubs. A number of these clubs had been secret conspiratorial societies in one form or another prior to 1820, and thus moderates readily branded *exaltados* as "Jacobins," warning that their demands for popular sovereignty would undermine liberal constitutionalism. Within months of the opening of the new Cortes, *moderatos* were attempting to obstruct radical mobilization and shut down the patriotic societies.[36] Riego encouraged the *exaltados*, and in doing so nurtured a cult around him that was bound to raise questions as to whether Spain had found its own Napoleon. Taking note of Riego's popularity, moderates feared that the Cortes might find itself confronted with a charismatic general who had ambitions of putting himself at the head of the government. This emerging conflict between representative government and popular revolution was complicated by royalists who refused to recognize constitutional government altogether. Royalist militias took their war to the provinces where they perpetrated violence on liberal supporters and patriots in the name of king, nation and religion. Liberals similarly engaged in localized forms of violence against political enemies. As the revolution got underway, the old hatreds and ideological conflicts of the Napoleonic Wars resurfaced, dividing entire communities that exacerbated factionalism.[37]

Moderato anxieties over the growing radicalism ran deeper than ideological divides and suspicion of the ambitious Riego, however. The Spanish revolution naturally drew the attention of the European powers, and it was doubtful whether the Holy Alliance would tolerate a liberal Spain. Preventing foreign intervention entailed convincing the powers that the revolution did not pose a threat to the status quo or legitimate monarchy.[38] This prospect was difficult, but it was complicated by the European-wide enthusiasm that greeted the 1820 uprising. European liberals welcomed the revolution and did not hide their hopes it might ignite a continental revolt against absolutist regimes. "Time and time again, we have forgotten Spain," exclaimed the French liberal Dominique de Pradt. "Now it calls to us."[39] Spain was fast becoming a model for European liberals and threatened to spread those dangerous ideas that the war on terror sought to suppress. This point was made evident just as the European powers were meeting to discuss the Spanish crisis. During that summer and the following spring, liberals in Portugal and Italy seized the initiative and staged uprisings against their respective governments while the liberal opposition in France grew more vociferous. For Metternich, the situation certainly appeared to confirm the existence of an orchestrated international plot and the hand of the dreaded *comité directeur*.

On the contrary, however, events in Italy were hardly part of an international conspiracy. In July, Luigi Minichini, a local priest and member of the Carbonari *vèndita* in Nola, organized his fellow Carbonaros to press the restored Bourbon monarch, Ferdinando IV, for constitutional reforms. The Carbonari had been planning a revolt for some time and had even taken the initiative in drawing up a constitution modeled on the 1812 Spanish constitution. Minichini led his group to Aviello where he encouraged military commanders to mutiny. The Spanish model was certainly fresh in their minds, but the Neapolitan generals were responding to local grievances resulting from mounting economic and political crises that the restored absolutist monarchy seemed incapable of resolving. The general Guglielmo Pepe, a Bonapartist supporter during the war, quickly took charge of the mutiny and in conjunction with Carbonarist leaders forced a dispirited Ferdinando IV to declare a constitution for Naples and Sicily. This "revolution" was by all standards tame. Elections to the parliament returned established notables and Papal claims to territory in Pontecorvo and Benevento were respected. The new government even worked to suppress more radical manifestations of revolt, demonstrating a concerted effort to maintain order and authority in southern Italy.[40]

Despite a relatively peaceful transfer of power, Metternich was not about to recognize a constitutional regime on the peninsula. He affirmed that the Neapolitan revolution was the work of secret societies and part of a larger plot orchestrated from abroad. In reality, Metternich was well aware that constitutionalism in the south would weaken Austria's hold over the continent. It posed a direct threat to the international power arrangements agreed upon in 1815 and, if allowed to stand, would limit Austrian influence in the region.[41] Thus, in February of 1821, Metternich convoked an international congress at Troppau and there negotiated the terms of Austrian intervention in Italy. Habsburg troops were ordered into Naples to restore the beleaguered Ferdinando IV. Pepe mounted a defense force to safeguard the Neapolitan revolution, but it proved no match for the 60,000-strong Austrian military. The defense collapsed and the Neapolitan revolution became the latest victim of the war on terror.

The defeat of Neapolitan liberalism did nothing to temper revolutionary zeal. In many ways, it reinforced it. Austrian intervention convinced many *exaltados* of the threat posed to Spain. Liberals were inclined to cast their revolution as an international crusade for liberty and constitutional government, identifying Spain as the moral center of European liberal revolt. As Austrian forces advanced on Naples, the radical deputy José Moreno Guerra urged his fellow liberals to offer encouragement and material support to the struggling Italians. "Naples is a part of Spain like Catalonia and we must assist it," he proclaimed.[42] The king was ill-disposed to send aid and *moderatos* had no desire to confirm Metternich's suspicions of an international conspiracy, lest Spain find itself confronting an Austrian intervention. However, radicals continued to press the issue and took measures to enforce their internationalist program. Spanish diplomats in Naples issued passports to Neapolitan liberals, offering men like Pepe and Minichini asylum. Exiles were subsequently given protection under Spanish law, enlisted in the Spanish army and ordered to fight for the liberal cause in Iberia.[43] Fiorenzo Galli, a Piedmontese officer who had made his way to Spain in 1821, did not mince words when buoying the spirits of his fellow countrymen. "What is there that a political organization dictated by humanity, founded on the right of the people, and administered by justice cannot do?"

he asked in a proclamation. "Italians come to Spain, or become Spaniards!"[44] Under threat in Italy, Italian liberals would find a welcome home in Spain, radicals assured.

The Spanish revolution provided the context for creating a liberal international against the conservatism of the Holy Alliance. Radicals made appeals to a common European movement to attract defenders from across the continent. "We are all rebels, revolutionaries and insurgents in the eyes of despotic leaders," the liberal Pedro Muños Arroyo contended. "The current war in Naples will be lead against us, against France, Portugal and all nations that value their independence and freedom."[45] *Exaltados* actively built a transnational movement, one capable of reinforcing Pan-European solidarity and attracting foreign fighters to Iberia. They communicated with secret societies and rebels abroad and sent delegations to France, England and Italy to bolster support for their cause. Italian commanders like Guglielmo Pepe and Giuseppe Pecchio headed exilic brigades in Spain that recruited internally and cooperated with prominent liberals abroad like Lafayette, who acclaimed the "sympathetic link between all nations denied liberty, the true civilization of peoples."[46] Carbonaros ran newspapers that generated support for the Spanish revolution and fortified connections from Portugal to Greece. By 1822, military battalions were secretly being organized across the Pyrenees to stir up revolt and mobilize resistance.[47] The activities corresponded with the rising prospect of military intervention and the suppression of the liberal regime in Spain. In October of 1822, Metternich once again summoned the powers at Verona and there planned to put an end to the liberal international. At Verona, the troublesome Spanish question was decided with France ordered to send a military force into Spain and suppress the Cortes.

French internationalists marshaled all their resources to obstruct the planned military expedition. In their estimation, the suppression of Spanish liberalism by the Bourbon government foreshadowed a similar fate for their own country, making the cause of Spain and France one and the same. Led by Colonel Charles Fabvier, a veteran of the Napoleonic Wars who had answered the call to fight in Spain, French battalions staged a daring last-ditch effort to save the Spanish revolution and, with it, the liberal international. Mounting their forces at the Pyrenees border, they confronted their compatriots directly and encouraged the troops to mutiny in the name of liberty and universal fraternity. Fabvier and his forces brandished patriotic symbols and sang revolutionary songs, insisting it was nobler to defend the ideals of liberty than to be pawns of absolutist oppression. These appeals fell on deaf ears. When the commanding officer ordered his troops to fire, they did so without reservation.[48] With Fabvier's plan a failure, French royalist forces proceeded to crush the Spanish revolution and put an end to the liberal experiment.

The Making of a Trans-Mediterranean Revolutionary Community

Although the suppression of the Spanish and Italian revolutions was disheartening, it did not spell the end of the liberal internationalism that emerged in the 1820s. Individuals committed to the cause of liberty and humanity found other theaters in which to act out the modern drama of revolution. Professional revolutionaries heeded the call of liberty wherever it may be found, often migrating from revolution to revolution and demonstrating the global scope of liberal internationalism. Cities like London, Paris and Brussels became centers of international revolutionary activity and provided places in which exiled liberals planned their next adventures and recruited adherents. Those who fled Spain and Naples lent their support to the Latin American revolutionary movements still underway, fraternizing with Guatemalan, Mexican and other Spanish American patriots. Liberals like Pradt and Pecchio supported the cause of Spanish America through their writings, depicting American independence as the final phase of a global revolutionary process destined to secure the rights of man throughout the world.[49] Some Italian exiles made the trip across the Atlantic and produced accounts of the struggles for liberty taking place in Spanish America for European audiences.[50] These activities served to reinforce the international dimensions of the liberal movement currently roiling global politics and crystallized the idea of a patriotic community united by common ideals of freedom and constitutionalism.

Yet freedom fighters did not need to travel to the New World to participate in this international community. Others remained closer to home, seeking to pursue the goals of liberal internationalism in the Mediterranean Basin.[51] North Africa became a destination for revolutionary exiles fleeing persecution and many Spanish and Italian insurgents made their way across the Mediterranean via Gibraltar, ending up in Tangiers, Tunisia and Egypt.[52] The Italian revolutionary Giuseppe Garibaldi spent time in Tunisia and Tangiers, and in between set sail across the Atlantic to take up the cause of liberation in Brazil. The exile Gaetano Fedriani, who arrived in Tunisia with Garibaldi, stayed on in the port city and was instrumental in setting up the "Young Italy" movement in North Africa during the 1830s. Such activities indicated the prominence cities like Tunis and Cairo were coming to play as organizational centers for exiled nationalists and liberals in the wake of the failed revolutions.[53] More to the point, these Trans-Mediterranean ties were part of a general reimagining of the Mediterranean region taking place in the early nineteenth century as Europeans came to see the sea as an interconnected and unified space linking three continents.[54]

In the wake of the Spanish and Italian debacles, attention turned to Greece where nationalism and liberalism came together to produce its own revolutionary moment. Greece was incorporated into the Ottoman Empire in the sixteenth century as the Ottomans expanded across Europe. However, this did not imply that the Greeks had acquiesced to Turkish rule. Greeks were conscious of the differences separating them from their imperial rulers. They spoke a different language, possessed a distinct culture and observed Orthodox Christianity as opposed to Islam, the official religion of the Ottoman Empire. Ottoman policies reinforced these differences. In managing its large multiethnic empire, the imperial state allowed each religious group (or *millet*) a fair amount of autonomy. The millet system organized communities around religious identity, discouraging an integrative or assimilationist approach that might reduce ethnic or confessional differences.[55] During the years of the Napoleonic Wars, this system was inflected with new ideas of nationalism and liberty preached by the

French as revolutionary forces established themselves in the Ionian Islands and Eastern Mediterranean.

The years of the French Revolution had impacted the Ottoman Empire in different ways across North Africa and in the Near East, drawing the foremost Muslim power into the political currents generated by the Age of Revolution.[56] The Napoleonic Wars had come directly to the Ottoman Empire with the invasion of Egypt in 1798 as French troops attempted to secure the Nile Valley. The empire had not been without its own internally generated revolutionary politics either. The reform-minded Sultan Selim III who came to power in 1789 was aware of Europe's new imperial designs on the Eastern Mediterranean and endeavored to pursue a policy of military modernizing and revive the declining fortunes of his empire. In the 1790s, his *Nazim-i Cedid* ("New Order" policy) intended to create a Western-style military, complete with European weaponry and training. The policy drew the ire of religious conservatives and especially the entrenched Janissary corps, who subsequently launched a coup in 1807 and unseated Selim.[57] The revolt against Selim's New Order signaled an early failure of Ottoman westernization, but it also signaled the impotence of Istanbul to rein in rowdy and conservative elements within the government and military. The capital seemed unable to exercise full control over its officials and territories, and this aspect was in many ways a more dangerous symptom of the decline of Ottoman power.

Certain Balkan nationalists were inclined to capitalize on this growing weakness. The influence of the French Revolution had not been lost on Greek nationalists who espoused the currents of romantic nationalism by writing poems to the glory of the Greek people and evoking their ancient past as the birthplace of Western civilization. The primary source of this new nationalist revival came from abroad. Many wealthy Greeks had left the region and established themselves in Britain and the United States. From these areas, they promoted the cause of Greek liberation and garnered international support. With aid from exilic Greeks, nationalists at home set up secret societies, the most prominent being Filiki Eteria (the Friendly Society). This society was instrumental in coordinating actions between Greek conspirators in the Balkans and circumnavigating Ottoman authorities. In 1820, the president of Filiki Eteria, Count Alexandros Ypsilantis, a former aide-de-camp to the Russian Tsar and Napoleonic War veteran, believed the time was ripe to foment a general Greek war of independence. He assumed that once the war began Russia would be compelled to intervene on behalf of its Orthodox brethren suffering under Turkish rule. His plan drew the support of the regional Ottoman potentate, Ali Pasha, who calculated that stoking the flames of Greek nationalism would strengthen his own local power base and furnish independence from Istanbul. The plan failed on both accounts. Ypsilantis's expectation of Russian aid never materialized and Ottoman forces brutally crushed the nascent Greek insurgence and deposed Ali Pasha. By 1821, the Greek war looked to be on the verge of extinction until a popular revolt largely inspired by Ottoman suppression reignited the movement and infused it with a second life.[58]

Greek exiles abroad encouraged strong public support for the cause against the Ottomans, and Europeans responded. Poets and writers across the continent expressed their sympathies for the Greek people, connecting them with the origins of Western civilization and Europe's heritage. This pronounced Philhellenism transformed the Greek war into another international crusade, one that attracted old liberal combatants just as much as the romantic intelligentsia. The London Greek Committee headed by Edward Blaquiere and Leicester Stanhope was instrumental in soliciting international aid, recruiting volunteers and organizing transport for combatants who wished to fight in the Balkans. Various public intellectuals also took a stance. The poet John Browning lent his pen to the cause, calling people to join the revolt and take up arms on behalf of the Greek people. The most notable of these figures was George Gordon, Lord Byron who in 1823 traveled to Greece with the assistance of the London Committee and died there a year later, becoming a martyr of the Greek cause and a symbol of the romantic struggle for liberty.[59] Although Byron's celebrity took center stage in the emotive outpouring of international support for and identification with Greek independence, there existed no shortage of Philhellenes in the 1820s. The Spanish liberal Francisco Martínez de la Rosa praised the "noble sons of Sparta and Athens" and identified Spain's own desire for liberty with that of the Greeks. Many Italian revolutionaries who had taken up arms in Spain sought to recoup the vigor of the internationalist cause in Greece after 1823. They spoke of a common Greco-Roman inheritance and hailed the Greek war as part of a common struggle in the Holy Alliance of peoples against tyranny. Both Fabvier and Pecchio were active in recruiting volunteers and pledged to fight for liberty in the Balkans.[60]

Rhetorical expressions of unity belied the actual picture on the ground. Certain internationalists looked askance at the London Greek Committee, claiming the organization monopolized the war effort by dictating how funds were used and what policies were pursued. Leicester Stanhope hesitated to give aid directly to Greek leaders, believing them corrupt, disorganized and too "Oriental" to lead an effective war effort. His perspective was seemingly confirmed as the Greek insurrection disintegrated into a brutal civil war by the mid-1820s. Greek combatants themselves were suspicious of the international volunteers arriving from abroad, finding them patronizing and motivated by altogether different goals than the Balkan Greek communities. Volunteers and native Greek battalions fought their own wars, and these tensions were not absent on the battlefield. Overall, however, these internal disputes did not eclipse the public image of a unified front in the war between a Western Christian people and Oriental Muslim "barbarism." The ideological and emotional connections linking Greece, Italy and Spain in the 1820s echoed through the numerous transnational revolutionary networks and societies organized during the period. Spanish and Italian patriots composed poems and songs celebrating their shared Mediterranean heritage with the Greeks, calling for a regeneration of Mediterranean peoples through a common struggle for emancipation and freedom. Liberal internationalism and Philhellenism provided the Spanish, Italian and Greek movements with a common ideological framework that drew together a broad spectrum of Bonapartists, republicans and liberals across the continent. Patriots celebrated international fraternity and depicted their efforts as part of a collective cause for national liberation and cosmopolitanism previously imagined in the Atlantic world. In their Mediterranean variant, these assumptions continued to reiterate the vision of an international revolutionary community and the common values it shared.[61]

Mazzini and Young Europe

Secret societies adhered to cosmopolitan principles that appealed to universal fraternity and revolutionary brotherhood. They also relied upon hierarchical command structures and secretive methods that aimed to circumvent the watchful eyes of state authorities and police spies. For professional revolutionaries and disobedient military officers, these tactics were not only useful, but essential to survival. They facilitated communication among loose-knit networks of revolutionary cells and mobilized resistance across national borders. Yet these tactics also alienated many republican nationalists who agreed with neither the unbridled cosmopolitanism nor military organizational structures popular among conspiratorial circles.[62] Post-revolutionary republicans maintained a strong attachment to principles of national self-determination and the nation-state. They believed that secret societies ought to serve as models of republican governance rather than resemble military juntas. More specifically, republican nationalists speculated on how to reconcile ideas of national sovereignty with revolutionary internationalism. If revolutionary cosmopolitanism emphasized allegiances that transcended the national community, republican patriots worried whether a Holy Alliance of peoples favored being a citizen of the world over one's own nation and *patrie*.

These considerations weighed heavily on Giuseppe Mazzini, a republican journalist and political activist dedicated to the cause of Italian unification first animated during the years of the French Revolution. In 1827, he joined the Carbonari with the expectation of fighting against all perceived obstacles to Italian unification, namely the Bourbon dynasty, the Austrians and the Papacy. Working with Buonarroti, he developed the disposition of the professional revolutionary, remarking on his constant need "to struggle, struggle every minute, otherwise I will commit suicide."[63] Yet his political principles and outlooks frequently clashed with the notorious Tuscan activist. Whereas Buonarroti favored secrecy and disciplined leadership, Mazzini put his faith in popular insurrection. In 1833, he wrote his "Rules for the Conduct of Guerilla Bands," a manual instructing revolutionaries in the methods of popular national resistance. His model derived from the Spanish resistance to Napoleon, insisting that guerilla uprisings constituted one of the principal means of nationalizing revolutionary movements. Guerilla war furnished "the military education of the people" and served as a "precursor to the nation," he contented. In Mazzini's estimation, militant patriotism would bind the national community together in a common struggle, providing the pretext for widespread national struggle.[64] Revolutionaries had to be conscious of the popular dimensions of resistance, never losing sight of the fact that their objective remained national in character.

Breaking with the Bebeuvist preference for a disciplined cadre of professional revolutionaries, Mazzini equally distanced himself from the Francophilia evident among many of his contemporaries. While France and 1789 remained important reference points in his revolutionary ideology, Mazzini did not believe that the revolutionary spark would ineluctably come from France. On the contrary, Mazzini placed his faith in a regenerated Italian people, calling for a national revolution that eschewed the terror

Figure 10 Giuseppe Mazzini © The British Library Board.

tactics of Jacobin sympathizers. Revolution implied struggle, but not violent dictatorship contrary to republican freedom. In maintaining this line, Mazzini eventually broke with the Carbonari in 1831, forming his own Young Italy faction. The movement professed a strong commitment to Italian unification, calling for armed struggle against the Habsburgs and Papacy. Despite its emphasis on national liberation, Young Italy did not abandon the internationalism of the previous decade altogether. In every respect, it blended currents of internationalism with Italian patriotism. "My Italianism consists not so much in working for Italian emancipation, as in working so that the Italian revolution, like the French of 1789, becomes a European revolution," Mazzini admitted in 1843. "I will try everything to make sure that the unrest spreads abroad."[65]

With its mix of patriotism and revolutionary messianism, Mazzini's program pitted itself against the parochial cultural nationalism that had taken hold in intellectual circles following the Napoleonic period. In contrast to romantics like Johann Gottfried Herder who emphasized language and tradition as the basis of nationality, Mazzini perpetuated a republican revolutionary tradition rooted in ideas of civic participation and rights. Common citizenship and cultural association brought people together into a higher national unity. In doing so, a people could communicate as a collective body and, consequently, form relationships with other nations. Nations did not exist in isolation, nor was a national community hermetically sealed off from others. Although nationality was a "sacred principle," it was never divorced from the general cause of humanity or commitment to liberty and the rights of man.[66] For Mazzini, the nation was a medium for cooperation and peaceful coexistence. His revolutionary nationalism anticipated the creation of a federation of nation-states linked by common republican principles, reflecting the wide-held aspiration of a Holy Alliance of peoples against a Holy Alliance of despots.[67] Seeking to give substance to this brand of national cosmopolitanism, Mazzini summoned a small international conference of revolutionaries to Berne in 1834. There, they signed a pact of fraternity that would become the founding document of a new revolutionary international, Young Europe. This umbrella organization was intended to unite the various secret and national societies in a congress of nations, proposing a new framework for revolutionary internationalism promising a "social transformation" vested in solid national and republican principles.[68]

Mazzini's Europe of nations marked a definitive moment in the development of the liberal international that had come of age in post-Napoleonic Europe. His proposed Young Europe drew upon longstanding themes of revolutionary cosmopolitanism and nationalism evident since 1789. These two principles had always coexisted uneasily alongside one another, at times translating into contradictory policies of nationalist self-assertion and imperial expansion. Young Europe set out to free itself of these inherent contradictions, imagining a form of patriotism that was at once national and cosmopolitan in spirit. Its syncretic qualities wove together strains of revolutionary thought, combining aspects of nationalism, republicanism and internationalism in equal measure. Its program, much like Mazzini's revolutionary ideology, reflected an age characterized by global nationalist revolution and migration, positing a political orientation sensitive to distinctive cultural identities yet committed to the advancement of universal values across borders.

Conclusion

The years following the Napoleonic Wars revealed the resilience of revolutionary ideas throughout Europe and the world. From the 1790s onward, governments progressively assumed powers aimed at suppressing radicalism and maintaining public order. The architecture for the modern police state had been apparent well before the Congress of Vienna. Restoration monarchies persistently upheld the fiction of a "return" to the past, even as they elaborated upon revolutionary and Napoleonic policies to combat popular and potentially destabilizing movements in their kingdoms. Monarchs who committed themselves to the post-revolutionary war on terror commonly found that their efforts met with mixed results. Metternich managed to preserve Habsburg control in Italy and suppress German nationalism, but it was questionable whether his police state could be maintained indefinitely. Moreover, the war on terror often proved counter-productive, turning liberals into revolutionaries and forcing moderate political elites underground. Radicals adapted to these new circumstances, drawing lessons from men like Babeuf and refining their methods of insurrection to accommodate the political realities of a post-Napoleonic order.

The changes that took shape within radical circles encouraged the creation of transnational revolutionary cells across Europe. These secret societies played an important role in transforming liberal revolt into an international phenomenon. Working with co-conspirators across national borders, radicals and liberals revived the revolutionary cosmopolitanism of the 1790s and gave it a distinctly new form in the process. As revolts broke out in Spain, Italy and Greece, leaders made appeals to new types of solidarities, associating their cause with larger movements stretching across the Mediterranean and Atlantic world. During the 1820s, the simultaneity of revolts provided a basis for imagining revolutionary communities that transcended borders and embodied the ideals of an embattled liberal constitutionalism. The liberal international encompassed a series of transnational social networks that were re-imagined to fit the contours of international struggle and solidarity. If these cosmopolitan associations re-oriented the battle between revolutionaries and counter-revolutionaries in the post-Napoleonic period, they also marked an important rethinking of the practice of revolutionary politics itself. As activists like Buonarroti and Mazzini attempted to direct these transnational networks, they contributed to the image of the professional revolutionary committed to insurrectionary politics and organization. These efforts stood as precursors to the vanguardism that would become fashionable later in the century, solidifying the image of the lone conspiratorial revolutionary as a hallmark of insurrectionary politics and revolt in the modern period.

CHAPTER 6
SOCIALISM AND SOCIAL PROTEST: FROM REFORM TO RADICALISM (1815–1848)

In 1840, Barthélemy Prosper Enfantin, a French social reformer known for his dramatic posturing and quasi-mystical sermonizing, saw fit to comment to a friend on what he took to be the most striking aspect of the current century. "The human function, evidently growing over the course of the half-century, and especially for the past twenty years, is precisely what, in our former social organization, was treated as minor and considered non-noble, imposed and the lot of slaves … It is industry."[1] His observation was accurate. The first half of the nineteenth century witnessed a profound shift in ideas regarding economic productivity and social relations across the continent. These changes also brought new challenges as cycles of rapid economic expansion and contraction and mass protests aggravated European societies. Writing three years after Enfantin, Karl Marx expressed his own ideas regarding transformations on the continent, citing the impoverishment of labor and social convulsions as hallmark features of an industrial era on the brink of revolution. "No class of civil society has the need for, or capacity of achieving, universal emancipation until it is compelled to by its immediate situation, by material necessity and its own chains," he warned, delivering his prophecy of impending worker insurrection and violent class struggle.[2]

Both outlooks possessed elements of truth and corresponded to the tensions roiling Europe in the 1840s. The post-revolutionary period inspired reflections on the feasibility of democratic government in the wake of the civil unrest unleashed during the 1790s. Elites attempted to find ways of balancing liberty and order, frequently resorting to exclusionary and illiberal tactics to do so. At the same time, economic modernization generated forms of working-class activism distinct from the *sans-culottism* of the revolutionary period. The changes wrought by capital accumulation, liberal politics and popular protest would divide European societies and nurture deep social cleavages that infuse revolutionary ideas of liberty and equality with new connotations and meanings. By the 1830s, the idea of class was becoming central to community building as elites claiming to defend the principle of liberty confronted calls for greater political inclusion and social equality.

Historians have conventionally explained nineteenth-century radicalism in relation to industrialization and the consequent "proletarianization" of labor that occurred. In this account, material and economic factors have been considered the driving forces behind political mobilization and social unrest.[3] This narrative has, however, been subject to re-evaluation in recent years as considerations for ideology and culture have supplanted former explanations rooted in purely socio-economic rationales. Certainly, revolutionary writers and political activists played an important role in shaping nominally working-class movements. The liberal revolutions of the 1830s saw elites employ perceptions of "bourgeois" and "middle class" capacity in Great Britain and France to validate the creation of exclusionary regimes committed to constitutional government and economic liberalism. Reacting to the rhetoric of bourgeois liberalism, revolutionaries and protest leaders took up egalitarian platforms that claimed to speak in the name of the oppressed and disenfranchised laboring classes. Class-based identification progressively became the predominant idiom of nineteenth-century politics. Although many radical and reformist platforms stemmed from different ideological positions and often pursued divergent goals, they all articulated themselves through an egalitarian idiom of class and social solidarity, fostering a new language of revolutionary identification that drew upon as much as shaped perceptions of industrialization and social conflict in the mid-nineteenth century.

Industrialization and Social Change

In the middle of the eighteenth century, it is estimated that China and Europe were roughly equal in terms of wealth and productivity. Within a century, however, Europe had pulled ahead significantly, outpacing Asia and creating a different type of economy capable of producing goods and generating capital at a pace unimagined in the 1700s.[4] The causes of this transformation were numerous: a century of steady population growth, increased urbanization, the growth of a nascent consumer culture and the development of new production methods. By the end of the eighteenth century, Europeans appeared to be working more, producing more and consuming more than they ever had in the past.[5] These changes characterized what has typically been considered an "industrial revolution," a term evoking images of assembly lines, mechanized production and factories. Yet this picture is one often shaped in retrospect. The term dates from the mid-nineteenth century and only acquired wide currency in the 1880s with the publication of Arnold Toynbee's *Lectures on the Industrial Revolution in England*. As states began investing in new methods of production, colonizing distant parts of the globe and staging large trade exhibitions like those in Hyde Park (1851) and Paris (1867) aimed at showing off their economic dynamism to international audiences, a general idea of irrevocable change seized the popular imagination. According to the writer Émile Montégut in 1855, industry and mechanization were now the defining characteristics of modern society. "It is through industry alone that our customs, habits, arts and even our revolutions are derived." For Montégut, the founders of modern society were not Rousseau, Voltaire or Thomas Paine, but rather inventors and economists like James Watt and Adam Smith.[6]

Modernity's immense potential was not lost on contemporary observers. Critics and writers hailed the "new era" opening for European civilization and wrote hymns to the marvels of modern science and human ingenuity. In 1835, the Scottish chemist and geologist Andrew Ure rhapsodized on the "blessing which physio-mechanical science has bestowed on society."⁷ Improvements in the "mechanical sciences," he believed, promised to free individuals from labor-intensive tasks, permitting them to pursue more creative and productive enterprises. There was no shortage of praise for the most conspicuous mark of modernity, the railroads, an alluring symbol of human triumph over nature and the natural world. "What is industry, if not a manifestation of the human spirit, domination exercised by the spirit over nature?" asked Michel Chevalier as he admired the displays of machinery and manufacturing at London's Great Exhibition in 1851. Impressed by the steam engines and industrial equipment he saw, Chevalier felt certain of modern civilization's "superiority" over the ancients. "It is there that the strength of humanity truly resides. [Europe] is today invested with the empire and depository of the future."⁸

Impressions of an industrial "revolution" driven by technological innovation inspired expectations of rapid and unprecedented change, but this vision remained more ideological than real. Change occurred incrementally over the course of the century. By the mid-nineteenth century, most work continued to be done by hand rather than machines. The majority of laborers were artisans, and many alternated between artisanal and agricultural sectors throughout the year.⁹ Nor did industrialization occur on a wide scale across the continent. Economic modernization was localized within an industrializing core encompassing Britain, France and western Germany. The surrounding periphery remained largely agrarian for much of the century. Even within industrializing countries, development was uneven.¹⁰ The most profound changes did not occur at the levels of mechanization and industry, but rather social and economic structures. The shift toward a more capitalist-oriented economy over the century resulted in the concentration of capital and production in fewer hands. Population growth created a more competitive labor market at a time when entrepreneurs were reorganizing manufacturing on a commercial basis. These economic changes occurred in tandem with the growth of state powers that could compel obedience and enforce policies—often violently—on uncompliant laborers.¹¹ In this environment, capital accumulation brought into existence a stratum of industrial elites while workers faced a range of new social and economic pressures that would alter their quality of life considerably.

The changing mindsets of manufacturers and entrepreneurs were inspired by the new doctrine of "economic liberalism," soon to be rebranded as *laissez-faire* capitalism. Drawing upon the theories of economists like Adam Smith, commercial magnates and business owners placed their faith in financial "management" and market forces, arguing that profits could be achieved through the "natural harmony" of interests. The "law of the market" became the supreme law, and economists like David Ricardo encouraged producers to maximize their profits through the efficient management of labor. His "iron law of wages" rationalized the maintenance of wages at subsistence levels, believing producers would invest surplus profits into manufacturing and, thereby, spur continual economic growth. While this formula made economic sense, it hardly boded well for workers who saw their wages decrease and livelihoods threatened as factories and mills supplanted the former cottage industries that had once been the backbone of the European economy. In a world in which labor was interpreted as a commodity, workers were forced to suffer the new ethos of competition, the logic of the market and employers seeking to maximize profits at nearly any cost.[12]

This change in attitudes was compounded by the new situation facing labor in the early nineteenth century. The French Revolution had disrupted the traditional guild systems and mutual aid networks on the continent. Guilds had regulated trades, offered certain protections to guild members and made funds available to workers in times of crisis. In the late eighteenth century, these worker-controlled institutions were attacked under the pretext of "economic liberty" as officials clamped down on popular movements and potential bases of *sans-culotte* radicalism. Revolutionary policies undermined the traditional economic and social support structures that existed and paved the way for future economic reforms conducive to speculation and capitalist investment. As guild controls collapsed, laborers found themselves without the securities such institutions once offered. With the end of the Napoleonic Wars, Europe faced an economic downturn that it was ill-equipped to handle. The reopening of continental markets meant greater competition. Mass demobilization saw markets contract at the exact moment a flood of workers was returning home in search of jobs and housing. These concurrent factors created a tenuous situation and fueled a new wave of radicalism from below as food riots and worker protests generated unrest.[13]

While elites celebrated industry and economic modernization as a progressive step in human development, they were also conscious of the horrors that modernity was capable of producing as well. Rural populations flocking to cities in search of work produced a mobile labor force, but equally contributed to overcrowding, disease and diminishing job prospects. As a result, industrial centers became panoramas of urban poverty and squalor exposing the darker side of industrial "progress." In 1844, Frederick Engels, who had taken a position as a clerk in his father's textile firm in Manchester, gave a bleak picture of nineteenth-century England. He noted filthy streets lined with ramshackle houses, canals filled with brown water and dreary mills where the inhabitants worked. "Everything which here arouses horror and indignation is of recent origin, belonging to the *industrial epoch*," he complained.[14] A stroll through Paris was hardly any better. In 1852, the writer Théophile Gautier remarked that "three-quarters of the streets are only networks of black and fetid filth." The sight of degraded laborers was just as harrowing. This "twilit population" had no connection to the city's prosperous residents "save for the death it receives from them … They are vanquished nations, forced under the earth to yield their place in the sun to a victorious people."[15] According to the socialist Victor Considérant, Paris appeared "an immense workshop of putrefaction where misery, disease and sickness work in concert."[16] In his estimation, these conditions furnished the context for a new preoccupation: reform. "The sense of social grievance is today developed more highly than it has ever been: pain in more acutely felt, evil speaks louder and there is everywhere the understanding of the urgent necessity of reform."[17]

Governments and social activists were hardly blind to this fact. The so-called "social question"—or how societies should respond to the problems generated by industry and modernization—was a hotly debated topic in France and Britain. Numerous government inquires and reports on the subject were conducted yielding a variety of possible solutions ranging from public works projects to state-sponsored colonization efforts abroad. However, many critics enamored by the new doctrine of economic liberalism remained suspicious of state intervention to solve these social ills. It would ruin industry and enervate the "productive spirit," they warned. Moral paternalism and religious instruction were acceptable, but government aid to improve material circumstances and check industry was anathema. Human society was based on "the principle of *competition*" and "individual exertion," the MP George Poulett Scrope explained. State assistance and oversight would only serve to hinder these attributes.[18] *Laissez-faire* was to be the guiding principle of social considerations just as much as economic ones.

Yet the "social question" could not be ignored, and by the middle of the century it would come to assume a central place in the major political debates of the day. It was not simply the growing litany of complaints and grievances relevant to issues of poverty and working conditions that compelled attention, but the means through which these concerns were coming to be expressed. As economic interests and the new conditions encountered by labor came to a head, politics became enmeshed in a battle between two opposing communities, a "bourgeois" class of producers and an exploited "proletariat" seeking social justice and redress. These two poles marked the frontlines of a new revolutionary conflict which although linked to the struggles of the past nonetheless found expression in new idioms of class warfare and solidarity.

A Bourgeois Revolution?

On July 23, 1830, King William IV stood before the British House of Commons and extoled "the general tranquility" that reigned over Europe since the mid-1820s.[19] His remarks proved premature. Political tensions were quickly unraveling in Switzerland, and within two weeks Paris was engaged in a revolt that would bring down the restored Bourbon monarchy. By the end of the year, nationalist revolutions had shaken the Netherlands and Poland, resulting in the creation of a new independent Belgian state and the violent suppression of Polish insurgents by the Russian military. It appeared that the revolutionary fervor of the 1820s would continue into the new decade, perpetuating the familiar scenario of democratic-national revolt and conservative reaction.

Although the revolutions of 1830 appeared to fit a familiar narrative, events in France nonetheless hinted at something new. During the 1820s, the Bourbon monarchy had worked to sideline liberal opponents, resorting to censorship and suppression when necessary. The death of Louis XVIII in 1824 and the ascension of his brother, the Comte d'Artois, to the French throne only aggravated the situation. Artois had been an inveterate counter-revolutionary during the 1790s, and upon taking the throne as Charles X he revealed that little had changed in his outlooks. In planning his coronation ceremony, Charles revived the traditional religious ceremonies used by the former French kings and wore the traditional gowns of the absolutist monarchs. Once on the throne, he scaled back the constitution granted by his brother, censored liberal-minded journals and curtailed free speech with new laws against blasphemy. By 1830, liberals feared a royal coup d'état was in the making. In late July, these pitched political battles spilled into the streets, provoking demonstrations. When the military was called in, a riot ensued. Knowing what angry Parisian mobs were capable of, Charles immediately packed his bags and fled to England. With the royal government gone, the opposition officially declared the Bourbons illegitimate and set to the task of creating a new government. France was once again in the throes of revolution.[20]

As barricades went up throughout the streets of Paris, a small group of liberal politicians and journalists gathered in the Parisian office of the prominent newspaper *Le National* and there planned a course of action. At the meeting, it was proposed that a junior branch of the royal family—the Orléanist line—be invited to take the throne and establish a new government. The journalist and future statesman Adolphe Thiers spelled out the issue clearly: "We need a new dynasty which owes the crown to us and which, because it owes it to us, is ready to accept the role assigned to it by the representative system."[21] It was believed that the Orléanist candidate Louis Philippe possessed a commitment to constitutional liberalism and would fit the bill of a "representative" monarch. More important perhaps, a candidate for the throne was needed quickly. In the heated atmosphere of Paris, calls for a republic had been heard and key republican advocates had already approached the Marquis de Lafayette to serve as president. Over the coming days, the liberals managed to avert a republican victory. Louis Philippe accepted the invitation extended by the liberals and took the throne as the "citizen king" of France. He even managed to obtain Lafayette's endorsement, thereby winning over republican support for an Orléanist regime.

It was not the details of the liberal revolution that were important so much as what the so-called "July Monarchy" represented. Liberals were a product of the post-revolutionary political atmosphere. They supported the principles of the French Revolution but hardly endorsed revolution itself. The Reign of Terror had been an abomination while the Napoleonic Empire had suppressed liberty through arbitrary and personal rule. In the aftermath of revolution and empire, political elites harbored strong misgivings over the practicality of democratic government while retaining mistrust for the "tyranny" that Bonapartism encouraged. Seeking a constitutional government of the center, liberals put their faith in a responsible and reasonable electorate that could sustain progressive society. In their calculation, elite political leadership was required to stand between king and people. Liberalism rejected popular participation and championed the rule of a limited political class endowed with the wealth, education and social pedigree essential for leadership. As the liberal Benjamin Constant argued, "Property alone makes men capable of the exercise of political rights. Proprietors alone can be citizens."[22] In short, liberal government signaled the ascension of property holders and tax payers to political power. The doctrine of "limited suffrage" restricted voting rights to those endowed with the capacity and capabilities for government, and according to French liberals these qualities were found in a new class rising to predominance in the post-revolutionary period: the bourgeoisie.[23]

True to its liberal creed, the July Monarchy offered itself as a government of the bourgeoisie. "We are the government of the bourgeoisie," the journalist and deputy

Charles de Rémusat proclaimed in 1834. "Without doubt, the revolution of 1830 has elevated the middle classes to a civil church [and] their true social rank."[24] Louis Philippe and his ministers expanded the voting franchise to include an additional 100,000 voters drawn from the "middle classes," investing bankers, financiers and newspaper moguls with the right to vote and hold office. State policies followed course, encouraging economic expansion and secular institutions to curb the power of Catholic conservatives. Louis Philippe himself cultivated an image as a bourgeois *par excellence*. He dressed in plain clothing rather than royal gowns; he gave avid speeches in support of industry and business. He supported family values and commonly appeared in public carrying an umbrella, the veritable symbol of the nineteenth-century bourgeois.[25] The discourse of liberal capacity offered a rationale for excluding workers and the poor from voting, and July Monarchy officials did not hesitate to express their inherent sense of middle-class elitism when disenfranchised workers called for democracy. When workers and artisans protested against such inequality, Prime Minister François Guizot callously replied *enrichissez-vous* ("get rich").[26]

The new discourse of limited suffrage equally acquired saliency in Great Britain during the early 1830s, although without the explicit aid of a revolution. Plots targeting government officials and radical efforts to stir up working-class rebellions after the Napoleonic Wars had alarmed the political classes, prompting concerns that Britain would face its own revolution if effective measures were not taken. While the aristocratic party (the Tories) was reluctant to endorse any measure of change to a system that favored landed interests, certain Whig opponents showed a willingness to countenance electoral reform as a panacea to revolt. Strategists reasoned that expanding the voting franchise to the "middle classes" would draw journalists and activists away from radical politics and ally them with the government, thereby dampening radicalism. This plan hinged, however, on making reform palatable to conservatives.[27] To this end, moderates needed to construct a "middle class" identity distinct from radicalism and assure critics that the middle classes were, in fact, a worthy ally of the Crown. Politicians and pamphlet writers spared no ink in extolling the moderate and progressive values of Britain's "middle class," arguing that this group was a product of the commercial prosperity and manufacturing enterprises of the nineteenth century. As a new social group, the middle class possessed its own political and economic interests that ought to be represented in parliament. Framed in the narrative of reform and social change, the entrance of this "middle class" into political life appeared natural and even desirable. "The seat of public opinion is in the middle ranks of life," one pamphleteer insisted, "that numerous class … possessing intelligence sufficient for the formation of a sound judgement, neither warped by interest nor obscured by passion."[28]

In 1832, the campaign for electoral reform proved successful, inaugurating a reform package that expanded the electorate to a new base of voters capable of paying a £10 tax qualification. An additional 300,000 property holders were added to the franchise, with one in seven Britons now able to vote and hold office.[29] Although the Whigs sold reform as a consequence of social change, the realities were far more complex. Urban riots and rural uprisings in Wales and the Midlands provided the backdrop against which the

Reform Bill of 1832 took shape.³⁰ As the Whig Thomas Babington Macaulay frankly admitted, it was not so much a "measure of reform" as a "measure of conservation" that had been achieved. The parliamentary system had been temporarily secured from the threat of popular radicalism, and Macaulay and his liberal allies intended to keep it that way. Liberals were not democrats. It was necessary to "exclude those whom it is necessary to exclude" and "admit those whom it is safe to admit," in Macaulay's opinion. "I oppose universal suffrage," he affirmed, "because I think it would produce a destructive revolution."³¹ Such assertions were analogous with outlooks across the Channel and echoed the pronouncement of French liberals like Guizot who unabashedly declared himself "a decided enemy of universal suffrage."³² In framing their brand of post-revolutionary liberalism, advocates endorsed a platform of natural elitism as an antidote to popular radicalism and anarchy. They defined the world and their constituencies in terms of economic and social distinction, and liberal theorists like Guizot and Augustin Thierry had few qualms in accommodating themselves to the realities of the "class struggle" they believed endemic to modern society.³³ Post-revolutionary politics had to engage this class struggle, ensuring that political power remained confined to the reasonable and moderate sections of society.

In justifying who was to be excluded and included, liberals readily injected politics with a class element, associating themselves directly with the new social groups of the "middle classes" or "bourgeoisie." These social categories were not self-evident in the early nineteenth century. Liberals may have tied their cause to the new industrial middle classes born from economic progress, but this narrative was one largely concocted by liberal ideologues. Many self-identified "bourgeois" citizens had few connections with industry and manufacturing. In certain instances, their social origins could be traced directly to established elite families. They were hardly the class of entrepreneurs, producers and industrialists that "bourgeois" rule implied.³⁴ "Bourgeois" or "middle class" hegemony was elaborated by liberal writers who saw in these social identities a new vision of community organized around concepts of class and social distinction. Class was, to use Benedict Anderson's phrase, an "imagined community." It created a new social constituency that could rationalize reform initiatives while simultaneously limiting their scope to a select stratum of individuals.³⁵ It was in this context, as post-revolutionary politics espoused the language of class to blunt radical democracy, that the 1830s marked a "bourgeois" revolution. Class became ingrained in the terms of political debate, providing a new foundation for political claims as well as calls to collective action.

Envisioning the Moral Community

The ideologies of economic and political liberalism would not go uncontested. As early as 1825, Thomas Hodgskin, a defender of worker organizations in England, challenged the exploitative behavior of employers in his book *Labour Defended against the Claims of Capital*. Others, like the French socialist Louis Blanc, similarly advanced arguments against the unbridled competition and profitmaking of business owners, insisting that capitalism robbed artisans of their independence and autonomy. These claims came to form the basis of a counter vision of post-revolutionary society that would bring together various ideas under the rubric of "socialism."

In certain instances, socialist proposals shared similarities with the paternalism and self-help initiatives advocated by middle-class liberals. In the early 1800s, the Welsh cotton manufacturer Robert Owen outlined his method of "benevolent management" as a means of reforming the industrial system through worker instruction and individual improvement. As a chief stock-holder in his father-in-law's firm at New Lanark in Scotland, Owen had an opportunity to implement changes he believed would increase worker productivity and quality of life, including reduced working hours and better working conditions. In his model village at New Lanark, housing and basic services were provided for families while workers were given a share of the profits made through the cooperative shops built on the grounds. Owen publicized his achievements in his book *A New View of Society* (1813), outlining an alternative business model that could be replicated elsewhere. In the coming years, Owen's ideas served as a basis for model societies created in Britain and North America in which common land ownership, communal farming and profit-sharing were put forward as solutions to the "social question" of the nineteenth century.[36]

French reformers were also active in these endeavors, although their inspiration had little connection to Owen's social experiments. The philosopher and social thinker Charles Fourier outlined his own profit-sharing community in which autonomous communes oversaw production and regulated communal life. In these so-called *phalanges* each member would be both a resident and shareholder in the enterprise. Local councils would assign work based on capacity and run communal kitchens that served locally produced foods while all profits were to be shared among *phalange* members. Fourier saw his model community as the true essence of equality, one running contrary to the supposed "equality" of the liberal market where the people had "no work, no bread, sells its life for five sous per day, [and] is dragged to the slaughter house with chains on its neck."[37] In practicing this form of "association," emphasis was placed upon the collective good and correcting the detrimental effects of individualism and competition encouraged by capitalism. In the *phalange*, social and class distinctions would break down as rich and poor socialized and toiled together. Collective work would, Fourier contended, secure a new bond of fraternity among man. Decadent and cruel "civilization" was to be replaced with "harmony," unbridled capitalism supplanted by association and the welfare of all.[38]

Attracting a dedicated core of followers, Fourier lived to see his philosophy put into practice. The Fourierists found adherents in both France and abroad. They set up *phalanges* in Condé-sur-Vesgre and Boussac, while other members went as far afield as Algeria, Italy and Romania to implement their model communities. By 1840, some sixteen *phalanges* had been founded in Iowa and across the north-eastern United States. None of these experiments lasted long and often collapsed due to internal fighting and economic hardship. One of the chief problems was that Fourierism failed to attract the support of workers and remained confined to idealistic educated elites. The French social reformer Étienne Cabet had more success in winning over artisans to his brand of "communism" based on democratic and egalitarian values. Like Fourier, Cabet hoped to eradicate the extreme inequalities created by capitalism. His "Icarian" societies were self-governing units where absolute equality would be perfected. He spread his ideas through his own newspaper, *Le Populaire*, and amassed a significant following among workers in Paris and Lyon. By 1846, he was working with Robert Owen to establish reformed communities in the United States.[39]

The model communities proposed by thinkers like Owen, Fourier and Cabet outlined a counter-vision to liberal capitalism, one that was broadly considered in terms of new "socialist" principles. Within these idealized communities, shared work and cooperative associations were envisioned as the vehicles for combatting the general denigration of labor occurring in the early nineteenth century. In many instances, they anticipated a complete social transformation that challenged not only existing social structures but gender hierarchies as well. "The extension of the privileges of women," Fourier wrote in 1808, "is the basic principle of all social progress."[40] Female emancipation and sexual liberation were considered part of a general social reform that would liberate the "new woman" from patriarchal domination. Women attracted by the proposal of equal sexual relations joined these movements hoping to realize aspirations for educational opportunities, collectivized family life and even legalized divorce central to feminist platforms since the 1790s. While social experiments held out the theoretical possibility of female participation and gender equality, these goals did not always develop at the grass-roots levels of the communities. Traditional ideas of gender and domesticity prevailed to the consternation of idealists, demonstrating the acceptance of ostensibly "bourgeois" values among the working classes.[41]

The issue of female emancipation almost destroyed the Saint-Simonians, one of the most conspicuous early socialist movements in France. During the late 1820s, the group permitted women to participate in a variety of activities from setting up communal houses to spreading propaganda. However, differences of opinion regarding divorce and sexual relations between members split the movement in 1831, creating two rival camps. Its survival spoke to the movement's popularity among former French Carbonarists and liberals who had been attracted to the teaching of the eccentric Henri de Saint-Simon, the movement's founder. The group had its own newspapers and in time would establish a network of adherents connected to the world of finance and high politics across Europe. While the early Saint-Simonians were committed to building model communities based on new social principles, the message preached by Saint-Simonians was quite distinct and attracted devotees interested in socialism as well as those given to new ideas concerning economic planning and management.[42]

Henri de Saint-Simon, a land speculator and philosopher, had been at the forefront of the social experimentation imagined in the wake of the French Revolution. Like many contemporaries, he believed that the revolution had fundamentally disrupted society and set the stage for a new phase of human existence. What was required was a new set of "general ideas" capable of regenerating mankind. It was not simply politics that interested Saint-Simon. He believed that human history was driven by alternating "organic" and "critical" cycles in which reigning ideas established periods of harmony before succumbing to contestation and crisis.[43] Following the French Revolution—a period in which existing values had been challenged—the task at hand was to construct a new organic harmony, one that could synthesize the social progress of the Enlightenment with the realities of an industrial-capitalist economy. According to Saint-Simon, this task required a radical reappraisal of society and a vision of the social whole as a "truly organized machine."[44] Everywhere he looked, this organization was lacking. Industry was inviting chaos; conflicts between employers and workers abounded; there existed little coordination between the economy and the government. Industrial society had the potential to herald an age of organized production and social progress like no other, Saint-Simon believed, but it would require integration on a mass scale and a willingness to create "a great society of industry" to sustain it.[45]

In order for this to occur, the state had to abandon its *laissez-faire* approach and become involved in management and planning. It would not merely supervise the economy and social relations, but actively take charge of all society's productive forces from the factories to the workers. As Prosper Enfantin, one of Saint-Simon's most dedicated acolytes and the future leader of the movement, claimed: "To begin the organization of industry it is necessary that the government give the example."[46] Saint-Simon criticized aristocratic landowners and proprietors who lived off the labor of others. These groups contributed nothing to society, in his opinion. Social organization would be better served by savants and technocrats endowed with the knowledge and skills to operate the great social machine. With the effective management of society and its resources, tensions between labor and employers would be resolved, productivity placed on a rational footing and a new social harmony realized. The answer to the problems facing modern society was, in sum, association, a term connoting both the coherent integration of industry and a just distribution of wealth and resources. "The war of the slaves has begun again, but thank God it is no longer a question of emancipation," Enfantin wrote. "Liberty has been conquered for all. It is *association* and *organization* for which the proletarian now calls."[47]

Whereas thinkers like Owen and Fourier sought to create autonomous communities apart from the current society, the Saint-Simonians envisioned a comprehensive reform of the existing system from the top down. Yet their emphasis on association and social harmony was consistent with other social experiments of the day. Moreover, like many of their contemporaries, the Saint-Simonians imparted a spiritual element to their calls for social reform. For all his talk of modern industry and scientific progress, Saint-Simon stressed the importance of religion in the regenerated world of the future.[48] Progress and science were imagined as the kernel of a new spirituality that would bind humanity together.[49] In gaining adherents, leading Saint-Simonians undertook proselytizing activities, winning over converts through the preaching of the Saint-Simonian doctrine at regular meetings. "Missionaries" interpreted their efforts in religious terms, typically barrowing the cultural forms and discourses of post-revolutionary religious revivalism.[50] Groups like the Fourierists and Owenites were no different. Socialists framed their ideas in terms consistent with millenarian religious outlooks, in some cases lauding economic equality as a Christian principle and depicting Jesus as the first socialist.[51]

Revolutionary Europe

The destruction wrought by the French Revolution and Napoleonic Wars inspired an acute sense of social dislocation and nurtured "a longing for what [was] missing," as Anita Brookner has argued.[52] Early socialist thinkers were part of this story. They aimed to restore a semblance of community in a world rife with uncertainty and convulsed by violent social change. "Community alone can achieve the happiness of mankind," Cabet claimed.[53] Their imagined communities represented mirror images of capitalist society. They spurned the unbridled competition, individualism and exploitation that surrounded them and attempted to sketch the contours of a new moral order built upon values of association and social harmony. "Community … is the most natural, simple and perfect mode of association," avowed the radical Alexandre Théodore Dézamy. "[It is] the sole and infallible means of combatting the obstacles that oppose the development of the social principle."[54] For Dézamy, like others, socialism and the equality it promised amounted to a new "communitarian code," one that would re-establish social relations and fulfill the emancipatory aspirations of the nineteenth century.

The Making of a Proletarian Identity

Early socialist visionaries sought to correct the injustices of capitalist society, but they were not radical revolutionaries. Most opposed violent struggle in achieving their goals. In their idealized societies, harmony rather than conflict took precedent. Relations between industry and workers need not be contentious, they argued. The reorganization of labor and production would lead to the development of mutual interests and cooperation between classes. This rationale depended upon groups putting aside class interests for the greater social good, a denouement that some believed was overly idealistic if not naïve.

In France, the July Monarchy showed itself strongly committed to its purported "bourgeois" supporters and routinely backed legislation favorable to business. Although these policies resulted in economic growth, their social consequences were devastating. The persistence of small-scale industries and manual labor required the intense exploitation of workers to sustain this growth. In 1831 and again in 1834, the regime showed no qualms suppressing demonstrations staged by silk workers in Lyon, nor did it have reservations about curtailing labor organizations and clubs frequented by artisans. Over the next decade, barricades would be raised periodically in Paris and other major French cities as workers and militants took to the streets demanding social and political reforms that liberals proved unwilling to countenance.[55] Unsurprisingly, protest assumed a marked class element. Militants challenged "bourgeois" rule with claims to represent disenfranchised workers. Confronted with a government that had consciously identified itself as bourgeois, opposition assumed an anti-bourgeois rhetoric.[56]

Republican clubs and societies took the lead in fomenting a radical revival during the mid-1830s as radicals met in secret and stockpiled arms in anticipation of revolt. Yet whereas the Jacobins of old had touted their revolutionary program in the name of "the people," neo-Jacobins were more inclined to associate their cause directly with a new class of artisans and day laborers identified as "the proletariat." During his trial in 1832, the republican conspirator Louis Auguste Blanqui candidly declared himself a "proletarian," that group "crushed by taxes for the benefit of … two or three hundred thousand idlers," as he explained.[57] As the scion of a middle-class family, Blanqui's proletarian credentials were questionable. However, his identification with a proletarian citizenry was indicative of the radical political culture growing up at mid-century as militant groups espoused socialist rhetoric, adopted names like "workers' equality" and organized into small cells labeled "workshops" (*ateliers*). A *declassé* intellectual, Blanqui refashioned himself as a working-class militant. Yet his brand of conspiratorial revolution hardly amounted to a worker movement. Blanqui was an inveterate revolutionary who elevated political violence to a religion. Effective revolutionary organization was the only valid means of founding a truly social republic, he contended. Like the Babeuvists and Carbonari, Blanquism relied upon a small cadre of radical conspirators willing to "submit all forces of the party to a single direction," as Théophile Guillard de Kersausie, head of the paramilitary *Société d'Action*, explained.[58] Neo-Jacobin rhetoric blended socialist ideas of class struggle with a republican revolutionary tradition, finding in this synthesis the validation for an egalitarian "social" republic that would abolish private property and religious institutions in the name of progress.[59]

Despite rising social tensions during the 1840s, neo-Jacobinism remained confined to the fringes of the French left. Moderate republicans endorsed less extreme solutions to the "social question" while distraught artisans sought immediate relief from economic hardship rather than the overthrow of the state. The journalist Louis Blanc drew liberally from the Fourierists and Saint-Simonians in his instance that labor was a natural "right" and the state ought to be the "supreme regulator of production." His program called for creating government-operated workshops that would provide jobs for the unemployed and ensure a basic level of subsistence for all citizens. State management was to be balanced with worker-elected "corporations" that would allow labor to influence economic and social policies. Blanc's welfare policies sketched the architecture for a republican state committed to labor yet not hostile to capital.[60] Empowering labor would lay the foundation for a more equitable social order, he reasoned. It was a message that resonated with artisans afflicted by new social and economic pressures. In many respects, his plan harkened back to the former guild system, envisioning state-run corporations organized by trade and infused with solid republican values.[61] While not necessarily radical, Blanc laid out a blueprint for a social republic that equated labor with citizenship and "the people." His ideas conformed with desires for "association" and cooperation popular among workers and interpreted republican values through the idiom of class solidarity and labor. For republican socialists like Blanc, labor was imagined as a new universal class, outfitting Rousseauvian notions of equality and the general will with a solid proletarian component.[62]

The range of socialist ideas that circulated throughout France revealed that socialism had neither a single doctrine nor core leadership. Moreover, it was never a movement directed explicitly by the working classes. Its consistency stemmed from the anti-bourgeois rhetoric popularized during the years of the July Monarchy. Liberalism defined

Figure 11 Louis Blanc © The British Library Board.

citizenship in economic terms, feeding impressions of an oppressive state dominated by capitalists. Politics and political language provided the context in which a worker culture and identity assumed form.[63] Republican spokesmen and radicals employed the language of class as they adapted their movements to fit changing circumstances. They informed workers about the common oppression they confronted and the common enemy they faced. These injunctions did more to construct a working-class identity than socioeconomic circumstances and served to foster perceptions of class-based solidarity that bound together a diverse range of political movements, trades and subcultures.

In Britain, there existed little conception of workers as a particular class prior to the late 1830s despite both a resurgent radicalism and awareness of the "social question" in the country. Certain liberal elites supported legislation aimed at ameliorating poverty and hardship, but the state-funded workhouses and poor laws that resulted from these early reform initiatives fell far short of their desired effects. Moreover, if the government tolerated paternalist reform initiatives spearheaded by the middle classes, it upheld its pathological mistrust of movements led directly by laborers. Radical newspapers were repeatedly targeted by authorities and meetings organized by artisans and trade workers suppressed. Workers found themselves shut out of politics and reliant on elites who, while perhaps well-intentioned, were more concerned with preventing social revolution than empowering workers and giving them a voice.

Seeking to change this situation, organizers formed the London Working Men's Association in 1836 and the following year drafted a "People's Charter" outlining fundamental grievances for parliament's consideration. Drawn up with the assistance of William Lovett, a former cabinet maker, and Henry Hetherington, the son of a London tailor, the Charter called for universal suffrage and the abolition of the property qualifications necessary for voting and holding office. Chartism sprang from the tradition of politically conscious artisan associations based in London since the 1790s and found support among a select group of radical politicians and newspaper editors disillusioned with promises of government reform.[64] The emphasis on political rather than direct social reform was a key feature of the movement, situating it within accepted ideas of representative government and parliamentary process familiar to Britain. The Irish lawyer and editor of the *Poor Man's Guardian*, James O'Brien, summed up the movement in 1837 when explaining to readers: "Knaves will tell you that it is because you have no property that you are unrepresented. I tell you, on the contrary, it is because you are unrepresented that you have no property."[65] Such rhetoric opposed the reign of property and monied interests on strictly constitutional grounds with the People's Charter presented as a new Magna Carta.

This orientation did not, however, preclude the possibilities for radicalism or imply Chartism was a movement directed by middle-class elites. The Irish Chartist Feargus O'Connor rejected cooperation with middle-class politicians to the dismay of men like Lovett, and instead favored a brand of working-class activism aimed at creating a mass party. By 1838, he had broken with the London Working Men's Association and formed his Great Northern Union, drawing together radical suffrage associations in places like Manchester, Leeds and Sheffield. Conscious of the difficulties he faced, O'Connor worked tirelessly to unify local groups and transform artisan radicalism into a spontaneous mass movement connected through a network of associations and newspapers. Known as the "apostle of the north," O'Connor helped found local Chartist organizations and gained the support of urban trade unions that would stitch together a national movement with a working-class base.[66] His fiery oratory was mixed with new tactics that included assembling workers in military formations, public drilling exercises and "torch light meetings" in which hundreds of artisans would assemble at night in deliberate and symbolic demonstrations of force. These tactics made "the people" a visible and public entity, underscoring the mass support Chartists claimed to enjoy. This display of what John Plotz has called "crowd power" marked a significant change in radical and popular political discourse. It replaced the disorderly revolutionary "mob" with organized manifestations of support, legitimating Chartist claims to represent "the people." It also suggested that "the people" was a coherent and recognizable entity which, much like the imagined "middle classes," was capable of participating in public debate and speaking on behalf of its own interests.[67]

The preference for mass public meetings and the creation of a "National Charter Association" put forward by O'Connor contrasted with the moderation advocated by men like Lovett. Arguments regarding whether to use "physical" or "moral" force divided the movement and often undermined its unified "national" front. In 1839, this split was made clear following the House of Common's refusal to consider the People's Petition submitted by Chartists leaders that summer. Riots erupted in Birmingham and west Wales. Protest organizers were jailed. In Newport, Chartists staged a mass march that transformed into an armed uprising. O'Connor and his ilk encouraged resistance while the moderate newspaper *The Chartist* urged readers to "pursue the course of peaceful agitation" and "press forward … under the watchwords of peace, law, order."[68] Despite these divisions, however, Chartism became the closest thing to a worker movement with a national reach. Its leaders claimed to speak for "the workers" and they provided a range of symbols and idioms to reinforce this imagined class unity.[69] One of Chartism's most striking qualities was its attempt to transcend purely political campaigns. Chartist organizations hosted recreational and religious activities that assisted in creating an "alternative culture" for workers. Instructional lecture programs, educational courses and even music recitals all contributed to the formation of a distinct working-class culture and identity which competed with the middle classes even as it replicated certain aspects of middle-class sociability regarding gender roles and masculine public identity.[70]

Chartism, just as much as French socialism, revealed the extent to which the new language of class identity was coming to transform the political landscape of the nineteenth century. The "laboring poor" and *sans-culottes* of the 1790s had, by the 1840s, assumed the garb of a proletarian class united in its aspiration for equality and fortified through a common struggle against the injustice of "bourgeois" rule. This imagined community encompassed an array of artisans and craft workers coming from various localities. In asserting a common identity and culture as laborers, it created the context for collective mobilization and the possibility of articulating a radical platform with universal implications. By the 1840s, the essential components were in place to convert these reformist and radical elements into a truly revolutionary movement.

Communism à la Marx

Early socialists proffered a number of labels to define their ideas and differentiate themselves from rivals. "Mutualists," "associationists" and "republican socialists" were all found on the left. Cabet preferred the term "communist" to describe his social philosophy of common ownership and social equality, a term often applied retrospectively to Babeuf and his followers.[71] Such ideas were not in short supply prior to the French Revolution, with writers like Jean Meslier and the Abbé Mably outlining utopian societies devoid of private ownership and regenerated through communal association.[72] However, communism (as a specific revolutionary ideology) has its origins in the nineteenth century and is particularly indebted to German thinkers like Moses Hess, Andreas Gottschalk and Friedrich Engels. It would, however, be Karl Marx who would leave his stamp on communist ideology and redefine Europe's revolutionary heritage.

Germany was in a state of agitation at the close of the Napoleonic period. "We owe an enormous amount to this wild and raging revolution that [has] ignited a great sea of fire in the mind," wrote Ernest Morritz Arndt in 1814.[73] Indeed, the years of revolutionary upheaval and war had animated an entire generation of German thinkers. Romantics and intellectuals anticipated the creation of a German *Vaterland*, a national community that would unite the German-speaking populations of Central Europe and solidify their status as a modern people. However, the post-revolutionary period took a different path. The Congress of Vienna preserved the assemblage of small states and free cities making up the German Confederation. Twenty-one of the thirty-seven principalities had population under 100,000. Hopes of a post-war liberal Germany were also frustrated, with political institutions kept under the control of regional monarchs and the nobility. Contrary to nationalist desires, Germany appeared medieval and backward. It was a patchwork of kingdoms; its political systems were aristocratic; and its industrial capacities remained underdeveloped. German intellectuals expressed a collective sense of disillusion and even inferiority as the post-Napoleonic era dawned. And yet, if elites felt betrayed by this state of affair, there was one area in which Germans were at the cultural forefront: philosophy.

German philosophers were among the leading thinkers of the period. By 1815, the French *philosophes* were beginning to appear outdated. Their ideas belonged to a pre-revolutionary world while many German philosophers were promoting ideas of romanticism and cultural nationalism. A general impression of Germany as a "*Land der Dichter und Denker*" (a country of poets and philosophers) emerged, giving Germans a sense of pride and distinctiveness.[74] As the poet Heinrich Heine wrote in 1844:

The Land belongs to the Russians and French
In the British the ocean is vested
But we in dream's airy regions possess
The mastery uncontested.[75]

Europeans esteemed the rise of the *deutsche Philosophen* who appeared in tune with the currents of post-revolutionary intellectual life, but one figure in particular stood out among others: Georg Wilhelm Friedrich Hegel.

Hegel was representative of a new brand of philosophical idealism popularized in Germany since the late eighteenth century. He had been a lecturer in Jena when the city was occupied by French forces in 1806 and managed to catch a glimpse of Napoleon briefly during the military campaign that year. He found the emperor an "extraordinary man whom it is impossible not to admire," as he told a friend.[76] The decade of Napoleonic dominance in Germany was a fruitful period for Hegel. As an idealist, he put a strong emphasis on the power of human understanding and, above all, reason. "Reason is the soul of the world it inhabits, its immanent principle, its most proper and inward nature, its universal," he argued.⁷⁷ In his estimation, reason was the primary force driving history, the "*Geist*" (Spirit) that impelled human development and actions across time. Man and the world, as Hegel understood them, were merely a medium through which this world spirit operated. Did not the French Revolution employ reason to regenerate and re-create society? Did not it demonstrate that human ideas and consciousness were the essential force behind all social existence? History was essentially rational, Hegel contended. It constituted a process by which human ideas actualized themselves and continually worked toward a higher fulfillment.⁷⁸

It was not that human development was simply driven by the power of ideas. Rather, it was the struggle of competing ideas and concepts that gave it its true force, what Hegel called the dialectic. In this schema, concepts begin with an affirmation (a thesis). However, this affirmation inevitably invites a negative concept (antithesis) signifying its opposite. According to Hegel, a concept and its negation would enter into struggle and eventually combine into a higher unity, or "synthesis." This synthesis, in turn, became a new thesis which produced its own antithesis and engendered a new dialectical struggle.⁷⁹ Hegel's vision of historical change may have appeared abstract, but this model was, in many respects, derived from the experience of the French Revolution. The revolution had marked a world-historical point of change, and it was this process of change and competing ideas that interested Hegel. The feudal, monarchial society of the Ancien Régime had served to produce its opposite, the Enlightenment with its notions of natural rights and freedom contrary to royal privilege and patriarchy. These two concepts had waged a violent war against one another, resulting in the French Revolution. However, this struggle had eventually reconciled itself in a new synthesis, a state in which the two aspects were combined and transformed into a higher combination. For Hegel, this higher synthesis was Napoleon with his mix of revolutionary and absolutist elements. The revolutionary emperor was the embodiment of the world spirit at the dawn of the nineteenth century, explaining Hegel's admiration for the man. For Hegel, Napoleon represented the world spirit incarnate, a manifestation of the conflicting ideals and aspirations lying beneath the surface of exterior realities.⁸⁰

Hegel's philosophy of history offered an explanatory model for violent historical change. It made sense of transformative events like the French Revolution and placed them within a narrative of continual social and human progress. This is not to suggest, however, that Hegel was an apologist for revolution. For Hegel, the French Revolution and the violence it unleashed were symptomatic of a deeper problem within modern society.⁸¹ In championing natural rights, revolutionaries had supported ideals of individual autonomy and freedom from the state. This ideological outlook not only justified the independence of "civil society" from the political sphere; it also justified the pursuit of self-interest. Theorists of capitalism may have lauded this development, but Hegel saw nothing natural or desirable in such a state of affairs. With the triumph of civil society came the predominance of personal and economic interest over the collective good, and the only corrective to this situation was law and governance derived from reason. In Hegel's view, the state alone was capable of resolving the competing interests and conflicts that civil society engendered.[82] The state represented a particular vision of community that could resist social fragmentation and disintegration. Freedom could be found *through* society rather than outside of it, with state institutions furnishing the ethical cohesion and communitarian "spirit" that civil society could not.

Hegel's philosophy, while not revolutionary in spirit, was nonetheless a product of the revolutionary environment in which it developed. It laid out a schema for historical change and collective action, seeing in human history a logic and purpose. Man's rational development progressed onward through higher and higher combinations, violently working toward the "absolute idea" and "end of history" when all conflict would be resolved. Such ideas appealed to a generation disillusioned with the present and captivated by the mythic aura of the French Revolution and Napoleon. Unsurprisingly, Hegelian philosophy came to play a dominant role in German universities during the post-revolutionary period, and it would be at one of these universities that a young philosophy student would begin to apply Hegel in new and very different ways.

Karl Marx was the son of a Rhineland barrister and assimilated Jew who hoped that his son would also take up a legal profession. At university in Bonn, however, the young Marx showed little inclination to follow in his father's footsteps. In fact, he showed little inclination to do much serious studying at all. He joined poetry and tavern clubs, took up gambling with his cohorts and even showed a taste for dueling. His youthful indiscretions were troubling, so much so that his father ordered him to continue his education in Berlin at an institution known for its rigor and discipline. The study of Hegelian philosophy was strongly entrenched in the Berlin curriculum, and it was there that Marx took to studying philosophy. While it was not law as his father had hoped, it was better than the carousing he had become known for in Bonn. In a complete about-face, Marx excelled at his studies. He became notorious for staying up late at night to write, even working himself to the point of exhaustion. It was a stimulating time to be in Berlin. During the late 1830s, the so-called "Young Hegelians" were in the ascent, and through club meetings and debating societies, Marx fraternized with young intellectuals enamored by materialist philosophy and critical of the recent illiberal turn in Prussian politics.

Although joining with the Young Hegelians, Marx soon discovered that he was not necessarily in agreement with their aims or methods. Philosophy, he came to believe, was overly abstract. Intellectuals and theorists were concerned with purely ethical and moral questions for their own sake but rarely considered the applications of their theorizing in the world at large. As Marx was coming to see it, purely academic questions were not enough. "Up until now the philosophers have only interpreted the world in various ways," he wrote in an often-quoted thesis from 1845; "the point, however, is to change it."[83] Hegel's emphasis on *Geist* and reason appeared removed from any meaningful social context. Philosophers could pontificate on the positive role of the state and its capacity for collective freedom, but for Marx such declarations appeared specious if not erroneous. It was not the state that united society, but actual social life. As he explained in 1845 in a book highly critical of the Young Hegelians, "in the real community, individuals obtain their freedom in and through their association."[84]

Figure 12 Karl Marx © The British Library Board.

Much like Hegel, Marx saw civil society as a destructive force and criticized liberalism for its preoccupation with political emancipation. "Political emancipation is a reduction of man to a member of civil society, to an egoistic independent individual on the one hand and to a citizen on the other hand," he contended.[85] However, Marx went further in his critique. If liberalism encouraged the uninhibited purist of private interests over the collective good, it also employed political institutions to enforce such values. The fragmentation, depravity and slavery of civil society were "the natural basis" of the modern state, he maintained.[86] In a society driven by personal interest, individuals came to think of themselves and treat others as means to individual ends. In his perceptive analysis of modern society, Marx recognized that the new political environment had a correlating impact on social relations, rendering them competitive and antagonistic in nature. The concept of *Gemeinwesen* (community) played a central role in Marx's thinking from any early age. Liberalism and capitalism effectively eroded social solidarity, in his opinion. Exploitation and inequality were pronounced symptoms of "the drastic dissolution of society" in the modern era.[87]

The insistence on a more active philosophy and growing consideration for the social question stemmed in part from Marx's journalistic preoccupations during the early 1840s. After finishing his studies in Berlin, he took a job editing the liberal *Rheinische Zeitung* where he reported on local agricultural issues and never missed an opportunity to criticize the policies of the Prussian state. Within five months of Marx's taking over the *Rheinische Zeitung*, the paper was suppressed. By this point, however, Marx himself had become weary of his editorial responsibilities and constant quibbling with officials, both of which distracted him from pursuing his critical and philosophical writings. "The government has given me back my freedom," he crowed after receiving news of the paper's closure.[88] As a philosopher, Marx always attached more importance to ideas over direct action, never aspiring to be a radical activist or revolutionary conspirator. "Practical attempts, even by the masses, can be answered with a cannon as soon as they become dangerous," he remarked in 1842, "but ideas that have overcome our intellect and conquer our convictions, ideas to which reason has riveted our conscience, are chains from which one cannot break loose without breaking one's heart."[89]

Marx established a reputation as a political firebrand, but he had not as yet committed himself firmly to socialism. This conversion would occur only after leaving Germany in 1843 when he relocated to Paris to write for the radical German émigré press and begin conducting research for a book on the French Revolution. In the French capital, Marx socialized with German political exiles, attended workers' meeting and established connections with the League of the Just, a conspiratorial group founded by Bebeuvists for the purposes of promoting worker revolution. Paris offered Marx a new world, and in collaborating with these groups Marx began to speak more openly about worker issues. Class struggle and revolutionary programs increasingly filled his writings as he studied socialist movements and reflected seriously upon their revolutionary potential.[90] Yet Marx came at this issue from a different perspective than his French counterparts. French radicals typically placed their hopes in political revolt. They plotted Jacobin-style coups to highjack the state and create a more just society. Marx was skeptical of such an approach. As a philosopher interested in economic and social issues, he felt that neo-Jacobin-style revolution was futile if the conditions for revolution were not in place first.

He was coming to understand that revolution could not only be political. It had to be a social revolution as well. "Revolution in general—the overthrow of the existing power and dissolution of previous relationships—is a political act," he claimed. "Socialism cannot be realized without a revolution. But when its organizing activity begins, when its peculiar aims, its soul, come forward, then socialism casts aside its political cloak."[91] Overthrowing the state and dictating laws would achieve little if society and social relationships themselves were not transformed. Revolutionaries needed a deeper appreciation for the social forces at play in Marx's opinion, and this was precisely what French radicals lacked. Marx went as far as to claim that the Reign of Terror had occurred precisely because the conditions for a real social revolution had not yet been ripe. The Jacobins had been compelled to enforce their policies through violence rather than implement them with broad support. This would certainly occur again were a coup orchestrated without first laying the groundwork for a vast social transformation.[92] What was currently laying the foundations for the type of social revolution envisaged by Marx were industrialization and the particular forms of social inequality and misery it generated.

In this opinion, Marx found a sympathizer in a fellow German political writer, Friedrich Engels. Engels had met Marx briefly in Cologne in 1842, but it was not until becoming reacquainted in Paris that their historic friendship would blossom. Engels came from Bremen, a small Rhenish town where his father owned a textile mill with a subsidiary branch in Manchester. Attending to his father's business in England, Engels used the opportunity to study British industrial society and familiarize himself with working-class movements like the Chartists.[93] "Class antagonisms [are] completely changing the aspect of political life," he concluded after noting the tenor of recent political debate in the country.[94] In the mid-1840s, his writing on British political economy appeared in a journal for which Marx wrote, sparking a correspondence and eventual partnership between the two German expatriates. Like many intellectuals of the mid-nineteenth century, Engels was critical of modernization's destructive tendencies, believing it dissolved established social relations and divided societies into property owners and those owning nothing but their labor.[95] Marx and Engels were, in many ways, complementary. Marx saw the working class in broad, abstract terms. For him, the proletariat was the product of larger social and economic changes that were taking place in the modern world. Engels took these abstractions and placed them in the real context of misery and factory life. These were the details that would, ultimately, authenticate Marx's ideas. It didn't hurt that Engels came from a prosperous family and had a source of funds the two could draw on to promote their ideas.

While socialism had initially been a French idea, Marx and Engels would put forward a new type of socialism, one that claimed to be scientific and grounded in an appreciation for social and economic realities. In their opinion, thinkers like Saint-Simon or Fourier were hopelessly "utopian." To believe that an idealistic social harmony was possible between workers and capitalists was to misconstrue the logic of capitalism or economic interest, Marx charged.[96] Capital and industrialization depended upon exploitation. Marx agreed with the theories of Smith and Ricardo, who insisted that wealth was made up of both labor and production. Yet Marx argued that while the workers produced they did not accrue the benefits of this production. They went to the capitalists who owned the means of production. This was a key point in understanding not just capitalism, but human societies in general. Control of resources and production were the lynchpins of social power. More to the point, every struggle for power or domination inevitably possessed a class or social element. "All struggles with the state, the struggle between democracy, aristocracy and monarchy, the struggle for franchises … are nothing but the illusory forms in which the real struggles of different classes are carried out among one another."[97] Given these circumstances, any hope of creating social harmony between classes and competing economic interests was a fiction.

In outlining his theories, Marx drew on his former Hegelian education. His understanding of social and historical change was heavily dependent upon Hegel's dialectic. Yet he did not intend to merely apply Hegel. He wanted to "turn Hegel on his head," as he claimed. This implied rejecting the notion of historical change driven by ideas. As Marx affirmed, "consciousness does not determine life, but life determines consciousness."[98] It was economic and material realties—not ideas—that drove historical change and structured the world. This proposition underpinned a materialist vision of history quite distinct from Hegel's idealism. "The nature of individuals ... depends on the material conditions which determine their production," Marx argued.[99] This key understanding could be boiled down into a simple conclusion: "the history of all hitherto existing societies is the history of class struggle."[100] Marx readily agreed with liberal theorists that class struggle was central to modern society. Furthermore, class struggle was the veritable motor of social and revolutionary change, as Marx saw it.

Oppressed classes would, over time, become "class conscious" and aware of their exploitation. This awakening provided the impetus for the overthrow of the existing order and the creation of new social and political institutions consistent with class interests and dominance. The French Revolution had, in Marx's assessment, been the moment of bourgeois emancipation as the non-noble middle classes cast off the constraints of an aristocratic, landed system to create the conditions for capitalism and civil society. The legal regimes, value systems and institutions that had been created over the eighteenth and nineteenth centuries were nothing more than "bourgeois prejudices" behind which lurked the interests and mechanisms of control that sustained bourgeois power. In the current period, it was now the industrial workers who would rise up in turn and overthrow their bourgeois oppressors. This conclusion was not mere speculation, but historical truth. The dialectical process commanded it. Social groups inevitably produced their opposing counterparts as they consolidated their economic interests. "What the bourgeoisie ... produces, above all, is their own grave diggers," Marx prophesized.[101] The task at hand was for the proletarian class to seize control of the means of production and secure their independence, enacting a "communist" revolution that would efface all existing social and economic relations. Violence was essential in this process, necessitating the creation of a dictatorship of the proletariat that would push through communist principles in its endeavor to realize this social revolution.

Marx clearly took his inspiration from the Enlightenment and French Revolution. Yet his vision of emancipation surpassed Enlightenment aspirations of eliminating the constraints that inhibited human freedom. He fused Enlightenment ideas of liberation with German historicist thinking, producing a revised model of revolution that at once found its validation in social realities and the logic of history. Revolutionary emancipation now appeared the culmination of a historical process determined by powerful material forces. If the "utopian" socialists continued to subscribe to humanitarian ideals and the abstract equality stemming from the Enlightenment, Marx insisted that socialism was the end product of history itself.[102] In line with his Hegelian scheme, the coming social revolution would usher in the foreordained "end of history" as social equality and the abolition of private property put an end to the class conflicts that drove change. "There is never a political movement which is not at the same time social," Marx dictated. "It is only in an order of things in which there are no more classes and class antagonisms that *social evolutions* will cease to be *political revolutions*."[103]

Enlightenment-inspired revolutions had also been republican revolutions. Revolutionaries supported ideas of democracy and nationalism with the aim of liberating oppressed peoples from the shackles of monarchy. Marx, however, was not a republican. His revolution spoke in the name of an oppressed social class, the proletariat. By its very nature, a national revolution denoted a "bourgeois" revolution. Patriotism and the nation-state only served to divide workers and mask the common oppression uniting them. Marx understood universal emancipation in its fullest context, foreseeing workers across the world, driven by material necessity, casting off their chains. The proletariat sought no "particular right," Marx claimed. Its redemption would only come about "through the redemption of the whole of humanity … [because] the proletariat represents the dissolution of society as a special order."[104] Because the proletariat represented a universal class, social revolution itself could only be imagined in the terms of international revolution. In its aspiration to abolish property and social distinction, the social revolution of the nineteenth century became a common one. Its principles of equality and equal distribution augured a new classless community and brand of "communism" at once egalitarian and international.

Despite his rhetoric of communist revolution, Marx did not support reckless adventurism. Social revolution could only occur when both "modern productive forces" and "bourgeois productive forms" were "in collision with each other." Patience and timing were essential.[105] "The old world must be brought right out into the light of day and the new one given a positive form," Marx insisted in 1843. "The longer that events allow thinking humanity time to recollect itself and suffering humanity time to assemble itself the more perfect will be the birth of the product that the present carries in its womb."[106] Spreading propaganda, organization and worker-led parties designed to politicize workers and agitate on their behalf were the effective instruments of preparation. To this end, Marx and Engels set to work organizing radicals across national borders. In 1846, they founded a network of communist correspondence committees to keep German, French and British socialists informed of each other's activities. The following year, the two took an active role in transforming the League of the Just into an enlarged Communist League. Contrary to neo-Jacobin expectations, Marx envisioned a more open and democratic structure for the league with the holding of annual congresses and an elected leadership. These efforts at organization proved invariably tricky, and typically resulted in feuds over the proper methods of communist revolution. More radical members tended to favor immediate insurrection and political revolt. However, Marx clung to his conviction in patience and proper timing.

Arguments often became heated, revealing the very fragile nature of radical movements in the 1840s. The question of when and how to strike was never resolved satisfactorily and remained a constant point of contention. To smooth over some of these conflicts, it was believed the Communist League required a clear profession of its goals and beliefs, if only to provide the organization with a public identity and to communicate its core ideological values to members. This responsibility fell to Marx and Engels who began drafting the work in late 1847. By January, the tract was finished and sent to London for publication. The title was unambiguous: *The Manifesto of the Communist Party*, a short and concise pamphlet that neatly summarized Marx's ideas on historical materialism and proletarian revolution.[107]

The timing of its publication was also fortuitous. When it appeared in press, the document was scarcely read outside a small circle of communist organizers and activists. However, it appeared at a moment when social tensions across the continent were reaching a fever pitch. As the pamphlet came off the presses, events in France were beginning to indicate that Marx's prophecy might, in fact, be accurate. That month, protests and street demonstrations brought down the government of Louis Philippe, generating a wave of radicalism that would ripple across the continent over the next year. Through chance, Marx and Engels' revolutionary manifesto now found a revolutionary environment, one that it had not necessarily created but which it could seek to influence.

Conclusion

Speaking before the Communist League in 1850, Marx confronted radicals calling for imminent revolution with an insightful reproof. "Just as Democrats abused the word 'people,' so now the word 'proletarian' has been degraded to a mere phrase."[108] Marx's insinuation that radicals did not understand the historical forces unfolding before them and the context of the true revolution at hand possesses a certain irony. He more than any other writer had been responsible for this "proletarianization" of "the people." Critics and working-class activists may have contributed to the invention of the "proletariat" as a social category, but Marx provided this group with a history and origin-story linked directly to the birth of industry and the modern world. His materialist history saw "bourgeois" and "proletariat" as the opposing poles of modernity and ascribed to the industrial worker the task of bringing forth a radically new community unparalleled in history. In the writings and theories of Marx, "the people" were effectively re-imagined as "the proletariat," providing a new source of legitimacy for political action.

Social historians have long emphasized the social and economic factors that drove revolt in the nineteenth century. This reading has largely agreed with Marxist appraisals, interpreting "proletarianization" as a consequence of modern industry and the common conditions it imposed on a destitute working class. However, the proletariat was always more fiction than reality. Social elites conjured this phantom whenever demonstrations arose. Activists appealed to the working class and proletariat in an effort to create a collective identity that transcended professional and regional attachments. In the broader perspective, socialist ideas were part of a systemic transformation in nineteenth-century identity and politics as the idiom of class became the dominant language for representing and interpreting the social world. Communist ideologues may have differed from their "utopian" counterparts in their methods and goals, but both contributed to the making of a working-class proletarian identity that reoriented radical politics and understandings of community. The assertion of a class-based community that could speak for "the people" gave embodiment to ideals of universal equality and contextualized many of the widespread political and social frustrations that accompanied the emergence of a liberal, capitalist order.

Revolutionary Europe

By the late 1840s, the social question had reached an impasse. A general sense of crisis appeared to loom across the continent. In 1848, the liberal Alexis de Tocqueville chided his fellow French politicians for their consistent intransigence and unwillingness to take seriously the brewing problems posed by working-class militancy. "Gentlemen allow me to tell you that I believe you are deceiving yourselves …," he warned that January. "I believe that at the present moment we are sleeping on a volcano."[109] Within a month, nobody would doubt that his caveat had been a valid one.

CHAPTER 7
THE INDIAN SUMMER OF ROMANTIC REVOLUTION: 1848 AND THE REASSESSMENT OF EUROPEAN RADICALISM

The year 1848 saw the outbreak of multiple revolutionary movements across continental Europe. The rapidity and widespread nature of these uprisings gave credence to fears of Jacobin conspiracies and the ominous *comité directeur*. Over the 1840s, tracts and pamphlets had routinely warned of worker revolts and conspiratorial plots, conjuring up the bloody memories of the *sans-culottes* and Terror. All too frequently, conservatives viewed the omnipresent "social question" through the prism of 1793, seeing in it a host of new Robespierres and Saint-Justs waiting to strike. The events of 1848 would seemingly validate these suspicions. Yet the social question sprang from deeper roots than the conflicts between artisans and employers waged in the cities. The revolutionary tide of 1848 was, in large part, a response to longstanding economic, social and political tensions that had been mounting for a decade. Their convergence, however, was the product of chance and fast-paced events on the ground rather than an orchestrated plot or the logical outcome of strict social forces.

The 1840s witnessed a severe agricultural crisis exacerbated by crop failures and a potato blight that ravaged the continent in 1845. Rising food prices and poverty spurred migrations to cities where workers competed for jobs with unskilled day laborers. Despite the shared hardships faced by agricultural and urban workers, the rural crisis was distinct. Across most of Europe, feudal and semi-feudal institutions remained intact. Peasants were subject to work obligations and Church taxes that diminished already meager incomes. Land was concentrated in the hands of the nobility and conflicts between lord and serf frequently translated into fights over access to forest and agricultural land. Even in areas where feudalism had been diminished, landless peasants engaged in forms of sharecropping while independent landholders relied on credit to sustain their livelihoods. The result was a European peasantry deeply in debt and squeezed by the mounting pressures of a subsistence economy in transition. Popularly referred to as the "hungry forties," the decade saw rural poverty and destitution on a wide scale. In 1847, a banking crisis compounded these anxieties, resulting in the contraction of credit and a general economic downturn that hit manufacturing and financial sectors. From the middle of the decade onwards, food riots and localized uprising periodically erupted in France, the Netherlands, Belgium, Italy and Germany.[1]

These systemic economic problems have traditionally been considered the cause of the widespread unrest in 1848. Numerous histories have noted the strains that modernization placed on traditional social and economic structures, generating protest movements driven by hunger and necessity.[2] Marxists in particular have emphasized the role of working-class mobilization in the unrest, seeing 1848 as a social revolution motivated by industrialization and declining living standards.[3] Examinations of the rural world have modified this focus on militant artisans and urban workers, indicating that revolutionary activities did extend beyond urban centers. Disruptions in rural areas conformed to older patterns of protest and resistance, making 1848 appear both a worker revolution and the last mass continental peasant uprising.[4] Certainly social and economic factors acted as a catalyst in mobilizing large groups of people, but they do not furnish a comprehensive explanation for the outbreak of the revolutions that agitated Europe throughout the year.

Attempting to find a causative explanation for the revolutions is difficult given that continental Europe was politically, socially and economically diverse. The liberal, industrializing regimes in France and Britain were quite distinct from the agrarian and feudal societies of Central and Eastern Europe. If "bourgeois" and "proletarian" actors were at the forefront of political movements in the West, liberal reformism came largely from the noble classes in the East.[5] In places like Hungary and Romania, the relative lack of industrialization meant a proletarian class was altogether absent.[6] Moreover, while most of the revolutions would espouse a nationalist tenor, nationalism was by no means well-developed throughout Europe. Locality, trade and religion remained more significant markers of identity outside elite circles. Multinational empires and regional dynasties rather than nation-states were the norm across much of the continent. The Habsburg domain encompassing Austria, Hungary, Bohemia and northern Italy was a baroque composite-state held together by varying dynastic and imperial loyalties. Germany and the Italian peninsula remained a mosaic of monarchial states and free cities which impeded nationalist movements just as much as inspired longings for national unity. In many respects, 1848 furnished a context to forge unitary states out of these complex arrangements as revolution heralded nationalist programs possessing the means of binding diverse populations together.

The initial wave of revolutionary activity was a series of autonomous domestic uprisings triggered by events in France.[7] The Russian writer Alexander Herzen expressed the outlook of many romantic intellectuals of the day when claiming that Paris was "the Jerusalem of revolutions."[8] Unrest in Paris had the potential to encourage imitation and evoke memories of the revolutionary wars that had once "liberated" Europe from its absolutist yoke. By early 1848, the July Monarchy was confronting pressures on a variety of fronts. Radical republicans had never endorsed the "bourgeois" liberalism of the government, but the economic crisis had shaken confidence among regime supporters and galvanized the political opposition. Critics called for reform and greater government accountability, ridiculing the narrow policies of Guizot and the Orléanists. Republicans held banquet campaigns designed to circumvent restrictions on political meetings. Under the pretext of apolitical dinner parties, opponents found means of organizing and rallying supporters to the cause of "liberty, equality and fraternity."[9] Eighteen years of liberal rule and class division had rekindled desires for national unity and association.

In a period characterized by growing social cleavages, the idea of a republic "one and indivisible" offered a model capable of reunifying a polarized society.[10]

On February 21, 1848, the government moved to shut down a large banquet meeting scheduled in Paris. When republicans arrived at the hall, they found the doors blocked by the police. With the meeting prohibited, participants took their message to the streets. The following day, a crowd gathered outside the ministry of justice. Protestors held placards with revolutionary slogans, shouting "Down with Guizot!" Soldiers were called in to disperse the crowd, and in a moment of confusion the troops fired into the crowd. With order breaking down, moderate republicans feared the situation would embolden radical revolutionaries to take action. The July Monarchy was completely discredited, eliciting calls for regime change. Over the next two days, barricades were erected in the streets and republicans made plans to create a provisional government. "As in 1830, the People are victorious," proclaimed a placard on a barricade outside the Collège de France, adding, "this time they will not lay down their arms."[11]

Given the tenor of such warnings, the incoming republicans were conscious of the need to appease Parisian workers and demands for a "social" republic. To this end, Louis Blanc was selected to head a commission charged with designing social legislation and making the "right to work" a reality. From the Hôtel de Ville, Blanc announced that the new republic would commit itself to the social question, provide jobs for the unemployed and found a new government on the principle of social and political equality. Within days, France had been transformed from a conservative monarchy into a revolutionary social republic.[12]

Over the coming weeks, protests began spreading into western Germany and Central Europe. According to Gustav von Struve, a Mannheim republican, the news from Paris was akin to an "electric spark." Not wasting any time, Struve and his fellow republican Friedrich Hecker organized public rallies in Baden and drew up a list of demands calling for freedom of the press and representative institutions. The *Märzforderungen* ("March demands") circulated rapidly throughout neighboring German states and became the centerpiece of reform programs in Bavaria, Württemberg and ultimately Berlin.[13] In Cologne, the communist Andreas Gottschalk drew up his own demands for social reform and set to work raising a citizens' militia. Agitation in cities quickly mixed with ongoing rural disturbances in the Odenwal and Black Forests where for the past year peasants had been resisting feudal and landed restrictions. Peasants armed with scythes and axes intimidated aristocratic landlords and occupied land. Faced with worker demonstrations, fiery political speeches and armed bands of peasants, German princes were quick to make concessions and express their sympathy with protestors.[14]

Vienna was no different. On February 29, a placard affixed to the Kärtner Gate declared "Within a month Prince Metternich will be overthrown! Long live constitutional Austria!"[15] The prediction proved accurate. On March 3, the journalist and nationalist Lajos Kossuth delivered a withering condemnation of Habsburg absolutism in the Hungarian diet, calling for a constitutional and autonomous Hungarian kingdom. The speech was immediately translated into German and distributed to enthusiastic Austrian democrats who began drafting petitions and organizing assemblies of their

Figure 13 Count Latour and the Vienna Uprising, 1848
© Nastasic/Getty Images.

own. University students and liberals applied pressure on the government while radicals mobilized workers and urged them to join in the demonstrations. Street protests compelled the government to dismiss Metternich, the detested icon of arch-conservatism in Austria and throughout Europe. This symbolic victory elicited celebrations in every European capital. It appeared that across the continent the old order was on the verge of crumbling. Journalists hailed 1848 as the *Völkerfrühling* ("spring time of nations"), a moment signaling the triumph of longstanding liberal and nationalist aspirations over absolutist tyranny. "No more shall we speak of oppressors and oppressed, no more hatred, no more rancor," declared a public letter drafted by the Venetian revolutionaries Daniele Manin and Nicolò Tommaseo that March. "We shall all be free; we shall all be brothers and friends."[16]

In almost every country from France to Romania crowds assembled and regimes capitulated. Censorship was lifted and radical newspapers printed petitions and called for the drafting of constitutions. Writers gave a voice to "the people" by turning out patriotic poems and proclaiming the birth of regenerated nations. Many went as far as to insist that 1848 marked a new era in history. All Europe's social problems would be solved; absolutism would be swept away; the people would take control of their own destinies. The idea of a "spring time of nations" provided a narrative context for the events shaking Europe, transforming a series of regional revolts and protests into a common European experience.[17]

The rapid collapse of the established order was, however, an illusion. The decentralized and weak nature of European state structures at mid-century precluded the possibility

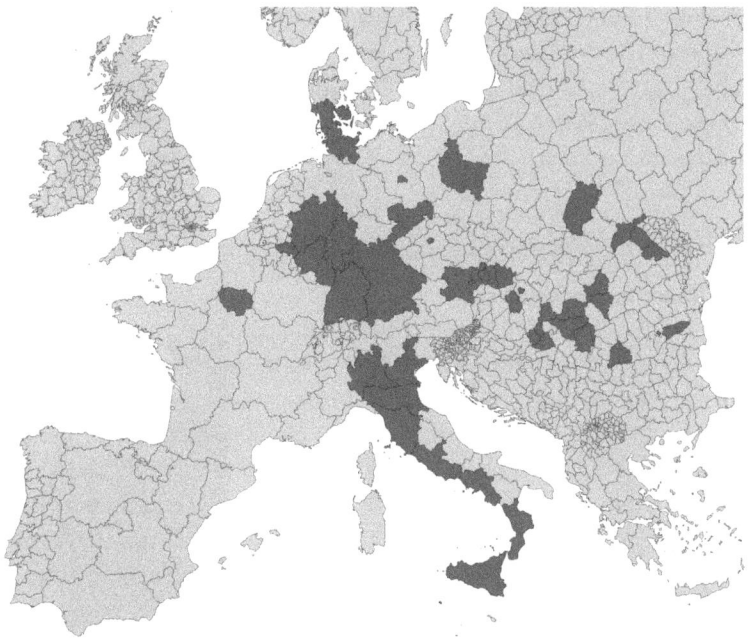

Map 7 Revolutionary disturbances in 1848 by region.

for quick, repressive measures. Rulers possessed neither the administrative machinery nor centralized control necessary to quell protests on such a scale.[18] Monarchs taking note of the street protests and rural disturbances also had the memories of the French Revolution in their minds. "Europe is facing the year 1793 again …," Metternich wrote to an Austrian diplomat on March 1. "We are headed toward horrible events."[19] Rather than assume an intransigent stance and potentially lose their heads, sovereigns believed it prudent to make concession and bide their time. Of course the memory of 1789 equally cast its spell on the protestors who interpreted 1848 through the prism of 1789 and the glorious triumph of "the people" over the crown. The Hungarian poet Sándor Petőfi wasted little time in setting up a "Committee of Public Safety" and a National Guard in Budapest once events took their course. Known for hanging portraits of Robespierre and Saint-Just on his wall, he could easily imagine himself taking up the mantle of a revolutionary vanguard.[20] This type of dramatic emulation was replicated throughout Europe that spring as intellectuals and politicians made grand declarations to the people and spoke of regenerating nations.[21]

What François Furet has called "the tyranny of revolutionary memory" exercised a powerful influence on both sides, but this should not undercut the novelty of the situation either.[22] Revolutions inspired revolutions, connecting disparate cities and movements in diverse ways. If Struve took his cue from Paris, the *Märzforderungen* he drafted provided a set of programmatic demands for other German states to follow. Kossuth's call for a Hungarian constitution inspired similar calls for liberalization in Vienna.[23] The wave of revolutions that crested in 1848 had its own cross-currents and would furnish new myths and heroic images.[24] Confronted with spontaneous street demonstrations, established regimes suffered a crisis of legitimacy. In this momentary power vacuum, revolutionaries discovered an opportunity to imagine alternative models of sovereignty which although inspired by memories of the French Revolution were, nonetheless, a product of their distinct moment.

Association and Solidarity

The quick retreat of the absolutist regimes set the stage for the election of national parliaments charged with the task of forming new governments and drafting constitutions. Most revolutionaries were not radical and sought to uphold property qualifications and the social order. France was unique in declaring universal manhood suffrage, but even republican moderates expressed reservations over enfranchising workers and peasants with the vote.[25] Romantic intellectuals may have celebrated the "cult of the people" with their veneration for the natural virtues of the common citizen and popular sovereignty, but for most these convictions were airy pronouncements that had little basis in real experience. On the surface, work proceeded quickly. The Habsburg Emperor Ferdinand I made tentative plans for a constituent assembly to liberalize the empire. In Prussia, King Friedrich Wilhelm grudgingly accepted a liberal ministry and the calling of a United Diet. In late March, the lawyer Daniele Manin declared a Venetian republic following streets demonstrations and clashes with Austrian authorities while the Hungarian Diet abolished feudalism and extended basic civil liberties to the entire population, setting the stage for an autonomous Hungarian Kingdom. German liberals gathered in Frankfurt also seized the initiative and announced the calling of a national assembly intent on realizing the longstanding dream of a unitary German state.

"Shouting! Firing! Frankfurt is awash in black, red and gold," reported Ludwig Bamberger, editor of the *Mainzer Zeitung*. "For the moment the city has an air of euphoria about it!"[26] This euphoria and effusion of nationalist sentiment were shared amongst most European cities as newly empowered legislatures began the work of consolidating the victories of 1848. However, the celebrations and enthusiasm were not confined to the parliaments. The legislatures constituted only one theater of the unfolding revolutions.

Throughout the 1840s, demands for "association" and the right to assemble had been a central grievance of the opposition. This concept was understood broadly, ranging from ideas of national fraternity and political organization to civic associations and clubs favoring particular social and financial interests. The civic organizations that did exist found themselves continually hampered by state censorship policies and laws restricting public meetings. Over the 1840s, critics repeatedly defended the right to express their ideas and participate in organizations, many of which did not have overtly political motives. The rapid collapse of authority across Europe offered an opportunity to act on these demands, and it was, therefore, unsurprising that a host of lawyers, intellectuals, journalist and civic advocates assumed leadership roles that March and April. As order broke down, existing civic networks provided a framework for channeling forms of social and political activism. They played a key role in drafting petitions, forming pressure groups and disseminating liberal and radical ideas. More importantly, these organizations provided links with other urban centers across the continent as reading societies and clubs became focal points of news and discussion that transcended local and national boundaries.[27]

The momentary end of censorship saw a surge in print. As one Viennese publicist exhorted, "The abolition of censorship now makes it possible for us to speak out, print, and circulate our wishes in thousands of sheets."[28] Of course this freedom extended beyond the purview of liberal reformers, offering a forum for the articulation of new radical and revolutionary voices. The *Neues Rheinische Zeitung* edited by Karl Marx in Cologne was one of the largest left-wing newspapers, with a press run of some 6,000. Other smaller journals across the continent equally encouraged support for democratic reforms and urged workers to take up arms against their class oppressors. Central and Eastern Europe saw a swell of new national publications as marginalized nationalities used the weakness of the Habsburg regime to put forward their own demands for autonomy and cultural recognition. The Czech journalist Karel Havlíček, editor of the *Pražské Noviny* (The Prague Newspaper), tellingly changed the name of his publication to *Národní noviny* (The National Newspaper) in April 1848. The journal was known for its bold Czech nationalism, and Havlíček himself was elected to the constituent assembly in Vienna.[29] Newspapers became the vehicles for mobilizing audiences, publicizing demands in the name of "the people" and keeping citizens informed of day-to-day politics. With censorship regimes paralyzed, almost any group or ideologue had the potential of using print to rally supporters and communicate political programs to a mass audience.[30]

This energized press was matched by an explosion of clubs and associations reflecting a range of ideological and political positions. Worker societies quickly carved out a place for themselves in the revolutionary public sphere. They spurred protestors into action and vocalized labor demands for social reform. Radical republican clubs led by Blanqui and others in Pairs routinely mobilized supporters and agitated for social revolution in the streets. Other worker clubs in France confined themselves to petitioning and applying pressure on the government to fulfill the promise of a social republic.[31] In Cologne, the Communist League headed by Marx and Stephan Born called for social revolution, although the League failed to organize workers at the national level and remained on the fringes of the German worker movement for the most part. More successful was the Congress of Craftsmen and Tradesmen convoked in Frankfurt in July and the *Allgemeine Deustche Arbeiterverbrüderung* (General German Worker Fraternity) headquartered in Berlin. The latter brought together an array of worker associations and ran its own newspaper, making it a formidable mouthpiece for labor demands. These bodies endorsed a more moderate agenda than the communists, pressing for social assurances and in some instances the re-establishment of guild protections against unbridled capitalism.[32]

Constitutionalists and democrats equally had their own organizational bodies, often building upon pre-established associations and networks such as the Viennese Legal-Political Reading Club or the former Carbonari cells in Naples and Sicily. These groups assisted in planning democratic congresses, scheduling mass rallies and staging patriotic events. A variety of trade organizations and interest groups took part, indicating that civil associations could be bastions of liberal ideas and values just as much as radical ones.[33] In fact, many clubs and associations functioned as nerve centers for liberal-constitutionalist movements and were exceedingly less radical than neo-Jacobin and militant socialist groups. The social ties and common interests these and other organizations encouraged contributed to the formation of nascent parties and factions, many of which sought to build cooperative relations between urban centers and the countryside in order to expand their support. In other instances, leaders attempted to unify the constellations of local clubs and organizations to generate truly national movements. The Central Association for the Preservation of the Accomplishments of March was set up in Germany, consisting of some 950 clubs and a half-million members. By early 1849, Mazzini was active merging the sundry democratic clubs of the Italian peninsula under a Central Committee based in Rome.[34]

The sheer number of political clubs and organizations that sprang up in 1848 testified to the widespread desires for "association" in the *Vormärz* period. Moreover, these various organizations often imparted a semblance of unity and common purpose to movements as activists mobilized support for social and political programs. Participants saw the clubs as the catalyst for political and social change. "The clubs are the living barricades of democracy," as the Paris-based Republican Club of Free Workers proclaimed.[35] Certainly, clubs were instrumental in popularizing revolutionary demands and organizing the crowds that demonstrated in the streets. They also spread revolutionary songs and slogans, creating a common language and stock of symbols from which protestors readily drew. As Jonathan Sperber has argued, the clubs and federations that took shape in 1848 marked a pioneering venture in mass political mobilization. These bodies were at the center of the rallies and protests, revealing a new form of citizen activism that not only infused political life during the 1848 revolutions, but also cemented the disparate uprisings into a national and transnational experience.[36]

The unity expressed by clubs did not, however, diminish existing social and political tensions latent within revolutionary programs. Liberal constitutionalists may have supported demands for rights and government accountability, but they hardly endorsed radical platforms calling for universal political rights and social reform. Not only did radical egalitarianism pose a threat to property owners. It also had the potential to push regimes toward reactionary positions that could jeopardize the initial gains made in March. Manin was indicative of the growing moderation among political leaders when he urged his republican followers in Venice to be "jealous guardians of order" if they wished to preserve freedom.[37] Desires by elites to keep conflicts contained within institutional structures often stood opposed to the emergent activism and popular mobilization evident among the clubs and workers. If the fervor of 1848 revealed longstanding aspiration for change, it also showed that social and political groups had

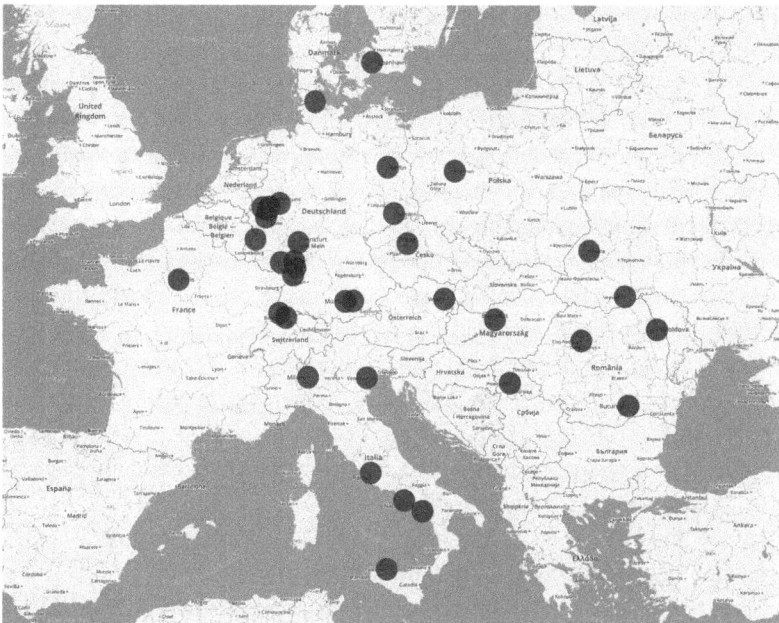

Map 8 Cities with major political unrest in 1848.

distinct interests which they hoped to pursue.[38] These tensions dissolved the initial sense of unity and raised one of the principal questions presented in moments of revolutionary agitation: who had the power to speak for "the people"? As events progressed, political elites became increasingly wary of popular mobilization, setting the stage for conflict among the revolutionaries themselves.

As in February, events in France set the tone. The provisional government's initial support for social reform had appeased urban workers and led them to believe that the July Monarchy would be replaced with a social-democratic republic favorable to labor. With Louis Blanc temporarily at the helm, the state opened national workshops that provided jobs and financial aid to workers. Although popular with urban artisans, his policies failed to win support from republican political elites or the rural peasantry. Peasants balked at the new taxes imposed to fund the state-sponsored workshops while republican moderates showed little inclination to back a social republic. With dwindling funds, a deepening economic crisis and growing opposition to social welfare reform, the provisional government found itself walking a precarious line by late spring. When the government moved to close down the national workshops that June, Parisian artisans responded by erecting barricades in the street.[39] The so-called "June Days," which saw French troops violently suppress a worker rebellion in the capital, cast a pall over the newly created Second Republic and led to a reactionary crackdown on clubs and political organizations in the name of public order.[40]

Over the next year, attempts to quash populist and working-class radicalism were multiplied across the continent. Austrian liberals won significant concessions from the imperial Habsburg government that spring, bringing into existence a constitution that sanctioned government accountability and limited political participation at the local levels of society. The backbone of the new liberal political culture that emerged in 1848 was the press and civic associations, both of which called for political reform while equally stressing their duty to guide the "culturally uneducated public regarding its interests."[41] From the start, the threat of radical democracy and worker mobilization threatened the legal constitutionalism of middle-class liberals, and measures were taken to rein in Viennese democrats and suppress riots in the capital. Worker and student organizers faced police harassment and opposition in the cities while the provinces were depoliticized through timely imperial decrees that abolished the primary grievance of the peasantry, the feudal system.[42] By the autumn of 1849, Viennese democrats were sufficiently isolated, permitting the Habsburg monarchy to re-impose its authority through military force. In Berlin, liberals refused to support worker participation in the National Guard and maintained their distance from the clubs and labor associations. When the Prussian monarch unilaterally closed down the National Assembly in early December and imposed his own constitution on the kingdom, many liberals accepted it, preferring monarchial order to the unknown of worker radicalism.

Although not strictly guided by class interests, liberals and political elites across Europe proved reluctant to endorse radical programs promising social emancipation and universal political rights. Liberals did wrench concessions from absolutist rulers that effectively brought an end to the traditional anciens régimes across much of Europe. Yet liberals remained "reluctant revolutionaries," confining their demands to the familiar language of institutional change and limited suffrage rather than popular mobilization. When push came to shove, these ideological cleavages fractured the unity of the various revolutionary movements, providing monarchs and princes with opportunities to re-impose their authority through force if necessary.

The Double-Edged Sword of Nationalism

If tensions between liberty and equality drove a wedge between revolutionaries during 1848–1849, nationalism was no different. The emancipatory power of nationalist rhetoric infused many of the movements that broke out during the "spring time of nations." Never reconciled to Austrian rule, Italian liberals and republicans found common cause in resisting Habsburg domination throughout the peninsula. The king of Piedmont-Sardinia, Charles Albert, used this resurgent patriotism to launch a war for Italian unification across the north, rallying nationalists against the Habsburgs with his battle cry of "*Italia ferà da sé*" (Italy will do it alone!). His efforts to carve out a Piedmont-dominated Italy and enlarge his kingdom soon collapsed when the Austrian military routed his forces and systematically crushed resistance movements in the major Italian cities.[43] Nonetheless, the Italian conflict did indicate the dangers that revolutionary nationalism posed for a multiethnic empire like the one presided over by the Habsburg dynasty, a fact that the situation in Hungary made all too evident.

The Hungarians had a long tradition of independence dating back to the Middle Ages. While the nobility had accepted the rule of the German Habsburg dynasty in the sixteenth century, they had nonetheless preserved their own unique identity as Magyars, an ethnic group with its own language and culture distinct from the Germans of the empire. This national particularism was prominent among the Magyar nobility who consistently resisted the centralizing policies of Vienna. During the 1840s, the journalist and lawyer Lajos Kossuth presented himself as the chief spokesman for the nationalist movement, forming an awkward alliance between liberals and the traditional noble classes.[44] In March of 1848, Kossuth led the charge in calling for Hungarian autonomy. Under the March Laws, the diet assumed control over all internal Hungarian politics. Feudalism was promptly abolished while a liberal-style constitution enfranchised property holders. The nobility gave its support to these measures since the Magyar nobles were the predominant land-owning class in the kingdom. Liberal in spirit, these reforms in essence validated a Hungarian government free from Viennese oversight and dominated by Magyar elites. More to the point, Kossuth and his allies had carried out this revolution through established institutional channels and compromise with the imperial bureaucracy. This "legal" revolution was not so much revolutionary as it was a renegotiation of the terms of Habsburg imperialism.[45]

Figure 14 Lajos Kossuth © The British Library Board.

Yet if Kossuth's Magyar autonomy movement appeared successful that spring, the Hungarian revolution would take its own unique turn. While a Hungarian national kingdom had been declared, in reality the idea of an ethnically homogenous and unified Hungarian state was a fiction. Hungary had a variety of ethnic groups within its borders. The Magyars were dominant in the north-west but were in fact a minority within the kingdom, which contained ethnic Romanians, Croats, Jews and Slavs. No sooner had Kossuth brokered a deal for Hungarian autonomy than these other ethnicities began making similar demands on the revolutionary Hungarian government, posing a threat to Magyar control. That spring, Serbs inhabiting the eastern region of Vojvodina presented a petition to the new Hungarian government requesting recognition of the Orthodox Church and the use of Serbo-Croatian as an official state language. Kossuth, under no illusions, knew that to concede to such demands would inspire other minorities to do likewise. "Hungary will break up or the sword will decide," he declared.[46] Enforcing this dictum, Kossuth began rounding up suspected revolutionaries in the Vojvodina and handed out death sentences to the Serbian nationalist leadership. A series of bloody reprisals followed soon after. In turn, the Hungarian army began a systematic suppression of Serb militants, plunging the eastern half of the kingdom into an ethnic war.

By June, Romanians within the Hungarian territories of Transylvania and the Banat similarly rose up in revolt against Magyar rule calling for union in a new Romanian nation. Much as in dealing with the Serb question, the Hungarian military opted for suppression, inciting a new round of ethnic warfare that further destabilized the kingdom.[47] These minority revolts were a blessing for Vienna, which provided military and logistical support to nationalist rebels. By the summer of 1848, the Hungarian revolution had dissolved into a bloody civil war divided along ethnic lines. The Hungarian state won by Kossuth was destroyed and, by 1849, Hungary was once again placed under German rule.[48]

While the Hungarian revolution was the most violent outburst of revolutionary nationalism, demands for liberty mixed with nationalist aspirations across Central and Eastern Europe. In Prague, a Pan-Slav Congress raised the issue of Bohemian autonomy and cultural rights, with the Czech nationalist Frantisak Palacký putting forward his idea of Austro-Slavism as a tenable solution. This proposal aimed at renegotiating the terms of Habsburg imperialism found little support among German liberals in Bohemia. Official refusal to countenance Czech cultural autonomy incited street protests that spurred repressive actions by the military.[49] The revolutions of 1848 forced Habsburg liberals to confront the challenges that nationalism posed to a multiethnic imperial society. German liberals in particular were placed in a difficult situation. Their support for rights and constitutional government could threaten their own status within the empire, especially in areas outside Austria where concessions to Slav nationalism threatened to transform Germans into a national minority.[50]

Even outside the explicit domains of the Habsburg Empire, the issue of German nationalism proved problematic. The calling of a German National Assembly that spring galvanized German nationalists. Liberals from across the German Confederation gathered in Frankfurt with the intention of writing a constitution for the German nation, an action which drew attention from Prussia, the Habsburgs and the various German princes. Yet it also elicited a response from German communities across Europe. In late March, Germans in the Danish territories of Schleswig-Holstein set up a provisional government and requested representation in the National Assembly. German populations in the Tyrol, Moravia and Polish areas soon followed suit. Many German nationalists sympathized with these demands, believing that support for Germans outside the confederation would provide a cause that transcended the various German states and unite liberals and democrats. It also corresponded with longstanding desires for a German Fatherland encompassing all German speakers scattered across the continent. Yet this envisaged greater Germany clearly raised questions that could strain international relations and possibly threaten war.[51] The issue of what constituted the German nation, its exact borders and the political character a unified Germany would take were by no means clear-cut as delegates arrived in Frankfurt. These questions would effectively divide the National Assembly over the next year.[52]

The issue of German minorities in Prussian-held Posen was a telling indication of the complexities that nationalist politics engendered. A territory located on Prussia's eastern periphery, Posen contained a substantial Polish population that co-existed uneasily alongside a German minority. Polish nationalists had not been immune to the currents of romantic nationalism. In 1830, a corps of Polish patriots had staged an abortive revolution against Russian authorities, temporarily seizing control of Warsaw before being summarily crushed and fleeing into exile. Despite this failure, staunch Polish nationalists never abandoned their faith that the Poles living in parts of Russia, Prussia and Austria would be reunified within a national homeland. Polish émigrés consisting of writers, intellectuals and former freedom fighters established themselves in all the major European capitals, lobbying governments on behalf of their oppressed brothers and writing poems to the heroism of the Polish people. Adam Mickiewicz, a poet and chief spokesperson for the Polish cause, famously compared his homeland to the Christ of nations, a county which, although presently effaced, would one day be resurrected and shine as a model of national fraternity for all the other peoples of the world.[53] Those lacking the eloquence and rhetorical gift of a poet like Mickiewicz turned their attention to consensus building and organizing a Polish Legion abroad that would fight for independence when the time arrived.

In the spring of 1848, a Polish National Committee was set up in Posen, provoking an outcry among German inhabitants. Fears of Polish domination prompted Posnian Germans to petition for entrance into the Frankfurt parliament. Liberals hesitated to support the proposal, drawing scathing criticism from greater German nationalists. Gustav von Struve chided his fellow delegates for their indecisiveness and accused them of "betraying our German brethren."[54] The issue was temporarily settled when the Prussian military reined in the Polish movement, fearing that militant patriots were bent on invading Russia and generating war between the two powers. This did not, however, translate into support for the Posnian German position. Berlin objected to Posen's entrance into the German Confederation, desiring to keep the territory under explicit Prussian jurisdiction. Frankfurt refused to rescind the invitation, however, hinting at the emergent tensions between Berlin and Frankfurt over the question of who had the power to legislate on German affairs.

Such frustrations were compounded by the Assembly's inability to convince the absolutist Prussian King Friedrich Wilhelm to accept the crown of a constitutional German state. The Assembly's failure to push through social reforms simultaneously alienated workers and radicals in the coming months, casting the future of a unified Germany in doubt. In the fall, socially motivated protests were renewed as calls for a "social republic" erupted in Cologne, Manheim and Düsseldorf. In Frankfurt itself, worker rallies turned violent, forcing the National Assembly to place the city under martial law. Clubs and societies were suppressed and the entire Rhineland placed in a state of siege. This disorder undermined faith in the abilities of the Frankfurt parliament and allowed the German princes to reassert their authority with the help of the Prussian military. By the fall of 1849, the hope of creating a constitutional and unified German state lay in ruins.

Nationalism proved to be a double-edged sword. Its emancipatory potential held the prospect of "liberating" peoples like the Hungarians and Germans, yet it also had the power to inspire calls for national autonomy and self-determination from competing groups. As such, it splintered revolutionary groups and unleashed latent ethno-national conflicts. Infighting and feuds over national rights and territory abounded, and rulers adeptly exploited these divisions to their benefit. Revolutionaries may have invoked the principles of *liberté, égalité* and *fraternité* first annunciated by the French Revolution, but there existed no consensus over how these values were to be realized or applied. As the initial spirit that had animated revolts in the spring of 1848 began to fade, revolutionaries of all stripes and persuasions found their competing ideas of community—whether rooted in notions of liberal citizenship, collective association or ethnic fraternity—in conflict, sowing the seeds of discord.

By the autumn of 1849, the revolutionary movements were effectively extinguished. The Habsburgs had successfully crushed revolts in Italy and Vienna and invoked Russian aid through the Holy Alliance to tame Hungary. The promise of a French social republic had been defeated, while across Germany democrats were being driven underground or fleeing into exile. There would be time for reflection afterwards, much brooding and blame to throw about. Yet the fact remained: the victory of the absolutist regimes marked the defeat of an entire generation of romantic revolutionaries and their vision of an age in which liberty and national fraternity reigned supreme.

Rewriting the Revolutionary Tradition

In December 1848, French voters went to the polls to elect the first president of the new republic. Following the catastrophe of the June Days and months of heated debates in the National Assembly, the country desired a period of repose. When the votes were tallied, the winner was Louis Napoleon, nephew of the former Emperor and a self-proclaimed "man of order." Thirty-three years after Waterloo, a Bonaparte was once again head of

France, and Louis Napoleon lived up to his pedigree. Within three years, he managed to suppress his political opposition, rally public support behind him and drive the republican left underground. In 1852, history seemed to be repeating itself when Louis Napoleon overthrew the Second Republic and proclaimed himself Emperor Napoleon III. Any lingering hopes of reviving the spirit of 1848 in France were swiftly extinguished with the creation of a new Bonapartist empire.

Observing this situation from London, Marx could only laugh sardonically. Reflecting on the failures of 1848, he accused revolutionaries of parodying the great events of the French Revolution and conjuring up the "old ghosts" of the past. Beholden to a veritable revolutionary "tradition," the generation of 1848 had only sought to imitate and mimic the heroic events of 1789 and the Convention. The appeals to the people and grand speeches celebrating national liberation had been nothing but playacting, a sad spectacle filled with the "time-honored disguises" and "barrowed language" of their predecessors. It was fitting that the revolution in France would be brought to its demoralizing end by a Bonapartist pretender. Yet there was a lesson in this farcical episode that Marx was certain to underscore. "The social revolution of the nineteenth century cannot draw its poetry from the past," he warned; "it can draw that only from the future."[55]

Of course, Marx was referring to the proletarian revolution of modern industrial society. In re-enacting the past, the revolutionaries of 1848 had fundamentally misunderstood the historic importance of their own epoch. Drawing their inspiration from previous ages, they were incapable of understanding the needs and consequences of the true social revolution at hand.

Unlike many of his fellow revolutionaries, Marx realized that a new revolution would inevitably be slow in coming. The restoration of order brought a severe crackdown on radical organizations. Political leaders fled into exile to avoid persecution. Radical journals and printers were suppressed across the continent. In addition to enacting these security measures, rulers also took the lessons of 1848 to heart. They proved surprisingly adaptive to the new political environment over the coming decade. Conservative governments made overtures toward liberal elites and brought them into governing coalitions. They reached out to industrialists and promoted economic policies in an effort to curb the unemployment and the social crises that drove workers to support radical socialist platforms. A brand of "neo-absolutism" emerged, bringing about what one historian has deemed a "revolution in government."[56] More effective administrations committed to industrial and economic growth led to renewed prosperity over the 1850s. In many ways, Napoleon III set the tone for this progressive authoritarianism, implementing impressive urbanization initiatives and public works programs that stimulated an economic boom in France lasting into the 1860s.

Napoleon III was also sensitive to nationalist sentiment and public opinion, never missing an opportunity to champion the cause of national revival either at home or abroad. Overall, conservative governments, once hostile to revolutionary nationalist aspirations, took up the banner of nationalism. Old dynasties began to cloak themselves in national garb, endorsing policies of "official nationalism" aimed at consolidating control over territories, strengthening state institutions and commanding the loyalties of subjects.⁵⁷ Unlike former populist and revolutionary nationalist movements, "nation-building" was state-driven and came from the top down rather than the bottom up. Conservatives grudgingly accepted certain revolutionary principles like national association and political suffrage, pressing them into the service of royal and conservative governance.⁵⁸ In 1860, the royal house of Piedmont-Sardinia would successfully unify the Italian Peninsula, creating a liberal Italian kingdom to the consternation of staunch republicans. Similarly, the Prussian chancellor Otto von Bismarck became the architect of German unity by the end of the decade, creating the German nation that liberals had failed to deliver in 1848. Contrary to liberal expectations, Bismarck's German Empire was carved out through a policy of "blood and iron" and used universal suffrage to prop up an illiberal Prussian monarchism.

These realities compelled radicals and liberals to re-orient their strategies and approaches. For his part, Marx remained committed to an international communist platform and clearly understood the need for a change in perspectives following the debacle of 1848. Early efforts to re-establish the Communist League were indicative of the challenges he and Engels faced. Neo-Jacobins and radicals persisted to adhere to the cult of the "revolutionary tradition," believing "the people" would fall in line and support them once revolution was underway. For Marx and Engels, this scenario was only another recipe for failure. Radicals too often remained ignorant of the material forces needed for a true social revolution, in their opinion. Revolutionary adventurism had to be discouraged, and this entailed sidelining groups like the Blanquists who continued to place their faith in spontaneous revolt.⁵⁹

During the 1850s, Marx endured his "sleepless night of exile" in London.⁶⁰ He and his family took a small, sparsely furnished apartment in Soho where they faced cold, scarcity and the ever-present threat of eviction. Added to financial hardship was the isolation bred by a life of exile. The émigré community that settled in England was wracked by petty and often personal squabbles as members doled out blame for the disasters and missed opportunities of 1848. By the mid-1850s, Marx, isolated and browbeaten, confessed to feeling "broken down."⁶¹ Exile was nothing but "a school of scandal and meanness," he complained.⁶² Nevertheless, his commitment to reinvigorating the worker movement and preparing the ground for his envisaged social revolution remained unshaken. Rather than being guided by a cadre of revolutionary idealists, workers needed to see themselves as the universal and oppressed class Marx insisted they were. Transcending the failures of 1848 required nurturing a proletarian consciousness among the working classes and instilling them with a new sense of community befitting the struggle ahead.

As luck would have it, the early 1860s offered just such an opportunity. The London Trades Council, a labor organization founded in 1860 by English trade unionists, was working to establish relations with foreign workers. Although the leadership was hardly radical and was concerned with routine labor grievances, political refugees in London saw the body as a possible vehicle for creating a broader revolutionary platform. French activists in particular were interested in transforming the organization into an international alliance. With their insistence, it was decided to convene a meeting at St. Martin's Hall in September 1864 to discuss common issues. The result was the creation of the International Workingmen's Association (IWMA), a body with a central committee based in London yet responsive to the plight of international labor. Marx was invited to join the organization and over the next few years would play a key role in assisting with its organization and drafting its main policy initiatives. While primarily working behind the scenes, he exercised a significant influence on the IWMA's general direction. Since the 1840s, Marx had been active in drawing together European workers and building relationships across national borders. Yet in the wake of 1848, the need for such an association appeared doubly urgent. The future revolution depended upon a class-conscious proletariat acting as a "class for itself," as Marx claimed. The IWMA was the imagined instrument for this outcome, one that through propaganda and organization would mold workers across nations into a unified class.[63]

Marx's energetic participation in the IWMA was not merely idealistic. The organization drew together an array of leftist groups, including Chartists, Owenites, Blanquists, Mazzinians and Polish radical democrats. While committed to democratic and social programs, these factions had distinct ideas of their own regarding revolutionary means and ends. The ideological feuds that had hamstrung the Communist League could easily be reignited. The French delegation was of particular concern. French socialists like Henri Tolain and Eugène Varlin had taken a leading role in establishing the IWMA and their followers were largely inspired by the ideas of Pierre-Joseph Proudhon, one of Marx's erstwhile antagonists dating back to his time in France.

A republican hailing from the Franche-Comté region bordering Switzerland, Proudhon came from a strong artisanal background with deep provincial roots. He participated in the revolutionary days of 1848 in Paris, although his specific ideas on "association" found little favor among republican leaders. His view of the world idealized the rural countryside, rejecting the luxuries and corrupting influences found in modern urban life. He criticized the Saint Simonians for their veneration of modern industry while accusing Fourier of encouraging capitalism through his imagined utopia. Expressing a hatred of mass production and capitalist modernization, Proudhon sought a more perfect world in a society free of authority and built upon the class of independent, self-sustaining peasants and artisans familiar to his native Franche-Comté. Noting the poverty and misery of these classes, Proudhon argued that modern capitalism was nothing short of "industrial and financial feudalism."[64] This provincial radicalism with strongly anti-modernist tendencies was balanced with a supreme faith in social progress and evolution. Indeed, progress for Proudhon was "the new instrument of war," as he claimed. It combatted religious dogma and former notions of subservience, leading toward a more just and egalitarian society. "Modern civilization, removed from traditions and examples, is irrevocably engaged in the path of revolution where neither historic precedents nor honest writing nor established faith are capable of guiding it."[65] Conscious of both the suffering and potential latent within modern society, Proudhon was a firm advocate of radical emancipation, contenting, "There is sufficient reason for revolution in the nineteenth century."[66]

His ideas were not fundamentally opposed to leading socialist thinkers critical of capital and wage labor. In 1840, Proudhon published his famous pamphlet *What Is*

Property?, answering this simple question with his unequivocal response: "property is theft!" What set Proudhon apart from his contemporaries, however, was his emphasis on what revolutionary action ought to achieve. In contrast to the domination of capital, he envisaged a new political order rooted in autonomous government and administration. "Politics is the science of freedom," he argued. "The government of man by man, under whatever name it is disguised, is oppression: the high perfection of society consists in the union of order and anarchy."[67] The kernel of this anarchist order was found in the immediate locality—the French *commune*—which served as the heart of self-governance and collective life. Contrary to the overbearing state with its police and army of bureaucrats, the commune was a "sovereign being" with the capacity to manage its own affairs.[68] Proudhon ultimately envisioned a small society of industrious craft workers and peasants collectively owning all industrial enterprises. They would negotiate and contract with one another, forming cooperatives and federations that would satisfy their material needs through a system of free and mutual exchange.[69] This brand of anarchism, typically referred to as "mutualism" among Proudhon's followers, furnished the basis for a social revolution that would empower laborers and permit them to "cast of their tutelage" and act "exclusively by themselves and for themselves."[70]

If these basic principles of mutualism were in line with Marx's political views, Marx was critical of Proudhon's ahistorical understanding of social theory and his naïve belief in social harmony that overlooked the realities of class interest and conflict.[71] His public criticism of Proudhon's books did not win favor with the French radical. Although the two remained in correspondence during the 1840s, a fundamental difference in outlooks precluded cooperation. If Marx felt Proudhon lacked intellectual rigor, Proudhon remained suspicious of Marx's overbearing and controlling disposition. When Marx wrote to him in 1846 inquiring whether he might participate in his communist association, Proudhon flatly expressed his reservations, replying, "let us not set ourselves up as the leaders of a new intolerance, let us not pose as the apostles of a new religion."[72] Almost twenty years later, little had changed.

The Proudhonists commanded a strong influence within the IWMA, one that Marx was eager to diminish to ensure that his conception of materialist social revolution predominated. To this end, he insisted upon drafting the preamble for the IWMA and drawing up the rules for membership. The organization was not to be a federation of political parties or trade unions, as the Proudhonists would have preferred. Rather, the General Council would serve as the chief organ, with individual members joining branches or sections in their home country. Marx scored a further victory by overriding Proudhonist demands for exclusive worker membership in the organization. The proposal would have excluded intellectuals like Marx from participating and left the Proudhonist faction consisting mainly of artisans predominant. Sidelining his French adversaries, however, forced Marx to ally with reform-minded English trade unionists. While successful, the tactic entailed compromise. Marx found himself persistently trying to convince parochial trade unionists to partake in "the guerilla fights between capitalism and labor" and expand their horizons beyond the limited world of trade grievances.[73]

Despite these endless frustrations, Marx succeeded in establishing his revolutionary socialism within the International. A marginal German émigré in the early 1860s, Marx acquired notoriety through his work with the IWMA and by the end of the decade managed to popularize his vision of class struggle and international worker revolution among a wider audience. Under Marx's aegis, the International would seek to put an end to the divisive "revolutionary sects" and create "a real organization of the working classes for struggle."[74] The dangers inherent in an outmoded "revolutionary tradition" had been made all too apparent after 1848. The new objectives emphasized worker self-emancipation and direct political engagement. Revolution was no longer the preserve of an intellectual elite acting out the dramas of the past, according to Marx. It belonged to the self-aware cosmopolitan proletariat who knew no tradition and had no past to venerate.

Envisioning Russia's Revolutionary Community

If Marx sought to escape the past by focusing attention on the international revolution ahead, Alexander Herzen had different ideas. A Russian social critic and reform-minded intellectual, Herzen had always idealized the French Revolution and believed it a model for his own country to emulate. Banding together with Russian intellectuals collectively known as "Westernizers," he became an advocate of European-style liberal and national reform, placing him at odds with the conservative imperial government of Tsar Nicholas I. Enduring banishment to central Russia and the persistent suspicion of the state during the 1830s and '40s, Herzen moved his family to Europe in 1847. The timing was propitious. He was in Italy when he received news of the revolutions breaking out across the continent and immediately headed to Paris. Like so many intellectuals that spring, Herzen intended to participate in the grand revolutionary drama of his generation and celebrate the victory of oppressed peoples over unjust regimes. Moreover, like so many that spring, this idealism quickly unraveled.[75]

In Paris, Herzen did not find the heroic people's army and barricades he imagined. The revolutionaries were disorganized and more preoccupied with petty arguments among themselves than leading a program of radical change. Former royalists and conservative bourgeois politicians were meanwhile joining the republican government, transforming it into an instrument of reaction. Confronted with a "revolutionary" republic dominated be old elites and an impotent "people," Herzen could only see 1848 as a calamity. The revolution "tore the bandage from my eyes," he claimed that May.[76] Over the next year, his disenchantment only grew as the revolutions crumbled one by one. "With profound sorrow I watched and recorded the success of the forces of dissolution and the decline of the republic, of France, of Europe," he wrote.[77] Like Marx, Herzen was conscious of the playacting and imitation that 1848 encouraged. He sarcastically pronounced judgment on the "revolutionary Don Quixote" that attempted to present himself as the "poet of the future" while time and time again evoking the memories of 1789, the Convention and the old Jacobin rhetoric. "They repeat the speeches that once moved hearts without realizing that for a long time these words have ceased to carry any significant meaning," he claimed.[78]

Yet for Herzen, these comedic interludes were few and far between. Where Marx saw parody, Herzen found a cosmic misfortune. The year 1848 revealed that his generation was composed of nothing more than "soulless orators." "Our blood is cold, it is only our ink which flows hot," he lamented. Revolutionaries had taken their inspiration from 1789 but they were ill-suited to consummate the great achievements of their predecessors. "You were playing at republic, playing at terror, at government, paying the fool in your clubs," Herzen charged.[79] Becoming increasingly pessimistic as the élan of 1848 diminished, he succumbed to despair. "The death of the old world carries us away," he wrote to a friend. "Recovery is no longer possible because our debilitated lungs can breathe nothing else than this infected air. We are headed toward inevitable ruin." If his generation had believed themselves capable of creating a new world, they had been sadly mistaken. "We are at once the corpse and the murderer, the disease and the prosector of the old world."[80] Romantic heroism and idealism turned out to be nothing more than a modern tragedy, leaving Herzen bitterly disillusioned.[81]

In 1851, Herzen, now officially an émigré, settled in London where he became a "detached spectator" of Russian and European politics.[82] Detachment did not, however, mean inactivity. During 1848, Herzen had also been a spectator. He had not participated in the movements and clubs nor had he engaged in politics. He had principally been a commentator, explaining his biting criticism of the failures of 1848, for which he bore no direct responsibility. In London he would do the same, lending his pen to the support of radical ideas with his insistence that to think and speculate was "already to act, to accomplish." Herzen was, in short, a revolutionary intellectual who saw his contribution to the cause of humanity in the realm of criticism rather than direct action.[83] His words were frequently inflammatory, such as his public support for Blanqui, the only true revolutionary who understood "it is useless to patch old things up, [and] that the primary task is to destroy what exists."[84] Yet such radicalism never translated into action. For all his fiery oratory, Herzen was a rational and sensible individual who weighed his actions carefully. He criticized bourgeois society and private property, yet lived off the income of his Russian estates. He preached upheaval and destruction, yet preferred journalism and the press to the barricades. Herzen perennially embodied the revolutionary intellectual confined to the realm of ideas and theory.

As well, in the wake of 1848, his youthful love affair with Europe slowly diminished. He abandoned his idealization of European revolution, arguing that "old" Europe was stuck in its ways and incapable of true change. Instead, he focused his attention on "young" Russia, orienting his writing toward the potential of a novel Russian revolutionary movement that would correct the decadence of the West. In 1856, he set up the Free Russian Press in London, an organ aimed at promoting "the free uncensored speech" of the Russian people.[85] If Russian public opinion remained stifled by the oppressive tsarist government at home, Herzen intended to offer an alternative forum abroad, smuggling pamphlets, books and newspapers back to his compatriots. Through the Free Russian Press, Herzen published the émigré newspaper *The Bell* committed to Russian views on government, feudalism and progressive socialist ideas. Running a press in exile was "the most practical revolutionary action that a Russian can take," he claimed. "The Russian printing press was my life's work ... With it I lived in the atmosphere of Russia; with it I was prepared and armed."[86]

For Herzen, "young Russia" pointed the way to the future. Such a claim struck many Europeans as odd, if not erroneous. Russia's entrenched feudal hierarchies and religious culture were reminiscent of Europe's bygone medieval age while its traditions of autocratic rule reflected the "despotism" familiar to Oriental societies. It lacked the industry and entrepreneurship ascendant in the West while Russia's vast multiethnic populace consisting of Slavs, Muslims and various Central Asian peoples appeared incompatible with any type of nation-state. According to many Europeans, Russia resembled an Asiatic backwater that had everything to learn from a progressive Europe but nothing to teach it. Conservative Slavophile nationalists routinely condemned the West, arguing that Russia had its own unique path to follow and should actively resist the materialism and liberalism of European modernity.[87] Herzen, however, argued otherwise. Russia's imputed backwardness was not a hindrance, but a virtue. Drawing upon certain ideas popularized by the Slavophiles, his "young Russia" blended notions of cultural nationalism with democratic-revolutionary ideology to produce a distinctly Russian brand of social revolution.

Turning away from European cities like Paris, Herzen focused attention on the Russian peasantry and, in particular, the agrarian peasant commune (*obshchina*) he believed native to Russian society. Since Peter the Great, the tsarist autocracy had attempted to modernize Russia in the Western mold. The effect had been an oppressive bureaucratic state with little attachment to the actual Russian people. "The historic forms of the state have never answered to the national ideals of the Slavs," as Herzen put it.[88] The autocracy was a Byzantine-Germanic import, alien to Slavic sensibilities. True Russia lay in the countryside, where peasants had little understanding or need of concepts like private property and administrative government. Communal farming and a shared understanding of community provided a readymade model for a brand of "agrarian communism" that did not necessitate the indignities and conflicts associated with capitalist modernization. The embourgeoisement of European society had been the fatal flaw that had corrupted and compromised Western radicalism.[89] Russia had, on the contrary, no bourgeoisie and could easily transition into a form of socialism only dreamed of by thinkers such as Proudhon and Fourier.[90] The question at hand was not how to modernize Russian industry and society but rather how to achieve the emancipation of Russian peasants without jeopardizing the communal principle. "Precisely in this lies the whole agonizing problem of the century," Herzen insisted, "precisely in this consists the whole [problem] of socialism."[91] The answer, he concluded, was communitarian socialism, a form of organization capable of reconciling individualism with the needs of the collective.

Herzen's faith in a pure socialism proposed a very specific idea of community rooted in the rural world and peasant society, not the urban masses. This reworked Russian nationalism drew its substance from native institutions like the *obshchina* and ultimately from an idealized image of the Russian "people," or *narod*. Soon branded as Russian "populism" or *narodnik* socialism, these ideas struck a chord with certain members of the Russian intelligentsia. The journalist Nikolai Gavrilovich Chernyshevsky equally praised the merits of agrarian socialism, and, like Herzen, advocated for the emancipation of the Russian peasantry from serfdom. More radical than Herzen, Chernyshevsky was instrumental in offering a model of Russian activism that Herzen, residing abroad in London, could not. In his novel *What Is to Be Done?* (1863), he chronicled the lives of men and women committed to building a new society on the foundations of the old regime. His rational and militant antagonists were driven by their moral strength and conviction. They socialized with the peasantry, adopted their moral values and practiced gender equality within their ranks. Above all, these "new people" pledged themselves to the cause of the *narodniki*. Although fictitious, Chernyshevsky's characters provided an archetype for aspiring radicals, giving them an image distinct from liberal and reform-minded contemporaries. As V.I. Lenin would later claim, *What Is to Be Done?* showed not only the way a revolutionary ought to think and act, but "what a revolution must be like, what its principles must be."[92]

The son of a priest with a talent for speaking plainly, Chernyshevsky presented a contrast to elite, aristocratic liberals like Herzen. Moreover, his writings responded directly to changes taking place in Russian society during the early 1860s. In 1855, Tsar Nicholas I, a notorious conservative committed to upholding autocracy and the Orthodox faith, died. The following year, Russia suffered a humiliating defeat in the Crimean War when a joint Ottoman-European coalition destroyed Russia's naval fleets in the Black Sea. Taken together, liberals insisted the time for change had come. Russia must either modernize or perish, they claimed. Fortunately, the new tsar, Alexander II, agreed, generating a momentary sense of optimism throughout the empire. Taking the throne, the first issue Alexander sought to tackle was Russia's feudal institutions, one of the chief impediments to modernization in the country. In 1857, a Committee of Peasant Affairs was established to draw up proposals. Four years later, an emancipation decree officially abolished serfdom throughout Russia.[93] Only six years in power, Alexander had fundamentally transformed the social and economic base of the empire, effacing the longstanding feudal institutions that had traditionally underpinned Russian society.

The politics of emancipation were a thorny issue. The government refused to appropriate aristocratic estates and redistribute land holding. Liberals and radicals alike criticized this measure, arguing it would create a class of peasant farmers dependent upon their former feudal landlords. Without the promise of land, the emancipation decree was toothless and changed little. These claims spurred young radicals into action, eliciting calls for a peasant revolution that would truly reform Russian society. Student demonstrations broke out in St. Petersburg and Moscow in the coming year, with radical organizers showing their commitment to agrarian socialism and veneration for the *narod*. Students formed *skhodki*—a term appropriated from traditional peasant village assemblies—to organize protests, draft petitions and publish their own newspapers with titles like *Herald of Free Opinion* and *Little Bell*, a homage to Herzen's own émigré newspaper. "Everyone felt an irresistible longing to show his worth in some desperately courageous and heroic action," as one student remarked.[94] The government responded in characteristic fashion, banning student organizations and intensifying state surveillance in the universities. Reform had its limits and radicalism was not to be tolerated.

Radicals were not deterred. In the coming decade, they formed secret organizations and movements to carry on the opposition. More striking, they acted out the populist program sketched by Chernyshevsky in *What Is to Be Done?* A small faction headed by Nikolai Ishutin set up cooperatives, lived ascetic lifestyles and worked to spread propaganda to the peasants of the countryside. The cooperatives were a model of association in action, including a bookbinding workshop and a seamstress cooperative run by female members like Vera Zasulich, who would later become a founding member of the first Marxist Russian group. Ishutin proved more radical than most and willing to countenance any means necessary to foment revolution against the state, including robbery and murder to obtain money.[95] Other leaders stressed long-term organization and network building to achieve their desired ends. In the early 1870s, students took to abandoning the universities, dressing in peasant garb and traveling out to the countryside to educate and radicalize peasants. The so-called "Going to the People" movement drew its inspiration directly from writers like Chernyshevsky and an idealized vision of peasant communitarianism uncorrupted by modernity. According to the revolutionary Sergei Kravchinsky, the *narodnichestvo* was "a kind of crusade," one revealing radicals' newfound fascination with folk nationalism and their profound emotional attachment to the *narodnik* cause.[96]

The movement proved a failure by the late 1870s. Intellectuals did not find the innate socialism they believed endemic to peasant society nor did they find a people willing to participate in the struggle against tsarist despotism. Peasants remained suspicious of urban elites dressing in folk costume and preaching ideas of radical social and gender equality. The image of the revolutionary, emancipated peasant cultivated by elites was always a fantasy, and contact between the intelligentsia and the real *narod* brought into sharp relief the material and cultural divides separating these groups.[97] Despite its shortcomings, the populist moment of the 1860s and 1870s marked a watershed in the creation and articulation of a Russian revolutionary tradition. Thinkers like Herzen and Chernyshevsky were successful in inspiring a strain of radicalism tailored to the unique contours of Russian society that gave young enthusiasts a sense of national mission and purpose distinct from the West. Blending nationalism and socialism in equal measure, the *narodnichestvo* navigated the disillusion following 1848 and proposed a novel means of social reintegration and community-building in the midst of modernity's atomizing and individualistic tendencies.[98]

Conclusion

Summing up the events of the "springtime of nations," the historian G.M. Trevelyan famously claimed that "1848 was the turning point at which modern history failed to turn."[99] This judgment subsequently became a mantra for historians of the twentieth century inclined to see the revolutionary year as a misguided failure led by romantic idealists. This assessment overlooks, however, the constitutive changes that 1848 did produce. Conservative government took up many of the exterior attributes of revolutionary programs, creating parliamentary and modernizing governments that diverged from old regime conservatism. The political ferment of 1848 equally left a legacy of civic participation and citizenship that would be revisited in the coming decades through nationalist platforms led from both the left and the right. Taken together, 1848 marked a watershed in nineteenth-century Europe and created the conditions for nation-building and mass political movements in the years ahead.

The collapse of revolutionary movements also compelled liberals and radicals to reassess their own strategies and ideologies. In the wake of 1848 émigrés and political thinkers were forced to reflect critically on the revolutionary tradition bequeathed by 1789 and the Jacobins. Marx and Herzen, both exiled in London, were symptomatic of the broader changes occurring among ideologues and demonstrated the potential for articulating new revolutionary programs in the post-1848 period. For Marx, escaping the constraints of "tradition" entailed fostering a cosmopolitan, class-based vision of community through organization and propaganda. Herzen sought refuge in the rural *obshchina*, turning away from the European revolutionary tradition that had inspired his youthful imagination. Both in their own ways responded to the experience of 1848 and the disillusion it bred. While Marx reimagined a universal and international community that transcended the nation, Herzen confronted the indigenous and local to discover the roots of an authentic Russia. These imagined communities spoke to the realities of political exile and estrangement that many former "forty-eighters" experienced. Desires for cosmopolitan acceptance or a nostalgic longing for home imprinted themselves on revolutionary programs, altering and redefining European radicalism in the process.

The changing nature of European radicalism was on full display by 1860 as the Italian question once again became the focus of European politics. Republican revolutionaries had failed to secure independence from Austria and unite the Italian peninsula during 1848–1849, and in the aftermath Italian nationalism, like many other revolutionary programs, was subject to reconsideration. Mazzini, a predominant figure of the Risorgimento who had headed a short-lived Roman Republic in 1849, set up a National Italian Committee in London bent on pursuing a familiar strategy. From England, he orchestrated a series of secret revolutionary plots, all of which ended in abysmal failures during the mid-1850s. Yet Mazzini's control over Italian nationalists was beginning to ebb. Critics impugned his tactics, arguing they were fruitless and counterproductive. Nationalists began looking to Piedmont and its liberal Prime Minister Camillo di Cavour, seeing diplomacy and realpolitik as an alternative to Mazzini's conspiratorial revolutionary methods. In 1857, Daniele Manin, then in Paris, helped organize the National Society, a body that would use its network of international contacts and newspapers to transform the Risorgimento from a revolutionary movement into a political one centered on the Piedmontese monarchy.[100] The cause of Italian unification, omnipresent since the days of the French Revolution, was undergoing a shift as leaders like Mazzini became increasingly marginalized.

With the covert aid of Napoleon III, Cavour generated a war with Austria in 1859 that placed the Italian question square on the table. The Piedmontese minister hoped to cobble together an Italian kingdom dominated by the liberal monarchy in Turin, progressively extending Piedmontese control over the entire peninsula. Cavour's policy was only partially successful in 1859, but events the next year proved auspicious when revolts erupted in Messina and Palermo against Bourbon rule in Sicily. The Sicilian uprisings held the prospect of linking the south with the unification movement occurring in the north, and nationalists were not about to let the opportunity slip through their fingers. In these circumstances, Giuseppe Garibaldi, the romantic revolutionary *par excellence*, found himself poised to take decisive action.

Garibaldi had collaborated with Mazzini's "Young Italy" movement during the 1830s and defended Italy against Austria in 1848. By this point, Garibaldi's revolutionary credentials were firmly established. During the 1840s, he had fought in Latin America alongside Italian exiles in Brazil and Uruguay, defending Montevideo and the Rio Grande Republic from authoritarianism. His Italian Legion became legendary as stories of Garibaldi's military exploits, daring maneuvers and inspiring leadership appeared in the international press. By 1848, Garibaldi had cultivated an image as a committed revolutionary well-suited to take a leading role in securing Italian independence from Austria and the Pope.[101] "He knows how to maintain a constant enthusiasm and trust among his soldiers," as one Italian volunteer remarked in 1849. It was not just soldiers who venerated Garibaldi either. The revolutionary general cut a striking image that fascinated European audiences. His portrait was reproduced in countless magazines and newspapers throughout the world while readers indulged in dramatic biographies chronicling his adventures. With his long hair and beard, brightly colored poncho and renowned horsemanship, Garibaldi appeared at once an exotic Southern American *gaucho*, a valiant soldier-hero and ardent Italian nationalist. As an itinerant and charismatic leader fighting for liberty and national emancipation, he embodied the romantic revolutionary tradition. "Garibaldi! What a man! What prestige!" a French newspaper extoled in 1859. "His name is on everybody's lips, in everybody's heart."[102]

Noticeably older and less flamboyant by 1860, Garibaldi, at fifty-three years of age, nonetheless still retained much of his cavalier and dramatic mystique. Rallying a battalion of volunteers with patriotic speeches and nationalist appeals, Garibaldi assembled his so-called "Thousands" and set sail for Sicily. The rapid success of his movement through Palermo and Naples astounded the Piedmont King Vittorio Emanuele, who feared that Garibaldi's popularity in the south might rival his own claims to Italian leadership. A committed patriot, however, Garibaldi had few qualms accepting the Piedmontese crown if it meant a unified Italian state. His submission to Vittorio Emanuele outside Rome that August was a telling indication of the changes that had occurred in Italian nationalist outlooks during the 1850s.[103] Mazzini's revolutionary republicanism, once the leading force of Risorgimento politics, had been eclipsed by the more pragmatic goals of Piedmontese constitutionalism and nation-building from above. Diplomacy and militarism, rather than revolutionary adventurism, had been the decisive factor in securing an Italian nation. Even a romantic revolutionary like Garibaldi had abandoned Mazzini and thrown his support behind Piedmont.

The doyen of romantic nationalists, Garibaldi remained a popular cult figure in the European imagination. Yet by the 1860s, his aging appearance and retirement from active political life were symbolic of a broader generational shift occurring across the continent. Writing in the 1870s, Garibaldi's secretary Giuseppe Guerzoni acknowledged that the famed revolutionary resembled "the ghost of a giant obliged to drag across the earth the weight of his past greatness."[104] The romantic revolutionary tradition with its pantheon of heroes, melodramatic patriotism and larger-than-life characters was entering its Indian summer. Everywhere, critics noted the old "ghosts" haunting Europe and actively attempted to reimagine the bounds of radical political engagement in the wake of 1848.

CHAPTER 8
THE REVOLUTIONARY TRADITION AT A CROSSROADS: THE ANARCHISTS (1865–1905)

"We recognize no other activity but the work of extermination," wrote the young Sergei Nechayev in 1869, "but we admit that the forms in which this activity will show itself will be extremely varied."[1] A student activist based in Saint Petersburg, Nechayev epitomized the conspiratorial revolutionary of the nineteenth century. He moved through underground circles, claimed to lead a secret organization called the People's Vengeance and drafted his own revolutionary "catechism" derived from Blanquist and Carbonarist principles. The revolutionary was, in his view, "a doomed man" whose every thought and action must be directed toward a single goal: the triumph of the revolution.[2] In his shady political dealings, Nechayev resorted to extortion, blackmail and even murder when it suited his interests, and his escapades eventually diminished the goodwill of fellow radical luminaries like Mikhail Bakunin and Herzen with whom he associated. Nechayev's idealistic and pathological militancy was characteristic of a neo-Jacobin minority in Russia and Europe. Nonetheless, his remarks exhibited a wider appreciation for the changes occurring across his own generation. In the following decades, passionate desires to "exterminate" unjust state institutions and power relationships did encourage activities that were "extremely varied" in their objectives. Although Nechayev's aggression and ruthlessness set him apart from many of his contemporaries, he was in tune with the currents and outlooks of his age.

The 1860s offered a reappraisal of radical politics. The creation of the International brought with it greater cooperation and renewed militancy. By the end of the decade, strikes in France, Spain and Italy signaled the rebirth of working-class movements and radicalized labor demands. Congresses organized by the International Workingmen's Association (IWMA) in Switzerland also reflected the changing perspectives of radical ideologues. Proudhonists stimulated a newfound appreciation for communal government and local forms of social organization. Russian thinkers attending congresses in Lausanne (1867) and Basel (1869) approached questions relevant to collective ownership and land distribution through the lens of *narodnik* socialism. Considerations on the peasant *obshchina* were blended with ideas of Marxist struggle and revolution, inclining radicals to take account of pre-capitalist communal ideas in addition to prevailing concerns with internationalist socialism and revolutionary government.[3] This "theoretical cross-fertilization" influenced leftist ideologies and paved the way for the elaboration of a distinct brand of radicalism that would crystallize in the emergent anarchist movement.[4]

Anarchism was a libertarian strand of nineteenth-century socialism. Most conspicuously, it rejected the state in favor of spontaneous and voluntary forms of political and economic association, professing a commitment to emancipatory and humanitarian values.[5] "To be governed," Proudhon contended, "is to be watched over, inspected, spied upon, directed, legislated at, numbered, regulated, enrolled, indoctrinated, preached at, controlled, checked, estimated, valued, censored, [and] commanded by men who have neither the right nor the wisdom nor the virtue to do so."[6] As an instrument of power and domination, the centralized state was the chief obstacle to both individual and collective liberation. The anarchist theorist Mikhail Bakunin put the matter bluntly: "It is necessary to abolish completely, in principle and in practice, everything that might be called political power, for so long as political power exists, there will always be rulers and ruled, masters and slaves, exploiters and exploited."[7] In line with his historical materialism, Marx saw the role of the state as progressive. Centralization marked an advance over localism and furnished the instrument through which the productive forces of society could be collectivized and, ultimately, democratized. Anarchists offered a counter-interpretation to this narrative, insisting that individuals were not instruments of some abstract historical process. Freedom did not have economic preconditions, and the state, far from being a progressive force, was a hindrance to the free and creative development of the individual and community.[8] "Apart from the expropriation and suppression of the bourgeoisie, the demolition of the State and all bourgeois institutions, there is no salvation," proclaimed Pyotr Kropotkin, a leading voice within anarchist circles of the 1880s.[9]

In its aversion to centralized authority and commitment to libertarian egalitarianism, anarchism offered a new vision of community and social revolution that found expression in both local and international dimensions. However, it remained the product of diverse intellectual and ideological influences, and as such never conformed to a strict doctrine or program of action. In many respects, the lived experiences of anarchist movements and agitators would have an immense impact on articulations of anarchist philosophy over the years, revealing that anarchism was a constantly evolving ideology receptive to changing circumstances on the ground.[10] This variability encouraged an array of tactics, strategies and divergent opinions rooted in opposition to all forms of centralized power and oppression, whether real or imagined. The newspapers *Le Révolté* revealed the multiple contexts in which anarchist opposition could be understood when discussing the movement's strategic initiatives in 1880: "Our action must be permanent revolt through writings, speeches, through daggers, rifles, dynamite, even perhaps through casting ballots. ..."[11] Given this injunction, anarchism amounted to both a critical attack on established sources of authority and a violent revolutionary revolt against it. Together, these dual resolutions would define the "anarchist moment" in Europe and across the world, giving the fin de siècle its own unique character and ambience.

The International Divided

Marx had found a worthy appointment in Proudhon and his followers. He managed, however, to contain the mutualist threat within the IWMA through a mix of backdoor politicking and compromise. This scenario was not to be repeated in the next round of tensions that roiled the International in the late 1860s as Marx confronted the Russian firebrand Mikhail Bakunin. Unlike the Proudhonists, Bakunin stressed the difference between political theory and practice and provided an example of anarchist fervor in action that others were keen to follow.

An aspiring Russian political philosopher, Bakunin had traveled to Paris in the 1840s where he mixed with leading radical thinkers of the day, among them Marx and Proudhon. His association with Polish refugees and plans to foment revolt in Russia provoked his expulsion from the country in late 1847. It was an opportune moment for an itinerant radical to be set loose. Over the course of the coming two years, Bakunin allied with worker groups in Germany and assisted with the Pan-Slav congress in Prague. His ideas transcended the modest aim of national autonomy advocated by most Slavic nationalists, revealing that Bakunin was already a hardline radical by this time. In his "Appeal to the Slavs" drafted in 1848, he insisted it was necessary to "overthrow from top to bottom" the existing social order. "The social question … appears to be first and foremost the question of the complete overturn of society."[12] Bakunin's political activities earned him a prison sentence and finally banishment to Siberia in 1857. His escape and subsequent travels through Japan and the United States became legendary, and by the time of his return to Europe in the 1860s Bakunin had achieved a conspicuous notoriety among continental circles. The Russian liberal and literary critic Vissarion Belinsky was taken by Bakunin's dedication to conspiratorial politics and imposing presence, although he questioned his actual merits as a humanitarian. "He loves ideas, not men," Belinsky remarked. "He wants to dominate with his personality, not to love."[13] Others were equally suspicious of such a grandiose and extremist personality. As one French observer put it, "Bakunin is invaluable the day of the revolution, but the next day it is absolutely necessary to have him shot."[14]

Bakunin's radicalism drew its substance from a variety of sources, blending Proudhonist anarchism and Marx's vision of social revolution and oppression. His emphasis on terrorism as a revolutionary tactic looked to Blanqui and the neo Jacobin tradition, despite the fact that he condemned dictatorship and insisted that republicanism led "by necessity to despotism."[15] Mixing various schools of thought, Bakunin was no imitator. He insisted that revolutionaries must possess a "heroic madness" and be a "militant church of democracy."[16] The mission of this "church" was to spread "the idea" to the people. The oppressed provided the raw revolutionary element, for they were "socialist without knowing it." Revolution was an educational experience that would bring these latent radical and socialist tendencies of the masses to the surface. "We must not teach the people, but lead them to revolt," he affirmed.[17] The failure of 1848 convinced Bakunin that the people could expect nothing from the bourgeoisie. They would have to take possession of their own destinies, and it was up to revolutionaries to provide them with the opportunities to do so. In London, he sought to encourage resistance among Polish nationalists, and once he had worn out his welcome there he set off for Italy where he joined with political émigrés and democrats in Tuscany and Naples.

His time spent in Italy would be transformative. His faith in nationalism as a revolutionary force began to dwindle following a failed Polish uprising in 1863.[18]

He equally became mistrustful of Marx, who he accused of "authoritarianism" and "ruining the workers by making theorists out of them."[19] Moreover, circumstances in Italy augured a re-evaluation of revolutionary politics. Italian republicans in the south had never fully been won over to Piedmontese leadership. They were critical of the administrative controls and taxation imposed by Turin and protested against the economic policies that were impoverishing southern farming communities. Like Bakunin's native Russia, southern Italy remained an agrarian society composed of peasants. Their destitution led Bakunin to believe that the peasantry, just as much as the industrial worker, could be a revolutionary agent. "One feels that electricity is gathering in the air, that the atmosphere is becoming charged," he wrote to Alexander Herzen with anticipation after arriving in Florence. "A storm is imminent."[20] Marx placed his faith in the proletariat. Yet according to Bakunin, this reverence for the urban proletariat translated into a working-class elitism. The situation in Italy indicated that another path to revolution could be imagined. Recruiting a small but dedicated cadre of Neapolitan followers consisting of lawyers, professionals and former Carbonaros and Garibaldino volunteers, Bakunin intended to win democrats over to his anti-authoritarian and anti-statist platform.

His objectives dovetailed with Marx and Engels, both of whom desired to diminish the appeal of Mazzini's republicanism and draw Italian workers to the IWMA. Believing that Bakunin's influence could dilute support for the Mazzinists, Marx encouraged Bakunin to sell the International as an alternative to Italian republicanism.[21] He and his collaborators issued a strong criticism of Mazzini, painting him as a bourgeois revolutionary willing to "sacrifice the freedom and well-being" of the popular masses for the sake of an "idealized" Italian nation-state.[22] Revolution and struggle were the only means of accomplishing true Italian liberation, the Bakuninists argued, and this was not to be found in the old Risorgimento leadership. Yet Bakunin was hardly prepared to submit to Marx and the IWMA either. Contrary to Marx's expectations, Bakunin founded his own International Brotherhood (later renamed the International Alliance of Socialist Democracy) modeled on the Carbonari and Free Masons. The Alliance had its own revolutionary catechism and oaths of loyalty requiring members to renounce the principle of nationality and pledge themselves to international socialism. Despite its similarities to the IWMA, Bakunin's International Alliance remained distant from the Marxists, Proudhonists and trade unionists in London. It aimed to serve as a revolutionary body independent of the organizing activities undertaken by the IWMA Central Council. "I am not a communist," Bakunin explained, "because communism … causes all the powers of society to be swallowed up by the State, because it leads necessarily to the centralization of property in the hands of the State, whereas I want the abolition of the State."[23]

Bakunin's loathing for centralized authority was a point of distinction as well as the basis of his political philosophy. "The State is the most flagrant, cynical and complete negation of humanity," he protested. "It shatters the universal solidarity of all men on the earth." National boundaries and government structures served to engender division and encourage aggression. In their place, Bakunin envisaged a federalist model of association that would promote the maximum freedom of the individual within the local community while fostering universal solidarity on an international level. "Federalist as to the interior, [the Social Democrat] wants international confederation, first by the spirit of justice, then because he is convinced that the social and economic revolution surpassing the artificial and deadly boundaries of states can only be realized ... by the collective action of all."[24] This plan for social reorganization required, however, a new type of revolution, according to Bakuninists. "We do not fear anarchy, we invoke it ...," asserted the founding proclamation of Bakunin's International Alliance. "The Revolution as we understand it will have to destroy the State and all the institutions of the State, radically and completely, from its very first day."[25]

Herein were a rival ideology and philosophy of revolution. Bakuninism was international in scope, militant in its application and committed to social emancipation. Yet it distinguished itself from Marxism on numerous levels. Its outreach to peasants and the agrarian world contrasted sharply with Marx's focus on the proletariat. Similarly, its mistrust of centralized authority and emphasis on spontaneous action equally set it apart. To the consternation of Marx and Engels, Bakunin perpetuated the revolutionary tradition's fetish for violence and even revered it. "Let us put our trust in the eternal spirit which destroys and annihilates," claimed Bakunin. "Our task is terrible: total, inexorable and universal destruction."[26] Marxist revolution urged workers to seize control of the state and transform society. Bakunin, to the contrary, urged his followers to eradicate the very instruments of power and coercion. Imminently more radical than the IWMA, the Alliance rejected state and nation in favor of free association and called for the collectivization of all productive forces, namely land and industry. These fundamental tenets became the basis for "anarchist collectivism," a radical philosophy that prized the community over the state, the social over the political, mutual aid and solidarity over capitalist individualism. In short, Bakunin sought to restore community as a structural unit of local social life, contending that capitalism and the state had atomized and enslaved humanity.[27]

Bakunin departed Italy in 1867 for Switzerland, but he left behind a dedicated group of Bakuninists who would sow the seeds of an Italian anarchist movement in the coming years. More significantly, his ideas began to spread to France and Spain. In 1868, Bakuninists profited from the precarious situation of the Spanish government. Decades of factionalism had left the kingdom unstable while longstanding economic problems spurred strikes and peasant uprisings. Military officials hoped to remedy these problems with necessary constitutional reforms, a solution that the government of Queen Isabella II refused to countenance. That September, officers launched a coup against the monarchy and established a more pliable government. Although liberals and centrists hailed it as *la gloriosa* (the "glorious revolution"), democratic republicans remained skeptical. These contentions set the stage for a new round of conflicts between royalists, republicans and the military, but they also provided conditions for the spread of worker radicalism. Catalonian artisans took the initiative in 1868 by setting up a Central Directory in Barcelona to agitate for worker rights and a federal republic. It quickly established relations with the International, forming the Federación Regional

Español (FRE) by 1870. The FRE constituted a blanket organization for Spanish worker groups. It was, however, French and Italian Bakuninists that assisted in organizing it, a factor that would have consequences for the future.[28]

Because the International was brought to Spain through the actions of Bakuninists, Spanish labor organizations developed along anarchist lines. Local unions were set up to ensure worker control and autonomy, thereby limiting the power of trade union leaders and the IWMA central committee. The structure of the FRE was designed to allow power to flow from the bottom up, and the newspapers run by worker groups promoted Bakuninist principles over Marxist communism. Bakunin's ideas spoke to the emerging industrial working class in Spain as well as the rural *bracero* (peasant laborers). They furnished these groups with a common vocabulary that nurtured an independent identity and radical platform distinct from liberal reformism. Despite the decentralized nature of the peasant and worker unions gathered under the FRE, Bakunin's Alliance enjoyed a fair amount of influence. *Aliancistas* loyal to Bakunin intended to pursue a revolutionary agenda and formed a hidden anarchist faction within the FRE that operated as a secret committee.[29]

This strategy had, in fact, been central to Bakunin's plan, although he always hid such aspirations behind a façade of cooperation and common principles. Writing to Marx in late 1868, Bakunin boasted that he was on the verge of fulfilling his internationalist goals. "I am now doing what you started to do more than twenty years ago … I know no other society, no other milieu than the world of the workers."[30] Marx, however, saw things differently. Bakunin presented a clear challenge to his own authority and leadership over the International, and he was not about to tolerate a potential rival. Over the next few years, Marx took steps to alienate Bakunin and pressed the General Council to purge the Bakuninists from its ranks, labeling the International Alliance a secret organization within the IWMA. By 1872, the split became irreconcilable when the Bakuninists were summarily expelled. This gesture appeared to confirm the charges of communist "authoritarianism" consistently levied by anarchists. Marx fired back, accusing the Alliance of seeking to replace the General Council with a "personal dictatorship."[31] The recriminations slung back and forth divided the left along both ideological and personal lines. In spite of common outlooks rooted in international organization and emancipation, radicals were unable to agree on what type of community they sought to create. The commanding personalities of leaders like Marx and Bakunin, moreover, did nothing to paper over these divisions.

The Paris Commune

The split between communists and anarchists occurred just as events in France rekindled leftist militancy. During the 1860s, student organizations, worker strikes and the growth of a republican opposition in the imperial legislature all signaled the waning popularity of Napoleon III's Second Empire. Blanqui, by now an elder-statesman of the revolutionary tradition, attracted a new generation of young followers who enthusiastically preached political violence and an aggressive atheism in the name of the coming social revolution.³² Beyond this neo-Jacobin revival, a mix of disgruntled intellectuals and activists—what the bohemian writer Jules Vallès deemed *réfractaires*— vented their spleen against the materialism and inequalities of bourgeois life. "Rather than accepting the place the world has offered them, [the *réfractaire*] desires to make it by them self," Vallès contended.³³ The poet, journalist and Blanquist sympathizer Eugène Vermersch was more explicit in this revolt against bourgeois life and values, informing his readers that violence was more effective than "writing a 1,000 page volume on capital or giving thirty speeches in the provinces."³⁴ French politics exhibited a broad range of pent up frustrations and contempt for Bonapartist authoritarianism by the late 1860s. This atmosphere revived political movements dormant since 1848, providing the tinder needed for a widespread conflagration.

The spark came in 1870. That July, the government of Napoleon III became embroiled in a war with Prussia through a series of diplomatic missteps. While the French military command assured the Emperor of a swift victory, the conflict did not go according to plan. Within a month, the French army had been driven back and the Prussian military was taking significant swaths of French territory. Napoleon III's blunder proved fatal. In September, the Second Empire collapsed under the weight of internal political opposition. Republicans immediately declared a Third Republic and created a government of national defense to take charge of the failing war effort. They made appeals to patriotism and used nationalist rhetoric to rally supporters, attempting to duplicate the heroic wars of the French Revolution nearly a century earlier. However, 1870 was not the French Revolution. Republicans may have preached "war to the end," but in reality they were fighting a losing cause, and as the weeks wore on this became evident. By January the new republic was forced to sue for peace and consent to territorial losses and a heavy war indemnity imposed by the new German Empire.³⁵

France was humiliated by the defeat. Moreover, during the war French citizens had suffered excessive hardship. Paris in particular had been subject to a four-month siege as the Germans attempted to starve the capital into submission. Parisians faced gas and fuel shortages throughout the winter. Food became scarce. Tales spread of resilient Parisians eating zoo animals and rats to survive.³⁶ City life was increasingly militarized as citizens joined National Guard battalions and workshops were converted into armament factories. Municipal officials oversaw food rationing and aid, assuming wartime government functions that impacted day-to-day life in the city. Men and women donned military uniforms and found new public roles assisting the defense campaign. Faced with this extreme situation, established institutions and social roles were subject to jarring reversals as Parisians endured the collective experience of wartime privation and suffering.³⁷

Things hardly improved after the war. The Parisian economy was in shambles and the government seemed to be drifting in a conservative direction. Elections returned former monarchists and provincial notables, generating anxieties over the very existence of the new republic. Heading the government was Adolphe Thiers, an Orléanist who had served under the July Monarchy. Thiers characteristically showed little sympathy for the capital, which requested aid and welfare benefits to recover from the siege. Soon enough, the old Parisian radicalism began to show its colors. Republicans and socialists organized clubs and made bold speeches in the streets. By early March, the government suspected that if the situation continued a revolt was bound to break out. Paris was famous for its revolutionary temper, and Thiers was not about to let chaos ensue. He was particularly concerned with the armaments in the city used during the defense. Should these fall into the hands of radicals, it could portend a showdown with the national government. Therefore, on March 18 the army was secretly sent into Paris at night to remove the weapons. The plan was to disarm the city and pre-empt any potential violence. It failed miserably. When the army tried to remove cannons stationed on the hills of Montmarte, the troops were surrounded by an angry mob, attacked and then butchered in the streets. It seemed to be the French Revolution all over again.[38]

Within days, activists of varying stripes—Proudhonists, Internationalists and neo-Jacobins—seized control of the city and declared Paris an autonomous commune. The Parisian National Guard assumed responsibility for defense while elections were called to form a municipal government run for the benefit of the working classes. Both the National Guard and the Paris section of the International already possessed organizational structures connected to local neighborhood committees. In essence, the Commune grew out of these pre-existing structures set up during the war.[39] Over the next two weeks, an Executive Commission was created to take control of the ministries and delegate power. Each arrondissement was given representation in the Communal Council, entailing a strong link between city districts (arrondissements) and the central authority. Citizens filled administrative and military posts, attending to public services ranging from social welfare programs like soup kitchens and the distribution of basic resources to education and defense. A Commission of Labor and Exchange pushed through reforms designed to empower producer-owned cooperatives and workshops organized along mutualist lines. Worker control, a longstanding goal of socialists, was momentarily realized as radicals created a government based upon principles of decentralized authority and collective management.[40] "Your revolution has a special character that distinguishes it from others," the newspaper *La Commune* informed its readers on March 19. "Its fundamental greatness is that it is made entirely by the people as a collective communal revolutionary up-taking, anonymous, unanimous, and for the first time without leaders."[41]

Central to this newfound sense of collective independence was the political empowerment the Commune offered to citizens. Parisians gathered in concert halls, workshops and churches throughout the city forming clubs and neighborhood associations. These multiple centers of power became forums for the expression of local concerns and opened up new areas for political engagement and activism. Just like the worker cooperatives and National Guard battalions, clubs facilitated the flow of power from below and ensured that delegates were directly accountable to their constituencies. The Paris Commune presented a radical alternative to established forms of government and power, mixing artisanal socialism with anarchist ideas of self-government and localized autonomy.[42] The new ethos of the revolutionary experiment was expressed in a manifesto issued by the Nicolas-des-Champs club of the Third Arrondissement that spring: "People, govern yourselves through public meeting, through your press."[43]

Generations of Marxist and social historians have debated whether and to what extent the Commune characterized a "proletarian" uprising led by workers against bourgeois authority.[44] While socialist goals were clearly evident among communard activists, what gave the Commune its distinct brand of radicalism was the diverse forms of emancipation it encompassed. With the collapse of French political authority, popular organizations and associations transcending narrow class-based affiliations sprang up across the city. They drew in manual laborers as well as professionals and bohemian intellectuals who identified with the alienation expressed by the working classes.[45] In this respect, the Commune marked a cultural revolution just as much as a political one. Workers and intellectuals mounted open challenges to bourgeois cultural hegemony and authority, taking control of public spaces and institutions that had previously been either monopolized by the state or denied to them.[46] On May 16, the people's "conquest of the public" assumed an epic quality when a large gathering of communards hoisted ropes around the towering statue of Napoleon on the Place Vendôme and brought the monument tumbling to the ground as an orchestra played the Marseillaise. This act not only dramatized the assertion of popular sovereignty over imperial authority. It witnessed "the people" collectively reshaping their own national memory and history. The destruction of the Vendôme Column gave symbolic form to the promise of a regenerated society over the inequalities and oppression of the past.[47]

Chief among those who ordered the destruction of the column was Gustave Courbet, head of the Arts Commission under the Commune and a leading figure of the "cultural" revolution taking place. That April, Courbet had made demands for the practice of cooperative autonomy within the artistic establishment. The French state traditionally exercised a great deal of influence over the arts through the Academy, the state-run École des Beaux-Arts and the annual Salon exhibition. As a proponent of the new social realist movement, Courbet loathed the insipid and highly stylized academic art sponsored by the Academy. He admired Proudhon and never hid his desires of applying Proudhonist principles to the art world. That April, he announced the creation of a democratically elected Fédération des Artistes with the aim of securing artist control over exhibitions, peer review committees and formal training in the schools. Courbet's plan to democratize the artistic establishment clearly aligned with the principles of autonomy championed by the Commune and reflected Courbet's strong anti-statist attitude and anarchist ideology.[48]

Challenges to established social, cultural and political norms similarly extended to the "female question." Associationist activities during the period of the Franco-Prussian War and Commune provided women with opportunities for civic engagement. Women partook in the crowds and clubs, and through this participation defined new public identities for themselves derived from their active support for the war and communal government. The revolutionary concept of *citoyenneté* was revived. Militants organized all-female battalions and served on local vigilance committees. Activists pressured the Labor Commission to abide by policies of gender equality regarding work and pay.

Elisabeth Dmitrieff, a Russian-born feminist active in the International, helped establish the Union des Femmes that April with the assistance of the IWMA, creating a body that openly advocated for a broad range of women's issues. Its activities attracted known feminists such as Léotilde Champsiex and Louise Michel, a provincial schoolteacher who routinely associated with members of the Parisian opposition. Serving in the Montmartre battalion and regularly clad in National Guard uniform, Michel epitomized the image of the female revolutionary, earning her the moniker the "red virgin." Her activism, social habits and even dress consciously flouted established gender roles and stereotypes of female domesticity, presenting a model of the new woman the revolution sought to create.[49]

Overall, the Commune did not produce any significant legislation specific to the condition of women. Moreover, not all communards embraced the cause of female emancipation nor saw it necessary to challenge traditional gender hierarchies. Nevertheless, the education and labor commissions did enact policies supportive of equal pay and female education. More broadly, the atmosphere of the Commune provided chances for female activism that reshaped discourses of social inclusion and citizenship. Women participated in the outbreaks of violence and the associational life of the clubs; they served the communal cause by taking jobs as ambulance nurses, canteen workers and soldiers. Through this participation, women were able to formulate conceptions of citizenship and claim a public role in the life of the Commune and, by extension, the larger revolutionary project.[50] As one journalist remarked, "It seems that [women] see this revolution as precisely their own, and in defending it they defend their own future."[51]

Given the various forms emancipation took during the spring of 1871, it is difficult to categorize the Commune as a "revolutionary government" on the model of the Convention. It possessed multiple points of authority and included socialists, republicans and anarchists of varying persuasions. Although it drew upon an established revolutionary tradition inclined to associate sovereignty with the assembly of citizens, it also promoted a specific idea of community rooted in local and urban forms of association that clearly possessed international implications. Upon extending citizenship to the German Internationalist Leo Fränkel, the government used the moment to iterate the Commune's commitment to universal values, declaring, "We consider that the flag of the Commune is that of the universal republic."[52] Such rhetoric clearly harkened back to the French Revolution and Anacharsis Cloots. However, the connotations associated with this "universal republic" had undergone significant transformations since the late eighteenth century. "Federation" had become a mantra of the republican and anarchist left. Radicals were proposing a novel type of social organization built upon networks of mutual aid societies, political clubs and cooperatives in place of state authority. These associations, organized at the municipal level, would function as self-governing collectivities and progressively extend outward to form an international confederation of autonomous municipalities and departments uniting humanity in an imagined universal republic.[53] It was a republican model "liberated" from the national mold, as the communard Élisée Reclus explained. "[The nation-state's] boundaries must be abolished, those limits and frontiers that make enemies out of sympathetic people … Our rallying cry is no longer 'Long Live the Republic' but 'Long Live the Universal Republic.'"[54] Concepts of individual freedom and local autonomy were never divorced from desires for international solidarity. The Commune fused these dual ideas of community together in a vision of an anarchist utopia consisting of self-regulating governments and worker-controlled industries. This formula of local liberty and international unity was believed to be the kernel of a reconstituted social order that would herald the true social republic. For the Internationalist Pierre Vésinier, the revolutionary attributes of this program were incontestable. "The Commune must replace the old world and became the base of a new world," he affirmed.[55]

In reality, however, this ideal was far from absolute. From the minute radicals seized power in March, the Commune was on a war footing. The French national government, reconvening in Versailles, had every intention of reasserting control over Paris and was willing to wage war to do so. By mid-April, Parisian officials began to fear that the decentralized nature of the communal government was ill-equipped to deal with the needs of defense. Calls for a Committee of Public Safety were put forward, sparking a debate regarding the very identity of the Commune itself. Neo-Jacobins had little qualms with authorizing a defense committee to manage the war effort. Almost from the start, Blanquists sought to exert control over National Guard battalions in preparation for a seizure of power carried out by radical paramilitaries.[56] Raoul Rigault, a student activist and devotee of Blanqui, had taken the post of Chief of Police in anticipation of just such a denouement. Others, however, heeded warnings about imitating the past and readily opposed those calling for "a new '93." Allusions to the Terror and Jacobin dictatorship ran the risk of alienating international sympathy for the communard cause and would only prove its detractors correct. Critics urged fellow communards to reject the violence of the past and emphasized the novelty of what the Commune sought to achieve. "Let us abandon revenge, retaliation, [and] violence," admonished Courbet; "let us establish a new order of events that belongs to us and that comes from us alone."[57] Opinion was divided, but as the Commune increasingly faced the threat of invasion, more radical propositions won out.

A five-member Committee of Public Safety was voted in early May and Blanquists seized the opportunity to round up any and all suspected enemies, holding priests and clerical officials as hostages.[58] This vicious anticlerical purge was a precursor of events to come. By late May, the war was brought into the heart of the city. National troops stormed Paris, taking back the city street by street. The so-called "bloody week" of May saw the wholesale slaughter of communard radicals as Paris was "bled white," according to the writer Edmond de Goncourt. In turn, communards responded by executing political prisoners, burning down any building they were forced to abandon and unleashing a violent reign of terror. This devastating civil war culminated in the Père Lachaise Cemetery on May 28, when the victorious government troops forced the last pockets of resistance to surrender. Upon surrendering, some 150 National Guardsmen were led unarmed into the cemetery, lined up against a wall and summarily shot. By the conclusion, approximately 15,000 Parisians had been killed. The city itself was in ruins, radicals had fled into exile or been shot and France was left deeply divided.

Revolutionary Europe

Lasting a mere seventy-two days, the Paris Commune was nonetheless a turning point in Europe's revolutionary heritage. Preoccupied with war and defense, communards had few opportunities to enact meaningful social legislation or establish concrete political institutions reflecting their radical programs. Differences between neo-Jacobins, socialists and anarchists equally militated against any type of uniform revolutionary project. Yet it was precisely this diversity that characterized the Commune's novelty. As Bakunin claimed, the Commune was a revolt against the *bête noire* of "authoritarian communism" as radicals renounced all theory and sought to regenerate society by "the spontaneous and continued action of the masses, the groups and associations of the people."[59] Ideas favoring local autonomy and collective participation were on full display, exhibiting an array of leftist activities that defied strict organization or firm leadership. Although short-lived, the Commune was an anarchist utopia that momentarily saw "the people" assume power over the institutions governing daily life. It infused desires for autonomy and local forms of community with political meaning, championing an idea of emancipation that was collectivist in practice while individualist in spirit.

Propaganda of the Deed

The Commune was a beginning, not an end, for many radicals. Anarchists watched with enthusiasm as the communards waged war against the state, and they collectively suffered the indignation of defeat that May. Publicists assured, however, that the communard cause was not in vain. Putting pen to paper that June, Bakunin drafted a lengthy eulogy of the failed uprising, hailing its achievements and condemning its brutal suppression. In his opinion, the coming social revolution would signal "the resurrection of Paris" as the solidarity of free people triumphed over the oppression of authority and enslavement.[60] Unfortunately, Bakunin never lived to see his prophesized revolution. He died in Bern, Switzerland, in 1876, living out his life in exile to the end. His revolutionary adventurism and commitment to radical freedom over the course of his life had made a name for Bakunin internationally. Yet none of his revolutionary exploits ever managed to bear substantial fruit. Herzen summed up Bakunin best, describing him as "a Columbus without an America."[61] Bakunin was however correct to see the Commune as the "point of departure for future revolutions." Revolutionaries of the coming decades would look back to the Commune as a source of inspiration. The Italian anarchist Andrea Costa was not exaggerating when he claimed "It was on the cadaver of the Commune—fecund in its ruins—that we pledged ourselves to the struggle between the old spirit and the new; it was from the blood of the slain communards that the omens were drawn."[62]

That the Paris Commune acquired international significance in its wake was hardly surprising. In the immediate aftermath of "bloody week," Marx delivered an address before the IWMA General Council declaring that the Commune was not a pale imitation of the French Revolution but a harbinger of the proletarian social revolution to come. Whether or not Marx was correct, radicals throughout Europe identified with the fallen communards and their cause, and for good reason. The Commune had never been a wholly French affair to begin with. In the spring of 1871, internationalists had flocked to Paris to participate in the revolution. Many of the activists who took up arms were allied with the IWMA. In demonstrations of international solidarity, workers in London staged marches in Hyde Park waving banners emblazoned with "Vive la Commune" and "Long Live the Universal Republic." The widespread support for the Commune and the publicity it attracted bolstered leftist activism and popularized anarchist ideas among an international audience. "Two months of fighting have done more than twenty-three years of propaganda," claimed the French anarchist Paul Brousse.[63]

Brousse was not mistaken, and this conclusion would illuminate a troubling tendency among anarchist thinkers. By its very nature, a political movement vested in ideas of decentralization and anti-authoritarianism did not lend itself to disciplined organization and leadership structures. Contrary to Marxist prescriptions of mass organization and

Figure 15 "Paris under the Commune," 1871 © The British Library Board.

propaganda, Bakuninists favored small conspiratorial coteries that would guide the people in determining their own future. As Bakunin instructed his disciples, "There is no need to recruit an army, since your army is the people. What we must form are *general staffs*, a network well-organized and inspired by the leaders of the popular movement."[64] As a consequence, anarchist cooperatives and networks tended to be diffuse and loose-knit. Given these circumstances, the question naturally arose how anarchists were expected to compete with communists and mobilize support for the revolutionary cause. According to Bakunin, the answer was in revolutionary action itself. "We must spread our principles, not with words but with deeds, for this is the most popular, the most potent and the most irresistible form of propaganda."[65]

This strategy constituted a central tenet of the emerging anarchist philosophy. The cult of violence and guerilla warfare were the essential tactics of the anarchist revolutionary. In the immediate aftermath of the Commune, anarchists in Spain were developing these very ideas. The struggles between Spanish monarchists and republicans had broken into a full-fledged civil war by 1873. Radical republican federalists encouraging calls for cantonal autonomy launched an armed resistance that summer in Cartegena that quickly spread through the south. Cantonalist insurgents seized control of municipalities and waged war against government forces. The FRE, wracked by internal squabbles between "authoritarian" and "anti-authoritarian" factions, surprisingly played a minimal role in these uprisings, although foreign anarchists attempted to rally supporters to the federalist platform.[66] Brousse, active in Barcelona, appealed to radicals, urging them to participate. "Revolutionary propaganda is made not only by the pen and spoken word …," he asserted; "it is above all made in the open, in the midst of the piled-up paving stones of the barricades."[67] The appeal failed, and the anarchists suffered a wave of repression at the hands of the Spanish state once the revolt was quelled, driving the FRE underground.

Between 1874 and 1877, a similar phenomenon occurred in Italy. Bakunin and his associates staged an abortive uprising in Bologna that rapidly fizzled out due to lack of mass support and organization. Over the next few years, the leaders of the Bakuninist wing Carlo Cafiero and Errico Malatesta worked to revive the movement and in 1877 planned to foment a guerilla peasant uprising in the mountainous region of the Benevento. The attempt was part of a strategy to use local revolts in encouraging mass revolutionary uprising. Rebels in a few villages heeded the call and proceeded to burn public records and proclaim a social republic, but they were quickly suppressed by authorities. Cafiero and Malatesta fled and the interior ministry used the disturbance to dissolve the Italian branch of the International and break up radical organizations.[68] Faced with state repression and the onset of an economic depression in 1873 that temporarily muted worker militancy, radicals were at a loss. Activists were eager to breathe new life into what they perceived to be a deteriorating situation. Falling back on the model of the Paris Commune, anarchists argued that only violent actions and dramatic gestures would keep the movement alive.

Such assessments found acceptance among anarchist luminaries based in Switzerland during the 1870s. Bakunin had first mobilized clockmakers in the Jura region and won them over to his anarchist ideas. Chaux-de-Fonds, the central town of the Jura

The Revolutionary Tradition at a Crossroads

Figure 16 Pyotr Alexeyevich Kropotkin © The British Library Board.

clock-making industry, became an ideological center of European anarchism over the decade that served as a magnet for political exiles and communard refugees. The Jura Federation, as the exilic community was branded, drew together a cosmopolitan group of intellectuals committed to "working out the practical and theoretical aspects of anarchist socialism" and trying to accomplish "something that will last," as Pyotr Kropotkin stated.[69] Kropotkin himself was one of the leading Jura personalities, having arrived in 1877. Son of an aristocratic family, Kropotkin abandoned a promising career in geography to pursue politics, falling in with Russian populists and eventually earning himself a jail sentence in 1874. By the 1880s, Kropotkin would become one of the foremost anarchist theorists of his generation. He gained a reputation as a radical thinker through articles published regularly in newspapers like the Jura *Bulletin*, the French newspaper *L'Avant-Garde* and his own *Le Révolté*. These articles furnished the basis for later books like *The Conquest of Bread* and *Mutual Aid*, both of which would contribute to a growing corpus of anarchist texts.

By the time Kropotkin took up residence in the Jura, the anarchist circle was on the verge of collapse. The cooperatives they had organized were failing and the anarchist sections possessed only a few resolute adherents. More disturbing was the leadership's noticeable lack of connection with the Swiss workers.[70] Conscious of the need to revive the movement, Kropotkin sought to gain support from larger audiences, and, as he claimed, "there is nothing like courage to win over the people." Words became "lost in the air like the empty chiming of bells." Action and vigorous political engagement were the essential components of a successful revolutionary movement. As he saw it, a single deed was better propaganda "than thousands of pamphlets."[71] This position was distilled into a simple philosophy: "propaganda of the deed." For Kropotkin, this "deed" was equated with heroic self-sacrifice and the demonstration of anarchist principles in action. "It is especially in taking an active part in the daily affairs of the commune that we can demonstrate in a visible and comprehensible manner all the evils of present-day society and the advantages of applying our economic and political principles," he instructed his cohorts in 1878 when publicizing the views of Paul Brousse. Local self-governance, as he saw it, offered "an excellent ground for the propaganda of collectivism."[72] This was not to say that Kropotkin did not also see the propagandistic value of violent uprisings and assassinations, both of which he endorsed alongside collectivist action.

These debates circulated among anarchist networks and took center stage at an international congress called in Berne in 1876. Militants worried over the declining stature of anarchism rallied to a program of violent action and guerilla tactics. "The insurrectionary deed" was "the most effective means of propaganda," Malatesta and Cafiero argued, because it alone animated "the living force of humanity."[73] Such views stemmed from anarchist understandings of human nature, which was believed to be fundamentally moral and good. Capitalism exercised a corrupting influence on the individual, making people selfish, greedy and dependent. Once people were liberated from the capitalist state, these vulgar impulses would disappear. It was this underlying belief in humanity that guided anarchist philosophy, and it was, at base, spontaneous revolutionary action alone that would liberate man's true nature. Inherent within this position was, however, an irresolvable contradiction that stabbed at the heart of militant revolutionary ideology: creating a world free of force and coercion condoned and even necessitated the use of unrestrained terror and violence to achieve it. In their quest for a more just world, revolutionaries endorsed shock, intimidation and murder against any and all perceived enemies of the people.

Not all anarchists agreed with these proposals. By the late 1870s, various anarchists were seeking to shift toward more conventional forms of organizations, fearing militant policies would only further alienate the movements and invite state repression. As well, conspirators like Malatesta and Cafiero preached spontaneous revolt and revolutionary violence, but they quickly learned that putting such ideas into practice was easier said than done. Their failed attempts offered a hard lesson in the gap separating ideology and reality, motivating a turn toward organization and publication in later years. Theorists such as Kropotkin made names for themselves celebrating the "propaganda of the deed," but in the end these prescriptions remained theoretical. Rarely did leading anarchist writers attempt to put their theories into action. Often times, it was others who lacked the eloquence and sophistication of writers like Kropotkin who took up the call to action. In 1886, Parisians stood aghast as a man sitting in the galleries of the Paris Stock Exchange threw a bottle of vitriol at the stockbrokers and fired gunshots in the name of anarchist revolution.[74] Occurrences such as these increasingly eclipsed the more benign and activist-oriented focus of anarchism, equating it with violence and terror in the popular imagination.

In 1891, a series of bombs were detonated outside the homes of government officials in Paris. Upon investigation it was discovered that this anonymous bombing campaign had been carried out by a single culprit: François Ravachol. Ravachol was a worker, although his employment record indicated he had never managed to hold down steady employment. To make ends meet, he turned to theft, murder and grave robbing. When questioned by authorities, he admitted to these unseemly activities with pride, depicting himself as a modern-day Robin Hood who stole from the rich. His bombing campaign had been motivated by revenge against an unjust bourgeois state, he told authorities at his trial. He openly identified as an anarchist, averring he was a political prisoner fighting inequality and oppression. The authorities were not swayed and Ravachol was executed. The Ravachol affair, however, became a *cause célèbre*. At meetings, French anarchists praised Ravachol as a martyr. He attained the status of a folk hero, inspiring a popular song, *La Ravachol*, with its refrain "Long live the sound of explosions, so it will be!" Over the next four years, other "inspired" individuals would perpetrate similar acts of terrorism, targeting police stations, cafés and even the chambers of the National Assembly where in 1893 Auguste Vaillant, a down-and-out work claiming to avenge Ravachol, detonated a homemade explosive filled with nails and shrapnel.[75]

Prominent anarchist theorists were loath to condone such behavior. Jean Grave, a leading anarchist publicist in Paris, affirmed his commitment to "complete and perpetual revolt" but discouraged anarchists from indulging in "unconscious revolt which strikes out blindly under the impulse of a momentary anger."[76] Kropotkin himself repudiated Ravachol, urging "it is not by these heroic acts that revolutions are made."[77] Anarchists across Europe denounced the unsettling trend of blind terror and destruction infecting the movement. "It is necessary that we are not ourselves auxiliaries to the current opinion which regards dynamite as synonymous with anarchism," Ricardo Mella implored his fellow Spanish anarchists in 1892.[78] Yet if leaders condemned blind terror, there remained little they could do to enforce this ruling. The movement had no centralized leadership and was dominated by autonomous militant groups free to pursue their own agendas.

Moreover, leading anarchist spokespeople were missing a key point. Ravachol and others were indicative of a new phenomenon: "closet anarchists." The advent of dynamite in the late 1880s placed the means of mass destruction in the hands of lone individuals and small groups. It was relatively easy to manufacture and transport, earning the epithet "the poor man's weapon." More generally, anarchist theory celebrated the lone revolutionary as a hero willing to carry out "the deed." This mentality was certainly appealing to isolated and impoverished individuals like Ravachol. Workers alienated from society, stricken by poverty and with little to look forward to in their daily lives discovered a sense of purpose in anarchism. Was it impossible to think that their act might be the spark that would ignite a world revolution; that they might be the one to redeem mankind and lead him toward salvation? Under the circumstances, sacrificing oneself on the altar of anarchism amounted to a noble act. For lone actors, anarchism could and did translate into an expression of rage at perceived injustices and inequalities.

For common criminals, it justified petty crimes and even murder against social betters in the name of higher ideals.[79]

During the 1880s and 1890s, similar acts were perpetrated across European cities. In Spain, small extremists associations (*grupitos*) were organized to execute acts of terror against public officials and state institutions. These *attentat*-style tactics resulted in carnage in September 1893 when anarchists threw a bomb during an official military inspection in Barcelona, killing bystanders and injuring the Spanish General Martínez Campos, the intended target of the attack. A month later, a second bomb was tossed in the Barcelona Opera House during an evening performance of Rossini's *William Tell*, killing twenty-two and wounding fifty. The following February, French anarchist Émile Henry detonated a bomb at the popular Café Terminus located in the Gare Saint-Lazare in Paris, killing one person and wounding dozens. These acts of terror against civilians deeply shocked European public opinion. The targets had not been politicians, but ordinary people socializing in public places. A wave of panic ensued and state authorities responded with severe crackdowns on all leftist and militant organizations. Anarchist leaders had warned against the inevitable backlash that terrorism would bring, and during the 1890s their fears proved warranted. Anarchists increasingly became seen as nothing but "miscreants who are now aspiring to terrorize the world" as one journalist wrote in 1894; "the very dregs of the population."[80]

Public opinion was also galvanized by the ability of terrorist perpetrators to target high-level officials. In 1894, an Italian anarchist stabbed and killed the French President Sadi Carnot during a scheduled public appearance in Lyon. Three years later, a gunman posing as an Italian journalist shot and killed the Spanish Prime Minister Antonio

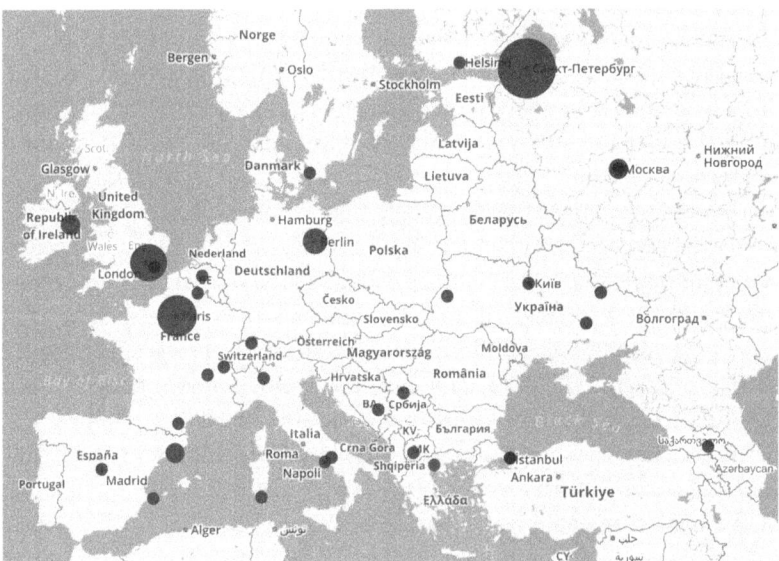

Map 9 Major acts of terrorism, 1856–1914. The size of the point indicates frequency of terrorist attempts.

Cánovas del Castillo while he was vacationing with his wife in the Basque Mountains. Anarchist assassins similarly claimed the lives of the Habsburg Empress Elisabeth and King Umberto I of Italy, and anarchist conspirators were implicated in two failed assassination attempts on the German Kaiser Wilhelm I. Between 1894 and 1916, six heads of states and various public officials would fall victim to the propaganda of the deed, among them the "great liberator" Tsar Alexander II.

Since the 1860s, Alexander had pushed through modernizing reforms that had abolished serfdom, reduced noble privilege and re-ordered various legal and governmental institutions in the empire. These reform packages had spurred young Russian populists into action, encouraging them to "go to the people" and develop the peasant socialism that *narodniks* believed natural to Russia. Student activism failed, however, to generate a mass movement while the rural peasantry proved reluctant to heed the guidance of urban elites dressed in peasant costume. By the 1870s, radicals expressed disillusion with their efforts to reform the people and were resentful of the autocracy's failure to make good on its promise of liberalization. In 1866, a radical associated with the Ishutin group fired on Tsar Alexander in the Summer Gardens, signaling a turn toward more extremist methods. The figure of the lone provocateur increasingly replaced grassroots organization as a means of affecting social change. Young radicals drafted revolutionary "catechism" preaching revolution and terror, giving rise to militants like Sergei Nechayev and his ilk.[81] Extremists and maximalists rhapsodized on the virtues of political violence to further social justice, rendering terror an integral part of the "moral economy" of Russian radicals.[82] In 1880, Nikolai Morozov outlined the new revolutionary movement at hand in a pamphlet with the provocative title "The Terrorist Struggle." Morozov's branding of combatants as "terrorists" (*terroristy*) was quite novel and suggested a method and ideology distinct from the more general "Terror" of the French Revolution.[83] It was also notable because Morozov belonged to *Narodnaia Volia* (The People's Will), an underground paramilitary organization committed to putting this form of "terrorism" into action.

The strategy of the *Narodnaia Volia* was simple: use assassinations and scare tactics to paralyze the autocracy and commence revolution. It was anarchism pure and simple, and in this respect secret radical organizations like *Narodnaia Volia* openly declared war on the imperial state. In March of 1881, Tsar Alexander was making a routine military inspection in Saint Petersburg when members of *Narodnaia Volia* threw a bomb into his carriage, blowing it to pieces. Alexander, his legs severed and his stomach disemboweled by the blast, was rushed to the Winter Palace. Two decades previous, he had signed the emancipation act in the very same building. Now the "great liberator" was receiving his last rites in it. Following the assassination, the new Tsar Alexander III ratcheted up state censorship and surveillance, engendering a war between the imperial bureaucracy and political extremists that would continue until the turn of the century.

This war on terror was one detail in a larger struggle between states and anarchist terrorism during the 1890s. In Spain, a special police unit—the *brigada social*—was created to investigate bombings and prosecute terrorists. Special laws passed in 1894 and 1896 permitted the government to disrupt anarchist activities and working-class organizations indiscriminately.[84] These actions were replicated and expanded upon elsewhere, in some cases compelling state authorities to create international policing agencies and cooperate with authorities abroad.[85] In November 1898, an international congress was convened in Rome by the European powers to address the anarchist threat, with proposals given for staunching the flow of anarchist periodicals and ending asylum for political prisoners that facilitated the creation of conspiratorial societies abroad. These cooperative efforts were largely unsuccessful, but it did not prevent states from pursuing independent measures to bolster internal security and insulate themselves from the "anarchist peril." Governments compiled registers of known anarchist suspects, preparing dossiers with biographic information, physical descriptions and profile photographs. Changes in state surveillance accompanied changes in immigration policy as well. In 1905, Britain, traditionally a haven for asylum seekers, passed the Aliens Act, which established a system of modern immigration control and facilitated extradition procedures for anarchist suspects.[86] Leftist organizations across the continent confronted severe laws that constrained their activities and subjected them to extralegal punishment. In meeting the challenges posed by the threat of international anarchist terror, authorities began to establish the architecture of a global security network that exists to this day.

The Making of an Anarchist Community

Beginning in the late 1870s, the anniversary of the Paris Commune became an annual celebration observed by partisans of the left. Leading radical figures gave speeches at these gatherings, expressing sympathy for oppressed workers and urging audiences to remember the communards. Revolutionary songs were sung and familiar slogans chanted. These fetes were staged in cities across the world as a testament to the international dimensions of radical liberation. The Commune became a collective symbol of the international left, a means of honoring fallen heroes and keeping the fight alive. Causes ranging from worker empowerment to feminism drew upon and perpetuated the symbols and rhetoric of radical internationalism, generating a "global radical movement" extending from Europe to the Middle East and Americas.[87] During the 1890s, the "red virgin" Louise Michel re-emerged as a spokeswoman for the international feminist movement by delivering speeches in France and England. After fighting in the Commune, Michel had been exiled to New Caledonia with other fellow communards. There, she had taken an interest in the plight of the native Canaque people and made connections between the colonized natives and the oppression of French workers.[88] This experience imparted a more global and universal scope to her radicalism. "The revolution is larger, it includes the world," she insisted in 1895; "it is not only against Caesars but against everything which limits the happiness of man."[89]

While the IWMA may have been suited for the task of directing a global radical movement, Marx and Engels abruptly moved to kill the organization in 1872. Weary of the ceaseless factionalism and infighting, Marx motioned to transfer the IWMA headquarters to New York, knowing quite well this decision would divide the organization and prompt its dissolution. The International limped on for another four years, but in the end Marx attained "the end of [his] slavery," as he put it.[90] By the 1870s, Anarchism was well-positioned to supplant the IWMA and brand itself as an "anti-authoritarian international." Bakuninists had successfully established branches in Spain and Italy, giving the socialist movements in these countries a patently anarchist character. Anarchism also had a flexible ideology sensitive to the particular circumstances found in proto-industrial countries. Unlike socialism, it was not exclusively oriented toward a skilled labor force. Its growing popularity among rural agitators gave it a broader appeal outside industrialized countries while migrant laborers—a growing portion of the global workforce by the late nineteenth century—espoused anarchist ideas and carried them across borders.[91] As the first transnational movement organized from below, anarchism progressed in tandem with the evolution of transnational labor migrations and global capitalism.[92]

Facing persecution and the threat of arrest at home, anarchist ideologues were equally mobile, and their peregrinations helped transform anarchism into a mass social movement with a global reach.[93] During the 1870s and 1880s, Italian anarchists left the peninsula and took up residence across Europe, the Americas and North Africa.[94] The internationalist Niccolò Converti fled Italy in 1887 to avoid imprisonment for his journalistic activities. Arriving in Tunisia, he founded the anarchist organ *L'Operaio*, which attracted an audience in both North Africa and southern Italy. Converti's experience was not unique. Fleeing Italy in 1878, Errico Malatesta went to Egypt where he would remain for the next five years. On the banks of the Nile, he discovered a thriving anarchist community directed by Italian migrant laborers and exiles. Political clubs in Alexandria discussed the latest international news while underground anarchist printers freely circulated newspapers in Cairo among the European population. By the turn of the century, Arab journalists were printing socialist articles and disseminating these ideas among a rising generation of Egyptian radicals and nationalists.[95] Departing Africa, Malatesta moved through Romania, Switzerland, France and England where he collaborated with anarchist exiles like himself. By the mid-1880s, he was busy setting up militant worker unions in Argentina.

The preoccupations of men like Converti and Malatesta revealed that Italian anarchism was a transnational movement spread through exile and diaspora.[96] Their activities challenged popular perceptions of Italian revolutionaries clinging to overly idealistic views of spontaneous uprising informed by earlier Carbonari and Mazzinist prescriptions. Failed uprisings and police pressure at home motivated anarchists to go abroad where they applied themselves to the hard work of political organization and journalism to mobilize supporters.[97] French, German, Belgian and Spanish radicals were no different.

England was a particularly popular destination for political refugees attempting to avoid capture. Some 3,500 people fled to England after the suppression of the Commune. This number increased as governments across Europe cracked down on radical organizations in the coming decades. French anarchists ran newspapers, participated in labor organizations and took jobs as language teachers, bakers and construction workers in London to make ends meet.[98] The London-based German Communist Workers' Education Society provided German socialists with a support network upon arrival, but it equally serviced French refugees and furnished an environment in which Poles, Russians, Italians, French and German radicals congregated.[99] Émigré socialization extended to organizing anarchist meetings, running mutual aid societies and publishing short-lived newspapers that were smuggled abroad when possible. The Rose Street Club in Soho and the Autonomie Club located on Charlotte Street were popular meeting places for London's polyglotic revolutionary community, but they were two among many. Clubs and meeting houses were an important aspect of exile life. Members and guests discussed politics, read newspapers and even put on plays and performances with anarchist themes. These extra-political activities played a key role not only in spreading anarchist ideas and forms of organization, but also in establishing a subculture and community shared among militants of different national backgrounds.[100]

By the 1880s, Paris sported a significant number of enclaves that nourished a strong anarchist culture through political clubs, cabaret performances and a host of popular newspapers. Between 1880 and 1900, approximately fifteen anarchist groups existed in the city comprising about 500 members in total. This relatively small membership belied, however, the extent and reach of anarchist influences in Europe's famed revolutionary capital.[101] Newspapers and print media circulated among the popular classes outside clubs and organizations. Jean Grave, a shoemaker and former communard, edited the newspaper *Le Révolté* from his headquarters in the Latin Quarter. With well-established connections to international anarchist luminaries like Elisée Reclus and Kropotkin, Grave commonly presented readers with the most up-to-date views on the anarchist movement and saw himself as a chief publicist for the cause both in France and abroad. His plain style of prose and use of colloquial speech attracted a broad international readership while his fiery rhetoric bristled with all the fury for which anarchists were becoming notorious.[102] Revolution, he informed readers, must bring about "a complete transformation of all social relations … a sweeping away of all present institutions."[103] Like many of his cohorts, Grave looked ahead to the coming storm, but he never abandoned his veneration for the French revolutionary tradition. Anarchism was interpreted as the logical extension of the great revolution, a movement heralding the completion of its lofty principles.[104]

Grave's network of friends and collaborators extended beyond the explicit world of politics to French artistic and literary circles. Grave's scandalous book *The Moribund Society and Anarchism* (1892) was prefaced by the writer and art critic Octave Mirbeau, a self-declared anarchist sympathizer. Critics like Mirbeau and Félix Fénéon championed movements such as neo-impressionism and social realism as veritable "anarchist" movements in their own rights. They linked rebellion against established art forms with the violence and search for social justice that anarchism embodied. In 1884, self-identified "anarchist" artists such as Paul Signac and Camille Pissarro joined together in the Société des Artistes Indépendants, a collective dedicated to aesthetic experimentation that would organize independent art exhibitions and put the principle of artist control into practice.¹⁰⁵ These efforts, harkening back to Courbet's Artist Federation during the Commune, celebrated the radical freedom promised by anarchism and inscribed it within the contexts of destabilizing aesthetic standards and artistic expression that fueled modernism and the avant-garde at the turn of the century.¹⁰⁶ The link between the arts and revolution was not lost on leading anarchist theorists either. Kropotkin readily urged artists and writers to apply their talents "in the service of the revolution." "The arts have a mission to accomplish for the achievement of the future society," he affirmed.¹⁰⁷

Anarchism was a cultural movement just as much as a political one.¹⁰⁸ This culture extended from elite to popular society, and in many instances had the potential to bridge the two. A common stock of myths, slogans, symbols and practices shaped an anarchist subculture shared by itinerant exiles and people coming from different national and social backgrounds. The press also played a critical role in broadcasting anarchist ideas and popularizing its heroes and martyrs to an international audience. In 1887, anarchists accused of detonating an explosive at Haymarket Square in Chicago during a labor protest were put on trial and hanged. Newspapers across the world carried stories of the trial and printed the defendants' impassioned speeches denouncing the state and all forms of social injustice. Portraits of the eight anarchist culprits were circulated in the press, depicting them as martyrs for the cause of universal freedom. Anarchists raised collections for the families of the martyrs while clubs across Europe organized public demonstrations of support, chanting slogans such as "Eternal praise to the Chicago martyrs! Love Live Anarchy! Long Live the Social Revolution!"¹⁰⁹ The event spurred an international day of recognition, with the first of May chosen by leftist organizations to commemorate victims of injustice and promote international solidarity.¹¹⁰ Commonly referred to as "May Day," International Workers' Day quickly became another commemorative ritual in the political culture of the global left.

Commemorations, newspapers, common practices of association and a shared corpus of works translated into multiple languages constituted the glue that bound the anarchist movement together across continents. These cultural forms helped create and sustain an imagined transnational community that reinforced ties between mobile revolutionaries across diverse centers of activity.¹¹¹ Even if the International had ceased to exist, anarchists continued to share in a common ideology and culture that transcended national borders, strengthening perceptions of a Universal Republic rooted in humanitarian and emancipatory values.

The Left and the Revolutionary Tradition Reconsidered

Celebrations of global fraternity and solidarity could not, however, expunge the persistent shadow of terror and political violence that lingered over anarchist politics. The brutal tactics directed against politicians and civilians alike put the left in a new situation. Socialists and labor organizers claiming to fight against injustice and inequality were compelled to denounce anarchist bombings as incompatible with their basic values. Terrorism proved counter-productive, as states began taking a harsher stance on all types of political organization, seeing worker protests and strikes as possible hotbeds of anarchist radicalism. As early as the 1880s, many leftists committed to improving labor conditions and achieving social equality were beginning to tone down their radical rhetoric. To save socialism and maintain it as a just cause required dissociating it from the anarchist rabble. It meant organizing workers, not blowing up buildings; pressing for incremental and tangible changes, not overthrowing society. In short, anarchist violence was pushing socialist leaders to reconsider their own tactics and objectives, generating support for "reformist," "legalitarian" and gradualist platforms.

Socialists subsequently organized respectable political parties that would seek to win votes and gain a voice in parliaments. Many of these leaders themselves were not necessarily factory workers, but journalists and politicians. While they still employed the rhetoric of class struggle and worker revolution, their actions were becoming less radical and more in tune with "bourgeois" parliamentary politics. Socialism was becoming a normalized political movement like any other, albeit one that spoke for workers and social reform. The social revolution would still come, they claimed, but in the distant future. In the meantime, it was better to work for practical goals at hand and improve the situation of workers who, as electoral reforms proceeded apace, were now becoming political constituents. To hardline radicals, this position was nothing short of a betrayal. However, it was difficult to argue with the results obtained by socialist moderates. In 1902, the historian and former republican Jean Jaurès assumed leadership of the French socialists. Elected to parliament, he assembled a strong collation under the *bloc des gauches* that was able to negotiate social legislation. The German Social Democratic Party was even more impressive. As a political party, it relied upon grassroots organization and trade union connections to become a leading party in the Reichstag. By 1912, it was the largest parliamentary party and achieved a variety of social and political reforms at the state level. While German socialists preached Marxist revolution, their actions were quite different: they organized social welfare programs for workers, sponsored adult education courses, opened libraries and had their own newspaper. Through these types of activities, they were able to command the loyalty of the German workers, making them an influential political presence in the German Reich.[112]

Even anarchist organizers saw the utility of distancing themselves from terrorist groups and directing their energies toward organization and collective action. Exiles in England had been impressed by the labor militancy of the late 1880s and the ability of trade union leaders to mobilize large shows of support. The Dock Strike of 1889 in which some 100,000 strikers took on employers and garnered national sympathy for their cause was commended by ideologues like Kropotkin and Malatesta and drew praise from radical newspapers like *Freedom*, *The Torch* and *The Tocsin* run by the French exile Charles Malato, who counseled his fellow anarchists to rethink their aversion to trade unions. "Enter them," he implored, "not so much to dissolve them but to transform them from top to bottom and raise an army of insurgents."[113]

French anarchists obliged. In 1895, French organizers formed the Confédération générale du travail (CGT), a labor federation focused on trade unionism. The CGT retained an anarchistic sentiment in its opposition to the state and its commitment to revolutionary liberation. However, its methods derived from trade union organization. Social theorists like Georges Sorel criticized revolutionary violence and the Jacobin tradition, arguing that one could not simply "liquidate the present order" through hasty methods and revolutionary tribunals.[114] Sorel gave this rejection of revolutionary violence and dictatorship a new term: *syndicalisme*. Syndicalism preached collective labor action, not lone adventurism. Rather than the propaganda of the deed, syndicalism saw the general strike as the most effective means of overthrowing capitalism and challenging the state. It proposed direct worker control and the re-organization of society around the structures of unions and labor councils, adhering to an anti-authoritarian platform that replaced the commune with the trade union. Syndicalists did not align themselves with the reform-minded socialists who collaborated with the government. They did, however, seek to organize labor with the goal of effecting revolutionary change. The strike was the means to this end. If controversies over "propaganda of the idea" and "propaganda of the deed" had divided anarchist circles of the 1880s and 1890s, syndicalism offered an alternative tactic and rhetoric that were anarchist in spirit and focused on positive social change through collective organization. By 1900, organizations like the CGT and the Federation of Workers in Spain were on the ascent and imparted a new radicalism to organized labor.[115]

It was evident that the left was in a period of transition. "Nowadays Parliamentary Socialists no longer entertain the idea of insurrection," Sorel claimed. "If they still occasionally speak of it, it is merely to give themselves airs of importance; they teach that the ballot-box has replaced the gun." Eschewing Jacobin-style revolutionary dictatorship as a means of viable social change, Sorel and his followers sought to outline a third way between the old revolutionary tradition and the moderate socialism and "middle-class cowardice" of parliamentarians.[116] This approach raised questions regarding the cult of violence and the very methods and ideologies central to European radicalism since 1789. The rhetoric and practices of radical movements were changing. The revolutionary script was undergoing a process of revision and re-evaluation.

On January 22, 1905, a crowd gathered at the Levallois-Perret Cemetery in Paris to pay their last respects to Louise Michel. The legendary "red virgin" of the Commune, Michel had been an icon of the radical left throughout the last quarter of the nineteenth century, and her funeral was certain to serve as a moment to commemorate the communard cause and by extension the revolutionary tradition itself. Although all the major left newspapers carried her obituary and those in attendance gave moving speeches, references to the Paris Commune and its legacy were noticeably muted. The socialist organ *L'Humanité* remarked tepidly on the importance of the Commune as "a period of transition between the era of traditional and classic revolution and the current era of social transformation." Others extolled the heroism of the communards. Yet many were hesitant to illustrate or draw out any concrete lessons that the experience of the Commune held for the current situation. If the Commune's symbolic importance was recognized, speakers nonetheless appeared to agree that it belonged to a former era and could not serve as a blueprint for the future. In a period when workers were forming their own political parties and labor organizers were pursuing legal avenues of opposition and reformist platforms, French critics were reluctant to revive the bloody memories of the Commune as a model of action.[117]

The French left was seemingly losing its appetite for revolution. By the turn of the century, the French Revolution was undergoing a process of "demystification" as leftist critics and intellectuals attempted to shape new forms of political engagement through party affiliations and strikes. They found it essential to distance themselves from the old revolutionary tradition and decenter the French Revolution as the common historical reference point of the left.[118] Coincidentally, the same day Michel was interred, workers in Russia began staging protests and defying state authority, portending a general political crisis for the tsarist autocracy. Such contrasts were certainly a telling sign of the times.

Conclusion

Writing toward the end of his life, Bakunin gave what might arguably be considered a succinct declaration of his radical political philosophy. "Revolution requires extensive and widespread destruction, a fecund and renovating destruction, since in this way, and only in this way, are new worlds born."[119] Bakunin came of age in a period where memories of the French Revolution continued to exercise a powerful influence over generations of radical thinkers and romantics. Yet by his death, the centrality of the French Revolution as a model was being eclipsed by more recent events and concerns. Bakunin himself had a part to play in this development. Political violence had been a staple of the revolutionary tradition since its origins. The wave of anarchist terror that consumed fin-de-siècle Europe was, however, unique and cast radical political practices in a new light. Anarchist terror was motivated by personal initiative just as much as concerted effort. Men like Vaillant and Ravachol were the face of a powerful idea capable of inspiring isolated individuals to act out the "propaganda of the deed." This phenomenon was distinct from the state-directed violence employed by the Jacobins, distinguishing revolutionary terror from the isolated radicalized "terrorists" who disrupted daily life and wreaked havoc on civilians.

Anarchist theorists attempted to distance themselves from such demonstrative violence, emphasizing anarchy's value as a political philosophy of activism and self-liberation. It was, as Kropotkin claimed, "more than a mere mode of action or a mere conception of freed society."[120] This, after all, was the shortcoming of Marxism, with its speculative theories and dialectical principles. Anarchy was a living idea based upon actual social principles. "Anarchy is no longer a utopia," insisted Kropotkin; "it is a philosophy which impresses itself on our age."[121]

This living philosophy was, ultimately, found in the social organization of communal life. "We recognize that in associating their efforts individuals will increase their well-being and develop their autonomy," explained Jean Grave in 1893. "We are therefore partisans of association."[122] At its core, anarchy proposed a novel idea of community rooted in localized forms of political, social and cultural autonomy. Yet this emphasis on local engagement and organization was never construed in a parochial sense.

"Never will we separate ourselves from the world to build a little chapel hidden off in some vast darkness," contended Elisée Reclus.[123] Anarchism remained committed to social revolution on a large scale, envisaging a world liberated from oppressive state structures and connected through common practices of self-management and mutual independence. These dual themes of the local and the global were key ideological components that constructed and sustained a transnational anarchist community during the late nineteenth and early twentieth centuries.

Taking courage from the experience of the 1871 Commune, radicals departed from the neo-Jacobin model of revolution and embraced currents of internationalism, collective ownership and decentralized power that would play a vital role in the leftist programs of the fin de siècle. And yet the devolved nature of the anarchist movement presented one of the most formidable challenges for militants. As individuals waged campaigns of terror in the name of anarchist principles, theorists were powerless to reprimand such acts as incorrect or heretical. Anarchists were bound by a vague set of principles that lacked a manifesto or central doctrine. Theorists could pronounce on the "propaganda of the deed," but they could not prevent others from interpreting this to include bombings, robbery and murder. The line between propaganda of the deed and terrorism perennially remained ill-defined and left a tainted legacy of violence and destruction that became increasingly difficult to reconcile with humanitarian and emancipatory values. In the end, anarchism came to occupy an ambivalent place in the politics of the left even as it awakened what Kropotkin deemed "the spirit of revolt" in those who dreamed of a new and liberated world.

CHAPTER 9
THE REVIVAL AND FAILURE OF REVOLUTIONARY CONSTITUTIONALISM: THE RUSSIAN AND OTTOMAN EMPIRES (1905–1914)

"It makes me sick to read the news!" wrote Tsar Nicholas II in October 1905. "Nothing but new strikes in schools and factories, murdered policemen, Cossacks and soldiers, riots, disorder, mutinies."[1] He was not exaggerating. Since the start of the year, Russia had been engulfed in a series of protests and pitched street battles that brought the empire to its knees. Across Russia, protestors called for a constitution and civil liberties. They spoke in the name of "the people" and made appeals to workers and democrats tired of the ineffective and oppressive tsarist autocracy. The various demonstrations and strikes revealed that the left had entered the age of mass politics. In this frenzied atmosphere, Marxists, democrats and nationalists all competed for loyalties and support. Above all, however, the salient cry resounding throughout Russia that year was for rights and representative government. A renewed age of constitutional revolution was being born.

Unlike the anarchist underground, constitutionalists did not seek the complete overthrow of society. On the contrary, they adhered to a program of political reform and changes to existing political structures. Although reform was intended to transform the locus of sovereignty and state power, it was not, in theory, interpreted as a radical break with the past.[2] Many activists looked back to the French Revolution with its demands for liberty and equality while minimalizing the role that terror and political violence had played in these.[3] In their support for political rights and responsible government, revolutionaries acknowledged the need for popular support and placed their faith in the broad attraction of such principles. As protests brought established models of sovereignty into question, revolutions opened up a new public space in which ideas of liberty and citizenship could be actualized. Even those who continued to stress conspiracy and top-down revolutionary tactics came to appreciate the importance of mass mobilization in the revolutionary process.

Geography also played a role in this latest revolutionary wave. Constitutional movements gained momentum in states on the European periphery undergoing economic and bureaucratic modernization. In Russia and the Ottoman Empire, absolutist regimes were developing industries and building state institutions similar to those found in Western Europe. Yet these modernizing initiatives were never intended to increase political freedoms or diminish personal power. If anything, they aimed to strengthen the power of the state. These objectives were, however, complicated by the fact neither Russia nor the Ottoman Empire were "nations" in any meaningful sense.

Revolutionary Europe

They were multiethnic empires that resisted unitary state and legal structures. This feature gave constitutional demands a particular character. Liberals and democrats opposed to absolutist rule saw constitutionalism as a way of diluting royal power, but they also understood that principles of common rights and citizenship could serve to bind together populations that had traditionally been separated and unaccustomed to thinking of themselves in national terms. As modernizing policies generated new social and political cleavages, revolutionary reformers became all the more convinced of the need for greater social cohesion. Constitutional revolution held out the prospect of imagining new concepts of sovereignty that sustained and hypostasized the idea of a unified body politic and people.

These goals were most pronounced among circles of political exiles that made their way to Europe. On the continent, democrats found the necessary freedoms to publish newspapers and vocalize their discontent with absolutist regimes reluctant to cede power. Young Turks, Russian Marxists and radical liberals built movements abroad, using the press and political networks to retain contact with their native countries. Life abroad also introduced exiles to new ideas as elites adapted their own platforms to evolving European and global models of revolution and resistance. This creativity and cross-fertilization gave the constitutionalist movements of the early twentieth century a measure of consistency despite their divergent aims and aspirations. As modernizing policies disrupted traditional social structures and power arrangements, elites in Russia, the Ottoman Empire and elsewhere came to believe in the transformative potential of revolutions grounded in basic principles and empowered through mass support. These efforts, they assured, would not only bring their respective societies into the "modern age." They would create a single, unified "people" from the detritus of benighted empires out of touch with the currents of modernity.

Tradition and Change in the Russian Empire

Russia was distinct from other European powers politically, socially and culturally. Whereas even the absolutist regimes in Central and Northern Europe had quasi-parliamentary systems, Russia was an autocracy. The tsar was the unquestionable sovereign authority who alone enacted laws and personally selected ministers to carry out his will. Autocratic ideologues legitimated this system of rule by invoking the tsar's paternal relationship with the people and his scared character. As head of the Orthodox Church, the sovereign was the guardian of "true Christianity" who, much like a suffering Christ, took upon himself the burdens of humanity.[4]

Given this strong link between church and state, Orthodoxy was integral to Russian identity. Yet social distinction was equally mapped according to a rigid hierarchy of orders (*soslóviia*). One's *soslóvie* indicated whether they were a noble, a clergy member or a peasant, with certain laws and privileges pertaining to each group. Until the 1860s, the peasants were bound to the aristocracy as serfs, providing cheap and exploitable labor. The result was that Russia's economy remained predominantly agrarian in a period of economic industrialization.⁵ *Soslóviia* also made distinctions based upon religious and ethnic identification, with the category of *inoródtsy* demarcating non-Christian subjects living within the imperial territory. Herein was another aspect of Russian uniqueness when compared with Western Europe. Stretching from Poland and the Ukraine to the Pacific coast, Russia was a vast multiethnic and multiconfessional empire populated by Slavs, Germans, Turkic populations, Caucasians, nomadic tribes and Asiatic peoples.⁶ In an age when the nation-state was becoming a symbol of political modernity and progress, Russia was a baroque imperial mosaic. "No other state on earth contains such a variety of inhabitants," wrote the ethnographer Heinrich Storch in 1797.⁷

Over the course of the eighteenth and nineteenth centuries, various efforts were undertaken to assimilate and consolidate the sprawling tsarist domain. In an attempt to "Russify" the administration, Catherine the Great had created a system of provincial governorates that would pave the way for the "enlightened" bureaucratic state.⁸ Yet these policies never resulted in the rational and uniform structures the government desired. By the late nineteenth century, Turkestan resembled a colony with a native administration and settler community similar to British India or French Algeria.⁹ Colonial policies and fears of ethnic separatism spurred a change toward cultural russification obliging schools and local governments to adopt the Russian language. Yet attempts to impose Russian culture provoked the inevitable pushback and served to politicize ethnic minorities, further exacerbating the situation.¹⁰ Outside of dynastic identification, there existed no strong sense of cohesion or community binding the empire. It remained disjointed and plagued by confusing administrative structures that often proved ineffective when it came to collecting taxes or enforcing law. Centrally appointed governors ruled over populations they hardly knew and saw as alien. As Prince Lvov, a local official in Tula remarked in the 1890s, "We know as much about the Tula countryside as we know about Central Africa."¹¹

For a minority of "enlightened" nobles, Russia's perceived backwardness was an obstacle to overcome.¹² They welcomed Alexander II's reforms of the 1860s, which abolished feudalism and established the groundwork for greater liberalization. The Zemstvo Statute of 1864 was in many ways a signature piece of this reform package. The act created elected provincial assemblies (*zemstva*) in most imperial districts. Reformers saw the zemstva as a vehicle for local self-governance and integration. The state, on the other hand, was guided by more practical considerations. The feudal system had to be replaced, and the imperial bureaucracy severely lacked the resources to administer such a vast empire on its own. Zemstva were charged with a variety of responsibilities, including maintaining roads, overseeing prisons, providing public services and running agricultural advisory boards. The problem with this plan was that the local assemblies had little control over taxation and few means of enforcing their policies. Reform amounted to empire on the cheap, with the costs and burdens of administration now delegated to the localities. Assemblies were typically dominated by the provincial nobility, the customary ally of the autocracy. As such, they were designed to reinforce the traditional power base of the autocracy in the countryside in addition to providing an administrative structure for post-emancipation Russia.¹³

Even with these strictures in place, the autocracy persisted to see the zemstva as a potential rival. In 1890, Alexander III set up a provincial bureau with the power to veto zemstvo appointments and constrain their budgetary powers. Governors were given significantly more influence over peasant judicial proceedings and elected village officials. These measures aimed to ensure that local spending and decision making remained in the hands of the nobility and that radical ideas did not permeate the lower levels of administration. Aspirations of integrating the provinces through local politics were given short shrift, demonstrating the autocracy's patent reluctance to carry through on the promise of reform as it attempted to preserve personal power and the old system of imperial rule.[14]

Despite such obstruction, the zemstvo reform did produce a substantial change in the autocratic structure. It opened new possibilities for engagement at the regional and municipal levels that had not previously existed. Teams of trained personnel were needed to run schools, supervise agricultural policies and administer populations. Progressive nobles committed to economic change saw opportunities in local autonomy, but so too did a generation of university-educated professionals inspired by desires to improve local institutions and transform rural life. The zemstva became magnets for civic and reform-minded individuals. So-called *"zemsty"* spearheaded various professional and public programs such as local medical and literary societies established to benefit the community. At a fundamental level, the *zemsty* regarded the aristocratic bureaucrats of the tsarist state with suspicion and saw themselves as true servants of the *narod* and the community. They were guided by a conception of a modern civic society composed of active citizens (*obschestvennost'*) which stood in stark contrast to the hierarchical and segregated society of noble privilege (*soslovnost'*). As one historian has remarked, this new "third element" of Russian society standing between the nobility and peasantry amounted to a "Russian variant of a middle class."[15]

Yet while reform empowered some groups, others continued to suffer as they had under the old system. Reformers contended that the abolition of serfdom would create a free and self-sufficient peasantry, but the realities of post-emancipation society were far from the ideal. Legal requirements forcing peasants to payback the state for their emancipation left most rural landholders deeply in debt. Systemic decline in agricultural prices across Europe during the 1870s and 1880s saw a reduction in rural incomes while population growth in the countryside diminished peasant landholding and created a surplus of agricultural labor in need of work. Many peasants remained subject to the provincial nobility despite the end of feudalism. Redemption payments left them dependent upon their former lords, who often controlled the local courts and institutions in their vicinity. Serfdom had an afterlife in which the local nobility continued to wield its coercive power over impoverished rural communities.[16]

In 1891, the dire situation in the provinces was brought to national attention when famine broke out across the arc of territory extending from the Black Earth region to the Black Sea. Epidemics of typhus and cholera followed, compounding the misery. The imperial bureaucracy struggled to manage the catastrophe, eliciting an energetic response from *zemsty* who coordinated relief efforts, took up public subscriptions and organized aid networks. Where the tsarist regime proved inadequate, a bourgeoning civil society filled the gap. More to the point, the intelligentsia expressed outrage at the government's seeming incompetence, entailing that the public efforts organized by the *zemsty* both activated Russian society and politicized it.[17]

What appeared a petrified political order on the surface was not, however, necessarily a completely stagnant one. Although four-fifths of the empire's population was rural, the state had begun taking an active role in developing industry. By mid-century, the Baltic provinces possessed modern ports and industrial centers. Cities like Saint Petersburg and Moscow had growing industrial sectors and the state was boosting mineral extraction in Ukraine and petroleum production in Transcaucasia. During the 1890s, the ambitious finance minister Sergei Witte outlined a state-sponsored modernization program with the intention of expanding the empire's rail infrastructure and encouraging foreign investment. Witte was conscious of the economic shortfalls afflicting the empire. Under his stewardship rapid industrialization became the objective and foreign capital the means to fulling it. In 1890, Russia had a little over 30,000 kilometers of rail track. By the end of the decade, this number had virtually doubled and work on the Trans-Siberian Railroad was well underway. Coal output in southern Russia jumped during these same years as did the production of steel and iron. The state participated directly in many of these endeavors, running most of the rail lines and owning a majority of the oilfields, mines and forest lands. By 1900, state industrial holdings accounted for nearly 25 percent of the government's annual income. At this same time, some 2.5 million people were employed in mining and industrial manufacturing, with another 500,000 employed in transportation. This impressive growth was, however, relative. The entire population of the empire stood at 129 million while less than 13 percent of the Russian population lived in urban areas. Russia's industrial labor force was a small minority when compared with the vast agrarian countryside populated by peasant farmers.[18]

Nonetheless, an industrial labor force was emerging, and rapid industrialization resulted in the labor conflicts familiar to Europe. Low wages, unsanitary conditions and poor living standards were common features of the worker experience. Peasants driven by rural poverty migrated to cities in search of factory work, creating overcrowding and slum-like neighborhoods in urban areas. In 1885, Russia got its first taste of worker discontent when widespread strikes broke out in Moscow. These disturbances were soon followed by others. In 1897, 30,000 workers employed in the cotton and spinning industry collectively walked out of their mills in a demonstration of trade solidarity. For the government, labor agitation posed a very real threat to stability. Also concerning was the fact that industrial workers were taking up radical ideas. With labor organizations and unions deemed illegal, labor groups had few channels through which to express their grievances and found common accord with underground revolutionaries. It was not unthinkable that migrant workers would return to their villages when their seasonal contracts expired and bring with them the radicalism they had been exposed to in the cities.[19]

On the whole, the government was sympathetic to plant and factory managers. The profits that came from private enterprise were central to the state's plan of fast-paced industrialization. The fact that roughly 40 percent of Russian industry was financed by foreign shareholders also influenced policy. If wages increased, foreign investors would simply move their businesses elsewhere. Cheap labor coming from the countryside was one of the primary attractions of investment. The government permitted entrepreneurs to make higher profits through exploitative practices and typically sided with employers. Authorities were not reluctant to use the army to suppress protests. A special police force was even created to monitor plants and keep a watchful eye on the more rowdy elements of the working classes.[20]

This is not to imply that urban workers were a socially homogenous group. Peasants from different regions retained their localism and typically congregated with other migrants from their home villages. There were also variations in the conditions of employment across trades and industrial sectors. Laborers could and did find a sense of identity through shared experiences and social interactions with fellow workers in their crafts. They defined themselves in opposition to their employers and plant managers, but also through their relationships to other workers and trades. In appealing to workers as a unified proletariat, radicals were going to have to find means of transforming this mixed and heterogeneous labor force into a unified social group through labor activism and political propaganda.[21]

The diversity found among workers was indicative of Russia's changing social landscape by the turn of the century. While institutions continued to reflect the former feudal hierarchies with their well-defined orders and estates, these categories were beginning to seem outmoded. They did not reflect the changes wrought by a mobile and industrialized labor force. Nor did they correspond to the emergent intelligentsia of provincial capitals participating in local assemblies and organizing civic associations.[22] In a broader context, the Russian Empire was a composite of varying interests and policies. In turn, it resembled a dynastic empire, a colonial regime and a nationalizing state. These competing polities were a reflection of Russia's historical development but also revealed deep fault lines running through the entire imperial edifice. What constituted the Russian community was never clear. As the tsarist government committed itself to rapid modernization in the image of the West, however, these tensions came into sharp relief and exposed the precarious position of the imperial autocracy.

The Genesis of Russian Marxism

With labor exhibiting its radical stripes, the Russian intelligentsia abandoned hopes of a peasant-led insurrection. In the closing decades of the century, certain theorists professed that it was the workers who were the true revolutionary force of the future. It was this precise subject which prompted the populist Vera Zasulich to write to Marx in 1881 regarding the potential of social democracy in Russia.[23] Zasulich was among a small number of Russian émigrés in Switzerland slowly coming to espouse a Marxist position. Socializing with notable German Social Democrats in Geneva and Zurich, exiles formed the first Russian Marxist group in 1883, Liberty of Labor. The group was headed by Georgi Plekhanov, a former populist-turned Marxist who could not abide the terrorist tactics of underground revolutionaries. Populists, he charged, refused to acknowledge the impact of Russian industrialization and persisted to cling to notions of peasant socialism that appeared out of touch with current realities. For him, it was the Russian proletariat—a concept that he developed and popularized in his writings—that would be the true revolutionary agent.[24] Plekhanov summed up his views succinctly in 1889, telling an international gathering of socialists: "The Russian revolution will either succeed as a workers' revolution or it will not succeed at all."[25]

For all their confidence, however, Russian Marxists had to admit that Russia appeared an odd choice for a Marxist-style proletarian revolution. Marxism rested upon a belief in material laws of historical development. It posited that societies moved through stages and that these stages were fundamental to the proper "consciousness" that drove revolt. With a nonexistent bourgeoisie and an underdeveloped industrial economy, Russia hardly fit the Marxist mold. Exiles emphasized, therefore, the need for a preliminary "bourgeois" revolution that would pave the way for Russian socialism. Plekhanov even insisted that workers should assist the advent of capitalism and aid their class enemies in securing bourgeois democracy. These ideological contortions naturally raised a number of questions. How were workers to relate to the mass of Russian peasants? Should workers collaborate with their natural class enemies? How much time was to pass before the first and second revolution? These and other matters frustrated Russian Marxists to no end, but they were not necessarily divorced from broader questions troubling Marxist ideologues or the wider context of European socialism at the end of the nineteenth century.[26]

Marxists relied on a set of canonical texts like the *Communist Manifesto* and the writings of Engels to hash out these issues, but they especially looked to the rising Social Democratic Party (SPD) in Germany as a source of inspiration. Marx and Engels had speculated that an independent worker party would bring about the merger of socialism with the labor movement, leading workers to the end goal of socialism. It was through this schema that workers would "conquer political power," as Marx had it.[27] During the 1890s, the SPD appeared the epitome of just such a worker party. Its organization and prominence were unmatched across Europe, and its efforts at mobilizing workers and sustaining the movement in exile made it a model to emulate.[28] The SPD was not only active in political agitation and parliamentary politics. It was also committed to forging a proletarian consciousness among German workers. Its various activities, ranging from newspaper printing to organizing cultural events, created a veritable "alternative culture" that was consciously attempting to bring forth the merger of socialist leadership with grassroots organization prophesized by Marx.[29] This active, party-led approach fed upon the political freedoms and liberties that "bourgeois" democracy afforded, entailing that the Marxist political strategy could only thrive in a liberal-capitalist society. It was unsurprising therefore that thinkers like Plekhanov supported the struggle for political freedom and insisted that social emancipation necessitated bourgeois liberty. For Russian intellectuals of the 1890s, the SPD, with its robust press, public meetings and well-oiled party machinery was the model *par excellence* of a Marxist party.[30]

This was true of the Liberty of Labor group as it was of other activists gravitating toward Marxism at this time. In 1898, the Russian Social Democratic Labor Party (RSDLP) was formed among émigré intellectuals in Germany and Switzerland. It attracted younger Marxist ideologues such as Julius Martov and the firebrand Vladimir Illyich Ulyanov, who soon adopted the name Lenin. Yet for all its hope of becoming a mass worker party, the RSDLP remained a clandestine circle of exiles with few connections to the workers. Headstrong and convinced of the correctness of their views, the various members quickly divided over key issues. Plekhanov steadfastly retained his Marxist orthodoxy, warning against the threat posed by reformist socialists who he branded "Economists." Others grappled with questions of allying with class enemies and the role of the peasants in the coming revolution, both of which encouraged abstract theorizing on the nature of proletarian revolt. For their part, Russian workers expressed interest in the RSDLP, although they were cold to the idea of local branches being dominated by intellectuals or the thought of obeying leaders abroad.[31]

Social Democrats (SDs) did have cause for optimism, however. The creation of the party corresponded with a wave of mass strikes and labor disturbances throughout Russia that bolstered radical projections of an imminent revolutionary upheaval. Yet these disturbances also brought to light further problems with which SDs would have to contend. By 1900, a populist revival was in full bloom led by the radical journalist Viktor Chernov. So-called Socialist Revolutionaries (SRs) modified the former *narodnik* platform, blending it with Marxist ideas of class struggle. Chernov urged workers and peasants—the "toiling people"—to unite for the purposes of obstructing capitalism and overthrowing the autocracy. These views found support in the countryside where SRs backed land reform and politicized the nagging "agrarian question," although the party's terrorist tactics and brash politics also attracted urban workers. Beginning in 1901, a series of violent attacks on government and public officials carried out by the SR "Combat Organization" brought the party to public notoriety, announcing a potential rival revolutionary faction that threatened to divide worker loyalties.[32]

Equally disturbing was the rise of national tensions creeping into labor unrest. Poland was a particular hotbed of strikes and agitation, with the city of Łódź popularly referred to as the "Polish Manchester." The recently formed Polish Socialist Party (PPS) had put national independence at the forefront of its program, refusing to collaborate with the RSDLP unless it recognized Polish national sovereignty and the right of the PPS to conduct all revolutionary activity on Polish soil. In Latvia, Georgia, the Ukraine and Azerbaijan, nationalist politics similarly fused with labor disturbances, setting a precedent that threatened to fragment the nascent SD movement. Noting the mobilizing potential of nationalism, Martov initially encouraged it as a means of spurring worker opposition against the state. In 1895, he advised Jewish workers to form their own party, insisting, "The growth of national and class consciousness must go hand in hand."[33] Two years later, Samuel Gozhanskii and Aaron Kremer took a leading role in creating the Bund, a party designed explicitly for Jewish Social Democrats in the western borderland. The Bund had its own official organ printed in Yiddish (*Der Arbeter Shtimme*) and an impressive network that stretched across cities like Vilna and Minks into the Polish territories. Its leaders accented Jewish cultural identity to compete with Zionism and provided Jews with a sense of cohesion and belonging rooted in distinct ideas of Jewish enlightenment and social life. When the RSDLP formed in 1898, the Bund joined the party as an autonomous entity.[34] Whether the RSDLP leadership liked it or not, it would have to confront the nationality question, and to this end the party manifesto drawn up in 1898 supported national self-determination as one of its chief goals.

Taking account of this situation, a core group of SDs, among them Lenin and Martov, felt the party was losing its cohesion. A former law student from Samara whose brother had been executed for seditious activity against the government, Lenin was by this time a devoted Marxist and political activist. In the early 1890s, he had organized Marxist circles in Saint Petersburg with the goal of forming a Social Democratic party in Russia comparable to the SPD. His political activities led to arrest and exile, and during his time abroad he joined with other émigré circles aspiring to direct a worker movement from Germany and Switzerland. Convinced of the need for greater organization and tactical deployment, Lenin and Martov established the newspaper *Iskra* (the Spark) with the assistance of the German SDs. The paper aimed to promote a comprehensive party program and defend social democracy from its critics.[35] As Lenin saw it, the RSDLP was losing ground to "the rubbish of populism and agrarianism."[36] Russian SDs had to augment their organizational strength. They had to build up a party structure and clearly define their mission in order to serve the worker movement.

Yet if Lenin desired to replicate the success of the SPD in Russia, the chances of achieving this goal were minimal. Building a mass national worker party was a fantasy in Russia's oppressive and illiberal political environment. In 1902, therefore, Lenin laid out a program of action in his pamphlet entitled *What Is to Be Done?*, a deliberate reference to Chernyshevsky's 1863 novel of the same name. Issues of organization and revolutionary activism were placed front and center, with Lenin regretting that "when we talk about organization, we literally talk in different tongues." He concluded that party structure was essential, lest the worker movement remain focused on battles over wages and working conditions. "Trade-union consciousness," which would only benefit the bourgeoisie, had to be combatted. To do so required a cadre of party leaders explicitly committed to revolutionary activity and agitation. As Lenin explained, "the struggle against the *political* police requires special qualities; it requires *professional* revolutionaries."[37] Under the tsarist autocracy, a mass party like the SPD had no chance of survival. It therefore fell to a small group of militant revolutionaries to ensure that the worker movement could in fact thrive underground and create the conditions for socialism.[38] Trade unionism alone would not achieve these ends. "Socialist consciousness cannot exist among the workers," Lenin argued. "This can be introduced only from without."[39]

Nothing in what Lenin proposed significantly deviated from Marxist principles or prevailing ideas of the party's world-historical "mission" in the march toward socialism. Yet at a time when many Marxist ideologues were calling for patience and urging followers to allow "objective" factors to take their natural course, Lenin suggested that willed action and "subjective" factors could accelerate the forces of history.[40] His call for revolutionary activism and "professional" revolutionaries restored Marxism to a revolutionary position.⁴¹ Lenin's emphasis on party organization and combatting fissiparous influences reflected the position of the RSDLP as it struggled against the autocracy. Centralized control, discipline and finely tuned organizational tactics: these were the essential needs of a party operating underground and constantly at war with the state. Mass democracy was to be replaced temporarily with a style of organization that Lenin would soon define as "democratic centralism."

The implications of Lenin's program would become clear the following year when the leadership convoked the second party congress to vote on a uniform party platform and iron out evident differences. Meeting in Brussels and London that summer, the RSDLP quickly divided over issues of party membership and questions of who would officially speak for the party. Demands for party centralization alienated groups like the Bund, who summarily walked out of the congress. However, the *Iskra* group was likewise divided. In a reversal, Martov refused to endorse Lenin's program and scoffed at his attempt to sideline opponents sitting on the *Iskra* editorial board. He placed his faith in a broad mass party, and Lenin's insistence on a strictly proletarian party seemed to preclude any hope of widening the party base. Lenin even found himself at odds with Plekhanov, whose insistence on a two-stage revolution clashed with Lenin's belief in nurturing labor militancy and fighting against capitalism. Each side attempted to mobilize support within the party, but in the end Lenin's position passed by a slim majority, earning Lenin and his supporters the title of Bolsheviks (the majority). Consequently, Martov and others assumed the position of a minority (Mensheviks). If the second congress had planned to unify the party, it had drastically backfired. The meeting engendered a schism that would remain central to the RSDLP for the remainder of its life.⁴²

The rift was by no means unbridgeable. Bolsheviks and Mensheviks continued to expound their positions within a common Marxist framework and the factions exhibited a fair amount of interdependence after 1903.⁴³ Yet the immediate fallout left its mark. Menshevik opponents did not hesitate to criticize Lenin's overbearing nature and desires for complete control over the party. In a private letter, Plekhanov readily compared Lenin to Robespierre. Pavel Axelrod, a founder of the Liberty of Labor group in the 1880s, was more assertive in his attacks. In the pages of *Iskra*, he blatantly compared the Bolsheviks to a "Jacobin Club" and warned of an impending dictatorship that would stifle all dissenting voices within the party.⁴⁴ These invectives "invented" what until then had not existed: a Russian Jacobin identity. It helped that Lenin himself espoused the label affixed to him by his enemies. "A Jacobin who is inseparably linked to the organized class-conscious proletariat *is* a revolutionary social democrat," he shot back defiantly.⁴⁵ If he was to be branded a Jacobin, then the Mensheviks were nothing more than perfidious Girondins.

New political identities sprang forth as each faction attempted to speak for the party. Yet oddly these divisions did not drastically hamper the party's expansion at the turn of the century. Local party committees were set up in Russia, Ukraine and the Caucasus. Committee leaders printed up the latest editions of *Iskra* and disseminated them to workers. They organized factory cells and oversaw recruitment in their jurisdictions. Although committees exhibited a great deal of regional variation and local leaders often pursued their own agendas in contravention of Lenin's expressed demand for party discipline, the RSDLP did make inroads within European Russia and the periphery. Much like the Jacobins of the early 1790s, the SDs built a party network with the potential to mobilize supporters. And as Lenin envisaged, it was a party capable of working in the shadows of an oppressive autocratic state.

An Ambiguous Revolution

The splintering and factionalism that divided the RSDLP were broadly symptomatic of Russian society in the late nineteenth century. Tsarist officials agonized over pernicious centrifugal forces just as much as conspirators. They grappled with problems of administrative integration, imperial assimilation and economic development, believing that modernization was the perceived antidote to the chronic difficulties facing the empire. Yet the tsar who took the throne in 1894, Nicholas II, was a conservative with a profound appreciation for tradition and Russia's autocratic heritage. Economic modernization proceeded apace, but existing social and political institutions remained unaltered. Industrialization fueled the nascent socialist movement, but it simultaneously gave rise to liberal groups demanding political reform and social change.[46] These competing and overlapping movements challenged the autocracy on numerous fronts but exposed the difficulties associated with forging a united opposition to the autocracy.

Liberals founded the loose-knit coalition Union of Liberation in 1903. While it sprang from the *zemsty* activists of the 1890s, its orientation was noticeably more left-leaning. The Union's program spoke of social and political reform, self-determination for imperial nationalities and appeals to social unity in the name of constitutional democracy. Constitutionalism became the watchword for Russian liberals. They sought a political program that could transcend the constraining factors of class and ethnicity and represent the Russian *narod* in all its diversity. Universal suffrage and rule of law were principles that every imperial subject could rally behind, or so it was believed at least.[47] Between 1904 and 1905, liberals were given a chance to test this premise.

In 1904, the tsarist government became embroiled in a war with Japan over claims to Manchuria. What was initially assumed to be a quick and easy military operation became a protracted and humiliating defeat for the Russian government that seemingly validated charges of government incompetence. At this critical moment, the SR Combat Organization carried out a well-timed assassination against Vyacheslav von Plehve, the minister of internal affairs, that summer. Nicholas II was conscious of the growing discontent and replaced Plehve with the more amenable Pyotr Sviatopolk-Mirsky, a man who favored reconciliation and was not averse to the reformist ideas of the *zemsty*.[48] Opponents took this as a sign of impending change. By November, liberals had organized a Zemstvo Congress in the capital with Mirsky's tacit consent, believing the assembly might provide a base from which a popular and elected government could be created. People throughout the country sent telegrams declaring their support for the congress. Newspapers publicized liberal goals and various groups allied themselves with the delegates. Imitating the French republicans of 1848, the Union of Liberation staged a banquet campaign with the objective of uniting the intelligentsia "around the constitutional banner."[49] At these gatherings, men and women gave critical speeches and shouted "Long Live the Constitutional Assembly!" Unions followed suit and staged strikes in solidarity with the liberals while student activists organized demonstrations in the streets. The congress even produced a resolution demanding greater local autonomies and a constitution. Russia was no longer the "personal property and fiefdom of the Tsar," delegates claimed. It was a nation with its own body politic.[50]

Constitutionalism became the basis of unity for an opposition movement spanning social and ideological lines. While Nicholas II made vague promises of "reform" to appease the sudden popular upsurge, he remained reticent when it came to talk of constitutional rule or limiting his personal power. Moreover, he relied on the tactic that had served his predecessors best. No sooner had he recognized the oppositional demands than he ordered authorities to begin clamping down on liberal organizations

Figure 17 Tsar Nicholas II and the Tsarina © The British Library Board.

to staunch popular mobilization. Liberals responded with increased agitation, intent on pressing their demands upon the reluctant monarch.

In early 1905, tensions between state and society came to a head. Neither the Marxists nor the liberals had very much to do with escalating the situation. Rather, the necessary spark came from an unlikely source: a Saint Petersburg priest and prison chaplain named Georgi Gapon. Father Gapon was an instrumental leader in the worker movement. Through meetings held in tea rooms across the capital, he had drawn together an Assembly of Russian Factory Workers dedicated to educating laborers and instructing them in methods of orderly protest. Certainly not a radical, Gapon preached loyalty to the tsar as a chief responsibility of the working classes. His goal was to draw workers away from radicals, and in this capacity the tsarist government was willing to tolerate and even occasionally fund his endeavors. Above all, Gapon believed in the traditional relationship between tsar and people and saw worker protest as a means of restoring this sacred bond. Pressuring the administration would encourage a policy of state-sponsored reform that was neither radical nor revolutionary.[51]

On January 9, Father Gapon led his followers in a march to the Winter Palace. There, workers made appeals to Nicholas II for higher wages, better working conditions and civil and political liberties. There was nothing overtly revolutionary in the gathering. However, greeting them at the palace was a line of soldiers. Upon seeing the crowd, the troops attempted to disperse the workers with rifle fire. In the process, some 150 protestors were shot dead. The opposition dubbed the event "Bloody Sunday." Reformers and workers alike criticized the handling of the protestors. More significantly, the event destroyed the popular image of the "good tsar" that had sustained the regime. Bloody Sunday sent the protest movement along a new dynamic. While the opposition of 1904 had been confined to political conflict, after Bloody Sunday protests disintegrated into lawlessness and violence on a large scale across the empire, fomenting a revolutionary situation that threw the autocracy into a momentary state of crisis.[52]

Workers from Saint Petersburg to Baku staged mass strikes and brought industry to a halt. For the most part, these strikes were spontaneous since the radicals were too weak to organize or play a leading role in them. Radical leaders such as Lenin, Plekhanov and Chernov were all in exile and could only watch in wonder from afar as this veritable "proletarian" revolution unfolded. Student organizations also partook in the disturbances and by February institutions of higher education were completely shut down. Liberals stepped up their organizational efforts and continued forming clubs with the anticipation of creating a constituent assembly. As tsarist authority melted away, various groups seized the initiative to vocalize their discontent. Protestors representing the Women's Union for Equality called for equal voting rights and pay. Trade unions coalesced in a national Union of Unions with the goal of rallying workers behind liberal demands. These political activities drew in nationalist grievances that overlapped with protest movements. Jews took to the streets in Warsaw and Poles set up barricades in Łódź that required military force to suppress. In August 1905, Tatar nationalists in the Volga region convoked a Union of Russian Muslims demanding a representative body of their own and greater autonomy in educational and cultural

Figure 18 Student Demonstration in Saint Petersburg, 1905 © DEA/BIBLIOTECA AMBROSIANA/Contributor/Getty Images.

affairs.[53] The many fault lines and inequalities dormant within Russian imperial society stunningly opened up a chasm and created poles of opposition around which militants and protestors now rallied.

The countryside was not immune to these disruptions. By the spring, riots and rent strikes were destabilizing rural districts. Peasants occupied landed estates and pillaged manor houses. As nobles fled and authority collapsed, peasants set up their own cooperatives and filled governmental posts in villages. In some areas, peasant "republics" were temporarily established that oversaw local services and enacted various types of agrarian social reform. Goaded by the SRs, that July peasant radicals declared a Peasant Union with the stated aim of directing rural affairs and linking peasants with the "all-nation struggle" for constitutional and political rights.[54] Suppressing these outbreaks proved exceedingly difficult. Soldiers—many of them conscripted from peasant ranks—refused to crush the riots. This development foreshadowed the wave of mutinies that would occur during the summer and fall as low morale and the humiliations of the Japanese war destabilized the military. In various locations, military discipline broke down and the autocracy lost control of the armed forces.[55]

Law and order dissolved as riots and vandalism became the order of the day. During late September and into October, Russian society was virtually paralyzed when unions organized a general strike across industries. The participation of the Railway Union was particularly effective as transport came to an abrupt halt. To coordinate activities, workers formed councils (*soviets*), which sprang up in approximately fifty cities. These elected worker bodies ran newspapers, carried out public services and even organized militias for public defense. The Saint Petersburg Soviet became the fulcrum of the soviet movement, creating an alternative authority and source of sovereignty against the autocracy. The revolution had inadvertently brought forth a revolutionary government with delegates elected at mass meetings held in factories and plants. Representatives were primarily union leaders and workers, although Bolshevik, Menshevik and SR agents also attended. Leon Trotsky, a Menshevik with a penchant for giving dramatic and fiery speeches, encouraged the Soviet to pursue a radical course of action, although he and his cohorts never managed to convince the leadership to accept the RSDLP party platform.[56] "There are no parties now" was the response they received, indicating the Soviet was not to be an instrument of revolutionary party politics.[57]

With the general strike in full effect, Nicholas II had little choice other than to concede. Ordering Count Witte to form a new cabinet, Nicholas issued his October Manifesto, promising a representative parliament (Duma), a constitution and political amnesty for exiles and prisoners. For many observers, the manifesto was far from an ideal solution. "There is a revolution going on," one journalist remarked to Witte during a press conference held the next day. "What the country needs is not promissory notes, but hard currency."[58] Yet "hard currency" was not forthcoming. Nevertheless, the opposition interpreted the October Manifesto as a clear victory for its cause. Upon hearing of its proclamation, people took to celebrating in the streets and printed lofty editorials in newspapers acclaiming Russia's entrance into the modern era. According to one report, the capital was in a "state of frantic and effervescing enthusiasm."[59] Within days, this enthusiasm quickly spilled over into violence and disorder.

Since the spring, conservative monarchists had been watching events unfold with anxiety. The October Manifesto made apparent that the tsar no longer possessed the ability to withstand the forces threatening Russian society. According to the monarchist Vladimir Gringmut, a self-proclaimed Russian traditionalist and devout Orthodox Christian, autocracy was the "alfa and omega of Russian state and public life." Every Russian had a moral obligation to defend the country from anarchy. Gringmut was symptomatic of the right-wing nationalism growing up over the course of 1905. He and fellow monarchists spearheaded a grassroots campaign to reunite a fractured Russian society around the traditional base of Orthodoxy and Autocracy. The Union of the Russian People was the most prominent monarchist party that took shape with branches springing up throughout Russia. At meetings, members sang "God save the tsar" and listened to energetic speeches. Those who did not attend the rallies could get a flavor for this inspired rhetoric in the various newspapers published by monarchist factions. Branches also organized paramilitary wings that took it upon themselves to harass strikers, beat up Jews and patrol city streets. In many instances, local authorities turned a blind eye to the violence perpetrated on radicals in the quest to save "Russia, one and indivisible."[60]

In actuality, the October Manifesto was designed to split the opposition. As expected, liberals immediately rallied behind it. As Pavel Miliukov, leader of the newly formed Kadet party, explained, "we are against those that pronounce the revolution 'continuous.'"[61] Constitutionalists were willing to hedge their bets with the promise of a Duma rather than risk a revolutionary uprising led by radicals. SDs denounced the Kadets as "traitors" and affirmed their commitment to revolutionary politics. To protect themselves from rightwing militants, local party committees employed similar strong-arm tactics, forming their own paramilitary units that exacerbated the street violence. Radicals were right to suspect the government. As the strikes lost momentum, officials began rounding up activists. In early December, the ring leaders of the Saint Petersburg Soviet were arrested. Fearing a general counter-revolutionary coup, Bolsheviks took control of the Moscow Soviet and urged workers to seize power. In their call to arms, they declared a "resolute and merciless war" upon the autocracy in the name of the proletariat.[62] The uprising lasted a mere week, and in its aftermath the leadership once against fled into exile.[63]

Despite the impressive organizational skills exhibited by the RSDLP in the closing months of 1905, the SDs misunderstood the import of the revolutionary events that year. The dominant discourse had been citizenship and constitutionalism, not socialism.[64] Any hope of creating an "all-nation struggle" faced an uphill battle. Political reform and constitutional rule were the central themes in the various overlapping protest movements that broke out in 1905. Once it appeared constitutionalism had prevailed, the opposition predictably fragmented, setting the stage for repression and counter-revolution. The October Manifesto made provisions for new freedoms, but authorities were given broad powers in determining what exactly constituted "seditious" activity.[65] Electoral laws for the Duma announced in early December strongly favored the nobility and conservative elements. The Duma itself was denied any constituent functions and was designed to be a purely advisory body. The Fundamental Law decreed in the spring of 1906 drove home the shortcomings of the revolution. The tsar was still recognized as an "autocrat" while ministers remained responsible to him alone. It was under these severely restrictive conditions that political opponents would have to pursue their liberal and nationalist agendas. A shaky "liberal" monarchy had been brought into existence as Russia limped toward a new age of constitutional rule.[66] Yet it was hard to deny that the revolution of 1905 had been an ambiguous one at best.

Confronting Ottoman Modernity

Every European newspaper reported on the events taking place in Russia. Headlines reading "Strikes in Petersburg" and "The Death of Tsardom" attracted readers curious about the fate of the empire. As 1906 progressed, radicals on the continent despaired at learning of Nicholas II's determination to scale back reforms and dissolved the Duma.

The drama of Russian constitutionalism had turned out to be yet another tragedy. Readers in the Ottoman Empire were particularly interested in these turbulent events, and not necessarily out of a sense of Schadenfreude either. Liberals hopeful for a constitutional regime of their own saw a lesson in Russia's constitutional experiment. "Seeing the events in Russia, we [Ottomans] should awaken …," urged one newspaper in November 1905. "If we do not know how a nation obtains its civil freedom, we should learn."[67] The injunction was clear. Russia's constitutional revolution was a potential "model" for its neighbor also suffering under the yoke of autocratic absolutism.

Much like Russia, the Ottoman Empire was a multiethnic and multiconfessional society. The empire had been stitched together over centuries of conquest and by 1900 stretched from the borders of Persia to Eastern Europe. The head of state claimed both temporal and spiritual powers, serving as the imperial sultan and the Caliph of the Muslim world. Although the ruling dynasty was Turkic and the official religion of the empire was Islam, this did not imply the empire was a Turkish state. "Ottoman" never correlated with an ethnic Turkish identity nor were Ottoman elites a homogenous group. Loyalty to the center rather than kinship or ethnic ties was the primary criterion that bound together a cosmopolitan imperial elite class. The empire itself was organized around the principle of the *millet* system which extended official recognition to religious minorities. Despite the empire's Islamic identity, Jews and Christians were permitted to worship freely and maintain their communities in exchange for paying a special tax. This brand of "tolerance" provided a framework for a supra-national imperial polity governing a diverse population, and bore a resemblance to the empires ruled by the Habsburg and Romanov dynasties.[68]

Yet by the nineteenth century, this imperial structure was showing signs of strain. Confronted with aggressive European expansion and national separatist movements, Ottoman officials were haunted by fears of imperial "decline" and proposed Western-style reforms as a panacea. Ottoman reformers, however, faced serious challenges. Entrenched elites resisted centralization from Istanbul while ethnic minorities espoused nationalist ideas emanating from Central Europe. Forward-looking political elites had hopes of strengthening the state. Yet they came up short when it came to fostering a sense of shared community among the empire's disparate power brokers and ethnic groups. Beginning in the 1840s, reformers endeavored to replace the old millet system with an idea of a modern Ottoman citizenry. They promoted a policy of "Ottomanism" (*osmanlilik*) that outlined a brand of imperial patriotism rooted in assurances of legal equality and civic attachment to a modernizing state. As the reformer Ali Suavi explained, "All the populations which today compose the Ottoman Empire constitute only one nationality: the Osmanli."[69] For all its progressive elements, Ottomanism was not revolutionary. It sought to rally the imperial community behind the reigning dynasty and bureaucracy, offering a unique style of "official" Ottoman nationalism believed capable of papering over existing ethno-national divisions.

Liberal-minded elites coming together under the banner of the "Young Ottomans" lent support to this program. Their name was suggestive of the novelty and sense of modernity these men coveted. In Muslim societies, youth traditionally implied inexperience and immaturity while age commanded respect and authority.[70] Reformers were intentionally employing the language of the revolutionary West, taking their cue from movements like Mazzini's Young Europe. They asserted the primacy of modern society over religious and authoritarian traditions. They backed Westernization where necessary but eschewed unconditionally aping European values as they brought the empire into the currents of "modern civilization."[71] Such aspirations, however, fell far short of their mark by mid-century. Promised reforms failed to materialize and conservative politicians suppressed talk of liberalism and secular citizenship. By the early 1870s, the reform movement had stalled. Worse still, the government increasingly appeared directionless as it grappled with a ballooning state deficit and outside pressures from the European powers.

The shortcomings of reform were all the more evident as uprisings and nationalist movements began to erode the empire. Serb, Greek and Bulgarian nationalists had little tolerance for Ottoman rule and were quick to support peasant unrest when it erupted in 1875. They fomented irredentist movements in Macedonia and Rumelia, seeking to chip away at the empire's western border and create independent nation-states in the Balkans. The intervention of foreign powers, most notably Russia and Britain, did little to curtail the violence that was unleashed, and even catalyzed it. Local conflicts quickly morphed into international crises. Frustrated by this situation, Young Ottomans mounted a protest movement and imposed a constitution on the reluctant Sultan Abdülaziz in 1876. However, this measure did little to halt the slide into the abyss. In 1878, Serbia gained independence from the empire. Austria occupied the province of Bosnia-Herzegovina while France and Britain gained a controlling influence over the Ottoman state debt, and hence the Ottoman economy. On all fronts, it looked as though the royal court was losing control. To make matters worse, in a moment of reaction the new Sultan Abdülhamid revoked the constitution and suppressed the Young Ottoman opposition. Following the crisis of 1875–1878, the message was clear: nationalism and great power politics posed an imminent threat to the existence of the empire and the state had little faith in constitutionalism as a remedy to the dire situation it faced.[72]

The Ottoman Empire certainly faced a more hostile environment after 1878. It was wracked by internal conflicts and on the verge of becoming a European protectorate. Neighboring Serbia had aspiration of carving out a Greater Serbian state in the region and kept close ties with Bosnia and adjacent Ottoman territories inhabited by ethnic Serbs. Greek nationalists were similarly determined to incorporate the Greek-speaking populations of Thrace and Anatolia into an enlarged Greek kingdom while Bulgaria continued to assert influence in Macedonia. Irredentist nationalism would pose a problem for Ottoman authority in the Balkans right up until the First World War. The situation inside the empire, moreover, hardly gave reformers cause for optimism. Having stifled the liberal opposition, Sultan Abdülhamid pursued a policy that blended modernization, absolutism and a marked Pan-Islamic ideology oriented toward the empire's Muslim population. While the state invested in railroads and attracted foreign investment in industry, it remained cold to political liberalization. Constitutional Ottomanism, the program liberals believed most capable of saving the empire, was a dead letter.[73]

Opponents kept the constitutionalist movement alive from abroad, publishing newspapers in London, Paris and Switzerland critical of the Hamidian regime. In exile, many democrats also expanded the scope of their ideas as they attempted to reach out to their fellow Ottoman citizens back home. Constitutionalism was combined with Islamic principles, linking concepts of parliamentary democracy with Quranic teachings. In translating Western concepts into an idiom that a Muslim Ottoman citizenry could accept and relate to, Hamidian opponents "invented" an Islamic constitutional tradition that drew upon both Ottoman and European influences.[74] Critics also began to rethink their former Ottomanist platform over the coming decades, bolstering a stronger sense of national patriotism. Namik Kemal, a leading voice among the Ottoman opposition camp, now spoke of the empire as the "fatherland" (*vatan*), incorporating elements of European nationalism into his rhetoric.[75] In time, these sentiments fused with currents of Pan-Turkic nationalism popularized by Tatar nationalists in the Russian Empire. As Turkism percolated into Ottomanist ideology, differing conceptions of the Ottoman community came to the surface.[76] Despite their commitment to constitutional liberalism, Ottomanist thinkers showed a willingness to endorse radicalized forms of nationalism, especially as ethno-national separatist movements ate away at the base of the empire.

These shifts occurred as the composition of the opposition movement changed. By the turn of the century, the older generation of Young Ottomans was being replaced with a new wave of exiles arriving on the continent. These men came from small circles formed within the Royal Medical School and War College of Istanbul. Their oppositional politics had drawn the wrath of the Hamidian state, forcing them to flee the country and join the Ottoman diaspora abroad. In 1895, they regrouped in Paris, taking the name the Committee of Union and Progress (CUP) under the direction of the activist and savant Ahmet Riza. Like earlier reform movements, the CUP was motivated by desires to salvage the empire. Outspoken émigrés were not reticent when it came to placing blame for the nationality problem squarely on the inept Hamidian government. "It is not shameful for us!" one newspaper thundered. "How can the Ottomans who once ruled the world become servants to their own shepherds, slaves and servants?"[77] Modernization and constitutionalism offered the remedy to this sad state, they contented. However, these "Young Turks" had little intention of serving as a mere voice of opposition abroad. From the start, the group demonstrated a talent for organizing and publicizing its message. Unlike their predecessors, the CUP leadership was a conspiratorial party. It acted as an umbrella organization for various political groups back home, the most important of which were factions within the military. Disillusioned with the sultan's ability to keep nationalism and the predatory European Powers at bay, military commanders back home were growing restless. For all their complaining, however, they lacked the organizational skills necessary to translate this disaffection into a political movement. The CUP provided the cohesion. It supplied the crucial organizational links that brought together officers and military cells with political elites in the capital.[78]

Allied with the military, many CUP leaders professed "revolution from above" as the party's operative strategy. They openly supported constitutionalism, but never lost sight of their end goals of administrative reform and centralization. Modernization and military reform: these were the elements that would strengthen the empire internally and provide the necessary unity for a multiethnic society. From abroad, Ottoman radicals also kept a close eye on international events, often developing their ideas in light of foreign influences. From the 1905 Russian revolution, they came to understand the power that elite demands could possess when backed by mass support. Events in Iran the following year impressed the CUP leaders, as Iranian protestors and religious authorities championed ideas of Islamic constitutionalism against the ruling Qajar dynasty in Persia. In drawing upon these contemporary lessons, CUP organizers consciously situated themselves within a "global wave" of constitutional revolution spanning from Europe to Asia. They adapted and modified these models to the particularities of the Ottoman context, coming to believe that military authority from above could organize and mobilize support for political change from below.[79] In outlining this revolutionary strategy, Young Turk radicals even considered political violence an effective means of revolutionary change, a position which had been largely absent among CUP ideologues a decade earlier.

This shift in perspective was also a response to events taking place within the Ottoman Empire itself. By the turn of the century, the Balkans was sliding into anarchy. Bulgarian and Russian agents persisted to aid secret guerilla bands and criminal organizations in Macedonia. Serbian support for underground nationalist cells in the region was suspected while Greek activists were urging co-nationals to "Hellenize" the region. In April 1903, a faction of anarchists calling themselves the Internal Macedonian Revolutionary Organization (IMRO) momentarily wreaked havoc in Salonica when it coordinated a series of brutal terrorist attacks across the city. Provocateurs dynamited a French ship in the harbor and proceeded to destroy city infrastructure, detonate explosives at popular hotels and cafés and blow up the Ottoman Bank. Through this reign of terror, the IMRO hoped to attract the attention of the European Powers and inflame ethnic strife in the region. It achieved both objectives.[80] Ottoman authorities retaliated, sparking resistance. The fighting became so intense that Muslims formed defense committees to protect themselves from rebel gangs. The Powers interpreted this latest surge in violence as a further sign of Ottoman decline and did not hesitate to intervene. That October, an international police force was charged with taking control of Macedonia and restoring the order the Ottoman regime could not provide. While the imperial government did not welcome the entrance of foreign powers into the affair, there was little it could do to prevent it.[81]

European intervention hardly improved the situation. The Turkish populations inhabiting the area were irate. They despised being supervised by a foreign police force and demanded that their sultan protect them from nationalist terrorism. In this growing chorus of discontent, the army as well showed signs of protest. The Turkish military stationed in Macedonia was growing hostile to bureaucrats in the capital. Troops had been waging a war against Balkan nationalists for over a decade, often times going for stretches without pay or adequate supplies. Under the circumstances, commanders stationed on the western fringe of the empire increasingly pursued policies independent of the military administration in Istanbul, revealing a disconnect between the government and its forces in the field. The Balkan garrisons became a hotbed of Young Turk sympathy, and the arrival of foreign forces in Macedonia only exacerbated these tensions. The army command spoke out openly against the weakness of the sultan who, they believed, could no longer hold the empire together. It was, they insisted, time for genuine reforms, and if the sultan did not consent he would have to go. In the summer of 1908, this situation reached a definitive head.

That July, Abdülhamid dispatched forces to Macedonia with the plan of removing rowdy commanders and reasserting his authority. When his men arrived, the troops garrisoned in the Balkans mutinied. Military commanders immediately began rallying soldiers and citizens to their side with calls for a constitution. In Salonica, crowds gathered in the streets shouting "Long Live the Constitution!" and "Long Live the Fatherland!" Officers and civil servants made impromptu speeches on squares and in cafés, threatening to march to Istanbul if their demands were not met. Abdülhamid had overplayed his hand and had few options available to him. The prospect of a widespread military mutiny would only invite further unrest and foreign intervention. The constitution of 1876 had to be reinstated and a parliamentary Chamber convened to appease opponents.[82] In Salonica, crowds celebrated the victory with parades and banner waving. A few days later, Enver Bey, a staff officer in the mutinous Third Army Corps, addressed an enthusiastic crowd on the newly christened Place de la Liberté and offered his expectations for the constitutional era about to dawn. "Citizens … we are all brothers," he stated. "There are no longer Bulgarians, Greeks, Serbs, Romanians, Jews, Muslims—under the same blue sky we are all equal, we are all proud to be Ottomans!"[83]

A charismatic figure with a knack for speechmaking, Enver Bey commanded attention as a chief spokesman for the new revolutionary vanguard committed to leading a decaying empire into the "modern era." Yet it remained uncertain whether the revolution would conform to the Ottomanist ideal presented in his speech that jubilant afternoon. Evolving between 1895 and 1908, the CUP strategy had envisioned a popular movement organized and controlled by the military. This plan had been executed in Macedonia, but could it be applied to the overall empire? Within a short period, this question would be answered with devastating consequences.

The Young Turk Revolution

The revolution begun in July was inspired by faith in a renewed Ottomanism emphasizing imperial loyalty and constitutional rule in the name of the Ottoman "people." That autumn, the theater of politics shifted from the Balkans to Istanbul, where crowds celebrated the regeneration of Ottoman society. State censorship was ignored as newspapers printed editorials and carried stories on the political events of the day. Public speeches and gathering were organized throughout the empire in which "all nations, all religions and all classes mixed together." Flag waving, chants of "Long Live the Constitution!" and even the singing of the Marseillaise were common occurrences. "What changes …!" remarked one observer. "Souls were suddenly set free. There is now a general neglect [for conventions] everywhere. We speak in raised voices and the street is animated with a candid and sincere sense of life."[84] After years of divisive authoritarian rule, Ottoman citizens were coming together in a moment of national fraternity to signal the rebirth of public life.

CUP spokesmen intent on sustaining mass support for the revolution repeatedly assured crowds that political reform would reunify a fractured community. Religious and legal equality, rights for women, secularization and economic improvement: these were the broad goals championed by Young Turk activists. Ottoman society was not incompatible with modernity and could be brought into line with the currents of "civilized" Europe, they argued.[85] Such pronouncements were aimed at foreign audiences just as much as domestic ones. It was imperative to allay European anxieties, and revolutionaries did their best to convince foreign governments that reform was in their best interest and that Christian minorities would be protected. Meeting with French representatives that October, Nazim Bey claimed that the empire was no longer a "purely Muslim power." He closely tied Ottoman regeneration with French values of secular liberalism, citing France as an intellectual and moral influence on the movement. "The new Turkey is the intellectual daughter of France and it wants to develop and prosper by its example," he stated.[86] Statements to this effect did not prevent other CUP leaders from reaching out to the empire's Muslim majority or hailing the revolution as a victory for Islamic civilization. Constitutionalists saw no contradiction in their support for civic Ottomanism and Islam, and in many ways these contradictions were inherent in the CUP strategy of mass mobilization. Difference of opinion within the Young Turk leadership and desires to win support from wide sections of the public brought forth these ideological divergences.[87]

This dualism was evident on the ground as well. The events of 1908 invigorated public life as voluntary associations and new journals sprang up and engaged citizens in a variety of activities. Political revolution brought forth a social revolution of sorts that saw a range of merchants, professionals and local notables take a leading role in politics.[88] In certain cases, the sudden swell of political activity cut across sectarian and class lines. In Macedonia, labor organizations drew in Bulgarians, Jews and Greeks that partook in strikes and work stoppages.[89] New elites from Anatolia to Syria lent support to Ottoman cosmopolitanism and publicized their message in the emergent public sphere. Through civic associations and the press, they promoted a shared vision of Ottoman modernity that drew upon Western models and gave new meaning to concepts of sovereignty and citizenship. Yet in other instances, activists appealed to ethnic and religious solidarity. Various Turkish and Arab spokespeople translated ideas of equality and rights into terms compatible with Quranic principles and customary religious discourses.[90] "Creative adaptation" was a hallmark feature of revolutionary activities ranging from CUP ideologues to provincial reformers in Jerusalem, Aleppo and Cairo. Yet it also highlighted potential points of division between Muslims and non-Muslims, especially in predominantly Muslim areas. Elites reformulated ideas of progress and modernity in an Islamic idiom, hoping to unite Arabs, Turks, Kurds and other Muslim groups into a common citizenry. To what extent these activities could draw in Christian populations was uncertain.

These discrepancies were not unresolvable as long as the initial euphoria of the revolution lasted and constitutional reform proceeded apace. Elections to the Chamber of Deputies were held in late 1908, ushering in a multiparty political system. The CUP won a majority of the seats and prepared to fight the government legally through the press and parliament. They applied pressure to force the resignation of top officials who enjoyed the favor of the sultan. The office of Grand Vizier was their first target. According to CUP deputies, it was the Chamber, as an extension of "the nation," that had the prerogative to appoint the highest imperial official, a claim foreshadowing later squabbles over ministerial and lower-level appointments. By submitting the issue to a vote, the CUP gave its demands an air of legality. As a precaution, however, they ordered a naval ship anchored in front of the Yildiz Palace with its guns trained on the sultan's residence.[91] Despite a stated commitment to parliamentary politics, the CUP continued to act like a conspiratorial party and was not above flexing its muscles to force compliance.

Strong-arm tactics went hand-in-hand with a full frontal assault on the state apparatus. The sultan's regime had been propped up by a cadre of imperial bureaucrats, many of whom were notorious for their corruption and malfeasance. Once in power, the CUP organized a purge that targeted key officials in the state and military bureaucracies with ties to the old regime. Hundreds of seasoned officials were released from service as hardline reformers declared war on "tyrants" and men "who did not place importance on the reforms of the people," as one critic asserted.[92] The old guard was replaced with new men backed by the CUP. Talaat Pasha, a member of the Salonica party branch, was charged with overseeing this administrative reshuffling in the summer of 1909 when he assumed the post of interior minister. The purges allowed the CUP to penetrate deep into the state administration, making government officials dependent upon the party central committee.[93] The party also expanded its networks and created organizational structures that competed with the state. Party branches assumed a more active role in the provinces and appropriated local functions, acting like a quasi-governmental organization. Liberals who had gathered around the *Ahrar* party headed by the reform-minded Prince Sabahaddin watched in horror as the CUP came to resemble a "government inside the government." Fears of a CUP dictatorship elicited calls for decentralization that divided constitutionalists and exposed growing divisions between reformist and revolutionary camps.[94]

Liberals were not the only ones agitated by the purges. Soldiers alarmed by the administrative reorganization rebelled against their new officers, demanding an end to partisan staffing policies and the reinstatement of military personnel. To add moral support to their ultimatum, soldiers petitioned the Şeyhülislam, the highest religious authority in the empire, whose support garnered the sympathy of thousands of religious students and Muslim officials. Organizing under the Society of Muhammad, conservative elements railed against the government's secular and "anti-Islamic" policies, calling for the restoration of the Caliph and Sharia law. In April 1909, pro-Hamidian protests surged when some 3,000 theological students and soldiers stormed the parliament in the Sultanhamet district of Istanbul and demanded the surrender of leading CUP politicians. Facing a potential counter-coup, CUP members regrouped in Salonica and assembled an "Army of Deliverance" that summarily crushed the conservative backlash. Mutinous soldiers and Islamists were arrested and executed. On April 27, Abdülhamid was officially deposed and replaced with his brother, who was to serve as little more than a puppet for the regime. Martial law and military force had "saved" the revolution, but the CUP no longer had illusions regarding its popularity. The party stepped up its purge of the bureaucracy but softened its secular and liberal agenda. Pacifying conservatives and Muslim opinion encouraged a more Islamist rhetoric, marking a significant shift in the political orientation of the Young Turks.[95]

This change in focus was equally dictated by the international conflicts convulsing the empire. European Powers exploited the instability generated by the revolution from the start, using it as a pretext to seize further Ottoman territory. In 1908, Austria annexed Bosnia, Bulgaria declared outright independence and Cretan insurgents announced union with Greece. The CUP's ability to defend the empire was immediately cast into doubt, and this doubt festered over the coming years. In 1911, Italy violated international law and launched an invasion of Ottoman Libya, forcing the Ottoman military to mount a resistance movement in conjunction with regional Arab clients. Pan-Islamic sentiment was employed to mobilize troops, strengthening the Islamic rhetoric of the military and government. Between 1912 and 1913, Greece, Bulgaria and Serbia occupied parts of Macedonia, effectively ending Ottoman rule in Europe. As these crises unfolded, the government became reliant on the military. Men like Enver Bey, who commanded forces in both Libya and the Balkans, progressively assumed a more direct role in state affairs, diminishing liberal rule.[96] In a more general sense, territorial losses reshaped perceptions of Ottomanism and the state as its Christian population shrank. After 1912, demographic realities dictated that the empire was now a primarily Turkish and Arab-speaking Muslim state.[97] If Ottomanism had constituted a strategy for binding together a multiethnic population, Islamism was now consistent with this objective.

Map 10 The area in dark grey indicates the losses incurred by the Ottoman Empire during the Balkan Wars, 1912–1913.

The persistent threat posed by secessionist nationalism also nurtured a pathological suspicion of ethnic minorities. CUP radicals were inclined to look upon ethnic Turks as the only reliable population in the empire. Consequently, a more pronounced sense of Turkish nationalism took root with organizations like *Türk Ocağı* (Turkish Hearth) exhorting a turn away from the previous Ottoman-centric worldview. Ziya Gökalp, a key advocate of Turkish nationalism within the CUP, was instrumental in promoting an ethnic nationalist ideology against minorities and Islamic clerics that would come to inform government policies in the years ahead. Ottoman regeneration was recast as a myth of "national revival" and the renunciation of cosmopolitan liberalism.[98] This reactionary utopianism found its way into state social and economic projects. Policy makers endeavored to create a Turkish-speaking middle class by resettling refugees and expelling undesirable Slavs, Armenians and Kurds. Interior Minister Talaat Pasha played a leading role in designing these policies as the state condoned ethnic cleansing to create a homogenous Anatolian core that would ideally provide a basis of support for a Turko-Islamic empire.[99] This defensive strategy revealed the extent to which the Young Turk revolution had morphed into a distinctly different type of modernizing project by 1914. The revolutionary élan of 1908 was extinguished as the government's nationalist platform alienated non-Turkish elites across the empire. As war and centrifugal ethno-national contentions spread, the cosmopolitan Ottomanism of 1908 fell to the wayside.

By January 1913, the constitutional government was utterly debilitated. Revolution, warfare and ethnic strife had enervated liberals, leaving them impotent. With the empire on the verge of complete collapse, CUP radicals resorted to a coup, with Enver seizing the war ministry and Talaat clamping down on internal affairs. Constitutionalism was put on ice as the "government of the pashas" took control of the fragile situation and pursued their modernizing revolution from above. Looking back at the period of the Young Turk revolution during the years of the First World War, the author Halid Ziya Uşakligil confessed that a persistent "shadow of sadness" loomed over his memories. "The new government promised us freedom and equality, reconstituted justice and civilization," he reflected. "The nation was celebrating nothing other than its own awakening." Yet nearly a decade of conflict and warfare had eclipsed the revolutionary enthusiasm generated in 1908. "There was no time for us to approach out goals by even a step," Uşakligil lamented. "Tragedies scattered across other nations during the course of a century were crowded together for us in the span of six years. New wounds were opened before the old ones had a chance to scar over, adding new agonies to old ones."[100] Writing in 1917, his words possessed the ring of an epitaph.

Conclusion

The nationalist, illiberal turn taken by the Young Turk revolution provides a cautionary tale of the dynamics latent within radical modernizing ideologies. This outcome, however, should not overshadow the aspirations present at its origin. Young Turk revolutionaries professed a commitment to cosmopolitan ideals and saw themselves as participants in a global wave of constitutional revolutions based upon broad principles of equality and national unity. At the turn of the century, constitutionalism had become a global doctrine attractive to many activists on the periphery of Europe who were conscious of the difficulties that a multiethnic citizenry and industrial underdevelopment posed for their societies. Modernizing states sought to transform diverse empires into national ones. However, as absolutist regime proved unreliable partners in this endeavor, elites showed themselves willing to entertain more radical options. They mobilized mass support behind promises of citizenship and representative government that acquired their own particular and local dimensions. From Saint Petersburg to Istanbul, crowds celebrated the entrance of "the people" into political life and the unity that constitutionalism promised, if only briefly. These festivities marked efforts at revolutionary community building rooted in shared visions of modern, progressive society.

Modernization, however, contained both centripetal and centrifugal potentialities. The Balkans became a staging ground for these two interrelated processes at the turn of the century as ethnic and national politics splintered communities and unleashed instability. As Ottoman authority in the region disintegrated, irredentism and the anarchic violence it bred were transformed into a European problem. Following Austria's annexation of Bosnia in 1908, Serbian nationalism increasingly took a more radical turn as South Slav and Bosnian patriots refused to countenance the loss of an ethnically Serb territory. Activists formed underground groups like Young Bosnia and the Black Hand that fomented agitation from Belgrade to Sarajevo. The Balkan Wars inspired a new sense of urgency as young nationalists took up arms and joined the Serbian military in its effort to "liberate" their fellow brothers. Emboldened by success on the battlefield, militants now endeavored to "liberate" Bosnia in a similar fashion.[101] Serbian military commanders were happy to accommodate. Over the coming year, they extended aid to terrorist organizations that might secure Greater Serbia or, at the very least, sabotage the Austrian administration. In the summer of 1914, this policy fueled the advent of a third Balkan War. On June 28, Franz Ferdinand, heir to the Austrian throne, arrived in Sarajevo to oversee a routine military inspection. That afternoon, he and his wife were shot dead by Gavrilo Princip, a student and Serb radical tied to the Bosnian political underground. Anarchist doctrinaires had repeatedly insisted that "propaganda of the deed" was more effective than a thousand political manifestos, a creed that Princip had clearly taken to heart.

Austria condemned the act, claiming it "opened the eyes of the entire civilized world" to the threat posed by an anarchic Balkan nationalism. The government's response was clear and unequivocal. "No civilized country possessed the right to stay the arm of Austria in this struggle with barbarism and political crime …" it concluded. "[We] cannot permit regicide to become a weapon that can be employed with impunity in political strife."[102] Having abetted revolutionary conspirators across its border, Serbia would receive its "just punishment." Austria was declaring a renewed war on terror, one that within months would metastasize into a global conflict.

CHAPTER 10
FORGING THE NEW REGIME: WAR AND REVOLUTION IN THE RUSSIAN EMPIRE (1914–1922)

The Balkan war that began in the summer of 1914 was unlike its antecedents. Through a mix of complex alliance systems, Great Power politics and misguided policies, Europe slid into one of the most devastating conflicts in modern history. Over the next four years, war would claim roughly 17 million lives, leaving European society devastated by its conclusion. As the conflict dragged on with no resolution in sight, states were compelled to mobilize all available resources and prepare for "total war." Between 1914 and 1918, governments exerted exceptional controls over industries to manage wartime economies while military authorities took charge of civilian affairs. At the same time, organized labor acquired greater bargaining powers in certain countries and women entered the workforce in unprecedented numbers. By 1918, state administrative capabilities were left significantly enhanced as total war encouraged bureaucratic restructuring and re-organization on a vast scale. In no uncertain terms, the First World War ushered in a radical economic, social and political transformation across Europe.[1]

This environment saw a corresponding radicalization of political movements and ideologies, and governments were not above exploiting these developments if possible. From the start, Germany spearheaded a far-reaching plan of subversion aimed at destabilizing its Entente enemies. The scope of these activities was impressive. German agents liaised with Polish, Flemish, Georgian and Ukrainian elites, bolstering nationalist resistance. Throughout Central and Eastern Europe, the military promoted "liberation" movements designed to dismember the Russian Empire. With an eye to Great Britain, German authorities aided the creation of an Irish Brigade assembled from prisoners of war (POWs) held in German war camps and funneled arms to republicans during the Easter Rebellion of 1916.[2] To obstruct the Entente war effort, German Under-Secretary of State Arthur Zimmerman coordinated "seditious undertakings" on a global scale and extended the war into the colonies. As part of this objective, the orientalist scholar and consular agent Max von Oppenheim was instructed to provoke anti-imperial jihadist movements within the British, French and Russian empires. Heading a propaganda bureau in Berlin, Oppenheim spent the war years working with shaykhs, Ottoman officials and Islamic insurgents from Morocco to India in an effort to "inflame the whole Muslim world."[3]

For the German Foreign Office, revolution was a strategic means of warfare. German war aims consciously stoked the flames of global insurrection, stimulating nationalist

Revolutionary Europe

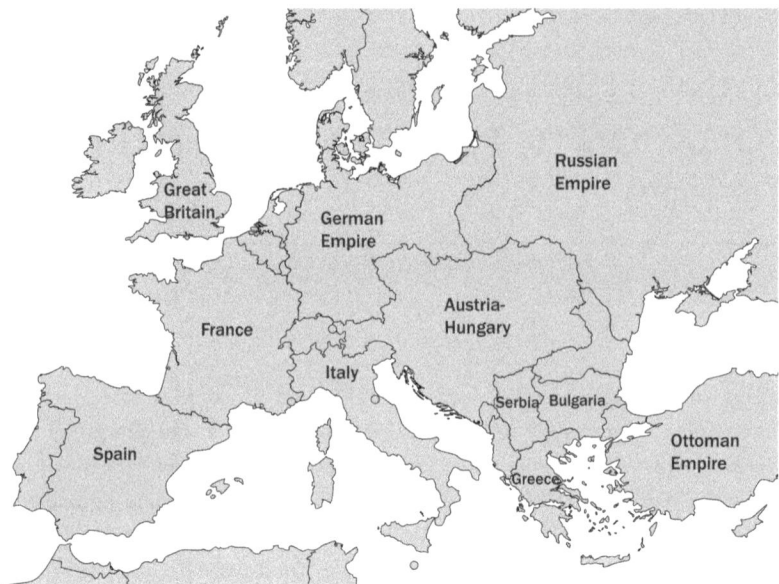

Map 11 Europe in 1914.

and anti-imperial movements that would extend into the postwar period.[4] Yet if military conflict abetted revolution, it also militarized revolutionary movements themselves. As war disrupted societies and established models of authority faltered, radicals were keen to exploit the crisis. They promoted rival conceptions of sovereignty that promised to restore unity to shattered societies. At the same time, radicals adapted their outlooks and strategies to the new conditions of total war, giving rise to circumstances that rationalized and even encouraged extreme forms of political violence. This pattern became most evident in Russia where war and the decay of state authority brought forth a revolutionary holocaust that would permanently transform Europe's revolutionary tradition.

Tsarist Authority in Crisis

Russia was ill-prepared to confront the German military in 1914. Facing munitions shortages and poorly organized supply lines, the Russian army endured a series of humiliating defeats along the western borderland that shook confidence in both the state and military. By September 1915, Austro-German forces had occupied the Baltic territories and large parts of Belorussia. As Austria pushed up from Galicia and German forces closed in from the Baltic, the Russian army was forced to abandon Poland and continue the fight within Russian territory. The retreat elicited criticism over the management of the war as progressive parties like the Kadets and Octoberists used the occasion to wrest concessions from the government. Unwilling to compromise,

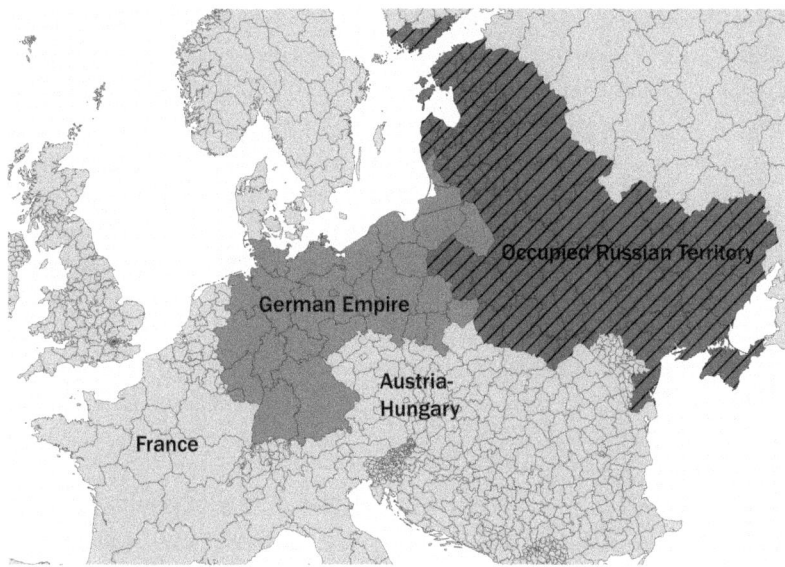

Map 12 Russian territory occupied by Germany during the First World War.

Tsar Nicholas suspended the Duma, provoking a constitutional crisis that only further aggravated the situation.

Political feuds inside the Duma were only one facet of the mounting crisis facing the empire as the war progressed. With Russia's military in retreat, sections of the empire came under enemy control. Abandoning these territories, commanders instituted a scorched earth policy. Whole villages were burned to the ground while livestock and material goods were requisitioned. To prevent the German military from conscripting civilians into the army, officials forcibly evacuated populations and relocated them to central Russia. By 1917, some six million refugees had been displaced. Resettled groups generated a host of ethnic and political tensions as they sought access to shelter and already strained resources.[5] Popular anger was particularly directed at Germans living within the empire. Officials and Russian nationalists argued that Russian-Germans posed a potential security threat to the country. The government passed legislation authorizing deportation and the confiscation of property belonging to German citizens. In cities, mobs attacked German neighborhoods and lynched people with German sounding last names as part of a general "struggle against German predominance."[6]

Wartime demands also destabilized Russian society as the state attempted to exploit all available manpower to the fullest extent. In 1914, the Russian military numbered around 1.4 million men. However, this number drastically increased as the conflict continued. In total, roughly 16 million people would be mobilized during the conflict, with the need for men and labor spurring aggressive conscription campaigns. Populations traditionally exempt from military service proved especially resistant to these demands. When the imperial government announced it was going to draft Central Asian subjects into labor battalions in June 1916, Kazak and Kyrghyz populations rose up in revolt. Prodded into action by protestors in Tashkent, bands of native insurgents began destroying infrastructure and launching attacks on Russian settler communities. Violent retribution followed as the military massacred entire villages.[7] The breakdown of order in Central Asia was symptomatic of a larger phenomenon. The war years and the demands they placed on the population eroded the traditional political and social relationships that held the multiethnic Russian Empire together. As civilian authorities fled combat zones, military commanders assumed control and took charge of ethnic minorities. Their domineering attitudes alienated native elites whose cooperation had long been essential to local stability. Martial law and military governance dissolved the links between state and imperial society. As authority crumbled in peripheral regions, opportunities arose for individuals and groups who could offer protection or provide basic services that the state could not. Such conditions reshaped understandings of authority and furnished contexts for imagining new forms of sovereignty that challenged imperial rule from the center.[8]

Managing the war became a crucial test of authority, one which often exposed the limitations of the imperial government. Like every European power, the Russian state mobilized its economy for war. Basic comestibles such as grain and meat were subject to procurement by state agencies. The newly created Council of Defense oversaw state-owned industries and had the power to force private enterprises to fulfill government contracts and ensure all necessary resources were channeled into war industries. These measures resulted in chronic shortages, inflation and food riots, all of which alarmed civilian organizations fearful that the government was giving priority to military affairs at the expense of social stability. Merchants and liberal elites attempted to compensate for government shortcomings by setting up an unofficial union of zemstva and urban municipalities (Zemgor) under Prince Georgy Lvov. Among other responsibilities, Zemgor associates attended to a variety of war-related activities ranging from organizing military supplies to providing medical services. In a similar fashion, the Moscow-based War Industries Committee was created the following year to supervise government work orders and coordinate with workers employed in war industries. These types of public initiatives challenged the state's exclusive control of the war effort and frequently instigated arguments regarding military and civilian jurisdiction. Yet more to the point, civilian actors were motivated by the perceived mismanagement of the war effort. They took a critical stance on state policies and endeavored to elaborate more efficient ones, often challenging state authority in the process.[9]

Requisitioning had a particularly adverse effect on the countryside where grain production was steadily declining. Peasants showed little inclination to comply with requisitioning, which many saw as an imposition placed on them by the cities. Coupled with an inadequate transport system for moving goods across the empire, urban and country relations broke down. Soldiers fighting at the front felt the pinch as scarcity and lack of supplies further undermined military morale. The capital, rechristened as the more Russian-sounding Petrograd, faced the continuous threat of food shortages by 1917.[10] Strikes, primarily concentrated in Moscow and Petrograd, began to rise in response to hunger, inflation and the general demands placed upon labor. More ominous, it was evident that worker militancy was acquiring political dimensions. Workers struck in 1915 when the Duma was temporarily suspended, and they did so again in December 1916 when the Duma attempted to press itself on the unpopular government.[11] Protestors could sympathize with the leader of the Progressive bloc, Pavel Milyukov, who assailed the state's handling of the war with the pointed question "Is this stupidity or treason?"[12] Weary of the troublesome Duma, Nicholas eventually closed it down indefinitely. Yet this was hardly a manageable solution. Growing criticism and lack of confidence were taking a toll on the government, prompting some within the higher echelons of society to contemplate regime change if necessary. It was not, however, the political elite who would ultimately provide the spark that would set the Russian Empire ablaze.

In 1917, International Women's Day—an important day of recognition in the socialist calendar—fell on February 23. Female textile workers used the occasion to take to the streets, protesting bread shortages and rising prices. The demonstration quickly drew in other workers. Over the coming days, 200,000 strikers occupied the streets of Petrograd waving banners, singing the Marseillaise and chanting "Down with the war! Down with the Tsar!" Crowds were emboldened when troops stationed in the capital flagrantly disobeyed orders to fire on the people and joined the demonstrators. With the military in open revolt, crowds stormed prisons and defaced symbols of the tsarist regime in a veritable anti-monarchist rage. Officials watched in disbelief as tsarist authority melted away overnight. The defection of the Petrograd garrison effectively transformed the February strikes into a revolutionary movement, one which showed signs of spreading to Moscow by the end of the week. Those observing the situation had few illusions concerning what was required to halt the slide into complete anarchy. Nicholas II had to abdicate and a new government be formed with popular support. Three centuries of Romanov rule was coming to end but what might replace it still remained unclear.[13]

Revolutionary Activism and Authority

It was presumed that Grand Duke Michael, brother of Nicholas II, would supplant the tsar and inaugurate a liberal monarchy. Michael, however, refused to take the throne without a popular mandate. This prospect was not completely out of the question. Days before Nicholas' formal abdication a Provisional Committee had formed in the Duma under the chairmanship of Prince Lvov, a longstanding liberal involved in the zemstvo movement since the 1880s. The body was in a position to assume power and serve as a caretaker government. Nine of its twelve members were Duma deputies, the majority of which were drawn from the Kadets.[14] Taking on the role of a provisional government, the Committee passed a string of legislation over the coming weeks that allowed for civil and political rights, universal suffrage and a general amnesty. Plans were made for a Constituent Assembly that would "crown the great Russian revolution," as Lvov claimed.[15] Contrary to initial expectations, Russia was to be a republic. In essence, the new program reiterated everything demanded in 1905 without the fear of counter-revolution coming from the Winter Palace.

February was not to be a replay of the abortive 1905 revolution. The collapse of the autocracy had been hastened by events in the streets, but the new regime hardly signified a "spontaneous" revolution in any meaningful sense of the word. A revolutionary government had not been forced upon the state by the protestors but rather organized and negotiated behind closed doors. The February revolution was, ultimately, one precipitated by political elites.[16] In one sense, this denouement assured a different outcome than what occurred in 1905. Yet it simultaneously raised doubts regarding the legitimacy of the government from the start. In the absence of a popular mandate, liberals fell back on promises of democratic reform, vesting their authority in the confidence of what their revolution could deliver. "The victorious revolution doubtless will bring a cleansing and renewal," one Kadet newspaper assured. The age of autocracy would be followed by "a time of independent activism" as former subjects came to see themselves as free citizens of a restored and sovereign national community.[17] Independent activism was, however, something that a regime with questionable legitimacy might also learn to fear, and this prospect too was evident from the start.

Concurrent with the declaration of a provisional government, organizers within the Central War Industries Committee exhibited the exact type of "independent activism" alluded to by liberals. Gathering workers and socialist deputies together, they revived the soviets of 1905 in order to manage the strikes convulsing the capital. Workers and soldiers gravitated toward these new organs, with some 3,000 deputies elected to the Petrograd Soviet alone. Socialist Revolutionaries (SRs) and Mensheviks made a strong showing in the new Soviet and secured a predominant position in its Executive Committee. Socialist spokesmen pegged February a "bourgeois" revolution and questioned whether liberals would in fact work in the interests of the people. Fear of counter-revolution from within the military encouraged a cooperative position vis-à-vis the provisional government. Yet the soviets let it be known that their support was conditional and should not be taken for granted. According to militants, it was the soviets that reflected the will of "the people." With hundreds of soviets established by the fall of 1917, the councils were a formidable political force with the potential to challenge the legitimacy of the provisional government and promote forms of democratic activism outside state institutions. As was evident, the February revolution had brought into existence two poles of sovereignty, establishing the conditions for "dual power" that would subsequently drive events in the capital.[18]

Liberals were conscious of the need to court popular support. In the euphoric days following Nicholas' abdication, they remained mute on the issue of the war and, in fact, believed that the war effort itself might provide a common patriotic platform capable of rallying the nation to the government. In the weeks following the February revolution, patriotism ran high. Even the soviet leaders were supporting the unpopular war effort, insisting the people's revolution needed to be defended from German invasion. In his proclamation "to the people of the world" published that March, the influential Menshevik Irakli Tsereteil addressed the international left with his appeal for a "fair peace without annexation." In the meantime, he urged Russians to throw their support behind the war. Touting the slogan "Defense of the Revolution," Tsereteil framed the conflict as a defensive war that would ultimately secure worker emancipation across Europe and the world.[19] If liberals believed they could harness this patriotic ebullience, they also remained conscious of the need to draw socialist leaders closer to the government in order to broaden their base of support. The provisional government may have been able to claim formal authority, but the soviet Executive Committee commanded the loyalties of workers and the garrisons.[20] Making overtures to the left, the government found an ally in Aleksandr Kerensky, a moderate SR and vice-chairman of the Petrograd Soviet. It was primarily through Kerensky's cooperation and rise within the government that dual power became a workable solution in the short-term, creating a weak but nonetheless vital connection between the central authority and popular movements.

"Dual power" has typically been used by historians to examine the conflicts over revolutionary sovereignty and authority that came to the fore in 1917. While applicable to events in Petrograd, this framework tends to obscure the multiple points of authority that emerged throughout the empire as the tsarist regime collapsed. The tensions that arose between the government and military were a telling indication of the complexities that revolutionary politics invited. Control of the military was of critical importance. The mutinies had provided the catalyst for the revolutionary momentum of February and liberals recognized the need to assert control over the military if they were to govern. On February 28, the government ordered troops to return to their barracks and obey commanding officers. The response, however, revealed the tenuous hold the government had over the military. Soldiers protested, complaining of inequality between soldiers and officers and the heavy-handed treatment meted out by superiors. The Petrograd garrison had already begun forming councils to speak on behalf of disgruntled soldiers and on March 14 the Petrograd Soviet energetically endorsed their program. Issuing Order Number 1, it demanded freely elected soviets be established within the army. The order was an affront to the provisional government. However, it had little choice other than to accept the directive, lest the government risk losing support among the troops. In the coming weeks, other barracks and regiments made similar demands, with soldiers requesting greater decision-making powers and democratization. While the Petrograd Soviet backed these demands, soldier councils and committees remained independent and tended to push diverse agenda responsive to particular situations.[21]

Evident tensions between central and localized authority manifested themselves across the empire. As imperial authority dissolved, militias sprang up and local actors took control of government offices to attend to immediate problems of resource management, law and policing. This radical decentralization was not part of a revolutionary program so much as a response to collapsing institutions and power structures at the local level. The Russian Empire had never been a cohesive and unified community. Its varying minorities and social groups had been held together by the imperial state and a common recognition of dynastic sovereignty. Once these broke down, Russian society fragmented into a constellation of autonomous bodies representing a range of interests and aspirations. Strongmen and newly minted citizens appeared ready and willing to

Figure 19 The Civil Guard in Petrograd, 1917 © DEA/G. DAGLI ORTI/Getty Images.

speak out on behalf of *their* constituents in the name of revolutionary emancipation. They appropriated the functions of government and attempted to provide the order that the state no longer could.[22]

Socialists hailed the worker soviets set up that spring as instruments of "revolutionary democracy," but these bodies were never defined by strict adherence to a particular revolutionary platform or ideology.[23] Worker radicalism was motivated more by growing production quotas and falling wages than by radical Marxist ideology. With the tsarist police gone, workers began to organize themselves. They formed factory committees, took control of plants and attacked hated foreman and managers. Armed worker brigades defended factories from looters and patrolled working-class neighborhoods in an effort to keep the public peace. Red Guard squads grew up in various Russian cities staffed by volunteers. These activities challenged the traditional social hierarchies and power relationships that laborers found so degrading. However, they also saw workers stepping into authoritative roles out of necessity and taking upon themselves political and organizational responsibilities that they alone could fulfill in the power vacuum opened by the revolution. As Chris Read has claimed, worker revolutionary and political consciousness was shaped through the evolution of everyday experiences. It was not ideologically predetermined.[24] Worker soviets reflected a broad range of interests shaped by factors such as trade, locality, sociability and circumstance. They provided channels through which organizers could influence worker radicalism and communicate with laborers, but they were hardly instruments that could be expected to follow directives and party initiatives blindly.

The empowerment that the revolution offered extended to gender hierarchies just as much as social ones. With the advent of war, conventional gender roles and identities were thrown into flux as men departed for the front and women filled jobs in industrial plants and rail industries. Women found opportunities to participate in the political agitation of the day, whether by protesting against food rationing or demanding an increase in family allowances provided by the state.[25] Militant feminists like Matriona Zalesskaia and Mariia Bochkareva made names for themselves organizing all-women militia units and embodying virtues of feminine self-sacrifice and patriotism. The government even encouraged the creation of female battalions as a means of "shaming" Russian men who performed poorly on the battlefield or attempted to skirt military responsibilities.[26] In general, the government was receptive to female activism. It granted certain civil liberties that opened up new avenues of social and political engagement for women. Yet activists rarely promoted ideas of explicit "female" emancipation. By and large, women espoused a discourse of class identity and solidarity, allying themselves with worker politics. They linked their struggle with the broader struggle of the oppressed masses, thereby claiming inclusion in an imagined universal community that transcended gender lines.[27]

This assimilation of particular and universal grievances proved more problematic in the countryside where peasants began forming their own committees and addressing longstanding rural complaints over land and poverty. Wartime demands on the provinces had driven a wedge between the government and countryside, portending a split between urban and rural interests. Peasants took control of communal and regional administrative organs, rejecting the authority of land captains and village elders alike. They put forward programs of agrarian reform and self-governance, in some cases hijacking land committees and summarily dividing up communal lands in accordance with their own notions of equality and the peasant moral economy. In many instances, SR activists took a leading role in these activities and goaded peasant radicalism. The provisional government treated acts of rebellion seriously. Cooperative urban-rural relations were essential to maintaining the grain supply that fed the cities and sustained the war. The government could not afford to ignore issues of agrarian reform and yet it had little taste for getting involved in rural politics. Land reform would not only alienate the landed elite. It would encourage desertion in the armed forces as peasant conscripts abandoned the front to claim land in their home regions. Unable to frame a coherent rural policy, the provisional government dithered. Consequently, both landowners and peasants began to look elsewhere.[28]

No less intractable, nationalism likewise posed a problem as war and revolution disrupted the empire.[29] Taking control of Latvia, White Russia and Poland, the German military pledged to "liberate" these territories from Russian rule. The *Ober Ost* command funneled aid to nationalists and Polish separatists with the goal of securing German influence in the region.[30] These policies had a ripple effect across the empire as movements for national autonomy broke out from Ukraine to the Caucasus. By early March, nationalists had convoked a Central Ukrainian Rada in Kiev to demand cultural and administrative autonomy within a re-worked Russian federation. The Kadets opposed making any national concessions before the Constituent Assembly was convened. More vocal opponents accused the Rada of being a German ploy to dismember the empire, an allegation that drew withering criticism from Ukrainian nationalists. Even the socialist newspaper *Izvestiia* lashed out at national autonomists, affirming unambiguously "the revolutionary democracy of Russia stands for the indivisibility of the state."[31] For populations subject to foreign occupation and general wartime hardships, national self-determination acquired a certain saliency as the empire buckled under the accumulated weight of protracted combat and political instability. In this context, "revolutionary democracy" had the potential to translate into forms of autonomy and independence that challenged the very foundations of imperial sovereignty.

Rebuffing national autonomists, government leaders showed themselves committed to preserving Russia as a great imperial power. The nationality question added yet another layer to an already tension-ridden situation as liberals contended with the hazards of revolutionary democracy. By the spring, the provisional government faced criticism for everything ranging from its handling of the provinces to its "imperialist" war policy. These criticisms were all the more alarming for a government lacking a popular mandate. As protests and strikes resumed, confidence in the government waned. The government needed to secure its authority and channel the aspirations unleashed that February into a model of revolutionary sovereignty that could sustain and unify the empire. Failing to do so would continually leave the government at the mercy of rival points of authority claiming to speak for "the people" and promising the "revolutionary democracy" that the government appeared unwilling to deliver.

The Bolsheviks Ascendant

The growing number of street protests and strikes that spring highlighted the government's weakened position as calls of "down with the provisional government" provoked panic among liberals. The need to re-establish confidence in the midst of rising inflation and a failing war effort was acutely felt, and Aleksandr Kerensky intended to rise to the occasion. Eloquent, pragmatic and possessing a flair for dramatic speechmaking, Kerensky was popular with workers and the liberal-minded intelligentsia. That March, his decision to join the government had boosted its legitimacy and won the tepid support of the soviets. "There is only one name that unites everyone," the socialite Zinaida Gippius claimed, "and that is the name of Kerensky."[32] Yet the "Kerensky cult" was not enough to sustain the government indefinitely, and the statesman knew it. Following street demonstrations that May, Kerensky understood the need to draw the left closer to the government and set out to form a new coalition with greater socialist participation. Appealing to the Soviet Executive Committee, he offered six ministerial positions to the Mensheviks and SRs which, after some deliberation, they accepted. Hedging their bets, the left believed it could push for reform within the government as a minority party. This assessment proved inaccurate, however. Socialists were given limited influence over government policy but strapped with full responsibility for any decisions made by the "bourgeois" government. They had tied their fate to the fortunes of the provisional government, and as confidence continued to erode so too did the credibility of the socialists.

The Bolsheviks proved the exception. At the start of the revolution, the party was unprepared to direct the popular movements. Its leadership was in exile and Bolshevik influence over workers in the major cities paled in comparison to the other socialist parties. In early April, however, the Bolsheviks received an impetus when Lenin returned to Russia. Since 1905, the Bolshevik firebrand had led his party from abroad, speaking at socialist congresses across Europe and writing prolifically. The start of the war found him in Switzerland where he published his views on the "imperialist" conflict and confidently prophesized on the coming proletarian revolution ahead.[33] His return to Russia was facilitated by the German government, which clearly understood the strategic value of releasing a radical like Lenin into the volatile political situation unfolding in the country. Germany intended to let loose the furies of radical revolution on the shaky provisional government. For his part, Lenin was happy to oblige.[34]

In his April Theses written en route to Russia, Lenin laid out his future plans for the Bolshevik party. Insisting that the war was a product of an imploding capitalist system, he proclaimed the start of a global socialist revolution in which he foresaw Russia inspiring other revolutionary movements abroad.[35] He denounced the Mensheviks and SRs for collaborating with the government and called for the transfer of power to the soviets, the only organs capable of inaugurating a truly revolutionary democracy. "All power to the soviets" was the resounding cry, a slogan that unconditionally staked the Bolsheviks to a policy of opposition.[36] These were strong words meant to rally party members to an uncompromising platform, and strong words and actions were needed if Lenin intended to lead. He was a virtual stranger to Russia, having spent the majority of his life abroad. "I know very little of Russia," he once confessed. "Simbirsk, Kazan, Petersburg, exile—that is all I know."[37] It was also difficult to ignore the fact that the Bolshevik party Lenin assumed control of in 1917 was not the same party he had left behind in 1905. If Lenin had imagined a tight-knit conspiratorial party, by 1917 this organizational structure was no longer the reality. After February, thousands of workers and soldiers had swelled the ranks of the Bolsheviks, transforming it from a revolutionary vanguard into a mass party. By the fall of 1917, it possessed over 350,000 members.[38]

Nor was Lenin's outlook necessarily the same as it had been in 1905 either. His thinking and political theories had matured during his years of exile, a fact made evident in his forthcoming work *State and Revolution*. Through debates with other prominent radicals, Lenin began to give serious consideration to the development and goals of a communist society. Like Marx and other prominent radical thinkers, Lenin believed that the Paris Commune of 1871 was a model for proletarian revolution that promised decentralized authority and worker control. Yet unlike many anarchists, Lenin was not concerned with the myth of the Commune as such. It was its practical applications that interested him, and more importantly its ultimate failure.[39] Taking his cue from Marx, Lenin argued that the Commune had failed to dispense with the instrument of bourgeois

Figure 20 Vladimir Ilyich Lenin © Keystone/Staff/Getty Images.

government: namely the state. The principal objective of proletarian revolution was not to assume control of the state; it aimed "to smash the bureaucratic-military machine" and create a new type of power and organization reflective of worker control.[40]

The proletariat would be wise to heed this lesson in the coming struggle, Lenin insisted. As he saw it, the state was a "special repressive force," one which the proletariat had to seize control of in order to push through its revolutionary program. While this injunction agreed with Jacobin political philosophy, Lenin showed that he was not simply the "Russian Jacobin" many of his critics claimed. This dictatorship of the proletariat was only a period of "political transition" in the evolution toward communism. In this transitional period, the state would attend to organizing industries and forming socialist citizens as people became "accustomed to observing the elementary rules of social life." Once this task of social leveling and renovation was accomplished, the state would "wither away" and provide the conditions for a radically new type of freedom. It was at this juncture the revolution could be considered achieved in the most meaningful sense. "Only in a Communist society, when the resistance of the capitalists has been completely crushed, when the capitalists have disappeared, when there are no classes … only then 'the state ceases to exist,' and it becomes possible to speak of freedom," he affirmed. "While the state exists there is no freedom. When there is freedom, there will be no state."[41]

Lenin was offering his adherents a vision of the anarchist utopia, albeit one achieved through Jacobin-style revolutionary tactics. His program laid out a strategy for how workers might seize control of the state while at the same time use it as an instrument in pursuing their own emancipatory goals. The advent of this coming revolution was, however, explained through the historical dialecticism and laws of Marxist theory. As a revolutionary program and ideology, therefore, Leninism adeptly synthesized competing revolutionary traditions and combined them into a new synthesis. It tied these various traditions to a radical revolutionary party with ambitions of leading the proletariat to the end goal of socialism.

In the short-term, Lenin and his allies framed an agenda promising worker control, land reform, national rights and a just end to the war. They aligned their message with the demands of activists and political organizers across the empire, and by doing so showed themselves willing to engage with the various revolutionary centers that had grown up since February. Workers and peasants had already begun formulating their own localized conceptions of soviet rule without the aid of the Bolsheviks. The task for Lenin and his cohorts was to harness this momentum and make the Bolsheviks *the* party of the revolution as it was broadly understood. Yet if the Bolsheviks courted popular support, such populist rhetoric did not signal a change in ideological perspective. Lenin never modified his position on party discipline or "democratic centralism." Bolshevik control and single-party rule by the proletariat remained the objective.[42] Party ideologues consistently spoke for the proletariat, but in the atmosphere of 1917 "proletariat" and "people" became easily fungible concepts in leftist discourse. Allusions to "the toiling people" and the working classes often functioned as shorthand for the Russian nation itself, equating revolutionary nationhood with the idea of a community of workers.[43] Bolshevik speeches and slogans gave the semblance of a popular democratic movement. Nonetheless, Lenin persistently saw the popular movements as a vehicle for achieving the aims of his revolutionary party speaking in the name of the proletariat. For Lenin, the party, as the embodiment of proletarian consciousness, was the true revolutionary force. The Bolsheviks were not representatives of popular opinion; they were the vanguard driven by historical necessity.[44]

Despite this robust activism, the Bolsheviks profited most from the government's diminishing credibility. In June, a disastrous military offensive in Galicia resulted in yet another humiliating retreat that generated riots in Petrograd. Kerensky responded to the unrest by announcing the creation of a "Government of Salvation" committed to protecting the state and inflicting "severe retribution" on the forces of social disorder. Carrying out this task fell to the new Supreme Commander-in-Chief, Lavr Kornilov. A seasoned military veteran with powerful conservative backers, Kornilov had a particular interpretation of what "salvation" implied for Russia. He had little patience for soldier committees and soviets, both of which were ruinous to the empire in his opinion. Conservatives looked favorably on the new appointment, seeing Kornilov as the man who could save Russia from socialism and imperial collapse. With their encouragement, Kornilov consolidated his position over the next month and warmed political elites to the idea of a military dictatorship. Kerensky had few illusions as to Kornilov's ultimate designs and in late August the situation reached a head when Kerensky accused the ambitious commander of plotting to overthrow the government. Refusing to step down, Kornilov decided to make a show of force. On August 27, he ordered troops into Petrograd with the intention of crushing the soviets, putting an end to dual power and installing himself at the head of the government. Kerensky had little choice but to turn to the soviets for assistance, urging railway workers to divert trains from the capital and halt the coup. The tactic worked but the damage had been done. In the wake of the Kornilov Affair, Kerensky and the government were completely discredited.[45]

The crisis equally tainted the Mensheviks and SRs, both of which had participated in the coalition government. That August and September, the Bolsheviks racked up electoral victories in the city dumas and councils. More importantly, they took a commanding position within the soviet executive committees. Political crisis and lack of faith in governing institutions produced a swell of radicalism from below as workers and soldiers turned to the Bolsheviks. Leon Trotsky was front and center in this grassroots Bolshevik resurgence. Whereas Lenin was distant and prone to abstraction at times, Trotsky possessed the qualities of a charismatic politician. As one of the principal speakers for the Bolsheviks in the Petrograd Soviet, he mastered the crowds with his oratory. Night after night, Trotsky appeared before workers and organizers, condemning Kerensky as a "counter-revolutionary" and leading the cry of "all power to the soviets!" Given the swell of support within the soviets, Lenin and the party leadership were confident that "all power to the soviets" would in actuality translate into "all power to the party," an assumption that had yet to be tested.[46] For the moment, however, the Bolshevik ascendency left the party in control of the Petrograd Soviet and the Red Guard. The time for action had arrived. "History will not forgive us if we do not assume power now," Lenin brazenly remarked.[47]

Many Bolshevik leaders were stunned by this latest declaration. The Congress of the Soviets was scheduled to meet on October 25. Settling the issue at the congress would invest any transfer of power with an air of legitimacy, not to mention ensure Menshevik and SR support for the action. Lenin, however, wanted to present the overthrow as a *fait accompli* to the congress rather than leave it open to debate and negotiation. The night before the congress, Trotsky mobilized military units and Red Guard battalions with warnings of an impending counter-revolutionary strike by the government. As Red Guard units seized control of key strategic points in the capital, Kerensky fled. The following day, Bolshevik forces stormed the Winter Palace and arrested the provisional government. Lenin had forced the issue, leaving the Bolsheviks in a strong position to dictate the new political program of soviet power. When the congress met, the Mensheviks and SRs denounced the act and walked out of the assembly. "Go where you ought to be," Trotsky famously called out after them, "into the dustbin of history."[48]

Trotsky's knack for extemporaneous yet memorable speeches conveyed an air of triumphant confidence as the Bolsheviks took power. However, as events would soon reveal, neither party was willing to consign themselves voluntarily to the dustbin of history. The Bolshevik revolution effectively ended "dual power" but it failed to create a single point of revolutionary sovereignty. The precious balancing act that dual power had invited was about to fragment into a thoroughgoing civil war pregnant with its own revolutionary and violent dynamics.

Consolidating Revolutionary Dictatorship

The October revolutionaries wasted little time validating their radical credentials. It was agreed elections for a Constituent Assembly would go ahead as planned. In the meantime, a governing body was required. With leading socialist delegates protesting the soviet congress, the Bolsheviks had a relatively free hand in determining the course of action. Over the next week, the congress passed a series of sweeping decrees authorizing an eight-hour workday, worker control of industries, the abolition of social classes and the expropriation of all land by the state. A Council of People's Commissars (Sovnarkom) was created to implement these measure, its fifteen members all Bolsheviks. Lastly, the congress announced it would begin conducting peace negotiations and seek a just end to the war. The dizzying speed with which the Bolsheviks acted stood in stark contrast to the staggered pace of reform under the provisional government.

Pushing through this program did not come without difficulties. Lenin's power grab and authoritarian temperament were dividing the party internally. In a preemptive strike on opponents, Lenin stacked the Executive Committee with loyalists and on November 5 imposed a ban on inter-party talks, effectively silencing any opposition. It was not, however, only party members who needed to be disciplined. Officials and civil servants were equally problematic. Immediately after the seizure of power, public officials walked out, mounted strikes and refused to obey what they saw as an illegal government. More alarming, the state bank and treasury refused the new government's demands for cash, without which it could not hope to operate. Rebuffed, the Bolsheviks resorted to demanding the money at gunpoint, putting an end to the issue. Yet the revolt of the bureaucracy was indicative of the government's tenuous position. Lenin and his associates had few means at their disposal of enforcing compliance other than overt force, and in the coming weeks force became their modus operandi. Resistant civil servants were arrested and new commissars were appointed to take their places. Naturally, these new appointees were party loyalists. In consolidating their power, the Bolsheviks hijacked the state administration.[49]

The Soviet Executive Committee was also targeted as decision making was progressively transferred to Sovnarkom. By early November, Sovnarkom was issuing decrees and imposing martial law without bothering to consult the Executive Committee. "Soviet power" turned out to be a farce, reducing the Executive Committee to nothing more than a "sorry parody of a revolutionary parliament," in the words of the Menshevik Nikolai Sukhanov.[50] Socialist opponents did not remain inactive. Indeed, the October Revolution drove a wedge between socialist parties and signaled a general realignment of the left. In an emergency meeting called by the Mensheviks in late November, Mikhail Liber, a leading spokesman for the Bund, condemned the Bolsheviks, professing they had "nothing in common with the class dictatorship of the proletariat." Liber's reference to "the right to insurrection" elicited murmurs, as it seemed he was declaring war on the Bolsheviks.[51] Martov proved more cautious when it came to outright confrontation. With the Constituent Assembly set to be called, popular democracy could be used to blunt the Bolshevik dictatorship, he believed. Martov could not help but consider the fate of the SRs who had revolted earlier that month. Mounting an anti-Bolshevik movement in Moscow, "right" SRs had declared a committee of public safety only to be summarily crushed by the newly created Military Revolutionary Committee. Bolsheviks were busy shutting down opposition newspapers and tarring opponents as "counter-revolutionaries" and "enemies of the people." The Constituent Assembly was the only feasible means of reversing this judgment.[52]

Having won previous elections in the soviets, Lenin felt confident that a second electoral victory was assured. Elections to the Constituent Assembly that November were widely interpreted as a national referendum on the Bolshevik government. In permitting the first freely democratic election in Russia's history, the Bolsheviks were calling upon the people to bestow the new soviet government with popular legitimacy. When all the votes were cast and the ballots counted, however, the result was a stunning defeat for the Bolsheviks, who won a mere 22 percent of the electorate. By far, the SRs were the clear victors with 39 percent of the vote, much of their support coming from rural areas. While the policies of the Bolsheviks were in line with worker and peasant demands, the elections revealed widespread reservation toward Lenin's single party dictatorship. Bolshevik popularity among urban workers and soldiers was not replicated in the countryside where the vast majority of voters resided. The rural areas remained SR strongholds and the election results proved it.[53] Learning the results of the election, Lenin had two choices. He could either share power with the other parties or ignore the elections and run the government without a mandate. He opted for the latter and dissolved the convention that January after a single meeting. According to Lenin, "class struggle" and the defeat of "bourgeois" enemies were required to consolidate soviet power. There was little need for "bourgeois" parliamentary government.[54] The message was clear. Rather than a popular revolution, the Bolshevik revolution would be a revolution by decree.

The closure of the assembly triggered protests and open rebellion. A general wave of arrests followed as "counter-revolutionaries"—Kadets, Mensheviks, SRs and others—were jailed and executed. Mensheviks and SRs had a strong presence in the soviets. Yet demobilized soldiers returning from the front and urban garrisons added a Bolshevik element to village life that was now poised to generate violent conflicts at the local level. Veterans formed paramilitary factions, set up their own Red Guard units and moved to eliminate political enemies.[55] To carry the war directly to the counter-revolutionaries, Sovnarkom created a secret police: the Cheka. Directed by Felix Dzerzhinsky, a Polish aristocrat converted to communism, the Cheka was given broad powers to liquidate class enemies and saboteurs. It was staffed by men "ready to do anything in defense of the revolution," as Dzerzhinsky claimed. "It is war now," he implored his men. "Face to face, a fight to the finish, life or death."[56] This agonal view of the world was one shared by many Bolsheviks as the revolution splintered.

The left opposition was not the only threat, nor was it the most dangerous. Remnants of the tsarist military were actively forming volunteer armies in the Baltic, Don and north Caucasus, and their anti-communist banner was drawing an array of supporters. Led by former aristocrats and imperial officials like Kornilov and Anton Denikin, the White opposition gave the appearance of a counter-revolutionary monarchist movement. In reality, however, it rallied traditionalist, patriots and Cossack regiments through appeals to Orthodox Christianity and cries of "Russia one and indivisible." Local populations welcomed the security that the White military bureaucracies provided at first as commanders restored temporary order to war-torn regions of the empire.[57] Although the movement was riven by constant infighting between the leading generals, many saw the Whites as the only alternative to Red Bolshevism. France, Britain and the United States supplied anti-Bolshevik forces with aid and weapons as the movement grew, making it a formidable threat by late 1918.[58]

Bolshevik ideologues agonized over whether the party should form a traditional army for defense or rely upon revolutionary partisans to carry out guerilla attacks on enemies. Trotsky took the initiative to mold the assemblage of citizen militias into a revolutionary Red Army, a decision that worried certain party members.[59] Trotsky's volunteer recruitment campaign was ultimately disappointing, forcing him to draft workers and peasants into military service. Recruits were given basic training and threatened with harsh disciplinary measures for insubordination or desertion. The soldier councils and elected military committees of 1917 were abolished to the dismay of many troops who had looked upon these institutions as the embodiment of revolutionary liberty. They found themselves once again placed under military officers and "specialists," many of them drawn from the ranks of the former tsarist army.[60] The demands incurred by defense were already exposing the gap between the promises of 1917 and the realities of running a revolutionary state.

With limited control over the provinces, the central committee relied upon distant soviets to mobilize support in the Crimea, Caucasus and Urals where White armies operated. This inability to command the situation directly produced one of the most infamous tragedies of the revolution. Since August, the royal family had been residing in the Urals. The provisional government evacuated the Romanovs from the capital in the summer of 1917 as uprisings threatened to topple Kerensky's government. With the Bolsheviks in power, the fate of the royal family was placed in the hands of the local soviet. By the summer of 1918, anti-Bolshevik forces were making gains in the Ural region and threatening to take Ekaterinburg, the town where Nicholas and his family were being held captive. As the Ural Soviet became uneasy, Iakov Yourovsky, the local Cheka boss, decided to dispense with the prisoners. On the night of July 16–17, Nicholas, his wife and five children were led to the basement of the Ipatiev House and informed they had been condemned to death by a revolutionary tribunal. The executioners fired their pistols at close range before bayonetting the bodies. According to the official announcement made by the Presidium of the Ural Region Soviet, Tsar Nicholas II had been guilty of violent crimes against the Russian people. In putting him to death, the Presidium had been "fulfilling the will the Revolution."[61]

The rationale was telling. For a government that lacked a popular mandate, the "will of the revolution" was the only thing capable of providing the Bolshevik dictatorship with any semblance of legitimate authority. Much as Robespierre and the Jacobins had claimed over a century before, revolution could be an end in itself. Of course, the Jacobins had demonstrated the inverse of this logic as well. If revolution was deemed an end in itself, it could also justify any end.

Revolutionary Europe

Militarized Socialism and Terror

Explanations for the civil war and the political violence it unleashed have proven to be a bone of contention among Russian historians no less than a judgment on the Russian Revolution itself. One camp has traced the roots of Bolshevik violence to the origins of the movement, citing Lenin's illiberal views and justification of force as core tenets of a Bolshevik ideology disposed toward extremism and authoritarian rule. The Soviet totalitarian state was, in this context, the logical outcome of the Bolshevik revolution.[62] Those presenting a counterpoint to this view have argued against strict ideological readings of the revolution, insisting that the experience of the civil war influenced the authoritarian and centralized nature of Bolshevik rule. Taking this line of argument, the civil war marked a "baptism by fire," as Sheila Fitzpatrick has claimed. Bolshevik leaders and administrators were forced to adapt their revolutionary government to the exigencies of war and political instability as they sought to maintain control over the country.[63]

In these debates, it is important to keep in mind the context in which the Russian Revolution unfolded. Unlike the French Revolution, the Russian Revolution evolved out of an ongoing global conflict the likes of which Europe had never seen. In many respects, the revolution can be considered part of a prolonged experience of militarization and combat, the coda to Russia's "long" First World War.[64] "Total war" had been the order of the day since 1914. Taking control of the state, the Bolsheviks found themselves in possession of a centralized administrative apparatus geared toward war and the management of national resources. The consolidation of Bolshevik power simply accelerated this process. To meet the demands of war and economic crisis, the Bolsheviks had to mobilize industry and agriculture. A Supreme Council of the National Economy was created with powers to confiscate, requisition and forcibly sequester any goods deemed necessary for production and distribution. Under this policy of "War Communism," the state built up an economic administration with nationalized industries and a monopoly over agricultural production. Although these policies were intended to address problems stemming from the war years, they were not devoid of ideological reasoning. Nationalizing industries and managing state production would, it was believed, lay the foundation for a socialist economy. Fighting the war and facilitating the transition to communism were not mutually incompatible.[65]

Whether a practical solution to economic necessity or a model of socialist transformation, War Communism had a profound impact on how ordinary men and women experienced the Bolshevik revolution. Factory workers found the promise of "worker control" violated as state-appointed economic commissariats began monitoring industries and subjecting factory labor to a disciplinary work regime. Grain requisitioning in the countryside sparked conflicts as peasants protested against the Bolshevik "food dictatorship" announced in 1918. Patrols scoured towns and villages in search of grain and other commodities, with those accused of hoarding labeled "enemies of the people" and subject to disciplinary measures. Violence broke out in the Black Earth and Volga regions as peasants refused to turn over food and resisted state requisitioning detachments.[66] Bolshevik ideologues translated peasant resistance into the Manichean terms of class struggle and counter-revolutionary subversion. According to Aleksandr Tsiurupa, the Commissar for Food from 1917 to 1921, state efforts to quell peasant unrest and forcibly extract grain from the countryside amounted to a "war on the rural bourgeoisie."[67]

The militarized atmosphere of the war years provided an environment in which a radical Bolshevik ideology could flourish, and this concurrence of war and revolution fueled political violence.[68] Prior to 1917, Lenin had outlined his views of revolution as a militarized conflict requiring "guerilla actions" and "mass violence" to succeed. Revolution was war, in his estimation, and the proletarian dictatorship was the instrument for implementing state terror on a mass scale.[69] The civil war merely offered the conditions under which this brand of "militarized socialism" and "system of organized violence" would find its truest expression.[70] As an ideological outlook, Marxism had the potential to rationalize acts of violence against imagined "class enemies" that posed an existential threat to socialist control. For Marx, the goal of social revolution was the dissolution of all classes and the realization of absolute equality across the social body.[71] Class struggle may have been the vehicle for social and political change, but it was not an end in itself. In imagining a community of workers as a universal class, Marxism encouraged a totalizing vision of society that eschewed social pluralism.[72] With the Bolsheviks claiming to represent the proletariat, any resistance to the party was interpreted as resistance to the revolution itself. Such logic possessed grave consequences for the future direction the Russian Revolution took.

Resistance exposed the absence of a developed "proletarian consciousness" among the population. Accordingly, the Cheka and the party would have to be its substitute and defender. The proletarian dictatorship thus became a disciplinary state.[73] Guided by Marxist principles, the Bolsheviks strove to enforce an absolute equality that refused to tolerate other social groups. Here was the Rousseauvian general will inflected with a pronounced sociological reasoning, and in the context of militarized social struggle the drive to forge a unified proletarian community justified, if not celebrated, the annihilation of class enemies. "War to the death against the rich and their hangers-on, the bourgeois intellectuals; war on the rogues, the idlers and the rowdies!" Lenin exhorted in late 1917. "All of them are the same brood—the spawn of capitalism, the offspring of aristocratic and bourgeois society."[74] It was through these measures alone that the universal worker community would be protected and the revolution safeguarded.

"Let blood flow like water," claimed a Cheka newspaper. "Only through the death of the old world can we liberate ourselves from the return of those jackals, [the bourgeoisie]."[75] Although such injunctions to cleanse the country of class enemies found expression at the top levels of power, oftentimes terror assumed its own localized dynamics. For the first year of the revolution, the Bolsheviks had only a tenuous hold over the provinces and areas outside the major cities. The Cheka may have been conceived of as an arm of the political state, but in reality the structure of the police force remained decentralized and in the hands of local party bosses throughout much of 1918. Local bosses pursued their own agendas, responding to pressures for "justice" and revenge exerted by the workers and soldiers they served. Attacks against social betters, the plundering of shops and homes belonging to "bourgeois" residents, violence directed against foreign ethnic groups: these and other acts constituted a Red Terror from below as communities sought retribution following years of oppression and social alienation. Only slowly would the Bolshevik central authorities come to exercise greater control over the Cheka and redirect it against politically defined enemies. At the close of the civil war, over 60,000 personnel were employed in the Cheka. By this point, the security forces were responsible for the deaths of some 280,000 people.[76] The Bolsheviks had been aware of their limited reach and endorsed independent action in the defense of the revolution where necessary. A decree of 1918 stated as much, authorizing the extermination of "counter-revolutionary rabble, without having to defer to anyone's authority at all."[77]

The Bolsheviks were conscious of what Trotsky in 1910 described as "the proletariat's unfulfilled feeling of revenge." This desire for vengeance was a powerful tool, he believed, one that the party ought to "stir up again and again" and exploit.[78] With conscription for the Red Army underway, Trotsky turned to drafting bourgeois labor from the populace in order to demonstrate this proletarian wrath firsthand. Former factory owners, professionals and priests were forced to take up menial tasks and perform labor before crowds of spectators. They dug ditches, cleaned out barracks and swept the streets in public displays that inverted familiar social hierarchies. Aristocrats—what the regime now labeled "former people"—were obligated to open up their homes and mansions to workers and share their households with strangers. These tactics were designed to humiliate and degrade nominal class enemies, but they also reflected Bolshevik assumptions that underpinned the logic of social and political violence during the revolution. Under the new regime, class was a key marker of identification. It dictated how one was to be treated and what rights, if any, they possessed.[79] These gestures symbolized the revolution's empowerment of the working class and its triumph over its oppressors. They exhibited the "justice" perpetrated by the socialist state and the values of the new society based upon the virtues of the proletarian masses. Through public degradation and collective punishment, the revolution became a lived experience. It gave shape and form to the worker community, crystallizing the dimensions of class and social identity inherent within notions of soviet citizenship.

Not all punishment was public theater, however. More frequently, disciplinary punishment and violence were ideologically conditioned responses to disorder and social fragmentation. As food shortages resulted and authority broke down, areas succumbed to crime waves and mob violence. Local militias were ill-suited to contain these outbursts, prompting the state to step in and impose a system of "proletarian justice" through the Cheka and revolutionary tribunals. Sentences were typically more lenient for workers and the poor, while groups branded "class enemies" faced harsh punishments and even death for a wide range of offenses. The justice system became an arm of state terror as the regime attempted to impose order on chaos and further solidify its vision of a class-based society through punishment and systematic retribution.[80]

One of the most pressing aspects of social fragmentation concerned the status of the Russian Empire itself. German occupation and the growth of nationalist movements during the war had eroded imperial authority. By 1918, the Ukrainian Rada was conducting independent peace negotiations with the Central Powers in a bid for complete independence. In Central Asia, tensions between Russian settlers and native populations were on the verge of igniting an ethnic war while Bolshevik control in Transcaucasia was being undermined in an ongoing struggle between Georgians, Armenians and Azeris. It did not help that White forces were operating in many of these areas, threatening complete collapse in the borderland provinces. To court the allegiance of national minorities, the Bolsheviks issued a declaration of minority rights in November 1917. The measure abolished all discriminatory legislation and recognized the right to national self-determination over "great Russian chauvinism."[81] While Lenin endorsed self-determination, he insisted that it must be subordinate to "proletarian self-determination." In other words, even if a national group opted for independent statehood, the Bolsheviks had a right to intervene on behalf of the "toiling masses" that populated these areas.[82] Joseph Stalin, the Commissar of Nationalities, gave a blunter assessment that January. "The principle of self-determination must be a means of struggle for socialism," he asserted, "and must be subordinate to the principles of socialism."[83] Simply put, the Bolsheviks intended to retain the empire and wed it to their emancipatory and anti-imperialist platform.

The status of imperial territories was of vital importance when it came to ending the war with the Central Powers. Germany had no plans of vacating the territories it occupied. The peace treaty signed at Brest-Litovsk in March 1918 stripped Russia of its western borderland and secured independence for Poland and the Baltic states under German protection. The Bolsheviks refused to accept this proposal and negotiations stalled until the German command applied military pressure. As German troops occupied eastern Ukraine and Belorussia and threatened to close in on Petrograd, the Bolsheviks fled to Moscow.[84] "It is a question of signing the peace terms now or signing the death sentence of the Soviet Government," Lenin conceded, dispelling any hopes the Bolsheviks might wage a "revolutionary war" against the German war machine.[85] As former imperial territories were relinquished under duress or declared independence of their own accord, Bolshevik promises of self-determination became meaningless. If the carrot had failed, the stick was the alternative.

Between 1918 and 1921, the imperial borderlands were transformed into a battleground between volunteer armies, local warlords, nationalists and Red battalions. In Ukraine, the Red Army carried out a vicious reign of terror against anti-Bolshevik forces. "Be merciless!" the commander Mikhail Muravëv instructed his men as they marched on Kiev. His declaration that Soviet power would only be established "with fire and sword" proved accurate, and when white forces under General Denikin marched through central and eastern Ukraine a year later they were just as ruthless.[86] In Central Asia, political violence fused with ethnic tensions stemming from years of colonial rule. Russian soldiers and settlers compared land-rich Kalmyk pastoralists in the Steppe to feudal landowners and whipped up a rabid nationalist hatred. Bands set fire to Kalmyk homes and unleashed a racially charged fury on non-Russian inhabitants of the region. In late 1917, Russian settlers aligning themselves with the Bolsheviks carried out a coup in Tashkent, setting up a Council of People's Commissars for Turkestan that looked to Petrograd for support. As a settler regime, it denied natives political rights and forbade them from serving in the soviets on the grounds that Muslims lacked the necessary "proletarian organization" to participate in a socialist government. Native elites withdrew to Kokand in the Ferghana Valley and there declared a rival autonomous Turkestani government. Unwilling to tolerate this affront, the Turkestani Soviet dispatched forces to Kokand. Soldiers carried out a campaign of murder and pillage before dousing the city in petrol and setting it ablaze. By the end of 1918, Basmachi guerilla bands composed of Bashir and Kyrghyz fighters were wreaking havoc across the Steppe in struggles against pro-Bolshevik forces.[87]

National and ethnic violence shaped the contours of revolutionary terror in the borderlands where the legacies of empire ran deep. These existing tensions equally informed Bolshevik responses as Moscow attempted to come to grips with anti-imperialist movements. When the hardline military approach proved ineffective, the Bolsheviks switched gears. Between 1919 and 1922, Moscow negotiated the creation of autonomous socialist soviet republics (ASSRs) for the Kazakhs, Tatars, Bashkirs and other native groups. The ASSRs guaranteed autonomy for former imperial peoples while integrating them into a communist party system tied to Moscow. This federal solution was amenable to ethnic elites and struck a balance between centralized rule and self-governance. After a prolonged period of revolutionary upheaval and war, the Bolsheviks managed to elaborate a unique brand of imperialism that reconciled aspirations for self-determination with the principles of socialism and democratic centralism. The creation of the Union of Socialist Soviet Republics (USSR) in 1922 brought the Russian Revolution to an effective close as the Bolsheviks suppressed the resistance movements and outlined a model of revolutionary sovereignty capable of binding a multinational society together.[88]

This restructured "empire of nations" embodied values of internationalism and self-determination central to the left. Yet if the Soviet Union was "nationalist in form," it was to be unquestionably "socialist in content." In the coming years, Bolshevik ideology was communicated through an idiom of national emancipation as native party members spread the gospel of Marxist-Leninism and assisted in the historic project of "building socialism."[89] If the Bolshevik Party championed the vision of a universal proletarian community, the Soviet Union was the personification of this universality. It presented an imagined community of peoples living out the Marxist dictum: "workers of the world unite."

Messianic Socialism

In spite of their professed atheism, the Bolsheviks were slow to attack the Orthodox Church, a traditional pillar of the tsarist autocracy. Through a series of decrees issued between 1917 and 1921, the regime chipped away at the religious establishment. It confiscated parish and monastic lands, rescinded state pensions for religious officials and placed religious schools under state control. Lenin had little desire to provoke a religious conflict while the civil war raged. Only after consolidating power did Lenin, Trotsky and the Bolsheviks launch a full assault on the Church. Beginning in 1922, "counter-revolutionary" priests and bishops were hauled before tribunals to answer for their "crimes." Parish churches were looted and public demonstrations of religion banned. The teaching of religion was made a criminal offense. A socialist society was a secular society, and the Church was the "last citadel" in the Bolsheviks' aggressive war against the past.[90]

The new regime replaced the messianic outlook of Orthodox Christianity with a variety of "messianic socialism," offering a surrogate religion that venerated the revolution, the proletarian state and its historic mission to spread the gospel of worker emancipation.[91] Although the proletarian revolution had begun in Russia, it was never intended to simply be a Russian revolution. The Bolsheviks saw themselves as taking the first step in fulfilling the world revolution prophesized by Marx. "Final victory is only possible on a word scale," Lenin explained to his colleagues, "and only by the joint efforts of the workers of all countries."[92] From the outset, the revolution was communicated in terms of a global struggle against capitalism that was destined to liberate the oppressed classes of all nations. As early as 1914, Lenin had pushed for an aggressive communist internationalism aimed at inciting civil wars and class struggle within European countries. Appalled by the pacifist stance taken by socialist parties across the continent, he argued for waging guerilla wars rather than patient reform.[93] His call to action went largely unheeded during the war years. However, with the collapse of the Central Powers in November 1918 the moment appeared ripe for spreading social revolution throughout Central and Eastern Europe as political and economic turmoil engulfed the region.

Germany was the most promising candidate. In the closing months of the war, Germany had been wracked by strikes and labor protests as the demands of "total war" generated social conflicts. As the German warfront crumbled, soldiers mutinied and workers imitated the Russian soviet movement by setting up *Räte* (councils) to air grievances and organize opposition. With the abdication of Kaiser Wilhelm on November 9, Germany was declared a republic and the Kaiserreich was brought to an unceremonious end. The German left was divided between Social Democrats (SPD) seeking a constitutional regime and Independent Socialist (USPD) calling for revolutionary democracy. While the leader of the SPD, Friedrich Ebert, had momentarily placed himself at the head of a "revolutionary" government, he and his cohorts planned to await the election of a National Assembly and establish a legitimate parliamentary regime. For the *Räte*, this scheme appeared too moderate and left the door open for compromise with the old nobility and military command. Mimicking Russian Communists with the slogan "all power to the councils!" radicals demanded a decentralized and egalitarian society that a "bourgeois" parliamentary regime could not deliver. As the SPD attempted to form a coalition government and push a constitutional agenda, the radicals walked out.[94]

In the closing days of 1918, it appeared that Germany might be on the verge of a soviet-style communist revolution. Observing the situation, Lenin dispatched Karl Radek to Berlin in an effort to stir the pot. A Jew from Lviv with a long history of activism in Polish and German socialist circles, Radek had made the acquaintance of Lenin in Switzerland. He accompanied the Bolshevik leader back to Russia in 1917 and eventually received an appointment as Vice-Commissar of Foreign Affairs. Radek's instructions were simple: engage with the German communists in Berlin and provoke revolution. He courted the most radical wing of the USPD, the insurrectionary Spartacus League led by Karl Liebknecht and Rosa Luxemburg. In early November, Liebknecht had aimed to lead the German radicals by declaring a Free Socialist Republic from the balcony of the Berlin Stadtschloss. The declaration failed to attract popular support, but this did not imply that the Spartacists abandoned their hope of a communist Germany. With its newspaper *The Red Flag*, the Spartacus League agitated for worker revolt and pushed the Social Democrats into a defensive crouch as they attempted to manage an orderly transfer of power. Strikes and protests were not enough, Liebknecht and his cohort argued. It was time to arm the workers, and the Bolsheviks were ready and willing to supply money and aid to this end.[95]

In the days leading up to the revolt, Rosa Luxemburg expressed doubts over a call to arms. It was too precipitous, she warned. The communists did not enjoy widespread support, and without popular support it was difficult to see how they could seize power.[96] Her warnings fell on deaf ears. On January 5, the communists staged their insurrection, coordinating the uprising with a massive worker strike in the capital. As Luxemburg predicted, the uprising was a disaster. The SPD turned to the military for assistance and urged war veterans to organize voluntary Freikorps battalions for national defense. It did not matter that the generals and veterans were conservative monarchists. Freikorp commanders crushed the strikes and rounded up the radical leadership. Liebknecht and Luxemburg were found hiding in an apartment and handed over to the Freikorps who exacted a brutal vengeance. Months later, Luxemburg's body was discovered floating in the Landwehr Canal with a bullet wound to the head. Liebknecht was similarly beaten and shot. The German communist leadership had been decapitated in one swift blow.[97] Severe repression followed and the beleaguered republicans increasingly found themselves reliant on former elites and generals with little taste for democracy. The German revolution was finished.[98]

In his haste to foment European revolution, Lenin failed to realize that postwar Germany was not 1917 Russia. German radicals borrowed the political vocabulary of the socialist labor movement but most were radical democrats at heart. Moreover, unlike the Russian provisional government, the German government had not hesitated to crush leftist attempts to undermine the state. Impatience and miscalculation resulted in a foreign policy debacle for the Soviets, an outcome that was reproduced in Hungary in the following months when Moscow encouraged the left socialist Béla Kun to take power in Budapest and establish a communist dictatorship. Kun had been a POW captured by Russia during the First World War. Upon his release by the Bolsheviks, Kun fought in the Russian civil war and assisted in forming a Hungarian section within the Russian Communist Party. He took up a radical stance, advocating the doctrine of the "revolutionary offensive" favored by Nikolai Bukharin, a Bolshevik politician and fervent proponent of active messianic socialism.[99] Returning to Hungary at the behest of the Soviets, Kun used money supplied by Moscow to put his "revolutionary offensive" into action. That March, Hungarian communists set up a soviet republic and imposed a program of rapid nationalization on land and industry. Kun also harbored aspirations of stirring revolutions in neighboring Czechoslovakia and Romania with the goal of recapturing Hungarian territory lost during the war. These aggressive tactics backfired. Facing mass protests and the threat of invasion from Romania, Kun turned to terror and intimidation. By August, the communist experiment had been thoroughly discredited and Kun fled into exile.[100] Once again, Soviet foreign policy objectives had miscarried.

At the moment Kun took power, however, the Soviets were already beginning to recalibrate their revolutionary strategy. With a Socialist International scheduled to be held in Berne that spring, Lenin decided to convoke his own international congress at the Kremlin. His aim was to split the left and direct the allegiances of radical communists toward Moscow. The Communist International (Comintern) gathered in March 1919, bringing together thirty-five delegates, most of whom were already stationed in Russia. Despite the small number of attendees, the Comintern signified a re-evaluation of Soviet foreign policy. Rather than relying upon POWs and foreign agents with questionable ties to labor movements abroad, the Bolsheviks opted to take an active role in building and training communist movements in order to promote Bolshevik-style revolutions on a global scale. As its opening resolution declared, the Comintern pledged to fight by force of arms "for the overthrow of the international bourgeoisie and the creation of an international Soviet Republic."[101] The organization was to function as the "world party of the proletariat" with Moscow serving as a revolutionary metropole. Grigory Zinoviev, the acting Comintern chairman, conveyed the messianic sentiment underpinning the new international movement when he called upon delegates to ignite "a general holy war" against capitalism in 1920.[102] Overly optimistic, Zinoviev conjectured that within a year all of Europe would be communist and the theater of struggle shifted to America and Asia.

For Lenin, the party had always been the revolutionary vanguard. The Soviet Union was now staking its claims as the vanguard of world revolution. As the "hearth" of socialism, it was charged with the mission of building and maintaining an international radical network consisting of European leftists, anti-colonial fights and Third World intellectuals to different degrees. Training, arms and funding for propaganda and party functions were all on offer, making Moscow a center of subversive world politics. Lofty declarations of internationalism and revolutionary fraternity aside, the Bolshevik leadership intended the Comintern to serve as an extension of the Russian Communist Party with branches subordinate to the Central Committee.[103] Democratic centralism, with its emphasis on party discipline and unity, constituted the acting policy and provided an organizational structure for a new breed of revolutionary politics. The communist party was envisaged as a global model for the left.[104] The objective of the Comintern was not to support international struggles for freedom as such, but rather to Bolshevize world revolution. The revolutionary tradition inherited from the French Revolution was being supplanted. The Bolsheviks were rewriting the revolutionary script for the drama of twentieth-century radical politics.

Conclusion

Taking advantage of the amnesty granted by the government in 1917, Pyotr Kropotkin returned to his native Russia after four decades of exile. Seventy-four years of age, the anarchist veteran saw much to admire in the soviet movement taking shape throughout the country. The soviets were emblematic of the free, self-governing communism he had advocated for over his political career, and throughout the summer of 1917 Kropotkin lent his pen in support of soviet freedom and the expectant future he foresaw for Russia. As the revolution progressed, however, optimism turned to despair. Following the Bolshevik seizure of power, Kropotkin found his ideas of mutual aid and federalism ignored. He was harassed by party officials and his anarchist meetings were broken up by the police. Everywhere he looked, party bosses and political committees were rapidly undermining the freedoms gained after February. The "state communism" favored by the Bolsheviks was an example of "how *not* to introduce communism," in Kropotkin's opinion.[105] Under the Soviet regime, he warned, "the very word *socialism* will become a curse." Kropotkin did not live long enough to see whether his prediction would prove accurate. He died in February 1921 and was buried in a secret funeral in defiance of Bolshevik authorities. Thousands of people attended and black anarchist flags were hung in commemoration. Within a year, the Russian anarchist movement would be non-existent, with many of its adherents fleeing into exile. Those who remained would fall victim to Bolshevik purges and terror.[106]

The Bolsheviks and anarchists had had their ideologically squabbles in the past, but after 1917 these divisions acquired a more lethal dimension. Lenin and the Bolsheviks brought into existence a single-party state, a dictatorship that fashioned itself as both a repository of the proletarian will and a guardian of the revolution that had elevated the working masses to its proper place in history. The revolutionary community imagined by the Bolsheviks was inspired by socialist ideas of worker solidarity and internationalism. However, it would be a community constructed through coercion, extreme violence and the obliteration of "former people." For a party that claimed to embody—rather than simply represent—"proletarian consciousness," minority opinion or deviation was anathema. To tolerate the minority was to tolerate "class enemies" and deny historical truth. In a worker state, only the unified will of the proletariat could prevail, and this will was expressed through the party alone. While the socialist revolution was always envisaged as a process, in time it became a permanent state of affairs as the Soviet regime anchored its *raison d'être* in the building of socialism and the defense of a revolutionary program constantly imagined to be threatened from without. It was a scenario for perpetual "revolutionary government," that concept first elaborated by the Jacobins during the Convention. Of course, the Jacobin dictatorship endured for fifteen months. The proletarian dictatorship would last over forty years, implementing a revolutionary terror that would claim millions of victims by its conclusion.

If the logics of Jacobinism and Bolshevism were comparable, the Bolshevik revolution was not a continuation of its French antecedent. Worker solidarity and internationalism offered a new ideological horizon that looked more to Marx and the Paris Commune of 1871 than it did to 1789 for inspiration. As a vanguard movement directed toward the future, the Bolsheviks consciously eschewed what Marx once referred to as the "poetry of the past." They placed their faith in the laws of history and the ideological certainty these offered rather than appealing to a revolutionary tradition. Supplanting concepts of natural rights and national sovereignty with a discourse of class identification, the Bolshevik revolution indicated the extent to which 1917 engendered its own revolutionary culture rooted in the party, international solidarity and the rhetoric of violent class struggle. These elements were written into the new revolutionary narrative. They not only sustained a vision of a multi-national Soviet community; they positioned Russia at the head of a global revolutionary movement prophesized to lead humanity to the end of history.

EPILOGUE: REVOLUTIONARY CURRENTS BEYOND EUROPE

Writing in 1907 with his typical air of certitude, Lenin insisted that Russian workers would never be appeased with promises of reform or parliamentary government. "The proletariat will uphold the revolutionary tradition," he pronounced confidently, indicating that when it came to the task of social and political transformation there could be no half-measures. As for his fellow Social Democrats, they too were beholden to a revolutionary "tradition" that had its origins in the late eighteenth century. "Present-day Social Democrats attach so much value to the great fruits of the French Revolution," observed Lenin, not without criticism.[1] Whether in action or thought, revolution was continually being evaluated in light of past precedents and examples that imparted a sense of continuity across an otherwise tumultuous long nineteenth century.

While hardly following a straight line, the path from 1789 to 1917 did trace the evolution of a European revolutionary tradition that influenced politics and political movements on the continent. European radicals possessed a set of shared discourses through which they articulated their revolutionary aspirations and programs. They had at their disposal a common stock of reference points, rituals, symbols and memories that accumulated over years and fashioned a distinct radical political culture and ideology. These shared traditions did not imply uniformity, since they could be and often were adapted to local circumstances and particular ideas of community as needed. Yet assumptions of a common genealogy could not be ignored either. Bakunin was not entirely incorrect when claiming that revolutionary socialism was "the latest offspring of the Great [French] Revolution."[2] Some feared the power exercised by the past, warning, as the anarchist Jean Grave did in 1893, that pale imitation would only serve to create "a barrier to the future."[3] Nearly a half-century earlier, Alexander Herzen had expressed similar reservations while chronicling the failed revolutions of 1848. "The traditions of the first revolution ... have been deeply engraved on our memories," he concluded as the revolutionary movements collapsed that year. Given the long shadow cast by the French Revolution over his generation, was it inevitable that revolutionaries sought to make "a copy in the name of an original" and nothing more?[4] For all its shortcomings, however, the revolutionary wave of 1848 did demonstrate that these memories and political rituals inherited from the past were a continent-wide phenomenon. Europe's revolutionary tradition and the radicalism it sustained were transnational in nature. "We have all been educated by revolutions," Alexis de Tocqueville remarked in 1851, a comment that would be no less valid in the early twentieth century as war and political upheaval profoundly transformed the continent once again.[5]

Revolutionary Europe

It was not simply that the recognition of a revolutionary tradition provided a measure of cohesion that reinforced radical solidarity. The collective memoires, practices and discourses that underpinned this tradition were constantly invoked through the acts of community building that radicals engaged in and sought to actualize. Songs, symbols, grand gestures, iconography and canonical texts, heroes and martyrs: these were just as important in shaping a common radical culture and identity on the continent as were the broader ideas and ideologies that informed radical politics. Together, they helped invent a tradition to which Europeans would continually appeal time and time again, whether in response to political crises or in seeking to mobilizing support against the reigning status quo.

It is, however, important to recognize that this revolutionary tradition was one among others and that revolution was not solely the preserve of Europeans. Over the course of the nineteenth century, radicalism assumed different forms across the globe. In certain instances, non-European activists were inclined to blend European influences with indigenous elements, if not look elsewhere altogether for inspiration. In Latin America, revolutionaries like Bolívar had drawn upon European and Western models early in the century as they attempted to carve out post-colonial nation-states. Yet by the 1840s, a new generation of activists showed themselves less enchanted with the Old World. Confronted with the realities of institutionalized slavery in the United States and renewed European colonial expansion, Latin Americans placed their hopes in the promise of Atlantic republicanism as an alternative to the racism and monarchical absolutism endemic to European societies. Looking toward their own political institutions and revolutionary traditions, they believed that the Rights of Man would find its most complete expression in the democratic republics of Spanish America, not Europe or the United States.[6] As one Columbian journalist claimed in 1864: "Europe is the past; America the future." Latin American republicans prided themselves on their robust political cultures, tolerance and commitment to fraternity for "all peoples and faiths."[7] This vision of Latin American vanguardism, rooted in the conviction that the post-colonial republics of the global south would establish a more perfect society free of racism and imminently more democratic than its North American or European counterparts, lasted well into the 1870s. During the mid-nineteenth century, Latin American radicals repeatedly published pamphlets and took up arms against authoritarian regimes in defense of their vision of republican modernity. Iconic revolutionary heroes like Garibaldi, who fought in South America during the1830s and 1840s, popularized the republican struggle among international audiences. These endeavors revealed that the values of liberty, equality and fraternity were neither geographically confined to Europe nor exclusive products of Western, European political cultures.

Having achieved formal independence from European rule, Afro-Caribbean and Latin American activists were perhaps at the forefront of a movement that would acquire a global resonance over the course of the nineteenth century: anti-colonial resistance. Yet following the age of Atlantic revolutions, the scope and terrain of this struggle shifted as European imperialism came to assert itself more forcefully in Asia and Africa. In 1857, Britain faced a massive uprising in India when units in the Third Native Cavalry revolted, setting off a chain of rebellions throughout the upper Ganges region and central Subcontinent. Provocation for the revolt stemmed from a variety of causes. The East India Company had progressively been eclipsing the traditional powers of the local Nawaab princes while the recruitment of British officers alienated local commanders who found themselves subject to overbearing foreign officials. What began as a localized mutiny that May rapidly metastasized into a widespread rebellion that would inspire calls for the restoration of Mughal sovereignty. The British reprisal was severe as the East India Company and British forces worked to re-establish control over the next year.[8] Although the anti-colonial elements of the rebellion became evident as British authority collapsed over the summer and fall of 1857 and the Islamic *ulama'* assisted in setting up a new Mughal emperor in Delhi, the rebellion itself was not framed in a revolutionary context. As Jürgen Osterhammel has argued, Indian rebels did not outline a new or alternative vision of society. Nor did they actively attempt to build a counter-state to supplant the British administration. Calls for the restoration of the Mughal Empire looked back to a pre-colonial tradition of leadership, highlighting a distinction between "rebellion" and social-political "revolution."[9]

Yet the fact that anti-colonial rebellions drew upon indigenous and "traditional" models of authority to mobilize resistance should not imply all movements were devoid of revolutionary implications. On the contrary, many of the resistance movements that roiled colonial empires in predominantly Muslim areas challenged tradition and hinted at the emergence of an alternative Islamic revolutionary discourse. Beginning in the eighteenth century, Sufi brotherhoods began to espouse an activist religious message emphasizing the reconstruction of Muslim society through the political and military defense of Islam. Often branded as "neo-Sufism," this form of Islamic revivalism fed into a variety of popular movements across Africa and Asia that would mix with anti-colonial platforms. In itself, the ideology of Sufi revivalism was not explicitly radical. However, Sufi organizational structures provided vehicles for mobilizing wide-scale resistance through the interconnected networks of religious lodges and schools overseen by Sufi orders. By instrumentalizing the brotherhoods, anti-colonial leaders were capable of tapping into these pre-existing networks for the purposes of forging cross-tribal alliances and building broader regional movements. In this environment, community leaders and militants effectively "politicized" Islam, employing traditional religious discourses and concepts of *jihad* to oppose European colonialism.[10]

During the nineteenth century, anti-colonial movements pressed traditional structures and discourses into service, in many cases to achieve new and potentially revolutionary ends. The Algerian resistance leader Abd al-Qādir enlisted the aid of Sufi brotherhoods and the Moroccan sultanate in his campaigns against the French military during the 1830s and 1840s. As Ottoman authority collapsed and left a power vacuum throughout much of Algeria, Abd al-Qādir undertook an ambitious state-building program that envisioned a Muslim community unified under the "pure law of God." His efforts enlisted Sufi networks and Moroccan bureaucratic structures to temporarily create an independent Algerian emirate with the powers of conscription and taxation. At its height, the emirate extended over two-thirds of Algeria and rallied supporters with calls of *jihad* against the French.[11] At approximately the same time, Imam Shamil was waging a comparable resistance movement against Russian forces in the Caucasus that would draw support from local branches of the Naqshbandiyya Sufi brotherhood. Like Abd al-Qādir, Shamil endeavored to create a centralized and modern government based upon the Qur'an and Sunna. He imagined a state built upon pure Islamic principles that could unite and mobilize the tribes of Chechnya and Dagestan.[12] In the 1880s, British forces found themselves similarly confronted with an uprising in the Sudan that would have revolutionary implications as combatants attempted to create a Mahdist state with the aid of regional Sufi *shykhs*.[13]

Anti-colonial resistance movements employed traditional and religious rhetoric to frame political agendas against European invaders, but appeals to traditional sources of authority often veiled overtly revolutionary intentions. European expansion into regions of Africa and Asia disrupted old power arrangements and destroyed established economic patterns. As such, imperialism catalyzed the breakdown of regional authority and created the conditions under which new forms of society and sovereignty could be imagined.[14] Muslim anti-colonial movements during the mid-nineteenth century encompassed acts of state-building and the reorganization of state–society relations. In many cases, militants appropriated and reformulated familiar concepts such as *jihad* (struggle) and *barakah* (spiritual authority) for new ends, linking them to modernizing projects. As the century wore on, moreover, various radical and reformist movements across the Near and Middle East began wedding modernist and Pan-Islamic currents to liberation and resistance platforms. Muslim intellectuals used the press and print media to spread their ideas and build transnational movements that were comparable in scope to the anarchist networks of the fin-de-siècle.[15] Mixing notions of secular progress with ideas of religious revivalism and unity, Islamic modernism developed a radical strain in the late nineteenth century that was just as critical of contemporary Muslim society as it was of the inimical influences of European imperialism.

Cairo was a chief nerve center of Islamic modernism, and it was in this milieu that one of the leading Islamic modernist thinkers would find his voice. Sayyid Jamāl al-Dīn al-Afghānī had gained a reputation as a reform-minded activist prior to his arrival in Egypt in 1871. His advocacy of Muslim unity and modernization drew both praise and criticism from Muslim elites. Yet in Cairo, he became an outspoken critic of European influence on the Egyptian government. In print and speech, Afghānī supported in turn nationalism, Pan-Islamic affiliation, violent jihadism and secular innovation. If his message was contradictory at times, his insistence on radical opposition to authoritarian regimes and European imperial power remained consistent. In 1879, he and his followers were expelled from Egypt for their open criticism of the reigning Khedive. They continued their political activities from Paris, publishing one of the first Islamic political newspapers with an international readership. Afghānī was forced to watch from afar as patriotic Egyptian nationalists led a revolt against the Khedival state in 1881. British intervention and the brutal suppression of the uprising did nothing to mitigate his anti-imperialist rhetoric. Over the next decade, Afghānī moved through Europe and the Muslim world, encouraging a vision of Islam as a global ideology of resistance against Western imperialism that would have repercussions in North Africa, the Ottoman Empire, Persia and India. Although never succeeding in his goal of igniting a Pan-Islamic revolution, Afghānī's efforts popularized the anti-colonial cause and inspired a generation of Salafist modernizers and radicals.[16]

In their most radical variants, Pan-Islamism and Islamic modernization constituted revolutionary forms of community building that stood opposed to Western hegemony and authoritarianism. By the twentieth century, these themes were serving as the driving ideology for guerrilla fighters in North Africa, as loose-knit groups like the Maghreb Unity Society organized international recruitment drives and dispatched insurgents to Morocco and Libya where they took up arms against French and Italian forces.[17] The Young Turk revolution further encouraged this brand of radicalism, providing a model of Islamic revolutionary modernization in action. Newspapers across the Muslim world hailed the event as a milestone in the development of Islamic civilization while European designs to dismember the empire aroused international indignation. This image of the Young Turks continued into the war years and became a central theme in propaganda aimed at encouraging Pan-Islamic uprisings in Entente colonial territories. As the German-Ottoman periodical *Die Islamische Welt* reported in 1917: "The rising development of the Ottoman Empire also means an uprising of the entire Islamic world."[18] Radical projects of Islamic modernization and unity found a place in the anti-colonial politics of the long nineteenth century. They were products of a Muslim revolutionary discourse that drew upon religious and traditional sources of authority in order to imagine a regenerated Islamic community liberated from colonial oppression.

Islamic modernism and Pan-Islamism were not the only forms of protest available to anti-colonial activists. Strikes and socialist-inspired worker demonstrations were on the rise across the world as were various other movements ranging from nationalism to transnational ideologies like Pan-Asianism and anarchism. All of this fed into a broader climate of anti-colonial protest, with movements acquiring radical overtones as the nineteenth century neared its close.[19] Non-Western states increasingly found themselves pressured to carry out reforms in order to maintain their independence and compete with European imperial powers. Governments that refused to abide often risked radicalizing domestic reform movements and alienating elites at home, creating conditions under which revolutions could occur. The Ottoman Empire provided one such example of this process at work, although it was hardly the first. Indeed, the Yung Turks themselves had looked to others for inspiration.[20] By the turn of the century, Japan had become the leading model of successful modernization by a non-Western power. It was also an international symbol for those protesting against Western imperial hegemony in the name of global equality.

During the late 1850s, Japanese elites had been divided over how best to manage relations with the West. Pressure exerted by foreign powers to open Japan to Western trade placed the reigning Tokugawa Bakufu in a perilous situation. Reform-minded elites urged modernizing initiatives that would strengthen Japan vis-à-vis predatory imperial powers. More radical reformers went further and attacked the entrenched feudal hierarchies that empowered high-level samurai and noble families, insisting privilege had made the government effete and ineffective. For their part, conservatives in the government refused to entertain reform and summarily purged the government of all opponents. Over the 1860s, conflict between these two factions intensified, provoking violence that tore the shogunate apart. Lower-level samurai were particularly active among the opposition, promoting values of meritocracy and state service that broke with Tokugawa traditions of obedience and loyalty favorable to the upper nobility (*daimyō*). Rather than loyalty to feudal lords, opponents preached loyalty to the emperor. In their perspective, the emperor could serve as a symbol of the Japanese community by embodying classical ideals of leadership and unity. Hardly democrats, so-called "restorationists" did nonetheless seek to transform the social and institutional landscape of Japan. In 1868, the Tokugawa shogunate collapsed and within five years those leading the imperial restoration (*ishin*) were actively dissolving the feudal order, creating a new state bureaucracy modeled on the West and devising a new national education system.[21]

The Meiji Ishin was framed as a return to ancient Japanese principles of imperial rule, but the coming years ushered in major changes in government and state–society relations that were nothing short of revolutionary. Meiji statesmen did not dispense with the imperial polity or traditional concepts of dynastic sovereignty. Yet within thirty years' time they managed to transform an assemblage of military fiefdoms into a modernizing imperial nation-state that claimed parity with the European powers.[22] Observers from the Americas to Asia invested the Ishin with political and world-historical significance. According to one commentator from Delhi, Japanese modernization proved to all people suffering the injustices of colonial rule that progress was not the sole preserve of Europe. "They have not only been able to accomplish the deeds that go to make a people civilized in the eyes of Europe, but they have done so without changing their creed, colour, descent or even their characteristics as an Asian nation," the author commended.[23] Others saw in the Ishin the promise of a new universal revolution focused on international equality and a turn away from the bourgeois liberalism of the West. The Russian populist and journalist Grigorii Blagosvetlov was convinced that events in Japan constituted a moment of rupture with the past. "In Japan, everything is being re-created anew," he remarked.[24] Other radical Russian thinkers were similarly excited about the new horizons opened by Japan's revolutionary turn and saw in it a model of transformation that could be adapted within a global, and hence human context.

These expectations were also shared by Japanese activists, many of whom socialized with Russian émigrés and other radical exiles who ended up in Asia. During the 1880s, the Freedom and People's Rights Movement pushed for constitutional and egalitarian reforms, arguing that the promises of the Ishin had yet to be fulfilled. The message of equality crept into various social and political movements across Japan, including peasant riots in the countryside, labor grievance in newly established industries and even anti-imperial movements critical of Japan's policies in Korea and China.[25] "By nature, human beings should be equal," proclaimed Fumiko Kaneko, a female anarchist whose plan to assassinate members of the imperial family led to her arrest and eventual suicide in prison in 1926.[26] An anarchist movement was well-established in Japan by the 1890s, especially as Japanese socialist renounced revolutionary tactics and committed themselves to worker organization and legal opposition. Japanese anarchists took inspiration from Russian populism and European radicals, but they also engaged with a variety of popular causes closer to home. Despite its origins, anarchism was never a purely Western product, and radicals did not see it as such. By the 1890s, it had become part of a global radical movement that was channeled into a variety of political causes, whether anti-imperial, anti-statist or libertarian-socialist in nature. Given its ideological flexibility and ability to adapt to local circumstances, anarchism was praised by adherents for its universal applications.[27] It was, moreover, this universality that bolstered a sense of solidarity among the international anarchist community and endowed anarchism with the status of a global political doctrine of the left.

By the turn of the century, Japanese radicals were coming to see their country's revolutionary awakening as part of a global process of emancipation and social development shared with others. If Russian populists had hailed the Meiji Ishin as a transformative moment in world history, Japanese anarchists repaid the compliment when it came to the Russian revolution of 1905. "Russia at the beginning of the twentieth century is like France at the beginning of the nineteenth century …," claimed the socialist-turned-anarchist Kōtoku Shūsui. "All the lost countries of the East look for a sign from the Russian Revolution."[28] The Meiji Ishin, 1905 Russia, the Young Turk Revolution: these became models and reference points within a global revolutionary tradition being elaborated outside the Western world. It was evident that the geography of radicalism was shifting as anti-imperial and internationalist currents infused leftist movements from Buenos Aires to Tokyo with a new energy, dissolving conceptual boundaries such as "East" and "West," "Modern" and "Backward" or "Civilized" and "Savage."

"The class-conscious European worker now has comrades in Asia," Lenin chortled when taking note of the upheavals destabilizing world politics by 1908. Whether events like the Young Turk Revolution were precursors to an international proletarian revolution had yet to be seen, but Lenin was perceptive when it came to politics in the Far East. There was no doubt that a "new spirit" was presenting itself in China, he claimed. The "old-style Chinese revolts" were on their way to becoming a modern democratic revolution, entailing that China now stood poised to enter the age of global revolution.[29]

China between Tradition and Radical Change

Writing from Hong Kong in 1907, the journalist Douglas Story reported that "for the first time in history" the Chinese people appeared to find themselves united as grievances against the government brought together "all sections of the community." As Story put it, "Unconsciously the Chinese have welded themselves into a nation."[30] The insistence that the Chinese were becoming a nation was novel, and many Europeans—let alone subjects of the Chinese imperial court—might have disagreed with Story's reading of events. A "Celestial Empire" in decline, perhaps; but it was difficult to see how China conformed to what most Europeans thought of as a national community.

The ruling Qing dynasty was Manchu, a northern people who had conquered and occupied China in the seventeenth century. The court relied upon a hereditary military caste organized through a Banner System that rewarded soldiers with salaries and land. While these banner people came from diverse origins, by the nineteenth century the majority Han population was coming to consider them as simply "Manchu," a foreign ethnicity ruling over a subjugated native Chinese population. The Qing dynasty itself did little to discourage this impression. Manchus had a separate administrative and legal status compared to the civilian Han population. They lived in segregated communities and received preferential treatment in terms of recruitment and official appointments. Qing expansion over the eighteenth and nineteenth centuries had been impressive, doubling the size of the empire and tripling China's population. Yet it had also made it an exceedingly diverse state, bringing Tibetans, Uighur, Muslims, Mongols, Burmese and Tai populations under Qing rule. Aside from the court which presided over the Manchu and Han, a Court of Colonial Affairs (*Lifan Yuan*) was responsible for dealing with the populations on the imperial peripheries.[31] Qing China was a multiethnic empire, and the Manchu court did not always prove effective at regulating ethnic relations within the imperial community.

Tensions between the court in Beijing and the south boiled over at mid-century in a calamitous civil war that devastated large parts of the empire between 1850 and 1864.

Figure 21 An image of the multi-ethnic Qing court in the final years of dynastic rule. The photograph shows a Tatar, Manchu and Han official. © The British Library Board.

Epilogue

The Taiping Heavenly Kingdom movement began in the Guangxi highlands before spreading to surrounding provinces and the Yangzi region. The mix of millenarian and Christian elements preached by Taiping leaders was effective in mobilizing supporters. Yet perhaps more significant, the movement appealed to the growing anti-Manchu sentiment taking root among Han Chinese of the south. The fighting that ensued was vicious, tearing entire regions apart. At its height, rebels set up a counter-state with a capital at Nanjing that presented a serious challenge to Manchu rule from the north. Crushing the rebellion further exposed the limits of Qing power. Unable to topple the Heavenly Kingdom on its own, the court was forced to rely upon local and regional authorities. Provincial governors cobbled together militias and armies that subsequently broke up rebel strongholds and restored order through brutal military campaigns. Once the conflict ended, local and provincial authorities were hesitant to relinquish their new powers. A shift in metropolitan-provincial power relations became noticeable, exposing the gap between the Manchu court and Han officials in the provinces. Moreover, the anti-dynastic rhetoric, certainly evident prior to the Taiping Rebellion, was heightened during the civil war, unleashing a racialized, anti-Manchu opposition that lingered into the coming years.[32]

Domestic opposition to the Qing was compounded with the ever-present fear of foreign invasion and colonial subjugation. In the wake of the so-called Opium Wars, Britain secured territorial rights over Chinese land and forcibly imposed trade policies on specified treaty ports beneficial to British merchants. Other European powers followed suit in the coming decades, subjecting the Qing to unequal trade agreements that slowly eroded the dynasty's economic and eventual political sovereignty. In 1894, Japan, eager

Map 13 The Qing Empire in the nineteenth century.

to extend its influence over mainland Asia, dealt a further humiliating blow to Qing prestige when it defeated Chinese forces in Korea. In addition to exposing the weakness of the Qing military, the Japanese forced the Chinese government to cede the Liaodong Peninsula and Taiwan, adding insult to injury. Europeans watched with a mix of awe and alarm as the Sino-Japanese War played out, and by its conclusion there was little doubt that the equilibrium of East Asia had shifted. With Japan entering the imperial game, the powers immediately began scrambling to secure further concessions and access to territory in the region.[33]

In 1900, these tensions produced a violent xenophobic backlash as peasants organized into secret societies and rose up across the north. Christian missionaries were a primary target of these "Boxer" rebels, although foreign schools and homes were also attacked. As the movement overtook Beijing, the imperial court lent support to the Boxer cause, calling upon the people to rid the country of foreigners and liberate China. Europeans would have none of it and quickly dispatched troops to the scene, although not before a German diplomat was shot dead and paraded through the streets. The Boxer Rebellion marked a turning point in Sino-European relations. Henceforth, China was treated as a "barbaric" state, and the peace settlement following the uprising effectively reduced China to a European dependency.[34] The Qing had attempted to co-opt a popular and radical anti-foreign movement for its own end, and the tactic had severely backfired. Rather than liberating China from foreigners, the Qing now found its empire on the verge of being partitioned among the imperial powers. The weakness of the dynasty was evident for all to see.

Elites were not blind to the impotence of the dynasty or the imminent threat of foreign occupation. Reform became the watchword of intellectuals and bureaucrats alike during the 1890s. The Cantonese scholar Kang Youwei was at the forefront of this initiative, insisting that industrialization and Westernization were both necessary to "rejuvenate" Chinese society and save it from colonial servitude. For inspiration, Kang turned to classical Chinese heritage, asserting that modernization was consistent with tradition. In 1897, Kang left little doubt as to his position when he published his book entitled *Confucius the Reformer* (1897). It was clear he envisioned a program for China similar to that of Meiji Japan. Yet it was also a program inspired by an idealized Chinese past in which enlightened local elites were free to set government policy uninhibited by a foreign northern court. "Self-government," whether applied to the provinces or the individual, was a central theme of Kang's thinking. He imagined a social revival led by autonomous provincial governors and an energized citizenry, and he was not afraid to provide a model for this type of active citizen either. During the Sino-Japanese War, he led students in anti-war demonstrations. Afterwards, he took a leading role in setting up study societies in Beijing and Shanghai to promote reform. China had a tradition of study societies dating back to the late Ming dynasty. Yet these societies were distinct in their attention to political concerns and Western ideas.[35] "Chinese substance, Western function" became a slogan touted in reform circles, suggesting that China need not abandon its cultural and historical identity in the pursuit of a modern state and society.[36]

Kang and his followers did have a specific vision for an imperial China. Rather than a state predicated upon militarized ethnic rule, they imagined a decentralized empire of autonomous provinces governed by enlightened statesmen. As a classically trained scholar, Kang had a deep veneration for the Confucian tradition as well as an appreciation for China's "natural" inclination toward voluntary association. He, like his disciple Liang Qichao, came from the southern province of Guangdong where Han proto-nationalism was taking shape against the Manchu court. The reformist camp valorized "local governance" (*xiangzhi*) and individual engagement with the locality. These elements would revive Chinese society, and they could only come about with a return to pure Chinese—read "Han"—tradition and the end of "foreign" dominance. "The Chinese state is the result of the conglomeration of localities," Liang argued. He traced this concept back through Chinese classical literature, finding in the past the "aspiration of local governance" evident in forms of philanthropy, study societies and mutual aid organizations.[37] In proposing a counter vision of the Chinese imperial community, reformers offered a liberalized, provincially based imperial system that was ultimately nationalist in sentiment. Such a polity might assist in resolving yet another pressing issue for reformers, namely how to "dissolve Manchu-Han differences," as the writer Zhang Yuanji phrased it.[38] In the final judgment, revitalizing civic life and effacing ethnic differences were believed necessary steps in uniting China against aggressive foreigners and restoring Chinese sovereignty.

Kang and other reformers did not present themselves as intransigent opponents of the Qing, but rather as potential allies in rejuvenating the state. Confronted with a dire situation, the young Guangxu Emperor was willing to oblige. In 1898, he invited Kang to the court and invested him with the authority to implement a reformist agenda. That summer, plans were drawn up to streamline the administration, reorganize ministries, revise the educational and judicial systems and encourage industrial activities. Given Kang's political views, it was not unthinkable that plans for a constitutional government and dispensing with the old Banner System might follow. The optimism was short-lived, however. That September, the Empress Dowager Cixi, a powerful woman committed to the existing Manchu imperial system, brought the ambitious "Hundred Days' Reform" to an abrupt end. In what amounted to a palace coup, Cixi placed her nephew the emperor under house arrest, purged the government and proceeded to hunt down advocates of reform. Kang Youwei and Liang Qichao saw which way the wind was blowing and fled to Japan. They had believed they could work with the government in modernizing the empire. After the Hundred Days' Reform, however, this expectation was dashed. Manchu rule itself was now the problem. "Without destruction there can be no construction …," Liang railed from Yokohama. "We must shatter at a blow the despotic and confused governmental system of some thousands of years."[39]

For the most part, Chinese opposition leaders were welcomed by Japanese reformers and radicals. Groups harboring Pan-Asian aspirations saw a benefit in cultivating ties with Chinese elites. Prominent Meiji political actors entertained hopes of organizing émigrés and creating a unified Chinese party that would look to Japan and promote Japanese interests on the mainland. In this atmosphere, Chinese exiles were permitted to run newspapers critical of the Qing and give public lectures. These activities attracted Chinese students currently studying in Japan, many of whom began mingling with Japanese anarchists and gravitating toward more radical platforms. In Tokyo, Chinese activists found new opportunities to organize and forge political networks. They also found themselves subject to new ideological influences.[40] Japanese journalists and book publishers provided access to translations of Western political works, and through them access to new concepts and ideas. Words such as *minzu* (nation), *minquan* (people's rights) and *gongheguo* (republic) now made their way into the Chinese political vocabulary. The term "revolution" (*geming*) was no different. Although familiar to Chinese political thinkers, "revolution" traditionally connoted the end of a dynastic cycle and the founding of a new ruling family in Chinese political discourse. The Japanese press, on the contrary, regularly used the Western term "revolution" to imply violent social and political upheaval. Chinese radicals espoused this concept and adapted it to their own movements, abandoning former terms such as "rebellion" and "popular protest" to describe their actions.[41]

New ideological concepts came to inform new political practices as well. Mimicking Russian populists and anarchists, Chinese students began forming secret societies. The militant Yang Yulin exemplified the radicalization of Chinese youth taking place at the dawn of the twentieth century. While studying in Japan, Yang participated in antiimperial Chinese movements and in 1903 assisted in setting up a joint Sino-Japanese Volunteer Corps to fight Russian encroachment in Manchuria. The organization was, however, a cover for establishing a Chinese revolutionary party. Yang also helped set up an expatriate Chinese press, editing the newspaper *Translations from Students Abroad* which openly advocated for revolution against the Qing regime.[42] Militant student groups typically organized according to their home provinces, exhibiting an emergent "provincial patriotism" that was not entirely national in scope.[43] Yet this did not preclude aspirations of national association either. In his work *New Hunan* written in 1903, Yang Yulin called upon his fellow Hunanese to give themselves over to the "spirit of destruction" as they built an anarchist style movement that would draw in the Chinese peasant classes.[44] The following year, Yang helped found the Society for China's Revival to promote the creation of revolutionary cells in Hunan province. In its tactics and ideology, Yang's program was a variant of Russian populism, emphasizing violence at the local level for the purposes of inspiring a national revolt.

These and other ideas were spread through newspapers and organizational links that spanned from Japan to Shanghai, a Chinese port city largely under European jurisdiction and relatively free of Qing oversight. Students returning from abroad also played a role in the dissemination of radical ideas, especially in areas around the lower Yangzi, Hunan and Guangdong provinces of the south. The revolutionary cells and militant organizations established in China were small, often provincial in their scope and largely autonomous. Yet through these conduits, radicals were coming to outline a new vision of Chinese society with broader implications. They dispensed with the multiethnic Qing state altogether and placed their hopes in a republic that would empower the Chinese people and encourage national revival.

In tandem with the rise of militant radicalism, anti-Manchu sentiments provided another factor of radical cohesion. As one newspaper remarked in 1903, "We will rid ourselves of this alien race of five million barbarians as easily as pulling up a rotten stump."[45] Manchu-Han relations had perennially been a problem for the Qing government. By the turn of the century, militants were mounting a nationalist, anti-imperialist movement that heightened awareness of Manchu domination and articulated it in racial terms. Western ideas of rights and liberty were applied within the context of Han emancipation. The young Sichuanese radical Zou Rong, recently returned from Japan, spelled out his aversion to Han subjugation in his influential pamphlet *The Revolutionary Army* (1903). He urged his fellow Han to overthrow and "annihilate" the Manchu race that enslaved them. "Take revolution as every man's duty," he commanded. "Consider it as necessary as your daily food."[46] The radical revolutionary Zhang Ji was no more sympathetic to the Qing. "Why do I find fault with the Manchu people?" he asked in 1903. "Because China belongs to the Chinese people."[47] Such injunctions fueled outright violence as well. In 1905, a member of the conspiratorial Restoration Society detonated an explosive in Beijing intending to kill five official commissioners the government was sending abroad as part of an exploratory committee for constitutional reform. More alarming was the assassination carried out by Xu Xilin the following year on the governor of Anhui. Radicalized in Japan before joining the Restoration Society, Xu Xilin freely admitted his act had been motivated by hatred for the Manchu, alerting the imperial government to the dangers that anti-Manchu sentiment posed as it mixed with revolutionary programs. "Expel the Manchus" was becoming an expression of a radical revolutionary nationalism that threatened to undermine the very basis of the Qing state and the imperial community it presided over.[48]

Despite their disorganized character, revolutionaries were coming to construct a radically different conception of Chinese sovereignty and community. The question was whether these various aspects and movements could be brought together to form a cohesive vanguard. The activist Sun Yat-sen believed they could and, moreover, that he was the individual to do it. Sun, like many of the leading Chinese reformers, came from Guangdong in the south. Often shunned by elites such as Kang Youwei due to his lack of a classical Chinese education, Sun turned to secret societies and forms of direct political engagement instead. At heart, he believed that rapid modernization was the only means of safeguarding Chinese sovereignty from Western imperialists. In working toward this end, Sun associated with the anti-dynastic and xenophobic secret societies across the south. He exhibited a talent for integrating these networks and bringing them under his leadership.[49] Qing authorities clamped down on Sun's activities following a series of abortive uprisings around Guangzhou. Like others, he fled into exile, moving through Hawaii, the United States, England and Japan. Each place he landed, Sun expanded his political networks. He cultivated ties with foreign Chinese communities that provided access to funds. He made contacts with Europeans and established safe heavens in Shanghai beyond the reach of Qing authority. Most important, he developed relations with militant student organizers in Japan. In 1905, with the aid of Japanese brokers, Sun met with young Chinese radicals in Tokyo and worked out an agreement that brought into existence a new Revolutionary Alliance, an organizational structure that promised to create a united revolutionary front with Sun at its head.

The alliance possessed an internal hierarchy and structure, giving it the semblance of a political party.[50] In reality, however, it was a loose-knit organization beset by infighting, regional differences and vying personalities. As such, the alliance was prone to centrifugal and autonomist influences from the start. Sun attempted to obviate this fractiousness by drafting a founding declaration of principles, the People's Three Principles. It committed alliance members to the overthrow of the Manchu, the restoration of Chinese sovereignty and the creation of a republic, and the equalization of land. Yet, most important, it stressed the need for Chinese unity. "If we do not earnestly espouse nationalism and weld together our four hundred million people into a strong nation," Sun urged, "there is a danger of China's being lost and our people being destroyed."[51] Although national unity was the message proffered by Sun, anti-Manchu sentiment proved to be the real ideological glue of the alliance and the leaders knew it. Under the Manchus, the Chinese were a "nationless" people. "China is the China of the Chinese," stated the alliance's manifesto. "Its government must return to the Chinese."[52] To this end, radicals invested their hopes in the idea of a republic that would remake social and political relations in the country. "Republicanism is carried out for the benefit of the many," explained the revolutionary Chen Tianhua in 1905, juxtaposing it against the personalized rule of the Qing imperial dynasty.[53] Many of these revolutionary principles were not new, radicals argued. Drawing upon the discourse of earlier reformers like Kang and Liang, writers championed forms of self-government and collective liberty believed "natural" to China. Republican democracy would simply extend these ancient Chinese principles into the modern age, Sun Yat-sen contended. The appeal of this revolutionary nationalism was its syncretic mix of indigenous tradition and modernity. These came together in the vision of a reconstituted Chinese community liberated from foreign oppression, "oppression" being understood in the double context of Manchu imperialism and Great Power colonialism.

The only problem was that the revolutionaries did not have a monopoly on anti-Manchu sentiment. It had been growing steadily over the course of the early twentieth century, especially as the Manchu government enacted a series of "new policies" intended to strengthen the central imperial administration. In the wake of the Boxer Rebellion, the Qing became painfully aware of the need for change. The court rapidly began restructuring the governmental ministries. It also began asserting greater control over the empire's fiscal resources, including tax collection and certain profitable industries. To offset opposition to these measures, the government made vague promises of political reform. In 1908, it authorized the creation of elected provincial assemblies as a step toward constitutionalism. The assemblies were intended to garner the support of local elites and cultivate loyalties to the dynasty. Contrary to Qing expectations, however, they quickly became forums for the expression of political grievances and anti-dynastic sentiment. For many Han, centralization was equivalent to the concentration of Manchu power. The court's persistent foot-dragging when it came to delivering on its constitutional promises appeared to validate these suspicions and eroded faith in the imperial regime.[54]

In the face of government restructuring, provincial complaints multiplied and generated calls for greater autonomy among local elites, demonstrating that the imperial vision put forward by Kang and the reformist camp had not died in 1898.[55] At the same time, popular movements grew up focused on overcoming China's reliance on foreign debts, recovering its sovereignty and "reviving" the people. Protestors staged boycotts against foreign goods. They organized against state efforts to appropriate provincial railroads and industries. These grievances and movements crystallized into a broad anti-dynastic opposition that some believed signaled a nationalist awakening in China.[56] Qing reforms proved insufficient, as the new *Beijing Women's News* warned in 1907. "Alas! Only when the nation was entirely lost did they know to reform! It's too late!"[57]

Notwithstanding these many points of opposition, it was a spontaneous army rebellion in the district of Wuchang that would provide the revolutionary spark in 1911. Contact between local revolutionary secret societies and soldiers stationed in Hubei province had created a radical wing within the Chinese military. In early October, military authorities uncovered the registry lists for these societies, thereby implicating all renegade soldiers in a conspiracy against the government. Faced with court martial and certain execution, soldiers launched an uprising on the night of October 10, with little preparation. By the following morning, they had seized control of the Wuchang barracks and were on their way to establishing a military government across Hubei. Local elites in the provincial assembly, hardly staunch Qing loyalists, lent their support to the uprising as imperial authority collapsed. With the movement gaining momentum, military commanders dispatched telegrams and propaganda to neighboring Hunan, Kwantung and Szechwan provinces, urging them to join the revolt. As the revolutionary movement spread, declarations were made in the name of the Military Government of the Republic of China.[58]

Although authorities in Wuchang were claiming to be the center of a new revolutionary republic, the unfolding of the revolution hinted at a different phenomenon altogether. Provinces across the south were breaking with the dynastic state. By November, fourteen provinces from the south and center had seceded, suggesting that 1911 was imagined by many as a "center-less" revolution that would liberate the provinces from Manchu rule.[59] Ethnic groups on the periphery of the empire were no less inclined to exploit the weakness of the government and make their own demands, often with the backing of foreign powers. That December, Mongolian separatists, provoked by Russia, announced independence, while Britain exerted pressure on the Chinese government to secure Tibetan autonomy. It was evident that the collapse of dynastic authority cast doubt on the viability of the entire multiethnic empire. Above all, the revolution exposed the difficulties associated with defining a unified Chinese state and polity and highlighted the ethnic fissures that had run through the heart of the old imperial system.[60]

The Revolutionary Alliance assembled by Sun Yat-sen was slow to mobilize as the revolution broke. Sun himself had been fundraising in the United States when the Wuchang mutiny occurred. Weeks later, members of the Revolutionary Alliance assembled in Shanghai, and there established a partnership with influential business elites that created a second revolutionary center. For Sun and his followers, the issue of authority was imperative. Provincial independence and regional rivalries threatened to undermine unity and invite foreign occupation. The challenge at hand was establishing a central government that could lead the revolutionary transition. Whether the Wuchang leadership or Shanghai would head the government was a point of tension, but not one that was insurmountable. Crisis was averted that December when Sun Yat-sen was elected president of a provisional republican government with a significant majority. Taking office in Nanking, he served for a mere forty-five days, conducting negotiations between the rebellious southern provinces and obtaining the formal abdication of the Manchu dynasty. His caretaker government was a republic in name only. Beneath the semblance of unity, regional power struggles and political disagreements sharply divided revolutionaries.[61] There existed little agreement on what type of government should replace the imperial system, whether it should be a federal republic of autonomous provinces or a centralized national republic with a strong executive. These and other issues were never fully resolved, leaving China in a precarious situation after the provisional government relinquished power later that year.

With Sun retreating from the political scene, the general Yuan Shikai assumed the presidency. Yuan had been instrumental in managing the abdication of the imperial dynasty and was seen as a strong leader capable of holding the country together. Yet as a military man who had served the imperial government in the past, it was uncertain to what extent he would uphold republican institutions. Almost from the start, battles over executive and parliamentary authority split the government as Yuan moved to secure his own power. Fearful for the republic's future, Song Jiaoren, one of the chief founders of the Revolutionary Alliance, worked to transform the alliance into an electoral force, rallying supporters to a new Nationalist Party (*Guomindang*). If the nationalists could secure a parliamentary majority, Song believed it was possible to check Yuan and safeguard the values of the revolution against reaction. The elections of 1913 marked an unprecedented moment in Chinese democracy. Some 100 parties participated with 40 million registered voters going to the polls. Guided by his hope of uniting republicans and democrats in a nationalist bloc, Song Jiaoren mobilized his followers and led the *Guomindang* to electoral victory. What should have been a moment of elation for republicans soon turned to tragedy when Song was assassinated that March. Song's death marked the beginning of a clamp down on the revolution as Yuan Shikai rapidly worked to establish a dictatorship. Provincial governors with questionable loyalties were dismissed. Shows of political opposition were summarily crushed. Yuan himself continued to run the government without bothering to consult parliament.[62]

Revolutionaries were put on the defensive as reactionary forces seriously crippled the republic and set the stage for decades of warlordism and violent civil war across China. Rather than unifying the Chinese people, the revolution of 1911 revealed fundamental disagreements over sovereignty and what constituted the Chinese community. Yet the shortcomings of the nationalist revolution should not eclipse its legacy. The revolution did put an end to a dynastic system that had been in place for two millennia, and in doing so ushered in a new political life and culture. The coming generation of Chinese activists understood the necessity of deploying popular support and mobilizing large groups in their efforts to challenge the inequalities and hierarchies of Chinese society.[63] In 1919, the May Fourth Movement saw massive anti-imperial protests staged against the government calling for Chinese cultural and social reform. Post-war anti-colonial movements and the Russian Revolution also provided new sources of inspiration for Chinese radicals. For all their importance in nurturing Chinese radicalism, nationalist and anarchist revolutionary models began to seem outdated after the First World War. Socialism appeared to be the future. Radicals consequently looked to the Bolsheviks and explored Marxism, reformulating the modernizing, anti-imperial movement of the late Qing and revolutionary period. In 1921, former nationalist-radicals Li Dazhao and Chen Duxiu assisted in founding the Chinese Communist Party, marking a new chapter in China's revolutionary tradition. "We are about to make our own start, meaning to follow in the footsteps of others," Li Dazhao proclaimed.[64] China would join the world revolution, party members insisted; but it would be Marxist-Leninism and the new world revolution announced from Moscow that would provide the guiding light.

Conclusion

In his *Essay on the History of Civil Society* published in 1767, the Scottish philosopher Adam Ferguson wrote, "The modern description of India is a repetition of the ancient, and the present state of China is derived from a distant antiquity, to which there is no parallel in the history of mankind. The succession of monarchs has been unchanged; but no revolutions have affected the state."[65] At the start of the twentieth century, Ferguson's static view of the East could only seem passé. In Asia as in Africa, tradition was being reinterpreted and "antiquity" replaced by modernizing initiatives led from both above and below. Radicals were reading Marx and anarchist theorists as they envisioned new social and political horizons for their respective communities. Nationalists challenged European colonial regimes and mobilized large crowds with demands for independence and sovereignty. Democrats and revolutionaries took inspiration from Japan, Moscow and Paris, but in doing so they also translated Enlightenment and revolutionary ideas into their own cultural idioms, appropriating and adapting them as needed. In the years immediately following the First World War, shared aspirations for "self-determination" and emancipation were channeled into anti-colonial nationalist and communist movements that would destabilize European empires right up until the era of decolonization.[66]

It was difficult to deny that the ideologies and praxis of modern revolution had arrived in the non-Western world by the dawn of the twentieth century. Yet it could not be said that these movements were imitations of Europe's own revolutionary heritage either. Radicals indigenized revolution and made it their own. In many instances, anti-colonial platforms pointed out the hypocrisies and inherent contradictions of Western Enlightenment political philosophy. Moreover, resistance to colonialism provided a common framework for imagining a distinctly different revolutionary tradition from that of Europe. Liberation was equated with the end of European hegemony; it entailed uniting the community in order to reclaim its sovereignty. Such aspirations fed into acts of radical community building that were both national and transnational in scope. Anti-colonial and revolutionary movements were dependent upon networks that cut across borders, if not continents. Transnational associations aided the spread of ideas and created common discourses and symbols vital to nurturing a revolutionary political culture. Through these ties, radicals were able to situate their activities within broader collective movements beyond their own communities, and in doing so increasingly articulated demands in universal terms that invested their speech and actions with a new authority.

Resistance to colonialism and the pursuit of collective liberty drew parallels with another universalist cause at the start of the nineteenth century: the Haitian Revolution. Later activists—among them C.L.R. James and Frantz Fanon—would identify the black liberation struggles of the Atlantic as a foundational moment in the global struggle against colonial subjugation and racism, tracing a revolutionary tradition outside the familiar European narrative. In the coming years, an anti-colonial revolutionary tradition would slowly be mapped, extending from the battles for freedom in colonial Saint-Domingue to the age of post-colonial nation building in the wake of the Second World War.[67] This tradition intersected with transnational and international liberation movements, encompassing programs as diverse as Pan-Africanism, revolutionary "Third Worldism" and Communist internationalism.[68]

If the long nineteenth century was a century of revolution, it was also an age of multiple revolutionary traditions that ran parallel to or intertwined with one another at various moments. Decentering Europe and examining the global parameters that framed nineteenth-century radicalism reveal the entangled histories that wove themselves through a tumultuous and transformative period. Tocqueville may have been correct when claiming "we have all been educated by revolutions." From the boulevards of Paris to the streets of Cairo and study societies of Beijing, revolution entered into the domain of social and political life. It not only furnished the impetus for imagining new models of sovereign authority when existing ones proved unsustainable or undesirable; it also offered programmatic scripts for action that could mobilize support and drive movements. "The Revolutionist—as I understand the word—has a creed, a faith," Mazzini once wrote.[69] This faith was found in the potential of revolutionary action to regenerate the community and recast social relations. It promised unity and universal association over the "fractious" forces of inequality and privilege, signifying what Mazzini called "the soul of all revolutions."[70] As economic transformation, imperialism and the spread of new ideas produced dislocations on a global scale, the revolutionary "creed" of the nineteenth century became a persuasive means of enacting radical change and resolving social conflicts across societies. Taking account of the multiple traditions and discourses that drove revolutions, their shared features and distinctive qualities, their interconnections across time and space is, ultimately, to see revolutionary community building for what it was: a product of and localized response to the global convulsions of the long nineteenth century.

NOTES

Introduction

1. Perry Anderson, "Modernity and Revolution," *New Left Review*, 1:144 (March–April 1984): 112.
2. Samuel Huntington, *Political Order and Changing Societies* (New Haven: Yale University Press, 1968), 264.
3. Paul Ginsborg, *Daniele Manin and the Venetian Revolution of 1848-49* (Cambridge: Cambridge University Press, 1979), 140.
4. Trygve R. Tholfsen, *Ideology and Revolution in Modern Europe: An Essay on the Role of Ideas in History* (New York: Columbia University Press, 1984); Roger Chartier, *The Cultural Origins of the French Revolution* (Durham: Duke University Press, 2004), 67; Jonathan Israel, *Revolutionary Ideas: An Intellectual History of the French Revolution from the Rights of Man to Robespierre* (Princeton: Princeton University Press, 2015).
5. Adam Schaff, "Marxist Theory of Revolution and Violence," *Journal of the History of Ideas*, 34:2 (April–June 1973): 263–70; William J. Davidshofer, *Marxism and the Leninist Revolutionary Model* (New York: Palgrave Macmillan, 2014).
6. Theda Skocpol, "France, Russia, China: A Structural Analysis of Social Revolutions," *Comparative Studies in Society and History*, 18:2 (April 1976): 175–210; Theda Skocpol, *States and Social Revolutions* (Cambridge: Cambridge University Press, 1979); Randall Collins, "Maturation of the State-Centered Theory of Revolution and Ideology," *Sociological Theory*, 11:1 (March 1993): 117–28; Jack A. Goldstone, *Revolutions and Rebellions in the Early Modern World* (Berkeley: University of California Press, 1991).
7. Bjørn Thomassen, "Notes towards an Anthropology of Political Revolutions," *Comparative Studies in Society and History*, 54:3 (2012): 679–706.
8. Alexander Motyl, *Revolutions, Nations, Empires* (New York: Columbia University Press, 1999), 23.
9. George Lawson, "Within and beyond the 'Fourth Generation' of Revolutionary Theory," *Sociological Theory*, 34:2 (2016): 106–27.
10. Colin J. Beck, "The Structure of Comparison in the Study of Revolution," *Sociological Theory*, 36:2 (2018): 136–37.
11. Keith Michael Baker and Dan Edelstein, "Introduction," *Scripting Revolution: A Historical Approach to the Comparative Study of Revolutions*, eds., Keith Michael Baker and Dan Edelstein (Stanford: Stanford University Press, 2015), 1–21.
12. Juan Pan-Montojo and Frederick Pedersen, "Introduction," *Communities in European History: Representations, Jurisdictions, Conflicts* (Pisa: Pisa University Press, 2007), ix–x.
13. Benedict Anderson, *Imagined Communities: Reflections on the Origin and Spread of Nationalism* (London: Verso, 2006).
14. Kristin Ross, *Communal Luxury: The Political Imaginary of the Paris Commune* (London: Verso, 2015).

Notes

15 For the concept of "interpretive communities," see: Stanley Fish, *Is There a Text in This Class? The Authority of Interpretative Communities* (Cambridge: Harvard University Press, 1980); Seth Cotlar, *Tom Paine's America: The Rise and Fall of Transatlantic Radicalism in the Early Republic*. Charlottesville: University of Virginia Press, 2011.

16 Andrean J. Pearce, *The Origins of Bourbon Reform in Spanish South America, 1700–1763* (New York: Palgrave Macmillan, 2014); John Lynch, *Bourbon Spain, 1700–1808* (Oxford: Basil Blackwell, 1989), 253.

17 Jeremy Adelman, "An Age of Imperial Revolutions," *The American Historical Review*, 113:2 (April 2008): 319–40.

18 See Mark Greengrass, ed., *Conquest and Coalescence: The Shaping of the State in Early Modern Europe* (London: E. Arnold, 1991).

19 Jack P. Greene, "State Formation, Resistance and the Creation of Revolution Traditions in the Early Modern Era," *Revolutionary Currents: Nation Building in the Transatlantic World*, eds., Michael A. Morrison and Melinda Zook (Lanham: Rowen and Littlefield, 2004), 1–4.

20 James Van Horn Milton, *The Rise of the Public in Enlightenment Europe* (Cambridge: Cambridge University Press, 2001); Mona Ozouf, "Public Opinion at the End of the Old Regime," *Journal of Modern History*, 60 (1988): 9–13.

21 Gabriel Paquette, "State-Civil Society Cooperation and Conflict in the Spanish Empire: The Intellectual and Political Activities of the Ultramarine *Consulados* and Economic Societies, c. 1780–1810," *Journal of Latin American Studies*, 39:2 (May 2007): 285–86.

22 Ashli White, *Encountering Revolution: Haiti and the Making of the Early Republic* (Baltimore: Johns Hopkins University Press, 2010), 21–22.

23 Victor M. Uribe-Uran, "The Birth of the Public Sphere in Latin America during the Age of Revolution," *Comparative Studies in Society and History*, 42:2 (April 2000): 438–45; Nathan Perl-Rosenthal, "Atlantic Cultures and the Age of Revolution," *The William and Mary Quarterly*, 74:4 (October 2017): 667–96.

24 Gordon S. Wood, *The Radicalism of the American Revolution* (New York: Vintage, 1991), 239.

25 Dorinda Outram, *The Enlightenment* (Cambridge: Cambridge University Press, 2013), 74.

26 Georges de Buffon, "Variétés dans l'espèce humaine," *Histoire Naturelle*, ed., J. Varloot (Paris: Gallimard, 1984), 142–43.

27 Michael Mosher, "Montesquieu on Empire and Enlightenment," *Empire and Modern Political Thought*, ed., Sankar Mathu (Cambridge: Cambridge University Press, 2012), 115–17; H. F. Augestein, ed., *Race: The Origins of an Idea, 1760–1850* (Bristol: Thoemmes Press, 1996).

28 Michael Lessnoff, *Social Contract* (London: Macmillan, 1986), 62.

29 Tholfsen, *Ideology and Revolution*, 47–49.

30 Robert Wolker, *Rousseau, the Age of Enlightenment and Their Legacies* (Princeton: Princeton University Press, 2012), 18.

31 Lessnoff, *Social Contract*, 79–80.

32 Wolker, *Rousseau*, 164.

33 Helena Rosenblatt, *Rousseau and Geneva: From the First Discourse to the Social Contract, 1749–1762* (Cambridge: Cambridge University Press, 1997), 212.

34 Asher Horowitz, *Rousseau, Nature and History* (Toronto: University of Toronto Press, 1987), 44–45.

35 Charles Edwyn Vaughan, "Introduction," *The Political Writings of Rousseau* (Cambridge: Cambridge University Press, 1915), 1:40–48; Jacob Talmon, *The Origins of Totalitarian*

Notes

Democracy (London: Secker and Warburg, 1960); Lester G. Crocker, *Rousseau's Social Contract: An Interpretive Essay* (Cleveland: Case Western Reserve University Press, 1968), 12–16, 163–64.

36 Horowitz, *Rousseau, Nature and History*, 15–16.
37 Wolker, *Rousseau*, 181.
38 Robert Zeretsky, *Boswell's Enlightenment* (Cambridge: Harvard University Press, 2015), 158.
39 Dena Goodman, *The Republic of Letters: A Cultural History of the French Enlightenment* (Ithaca: Cornell University Press, 1994), 38–52.
40 Robert Darnton, "The High Enlightenment and the Low-Life Literature in Pre-Revolutionary France," *Past and Present*, 51 (1971): 81–115.

Chapter 1

1 Thomas Paine, "The Rights of Man," *Common Sense, Rights of Man, and Other Essential Writings* (New York: Signet, 2003), 256.
2 Baker, "Revolutionizing Revolution," *Scripting Revolution*, 85.
3 R. R. Palmer, *The Age of Democratic Revolution: A Political History of Europe and America, 1760–1800* (Princeton: Princeton University Press, 2014).
4 Greene, "State Formation," *Revolutionary Currents*, 1–2; Adelman, "An Age of Imperial Revolutions," 319–40.
5 Colin Jones, "Bourgeois Revolution Revivified: 1789 and Social Change," *Rewriting the French Revolution*, ed., Colin Lucas (Oxford: Oxford University Press, 1991), 69–118.
6 Douglas Brandburn. *The Citizenship Revolution: Politics and the Creation of the American Union, 1774–1804* (Charlottesville: University of Virginia Press, 2009); Peter Sahlins, *Unnaturally French: Foreign Citizens in the Old Regime and After* (Ithaca: Cornell University Press, 2004).
7 Marchamont Nedham, *The Excellencie of a Free State*, ed., Balir Worden (Indianapolis: Liberty Fund, 2011), MP91.
8 Ferdinand Tönnies, ed., *Behemoth, or the Long Parliament* (New York: Barnes and Noble, 1969), 204.
9 Steve Pincus, *1688: The First Modern Revolution* (New Haven: Yale University Press, 2009).
10 Ilan Rachum, "The Meaning of 'Revolution' in the English Revolution, 1648–1660," *Journal of the History of Ideas*, 56:2 (April 1995): 195–215.
11 Richard Bourke, *Empire and Revolution: The Political Life of Edmund Burke* (Princeton: Princeton University Press, 2015), 9; Harris, "Did the English Have a Script for Revolution in the Seventeenth Century?" *Scripting Revolution*, 34–38.
12 William Byrd to Daniel Horsmanden, August 8, 1690, "Letters of William Byrd, First," *Virginia Magazine of History and Biography*, 26:4 (October 1918): 392.
13 John Murrin, "A Roof without Walls: The Dilemma of American National Identity," *Beyond Confederation: Origins of the Constitution and American National Identity*, eds., Richard Beeman, Stephen Botein and Edward C. Carter (Chapel Hill: University of North Carolina Press, 1987); T. H. Breen, "An Empire of Goods: The Anglicanization of Colonial America, 1690–1776," *Journal of British Studies*, 25 (1986): 467–99.
14 David Armitage, *The Ideological Origins of the British Empire* (Cambridge: Cambridge University Press, 2000), 181–82; Ian K. Steele, *The English Atlantic, 1675–1740: An Exploration of Communication and Community* (Oxford: Oxford University Press, 1986).

Notes

15 Colin Kidd, *British Identities before Nationalism: Ethnicity and Nationhood in the Atlantic World, 1600–1800* (Cambridge: Cambridge University Press, 1999), 265–70.

16 Frank Ankersmit, "Edmund Burke, Historicism and History," *Revolutionary Histories: Transatlantic Cultural Nationalism, 1775–1815*, ed., W. M. Verhoeven (Basingstoke: Palgrave, 2002), 197.

17 Jack P. Greene, "Empire and Liberty," *Exclusionary Empire: English Liberty Overseas, 1600–1900* (Baltimore: Johns Hopkins University Press), 2009, 2–3.

18 Greene, *Exclusionary Empire*, 60.

19 Anthony Pagden, "Fellow Citizens and Imperial Subjects: Conquest and Sovereignty in Europe's Overseas Empires," *History and Theory*, 44:4 (December 2005): 33.

20 Steven Sarson, *British America, 1500–1800: Creating Colonies, Imagining and Empire* (New York: Oxford University Press, 2005), 203–04.

21 Pierre Serna, "Every Revolution Is a War of Independence," *The French Revolution in Global Perspective*, eds., Suzanne Desan, Lynn Hunt and William Max Nelson (Ithaca: Cornell University Press, 2013), 168.

22 Jack P. Greene, *Peripheries and Centers: Constitutional Development in the Extended Polities of the British Empire and the United States, 1607–1788* (Athens: University of Georgia Press, 1986), 12–18.

23 David S. Lovejoy, "The Two American Revolutions, 1689 and 1776," *Three British Revolutions: 1641, 1688, 1776*, ed., J. G. A. Pocock (Princeton: Princeton University Press, 1980), 254.

24 Michael Kammen, *Deputies and Liberties: The Origins of Representative Government in Colonial America* (New York: Knopf, 1969), 11–12; Greene, *Exclusionary Empire*, 53.

25 Jack P. Greene, "The American Revolution," *The American Historical Review*, 105:1 (February 2000): 94–95.

26 Sarson, *British America*, 208–10; Elizabeth Mancke, "Empire and State," *The British Atlantic World, 1500–1800*, eds., David Armitage and Michael J. Braddick (Houndmills: Palgrave Macmillan, 2002), 192–93.

27 Eliga G. Gould, *The Persistence of Empire: British Culture in the Age of the American Revolution* (Chapel Hill: University of North Carolina Press, 2000), 68.

28 Patrick Griffin, *America's Revolution* (Oxford: Oxford University Press, 2013), 75–76.

29 Thomas Jefferson, *A Summary View of the Rights of British America* (London: G. Kearsly, 1774), 19.

30 Mancke, "The Language of Liberty in British North America," *Exclusionary Empire*, 25–49.

31 John Phillip Reid, *Constitutional History of the American Revolution: The Authority of Rights* (Madison: University of Wisconsin Press, 2003).

32 *Georgia Gazette*, September 6, 1769; Herbert Aptheker, *The American Revolution, 1763–1783: A History of the American People* (New York: International Publishers, 1985), 107.

33 Cato, "To the People of Pennsylvania," *Dunlap's Pennsylvania Packet or, the General Advertiser*, April 29, 1776.

34 *The Norwich Packet and the Connecticut, Massachusetts, New-Hampshire, and Rhode-Island Weekly Advertiser*, January 22, 1776.

35 Dror Wahrman, *The Making of the Modern Self: Identity and Culture in Eighteenth-Century England* (New Haven: Yale University Press, 2004), 246.

36 "To the People of Great Britain," *The Constitutional Gazette*, February 3, 1776.

37 Paine, "Common Sense," *Common Sense, Rights of Man, and Other Essential Writings*, 20, 46.
38 Robert A. Ferguson, *The American Enlightenment, 1750-1820* (Cambridge: Harvard University Press, 1997), 36-37; Wahrman, *The Making of the Modern Self*, 250.
39 Griffin, *America's Revolution*, 134-38.
40 Marie-Jeanne Rossignol, "A Black Declaration of Independence? War, Republic and Race in the United States of America, 1775-1787," *Republics at War, 1776-1840: Revolutions, Conflicts and Geopolitics in Europe and the Atlantic World*, eds., Pierre Serna, Antonio De Francesco and Judith Miller (Houndmills: Palgrave Macmillan, 2013), 111-22.
41 Greene, "The American Revolution": 100-01; Joyce E. Chaplin, "Race," *The British Atlantic World*, 171-72.
42 Maya Jasanoff, "Revolutionary Exiles: The American Loyalists and French Émigré Diasporas," *The Age of Revolution in Global Context, c. 1760-1840*, eds., David Armitage and Sanjay Subrahmanyam (Houndmills: Palgrave Macmillan, 2010), 38-51.
43 Ilan Rachum, "From 'American Independence' to the 'American Revolution,'" *Journal of American Studies*, 27:1 (April 1993): 37-81.
44 Thomas Paine, *A Letter Addressed to the Abbé Raynal on the Affairs of North America* (London: W. T. Sherwin, 1817), 37.
45 Paine, *A Letter Addressed to the Abbé Raynal*, 8.
46 Durand Echeverria, *Mirage in the West: A History of the French Image of American Society to 1815* (Princeton: Princeton University Press, 1957), 77.
47 Simon Schama, *Citizens: A Chronicle of the French Revolution* (New York: Vintage, 1990), 49.
48 Lenore Lofte, *Passion, Politics and Philosophie: Rediscovering J.-P. Brisso*t (Westport: Greenwood, 2002), 186-87.
49 Janet Polasky, *Revolutions without Borders: The Call to Liberty in the Atlantic World* (New Haven: Yale University Press, 2016), 36.
50 George Washington to Crèvecoeur, April 10, 1789, Washington Papers, Presidential Series, vol. 2. Charlottesville: University of Virginia Press, Rotunda, 2008.
51 Abbé Raynal, *The Revolution of America* (London: L. Davis, 1781), 173.
52 Arthur Young, *Travels in France, 1787-89*, ed., Constantia Maxwell (Cambridge: Cambridge University Press, 1929), 85.
53 Sewell, "The French Revolution and the Emergence of the Nation Form," *Revolutionary Currents*, 103.
54 David A. Bell, *The Cult of the Nation in France: Inventing Nationalism, 1680-1800* (Cambridge: Harvard University Press, 2003), 74.
55 Serna, "Every Revolution Is a War of Independence," *French Revolution in Global Perspective*, 176-77.
56 Saliha Belmessous, *Assimilation and Empire: Uniformity in French and British Colonies, 1541-1954* (Oxford: Oxford University Press, 2013), 27.
57 Nicholas Henshall, *The Myth of Absolutism: Change and Continuity in Early Modern European Monarchy* (New York: Routledge, 1996); Jean-Frédéric Schaub, "The European Old Regime and the Imperial Question: A Modernist View of a Contemporary Question," *Nationalizing Empires*, eds., Stefan Berger and Alexei Miller (Budapest: Central European University Press, 2014), 569.
58 Timothy Blanning, *The French Revolution: Aristocrats versus Bourgeois?* (London: Macmillan, 1989), 17.

Notes

59 Gwynne Lewis, *The French Revolution: Rethinking the Debate* (New York: Routledge, 1999), 6.
60 Serna, "Every Revolution Is a War of Independence," *French Revolution in Global Perspective,* 174–79.
61 Sahlin, *Unnaturally French*, 19–60.
62 Gail Bossenga, *The Politics of Privilege: Old Regime and Revolution in Lille* (Cambridge: Cambridge University Press, 1991).
63 Bell, *The Cult of the Nation*, 63.
64 Chartier, *The Cultural Origins of the French Revolution*, 111–35.
65 Tholfsen, *Ideology and Revolution*, 57.
66 Jeremy Popkin, *Revolutionary News: The Press in France, 1789-1799* (Durham: Duke University Press, 1990), 25–26.
67 Schama, *Citizens*, 303.
68 Quoted in Tholfson, *Ideology and Revolution*, 61.
69 Emmanuel Sieyès, "What Is the Third Estate?" *French Philosophers of the Eighteenth Century* (Philadelphia: University of Pennsylvania Press, 1899), 6:32–35. For an examination of Sieyès' political thought on representative government, see: Michael Sonenscher, ed., *Emmanuel Joseph Sieyès: Political Writings* (Indianapolis: Hackett Publishing, 2003).
70 Sieyès, "What Is the Third Estate?" *French Philosophers*, 6:35.
71 Derek Jarrett, *Three Faces of Revolution: Paris, London and New York in 1789* (London: G. Philip, 1989), 92–93.
72 Keith Michael Baker, "The Idea of a Declaration of Rights," *The French Revolution: Recent Debates and New Controversies*, ed., Gary Kates (London: Routledge, 1998), 108.
73 Tholfsen, *Revolution and Ideology*, 59.
74 Baker, "Declaration of Rights," 101.
75 David E. A. Coles, *The French Revolution* (Victoria: Friesen, 2014), 90–96.
76 Henry Cabot Lodge, *The History of Nations* (New York: P. F. Collier, 1913), 56.
77 William Sewell, Jr., "Historical Events as Transformations of Structures: Inventing Revolution at the Bastille," *Logics of History: Social Theory and Social Transformation* (Chicago: University of Chicago Press, 2005), 225–70.
78 Baker, "Declaration of Rights," 110.
79 Tholfsen, *Ideology and Revolution*, 62.
80 Adam Zamoyski, *Phantom Terror: The Threat of Revolution and the Repression of Liberty, 1789-1848* (London: William Collins, 2014), 11.
81 August 4, 1789, J. Madival and E. Laurent, eds. *Archives parlementaires de 1789 à 1860: recueil complet des débats législatifs et politiques des Chambres françaises* (Paris: Librairie administrative de P. Dupont, 1862), 8:344.
82 See article I, III, IV, XVII. Also see: Baker, "Declaration of Rights"; Lewis, *The French Revolution*, 31.
83 Pierre Birnbaum, *The Idea of France* (New York: Hill and Wang, 2001), 58.
84 Philip Ziesche, "Exporting American Revolutions: Gouverneur Morris, Thomas Jefferson and the National Struggle for Universal Rights in Revolutionary France," *Journal of the Early Republic*, 26:3 (Fall 2006): 431–36.
85 Baker, "Declaration of Rights," 117.

Chapter 2

1. Jasanoff, "Revolutionary Exiles," 38, 51.
2. Jarrett, *Three Faces of Revolution*, 176.
3. Micha Alpaugh, "The Politics of Escalation in French Revolutionary Protest: Political Demonstrations, Non-Violence and Violence in the *Grandes Journées* of 1789," *French History*, 23:3 (2009): 336–59.
4. Baker, "Declaration of Rights," 135.
5. Alma Söderhjelm, *Le Régime de la Presse pendant la Révolution française* (Geneva: Slatkine, 1971), 1:81–82.
6. Polasky, *Revolutions without Borders*, 111–16.
7. Popkin, *Revolutionary News*; Jack Censer, *Prelude to Power: The Parisian Radical Press, 1789–1791* (Baltimore: Johns Hopkins University Press, 1979).
8. David P. Jordan, "The Robespierre Problem," *Robespierre*, eds., Colin Haydon and William Doyle (Cambridge: Cambridge University Press, 1999), 20.
9. "Protestaion contre la loi martiale," *L'Ami du Peuple*, November 10, 1789.
10. Schama, *Citizens*, 146–47.
11. Jacques Godechot, *Histoire générale de la Presse française* (Paris: Presses Universitaires de France, 1969), 1:493–94; J. Gilchrist and W. J. Murray, *The Press in the French Revolution* (New York: St. Martin's Press, 1971).
12. Polasky, *Revolutions without Borders*, 112.
13. Michael Kennedy, *The Jacobin Clubs in the French Revolution: The First Years* (Princeton: Princeton University Press, 1982), 26, 45; R. B. Rose, *The Making of the Sans-Culottes: Democratic Ideals and Institutions in Paris, 1789–92* (Manchester: Manchester University Press, 1983), 96–116.
14. Laura Mason, *Singing the French Revolution: Popular Culture and Politics, 1787–1799* (Ithaca: Cornell University Press, 1996), 61–90; Mona Ozouf, *Festivals of the French Revolution*, trans., Alan Sheridan (Cambridge: Harvard University Press, 1988), 33–60.
15. Emmet Kennedy, *A Cultural History of the French Revolution* (New Haven: Yale University Press, 1989), 329–31.
16. Sewell, "The French Revolution," *Revolutionary Currents*, 95.
17. William Max Nelson, "Colonizing France," *The French Revolution in Global Perspective*, 76.
18. Tholfsen, *Ideology and Revolution*, 67.
19. Sophie Wahnich, *L'impossible citoyen: L'étranger dans le discours de la Révolution française* (Paris: Albin Michel, 1997), 59.
20. Jacques Godechot, "The New Concept of the Nation and Its Diffusion in Europe," *Nationalism in the Age of the French Revolution*, eds., Otto Dann and John Dinwiddy (London: Hambledon Press, 1988), 17.
21. Sewell, "The French Revolution," *Revolutionary Currents*, 104.
22. Marie-Vic Ozouf-Marignier, *La formation des départments: La représentation du territoire français à la fin du 18e siècle* (Paris: Etudes des Hautes Etudes en Science Social, 1989).
23. Birnbaum, *The Idea of France*, 45.
24. Ozouf-Marignier, *La Formation des départements*, 65.

Notes

25 Clive Emsley, "Nationalist Rhetoric and Nationalist Sentiment in Revolutionary France," *Nationalism in the Age of the French Revolution*, 40.

26 Kennedy, *The Jacobin Clubs*, 13–14, 30; David Andress, *The Terror: The Merciless Wars for Freedom in Revolutionary France* (New York: Farrar Strauss Giroux, 2006), 33–34.

27 December 5, 1790, *Archives Parlementaires*, 21:249.

28 October 22, 1789, *Archives Parlementaires*, 9:479.

29 April 28, 1791, *Archives Parlementaires*, 25:387.

30 Kennedy, *The Jacobin Clubs*, 44, 166.

31 David Andress, *The French Revolution and the People* (London: Hambledon, 2006), 157.

32 Geoffrey Best, *War and Society in Revolutionary Europe, 1770–1870* (Leicester: Leicester University Press, 1982), 65; Annie Crépin, *Deféndre la France: Les français, la guerre et le service militaire de la guerre de Sept Ans à Verdun* (Rennes: Presses Universitaires de Rennes, 2005), 6–8.

33 Antonio De Francesco, "The American Origins of the French Revolution," *Republics at War*, 31–35.

34 Annie Jourdan, *La Révolution, une exception française?* (Paris: Flammarion, 2004), 220.

35 Florence Gauthier, "Universal Rights and National Interest in the French Revolution," *Nationalism in the Age of the French Revolution*, 31; De Francesco, "The American Origins of the French Revolution," 34.

36 See: Jean-Paul Bertaud, *Guerre et Société en France de Louis XIV à Napoléon* (Paris: Armand Colin, 1998); Pierre Serna, "War and Republic: Dangerous Liaisons," *Republics at War*, 10–11.

37 Adrian Jones, "Towards a New Structural Theory of Revolution: Universalism and Community in the French and Russian Revolutions," *The English Historical Review*, 107:425 (October 1992): 876–79.

38 Wood, *The Radicalism of the American Revolution*, 221.

39 Ian Coller, "Citizen Chawich: Arabs, Islam and Rights in the French Revolution," *French History and Civilization*, 5 (2012): 45–46.

40 Polasky, *Revolutions without Borders*, 67.

41 April 26, 1793, *Archives Parlementaires*, 63:394.

42 Paine, "The Rights of Man," *Common Sense, Rights of Man, and Other Essential Writings*, 147, 169.

43 Ibid., 160, 256.

44 *New York Journal*, May 10, 1794.

45 Seth Cotlar, *Tom Paine's America: The Rise and Fall of Transatlantic Radicalism in the Early Republic* (Charlottesville: University of Virginia Press, 2011), 51–53, 68–69.

46 Joel Barlow, "A Letter Addressed to the People of Piedmont," *The Political Writings of Joel Barlow* (New York: Mott and Lyon, 1796), 205, 216.

47 Anacharsis Cloots, *La République Universelle* (Paris: Marchands de Nouveautés, 1795), 6.

48 Gautier, "Universal Rights and National Interests," *Nationalism in the Age of the French Revolution*, 30–31.

49 Desan, "Foreigners, Cosmopolitanism and French Revolutionary Universalism," *The French Revolution in Global Perspective*, 88.

50 Whanich, *L'impossible citoyen*, 197–200.

51 Paul R. Hanson, *The Jacobin Republic under Fire: The Federalist Revolt in the French Revolution* (University Park: The Pennsylvania State University Press, 2003).

52 Andress, *The Terror*, 161.
53 Emsley, "Nationalist Rhetoric and Nationalist Sentiment," *Nationalism in the Age of the French Revolution*, 50–52.
54 Andress, *The Terror*, 179.
55 Andress, *The French Revolution and the People*, 231.
56 Timothy Tackett, *The Coming of the Terror in the French Revolution* (Cambridge: Harvard University Press, 2017); Andress, *The Terror*.
57 François Furet, *Interpreting the French Revolution* (Cambridge: Cambridge University Press, 1981).
58 Tholfsen, *Ideology and Revolution*, 68–69.
59 Lynn Hunt, "The Rhetoric of Revolution in France," *History Workshop*, 15 (Spring 1983): 88.
60 Maximilien Robespierre, "On the Principles of Political Morality," *Robespierre: Virtue and Terror*, ed., Slavoj Žižek (New York: Verso, 2007), 115.
61 Jeremy D. Popkin, *A Short History of the French Revolution* (London: Routledge, 2015), 72.
62 Dan Edelstein, "From Constitutional to Permanent Revolution, 1649 and 1793," *Scripting Revolutions*, 127–29.
63 Michael C. Frank, *The Cultural Imaginary of Terrorism in Public Discourse, Literature and Film* (London: Routledge, 2017), 38.
64 Dan Edelstein, "Do We Want a Revolution without Revolution? Reflections on Political Authority," *French Historical Studies*, 25:2 (Spring 2010): 269–89.
65 Mona Ozouf, "La Révolution française et la formation de l'homme nouveau," *L'Homme régénéré. Essais sur le Révolution française* (Paris: Gallimard, 1989), 115–57.
66 Kennedy, *A Cultural History*, 205–07.
67 Michel Vovelle, *The Revolution against the Church: From Reason to the Supreme Being* (Cambridge: Polity Press, 1991).
68 Lynn Hunt, *Politics, Culture and Class in the French Revolution* (Berkeley: University of California Press, 1984).
69 Kennedy, *A Cultural History*, 250.
70 Warren Roberts, *Jacques-Louis David, Revolutionary Artist: Art, Politics and the French Revolution* (Chapel Hill: University of North Carolina Press, 1992).
71 Schama, *Citizens*, 749; Ozouf, *Festivals*; James A. Leith, *Space and Revolution: Projects for Monuments, Squares, and Public Buildings in France, 1789–1799* (Montreal: McGill-Queen's University Press, 1991).
72 September 20, 1793, *Archives Parlementaires*, 74:550.
73 Matthew Shaw, *Time and the French Revolution: The Republican Calendar, 1789–Year XIV* (Woodbridge: Boydell Press, 2011); Sanja Perovic, *The Calendar in Revolutionary France: Perceptions of Time in Literature, Culture, Politics* (Cambridge: Cambridge University Press, 2012), 3–16.
74 Eli Sagen, *Citizens and Cannibals: The French Revolution, the Struggle for Modernity and the Origins of Ideological Terror* (Lanham: Rowen and Littlefield, 2001); Ferenc Fehér, ed., *The French Revolution and the Birth of Modernity* (Berkeley: University of California Press, 1990); Hunt, *Politics, Culture and Class*.
75 De Francesco, "The American Origins of the French Revolution," 35.

Notes

76 Lewis, *The French Revolution*, 106.
77 Andress, *The French Revolution and the People*, 215.
78 Nelson, "Colonizing France," *The French Revolution in Global Perspective*, 79.
79 Keith Michael Baker, "Introduction," *The Political Culture of the Old Regime* (Oxford: Pergamon, 1987), xxiii.
80 June 24, 1793, *Archives Parlementaires*, 67:267.
81 For contrasting views, see: Polasky, *Revolutions without Borders*; Wahnich, *L'impossible citoyen*.
82 Bell, *Cult of the Nation*, 160–61.

Chapter 3

1 Peter Sahlins, "The Eighteenth-Century Citizenship Revolution in France," *Migration Control in the North Atlantic World: The Evolution of State Practices in Europe and the United States from the French Revolution to the Inter-War Period*, eds., Andreas Fahrmeir, Olivier Faron and Patrick Weil (New York: Berghahn Books, 2003), 11–24; Carolyn E. Fick, "The Haitian Revolution and the Limits of Freedom: Defining Citizenship in the Revolutionary Era," *Social History*, 32:4 (November 2007): 394–95.
2 Jennifer Ngaire Heuer, *The Family and The Nation: Gender and Citizenship in Revolutionary France, 1789–1830* (Ithaca: Cornell University Press, 2005), 3–4.
3 Rose, *The Making of the Sans-Culottes*, 40.
4 Eric Hazan, *A People's History of the French Revolution* (London: Verso, 2014), 57–84; Micha Alpaugh, *Non-Violence and the French Revolution: Political Demonstrations in Paris, 1787–1795* (Cambridge: Cambridge University Press, 2015), 75–100.
5 Rose, *The Making of the Sans-Culottes*, 62.
6 Andress, *The Terror*, 174.
7 Suzanne Desan, "Constitutional Amazons: Jacobin Women's Clubs in the French Revolution," *Re-Creating Authority in Revolutionary France*, eds., Bryant T. Ragan and Elizabeth A. Williams (New Brunswick: Rutgers University Press, 1992), 23.
8 Katie L. Jarvis, "The Cost of Female Citizenship: How Prince Controls Gendered Democracy in Revolutionary France," *French Historical Studies*, 41:4 (October 2018): 664–69.
9 November 29, 1792, *Archives Parlementaires*, 27:664.
10 Louis-Antoine de Saint-Just, "Republican Institutes," *Readings in European History*, ed., J. H. Robinson (New York: Ginn and Company, 1906), 2: 452–53.
11 November 29, 1792, *Archives Parlementaires*, 27:665.
12 February 12, 1793, *Archives Parlementaires*, 58:475.
13 Alan Forrest, *The French Revolution and the Poor* (Oxford: Oxford University Press, 1981), 82–85.
14 George Rudé, *The Crowd in the French Revolution* (Oxford: Oxford University Press, 1959), 125–33.
15 Seth Cotlar, "Languages of Democracy in America from the Revolution to the Election of 1800," *Re-Imaging Democracies in the Age of Revolutions: America, France, Britain and Ireland, 1750–1850*, eds., Joanna Innes and Mark Philp (Oxford: Oxford University Press, 2013), 24.

16 Terry Bouton, *Taming Democracy: The People, the Founders and the Troubled End of the American Revolution* (New York: Oxford University Press, 2007), 32, 43–54, 106.

17 Patrick Griffin, *American Leviathan: Empire, Nation and Revolutionary Frontier* (New York: Hill and Wang, 2008), 184.

18 Leonard L. Richards, *Shay's Rebellion: The American Revolution's Final Battle* (Philadelphia: University of Pennsylvania Press, 2002).

19 Bounton, *Taming Democracy*, 220.

20 Jennifer Mori, *Britain in the Age of the French Revolution, 1785–1820* (London: Routledge, 2000), 31–73; J. R. Dinwiddy, *Radicalism and Reform in Great Britain, 1780–1850* (London: Hambledon, 1992), 169–94.

21 Gwyn A. Williams, *Artisans and Sans-Culottes: Popular Movements in France and Britain during the French Revolution* (London: Libris, 1989), 61.

22 Zamoysky, *Phantom Terror*, 53–55; Polasky, *Revolutions without Borders*, 127–28.

23 Williams, *Artisans and Sans-Culottes*, 77.

24 John Thornton, *Africa and Africans in the Making of the Atlantic World, 1400–1800* (Cambridge: Cambridge University Press, 1998).

25 Ira Berlin, *Generations of Captivity: A History of African-American Slaves* (Cambridge: Harvard University Press, 2003), 72–73.

26 Joyce E. Chaplin, "Race," *The British Atlantic World*, 154.

27 Peter H. Wood, "The Dream Deferred: Black Freedom Struggles on the Eve of White Independence," *In Resistance: Studies in African, Caribbean and Afro-American History*, ed., Gary Y. Okihiro (Amherst: University of Massachusetts Press, 1986), 166–87.

28 Peter A. Dorsey, *Common Bondage: Slavery as Metaphor in Revolutionary America* (Knoxville: University of Tennessee Press, 2009).

29 Ira Berlin, *Many Thousands Gone: The First Two Centuries of Slavery in North America* (Cambridge: Harvard University Press, 1998), 228–355.

30 Rossignol, "A Black Declaration of Independence? War, Republic and Race in the United States of America, 1775–1787," *Republics at War*, 114–18; Gary B. Nash, *The Forgotten Fifth: African Americans in the Age of Revolution* (Cambridge: Harvard University Press, 2006), 1–66.

31 Sylvia R. Frey, *Water from a Rock: Black Resistance in a Revolutionary Age* (Princeton: Princeton University Press, 1993), 54–92.

32 Nash, *The Forgotten Fifth*, 46; Simon Schama, *Rough Crossings: Britain, the Slaves and the American Revolution* (New York: Harper Perennial, 2007).

33 William Fox, "An Address to the People of Great Britain," *Slavery: Abolition and Emancipation: Writings in the British Romantic Period*, ed., Peter J. Kitson (London: Pickering and Chatto, 1999), 2:155.

34 Ibid., 2:160.

35 Adam Hochschild, *Bury the Chains: Prophets and Rebels in the Fight to Free an Empire's Slaves* (New York: Houghton Mifflin, 2005).

36 Polasky, *Revolutions without Borders*, 88–92.

37 See: Lawrence C. Jennings, *French Anti-Slavery: The Movement for the Abolition of Slavery in France, 1802–1848* (Cambridge: Cambridge University Press, 2000).

38 Silyane Larcher, *L'autre citoyen: l'idéal républicaine et les Antilles après l'esclavage* (Paris: Armand Colin, 2014), 41.

39 Malick W. Ghachem, "The Antislavery Script," *Scripting Revolutions*, 156.

Notes

40 Jürgen Osterhammel, *The Transformation of the World: A Global History of the Nineteenth Century* (Princeton: Princeton University Press, 2014), 529.

41 Frédéric Régent, *Esclavage, métissage, liberté: La Révolution française en Guadeloupe* (Paris: Grasset, 2004), 36–38; Sidney Mintz, "La vie des esclaves sur les plantations sucrièrs des Caraïbes: Quelques questions non résolves," *Histoire et identités sans la Caraïbe: Trajectoires plurielles*, eds., Mamadou Diouf and Wulbe Bosma (Paris: Karthala-Sephis, 2004).

42 Malick W. Ghachem, *The Old Regime and the Haitian Revolution* (Cambridge: Cambridge University Press, 2012), 240–41.

43 Larcher, *L'Autre citoyen*, 44–45; Laurent Dubois, *Avengers of the New World: The Story of the Haitian Revolution* (Cambridge: Harvard University Press, 2004), 72–84.

44 David Geggus, "Racial Equality, Slavery and Colonial Secession during the Constituent Assembly," *American Historical Review*, 94:5 (December 1989): 1290–1308.

45 John D. Garrigus, *Before Haiti: Race and Citizenship in French Saint-Domingue* (Houndmills: Palgrave Macmillan, 2006), 234.

46 October 22, 1789, *Archives Parlementaires*, 16:476.

47 October 22, 1789, *Archives Parlementaires*, 16:477.

48 Larcher, *L'autre citoyen*, 47–48.

49 Abbé Grégoire, "Memoir in Favor of the People of Color or Mixed–Race of Saint Domingue," *The French Revolution and Human Rights: A Brief Documentary History*, ed., Lynn Hunt (New York: St. Martin's Press, 1996), 105–06.

50 Deborah Jenson, "Toussaint Louverture, Spin Doctor?: Launching the Haitian Revolution in the French Media," *Tree of Liberty: Cultural Legacies of the Haitian Revolution in the Atlantic World*, ed., Doris Lorraine Garraway (Charlottesville: University of Virginia Press, 2008), 45–46.

51 Frédéric Régent, "From Individual to Collective Emancipation," *Republics at War*, 167.

52 Ibid., 167–69.

53 May 13, 1791, *Archives Parlementaires*, 26:59–60; Larcher, *L'autre citoyen*, 51–54.

54 "Law on the Colonies," May 29, 1791, *Slave Revolution in the Caribbean, 1789-1804*, eds., Laurent Dubois and John Garrigus (London: Palgrave, 2006), 85.

55 May 13, 1791, *Archives Parlementaires*, 26:56.

56 "Law on the Colonies," 85.

57 Dubois, *Avengers of the New World*, 135–36.

58 Polasky, *Revolutions without Borders*, 164.

59 Jeremy Popkin, *Facing Racial Revolution: Eyewitness Account of the Haitian Insurrection* (Chicago: University of Chicago Press, 2007), 22–24.

60 White, *Encountering Revolution*; Tim Matthewson, "Jefferson and Haiti," *The Journal of Southern History*, 61:2 (May 1995): 212–14.

61 Popkin, *Facing Racial Revolution*, 30.

62 David Geggus, *Slavery War and Revolution: The British Occupation of Saint-Domingue, 1793-1798* (Oxford: Oxford University Press, 1982), 83, 395–99.

63 Fick, "The Haitian Revolution," 397.

64 "The Emancipation Proclamation of 29 August 1793," *The Haitian Revolution: A Documentary History*, ed., David Geggus (Indianapolis: Hackett, 2014), 107.

65 Miranda Spieler, "Abolition and Reenslavement in the Caribbean," *The French Revolution in Global Perspective*, 133; Laurent Dubois, *A Colony of Citizens: Revolution and Slave Emancipation in the French Caribbean, 1787–1804* (Chapel Hill: University of North Carolina Press, 2004), 170–74.

66 Régent, "From Individual to Collective Emancipation," *Republics at War*, 178.

67 Fick, "The Haitian Revolution," 401.

68 Polasky, *Revolutions without Borders*, 242.

69 Laurent Dubois, "The Price of Liberty: Victor Hugues and the Administration of Freedom in Guadeloupe, 1794–1798," *The William and Mary Quarterly*, 56:2 (April 1999): 363–92; Spieler, "Abolition and Reenslavement in the Caribbean," *French Revolution in Global Perspective*, 133–35.

70 Larcher, *L'autre citoyen*, 20–23.

71 Immanuel Wallerstein, "Citizens All? Citizens Some! The Making of the Citizen," *Comparative Studies in Society and History*, 45:4 (October 2003): 650–79.

72 Grégoire, "Letter to the Citizens of Color and Free Blacks," *The Haitian Revolution*, 48.

73 See: Alyssa Goldstein Sepinwall. "Eliminating Race, Eliminating Difference: Blacks, Jews and the Abbé Grégoire," *The Color of Liberty: Histories of Race in France*, eds., Sue Peabody and Tyler Stovall (Durham: Duke University Press, 2003), 28–37.

74 Tholfsen, *Ideology and Revolution*, 28.

75 Rose, *The Making of the Sans-Culottes*, 40.

76 Doris Y. Kadish and Françoise Massardier-Kenney, eds., *Translating Slavery: Gender and Race in French Women's Writings* (Kent: Kent State University Press, 1994); Christopher L. Miller, *The French Atlantic Triangle: Literature and Culture of the Slave Trade* (Durham: Duke University Press, 2008), 99–175.

77 Olympe de Gouges, "Reflections on Negroes," *Women's Political and Social Thought*, eds., Hilda L. Smith and Bernice A. Carroll (Bloomington: University of Indiana Press, 2000), 133.

78 Susan Desan, "Women's Experience of the French Revolution," *Literate Women and The French Revolution of 1789*, ed., Catherine R. Montfort (Birmingham: Summa, 1994), 19–31; Dominique Godineau, *The Women of Paris and Their Revolution* (Berkeley: University of California Press, 1988).

79 Susan G. Bell and Karne M. Offen, *Women, the Family and Freedom: Debates in Documents, 1750–1880* (Stanford: Stanford University Press, 1983), 1:29–37.

80 Anne E. Duggan, *Salonnières, Furies and Fairies: The Politics of Gender and Cultural Change in Absolutist France* (Newark: University of Delaware Press, 2005), 25–48; Goodman, *The Republic of Letters*, 90–134.

81 Polasky, *Revolutions without Borders*, 172–73, 189.

82 Carole Pateman, *The Disorder of Women: Democracy, Feminism and Political Theory* (Stanford: Stanford University Press, 1988); Annie K. Smart, *Citoyennes: Women and the Ideal of Citizenship in Eighteenth-Century France* (Newark: University of Delaware Press, 2011); Joan B, Landes, *Women and the Public Sphere in the Age of the French Revolution* (Ithaca: Cornell University Press, 1988).

83 Suzanne Desan, *The Family on Trial in Revolutionary France* (Berkeley: University of California Press, 2006); Heuer, *The Family and the Nation*.

Notes

84 Sophie Mousset, *Women's Rights and the French Revolution: A Biography of Olympe de Gouges* (New Brunswick: Transaction, 2007), 1; John Cole, *Between the Queen and the Cabby: Olympe de Gouges's Rights of Women* (Montreal: McGill-Queen's University Press, 2011); Karen Green, *A History of Women's Political Thought in Europe, 1700–1800* (Cambridge: Cambridge University Press, 2014), 227–31.
85 Polasky, *Revolution without Borders*, 75.
86 Rose, *The Making of the Sans-Culottes*, 110–11; Desan, "Constitutional Amazons," 18–19.
87 Desan, "Women's Experience of the French Revolution," *Literate Women and the French Revolution*, 20.
88 Smart, *Citoyennes*, 3–4; Desan, "Constitutional Amazons," 25–30.
89 Godineau, *The Women of Paris*, 97–133; Rose, *The Making of the Sans-Culottes*, 114; Olwen H. Hufton, *Women and the Limits of Citizenship in the French Revolution* (Toronto: University of Toronto Press, 1992), 22–29.
90 Andress, *The Terror*, 157–58.
91 Jarvis, "The Cost of Female Citizenship," 648–50.
92 Hufton, *Women and the Limits of Citizenship*, 37–38; Godineau, *The Women of Paris*, 158–74.
93 Sarah E. Melzer and Leslie W. Rabine, eds., *Rebel Daughters: Women and the French Revolution* (Oxford: Oxford University Press, 1992).

Chapter 4

1 Andress, *The Terror*, 333.
2 Clarence Crane Brinton, *The Anatomy of Revolution* (New York: Prentice Hall, 1965), 205–36.
3 Bailey Stone, *The Anatomy of Revolution Revisited: A Comparative Analysis of England, France and Russia* (Cambridge: Cambridge University Press, 2014), 395–470.
4 Andrew Jainchill, *Reimagining Politics after the Terror: The Republican Origins of French Liberalism* (Ithaca: Cornell University Press, 2008).
5 Bronislaw Baczko, *Ending the Terror: The French Revolution after Robespierre* (Cambridge: Cambridge University Press, 1994), 33.
6 Williams, *Artisans and Sans-Culottes*, 81–94.
7 Marisa Linton, *Choosing Terror: Virtue, Friendship and Authenticity in the French Revolution* (Oxford: Oxford University Press, 2013), 269.
8 Mette Harder, "A Second Terror: The Purges of French Revolutionary Legislators after Thermidor," *French Historical Studies*, 38:1 (2015): 33–60; Howard G. Brown, "Politics, Professionalism and the Fate of Army Generals after Thermidor," *French Historical Studies*, 19:1 (Spring 1995): 133–52.
9 Howard Brown, *Ending the French Revolution: Violence, Justice and Repression from the Terror to Napoleon* (Charlottesville: University of Virginia Press, 2006), 253.
10 Jainchill, *Reimagining Politics after the Terror*, 17.
11 Williams, *Artisans and Sans-Culottes*, 92–94.
12 Isser Woloch, *Jacobin Legacy: The Democratic Movement under the Directory* (Princeton: Princeton University Press, 1970).

Notes

13 R. R. Palmer, *The Age of Democratic Revolution* (Princeton: Princeton University Press, 1964), 2:236–37.

14 Murray Bookchin, *The Third Revolution: Popular Movements in the Revolutionary Era* (London: Cassell, 1998), 2:7.

15 Zamoyski, *Phantom Terror*, 74.

16 Godechot, "The New Concept of the Nation and Its Diffusion," *Nationalism in the Age of the French Revolution*, 19.

17 Sylvie Kleinman, "Tone and the French Expeditions to Ireland, 1796–1798: Total War or Liberation?" *Republics at War*, 88–98.

18 Jerzy W. Borejsza, "The French Revolution in Relation to Poland and East-Central Europe," *The Global Ramifications of the French Revolution*, eds., Joseph Klaits and Michael C. Haltzel (Cambridge: Cambridge University Press, 2002), 56–60.

19 T. C. W. Blanning, *The French Revolution in Germany: Occupation and Resistance in the Rhineland, 1791–1802* (Oxford: Oxford University Press, 1982); Arno Störkel, "The Defenders of Mayence in 1792: A Portrait of a Small European Army at the Outbreak of the French Revolutionary Wars," *War and Society*, 12:2 (October 1994): 1–21.

20 Franz Dumont, "The Rhineland," *Nationalism in the Age of the French Revolution*, 169.

21 Jainchill, *Reimagining Politics after the Terror*, 151–86; Pierre Serna, "War and Republic: Dangerous Liaisons," *Republics at War*, 17.

22 Polasky, *Revolutions with Borders*, 243–44.

23 Marco Meriggi, "Italy," *Nationalism in the Age of the French Revolution*, 201–02.

24 Jainchill, *Reimagining Politics after the Terror*, 172–78; Godechot, "The New Concept of the Nation," *Nationalism in the Age of the French Revolution*, 23–24.

25 Marc Belissa, Repenser l'ordre européen (1795–1802): De la société des rois aux droits des nations (Paris: Krimé, 2006), 310–11.

26 Jainchill, *Reimagining Politics after the Terror*, 172.

27 Jacques Frémeaux, *La France et L'Islam depuis 1789* (Paris: Presses Universitaires de France, 1991), 35–48.

28 Maya Jasanoff, *Edge of Empire: Conquest and Collecting in the East, 1750–1840* (London: Harper Perennial, 2006), 127–38; André Raymond, *Egyptiens et Français au Caire, 1798–1801* (Cairo: IFAO, 1998), 214–15; Juan Cole, "Playing Muslim: Bonaparte's Army of the Orient and Euro-Muslim Creolization," *The Age of Revolutions in Global Context*, 129–41.

29 Nicole Dhombres and Jean Dhombres, *Naissaince d'un pouvoir: Sciences et savants en France, 1793–1824* (Paris: Payot, 1989), 103–05.

30 Ian Coller, *Arab France: Islam and the Making of Modern Europe, 1798–1831* (Berkeley: University of California Press, 2011), 29.

31 Isser Woloch, *Napoleon and His Collaborators: The Making of a Dictatorship* (New York: W. W. Norton, 2002).

32 David P. Jordan, *Napoleon and the Revolution* (New York: Palgrave Macmillan, 2012), 71.

33 Alexander Grab, *Napoleon and the Transformation of Europe* (New York: Palgrave Macmillan, 2003), 34–59.

34 Michael Broers, *Europe under Napoleon, 1799–1815* (New York: St. Martin's Press, 1996), 50–92.

35 Susan Punzel Conner, *The Age of Napoleon* (Westport: Greenwood Press, 2004), 48–49.

Notes

36 Philip G. Dwyer, "Napoleon and the Foundation of the Empire," *The Historical Journal*, 53:2 (2010): 339–58.

37 Michael Broers, "The First Napoleonic Empire, 1799–1815," *Nationalizing Empires*, 103–23; D. G. Wright, *Napoleon and Europe* (New York: Longman, 1984), 24–61.

38 Annie Jourdan, *L'Empire de Napoléon* (Paris: Flammarion, 2000), 124–25.

39 Stuart Woolf, "The Construction of a European World-View in the Revolutionary and Napoleonic Years," *Past and Present*, 137 (November 1992): 74–101.

40 Stuart Woolf, "French Civilization and Ethnicity in the Napoleonic Empire," *Past and Present*, 124 (August 1989): 113.

41 Fick, "The Haitian Revolution," 409–10.

42 Labor Decree, October 12, 1800, Geggus, *The Haitian Revolution: A Documentary History*, 153–54.

43 Régent, "From Individual to Collective Emancipation," *Republics at War*, 178–80; David Armitage, "The Declaration of Independence in World Context," *OAH Magazine of History*, 18:3 (April 2004): 61–66.

44 Philippe R. Rirard, *The Slaves Who Defeated Napoleon: Toussaint Louverture and the Haitian War of Independence, 1801–1804* (Tuscaloosa: The University of Alabama Press, 2011), 11–32; Lorelle D. Semley, "To Live and Die, Free and French: Toussaint Louverture's 1801 Constitution and the Original Challenge of Black Citizenship," *Radical History Review*, 115 (2013): 65–90.

45 Joseph M. Fradera, "L'escalvage et la logique constitutionnelle des empires," *Annales: Histoire, Sciences Sociales*, 3 (May–June 2008): 534–36.

46 Ronald Angelo Johnson, *Diplomacy in Black and White: John Adams, Toussaint Louverture, and Their Atlantic World Alliance* (Athens: University of Georgia Press, 2014), 183.

47 Matthewson, "Jefferson and Haiti," 232–47; White, *Encountering Revolution*, 164–70; James Alexander Dun, *Dangerous Neighbors: Making the Haitian Revolution in Early America* (Philadelphia: University of Pennsylvania Press, 2016).

48 Biancamaria Fontana, "The Napoleonic Empire and the European Nations," *The Idea of Europe: From Antiquity to the European Union*, ed., Anthony Pagden (Cambridge: Cambridge University Press, 2002), 125–28.

49 Patrick Geary, *The Myth of Nations: The Medieval Origins of Europe* (Princeton: Princeton University Press, 2003), 23–26.

50 Johan G. Fichte, *Address to the German Nation*, trans., G. A. Kelly (New York: Harper and Row, 1968), 45, 12.

51 Zamoysky, *Phantom Terror*, 199–200.

52 Karen Hagemann, *Revisiting Prussia's Wars against Napoleon: History, Culture and Memory* (Cambridge: Cambridge University Press, 2015), 61–74.

53 Barbara H. Stein and Stanley J. Stein, *Crisis in an Atlantic Empire: Spain and New Spain, 1808–1810* (Baltimore: Johns Hopkins University Press, 2014), 7–44.

54 Pedro Rújula, "International War, National War, Civil War: Spain and Counterrevolution," *Republics at War*, 247.

55 Ronald Fraser, *Napoleon's Cursed War: Spanish Popular Resistance in the Peninsular War, 1808–1814* (London: Verso, 2008).

56 Pearce, *The Origins of Bourbon Reform*; Lynch, *Bourbon Spain*, 253; Jeremy Adelman, *Sovereignty and Revolution in the Iberian Atlantic* (Princeton: Princeton University Press, 2006), 24.

57 Paquette, "State-Civil Society," 263–98; Uribe-Uran, "The Birth of the Public Sphere in Latin America," 438–45.

58 Anthony Pagden, *Spanish Imperialism and the Political Imagination: Studies in European and Spanish-American Social and Political Theory, 1513–1830* (New Haven: Yale University Press, 1990), 118.

59 Jaime E. Rodríguez O., *The Independence of Spanish America* (Cambridge: Cambridge University Press, 1998), 2–5.

60 Adelman, *Sovereignty and Revolution*, 186.

61 Richard Herr, "The Constitution of 1812 and the Spanish Road to Parliamentary Monarchy," *Revolution and the Meaning of Freedom in the Nineteenth Century*, ed., Isser Woloch (Stanford: Stanford University Press, 1996), 65–102.

62 Jaime E. Rodríguez O., "New Spain and the 1808 Crisis of the Spanish Monarchy," *Mexican Studies*, 24:2 (Summer 2008): 245–87.

63 John Charles Chasteen, *Americanos: Latin America's Struggle for Independence* (New York: Oxford University Press, 2008), 3–10.

64 Joseph M. Fradera, "The Empire, The Nation and the Homelands: Nineteenth-Century Spain's National Idea," *Region and State in Nineteenth-Century Europe: Nation-Building, Regional Identities and Separatism*, eds., Joost Augusteijn and Eric Storm (Houndmills: Palgrave Macmillan, 2012), 132–33; Adelman, *Sovereignty and Revolution*, 192–93.

65 Gabriel Paquette, "The Dissolution of the Spanish Atlantic Monarchy," *The Historical Journal*, 52:1 (March 2009): 199–202.

66 Simón Bolivar, "The Jamaica Letter," September 6, 1815, *El Libertador: The Writings of Simón Bolivar*, ed., David Bushnell (Oxford: Oxford University Press, 2003), 14.

67 Pagden, *Spanish Imperialism*, 136–38.

68 Simón Bolivar, "The Cartagena Manifesto," December 15, 1812, *El Libertador*, 6.

69 John Rydjord, "The French Revolution in Mexico," *Hispanic American Historical Review*, 9:1 (1929): 82.

70 Alan Knight, "Democratic and Revolutionary Traditions in Latin America," *The Bulletin of Latin American Research*, 20:2 (April 2001): 158–59; Chasteen, *Americanos*, 3–4.

71 Adelman, "An Age of Imperial Revolutions," 319–40.

72 Leon Howard, "Joel Barlow and Napoleon," *Huntington Library Quarterly*, 2:1 (October 1938): 50.

73 Gary B. Nash, "Sparks from the Altar of '76: International Repercussions and Reconsiderations of the American Revolution," *The Age of Revolutions in Global Context*, 1–19.

74 Cotlar, *Tom Paine's America*, 2–3; Griffin, *America's Revolution*, 257–59.

Chapter 5

1 Françoit Furet, "The Tyranny of Revolutionary Memory," *Fictions of the French Revolution*, ed., Bernadette Fort (Evanston: Northwestern University Press, 1991), 155.

2 François-René de Chateaubriand, *The Memoirs of Chateaubriand*, ed., Robert Baldick (New York: Knopf, 1961), 2:38–39.

3 David A. Bell, *The First Total War: Napoleon's Europe and the Birth of Warfare as We Know It* (Boston: Houghton Mifflin, 2007).

Notes

4 Bourke, *Empire and Revolution*, 703–76.
5 Joseph de Maistre, *Essai sur le principe générateur des constitutions politiques et des autres institutions humaines* (Paris: La Société Typographique, 1814).
6 Darrin M. McMahon, *Enemies of the Enlightenment: The French Counter-Enlightenment and the Making of Modernity* (Oxford: Oxford University Press, 2001), 121–88.
7 Michael Borers, *Europe after Napoleon: Revolution, Reaction and Romanticism, 1814–1848* (Manchester: Manchester University Press, 1996), 9–18.
8 Martin Lyons, *Post-Revolutionary Europe, 1815–1856* (New York: Palgrave Macmillan, 2006), 22–37.
9 David Laven and Lucy Riall, eds., *Napoleon's Legacy: Problems of Government in Restoration Europe* (Oxford: Berg, 2000).
10 Zamoysky, *Phantom Terror*, 172.
11 See: Donald E. Emerson, *Metternich and the Political Police: Security and Subversion in the Habsburg Monarchy, 1815–1830* (The Hague: Martinus Nijhoff, 1968); His-Huey Liang, *The Rise of Modern Police and the European State System from Metternich to the Second World War* (Cambridge: Cambridge University Press, 1992), 18–81; Robert Justin Goldstein, *Political Repression in Nineteenth-Century Europe* (London: Routledge, 2010), 91–109.
12 Isaac Land, ed., *Enemies of Humanity: The Nineteenth-Century War on Terrorism* (New York: Palgrave Macmillan, 2008); Zamoysky, *Phantom Terror*, 48–81; Alan Sked, *Metternich and Austria: An Evaluation* (New York: Palgrave Macmillan, 2008), 123–77.
13 Alan Spitzer, *Old Hatred and Young Hopes: The French Carbonari against the Bourbon Regime* (Cambridge: Harvard University Press, 1971), 20–22.
14 Alfred de Vigny, *The Military Condition*, trans. Marguerite Barnett (London: Oxford University Press, 1964), 10, 201.
15 Richard Stites, *The Four Horsemen: Riding to Liberty in Post-Napoleonic Europe* (Oxford: Oxford University Press, 2014), 60–63.
16 Elizabeth Einstein, *The First Professional Revolutionary: Filippo Michele Buonaratti* (Cambridge: Harvard University Press, 1959).
17 Samuel Bernstein, *French Political and Intellectual History* (London: Transaction Books, 1984), 99.
18 Karma Nabulsi, "Patriotism and Internationalism in the 'Oath of Allegiance' to Young Europe," *European Journal of Political Theory*, 5:1 (2006): 61–70.
19 Maurizio Isabella, "Mazzini's Internationalism in Context: From Cosmopolitan Patriotism of the Italian Carbonari to Mazzini's Europe of the Nations," *Giuseppe Mazzini and the Globalization of Democratic Nationalism, 1830–1920*, eds., C. A. Bayly and Eugenio F. Biagini (Oxford: Oxford University Press, 2008), 39–40.
20 John A. Davis, *Naples and Napoleon: Italy and the European Revolutions (1780–1860)* (Oxford: Oxford University Press, 2006), 265–66.
21 Zamoysky, *Phantom Terror*, 170–72.
22 Davis, *Naples and Napoleon*, 297.
23 Sudhir Hazareesingh, *The Legend of Napoleon* (London: Granata, 2004), 105–06.
24 James H. Billington, *Fire in the Minds of Men: Origins of the Revolutionary Faith* (London: Transaction, 1999), 136–38; Spitzer, *Old Hatred and Young Hopes*, 212–41.
25 Zamoysky, *Phantom Terror*, 208–15; James M. Brophy, *Popular Culture and the Public Sphere in the Rhineland, 1800–1850* (Cambridge: Cambridge University Press, 2007), 69–70.

26 McMahon, *Enemies of the Enlightenment*, 154.
27 Letter to James Monroe, July 20, 1820, *Mémoires, correspondance et manuscrits du Général Lafayette* (Paris: H. Fournier Aîné, 1838), 6:93.
28 "Sur le Projet de Loi relatif aux élections," *Mémoires, correspondance et manuscrits*, 6:76.
29 Spitzer, *Old Hatred and Young Hopes*, 84–137.
30 Zamoysky, *Phantom Terror*.
31 Sylvia Neely, *Lafayette and the Liberal Ideal, 1814–1824: Politics and Conspiracy in an Age of Restoration* (Carbondale: Southern Illinois University Press, 1991), 165.
32 Stites, *The Four Horsemen*, 57–60.
33 Charles Esdaile, "Enlightened Absolutism versus Theocracy in the Spanish Restoration," *Napoleon's Legacy*, 70–78.
34 Michael P. Costeloe, *Response to Revolution: Imperial Spain and the Spanish American Revolution, 1810–1840* (Cambridge: Cambridge University Press, 1986), 57–58.
35 Stites, *The Four Horsemen*, 65.
36 Christiana Brennecke, *Von Cádiz nach London: Spanischer Liberalismus im Spannungsfeld von nationaler Selbstbestimmung, Internationalität und Exil, 1820–1833* (Göttingen: Vandenhoeck und Ruprecht, 2010), 63–64.
37 Charles Esdaile, *Spain in the Liberal Age, 1808–1939* (Oxford: Blackwell, 2000), 42–60.
38 Zamoysky, *Phantom Terror*, 237–38.
39 Brennecke, *Von Cádiz nach London*, 48.
40 Davis, *Naples and Napoleon*, 297–311.
41 Emerson, *Metternich and the Political Police*, 87–88.
42 Stites, *The Four Horsemen*, 93.
43 Brennecke, *Von Cádiz nach London*, 49–50.
44 Maurizio Isabella, *Risorgimento in Exile: Italian Émigrés and the Liberal International in the Post-Napoleonic Era* (Oxford: Oxford University Press, 2009), 34.
45 Brennecke, *Von Cádiz nach London*, 55.
46 "Sur une rectification du procès-verbal relative a l'occupation du Royaume de Naples," *Mémoires, correspondance et manuscrits*, 6:95–96.
47 Spitzer, *Old Hatred and Young Hopes*, 198–99.
48 Neely, *Lafayette and the Liberal Ideal*, 239–40; Stites, *The Four Horsemen*, 104–05.
49 See: Dominque de Pradt, *Des colonies de la révolution actuelle de l'Anerique* (Paris: F. Brechet, 1817); Giuseppe Pecchio, "Guatemala," *New Monthly Magazine*, 14 (1825): 578–93. In general, see: Matthew Brown and Gabrielle Paquette, eds., *Connections after Colonialism: Europe and Latin America in the 1820s* (Tuscaloosa: University of Alabama Press, 2013).
50 For example, see: Giacomo Constantino Beltrami, *Le Mexique* (Paris: Delaunay, 1830).
51 Maurizio Isabella and Konstantina Zanou, eds., *Mediterranean Diasporas: Politics and Ideas in the Long Nineteenth Century* (London: Bloomsbury, 2016).
52 Jean-Louis Miège, "Les réfugiés politiques à Tanger, 1796–1875," *Revue Africaine*, 101 (1957): 134–36.
53 Julia Clancy-Smith, *Mediterraneans: North Africa and Europe in an Age of Migration, 1800–1900* (Berkeley: University of California Press, 2011), 83–84.

Notes

54 Peregrine Horden and Nicholas Purcell, "The Mediterranean and the New Thalassology," *American Historical Review*, 111:3 (2006): 722–40.

55 See: Karen Barkey, *Empire of Differences: The Ottomans in Comparative Perspective* (Cambridge: Cambridge University Press, 2008).

56 Ian Coller, "Barbary and Revolution: France and North Africa, 1789–1798," *French Mediterraneans: Transnational and Imperial Histories*, eds., Patricia Lorcin and Todd Shepherd (Lincoln: University of Nebraska Press, 2016), 52–75; Fatih Yesil, "Looking at the French Revolution through Ottoman Eyes: Ebubekir Ratid Efendi's Observations," *Bulletin of the School of Oriental and African Studies*, 70:2 (2007): 283–304.

57 Bernard Lewis, *The Emergence of Modern Turkey* (Oxford: Oxford University Press, 2002), 40–73.

58 Douglas Dakin, *The Greek Struggle for Independence, 1821–1833* (Berkeley: University of California Press, 1973), 41–69; Lucien J. Fray, *Russia and the Making of Modern Greek Identity, 1821–1844* (Oxford: Oxford University Press, 2015), 31.

59 Roderick Beaton, *Byron's War: Romantic Rebellion, Greek Revolution* (Cambridge: Cambridge University Press, 2013).

60 Stites, *The Four Horsemen*, 229–37.

61 Isabella, *Risorgimento in Exile*, 65–89.

62 Nabulsi, "Patriotism and Internationalism," 64.

63 Roland Sarti, "Giuseppe Mazzini and Young Italy," *Giuseppe Mazzini and the Globalization of Democratic Nationalism*, 290.

64 Stefano Recchia and Nadia Urbinati, "Giuseppe Mazzini's International Political Thought," *The Cosmopolitanism of Nations: Giuseppe Mazzini's Writings on Democracy, Nation Building and International Relations* (Princeton: Princeton University Press, 2009), 23–24.

65 Sarti, "Giuseppe Mazzini and Young Italy," *Giuseppe Mazzini*, 296.

66 Maurizio Viroli, *For Love of Country: An Essay on Patriotism and Nationalism* (Oxford: Clarendon, 1995), 150–51.

67 Ariane Chebel D'Appollonia, "European Nationalism and European Union," *The Idea of Europe*, 182.

68 Nabulsi, "Patriotism and Internationalism," 66–68.

Chapter 6

1 Prosper Enfantin, "Letter to François Barthélemy Arlès-Dufour," September 19, 1840, *Œuvres de Saint-Simon et d'Enfantin* (Aalen: Otto Zeller, 1964), 2:22.

2 Tholfsen, *Ideology and Revolution*, 82.

3 Ira Katznelson and Aristide R. Zolberg, eds., *Working-Class Formation: Nineteenth-Century Patterns in Western Europe and the United States* (Princeton: Princeton University Press, 1986); John M. Merriman, ed., *Consciousness and Class Experience in Nineteenth-Century Europe* (New York: Holmes and Meier, 1979).

4 Kenneth Pomeranz, *The Great Divergence: China, Europe and the Making of the Modern World Economy* (Princeton: Princeton University Press, 2001).

5 Jan De Vries, "The Industrial Revolution and the Industrious Revolution," *The Journal of Economic History*, 54:2 (June 1994): 249–70.

6   Émile Montégut, "Perspectives sur le temps present de la toute-puissance de l'industrie," *Revue des Deux Mondes* (Paris: Bureau de la Revue des Deux Mondes, 1855), 9:1003–04.

7   Peter Capuano, *Changing Hands: Industry, Evolution and the Reconfiguration of the Victorian Body* (Ann Arbor: University of Michigan Press, 2015), 54.

8   Michel Chevalier, *Exposition Universelle de Londres en 1851* (Paris: L. Mathias, 1851), 35, 14.

9   Raphael Samuel, "Mechanization and Hand Labour in Industrial Britain," *The Industrial Revolution and Work in Nineteenth-Century Europe*, ed., Lenard R. Berlanstein (New York: Routledge, 1992), 26–43; William Sewell, Jr., "Uneven Development: The Autonomy of Politics and the Dockworkers of Nineteenth-Century Marseille," *American Historical Review*, 93 (1988): 604–37; Michael P. Hanagan, *Nascent Proletarians: Class Formation in Post-Revolutionary France* (Oxford: Basil Blackwell, 1989).

10 Ivan T. Berend and György Ránki, *The European Periphery and Industrialization, 1780–1914* (Cambridge: Cambridge University Press, 1982).

11 Clive H. Church, *Europe in 1830: Revolution and Political Change* (London: George Allen and Unwin, 1983), 10–11; Charles Tilly, "Social Change in Modern Europe: The Big Picture," *The Industrial Revolution and Work*, 44–60.

12 Henry William Spiegel, *The Growth of Economic Thought* (Durham: Duke University Press, 1991), 221–337; Boyd Hilton, *A Mad, Bad and Dangerous People? England 1783–1846* (Oxford: Clarendon Press, 2006), 343–45.

13 Linda Vardi, "The Abolition of Guilds during the French Revolution," *French Historical Studies*, 15:4 (Autumn 1988): 704–17; Rose, *The Making of the Sans-Culottes*, 14; D. G. Wright, *Popular Radicalism: The Working-Class Experience, 1780–1880* (London: Longman, 1988), 64–65.

14 Friedrich Engels, *The Conditions of the Working Class in England in 1844* (New York: Cosimo, 2008), 53.

15 Théophile Gautier, *Caprices et Zizags* (Paris: Victor Lecou, 1852), 309, 312.

16 Pamela M. Pilbeam, *French Socialist before Marx: Workers, Women and the Social Question in France* (Montreal: McGill-Queen's University Press, 2000), 24.

17 Jacob Talmon, *Political Messianism: The Romantic Phase* (London: Secker and Warburg, 1960), 135.

18 Hilton, *A Mad, Bad and Dangerous People*, 350.

19 Robert William Seton-Weston, *Britain in Europe 1789 to 1914* (Cambridge: Cambridge University Press, 1955), 148.

20 Church, *Europe in 1830*, 71–78; Pamela Pilbeam, *The 1830 Revolution in France* (Houndmills: Macmillan, 1991), 60–98.

21 J. P. T. Bury and R. P. Tombs, *Theirs, 1797–1877: A Political Life* (London: Allen and Unwinn, 1986), 35.

22 Biancamaria Fontana, *Benjamin Constant and the Post-Revolutionary Mind* (New Haven: Yale University Press, 1991), 75.

23 Alan S. Kahan, *Liberalism in Nineteenth-Century Europe: The Political Culture of Limited Suffrage* (Houndsmill: Palgrave Macmillan, 2003), 21–65; Pierre Rosanvallon, *Le Moment Guizot* (Paris: Gallimard, 1985), 99–114; Sarah Maza, *The Myth of the French Bourgeoisie: An Essay on the Social Imaginary, 1750–1850* (Cambridge: Harvard University Press, 2003), 147–50.

24 Archives Nationales 87 AP 15, "Discours pronounce par M. De Rémusat," March 14, 1834.

Notes

25 Katherine A. Lynch, *Family, Class and Ideology in Early Industrial France. Social Policy and the Working-Class Family, 1825–1848* (Madison: University of Wisconsin Press, 1988), 18–20; Philippe Perrot, *Fashioning the Bourgeoisie: A History of Clothing in the Nineteenth Century* (Princeton: Princeton University Press, 1994), 15–35.

26 George Charles Riche III, *Frederic Bastiat: A Man Alone* (New Rochelle, NY: Arlington House, 1971), 63.

27 Eric Evans, *Parliamentary Reform in Britain, 1770–1918* (Cambridge: Cambridge University Press, 1999), 18–25; Hilton, *A Mad, Bad and Dangerous People*, 420–38.

28 Dror Wahrman, *Imagining the Middle Class: The Political Representation of Class in Britain, c. 1780–1840* (Cambridge: Cambridge University Press, 1995), 269.

29 Wright, *Popular Radicalism*, 88.

30 Edward Royale, *Revolutionary Britannia? Reflections on the Threat of Revolution in Britain, 1789–1848* (Manchester: Manchester University Press, 2000), 70–89.

31 Thomas Babington Macaulay, *A Speech Delivered in the House of Commons on the Debate of Wednesday, March 2, 1831* (London: James Ridgway, 1831), 8–9.

32 Peter Davies, *The Debate on the French Revolution* (Manchester: Manchester University Press, 2006), 66.

33 Pierre Bouretz, "L'héritage des Lumières," *François Guizot et la culture politique de son temps*, ed., Mariana Valensise (Paris: Gallimard, 1991), 37–54; Rosanvallon, *Le Moment Guizot*, 109–14.

34 Peter N. Stearns, *Paths to Authority: The Middle Class and the Industrial Labor Force in France, 1820–1848* (Urbana: University of Illinois Press, 1978), 108–10; Jesús Cruz, "An Ambivalent Revolution: The Public and Private in the Construction of Liberal Spain," *Journal of Social History*, 30:1 (Autumn 1996): 5–27.

35 Jeremy D. Popkin, *Press, Revolution and Social Identities in France, 1830–1835* (University Park: Pennsylvania State University Press, 2002), 70; Maza, *The Myth of the French Bourgeoisie*; Wahrman, *Imagining the Middle Class*.

36 Ian Donnachie, *Robert Owen: Owen of New Lanark and New Harmony* (London: Tuckwell, 2000); Malcolm Chase, *The People's Farm: English Radical Agrarianism* (Oxford: Clarendon Press, 1988), 121–89.

37 Talmon, *Political Messianism*, 133.

38 Jonathan Beecher, *Charles Fourier: The Visionary and His World* (Berkeley: University of California Press, 1986), 241–96; Pamila Pilbeam, "Dream Worlds? Religion and the Early Socialists in France," *The Historical Journal*, 43:2 (January 2000): 502.

39 Carl J. Guarneri, *The Utopian Alternative: Fourierism in Nineteenth-Century America* (Ithaca: Cornell University Press, 1991); Pilbeam, *French Socialists before Marx*, 121–26; Robert P. Sutton, *Les Icariens: The Utopian Dream in Europe and America* (Urbana: University of Illinois Press, 1994).

40 Charles Fourier, *The Theory of the Four Movements*, eds., Gareth Stedman Jones and Ian Patterson (Cambridge: Cambridge University Press, 1996), 132.

41 Pilbeam, "Dream Worlds": 502–03; Hilton, *A Mad, Bad and Dangerous People*, 491.

42 Pamela Pilbeam, *Saint-Simonians in Nineteenth-Century France: From Free Love to Algeria* (London: Palgrave Macmillan, 2014).

43 Talmon, *Political Messianism*, 41–43.

44 Henri de Saint-Simon, "De la physiologie appliquée à l'amélioration des institutions sociales," *Œuvres de Claude-Henri de Saint-Simon* (Paris: Anthropos, 1966), 5:177.

Notes

45 Saint-Simon, "L'Industrie," *Œuvres de Claude-Henri de Saint-Simon*, 1:68–69.
46 Prosper Enfantin, "Letter to Arlès," October 1, 1840, *Œuvres*, 2:38.
47 Prosper Enfantin, "Letter to Arlès," September 19, 1840, *Œuvres*, 2:30.
48 Saint-Simon, "Introduction aux travaux scientifique du XIXe siècle," *Œuvres de Claude-Henri de Saint-Simon*, 6:170.
49 Michèle Riot-Sarcey, "L'affirmation d'une doctrine et l'organisation d'une religion alternative," *Le siècle des Saint-Simoniens du Nouveau Christianisme au canal de Suez*, eds., Nathalie Coilly and Philippe Régnier (Paris: Bibliothèque Nationales, 2006), 44–47.
50 Talmon, *Political Messianism*, 75–76.
51 Pilbeam, "Dream Worlds": 499–515; Edward Berenson, *Populist Religion and Left-Wing Politics in France, 1830–1852* (Princeton: Princeton University Press, 1984); J. F. C. Harrison, *Robert Owen and the Owenites in Britain and America: The Quest for the New Moral World* (London: Routledge, 1969), 91–139.
52 Anita Brookner, *Romanticism and Its Discontents* (New York: Farrar, Straus and Giroux, 2000), 3.
53 Étienne Cabet, *Comment je suis communiste* (Paris: Chez Souverain, 1840), 9.
54 Talmon, *Political Messianism*, 164.
55 Jean Tulard, *Les Révolutions* (Paris: Fayard, 1985), 362–66; Howard Pinkney, *Decisive Years in France, 1840–1847* (Princeton: Princeton University Press, 1986), 23–49; Berenson, *Populist Religion*, 34–35; Jill Harsin, *Barricades: The War on the Streets in Revolutionary Paris, 1830–1848* (New York: Palgrave, 2002).
56 Maza, *The Myth of the French Bourgeoisie*, 170–80.
57 Max Nomad, *Apostles of Revolution* (Boston: Little, Brown and Company, 1939), 17.
58 Harsin, *Barricades*, 75.
59 Alan Spitzer, *The Revolutionary Theories of Louis Auguste Blanqui* (New York: Columbia University Press, 1957); Pilbeam, *French Socialism before Marx*, 30–34.
60 William Sewell, Jr., "Corporations Républicaines: The Revolutionary Idiom of Parisian Workers in 1848," *Comparative Studies in Society and History*, 21:2 (April 1979): 195–203.
61 William Sewell, Jr., *Work and Revolution in France: The Language of Labor from the Old Regime to 1848* (Cambridge: Cambridge University Press, 1980).
62 Talmon, *Political Messianism*, 164–72.
63 Gareth Stedman Jones, *Languages of Class: Studies in English Working Class History, 1832–1982* (Cambridge: Cambridge University Press, 1983)
64 Hilton, *A Mad, Bad and Dangerous People*, 611; Wright, *Popular Radicalism*, 117.
65 Royale, *Revolutionary Britannia*, 93.
66 Humphrey Southall, "Agitate! Agitate! Organize! Political Travelers and the Construction of a National Politic, 1839–1880," *Transactions of the Institute of British Geographers*, 21:1 (1996): 177–93.
67 John Plotz, "Crowd Power: Chartism, Carlyle, and the Victorian Public Sphere," *Representations*, 70 (Spring 2000): 87–94.
68 Royale, *Revolutionary Britannia*, 103.
69 James A. Epstein, *Radical Expression: Political Language, Ritual and Symbol in England, 1790–1850* (Oxford: Oxford University Press, 1994), 150–57.

Notes

70 Wright, *Popular Radicalism*, 139–40; E. P. Thompson, *The Making of the English Working Class* (New York: Pantheon, 1963), 398–99; Dorothy Thompson, *The Chartists: Popular Politics in the Industrial Revolution* (New York: Pantheon, 1984), 120–51.
71 R. B. Rose, *Gracchus Babeuf: The First Revolutionary Communist* (Stanford: Stanford University Press, 1978).
72 Tholfsen, *Ideology and Revolution*, 48–49.
73 David Blackbourn, *History of Germany, 1780–1918* (Oxford: Blackwell, 2003), 37.
74 Mary Fulbrook, *A Concise History of Germany* (Cambridge: Cambridge University Press, 1991), 94.
75 Heinrich Heine, "Germany, A Winter Tale," *The Poems of Heine*, trans., Edgar Alfred Bowring (London: Bell and Daldy, 1866), 339.
76 Terry Pinkard, *Hegel: A Biography* (Cambridge: Cambridge University Press, 2000), 228.
77 Robert Stern, *The Routledge Guidebook of Hegel's Phenomenology of Spirit* (London: Routledge, 2013), 103.
78 Talmon, *Political Messianism*, 203.
79 Michael Rosen, *Hegel's Dialectic and Its Criticism* (Cambridge: Cambridge University Press, 1982).
80 Robert C. Salmon, *In the Spirit of Hegel* (Oxford: Oxford University Press, 1983), 36–38.
81 Paul Thomas, *Karl Marx and the Anarchists* (London: Routledge, 1980), 25–31.
82 Shlomo Avineri, *Hegel's Theory of the Modern State* (Cambridge: Cambridge University Press, 1972); Z. A. Pelczynski, ed., *The State and Civil Society: Studies in Hegel Political Philosophy* (Cambridge: Cambridge University Press, 1984).
83 Karl Marx, "Theses on Fuererbach," *Selected Writings*, ed., David McLellan (Oxford: Oxford University Press, 2000), 173.
84 Thomas, *Karl Marx*, 61.
85 Thomas, *Karl Marx*, 63.
86 Marx, "Critical Remarks on the Article: 'The King of Prussia and Social Reform,'" *Selected Writings*, 135.
87 Thomas, *Karl Marx*, 46.
88 Edmund Wilson, *To the Finland Station: A Study in the Writing and Acting of History* (London: Macmillan, 1972), 148.
89 Marx, "Communism and the Augsburger Allgemeine Zeitung," *Selected Writings*, 25–26.
90 Jacques Grandjonc, *Marx et les communistes allemands à Paris* (Paris: F. Maspero, 1974).
91 Marx, "Critical Remarks," *Selected Writings*, 137.
92 Hal Draper, *Karl Marx's Theory of Revolution* (New York: Monthly Review Press, 1986), 3:362–64.
93 Tristram Hunt, *The Frock-Coated Communist: The Revolutionary Life of Friedrich Engels* (London: Allen Lane, 2009), Chapter 3.
94 Wilson, *To the Finland Station*, 162.
95 Richard F. Hamilton, *The Bourgeois Epoch: Marx and Engels on Britain, France and Germany* (Chapel Hill: University of North Carolina Press, 1991), 25–30.
96 Thomas, *Karl Marx*, 199–200.
97 Marx, "The German Ideology," *Selected Writings*, 185–86.

98   Marx, *Selected Writings*, 141.
99   Marx, "The German Ideology," *Selected Writings*, 177.
100 Karl Marx and Friedrich Engels, *The Manifesto of the Communist Party* (Chicago: Charles H. Kerr, 1910), 12.
101 Ibid., 29.
102 Tholfsen, *Ideology and Revolution*, 75–82.
103 Marx, "The Poverty of Philosophy," *Selected Writings*, 232.
104 Wilson, *To the Finland Station*, 172–73.
105 David McLellan, *The Thought of Karl Marx* (London: Macmillan, 1980), 62.
106 Anne M. Woodall, *What Price the Poor? William Booth, Karl Marx and the London Residium* (Burlington: Ashgate, 2006), 123.
107 Michael Löwy, *The Theory of Revolution in the Young Marx* (Chicago: Haymarket Books, 2005), 139–47.
108 Marx, "Speech to the Central Committee of the Communist League," *Selected Writings*, 326.
109 Alexis de Tocqueville, *On Democracy, Revolution and Society*, eds., John Stone and Stephen Mennell (Chicago: University of Chicago Press, 1980), 11.

Chapter 7

1   Peter Jones, *The 1848 Revolution* (Essex: Longman, 1981), 15, 28–29; Jonathan Sperber, *The European Revolutions, 1848–1851* (Cambridge: Cambridge University Press, 1994), 40–43.
2   Priscilla Robertson, *The Revolutions of 1848: A Social History* (Princeton: Princeton University Press, 1952); P. H. Noyes, *Organization and Revolutions: Working Class Associations in the German Revolutions of 1848–1849* (Princeton: Princeton University Press, 1966); Jones, *The 1848 Revolution*.
3   E. J. Hobsbawm, *The Age of Capital, 1848–1875* (London: Abacus, 1977), 28.
4   Sperber, *The European Revolutions*, 54.
5   Laszlo Deme, "Echoes of the French Revolution in 1848 Hungary," *East European Quarterly*, 25:1 (Spring 1991): 103.
6   Claus Møller Jørgensen, "Transurban Interconnectivities: An Essay on the Interpretation of the Revolutions of 1848," *European Review of History*, 19:2 (April 2012): 206–07.
7   Kurt Weyland, "The Diffusion of Revolution: 1848 in Europe and Latin America," *International Organization*, 63:3 (Summer 2009): 391–423.
8   Alexander Herzen, "Letter XIV," December 31, 1851, *Lettres de France et d'Italie* (Geneva: Imprimerie Czerniecki, 1871), 292.
9   William Fortescue, *France and 1848: The End of Monarchy* (London: Routledge, 2005), 58–60.
10 Christine Guionnet, *L'Apprentissage de la politique modern: Les élections municipales sous la Monarchie de Juillet* (Paris: Harmattan, 1997), 310.
11 Alfred Delvau, *Les Murailles Révolutonnaires de 1848* (Paris: E. Picard, 1868), 1:21.
12 Roger V. Gould, *Insurgent Identities: Class, Community and Protest in Paris from 1848 to the Commune* (Chicago: University of Chicago Press, 1995), 38–40.

Notes

13 Wolfram Siemann, *The German Revolution of 1848–49* (London: Macmillan, 1998), 58.
14 Hans Joachim Hahn, *The 1848 Revolutions in German-Speaking Europe* (London: Routledge, 2001), 46–65.
15 R. John Rath, *The Viennese Revolution of 1848* (Austin: University of Texas Press, 1977), 34.
16 Ginsborg, *Daniele Manin*, 116.
17 Axel Körn, ed., *1848-A European Revolution? International Ideas and National Memories of 1848* (Houndmills: Palgrave Macmillan, 2000).
18 Sperber, *The European Revolutions*, 27.
19 Weyland, "The Diffusion of Revolution," 414.
20 Deme, "Echoes of the French Revolution," 105.
21 J. L. Talmon, *Romanticism and Revolt: Europe 1815–1848* (London: Thames and Hudson, 1967), 168.
22 Furet, "The Tyranny of Revolutionary Memory," *Fictions of the French Revolution*, 151–60.
23 Jørgensen, "Transurban Interconnectivities," 208.
24 Osterhammel, *The Transformation of the World*, 546.
25 J. A. W. Gunn, "French Republicans and the Suffrage: The Birth of the Doctrine of False Consciousness," *French History*, 22:1 (March 2008): 28–50.
26 Siemann, *The German Revolution*, 176.
27 Jørgensen, "Transurban Interconnectivities," 206–07.
28 Rath, *The Viennese Revolution*, 80.
29 Stanley Z. Pech, *The Czech Revolution of 1848* (Chapel Hill: University of North Carolina Press, 1969), 33–34, 89, 118–21.
30 Sperber, *The Revolutions of 1848*, 151–52.
31 Harsin, *Barricades*, 285–88; Peter H. Amann, *Revolution and Mass Democracy: The Paris Club Movement in 1848* (Princeton: Princeton University Press, 1975), 111–43.
32 Siemann, *The German Revolution of 1848*, 90–91.
33 Jørgensen, "Transurban Interconnectivities," 210.
34 R. S. Alexander, *Europe's Uncertain Path, 1815–1914: State Formation and Civil Society* (Oxford: Wiley-Blackwell, 2012), 116; Jonathan Sperber, *Rhineland Radicals: The Democratic Movement and the Revolution of 1848–1849* (Princeton: Princeton University Press, 1991), 191–03.
35 Amann, *Revolution and Mass Democracy*, 33.
36 Sperber, *The Revolutions of 1848*, 165–67.
37 Ginsborg, *Daniele Manin*, 88.
38 Jones, *The 1848 Revolutions*, 58–60; Jørgensen, "Transurban Interconnectivities," 210–11; Robertson, *Revolutions of 1848*.
39 Mark Traugott, *Armies of the Poor: Detriments of Working-Class Participation in the Parisian Insurrection of June 1848* (Princeton: Princeton University Press, 1985); Charles Tilly and Lynn H. Lees, "The People of June, 1848," *Revolution and Reaction: 1848 and the Second French Republic*, ed., Roger Price (London: Croom Helm, 1975), 176–77.
40 Amann, *Revolution and Mass Democracy*, 294–323.

41 Pieter M. Judson, *Reluctant Revolutionaries: Liberal Politics, Social Experience and National Identity in the Austrian Empire, 1848–1914* (Ann Arbor: University of Michigan Press, 1996) 34–48; John Deak, *Forging a Multinational State: State Making in Imperial Austria from the Enlightenment to the First World War* (Stanford: Stanford University Press, 2015), 72–79.

42 Lewis Namier, *1848: The Revolution of the Intellectuals* (London: Geoffrey Cumberlege, 1944), 22–23.

43 Sperber, *The European Revolutions*, 127–28; Ginsborg, *Daniele Manin*, 142–52.

44 Fikhert Adanir, "Religious Communities and Ethnic Groups under Imperial Sway: Ottoman and Habsburg Lands in Comparison," *The Historical Practice of Diversity: Transcultural Interactions from the Early Modern Mediterranean to the Postcolonial World*, ed., Dirk Hoerder (New York: Berghahn, 2003), 68.

45 István Deák, *The Lawful Revolution: Louis Kossuth and the Hungarians, 1848–1849* (New York: Columbia University Press, 1979).

46 Benyamin Neuberger, "National Self-Determination and Democracy," *Nationalism and Democracy: Dichotomies, Complementarities, Oppositions*, eds., André Lecours and Luis Moreno (London: Routledge, 2010), 75.

47 Ivan T. Berend, *History Derailed: Central and Eastern Europe in the Long Nineteenth Century* (Berkeley: University of California Press, 2003), 111–14.

48 Adanir, "Religious Communities and Ethnic Groups," 68–69.

49 Pech, *The Czech Revolution*, 123–38; Jones, *The 1848 Revolutions*, 44.

50 Judson, *Reluctant Revolutionaries*, 59–65.

51 Siemann, *The German Revolution*, 144–45.

52 Brian E. Vick, *Defining Germany: The 1848 Frankfurt Parliament and National Identity* (Cambridge: Harvard University Press, 2002).

53 Michael Burleigh, *Earthly Powers: The Clash of Religion and Politics in Europe from the French Revolution to the Great War* (New York: HarperCollins, 2005), 174–75.

54 Namier, *1848*, 70.

55 Karl Marx, *The Eighteenth Brumaire of Louis Bonaparte*, trans., Daniel De Leon (Chicago: Charles H. Kerr, 1905), 5–7.

56 Cristopher Clark, "After 1848: The European Revolution in Government," *Transactions of the Royal Historical Society*, 22 (December 2012): 171–97.

57 Benedict Anderson, *Imagined Communities: Reflections on the Origins and Spread of Nationalism* (London: Verso, 1996), 83–111; Daniel L. Unowsky, *The Pomp and Politics of Patriotism: Imperial Celebrations in Habsburg Austria, 1848–1916* (West Lafayette: Perdue University Press, 2006); Berger and Miller, *Nationalizing Empires*.

58 Otto Pflanze, "Nationalism in Europe, 1848–1871," *The Review of Politics*, 28:2 (April 1966): 129–43.

59 Christine Lattek, *Revolutionary Refugees: German Socialism in Britain, 1840–1860* (London: Routledge, 2006), 48–82; McLellan, *The Thought of Karl Marx*, 51–62.

60 McLellan, *The Thought of Karl Marx*, 68.

61 Wilson, *To the Finland Station*, 244–57.

62 Martin Conway, "Legacies of Exile," *Europe in Exile: European Exile Communities in Britain, 1940–1945*, eds., Martin Conway and Jose Gotovich (New York: Berghahn, 2001), 255.

Notes

63 Billington, *Fire in the Minds of Men*, 294; Thomas, *Karl Marx and the Anarchists*, 256–60.
64 Pierre-Joseph Proudhon, "De la capacité politique des classes ouvrières," *Œuvres complètes* (Paris: Marcel Rivière, 1924), 4:261.
65 Proudon, "Philosophie du progrès," *Œuvres complètes*, 13: 60, 40.
66 Proudhon, "Idée générale de la Révolution au XIXe siècle," *Œuvres complètes*, 3:154.
67 James Joll, *The Anarchists* (London: Eyre and Spottiswoode, 1964), 54.
68 Proudhon, "De la capacité politique," *Œuvres complètes*, 4:285.
69 Murray Bookchin, *The Spanish Anarchists: The Heroic Years, 1868–1936* (New York: Free Life Editions, 1977), 19–22.
70 Proudhon, "De la capacité politique," *Œuvres complètes*, 4:244.
71 McLellan, *The Thought of Karl Marx*, 40.
72 Proudhon to Marx, May 17, 1846, *Correspondance de P.-J. Proudhon* (Paris: A. Lacroix, 1875), 2:199.
73 Thomas, *Karl Marx and the Anarchists*, 275; Billington, *Fire in the Minds of Men*, 294–95.
74 Löwy, *The Theory of Revolution in the Young Marx*, 156.
75 Edward Acton, *Alexander Herzen and the Role of the Intellectual Revolutionary* (Cambridge: Cambridge University Press, 1979), 40–42.
76 Martin Malia, *Alexander Herzen and the Birth of Russian Socialism* (New York: Gosset and Dunlap, 1965), 371.
77 Alexander Herzen, *My Past and Thoughts*, trans., Constance Garnett (Berkeley: University of California Press, 1973), 347.
78 Herzen, "Letter XIII," July 1, 1851, *Lettres de France et d'Italie*, 280.
79 Alexander Herzen, "From the Other Shore," *Selected Philosophical Works* (Moscow: Foreign Language Publishing House, 1956), 435–36.
80 Herzen, "Letter XIII," July 1, 1851, *Lettres de France et d'Italie*, 285.
81 Judith E. Zimmerman, *Midpassage: Alexander Herzen and European Revolution, 1847–1852* (Pittsburgh: University of Pittsburgh Press, 1989), 88–89.
82 Monica Partridge, "Alexander Herzen and the English Press," *The Slavonic and East European Review*, 36:87 (June 1958): 453.
83 Acton, *Alexander Herzen*, 106.
84 Malia, *Alexander Herzen*, 378.
85 Partridge, "Alexander Herzen and the English Press," 455.
86 Abbot Gleason, *Young Russia: The Genesis of Russian Radicalism in the 1860s* (Chicago: University of Chicago Press, 1980), 84, 86.
87 Laura Engelstein, *Slavophile Empire: Imperial Russia's Illiberal Past* (Ithaca: Cornell University Press, 2009); Susanna Rabow-Edling, *Slavophile Thought and the Politics of Cultural Nationalism* (Albany: State University of New York Press, 2006).
88 Alexander Herzen, *From the Other Shore and the Russian People and Socialism* (New York: World Publishing Company, 1963), 175.
89 Sidney Monas, "The Twilit Middle Class of Nineteenth Century Russia," *Between Tsar and People: Educated Society and the Quest for Public Identity in Late Imperial Russia*, eds., Edith W. Clowes, Samuel D. Kassow and James L. West (Princeton: Princeton University Press, 1991), 2–29.

90	Acton, *Alexander Herzen*, 402–05.
91	Gleason, *Young Russia*, 22.
92	Gleason, *Young Russia*, 297–98; Joseph Frank, *Through the Russian Prism: Essays on Literature and Culture* (Princeton: Princeton University Press, 1990), 187–201; Derek Offord, *Nineteenth-Century Russia: Opposition to Autocracy* (London: Routledge, 2013), 55–59.
93	David Moon, *The Abolition of Serfdom in Russia, 1762–1907* (London: Routledge, 2014), 56–83; David Saunders, *Russia in the Age of Reaction and Reform, 1801–1881* (London: Routledge, 1992), 204–38.
94	Gleason, *Young Russia*, 141, 128–33.
95	Barbar Alpern Engle, *Mothers and Daughters: Women of the Intelligentsia in Nineteenth-Century Russia* (Evanston: Northwestern University Press, 2000), 87–88; Barbara Alpern Engle and Clifford N. Rosenthal, eds., *Fiver Sisters against the Tsar: The Memoirs of Five Young Anarchist Women of the 1870s* (New York: Routledge, 1992), 59–94.
96	Tibor Szamuely, *The Russian Tradition* (New York: McGraw-Hill, 1974), 281.
97	Richard Wortman, *The Crisis of Russian Populism* (Cambridge: Cambridge University Press, 1967), 17–19.
98	Gleason, *Young Russia*, 23.
99	George W. Fasel, *Europe in Upheaval: The Revolutions of 1848* (New York: Rand McNally, 1970), 168.
100	Raymond Grew, *A Sterner Plan for Italian Unity: The Italian National Society in the Risorgimento* (Princeton: Princeton University Press, 1963), 154–55; Lucy Riall, *The Italian Risorgimento: State, Society and National Unification* (London: Routledge, 1994), 14–15.
101	Christopher Hibbert, *Garibaldi and His Enemies: The Clash of Arms and Personalities in the Making of Italy* (New York: Penguin, 1966), 17–44.
102	Lucy Riall, *Garibaldi: Invention of a Hero* (New Haven: Yale University Press, 2008), 85, 189.
103	Denis Mack Smith, *Cavour and Garibaldi 1860: A Study in Political Conflict* (Cambridge: Cambridge University Press, 1954).
104	Riall, *Garibaldi*, 363.

Chapter 8

1	Joll, *The Anarchists*, 78.
2	Gleason, *Young Russia*, 359.
3	Woodford McClellan, *Revolutionary Exiles: The Russians in the First International and the Paris Commune* (New York: Taylor and Francis, 1979); Alan Kimball, "The First International and the Russian Obshchina," *Slavic Review*, 32:3 (September 1973): 491–514.
4	Ross, *Communal Luxury*, 26–29.
5	Robert Graham, *Anarchism: A Documentary History of Libertarian Ideas* (New York: Black Rose Books, 2005), 1:xiii–xiv.
6	Pierre-Joseph Proudhon, *The General Idea of Revolution in the Nineteenth Century* (London: Freedom Press, 1923), 239.

Notes

7   Mikhail Bakunin, *Stateless Socialism: Anarchism* (The Anarchist Library, 2009), 5.
8   Bookchin, *The Spanish Anarchists*, 26–27.
9   George Woodcock and Ivan Avakumović, *The Anarchist Prince: A Biographical Study of Peter Kropotkin* (New York: Kraus, 1970), 160.
10 Ross, *Communal Luxury*, 89–92.
11 "L'Action," *Le Révolté*, December 25, 1880.
12 Mikhail Bakunin, "Appeal to the Slavs," *Bakunin on Anarchy*, ed., Sam Dolgoff (New York: Vintage, 1971), 68.
13 Joll, *The Anarchists*, 68.
14 E. H. Carr, *Michael Bakunin* (New York: Vintage, 1961), 157.
15 Mikhail Bakunin, "Fédéralisme, Socialisme et Antithéologisme," *Œuvres* (Paris: P. V. Stock, 1907), 1:43.
16 Nunzio Pernicone, *The Italian Anarchists, 1864–1892* (Princeton: Princeton University Press, 1993), 19.
17 Joll, *The Anarchists*, 75.
18 Franco Venturi, *Roots of Revolution: A History of the Populist and Socialist Movements in Nineteenth-Century Russia* (New York: Grosset and Dunlop, 1966), 54–56.
19 Joll, *The Anarchists*, 69.
20 Letter to Herzen and Ogareff, March 4, 1864, *Correspondance de Michel Bakounine: Lettres à Herzen et à Ogareff*, ed., Michel Dragomanov (Paris: Perrin, 1896, 200).
21 Joll, *The Anarchists*, 74.
22 Bakunin, "Fédéralisme, Socialisme et Antithéologisme," *Œuvres*, 1:84.
23 Pernicone, *Italian Anarchists*, 24–28.
24 Bakunin, "Fédéralisme, Socialisme et Antithéologisme," *Œuvres*, 1:150, 42.
25 "The Program of the International Brotherhood," *Bakunin on Anarchy*, 152.
26 Thomas, *Karl Marx and the Anarchists*, 298.
27 Bookchin, *The Spanish Anarchists*, 28–29.
28 George Richard Esenwein, *Anarchist Ideology and the Working-Class Movement in Spain, 1868–1898* (Berkeley: University of California Press, 1989), 16–18.
29 Bookchin, *The Spanish Anarchists*, 14–15, 54–55; Esenwein, *Anarchist Ideology*, 6.
30 Joll, *The Anarchists*, 84.
31 Thomas, *Karl Marx and the Anarchists*, 321–22.
32 Patrick H. Hutton, *The Cult of the Revolutionary Tradition: The Blanquists in French Politics, 1864–1893* (Berkeley: University of California Press, 1981), 17–58.
33 Jules Vallès, "Les Réfractaires," *Œuvres* (Paris: Gallimard, 1975), 1:138.
34 Jerrold Seigel, *Bohemian Paris: Culture, Politics and the Boundaries of Bourgeois Life, 1830–1930* (Baltimore: Johns Hopkins University Press, 1986), 190.
35 J. P. T. Bury, *Gambetta and the National Defense: A Republican Dictatorship in France* (Westport: Greenwood Press, 1971); Stéphan Audoin-Rouzeau, *1870: La France dans la guerre* (Paris: Armand Colin, 1989); Michael Howard, *The Franco-Prussian War: The German Invasion of France, 1870–1871* (London: Routledge, 2001).
36 Rebecca Spang, "And They Ate the Zoo: Relating Gastronomic Exoticism in the Siege of Paris," *MNL*, 107 (1992): 752–73.

Notes

37 Hollis Clayson, *Paris in Despair: Art and Everyday Life under Siege* (Chicago: University of Chicago Press, 2002); Audoin-Rouzeau, *1870*, 273-74.

38 Samuel M. Osgood, *French Royalism under the Third and Fourth Republics* (The Hague: Martinus Nijhoff, 1960), 1-34; J. P. T. Bury and R. P. Tombs, *Thiers, 1797-1877: A Political Life* (London: Allen and Unwin, 1986), 199-202; Gay L. Gullickson, *Unruly Women of Paris: Images of the Commune* (Ithaca: Cornell University Press, 1996), 27-38.

39 Ross, *Communal Luxury*, 19-20.

40 Martin Phillip Johnson, *The Paradise of Association: Political Culture and Popular Organizations in the Paris Commune of 1871* (Ann Arbor: University of Michigan Press, 1996), 89-125; Donny Gluckstein, *The Paris Commune: A Revolution in Democracy* (Chicago: Haymarket Books, 2011), 19; April Carter, *The Political Theory of Anarchism* (London: Routledge, 1971), 60-62.

41 Gluckstein, *The Paris Commune*, 5.

42 Ross, *Communal Luxury*, 18-19; Bookchin, *The Third Revolution*, 2:219-50; Johnson, *The Paradise of Association*, 131-63.

43 Gluckstein, *The Paris Commune*, 37.

44 Edward S. Mason, *The Paris Commune: An Episode in the History of the Socialist Movement* (New York: H. Fertig, 1930); Jacques Rougerie, *Paris Libre, 1871* (Paris: Seuil, 1971); William Serman, *La Commune de Paris* (Paris: Fayard, 1986); Gould, *Insurgent Identities*.

45 Seigel, *Bohemian Paris*, 182-200.

46 Kristin Ross, *The Emergence of Social Space: Rimbaud and the Paris Commune* (Minneapolis: University of Minnesota Press, 1989).

47 David A. Shafer, *The Paris Commune* (Houndmills: Palgrave, 2005), 167.

48 Ganzalo J. Sánchez, *Organizing Independence: The Artists Federation of the Paris Commune and Its Legacy, 1871-1889* (Lincoln: University of Nebraska Press, 1997), 48-58.

49 Carolyn J. Eichner, *Surmounting the Barricades: Women in the Paris Commune* (Bloomington: Indiana University Press, 2004).

50 Shafer, *The Paris Commune*, 145-55.

51 Sylvie Vraibant, *Elisabeth Dmitrieff, aristocrate et pétroleuse* (Paris: Belfond, 1992), 114.

52 Gluckstein, *The Paris Commune*, 30.

53 Johnson, *The Paradise of Association*, 4-5.

54 Ross, *Communal Luxury*, 22.

55 Shafer, *The Paris Commune*, 128.

56 Johnson, *The Paradise of Association*, 18-21.

57 Dominica Chang, "Un Nouveau '93: Discourses of Mimicry and Terror in the Paris Commune of 1871," *French Historical Studies*, 36:4 (Fall 2013): 641.

58 Hutton, *The Cult of the Revolutionary Tradition*, 59-99.

59 Bakunin, "The Paris Commune and the Idea of the State," *Bakunin on Anarchy*, 268.

60 Ibid., 265.

61 Paul Avrich, *Anarchist Portraits* (Princeton: Princeton University Press, 1988), 14.

62 Nunzio Pernicone, *Italian Anarchism, 1864-1892* (Princeton: Princeton University Press, 1993), 35.

63 Caroline Cahm, *Kropotkin: The Rise of Revolutionary Anarchism, 1872-1886* (Cambridge: Cambridge University Press, 1989), 78.

Notes

64 Joll, *The Anarchists*, 90–91.
65 Bakunin, "Letter to a Frenchman on the Present Crisis," *Bakunin on Anarchy*, 195–96.
66 Bookchin, *The Spanish Anarchists*, 74–87; Esenwein, *Anarchist Ideology*, 44–47.
67 Caham, *Kropotkin*, 76–77.
68 Pernicone, *Italian Anarchism*, 84–95.
69 Pyotr Kropotkin, *Memoirs of a Revolutionist* (New York: Dover, 1971), 398.
70 Woodcock and Avakumović, *The Anarchist Prince*, 155–56.
71 Pyotr Kropotkin, "The Spirit of Revolt," *Kropotkin's Revolutionary Pamphlets*, ed., Roger N. Baldwin (New York: Dover, 1970), 38–40.
72 "Congrès annuel de la Fédération Jurassienne," *L'Avant-Garde*, August 12, 1878.
73 Richard Hostetter, *The Italian Socialist Movement: Origins, 1860–1882* (Princeton: Princeton University Press, 1958), 368.
74 Albert Parry, *Terrorism: From Robespierre to the Weather Underground* (Mineola: Dover, 1976), 87.
75 Richard Bach Jensen, *The Battle against Anarchist Terrorism: An International History, 1878–1934* (Cambridge: Cambridge University Press, 2014), 34; John Merriman, *The Dynamite Club: How a Bombing in Fin-de-Siècle Paris Ignited the Age of Modern Terror* (New Haven: Yale University Press, 2016).
76 Alexander Varias, *Paris and the Anarchists: Aesthetes and Subversives during the Fin-de-Siècle* (Basingstoke: Macmillan, 1997), 87.
77 Bookchin, *The Spanish Anarchists*, 128.
78 Esenwein, *Anarchist Ideology*, 172.
79 Barbara Tuchman, *The Proud Tower: A Portrait of the World before the War, 1890–1914* (New York: Random House, 1994), 67–126.
80 Nhat Hong, *The Anarchist Beast: The Anti-Anarchist Crusade in Periodical Literature, 1894–1906* (Minneapolis: Soil of Liberty, 1970), 16.
81 Gleason, *Young Russia*, 318–56.
82 Susan K. Morrissey, "The Apparel of Innocence: Toward a Moral Economy of Terrorism in Late Imperial Russia," *The Journal of Modern History*, 84:3 (September 2012): 607–42.
83 Claudia Verhoeven, "The Making of Russian Revolutionary Terror," in Land, *Enemies of Humanity*, 100–01.
84 Esenwein, *Anarchist Ideology*, 167.
85 Richard Back Jensen, "The Secret Agent, International Policing and Anarchist Terrorism, 1900–1914," *Terrorism and Political Violence*, 29:4 (2017): 735–71.
86 Constance Bantman, *The French Anarchists in London, 1880–1914: Exile and Transnationalism in the First Globalisation* (Liverpool: Liverpool University Press, 2013), 47–48, 153–54.
87 Ilham Khuri-Makdisi, *The Eastern Mediterranean and the Making of Global Radicalism, 1860–1914* (Berkeley: University of California Press, 2013), 16–20; Carolyn J. Eichner, "Vive la Commune! Feminism, Socialism and Revolutionary Revival in the Aftermath of the 1871 Paris Commune," *Journal of Women's History*, 15:2 (2003): 68–98.
88 Alice Bullard, *Exile to Paradise: Savagery and Civilization in Paris and the South Pacific, 1790–1900* (Stanford: Stanford University Press, 2000), 60–96.

89   Varias, *Paris and the Anarchists*, 70.

90   Thomas, *Karl Marx and the Anarchists*, 329.

91   Khuri-Makdisi, *The Eastern Mediterranean*, 19–20; José Moya, "Immigrants and Associations: A Global and Historical Perspective," *Journal of Ethnic and Migration Studies*, 31:5 (2005): 839–42.

92   Carl Levy, "Anarchism, Internationalism and Nationalism in Europe, 1860–1939," *Australian Journal of Politics and History*, 50:3 (2004): 330–42; Steven Hirsch and Lucien van der Walt, *Anarchism and Syndicalism in the Colonial and Postcolonial World, 1870–1940: The Praxis of National Liberation, Internationalism and Social Revolution* (Leiden: Brill, 2010).

93   Benedict Anderson, *Under Three Flags: Anarchism and the Anti-Colonial Imagination* (London: Verso, 2005).

94   Carl Levy, "The Rooted Cosmopolitan: Errico Malatesta, Syndicalism, Transnationalism and the International Labour Movement," *New Perspectives on Anarchism, Labour and Syndicalism: The Individual, the Nation and the Transnational*, eds., David Berry and Constance Bantman (New Castle: Cambridge Scholars, 2010), 74–76.

95   Ilham Khuri-Makdisi, "Fin-de-Siècle Egypt: A Nexus for Mediterranean and Global Radical Networks," *Global Muslims in the Age of Steam and Print*, eds., James L. Gelvin and Nile Green (Berkeley: University of California Press, 2014), 89–90.

96   Donna Gabaccia, *Italy's Many Diasporas* (London: University College London Press, 2000), 107.

97   Davide Turcato, "Italian Anarchism as a Transnational Movement, 1885–1915," *International Review of Social History*, 52 (2005): 407–44.

98   Bantman, *The French Anarchists*, 44–102.

99   William J. Fishman, *East-End Jewish Radicals, 1875–1914* (Nottingham: Five Leaves, 2004), 30; Lattek, *Revolutionary Refugees*, 226.

100 Pietro Di Paola, *The Knights Errant of Anarchy: London and the Italian Anarchist Diaspora (1880–1917)* (Liverpool: Liverpool University Press, 2013), 39–52, 182–83.

101 Varias, *Paris and the Anarchists*, 5–18.

102 Louis Patsouras, *The Anarchism of Jean Grave: Editor, Journalist and Militant* (New York: Black Rose Press, 2003).

103 Jean Grave, "La Révolution et le paysan," *Les Temps Nouveaux*, May 27, 1899.

104 C. Alexander McKinley, *Illegitimate Children of the Enlightenment: Anarchists and the French Revolution, 1880–1914* (New York: Peter Lang, 2008).

105 Reg Carr, *Anarchism in France: The Case of Octave Mirbeau* (Manchester: Manchester University Press, 1977); David Weir, *Anarchy and Culture: The Aesthetic Politics of Modernism* (Amherst: University of Massachusetts Press, 1997); David Sweetman, *Explosive Acts: Toulouse-Lautrec, Oscar Wilde, Felix Feneon and the Art and Anarchy of the Fin de Siecle* (New York: Simon and Schuster, 2000).

106 Roger Shattuck, *The Banquet Years: The Origins of the Avant-Garde in France, 1885 to World War I* (New York: Random House, 1955), 22.

107 Varias, *Paris and the Anarchists*, 24.

108 Richard Sonn, *Anarchism and Cultural Politics in Fin de Siècle France* (Lincoln: University of Nebraska Press, 1989).

Notes

109 Esenwein, *Anarchist Ideology*, 159.
110 Temma Kaplan, "Civic Rituals and Patterns of Resistance in Barcelona, 1890–1930," *The Power of the Past*, eds., Pat Thane, Geoffrey Crossick and Roderick Floud (Cambridge: Cambridge University Press, 1984), 173–94.
111 Di Paola, *The Knights Errant of Anarchy*, 9–10.
112 Geoffrey Kurtz, *Jean Jaurès: The Inner Life of Social Democracy* (University Park, Pennsylvania State University Press, 2014); K. Steven Vincent, *Between Marxism and Anarchism: Benoît Malon and French Reformist Socialism* (Berkeley: University of California Press, 1992); Guenther Ross, *The Social Democrats in Imperial Germany: A Study in Working Class Isolation and National Integration* (Totowa: Bedminster Press, 1963).
113 Bantman, *The French Anarchists*, 101.
114 Jeremy Jennings, "Syndicalism and the French Revolution," *Journal of Contemporary History*, 26:1 (January 1991): 71–96.
115 Bookchin, *The Spanish Anarchists*, 132–35; Kenneth H. Tucker, *French Revolutionary Syndicalism and the Public Sphere* (Cambridge: Cambridge University Press, 1996), 13–31.
116 Georges Sorel, *Reflections on Violence*, trans., Thomas Ernest Hulme (London: George Allen and Unwin, 1915), 54, 72.
117 Casey Harison, "The Paris Commune of 1871, the Russian Revolution of 1905, and the Shifting of the Revolutionary Tradition," *History and Memory*, 19:2 (Fall/Winter 2007): 5–42.
118 Jennings, "Syndicalism and the French Revolution," 72.
119 Bakunin, "Statism and Anarchy," *Bakunin on Anarchy*, 334.
120 Woodcock and Avakumović, *The Anarchist Prince*, 165.
121 Cahm, *Kropotkin*, 2.
122 Jean Grave, *La Société au lendemain de la Révolution* (Paris: Bureau de la Révolte, 1893), 5.
123 Ross, *Communal Luxury*, 121.

Chapter 9

1 Ann Erickson Healy, *The Russian Autocracy in Crisis, 1905–1907* (Hamden: Archon, 1976), 24.
2 Nader Sohrabi, "Historicizing Revolutions: Constitutional Revolutions in the Ottoman Empire, Iran and Russia, 1905–1908," *American Journal of Sociology*, 100:6 (May 1995):1385.
3 Dmitry Shlapentokh, *The French Revolution in Russian Intellectual Life, 1865–1905* (Westport: Praeger, 1996), 94–99.
4 Marc Szeftel, "Church and State in Imperial Russia," *Russian Orthodoxy under the Old Regime*, eds., Robert L. Nichols and Theofanis George Stavrou (Minneapolis: University of Minnesota Press, 1978), 127–41.
5 Richard Pipes, *Russia under the Old Regime* (New York: Penguin, 1993), 172–90; Gregory L. Freeze, "The Soslovie (Estate) Paradigm and Russian Social History," *American Historical Review*, 91:1 (1986): 11–36.
6 John W. Slocum, "Who, and When, Were the Inorodtsy? The Evolution of the Category of 'Aliens' in Imperial Russia," *The Russian Review*, 57:2 (April 1998): 173–90; Andreas Kappeler, *The Russian Empire: A Multi-Ethnic History* (London: Routledge, 2001).

7   Ronald Grigor Suny, "The Empire Strikes Out: Imperial Russia, National Identity and Theories of Empire," *A State of Nations: Empire and Nation Making in the Age of Lenin and Stalin*, eds., Ronald Grigor Suny and Terry Martin (Oxford: Oxford University Press, 2001), 42.

8   Willard Sunderland, *Taming the Wild Field: Colonization and Empire on the Russian Steppe* (Ithaca: Cornell University Press, 2004), 60–62, 111–12.

9   Alexander Morrison, "Russian Rule in Turkestan and the Example of British India, *c.* 1860–1917," *The Slavonic and East European Review*, 84:4 (October 2006): 666–707.

10 Edward C. Thaden, ed., *Russification in the Baltic Provinces and Finland, 1855–1914* (Princeton: Princeton University Press, 1981); Theodore R. Weeks, *Nation and State in Late Imperial Russia: Nationalism and Russification on the Western Frontier, 1863–1914* (Dekalb: Northern Illinois University Press, 2008); Robert P. Geraci, *Window on the East: National and Imperial Identities in Late Tsarist Russia* (Ithaca: Cornell University Press, 2001), 227–29, 256–61.

11 Orlando Figes, *A People's Tragedy: The Russian Revolution, 1891–1924* (London: Pimlico, 1997), 46.

12 W. Bruce Lincoln, *In the Vanguard of Reform: Russia's Enlightened Bureaucrats, 1825–1861* (Dekalb: University of Northern Illinois Press, 1982).

13 Hans Rogger, *Russia in the Age of Modernization and Revolution, 1881–1917* (London: Routledge, 1983), 59–61.

14 Thomas S. Pearson, *Russian Officialdom in Crisis: Autocracy and Local Self-Government, 1861–1900* (Cambridge: Cambridge University Press, 2004), 164–242; Figes, *A People's Tragedy*, 52–54.

15 Charles E. Timberlake, "The Zemstvo and the Development of a Russian Middle Class," *Between Tsar and People*, 168; Valeriia A. Nardova, "Municipal Self-Government after the 1870 Reform," *Russia's Great Reforms, 1855–1881*, eds., Ben Eklof, John Bushnell and Larissa Zakharova (Bloomington: Indiana University Press, 1994), 182–84; Thomas Earl Porter and Scott Seregny, "The Zemstvo Reconsidered," *The Politics of Local Government in Russia*, eds., Alfred B. Evans and Vladimir Gel'man (Oxford: Rowman and Littlefield, 2004), 19–24; Terence Emmons and Wayne S. Vucinich, eds., *The Zemstvo in Russia: An Experiment in Local Self-Governance* (Cambridge: Cambridge University Press, 1982).

16 James Simms, "The Crisis in Russian Agriculture at the End of the Nineteenth Century: A Different View," *Slavic Review*, 3 (1977): 377–98; Rogger, *Russia in the Age of Modernization*, 71–95; Figes, *A People's Tragedy*, 97–98.

17 Richard G. Robbins, *Famine in Russia, 1891–1892: The Imperial Government Responds to Crisis* (Cambridge: Cambridge University Press, 1975); Figes, *A People's Tragedy*, 158–62.

18 Rogger, *Russia in the Age of Modernization*, 100–08; Tim McDaniel, *Autocracy, Modernization and Revolution in Russia and Iran* (Princeton: Princeton University Press, 2014), 72–74; William L. Blackwell, *The Industrialization of Russia: An Historical Perspective* (New York: Crowell, 1970), 47; J. L. H. Keep, *The Rise of Social Democracy in Russia* (Oxford: Clarendon Press, 1963), 6–11.

19 Victoria E. Bonnell, ed., *The Russian Worker: Life and Labor under the Tsarist Regime* (Berkeley: University of California Press, 1983).

20 John P. Mckay, *Pioneers for Profit: Foreign Entrepreneurship and Russian Industrialization, 1885–1913* (Chicago: University of Chicago Press, 1970).

Notes

21 Mark D. Steinberg, *Moral Communities: The Culture of Class Relations in the Russian Printing Industry, 1867–1907* (Berkeley: University of California Press, 1992); Smith, *Russia in Revolution*, 40–41.

22 Elise Kimerling Wirtschafter, *Social Identity in Imperial Russia* (DeKalb: Northern Illinois University Press, 1997); Catherine Evtuhov, *Portrait of a Russian Province: Economy, Society and Civilization in Nineteenth-Century Nizhnii Novgorod* (Pittsburgh: University of Pittsburgh Press, 2011).

23 Jay Bergman, *Vera Zasulich: A Biography* (Stanford: Stanford University Press, 1983), 78–86.

24 Samuel H. Baron, *Plekhanov: The Father of Russian Marxism* (Stanford: Stanford University Press, 1963).

25 Keep, *The Rise of Social Democracy*, 20.

26 Bruno Naarden, *Socialist Europe and Revolutionary Russia: Perception and Prejudice, 1848–1923* (Cambridge: Cambridge University Press, 2002), 95–100.

27 Gareth Stedman Jones, *Karl Marx: Greatness and Illusion* (London: Allen Lane, 2017), 465.

28 Gary P. Steenson, *After Marx, before Lenin: Marxism and Socialist Working-Class Parties in Europe, 1884–1914* (Pittsburgh: University of Pittsburgh Press, 1991), 80.

29 Vernon L. Lidtke, *The Alternative Culture: Socialist Labor in Imperial Germany* (Oxford: Oxford University Press, 1985).

30 Lars T. Lih, *Lenin Rediscovered: What Is to Be Done? In Context* (Chicago: Haymarket Books, 2008), 5–7, 65–73.

31 Keep, *The Rise of Social Democracy*, 54–60; Allan K. Wildman, *The Making of a Workers' Revolution: Russian Social Democracy, 1891–1903* (Chicago: University of Chicago Press, 1967).

32 Maureen Perrie, *The Agrarian Policy of the Russian Socialist-Revolutionary Party from Its Origins through the Revolution of 1905–07* (Cambridge: Cambridge University Press, 1976).

33 Keep, *The Rise of Social Democracy*, 44.

34 Joshua D. Zimmerman, *Poles, Jews and the Politics of Nationality: The Bund and the Polish Socialist Party in Latin Imperial Russia, 1892–1914* (Madison: University of Wisconsin Press, 2004); Zvi Gitelman, *A Century of Ambivalence: The Jews of Russia and the Soviet Union, 1881 to the Present* (New York: Schocken, 1988), 23; Aleksandr Lokshin, "The Bund in the Russian-Jewish Historical Landscape," *Russia under the Last Tsar: Opposition and Subversion, 1894–1917*, ed., Anna Geifman (Oxford: Blackwell, 1999), 52–63.

35 Lih, *Lenin Rediscovered*, 160–61.

36 Keep, *The Rise of Social Democracy*, 77.

37 V. I. Lenin, *What Is to Be Done?* (The Marxist Internet Archive), 17, 69.

38 Lih, *Lenin Rediscovered*, 557–58.

39 Adam Bruno Ulam, *The Bolsheviks: An Intellectual and Political History of the Triumph of Communism in Russia* (Cambridge: Harvard University Press, 1998), 178.

40 Smith, *Russia in Revolution*, 43.

41 Figes, *A People's Tragedy*, 146.

42 Keep, *The Rise of Social Democracy*, 110–36; Ulam, *The Bolsheviks*, 192–93.

43 André Liebich, "The Mensheviks," *Russia under the Last Tsar*, 27–28; Abraham Ascher, *Pavel Axelrod and the Development of Menshevism* (Cambridge: Harvard University Press, 1972), 213–14.

44 Robert Mayer, "Lenin and the Jacobin Identity in Russia," *Studies in Eastern European Thought*, 51:2 (June 1999): 141–46.

45 Keep, *The Rise of Social Democracy*, 144.

46 Abraham Ascher, *The Revolution of 1905* (Stanford: Stanford University Press, 1994), 1:29.

47 Melissa Stockdale, "Liberalism and Democracy: The Constitutional Democratic Party," *Russia under the Last Tsar*, 155–57.

48 Shmuel Galai, *The Liberation Movement in Russia, 1900–1905* (Cambridge: Cambridge University Press, 1973), 207–08.

49 Ascher, *The Revolution of 1905*, 1:66.

50 Figes, *A People's Tragedy*, 172–73.

51 Walter Sablinsky, *The Road to Bloody Sunday: The Role of Father Gapon and the Petersburg Massacre of 1905* (Princeton: Princeton University Press, 1976).

52 Keep, *The Rise of Social Democracy*, 155–56; Figes, *A People's Tragedy*, 179; Ascher, *The Revolution of 1905*, 1:101.

53 Smith, *Russia in Revolution*, 49–51; Scott Ury, *Barricades and Banners: The Revolution of 1905 and the Transformation of Warsaw Jewry* (Stanford: Stanford University Press, 2012), 91–138; Jacob M. Landau, *The Politics of Pan-Islamism: Ideology and Organization* (Oxford: Clarendon Press, 1994), 152–54.

54 Scott J. Seregny, "A Different Type of Peasant Movement: The Peasant Unions in the Russian Revolution of 1905," *Slavic Review*, 47:1 (Spring 1988): 61–67.

55 John Bushnell, *Mutiny Amid Repression: Russian Soldiers in the Revolution of 1905–1906* (Bloomington: Indiana University Press, 1985).

56 Ascher, *The Revolution of 1905*, 1:211–42; Keep, *The Rise of Social Democracy*, 233–35; Beryl Williams, "1905: The View from the Provinces," *The Russian Revolution of 1905: Centenary Perspectives*, ed., Jonathan D. Smele (Abingdon: Routledge, 2005), 35–54.

57 Smith, *Russia in Revolution*, 52.

58 Rogger, *Russia in the Age of Modernization*, 215.

59 Healy, *The Russian Autocracy in Crisis*, 15.

60 Don C. Rawson, *Russian Rightists and the Revolution of 1905* (Cambridge: Cambridge University Press, 1995), 24, 56–65, 127–31.

61 Rogger, *Russia in the Age of Modernization*, 218.

62 Keep, *The Rise of Social Democracy*, 250.

63 Laura Engelstein, *Moscow 1905: Working-Class Organization and Political Conflict* (Stanford: Stanford University Press, 1982).

64 Smith, *Russia in Revolution*, 59–62.

65 Ascher, *The Revolution of 1905*, 1:107–10.

66 Rogger, *Russia in the Age of Modernization*, 218–19.

67 Murat Yaşar, "Learning the Ropes: The Young Turk Perception of the 1905 Russian Revolution," *Middle Eastern Studies*, 50:1 (2014): 124.

68 Karen Barkey, *Empire of Difference: The Ottomans in Comparative Perspective* (Cambridge: Cambridge University Press, 2008); Adanir, "Religious Communities and Ethnic Groups under Imperial Sway: Ottoman and Habsburg Lands in Comparison," in Hoerder, *The Historical Practice of Diversity*, 59–73.

Notes

69 Roderic H. Davidson, *Reform in the Ottoman Empire, 1856–1876* (Princeton: Princeton University Press, 1963), 222.

70 Bernard Lewis, *What Went Wrong? Western Impact and Middle Eastern Response* (Oxford: Oxford University Press, 2002), 58.

71 Şerif Mardin, *The Genesis of Young Ottoman Thought* (Princeton: Princeton University Press, 1962); Ariel Salzmann, "Citizens in Search of a State: The Limits of Political Participation in the Late Ottoman Empire," *Extending Citizenship, Reconfiguring States*, eds., Michael Hanagan and Charles Tilly (Lanham: Rowan and Littlefield, 1999), 38–45; Feroz Ahmad, *The Making of Modern Turkey* (New York: Routledge, 1993), 24–26.

72 Michael A. Reynolds, *Shattering Empires: The Clash and Collapse of the Ottoman and Russian Empires, 1908–1918* (Cambridge: Cambridge University Press, 2011), 14–18; Fatma Müge Göçek, "The Decline of the Ottoman Empire and the Emergence of Greek, Armenian, Turkish and Arab Nationalisms," *Social Constructions of Nationalisms in the Middle East*, ed., Fatma Müge Göçek (Albany: State University of New York Press, 2002), 15–83.

73 Kemal H. Karpat, *The Politicization of Islam: Reconstructing Identity, State, Faith and Community in the Late Ottoman State* (Oxford: Oxford University Press, 2001); Selim Deringil, *The Well-Protected Domains: Ideology and the Legitimation of Power in the Ottoman Empire, 1876–1909* (London: I.B. Tauris, 2011).

74 Mardin, *The Genesis of Young Ottoman Thought*, 18–19; Nader Sohrabi, "Global Waves, Local Actors: What the Young Turks Knew about Other Revolutions and Why It Mattered," *Comparative Studies in Society and History*, 44:1 (January 2002): 60.

75 Mardin, *The Genesis of Young Ottoman Thought*, 328.

76 Karpat, *The Politicization of Islam*, 303–06; Howard Eissenstat, "Modernization, Imperial Nationalism and the Ethnicization of Confessional Identity in the Late Ottoman Empire," *Nationalizing Empires*, 448–49.

77 Sohrabi, "Global Waves," 64.

78 M. Şükrü Hanioğlu, *Preparation for a Revolution: The Young Turks, 1902–1908* (New York: Oxford University Press, 2001).

79 Sohrabi, "Global Waves," 45–79; Yaşar, "Learning the Ropes," 114–28.

80 Mark Mazower, *Salonica, City of Ghosts: Christians, Muslims and Jews, 1430–1950* (London: Harper Perennial, 2004), 263–68.

81 Nadine Akhund, "Stabilizing a Crisis and the Mürzsteg Agreement of 1903: International Efforts to Bring Peace to Macedonia," *The Hungarian Historical Review*, 3:3 (2014): 587–608.

82 Aykut Kansu, *The Revolution of 1908 in Turkey* (Leiden: Brill, 1997), 73–112.

83 Mazower, *Salonica*, 275.

84 "Courrier de Constantinople," *Correspondance d'Orient*, October 1, 1908.

85 Cemil Aydin, *The Politics of Anti-Westernism in Asia: Visions of World Order in Pan-Islamic and Pan-Asian Thought* (New York: Columbia University Press, 2009), 95–99.

86 "France et Turquie," *Correspondance d'Orient*, November 1, 1908.

87 Landau, *The Politics of Pan-Islamism*, 90.

88 Fatma Müge Göçek, *Rise of the Bourgeoisie, Demise of the Empire: Ottoman Westernization and Social Change* (Oxford: Oxford University Press, 1996), 109–10.

89 Mazower, *Salonica*, 287–89.

90 Keith David Watenpaugh, *Being Modern in the Middle East: Revolution, Nationalism, Colonialism and the Arab Middle Class* (Princeton: Princeton University Press, 2006), 67–101.

91 Sohrabi, "Historicizing Revolutions," 1402.

92 Michelle Campos, *Ottoman Brothers: Muslims, Christians and Jews in Early Twentieth-Century Palestine* (Stanford: Stanford University Press, 2011), 94.

93 Fatma Müge Göçek, *The Transformation of Turkey: Redefining State and Society from the Ottoman Empire to the Modern Empire* (London: I.B. Tauris, 2011), 79–80.

94 Sohrabi, "Historicizing Revolutions," 1402.

95 Eric J. Zürcher, *Turkey: A Modern History* (London: I.B. Tauris, 1993), 102–03; Sean McMeekin, *The Berlin-Baghdad Express: The Ottoman Empire and Germany's Bid for World Power* (Cambridge: Harvard University Press, 2010), 74–75.

96 Aydin, *The Politics of Anti-Westernism*, 95–99; Karpat, *The Politicization of Islam*, 369–70.

97 C. Ernest Dawn, *From Ottomanism to Arabism: Essay on the Origins of Arab Nationalism* (Urbana: University of Illinois Press, 1973).

98 Ümit Kurt and Doğan Gürpinar, "The Balkan Wars and the Rise of the Reactionary Modernist Utopia in Young Turk Thought," *Nations and Nationalism*, 21:2 (2015): 348–68.

99 Ahmad, *The Making of Modern Turkey*, 42–46; Zürcher, *Turkey*, 129; Taner Akçam, "The Young Turks and the Plans for the Ethnic Homogenization of Anatolia," *Shatterzone of Empires: Coexistence and Violence in the German, Habsburg, Russian and Ottoman Borderlands*, eds., Omer Bartov and Eric D. Weitz (Bloomington: Indiana University Press, 2013), 258–82.

100 Halid Sia, "Gedanken zur turkischen Freiheitsfeier," *Die Islamischer Welt*, 9 (August 1917), 523–25.

101 Edin Hajdarpasic, *Whose Bosnia? Nationalism and Political Imagination in the Balkans, 1840–1914* (Ithaca: Cornel University Press, 2015), 127–60.

102 *The German White Book* (Germany: Auswärtiges Amt, 1915), 4.

Chapter 10

1 Roger Chickering and Stig Förster, eds., *Great War, Total War: Combat and Mobilization on the Western Front, 1914–1918* (Cambridge: Cambridge University Press, 2000); Pierre Purseigle, "The First World War and the Transformations of the State," *International Affairs*, 90:2 (2014): 249–64.

2 Michael Foy and Brian Barton, *The Easter Rising* (Stroud: The History Press, 2011), 25–28.

3 McMeekin, *Berlin-Baghdad Express*, 86.

4 Fritz Fischer, *Germany's Aims in the First World War* (New York: W. W. Norton, 1967), 115–20.

5 Peter Gatrell, *A Whole Empire Walking: Refugees in Russia during World War I* (Bloomington: Indiana University Press, 1999).

6 Eric Lohr, *Nationalizing the Russian Empire: The Campaign against Enemy Aliens during World War I* (Cambridge: Harvard University Press, 2003).

7 Edward D. Sokol, *The Revolt of 1916 in Russian Central Asia* (Baltimore: Johns Hopkins University Press, 1954).

8 Joshua A. Sanborn, *Imperial Apocalypse: The Great War and the Destruction of the Russian Empire* (Oxford: Oxford University Press, 2014), 37–64.

Notes

9   Peter Gatrell, *Russia's First World War: A Social and Economic History* (New York: Routledge, 2014), 42–43; Lewis Sigelbaum, *The Politics of Industrial Mobilization in Russia, 1914–1917: A Study of the War Industries Committees* (Basingstoke: Macmillan, 1983), 165.

10 Christopher Read, *From Tsar to Soviets: The Russian People and Their Revolution, 1917–1921* (New York: Oxford University Press, 1996), 100–01; Rogger, *Russia in the Age of Modernization*, 258–59.

11 Smith, *Russia in Revolution*, 98; Barbara Alpern Engel, "Not by Bread Alone: Subsistence Riots in Russia during World War One," *Journal of Modern History*, 69:4 (December 1997): 696–721.

12 Laura Engelstein, *Russia in Flames: War, Revolution, Civil War, 1914–1921* (Oxford: Oxford University Press, 2018), 96.

13 Figes, *A People's Tragedy*, 308–15; Rogger, *Russia in the Age of Modernization*, 266–67.

14 William G. Rosenberg, *Liberals in the Russian Revolution: The Constitutional Democratic Party, 1917–1921* (Princeton: Princeton University Press, 1974).

15 Figes, *A People's Tragedy*, 361.

16 Read, *From Tsar to Soviets*, 44.

17 "The Liberals on The Democracy's Responsibility," *Competing Voices from the Russian Revolution*, ed., Michael C. Hickey (Oxford: Greenwood, 2011), 93.

18 Tsuyoshi Hasegawa, *The February Revolution, Petrograd, 1917: The End of the Tsarist Regime and the Birth of Dual Power* (Leiden: Bill, 2017); Rex A. Wade, *The Russian Revolution, 1917* (Cambridge: Cambridge University Press, 2005), 53–86.

19 Stone, *The Anatomy of Revolution Revisited*, 236.

20 William G. Rosenberg, "Social Mediation and State Construction(s) in Revolutionary Russia," *Social History*, 19:2 (1994): 169–88.

21 Allan K. Wildman, *The End of the Russian Imperial Army: The Old Army and the Soldiers' Revolt* (Princeton: Princeton University Press, 1980), 187, 292–93.

22 Sanborn, *Imperial Apocalypse*, 193–95; Figes, *A People's Tragedy*, 359–60.

23 Smith, *Russia in Revolution*, 107–09.

24 Read, *From Tsar to Soviets*, 79–91.

25 Sarah Badcock, "Women, Protests and Revolution: Soldiers' Wives in Russia during 1917," *International Review of Social History*, 49:1 (2004): 47–70.

26 Laurie S. Stoff, *They Fought for the Motherland: Russia's Women Soldiers in World War I and the Revolution* (Lawrence: University Press of Kansas, 2006).

27 Smith, *Russia in Revolution*, 139–41.

28 Graeme J. Gill, *Peasants and Government in the Russian Revolution* (Basingstoke: Macmillan, 1979), 46–88; Aaron B. Retish, *Russia's Peasants in Revolution and Civil War: Citizenship, Identity and the Creation of the Soviet State, 1914–1922* (Cambridge: Cambridge University Press, 2008), 64–129.

29 Ronald G. Suny, "Nationalism and Class in the Russian Revolution: A Comparative Discussion," *Revolution in Russia: Reassessments of 1917*, eds., Edith Rogovin Frankel, Jonathan Frankel and Baruch Knei-Paz (Cambridge: Cambridge University Press, 1992), 219–46.

30 Shelly Baranowski, *Nazi Empire: German Colonialism and Imperialism from Bismarck to Hitler* (Cambridge: Cambridge University Press, 2011), 88–90.

Notes

31 Sanborn, *Imperial Apocalypse*, 215.
32 Figes, *A People's Tragedy*, 338.
33 V. I. Lenin, "Socialism and War," *Collected Works* (Moscow: Progress Publishers, 1974), 21:301–03.
34 Catherine Merridale, *Lenin on the Train* (London: Allen Lane, 2016).
35 Lenin, "Theses," *Collected Works*, 24:23–26.
36 Lenin, "Resolution on the Soviets of Workers' and Soldiers' Deputies," Seventh All-Russian Conference of the R.S.D.L.P, *Collected Works*, 24:295.
37 Figes, *A People's Tragedy*, 386.
38 Smith, *Russia in Revolution*, 113; Robert Service, *The Bolshevik Party in Revolution: A Study in Organizational Change* (Basingstoke: Macmillan, 1979).
39 Harison, "The Paris Commune of 1871," 7–8.
40 Lenin, "The State and Revolution," *Collected Works*, 25:420. More generally, see: David W. Lovell, *From Marx to Lenin: An Evaluation of Marx's Responsibility for Soviet Authoritarianism* (Cambridge: Cambridge University Press, 1984), 172–74.
41 Lenin, "The State and Revolution," *Collected Works*, 25:467.
42 Shelia Fitzpatrick, *The Russian Revolution* (Oxford: Oxford University Press, 2001), 65–66; Read, *From Tsar to Soviets*, 145–46.
43 Smith, *Russia in Revolution*, 137–38.
44 Paul Le Blanc, *Lenin and the Revolutionary Party* (Chicago: Haymarket Books, 1993).
45 Wade, *The Russian Revolution*, 194–95; Brian D. Taylor, *Politics and the Russian Army: Civil-Military Relations, 1689–2000* (Cambridge: Cambridge University Press, 2003), 107–17.
46 Alexander Rabinowitch, *The Bolsheviks Come to Power: The Revolution of 1917 in Petrograd* (Chicago: Haymarket Books, 2004), 83–190; Figes, *A People's Tragedy*, 457–60; Sanborn, *Imperial Apocalypse*, 226–27.
47 Lenin, "The Bolsheviks Must Assume Power," *Collected Works*, 26:21.
48 Wade, *The Russian Revolution*, 239–40; Smith, *Russia in Revolution*, 150–51.
49 Thomas H. Rigby, *Lenin's Government: Sovnarkom, 1917–1922* (Cambridge: Cambridge University Press, 1979), 1–52.
50 Figes, *A People's Tragedy*, 506.
51 Jane Burbank, *Intelligentsia and Revolution: Russian Views of Bolshevism, 1917–1922* (Oxford: Oxford University Press, 1986), 35.
52 Mark D. Steinberg, *Voices of Revolution, 1917* (New Haven: Yale University Press, 2001), 260–62.
53 Smith, *Russia in Revolution*, 155; Oliver Henry Radkey, *Russia Goes to the Polls: The Election of the All-Russian Constituent Assembly, 1917* (Ithaca: Cornell University Press, 1989).
54 Lenin, "Draft Decree on the Dissolution of the Constituent Assembly," *Collected Works*, 26:354–36.
55 Scott Baldwin Smith, *Captives of Revolution: The Socialist Revolutionaries and the Bolshevik Dictatorship, 1918–1923* (Pittsburgh: Pittsburgh University Press, 2011), 1–88; Vladimir N. Brovkin, *The Mensheviks after October: Socialist Opposition and the Rise of the Bolshevik Dictatorship* (Ithaca: Cornell University Press, 1987), 15–75.
56 George Leggett, *The Cheka: Lenin's Political Police* (Oxford: Clarendon, 1981), 17.

Notes

57 S. Karpenko, "The White Dictatorships' Bureaucracy in the South of Russia: Social Structure, Living Conditions and Performance (1918–1920)," *Soviet and Post-Soviet Review*, 37:1 (2010): 84–96; Peter Kenez, *Civil War in South Russia, 1918: The First Year of the Volunteer Army* (Berkeley: University of California Press, 1971).

58 Ian C. D. Moffat, *The Allied Intervention in Russia: The Diplomacy of Chaos* (Houndmills: Palgrave Macmillan, 2015).

59 Earl F. Ziemke, *The Red Army, 1918–1941: From Vanguard of World Revolution to US Ally* (London: Frank Cass, 2004), 35–36.

60 Mark von Hagen, *Soldiers in the Proletarian Dictatorship: The Red Army and the Soviet Socialist State, 1917–1930* (Ithaca: Cornell University Press, 1990); Francesco Benvenuti, *The Bolsheviks and the Red Army, 1918–1922* (Cambridge: Cambridge University Press, 1988).

61 John D. Klier and Helen Mingay, *The Search for Anastasia* (London: Smith Gryphon, 1995), 46.

62 Figes, *A People's Tragedy*; Richard Pipes, *The Russian Revolution* (New York: Vintage, 1991).

63 Fitzpatrick, *The Russian Revolution*, 71–72.

64 Evan Mawdsley, "Revolution, Civil War and the 'Long' First World War in Russia," *Journal of Military and Strategic Studies*, 16:2 (2015): 208–26.

65 Silvana Malle, *The Economic Organization of War Communism, 1918–1921* (Cambridge: Cambridge University Press, 1985); Thomas F. Remington, *Building Socialism in Bolshevik Russia: Ideology and Industrial Organization, 1917–1921* (Pittsburgh: University of Pittsburgh Press, 1984).

66 Smith, *Captives of Revolution*, 68–70.

67 Smith, *Russia in Revolution*, 226.

68 Peter Holquist, "Violent Russia, Deadly Marxism? Russia in the Epoch of Violence, 1905–21," *Kritika: Explorations in Russian and Eurasian History*, 4:3 (Summer 2003): 627–52.

69 James Ryan, "Revolution Is War: The Development of the Thought of V.I. Lenin on Violence, 1899–1907," *The Slavonic and East European Review*, 89:2 (April 2011): 250–51.

70 Hagen, *Soldiers in the Proletarian Dictatorship*, 6–7, 332–34.

71 Touraine, "The Idea of Revolution," 125–26.

72 Igal Halfin, *From Darkness to Light: Class, Consciousness, and Salvation in Revolutionary Russia* (Pittsburgh: University of Pittsburgh Press, 2000).

73 Read, *From Tsar to Soviets*, 211–12.

74 Lenin, "How to Organize Competition?" *Collected Works*, 26:411.

75 Gregory Claeys, *Dystopia: A Natural History* (Oxford: Oxford University Press, 2017), 133.

76 Figes, *A People's Tragedy*, 525; Laggett, *The Cheka*, 467.

77 Claeys, *Dystopia*, 133.

78 Leon Trotsky, *Marxism and Terrorism* (Atlanta: Pathfinder Press, 1995), 12.

79 Sheila Fitzpatrick, "Lives and Times," In *The Shadow of Revolution: Life Stories of Russian Women from 1917 to the Second World War*, eds., Sheila Fitzpatrick and Yuri Slezkine (Princeton: Princeton University Press, 2000), 12; Figes, *A People's Tragedy*, 529.

80 Matthew Rendle, "Revolutionary Tribunals and the Origins of Terror in Early Soviet Society," *Historical Research*, 84:226 (2011): 693–721.

81. Jeremy Smith, *The Bolsheviks and the National Question, 1917–1923* (Basingstoke: Macmillan, 1999), 7–28.
82. Richard Pipes, *Russia under the Bolshevik Regime, 1919–1924* (London: Fontana, 1995), 150.
83. Smith, *Russia in Revolution*, 184.
84. Borislav Chernev, *Twilight of Empire: The Brest-Litovsk Conference and the Remaking of East-Central Europe, 1917–1918* (Toronto: University of Toronto Press, 2017); Mark von Hagen, *War in a European Borderland: Occupations and Occupation Plans in Galicia and Ukraine, 1914–1918* (Seattle: University of Washington Press, 2007).
85. Figes, *A People's Tragedy*, 547.
86. Smith, *Russia in Revolution*, 201.
87. Pipes, *Russia under the Bolshevik Regime*, 156–57; Jeff Sahadeo, *Russian Colonial Society in Tashkent, 1865–1923* (Bloomington: Indiana University Press, 2007), 187–228; Peter Hopkirk, *Setting the East Ablaze: Lenin's Dream of an Empire in Asia* (London: Hodder and Stoughton, 2012).
88. Francine Hirsch, *Empire of Nations: Ethnographic Knowledge and the Making of the Soviet Union* (Ithaca: Cornell University Press, 2005).
89. Yuri Sleskine, "The USSR as a Communal Apartment, or How a Socialist State Promoted Ethnic Particularism," *Slavic Review*, 53:2 (Summer 1994): 414–52; Terry Martin, *The Affirmative Action Empire: Nations and Nationalism in the Soviet Union, 1923–1939* (Ithaca: Cornell University Press, 2001).
90. Jonathan W. Daly, "Storming the Last Citadel: The Bolshevik Assault on the Church, 1922," *The Bolsheviks in Russian Society: The Revolution and the Civil Wars*, ed., Vladimir N. Brovkin (New Haven: Yale University Press, 1997), 235–68.
91. Geoffrey Hosking, *Ruler and Victims: The Russians and the Soviet Union* (Cambridge: Harvard University Press, 2006), 26–35.
92. Lenin, "Report on Foreign Policy," May 14, 1918, *Collected Works*, 27:373.
93. Pipes, *Russia under the Bolshevik Regime*, 173.
94. Mark Jones, *Founding Weimar: Violence and the German Revolution of 1918–1919* (Cambridge: Cambridge University Press, 2016); Gabriel Kuhn, *All Power to the Councils! A Documentary History of the German Revolution of 1918–1919* (Oakland: PM Press, 2012), 27–28.
95. Ralf Hoffrogge, *Working-Class Politics in the German Revolution: Richard Müller, the Revolutionary Shop Stewards and the Origins of the Council Movement* (Leiden: Brill, 2015), 61–65.
96. Paul Frölich, *Rosa Luxemburg: Ideas in Action* (Chicago: Haymarket, 2010), 277–78.
97. Jones, *Founding Weimar*, 173–250.
98. Reinhard Rürup, "Problems of the German Revolution, 1918–19," *Journal of Contemporary History*, 3:4 (October 1968): 109–35.
99. Jon Jacobson, *When the Soviets Entered World Politics* (Berkeley: University of California Press, 1994), 46–47.
100. Pipes, *Russia under the Soviet Regime*, 169–71.
101. "Statutes of the Communist International Adopted at the Second Comintern Congress," August 4, 1920, *The Communist International, 1919–1943: Documents*, ed., Jane Degras (Oxford: Oxford University Press, 1956), 1:163.

Notes

102 Smith, *Russia in Revolution*, 306.
103 Pipes, *Russia under the Soviet Regime*, 176,
104 A. James McAdams, *Vanguard of the Revolution: The Global Idea of the Communist Party* (Princeton: Princeton University Press, 2017).
105 Kropotkin, "The Russian Revolution and the Soviet Government," *Kropotkin's Revolutionary Pamphlets*, 254.
106 Burbank, *Intelligentsia and Revolution*, 99–105.

Epilogue

1 Lenin, "The Agrarian Programme of Social-Democracy in the First Russian Revolution," *Collected Works*, 13:324–28.
2 Bakunin, "Federalism, Socialism, Anti-Theologism," *Bakunin on Anarchy*, 117.
3 Grave, *La société au lendemain de la Revolution*, 18.
4 Herzen, "Letter XI," June 1, 1849, *Lettres de France et d'Italie*, 253–54.
5 Alexis de Tocqueville to N. W. Senior, Esquire, July 27, 1851, *Memoir, Letters and Remains of Alexis de Tocqueville* (London: Macmillan, 1861), 2:169.
6 James E. Sanders, "Atlantic Republicanism in Nineteenth-Century Columbia: Spanish America's Challenge to the Contours of Atlantic History," *Journal of World History*, 20:1 (March 2009): 131–50; Caitlin Fitz, *Our Sister Republics: The United States in an Age of American Revolution* (New York: W. W. Norton, 2016).
7 James E. Sanders, "The Vanguard of the Atlantic World: Contesting Modernity in Nineteenth-Century Latin America," *Latin American Research Review*, 46:2 (2011): 105, 112.
8 Peter Hardy, *The Muslims of British India* (Cambridge: Cambridge University Press, 1972), 62–77; Clare Anderson, *The Indian Uprising of 1857-58: Prisons, Prisoners and Rebellions* (London: Ashgate, 2007).
9 Osterhammel, *The Transformation of the World*, 551.
10 R. S. O'Fahey and Bernd Radyke, "Neo-Sufism Reconsidered," *Der Islam: Journal of the History and Culture of the Middle East*, 70:1 (January 1993): 52–87; Reinhard Schulze, "Die Politisierung des Islam im 19 Jahrhundert," *Die Welt des Islams*, 22 (1982): 106–08.
11 James McDougall, *A History of Algeria* (Cambridge: Cambridge University Press, 2017), 64–73; Amira K. Bennison, *Jihad and Its Interpretations in Pre-Colonial Morocco: State-Society Relations during the French Conquest of Algeria* (London: Routledge, 2002), 12–18.
12 Karpat, *The Politicization of Islam*, 35–40; Alexander Knysh, "Sufism as an Explanatory Paradigm: The Issue of the Motivations of Sufi Resistance Movements in Western and Russian Scholarship," *Die Welt des Islams*, 42:2 (2002): 139–73; Moshe Gammer, *Muslim Resistance to the Tsar: Shamil and the Conquest of Chechnia and Daghestan* (London: Frank Cass, 1994).
13 Kim Searcy, *The Formation of the Sudanese Mahdist State: Ceremony and Symbols of Authority, 1882–1898* (Leiden: Brill, 2011).
14 Benjamin D. Hopkins, "Islam and Resistance in the British Empire," *Islam and the European Empires*, ed., David Motadel (Oxford: Oxford University Press, 2014), 163–64.

15 Aydin, *The Politics of Anti-Westernism*, 51–67; 162–70; James L Gelvin and Nile Green, "Introduction," *Global Muslims in the Age of Steam and Print* (Berkeley: University of California Press, 2014), 11–14.

16 Umar Ryad, "Anti-Imperialism and the Pan-Islamic Movement," *Islam and Empire*, 132–38; Landau, *The Politics of Pan-Islamism*, 15–21; Christopher de Bellaigue, *The Islamic Enlightenment: The Modern Struggle between Faith and Reason* (London: Vintage, 2017), 217–30.

17 Edmund Burke III, "Pan-Islamism and Moroccan Resistance to French Colonial Penetration," *The Journal of African History*, 13:1 (1972): 103–09; Olide Moreau, "Aref Taher Bey: An Ottoman Military Instructor Bridging the Maghreb and the Ottoman Mediterranean," *Subversives and Mavericks in the Muslim Mediterranean: A Subaltern History*, eds., Olide Moreau and Stuart Schaar (Austin: University of Texas Press, 2016), 60–61.

18 Menemenli-Zade Edherm Bey, "Das Osmanische Reich und die islamische Kultur," *Die Islamische Welt*, 5 (April 1917), 264.

19 Khuri-Makdisi, *The Eastern Mediterranean and the Making of Global Radicalism*, 19–25; Aydin, *The Politics of Anti-Westernism in Asia*, 3–13.

20 Renée Worringer, *Ottomans Imagining Japan: East, Middle East and Non-Western Modernity at the Turn of the Twentieth Century* (New York: Palgrave Macmillan, 2014), 109–82.

21 Thomas H. Huber, *The Revolutionary Origins of Modern Japan* (Stanford: Stanford University Press, 1981); Albert M. Craig, *Chōshū in the Meiji Restoration* (Lanham: Lexington Books, 2000).

22 Mark Ravina, *To Stand with the Nations of the World: Japan's Meiji Restoration in World History* (Oxford: Oxford University Press, 2017).

23 S. M. R. Ali, "The East and the West," *The Islamic Review*, 4:1 (May 1913): 154.

24 Sho Konishi, "Reopening the 'Opening of Japan': A Russian-Japanese Revolutionary Encounter and the Vision of Anarchist Progress," *American Historical Review*, 112:1 (February 2007): 108.

25 Roger W. Bowen, *Rebellion and Democracy in Meiji Japan: A Study of Commoners in the Popular Rights Movement* (Berkeley: University of California Press, 1980); Irokawa Daikichi, *The Culture of the Meiji Period*, trans., Marius B. Jansen (Princeton: Princeton University Press, 1985), 19–68.

26 Makiso Hane, *Peasants, Rebels, Women and Outcastes: The Underside of Modern Japan* (New York: Rowan and Littlefield, 2003), 248.

27 Robert Thomas Tierney, *Monster of the Twentieth Century: Kōtoku Shūsui and Japan's First Anti-Imperialist Movement* (Berkeley: University of California Press, 2015); Sho Konishi, *Anarchist Modernity: Cooperatism and Japanese-Russian Intellectual Relations in Modern Japan* (Cambridge: Harvard University Press, 2013); Nadine Willems, "Transnational Anarchism, Japanese Revolutionary Connections and the Personal Politics of Exile," *The Historical Journal*, 61:3 (2018): 719–41.

28 Martin Bernal, "The Triumph of Anarchism over Marxism, 1906–1907," *China in Revolution: The First Phase, 1900–1913*, ed., Mary Clabaugh Wright (New Haven: Yale University Press, 1968), 125.

29 Lenin, "Inflammable Material in World Politics," *Collected Works*, 15:185.

30 Mary Clabaugh Wright, "The Rising Tide of Change," *China in Revolution*, 30.

Notes

31 Pamela Kyle Crossley, Helen S. Siu and Donald S. Sutton, eds., *Empire at the Margins: Culture, Ethnicity and Frontier in Early Modern China* (Berkeley: University of California Press, 2006); Edward J. M. Rhoads, *Manchu and Han: Ethnic Relations and Political Power in Late Qing and Early Republican China, 1861–1928* (Seattle: University of Washington Press, 2000), 34–68.

32 William T. Rowe, *China's Last Empire: The Great Qing* (Cambridge: Harvard University Press, 2009), 178–200; Tobie Meyer-Fong, "Where the War Ended: Violence, Community and Commemoration in China's Nineteenth-Century Civil War," *American Historical Review*, 120:5 (December 2015): 1724–38.

33 Robert Bickers, *The Scramble for China: Foreign Devils in the Qing Empire, 1832–1914* (London: Penguin, 2016).

34 Odd Arne Westad, *Restless Empire: China and the World since 1750* (London: Vintage, 2013), 127–30; Diana Preston, *The Boxer Rebellion* (New York: Berkeley Books, 2000).

35 Rowe, *China's Last Empire*, 238–39; Frederic Wakeman, *The Fall of Imperial China* (New York: The Free Press, 1975), 199–206.

36 Mizoguchi Yūzō, "The Chaotic Late Qing and Early Republican Periods," *Inter-Asia Cultural Studies*, 17:4 (2016): 587.

37 Ibid., 577.

38 Rhoads, *Manchu and Han*, 65.

39 Liang Qichao, "Renewing the People," *Sources of Chinese Tradition*, eds., William Theodore de Barry and Richard Lufrano (New York: Columbia University Press, 2000), 2:292–93.

40 Paula Herrell, *Sowing the Seeds of Change: Chinese Students, Japanese Teachers, 1895–1905* (Stanford: Stanford University Press, 1992); Douglas R. Reynolds, *China, 1898–1912: The Xinheng Revolution and Japan* (Cambridge: Harvard University Press, 1993).

41 Marie-Claire Bergère, *Sun Yat-sen*, trans., Janey Lloyd (Stanford: Stanford University Press, 1998), 60; Rowe, *China's Last Empire*, 265–66.

42 Chun-Tu Hsueh, *Huang Hsing and the Chinese Revolution* (Stanford: Stanford University Press, 1961), 91; Herrell, *Sowing the Seeds of Change*, 146–63.

43 Stephen R. Platt, *Provincial Patriots: The Hunanese and Modern China* (Cambridge: Harvard University Press, 2007), 117–21.

44 Bernal, "The Triumph of Anarchism," *China in Revolution*, 120.

45 Herrell, *Sowing the Seeds of Change*, 151.

46 Rowe, *China's Last Empire*, 269.

47 Rhoads, *Manchu and Han*, 13.

48 Zhang Kaiyuan, "The Slogan 'Expel the Manchus' and the Nationalist Movement in Modern Chinese History," *The 1911 Revolution in China*, eds., Etō Shinkichi and Harold Z. Schiffrin (Tokyo: University of Tokyo Press, 1984), 33–34.

49 Bergère, *Sun Yat-sen*, 49–51; Rowe, *China's Last Empire*, 272.

50 Harold Z. Schiffrin, *Sun Yat-sen: Reluctant Revolutionary* (Boston: Little Brown, 1980), 362.

51 Sun Yat-sen, "The Three People's Principles," *Sources of Chinese Tradition*, 2:321.

52 Bergère, *Sun Yat-sen*, 157–58.

53 Yūzō, "The Chaotic Late Qing," 594.

54 Rowe, *China's Last Empire*, 257–79; John Fincher, "Political Provincialism and the National Revolution," *China in Revolution*, 185–226.
55 Yūzō, "The Chaotic Late Qing," 580–83.
56 Wright, "The Rising Tide of Change," *China in Revolution*, 8–32.
57 Rhoads, *Manchu and Han*, 114.
58 Vidya Prakash Dutt, "The First Week of Revolution: The Wuchang Uprising," *China in Revolution*, 385–415; Wakeman, *The Fall of Imperial China*, 248–49.
59 Yūzō, "The Chaotic Late Qing," 574–75.
60 Westad, *Restless Empire*, 146–50.
61 Bergère, *Sun Yat-sen*, 216–20; Chen Xiqi, "Sun Yat-sen and the Founding of the Provisional Nanjing Government," *The 1911 Revolution in China*, 209–23.
62 Bergère, *Sun Yat-sen*, 224–27; Rey-Ching Lu, *Chinese Democracy and Elite Thinking* (New York: Palgrave Macmillan, 2011), 38–42.
63 David Strand, *An Unfinished Republic: Leading by Word and Deed in Modern China* (Berkeley: University of California Press, 2011).
64 Westad, *Restless Empire*, 154.
65 Adam Ferguson, *An Essay on the History of Civil Society* (London: T. Cadell, 1793), 186–87.
66 Erez Manela, *The Wilsonian Moment: Self-Determination and the International Origins of Anticolonial Nationalism* (Oxford: Oxford University Press, 2007); Kevin B. Anderson, *Marx and the Margins: On Nationalism, Ethnicity, and Non-Western Societies* (Chicago: University of Chicago Press, 2010).
67 Adom Getachew, "Universalism after the Post-Colonial Turn: Interpreting the Haitian Revolution," *Political Theory*, 44:6 (2016): 821–45.
68 Minkah Makalani, *In the Cause of Freedom: Radical Black Internationalism from Harlem to London, 1917–1939* (Chapel Hill: University of North Carolina Press, 2011); Jeffery James Bryne, *Mecca of Revolution: Algeria, Decolonization and the Third World Order* (Oxford: Oxford University Press, 2016).
69 Giuseppe Mazzini, "Autobiographical Notes," *Life and Writing of Joseph Mazzini* (London: Smith, Elder and Co., 1890), 1:209.
70 Mazzini, "Essay on the Causes Which Have Hitherto Impeded the Development of Liberty in Italy," *Life and Writings*, 1:131.

SELECTED BIBLIOGRAPHY

Revolution (General)

Perry Anderson. "Modernity and Revolution." *New Left Review*, 1:144 (March–April 1984): 96–113.
Keith Michael Baker and Dan Edelstein, eds. *Scripting Revolution: A Historical Approach to the Comparative Study of Revolutions*. Stanford: Stanford University Press, 2015.
Colin J. Beck. "The World-Cultural Origins of Revolutionary Waves: Five Centuries of European Contention." *Social Science History*, 35:2 (Summer 2011): 167–207.
Randall Collins. "Maturation of the State-Centered Theory of Revolution and Ideology." *Sociological Theory*, 11:1 (March 1993): 117–28.
William J. Davidshofer. *Marxism and the Leninist Revolutionary Model*. New York: Palgrave Macmillan, 2014.
John Foran, ed. *Theorizing Revolutions*. London: Routledge, 1997.
John R. Gillis. "Political Decay and the European Revolutions, 1789–1848." *World Politics*, 22:3 (April 1970): 344–70.
Adrian Jones. "Towards a New Structural Theory of Revolution: Universalism and Community in the French and Russian Revolutions." *The English Historical Review*, 107:425 (October 1992): 862–900.
George Lawson. "Within and beyond the 'Fourth Generation' of Revolutionary Theory." *Sociological Theory*, 34:2 (2016): 106–27.
Alexander Motyl. *Revolutions, Nations, Empires*. New York: Columbia University Press, 1999.
Adam Schaff. "Marxist Theory of Revolution and Violence." *Journal of the History of Ideas*, 34:2 (April–June 1973): 263–70.
Theda Skocpol. *States and Social Revolutions*. Cambridge: Cambridge University Press, 1979.
Bailey Stone. *The Anatomy of Revolution Revisited: A Comparative Analysis of England, France and Russia*. Cambridge: Cambridge University Press, 2014.
Trygve R. Tholfsen. *Ideology and Revolution in Modern Europe: An Essay on the Role of Ideas in History*. New York: Columbia University Press, 1984.
Bjørn Thomassen. "Notes towards an Anthropology of Political Revolutions." *Comparative Studies in Society and History*, 54:3 (2012): 679–706.
Alain Touraine. "The Idea of Revolution." *Theory, Culture and Society*, 7 (1990): 121–41.

The French Revolution

Micah Alpaugh. *Non-Violence and the French Revolution: Political Demonstrations in Paris, 1787–1795*. Cambridge: Cambridge University Press, 2014.
David Andress. *The French Revolution and the People*. London: Hambledon, 2006.
David Andress. *The Terror: The Merciless Wars for Freedom in Revolutionary France*. New York: Farrar Strauss Giroux, 2006.
Keith Michael Baker. *Inventing the French Revolution. Essays on French Political Culture in the Eighteenth Century*. Cambridge: Cambridge University Press, 1990.

Selected Bibliography

Howard Brown. *Ending the French Revolution: Violence, Justice and Repression from the Terror to Napoleon*. Charlottesville: University of Virginia Press, 2006.
Roger Chartier. *The Cultural Origins of the French Revolution*. Durham: Duke University Press, 2004.
Suzanne Desan. *The Family on Trial in Revolutionary France*. Berkeley: University of California Press, 2004.
Suzanne Desan, Lynn Hunt and William Max Nelson, eds. *The French Revolution in Global Perspective*. Ithaca: Cornell University Press, 2013.
Dan Edelstein, "Do We Want a Revolution without Revolution? Reflections on Political Authority." *French Historical Studies*, 25:2 (Spring 2010): 269-89.
Alan Forrest. *The French Revolution and the Poor*. Oxford: Oxford University Press, 1981.
François Furet. *Interpreting the French Revolution*. Cambridge: Cambridge University Press, 1981.
Dominique Godineau, *The Women of Paris and Their Revolution*. Berkeley: University of California Press, 1988.
Paul R. Hanson. *The Jacobin Republic under Fire: The Federalist Revolt in the French Revolution*. University Park: The Pennsylvania State University Press, 2003.
Jennifer Ngaire Heuer. *The Family and the Nation: Gender and Citizenship in Revolutionary France, 1789-1830*. Ithaca: Cornell University Press, 2005.
Olwen H. Hufton. *Women and the Limits of Citizenship in the French Revolution*. Toronto: University of Toronto Press, 1992.
Lynn Hunt. *Politics, Culture and Class in the French Revolution*. Berkeley: University of California Press, 1984.
Jonathan Israel. *Revolutionary Ideas: An Intellectual History of the French Revolution from the Rights of Man to Robespierre*. Princeton: Princeton University Press, 2015.
Andrew Jainchill. *Reimagining Politics after the Terror: The Republican Origins of French Liberalism*. Ithaca: Cornell University Press, 2008.
Gary Kates, ed. *The French Revolution: Recent Debates and New Controversies*. London: Routledge, 1998.
Emmet Kennedy. *A Cultural History of the French Revolution*. New Haven: Yale University Press, 1989.
Joan B. Landes. *Women and the Public Sphere in the Age of the French Revolution*. Ithaca: Cornell University Press, 1988.
Marisa Linton. *Choosing Terror: Virtue, Friendship and Authenticity in the French Revolution*. Oxford: Oxford University Press, 2013.
Colin Lucas, ed. *Rewriting the French Revolution*. Oxford: Oxford University Press, 1991.
Laura Mason. *Singing the French Revolution: Popular Culture and Politics, 1787-1799*. Ithaca: Cornell University Press, 1996.
Peter McPhee. *The French Revolution, 1789-1799*. Oxford: Oxford University Press, 2002.
Mona Ozouf. *Festivals of the French Revolution*, trans., Alan Sheridan. Cambridge: Harvard University Press, 1988.
Jeremy Popkin. *Revolutionary News: The Press in France, 1789-1799*. Durham: Duke University Press, 1990.
R. B. Rose. *The Making of the Sans-Culottes: Democratic Ideals and Institutions in Paris, 1789-92*. Manchester: Manchester University Press, 1983.
Eli Sagen. *Citizens and Cannibals: The French Revolution, the Struggle for Modernity and the Origins of Ideological Terror*. Lanham: Rowen and Littlefield, 2001.
Simon Schama. *Citizens: A Chronicle of the French Revolution*. New York: Vintage, 1990.
Timothy Tackett. *Becoming Revolutionary: The Deputies of the French National Assembly and the Emergence of a Revolutionary Culture (1789-1970)*. Princeton: Princeton University Press, 1996.

Selected Bibliography

Timothy Tackett. *The Coming of the Terror in the French Revolution*. Cambridge: Harvard University Press, 2017.
Isser Woloch. *The New Regime: Transformations of the French Civic Order, 1789–1820s*. New York: W. W. Norton, 1994.

The Age of Atlantic Revolution

Jeremy Adelman. *Sovereignty and Revolution in the Iberian Atlantic*. Princeton: Princeton University Press, 2006.
David Armitage and Michael J. Braddick, eds. *The British Atlantic World, 1500–1800*. Houndmills: Palgrave Macmillan, 2002.
David Armitage and Sanjay Subrahmanyam, eds. *The Age of Revolution in Global Context, c. 1760–1840*. Houndmills: Palgrave Macmillan, 2010.
Terry Bouton. *Taming Democracy: The People, the Founders and the Troubled End of the American Revolution*. New York: Oxford University Press, 2007.
Douglas Brandburn. *The Citizenship Revolution: Politics and the Creation of the American Union, 1774–1804*. Charlottesville: University of Virginia Press, 2009.
John Charles Chasteen. *Americanos: Latin America's Struggle for Independence*. New York: Oxford University Press, 2008.
Michael P. Costeloe. *Response to Revolution: Imperial Spain and the Spanish American Revolution, 1810–1840*. Cambridge: Cambridge University Press, 1986.
Seth Cotlar. *Tom Paine's America: The Rise and Fall of Transatlantic Radicalism in the Early Republic*. Charlottesville: University of Virginia Press, 2011.
Robert B. Dishman. *Burke and Paine on Revolution and the Rights of Man*. New York: Scribner, 1971.
Laurent Dubois. "The Price of Liberty: Victor Hugues and the Administration of Freedom in Guadeloupe, 1794–1798." *The William and Mary Quarterly*, 56:2 (April 1999): 363–92.
Laurent Dubois. *Avengers of the New World: The Story of the Haitian Revolution*. Cambridge: Harvard University Press, 2004.
Laurent Dubois. *A Colony of Citizens: Revolution and Slave Emancipation in the French Caribbean, 1787–1804*. Chapel Hill: University of North Carolina Press, 2004.
James Alexander Dun. *Dangerous Neighbors: Making the Haitian Revolution in Early America*. Philadelphia: University of Pennsylvania Press, 2016.
Carolyn E. Fick. "The Haitian Revolution and the Limits of Freedom: Defining Citizenship in the Revolutionary Era." *Social History*, 32:4 (November 2007): 394–414.
Sylvia R. Frey. *Water from a Rock: Black Resistance in a Revolutionary Age*. Princeton: Princeton University Press, 1993.
Doris Lorraine Garraway, ed. *Tree of Liberty: Cultural Legacies of the Haitian Revolution in the Atlantic World*. Charlottesville: University of Virginia Press, 2008.
John D. Garrigus, *Before Haiti: Race and Citizenship in French Saint-Domingue*. Houndmills: Palgrave Macmillan, 2006.
David Geggus. "Racial Equality, Slavery and Colonial Secession during the Constituent Assembly." *American Historical Review*, 94:5 (December 1989): 1290–1308.
Malick W. Ghachem. *The Old Regime and the Haitian Revolution*. Cambridge: Cambridge University Press, 2012.
Jacques Godechot. *France and the Atlantic Revolution of the Eighteenth Century*, trans., Herbert Rowen. New York: Free Press, 1965.
Eliga G. Gould. *The Persistence of Empire: British Culture in the Age of the American Revolution*. Chapel Hill: University of North Carolina Press, 2000.

Jack P. Greene. "The American Revolution." *The American Historical Review*, 105:1 (February 2000): 93–102.
Patrick Griffin. *America's Revolution*. Oxford: Oxford University Press, 2013.
Alan Knight. "Democratic and Revolutionary Traditions in Latin America." *The Bulletin of Latin American Research*, 20:2 (April 2001): 147–86.
Michael A. Morrison and Melinda Zook, eds. *Revolutionary Currents: Nation Building in the Transatlantic World*. Lanham: Rowen and Littlefield, 2004.
R. R. Palmer. *The Age of Democratic Revolution: A Political History of Europe and America, 1760–1800, Updated Edition*. Princeton: Princeton University Press, 2014.
Nathan Perl-Rosenthal. "Atlantic Cultures and the Age of Revolution." *The William and Mary Quarterly*, 74:4 (October 2017): 667–96.
Janet Polasky. *Revolutions without Borders: The Call to Liberty in the Atlantic World*. New Haven: Yale University Press, 2016.
Jeremy Popkin. *Facing Racial Revolution: Eyewitness Account of the Haitian Insurrection*. Chicago: University of Chicago Press, 2007.
Philippe R. Rirard. *The Slaves Who Defeated Napoleon: Toussaint Louverture and the Haitian War of Independence, 1801-1804*. Tuscaloosa: The University of Alabama Press, 2011.
Jaime E. Rodríguez O. *The Independence of Spanish America*. Cambridge: Cambridge University Press, 1998.
Victor M. Uribe-Uran. "The Birth of the Public Sphere in Latin America during the Age of Revolution." *Comparative Studies in Society and History*, 42:2 (April 2000): 425–57.
W. M. Verhoeven, ed. *Revolutionary Histories: Transatlantic Cultural Nationalism, 1775–1815*. Basingstoke: Palgrave, 2002.
Ashli White. *Encountering Revolution: Haiti and the Making of the Early Republic*. Baltimore: Johns Hopkins University Press, 2010.
Gordon S. Wood. *The Radicalism of the American Revolution*. New York: Vintage, 1991.
Philipp Ziesche. *Cosmopolitan Patriots: Americans in Paris in the Age of Revolution*. Charlottesville: University of Virginia Press, 2010.

Revolutionary Europe and the Age of Napoleon

David A. Bell. *The First Total War: Napoleon's Europe and the Birth of Warfare as We Know It*. Boston: Houghton Mifflin, 2007.
T. C. W. Blanning. *The French Revolution in Germany: Occupation and Resistance in the Rhineland, 1791–1802*. Oxford: Oxford University Press, 1982.
Rafe Blaufarb. *Bonapartists in the Borderlands: French Exiles and Refuges in the Gulf Coast, 1815–1835*. Tuscaloosa: University of Alabama Press, 2005.
Michael Broers. *Europe under Napoleon, 1799–1815*. New York: St. Martin's Press, 1996.
Michael Broers. *The Napoleonic Mediterranean: Enlightenment, Revolution and Empire*. London: I.B. Tauris, 2017.
Christophe Belaubre, ed. *Napoleon's Atlantic: The Impact of Napoleonic Empire in the Atlantic World*. Leiden: Brill, 2010.
Roger Chickering and Stig Forester, eds. *War in an Age of Revolution, 1775–1815*. Cambridge: Cambridge University Press, 2010.
Susan Punzel Conner. *The Age of Napoleon*. Westport: Greenwood Press, 2004.
John A. Davis. *Naples and Napoleon: Italy and the European Revolutions (1780–1860)*. Oxford: Oxford University Press, 2006.
J. R. Dinwiddy. *Radicalism and Reform in Great Britain, 1780–1850*. London: Hambledon, 1992.

Selected Bibliography

Philip G. Dwyer. "Napoleon and the Foundation of the Empire." *The Historical Journal*, 53:2 (2010): 339–58.
Alexander Grab. *Napoleon and the Transformation of Europe*. New York: Palgrave Macmillan, 2003.
Michael J. Hughes. *Forging Napoleon's Grande Armée: Motivation, Military Culture and Masculinity in the French Army, 1800–1808*. New York: New York University Press, 2012.
David P. Jordan. *Napoleon and the Revolution*. New York: Palgrave Macmillan, 2012.
Annie Jourdan. *L'Empire de Napoléon*. Paris: Flammarion, 2000.
Jennifer Mori. *Britain in the Age of the French Revolution, 1785–1820*. London: Routledge, 2000.
Edward Royale. *Revolutionary Britannia? Reflections on the Threat of Revolution in Britain, 1789–1848*. Manchester: Manchester University Press, 2000.
Pierre Serna, Antonio De Francesco and Judith Miller, eds. *Republics at War, 1776–1840: Revolutions, Conflicts and Geopolitics in Europe and the Atlantic World*. Houndmills: Palgrave Macmillan, 2013.
Isser Woloch. *Napoleon and His Collaborators: The Making of a Dictatorship*. New York: W. W. Norton, 2002.
Stuart Woolf. "French Civilization and Ethnicity in the Napoleonic Empire." *Past and Present*, 124 (August 1989): 96–120.
Stuart Woolf. *Napoleon's Integration of Europe*. New York: Longman, 1993.

Post-Revolutionary Europe

C. A. Bayly and Eugenio F. Biagini, eds. *Giuseppe Mazzini and the Globalization of Democratic Nationalism, 1830–1920*. Oxford: Oxford University Press, 2008.
Roderick Beaton. *Byron's War: Romantic Rebellion, Greek Revolution*. Cambridge: Cambridge University Press, 2013.
Edward Berenson. *Populist Religion and Left-Wing Politics in France, 1830–1852*. Princeton: Princeton University Press, 1984.
Michael Broers. *Europe after Napoleon: Revolution, Reaction and Romanticism, 1814–1848*. Manchester: Manchester University Press, 1996.
James M. Brophy. *Popular Culture and the Public Sphere in the Rhineland, 1800–1850*. Cambridge: Cambridge University Press, 2007.
Malcolm Chase. *The People's Farm: English Radical Agrarianism*. Oxford: Clarendon Press, 1988.
Clive H. Church. *Europe in 1830: Revolution and Political Change*. London: George Allen and Unwin, 1983.
Douglas Dakin. *The Greek Struggle for Independence, 1821–1833*. Berkeley: University of California Press, 1973.
Ian Donnachie. *Robert Owen: Owen of New Lanark and New Harmony*. London: Tuckwell, 2000.
Michael P. Hanagan. *Nascent Proletarians: Class Formation in Post-Revolutionary France*. Oxford: Basil Blackwell, 1989.
Jill Harsin. *Barricades: The War on the Streets in Revolutionary Paris, 1830–1848*. New York: Palgrave, 2002.
Sudhir Hazareesingh. *The Legend of Napoleon*. London: Granata, 2004.
Patrick H. Hutton. *The Cult of the Revolutionary Tradition: The Blanquists in French Politics, 1864–1893*. Berkeley: University of California Press, 1981.
Maurizio Isabella. *Risorgimento in Exile: Italian Émigrés and the Liberal International in the Post-Napoleonic Era*. Oxford: Oxford University Press, 2009.

Isaac Land, ed. *Enemies of Humanity: The Nineteenth-Century War on Terrorism*. New York: Palgrave Macmillan, 2008.
David Laven and Lucy Riall, eds. *Napoleon's Legacy: Problems of Government in Restoration Europe*. Oxford: Berg, 2000.
Martin Lyons. *Post-Revolutionary Europe, 1815–1856*. New York: Palgrave Macmillan, 2006.
Sylvia Neely. *Lafayette and the Liberal Ideal, 1814–1824: Politics and Conspiracy in an Age of Restoration*. Carbondale: Southern Illinois University Press, 1991.
Pamela M. Pilbeam. *The 1830 Revolution in France*. Houndmills: Macmillan, 1991.
Richard Stites. *The Four Horsemen: Riding to Liberty in Post-Napoleonic Europe*. Oxford: Oxford University Press, 2014.
Jacob L. Talmon. *Romanticism and Revolt: Europe 1815–1848*. London: Thames and Hudson, 1967.
Adam Zamoyski. *Phantom Terror: The Threat of Revolution and the Repression of Liberty, 1789–1848*. London: William Collins, 2014.

The Revolutions of 1848

Peter H. Amann, *Revolution and Mass Democracy: The Paris Club Movement in 1848*. Princeton: Princeton University Press, 1975.
István Deák. *The Lawful Revolution: Louis Kossuth and the Hungarians, 1848–1849*. New York: Columbia University Press, 1979.
Laszlo Deme. "Echoes of the French Revolution in 1848 Hungary." *East European Quarterly*, 25:1 (Spring 1991): 101–15.
George W. Fasel. *Europe in Upheaval: The Revolutions of 1848*. New York: Rand McNally, 1970.
William Fortescue. *France and 1848: The End of Monarchy*. London: Routledge, 2005.
Paul Ginsborg. *Daniele Manin and the Venetian Revolution of 1848–49*. Cambridge: Cambridge University Press, 1979.
Hans Joachim Hahn. *The 1848 Revolutions in German-Speaking Europe*. London: Routledge, 2001.
Peter Jones. *The 1848 Revolution*. Essex: Longman, 1981.
Claus Møller Jørgensen. "Transurban Interconnectivities: An Essay on the Interpretation of the Revolutions of 1848." *European Review of History*, 19:2 (April 2012): 201–27.
Axel Körn, ed. *1848–A European Revolution? International Ideas and National Memories of 1848*. Houndmills: Palgrave Macmillan, 2000.
Lewis Namier. *1848: The Revolution of the Intellectuals*. London: Geoffrey Cumberlege, 1944.
Roger Price, ed. *Revolution and Reaction: 1848 and the Second French Republic*. London: Croom Helm, 1975.
Mike Rapport. *1848: Year of Revolution*. New York: Basic Books, 2008.
R. John Rath. *The Viennese Revolution of 1848*. Austin: University of Texas Press, 1977.
Priscilla Robertson. *The Revolutions of 1848: A Social History*. Princeton: Princeton University Press, 1952.
Wolfram Siemann. *The German Revolution of 1848–49*. London: Macmillan, 1998.
Jonathan Sperber. *Rhineland Radicals: The Democratic Movement and the Revolution of 1848–1849*. Princeton: Princeton University Press, 1991.
Jonathan Sperber. *The European Revolution, 1848–1851*. Cambridge: Cambridge University Press, 1994.
Mark Traugott. *Armies of the Poor: Detriments of Working-Class Participation in the Parisian Insurrection of June 1848*. Princeton: Princeton University Press, 1985.

Selected Bibliography

Brian E. Vick. *Defining Germany: The 1848 Frankfurt Parliament and National Identity*. Cambridge: Harvard University Press, 2002.
Kurt Weyland. "The Diffusion of Revolution: 1848 in Europe and Latin America." *International Organization*, 63:3 (Summer 2009): 391–423.

The Paris Commune

Dominica Chang. "Un Nouveau '93: Discourses of Mimicry and Terror in the Paris Commune of 1871." *French Historical Studies*, 36:4 (Fall 2013): 629–48.
Hollis Clayson. *Paris in Despair: Art and Everyday Life under Siege*. Chicago: University of Chicago Press, 2002.
Carolyn J. Eichner. *Surmounting the Barricades: Women in the Paris Commune*. Bloomington: Indiana University Press, 2004.
Donny Gluckstein. *The Paris Commune: A Revolution in Democracy*. Chicago: Haymarket Books, 2011.
Roger V. Gould. *Insurgent Identities: Class, Community and Protest in Paris from 1848 to the Commune*. Chicago: University of Chicago Press, 1995.
Gay L. Gullickson. *Unruly Women of Paris: Images of the Commune*. Ithaca: Cornell University Press, 1996.
Casey Harison. "The Paris Commune of 1871, the Russian Revolution of 1905, and the Shifting of the Revolutionary Tradition." *History and Memory*, 19:2 (Fall/Winter 2007): 5–42.
Martin Phillip Johnson. *The Paradise of Association: Political Culture and Popular Organizations in the Paris Commune of 1871*. Ann Arbor: University of Michigan Press, 1996.
Edward S. Mason. *The Paris Commune: An Episode in the History of the Socialist Movement*. New York: H. Fertig, 1930.
Woodford McClellan. *Revolutionary Exiles: The Russians in the First International and the Paris Commune*. New York: Taylor and Francis, 1979.
Kristin Ross. *The Emergence of Social Space: Rimbaud and the Paris Commune*. Minneapolis: University of Minnesota Press, 1989.
Kristin Ross. *Communal Luxury: The Political Imaginary of the Paris Commune*. London: Verso, 2015.
David A. Shafer. *The Paris Commune*. Houndmills: Palgrave, 2005.

Socialism and Anarchism

Benedict Anderson. *Under Three Flags: Anarchism and the Anti-Colonial Imagination*. London: Verso, 2005.
Constance Bantman. *The French Anarchists in London, 1880–1914: Exile and Transnationalism in the First Globalisation*. Liverpool: Liverpool University Press, 2013.
Murray Bookchin. *The Spanish Anarchists: The Heroic Years, 1868–1936*. New York: Free Life Editions, 1977.
Caroline Cahm. *Kropotkin: The Rise of Revolutionary Anarchism, 1872–1886*. Cambridge: Cambridge University Press, 1989.
Sam Dolgoff, ed. *Bakunin on Anarchy*. New York: Vantage, 1971.
Barbara Alpern Engle and Clifford N. Rosenthal, eds. *Fiver Sisters against the Tsar: The Memoirs of Five Young Anarchist Women of the 1870s*. New York: Routledge, 1992.

George Richard Esenwein. *Anarchist Ideology and the Working-Class Movement in Spain, 1868–1898*. Berkeley: University of California Press, 1989.
Jeremy Jennings. "Syndicalism and the French Revolution." *Journal of Contemporary History*, 26:1 (January 1991): 71–96.
Richard Bach Jensen. *The Battle against Anarchist Terrorism: An International History, 1878–1934*. Cambridge: Cambridge University Press, 2014.
James Joll. *The Anarchists*. London: Eyre and Spottiswoode, 1964.
Gareth Stedman Jones. *Languages of Class: Studies in English Working-Class History, 1832–1982*. Cambridge: Cambridge University Press, 1983.
Gareth Stedman Jones. *Karl Marx: Greatness and Illusion*. London: Allen Lane, 2017.
Alan Kimball. "The First International and the Russian Obshchina." *Slavic Review*, 32:3 (September 1973): 491–514.
Christine Lattek. *Revolutionary Refugees: German Socialism in Britain, 1840–1860*. London: Routledge, 2006.
C. Alexander McKinley. *Illegitimate Children of the Enlightenment: Anarchists and the French Revolution, 1880–1914*. New York: Peter Lang, 2008.
David McLellan. *The Thought of Karl Marx*. London: Macmillan, 1980.
Pietro Di Paola. *The Knights Errant of Anarchy: London and the Italian Anarchist Diaspora (1880–1917)*. Liverpool: Liverpool University Press, 2013.
Louis Patsouras. *The Anarchism of Jean Grave: Editor, Journalist and Militant*. New York: Black Rose Press, 2003.
Nunzio Pernicone. *The Italian Anarchists, 1864–1892*. Princeton: Princeton University Press, 1993.
Pamela M. Pilbeam. *French Socialist before Marx: Workers, Women and the Social Question in France*. Montreal: McGill-Queen's University Press, 2000.
Richard Sonn. *Anarchism and Cultural Politics in Fin de Siècle France*. Lincoln: University of Nebraska Press, 1989.
Paul Thomas. *Karl Marx and the Anarchists*. London: Routledge, 1980.
Davide Turcato. "Italian Anarchism as a Transnational Movement, 1885–1915." *International Review of Social History*, 52 (2005): 407–44.
Alexander Varias. *Paris and the Anarchists: Aesthetes and Subversives during the Fin-de-Siècle*. Basingstoke: Macmillan, 1997.

The Ottoman Empire and the Young Turk Revolution

Michelle Campos. *Ottoman Brothers: Muslims, Christians and Jews in Early Twentieth-Century Palestine*. Stanford: Stanford University Press, 2011.
Roderic H. Davidson. *Reform in the Ottoman Empire, 1856–1876*. Princeton: Princeton University Press, 1963.
Selim Deringil. *The Well-Protected Domains: Ideology and the Legitimation of Power in the Ottoman Empire, 1876–1909*. London: I.B. Tauris, 2011.
Fatma Müge Göçek. *Rise of the Bourgeoisie, Demise of the Empire: Ottoman Westernization and Social Change*. Oxford: Oxford University Press, 1996.
M. Şükrü Hanioğlu. *Preparation for a Revolution: The Young Turks, 1902–1908*. New York: Oxford University Press, 2001.
Aykut Kansu. *The Revolution of 1908 in Turkey*. Leiden: Brill, 1997.
Ümit Kurt and Doğan Gürpinar. "The Balkan Wars and the Rise of the Reactionary Modernist Utopia in Young Turk Thought." *Nations and Nationalism*, 21:2 (2015): 348–68.

Selected Bibliography

Şerif Mardin. *The Genesis of Young Ottoman Thought*. Princeton: Princeton University Press, 1962.
Nader Sohrabi. "Historicizing Revolutions: Constitutional Revolutions in the Ottoman Empire, Iran and Russia, 1905–1908." *American Journal of Sociology*, 100:6 (May 1995): 1383–1447.
Nader Sohrabi. "Global Waves, Local Actors: What the Young Turks Knew about Other Revolutions and Why It Mattered." *Comparative Studies in Society and History*, 44:1 (January 2002): 45–79.
Keith David Watenpaugh. *Being Modern in the Middle East: Revolution, Nationalism, Colonialism and the Arab Middle Class*. Princeton: Princeton University Press, 2006.
Murat Yaşar. "Learning the Ropes: The Young Turk Perception of the 1905 Russian Revolution." *Middle Eastern Studies*, 50:1 (2014): 114–28.

Russia and the Russian Revolution

Abraham Ascher. *The Revolution of 1905*. 2 volumes. Stanford: Stanford University Press, 1994.
Sarah Badcock. "Women, Protests and Revolution: Soldiers' Wives in Russia during 1917." *International Review of Social History*, 49:1 (2004): 47–70.
Francesco Benvenuti. *The Bolsheviks and the Red Army, 1918–1922*. Cambridge: Cambridge University Press, 1988.
Victoria E. Bonnell, ed. *The Russian Worker: Life and Labor under the Tsarist Regime*. Berkeley: University of California Press, 1983.
Vladimir N. Brovkin. *The Mensheviks after October: Socialist Opposition and the Rise of the Bolshevik Dictatorship*. Ithaca: Cornell University Press, 1987.
Vladimir N. Brovkin, ed. *The Bolsheviks in Russian Society: The Revolution and the Civil Wars*. New Haven: Yale University Press, 1997.
Jane Burbank. *Intelligentsia and Revolution: Russian Views of Bolshevism, 1917–1922*. Oxford: Oxford University Press, 1986.
John Bushnell. *Mutiny amid Repression: Russian Soldiers in the Revolution of 1905–1906*. Bloomington: Indiana University Press, 1985.
Barbara Alpern Engel. "Not by Bread Alone: Subsistence Riots in Russia during World War One." *Journal of Modern History*, 69:4 (December 1997): 696–721.
Laura Engelstein. *Moscow 1905: Working-Class Organization and Political Conflict*. Stanford: Stanford University Press, 1982.
Laura Engelstein. *Russia in Flames: War, Revolution, Civil War, 1914–1921*. Oxford: Oxford University Press, 2018.
Orlando Figes. *A People's Tragedy: The Russian Revolution, 1891–1924*. London: Pimlico, 1997.
Shelia Fitzpatrick. *The Russian Revolution*. Oxford: Oxford University Press, 2001.
Abbot Gleason. *Young Russia: The Genesis of Russian Radicalism in the 1860s*. Chicago: University of Chicago Press, 1980.
Neil Harding. *Lenin's Political Thought: Theory and Practice in the Democratic Socialist Revolution*. Chicago: Haymarket Books, 2009.
Tsuyoshi Hasegawa. *The February Revolution, Petrograd, 1917: The End of the Tsarist Regime and the Birth of Dual Power*. Leiden: Bill, 2017.
Michael C. Hickey, ed. *Competing Voices from the Russian Revolution*. Oxford: Greenwood, 2011.
Peter Holquist. "Violent Russia, Deadly Marxism? Russia in the Epoch of Violence, 1905–21." *Kritika: Explorations in Russian and Eurasian History*, 4:3 (Summer 2003): 627–52.

S. Karpenko. "The White Dictatorships' Bureaucracy in the South of Russia: Social Structure, Living Conditions and Performance (1918–1920)." *Soviet and Post-Soviet Review*, 37:1 (2010): 84–96.

Ronald I. Kowalski. *The Bolshevik Party in Conflict: The Left Communist Opposition of 1918*. Basingstoke: Macmillan, 1991.

Lars T. Lih. *Lenin Rediscovered: What Is to Be Done? In Context*. Chicago: Haymarket Books, 2008.

Martin Malia. *Alexander Herzen and the Birth of Russian Socialism*. New York: Gosset and Dunlap, 1965.

David R. Marples. *Lenin's Revolution: Russia, 1917–1921*. London: Routledge, 2000.

Evan Mawdsley, "Revolution, Civil War and the 'Long' First World War in Russia," *Journal of Military and Strategic Studies*, 16:2 (2015): 208–26.

Richard Pipes. *The Russian Revolution*. New York: Vintage, 1991.

Richard Pipes. *Russia under the Bolshevik Regime, 1919–1924*. London: Fontana, 1995.

Christopher Read. *From Tsar to Soviets: The Russian People and Their Revolution, 1917–1921*. New York: Oxford University Press, 1996.

Matthew Rendle. "Revolutionary Tribunals and the Origins of Terror in Early Soviet Society." *Historical Research*, 84:226 (2011): 693–721.

Aaron B. Retish. *Russia's Peasants in Revolution and Civil War: Citizenship, Identity and the Creation of the Soviet State, 1914–1922*. Cambridge: Cambridge University Press, 2008.

Hans Rogger. *Russia in the Age of Modernization and Revolution, 1881–1917*. London: Routledge, 1983.

James Ryan. *Lenin's Terror: The Ideological Origins of Early Soviet State Violence*. London: Routledge, 2012.

Joshua A. Sanborn. *Imperial Apocalypse: The Great War and the Destruction of the Russian Empire*. Oxford: Oxford University Press, 2014.

S. A. Smith. *Russia in Revolution: An Empire in Crisis, 1890–1928*. Oxford: Oxford University Press, 2017.

Scott Baldwin Smith. *Captives of Revolution: The Socialist Revolutionaries and the Bolshevik Dictatorship, 1918–1923*. Pittsburgh: Pittsburgh University Press, 2011.

Mark D. Steinberg. *Voices of Revolution, 1917*. New Haven: Yale University Press, 2001.

Laurie S. Stoff. *They Fought for the Motherland: Russia's Women Soldiers in World War I and the Revolution*. Lawrence: University Press of Kansas, 2006.

Rex A. Wade. *The Russian Revolution, 1917*. Cambridge: Cambridge University Press, 2005.

INDEX

Abd al-Qādir 271
Abdülhamid: and authoritarianism 232; opposition to 235; and overthrow 238; and political policy 232
Abolitionism 66–67
Absolutism: and corporatism 7; and empire 6–7; and France 24–26; and state-building 5–6
Al-Afghānī, Sayyid Jamāl al-Dīn 272–73
Alexander I (Russia) 115
Alexander II (Russia): assassination of 205; and political reform 182
Alexander III (Russia) 205
Ali Pasha 128
American Revolution: and American sovereignty 19–20; and colonial protest 17–18; and farmers 62; and French Revolution 34, 44; and influence of in Europe 22–23, 44, 109; and military conflict 21; and radicalism 63; and rights 16–18, 62–63; and slavery 21, 65–66, 109
Anarchism: and aesthetics 208–09; and collectivism 191; critique of state powers 188, 195; definition of 187–88; and development of ideology 177–78, 188–89; and federalism 191, 196–97; and international scope 207–08, 213, 273, 275, 280; and local association 4, 178, 190–91, 194–95; and organization 200; and political violence 199, 200, 202–03, 205, 213; and suppression of 205–06
Anti-colonial resistance 105–06, 108, 286
Antoinette, Marie 35
Arab Spring 2
Aristocrats 33, 37, 69, 260. *Also see* Nobility; Émigrés
Artisans: and radical politics 60, 65, 85, 162; and social impact of modernization 138, 161
Assembly of Notables (1787) 27
Atlantic: and empire 6, 16, 67, 97–98; and plantation economy 7, 98; and republicanism 64, 270; and revolution 23, 48, 59, 65; and slave trade 7–8, 65
Austria 89, 113, 173; and Balkan policy 232, 238, 240; and occupation of Bosnia 232; and revolution 163–64, 169–70, 184; and state policies 116, 172; and war 94, 185, 242. *Also see* Habsburgs

Babeuf, François-Noël: influence of 89, 118, 150; and social equality 85–86
Bakunin, Mikhail: and ideological outlook 189–90; and relations with Marx 190–92; and revolutionary politics 189, 190, 192, 198, 200; and view on the Paris Commune 198; and views on revolution 191, 200, 212, 269; and views on the state 188, 190
Balkans 108, 232; and nationalist conflict 128–29, 234, 238, 240
Barlow, Joel 49, 108–09
Bastille. *See* French Revolution
Batavian Republic 87–88
Bismarck, Otto von 176
Blackstone, William 15
Blanc, Louis: and republican socialism 142, 147; and Second Republic 163, 169
Blanqui, Louis Auguste 118, 180; and influence of 197; and Jacobin tradition 167, 189; and revolutionary socialism 147
Blanquists 176, 177, 187, 193; and role in Paris Commune 197
Blaquiere, Edward 128
Bohemia: and Czech nationalism 167, 172; and Habsburg rule 5
Böhmer, Georg Wilhelm 87
Bolivar, Simón 106, 270
Bolshevik Party: and activities during 1905 revolution 229–30; and comparison to Jacobins 224; and elections 256; and empire 260–62; founding of 224; and influence abroad 285; and national minorities 261–62; opposition to 255, 257, 261; and political violence 258, 260; and relationship with workers 253; and revolutionary politics 251, 253, 255, 257, 259, 262–63; and rise to power 251, 254; and seizure of power 254–56; and support for international revolution 263–65; and war 257–58, 261
Bonaparte, Louis-Napoleon (Napoleon III): and fall from power 192–93; rise to power of 174–75; and unification of Italy 185
Bonaparte, Napoleon (Napoleon I): and Atlantic colonies 96–97; and bureaucratic reform 93–94, 116; and coup of Brumaire 92; defeat of 112–13, 116; and Egyptian campaign 90–92; and Italy 89; legacy of 119; and revolution 92–93, 108, 111; rise of 90. *Also see* Napoleonic Empire
Bosnia 232, 238; and radical nationalism 240
Bourbons: and France 24, 26, 54; and overthrow 140; and restoration 117, 120; and Spain 101

Index

Bourgeoisie: and class struggle 157, 159, 188, 223, 259, 265; and middle-class politics 136, 140–42
Boxer Rebellion 278, 282
Brissot, Jacques Pierre: and abolitionism 67, 69, 70, 71; and Girondin opposition 49–50; and influence of American Revolution 23; and journalism 37; and revolutionary politics 39, 44, 49, 55; and revolutionary war 44, 75; and support for the Genevan revolution 23
Brousse, Paul 199, 200, 202
Bulgaria 232, 234, 235, 236, 238
Bund: and criticism of Bolsheviks 255; and Jewish socialism 222–23, 224
Buonarroti, Filippo: and activities during the French Revolution 88; association with Babeuf 89, 118; and Italian nationalism 88–89; and post-revolutionary activities 117–18, 119, 130
Burke, Edmund: and British liberty 16; and views on French Revolution 86, 113
Byron, George Gordon, Lord: and Greek revolution 129

Cabet, Étienne 144, 146, 150
Cafiero, Carlo 200, 202
Carbonari: foundation of 118–19; in France 119; and role in Neapolitan revolution 124–25; underground activities 120, 147, 168
Carlos III (Spain) 6
Carlsbad Decrees 120
Catholic Church: and the old regime 5; and Papal states 88, 125, 130; and reaction to French Revolution 42
Cattaneo, Carlo 1
Charles X (France): and conservative policies 139–40; and émigré court 35
Chartism: founding of 149; and working-class mobilization 149–50
Chateaubriand, François-René de 112
Chernyshevsky, Nikolai Gavrilovich 182–83
China: and communism 285; and multi-ethnic empire 276, 281, 283; and nationalism 279, 281–82, 284; and 1911 revolution 283–84; and radical politics 279–81; and reform 279–80, 281–82, 283; and relations with Europe 136, 277–78; and social unrest 277, 278
Citizenship: and "active" citizenship 32, 76, 85; and cosmopolitanism 23–24, 48, 130; and emancipated slaves 66, 75, 76, 98; and female emancipation 77–78, 195–96; and limited suffrage 142; and militarism 44, 80; and republicanism 11, 66, 106–07; and revolution 13, 33, 59, 69–70, 235; and rights 13
Civil society: and associations 166–67; and the Enlightenment 8; and political clubs 168
Civil war: and American Revolution 21; and England (1642–1648) 14; and French colonies 72; during French Revolution 50–51; during Russian Revolution 258
Cixi (Empress Dowager) 279
Clarkson, Thomas 67
Cloots, Anacharsis: and revolutionary cosmopolitanism 48, 52, 196; and revolutionary war 49
Club Massiac 69
Committee of Public Safety: and American Revolution 21; and French Revolution 51, 52, 88; and Hungarian Revolution 165; and Paris Commune 197; and political violence 83; and Russian Revolution 256
Committee of Union and Progress (CUP): and coup 239; founding of 233; and Islam 236–37; and revolutionary ideology 233–34; and revolutionary politics 235–36, 237
Communism: and agrarianism 181; criticism of 190, 266; and early proponents of 144, 150; evolution toward 252, 258; and influence of Marx 151, 158
Communist International (Comintern) 265
Communist League 158, 159, 167, 176, 177
Communist Manifesto. See Manifesto of the Communist Party
Condorcet, Nicolas de 67
Confédération générale du travail (CGT) 210, 211
Congress of Vienna 113, 114–15, 132, 151
Conservatism 111, 113, 161, 176
Constant, Benjamin: and liberal politics 140; and opposition to Napoleon 100
Cordelier Club 39, 43, 60
Courbet, Gustave 195, 197, 209
Crèvecoeur, Hector St. Jean 23, 24

D'Aelders, Etta Palm 39, 79–80, 81
D'Artois, Comte. See Charles X (France)
David, Jacques-Louis 54–55
Declaration of Independence (1776) 20, 21, 65
Democracy 3, 156, 189, 221; and demands for 141, 157, 248; and political mobilization 168, 170, 224, 225, 255, 258; and suppression of 142, 264
Deschamps, Léger Marie 10
Desmoulins, Camille 30, 41, 42
Dessalines, Jean-Jacques 99
Dézamy, Alexandre Théodore 146
Diderot, Denis 10, 26
Directory (France): and expansion 88–89; founding of 84–85; and military policy 88, 89–90; overthrow of 92; suppression of radicalism 86, 116
Dmitrieff, Elisabeth 196
D'Outrepont, Charles Lambert 23
Dumont, Étienne 35

345

Index

East India Company (British) 6, 90, 270
Egypt: and anarchist movement 207; and Islamic modernism 272–73; and Napoleon 90–92
Émigrés: and Atlantic colonies 73, 111; and the French Revolution 35, 45–46, 111; and revolutionary exiles 86, 88, 127, 176, 216, 233, 251, 274
Enfantin, Barthélemy Prosper 135, 145
Engels, Fredrich: and political organization 158, 176, 190; and views on industrial society 156; and views on worker organization 221
Enlightenment: and the Atlantic 8–9; and cosmopolitanism 9; and the *philosophes* 8–9, 12, 151; and the public sphere 8; and revolution 3, 12, 28, 31;
Enver Bey 235, 238, 239
Estates General (France) 15, 24, 37, 41; calling of 27, 29; and grievances of women 77; and issue of slavery 69

Ferdinando IV (Naples) 125
Fernando VII (Spain): and counter-revolutionary policies 122–23; and Napoleonic invasion 101; and post-revolutionary restoration 121–22
Fichte, Johan Gottlieb 100–01
Findley, William 62–63
First World War: outbreak of 240; and total war 241, 242
Fitzgerald, Edward 87
Fourier, Charles 143–44, 145, 156, 181; and criticism of 177
Fox, William 66
France: and economy 27, 137, 175; and empire 17, 22, 67–68, 90, 94; and nationalism 32–33, 162; and political institutions 35, 47, 52, 74, 93–94, 166, 175; and social unrest 31, 64, 73, 139, 162–63, 167, 169, 193–98; and society 31, 50, 71; and territorial formation 24–25, 87. *Also see* French Revolution; Napoleonic Empire; Paris Commune
Franco-Prussian War (1870) 193
Frankfurt Parliament (1848) 166, 172–74
Franklin, Benjamin 22
Franz Ferdinand 240
French and Indian War (1754–1763) 17, 22
French Revolution: and abolition of feudalism 31; causes of 26–27, 31; and challenge to royal authority 29–30; changing conception of revolution 31, 33; and counter-revolution 35–36, 51; creation of a revolutionary calendar 55; creation of National Assembly 29; and culture 54–55; and de-Christianization 54, 56; and drafting of the constitution 33; and empire 69, 71–72, 74–75; and the French clergy 35–36; and institutional change 39–40, 41; and international scope of 31, 33, 47–48; and militarism 45–46, 87–88; as model 2; and national sovereignty 29, 31, 32–33, 40–41; and overthrow of monarchy 46; and political clubs 38–39, 43; and political rights 32–33; and popular mobilization 30–31, 36, 39, 42; and the press 37; and repressive measures 43–44; and revolutionary festivals 40, 47–48, 55; and storming of the Bastille 30; and violence 30, 33, 37, 46, 51–52; and women 36, 61, 77; and workers 60. *Also see* Estates General (France); Jacobins; Revolution; Rights of Man and Citizen; Sans-Culottes

Gapon, Georgi 227
Garibaldi, Giuseppe: and exile in North Africa 127; and Italian unification 185–86; and revolutionary activity abroad 185, 270
Geneva 10, 23, 220
Gens de couleur: and equality with whites 70, 73; and political activism 71, 72; and reaction to slave revolts 96; status of 69
George III (Britain) 21
Germany: and Napoleon 95, 100; and nationalism 100–01, 119–20, 151, 172–73, 176; and post-revolutionary settlement 114, 151, 162; and revolution 87–88, 120, 163, 263–64; and social unrest 167; and war plans 241
Girondins: and reaction to radicalism 49; and rebellion against government 49–50; and targets of terror 52; and war 44–45
Glorious Revolution (1688) 14–15
Gottschalk, Andreas 151, 163
Gouges, Olympe de: execution of 81; and rights of women 79–80; and slavery 77
Grave, Jean 212, 269; and views on revolution 203, 208
Great Britain: and conceptions of liberty 15–16, 19; and dock strike 210; and idea of commonwealth 17–18; and imperial conflict with France 22, 74, 90–91; and imperial identity 15–16; and imperial policy in North America 17–18; and social unrest 63–65, 141–42, 149
Greece: and Balkan Wars 238; and war of independence 127–29
Grégoire, Henri 56; and slavery 71, 76
Gringmut, Vladimir 229
Guizot, François 141, 162, 163
Guomindang 284

Habsburgs: dynastic monarchy 5–6; and French Revolution 87–88; and liberalization 166; and multi-ethnic empire 116, 162; and nationalism 170, 172; and post-revolutionary aims 132; and revolution 170
Haiti: founding of 99; and revolutionary independence 108; and revolutionary legacy 286. *Also see* Saint-Domingue
Hardy, Thomas 64

346

Haymarket Square 209
Hébert, Jacques 52
Hecker, Friedrich 163
Hegel, Georg Wilhelm Friedrich: and influence on Marx 153–54, 156; and philosophical idealism 152–53; and view on civil society 153
Herzen, Alexander: and relations with Bakunin 187, 190, 198; and Russian politics 180–81, 183, 184; and socialism 181–82; and views on Europe 162, 179–80; and views on revolution 179–80, 269
Hobbes, Thomas 14
Hollis, Thomas 14
Holy Alliance: and holy alliance of people 121, 129, 130, 132; and Hungarian revolution 174; and post-revolutionary alliance system 115, 116, 121; and Spanish crisis 124, 126
Hume, David 14
Hungary: and communist revolution 264–65; and feudalism 162, 166; and Habsburg rule 5; and nationalism 172; and revolution 165, 171–72
Hutchinson, Thomas 17

Imam Shamil 272
Indian Rebellion (1857) 270–71
Industrialization: causes of 136–37; and conceptions of "industrial revolution" 137–38; and social impact of 135–36, 138
International Workingmen's Association (IWMA) 187, 207; conflicts within 178, 188, 190, 192; dissolution of 206–07; founding of 176–77; and Paris Commune 196, 198, 199
Ireland: and republicanism 87, 241
Islam: and French occupation of Egypt 91; and radicalism 271–73. *Also see* Ottoman Empire
Italy: and the anarchist movement 190, 200; and French Revolution 88–89; and Napoleonic Empire 95; and revolution 164; and revolutionary nationalism 130–31, 162, 170, 184–86; and unification 176, 185–85

Jacobins: and dictatorship 52–53, 54; and economic policies 60–61; and factionalism 47; and nationalism 52–53; and neo-Jacobinism 118, 147; and political organization 41–42; and radicalism 49; and revolutionary government 53–54, 83; and revolutionary politics 42, 45, 75; and slavery 75–76; and support for revolution abroad 86–87; suppression of 84–85; and use of political violence 51, 53; and xenophobia 49
Japan: and radical politics 274–75; and war with China 278; and war with Russia 225
Jefferson, Thomas: and American independence 20; and colonial opposition 18; and Haitian Revolution 74, 99, 109; and influence on French Revolution 37; and relationship with Thomas Paine 109

Joly, Étienne-Louis Hector de 70, 71
Journalism: and revolutionary politics 37–38, 182; and spread of ideas 167; and revolutionary exiles 180
July Monarchy (France): and collapse of 162–63, 169; founding of 140; and social policies 141, 146

Kadets 230, 242, 245, 250, 256
Kang Youwei: and Confucian influences 278–79, 281; and reform 279, 282, 283
Kerensky, Aleksandr: and criticism of 254; and the provisional government 247, 250, 254; and reaction to radicalism 253
Kornilov, Lavr 253–54, 256
Kościuszko, Thaddeus 87
Kossuth, Lajos: and Hungarian autonomy 163, 171, 172; and nationalism 171; and revolutionary politics 171, 172
Kropotkin, Pyotr 208, 210; and criticism of political violence 203; and ideological outlook 188, 201–02, 212; and the Russian Revolution 266; and views on revolution 209, 213

Lafayette, Gilbert du Mortier, Marquis de: and command of the National Guard 37, 43; and conspiratorial politics 120; and constitutional monarchy 43; and July Revolution 140; and liberal opposition 119–20, 121; and revolutionary politics 39, 126; and slavery 67, 109
Le Chapelier laws (1791) 42–43
League of the Just 155, 158
Leclerc, Charles Emmanuel 98–99
Legitimism 113
Lenin, Vladimir Illyich: and difference of opinion with socialists 224, 269; and exile 227, 251; and ideological outlook 182, 223, 251–53, 263; and internationalism 263, 265, 275; and the nationality question 261; and party organization 223–25, 251, 253, 256, 265; and political activities 222, 223, 263; and political violence 259; and revolutionary politics 251, 254–55, 261; and seizure of power 255–56; and views on worker movement 223, 269
Léon, Anne-Pauline 80, 81
Liang Qichao 279, 282
Liberal international 133; and post-revolutionary politics 119, 121, 126, 127, 129
Liberalism: and fears of radicalism 124, 170; and political ideology 136, 140–42, 148, 225; and post-revolutionary France 120–21; and revolutionary politics 111–12, 123–24, 135, 168, 227–28
Liebknecht, Karl 264
Locke, John: and ideas of rights 15; and influence on

Index

American Revolution 18, 19, 20; and theories of government 10–11, 53
London Corresponding Society 64–65
Louis XIV (France) 24
Louis XV (France) 26
Louis XVI (France): and the colonies 73; execution of 47, 54; and financial problems 26–27; and flight to Varennes 43–44; and French Revolution 35, 40
Louis XVIII (France) 120, 139
Louis Philippe 140–41
Loustalot, Elysée 38
Louverture, Toussaint: arrest of 99; and militarism 75; and revolutionary nationhood 108; and views on black emancipation 97–98
Lovett, William 149, 150
Luxemburg, Rosa 264
Lvov, Georgy 217, 244, 245

Macaulay, Thomas Babington 142
Mainz 87, 120
Maistre, Joseph de 113
Malatesta, Errico 200, 202, 207, 210
Manifesto of the Communist Party 1, 158–59, 221
Manin, Daniele 164; and Italian unification 184; and Venetian Republic 166, 168
Marat, Jean-Paul: assassination of 51; and journalism 38; and martyrdom 55; and slavery 65
Marseillaise 195, 235, 245
Martin, Claude-Charles 60
Martov, Julius 222; and disagreement with Lenin 224, 255; and views on Russian worker movement 223
Marx, Karl 118, 151, 159; and commentary on Paris Commune 198; and critique of capitalism 156; and critique of revolutionary tradition 175, 184; early thought of 153–54; and exile 175–76; and internationalism 158, 176–78; and interpretation of French Revolution 155, 157; and political activities 158, 167, 191; and proletarian identity 159; and relationship with Bakunin 191–92; and relationship with Engels 156; and role in the International 177–78, 190–91, 206–07; view on the state 188; and views on social revolution 135, 155–56, 175
Marxism: and class struggle 159; and conceptions of revolution 1–2, 156–58, 162, 191; and development in China 285; and development in Russia 183, 220–25, 253, 259; and difference from anarchism 187–88, 191, 200, 207, 212; and German radicalism 210; and nationalism 158; and social equality 3, 157–58; and violence 157, 259–60
Mathers, Increase 16
Mazzini, Giuseppe: and affiliation with Italian secret societies 130, 133; and foundation of Young Europe 132, 232; and influence of 177; and revolutionary nationalism 130–31, 184; and revolutionary politics 168, 184–85, 186, 190, 207, 286; and Young Italy 185
Mediterranean: and international revolution 127, 129; and Napoleonic period 90–91
Meiji Ishin 273–74, 275
Mensheviks: activities in 1905 revolution 229; and collaboration with government 250, 254; found of 224; and opposition to Bolsheviks 224, 254, 255; and revolutionary politics 246; suppression of 256
Mercier, Louis-Sébastien 22
Méricourt, Théroigne de 80, 81
Metternich, Klemens von: dismissal of 163–64; and German policy 120; and Italian policy 125; and police state 115, 121; and post-revolutionary diplomacy 115–16, 126; and reaction to revolution 115–16, 125, 165; and resistance to Napoleon 114–15; and Spanish crisis 124–25
Michel, Louise 196, 206, 211
Minichini, Luigi 124–25
Monarchy: and nationalism 175–76; and the restoration of 113–14, 116, 121, 132
Morris, Gouverneur 21, 33
Mounier, Jean Joseph 27, 29; and the *monarchiens* 32–33

Napoleonic Empire: founding of 94; ideological origins of 91–92; impact of 113–14; imperial policies in Europe 94–96; and Peninsular War 101–02; resistance to 100–02, 130. *Also see* Bonaparte, Napoleon (Napoleon I)
Narodnaia Volia 205
National Convention: establishment of 46; and fear of radicalism 49–50. *Also see* French Revolution; Jacobins
National Guard: creation of in France 30; during Franco-Prussian War 193; and the French Revolution 36–37, 42, 43; and radicalism 46, 170, 194
Nationalism: and political conflict 172, 174 and popular sovereignty 14, 28; and resistance 100–01
Natural Rights 9–10, 32, 48
Neapolitan Revolution (1820) 124–25
Nechayev, Sergei 187, 205
Nedham, Marchamont 14
Nicholas II (Russia) 215, 225, 227; and abdication of 245, 246; and activities during 1905 revolution 226, 229; and dealings with the Duma 229–30, 243, 245; and execution of 257; and political outlook 225
Nobility: and political power 27, 151, 218, 230, 263, 274; and predominance of 161, 218; and reform

348

Index

26, 171; and relationship with monarchs 5, 25, 26, 102, 171; social privilege 7, 25–26, 28
North Africa 4, 273; and revolutionary exiles 127, 207

O'Connor, Feargus 149–50
Ogé, Vincent 70, 72
Oliver, Andrew 17–18
Oppenheim, Max von 241
Ottoman Empire: and Arabs 236, 238; and Egypt 90; and Greek revolution 128; and Islam 232, 233, 241; and liberal reform 231–32; and modernization 232; as multi-ethnic empire 127–28, 231, 238; and nationalism 232; and political opposition 233; and relations with Europe 232, 238; and Turkic nationalism 233, 239
Owen, Robert 143, 144, 145

Paine, Thomas 13, 34, 136; and American Revolution 21–22; and *Common Sense* 19–20; and French National Assembly 48–49; and international influence 48, 63, 103; and return to United States 109–10; and *Rights of Man* 48, 64
Paris Commune: and anarchism 194, 196–97, 198; and French Revolution 46; outbreak of (1871) 194; and radicalism of 197–98; and suppression of 197–98
Parlement (France) 26, 27
Pecchio, Giuseppe 126; and Greek independence 129; and support for Spanish American liberty 127
Pepe, Guglielmo 125–26
Plekhanov, Georgi: and ideological differences with Lenin 224; and political outlook 221, 222, 227
Poland: and Napoleon 95; and nationalist movement 173, 189; and radical politics 177, 189, 222; and revolution 87, 137, 189
Postlethwayt, Malachy 17
Pradt, Dominique de 124, 127
Proudhon, Pierre-Joseph 181; and influence of 178–79, 195; and political thought 177–78, 188; and relation with socialists 177, 178, 189
Prussia: and absolutism 5; and German nationalism 101, 173–74; and liberalization 166; and suppression of revolution 23, 174

Qing: and decline 278; as dynastic power 276, 281; opposition to 277, 280, 282–83

Raimond, Julien 70, 71
Ravachol, François 203, 212
Raynal, Guillaume Thomas 21, 23
Reclus, Élisée 196, 208, 213
Red Army 257, 260–61
Red Guard 248, 254, 256
Reform Bill (1832) 141–42
Republicanism 11, 189, 270; and China 282; and empire 88–89; and equality 62, 66, 75; and nationalism 77; and radical politics 22, 63, 118, 167; and social policies 61
Revolution: and community 3–5; and conceptions of restoration 14–15, 19, 29; and modernity 5; and professional revolutionaries 118, 121, 127, 130, 223; and revolutionaries 187, 286; as "script" 2, 57; as social revolution 61, 155, 157–58, 162; and structural interpretation 1–2; theories of 1–3; and tradition 3, 175, 184, 269–70; and waves of 106, 165–66, 215, 234, 240, 269
Ricardo, David 137, 156
Riego, Rafael del 123–24
Rigaud, André 97
Rights of Man and Citizen 1, 270; declaration of 32; and national sovereignty 41; and slavery 67, 72
Riza, Ahmet 233
Robespierre, Maximilien: arrest and execution of 83; and fears of counter-revolution 44–45; and influence of Rousseau 52; and modernity 55, 57; and opposition to the Girondins 44, 49; and revolutionary government 54; revolutionary principles 42, 76, 77; and slavery 72; and views on political violence 53, 81
Romania 143, 162, 164, 265
Rousseau, Jean-Jacques: and civic religion 40; the general will 11, 147, 259; and influence on the French Revolution 26, 28–29, 32–33, 42, 52, 56; and influence on revolutionary thought 88–89, 106, 113, 136; and romanticism 100; and theories on government 10–11, 100; and views on women 78
Russia: and 1905 revolution 226–30, 275; and autocracy 216, 246; and liberalism 182, 218–19, 225, 227–28, 246; and modernization 219–20; as multi-ethnic empire 217, 244, 272; and the peasantry 183, 219–20, 221–22, 228; and radical politics 182–83, 205–06; and reform 217–18; and serfdom 182, 218; and social hierarchies 216–17; and socialism 181–82, 187, 225
Russian Revolution: causes of 245–46; and the church 262–63; and constitutional assembly 245, 255–56; and counter-revolution 246, 254, 256–57, 261; and dual power 246–47, 254; and empire 244, 249–50, 260–62; and industries 244, 246, 258; and internationalism 263–64, 267; and nationalism 249–50; and peasant radicalism 249, 253, 256; and political activism 246–47, 250, 253; and provisional government 245–46, 250–51, 254, 257; and soldiers 247, 256, 257; and violence 258–60; and war 243, 253, 261; and war communism 258; and women 249; and workers 244–45, 246, 248, 260. *Also see* Bolshevik Party
Russian Social Democratic Labor Party (RSDLP): and founding of 222; and leftist politics 223, 224, 225, 229–30

349

Index

Saint-Domingue: and Atlantic world 9; and autonomy 69, 98; and emancipation 74-75, 96-97; and French imperialism 68, 97; and independence 99; and Napoleon 97-98; and revolutionary politics 69-71, 72, 73; and slave revolt 72; and social composition 67-68. *Also see* Haiti

Saint-Just, Louis Antoine de: arrest and execution of 83-84; and revolutionary government 53, 81; and revolutionary nationalism 41; and social policies 61

Saint-Simon, Henri de 144-45

Sand, Karl 121

Sans-Culottes 51, 61, 65, 138, 150, 161; and political activism 60; and radicalism 39, 44, 49-50, 52, 64, 86; the sections 46; suppression of 84-85; and women 80-81

Scrope, George Poulett 139

Secret societies 3; and post-Napoleonic Europe 117-18, 120

Ségur, Louis-Philippe Comte de 22

Selim III 91, 128

September Massacres (1792) 46-47

Serbia: and Balkan policy 232, 238, 240; and independence 232; nationalist conflict 172, 234

Shawish, Al-Kahin Diyunysius 47

Shay, Daniel 63

Sieyès, Emmanuel Joseph: and conception of the nation 28-29, 32; and creation of French departments 40-41; and opposition 28-29; and revolutionary politics 33, 34, 39, 52

Slave trade: and Caribbean 65, 67; criticism of 66; and the old regime 7

Slaves: and legal status 7-8, 69, 72; and revolt 73; and revolutionary emancipation 21, 66-67, 75, 98-99

Socialism: and critiques of capitalism 142-43, 147-48; and influence of religion on 145; and Narodnik movement 183, 187, 222; and political parties 210-11; and principle of association 143-44, 145-46, 147, 149, 150; and social equality 61-62, 143-44; and worker mobilization 146-47, 149-50; and "utopian" ideologies 143-44, 156

Social Democratic Party of Germany (SPD): influence of 221, 223; and political orientation of 210, 263, 264

Socialist Revolutionaries (SRs) 222, 246; and collaboration with government 251, 254; disagreement with Bolsheviks 254, 255, 256; influence among Russian peasantry 222, 228, 256; and political violence 222

Société des Amis des Noirs 67, 69, 71. *Also see* abolitionism

Society of United Irishmen 87

Sons of Liberty 17, 21

Sonthonax, Léger-Félicité 74-75

Sorel, Georges 211

Sovereignty 3; and empire 17, 106-07; and popular sovereignty 14, 20, 29; and revolution 13, 29, 38, 166

Soviet 229, 260; and the Bolsheviks 254, 255-56, 261; and establishment of Soviet Union (USSR) 262; and execution of the tsar 257; and German revolution 263; and localized government 253; and radical politics 229, 246, 247; and revolutionary organization 247, 250; role in 1905 revolution 229-30

Spain: and anarchism 192, 200, 204-05; and the Cortes 103-04, 105, 121, 124, 126; and liberalism 102, 104, 123-24; and monarchy 5, 102; and Napoleonic Wars 101-02; and nationalism 102, 104; and social unrest 191-92; and the Trienio Liberal 123-26

Spanish America: and American identity 107; and autonomist movements 104-05; and independence movements 106; and Napoleonic Wars 102-03; and relationship with metropole 102-03, 105; and royal governance 6, 102

Staël, Germaine de 100

Stalin, Joseph 261

Stanhope, Leicester 129

Stein, Heinrich Friedrich Karl, Baron vom 101

Struve, Gustav von 163, 165, 173

Sun Yat-sen: as president 284; and revolutionary alliance 281-82, 283

Switzerland 76, 139, 177, 187, 264; and anarchism 200-01; and political exiles 117, 207, 220, 222-23, 233, 251

Syndicalism 211

Taiping Heavenly Kingdom 277

Talaat Pasha 237, 239

Tashkent 244, 261-62

Terror 3, 161, 203-04; and "cultural terror" 56; and the French Revolution 51-52, 81, 83; and post-revolutionary war on terror 116-17, 119, 121, 124-25, 205, 240; and "red" terror 259-60; and "white" terror 117; and terrorism 202-03, 205

Third Estate (France) 26, 27; and opposition to absolutism 28-29

Tocqueville, Alexis de 160, 269, 286

Tooke, John Horne 63

Trotsky, Leon 260, 263; and formation of Red Army 257; and political activities of 229, 254

Ukraine 217, 219, 224; and Napoleonic Wars 100; and nationalism 222, 249-50; and occupation of 261-62

United States: founding of 18-20; and response to Atlantic revolution 74; revolutionary legacy 109-10; and utopian socialist communities 144

350

Vendée 42, 50, 80
Viscardo, Juan Pablo 103
Völkerfrühling (1848) 164, 170, 183
Voltaire (François-Marie Arouet) 11, 13, 14, 25; and influence on revolution 113, 136

War: and aftermath of Napoleonic Wars 116–17; and the militarization of society 56, 193, 258; and Napoleonic Wars 94, 96, 98; and patriotism 44–45, 80; and requisitioning 60, 83, 258; and revolution 53, 56, 66, 75–76, 194–95, 259; and revolutionary defence 52, 86–87, 247
Washington, George 21, 22, 23, 47, 106
Wedekind, Georg 87
Whiskey Rebellion 62
William IV (Britain) 139
Witte, Sergei 219, 229
Wolfe Tone, Theobald 87
Women: and political activism 36, 61, 79–81, 195–96, 249; and revolutionary politics 236, 249; and social roles 193, 241, 249; and socialism 144, 182

Young, Arthur 24
Young Europe 132, 232
Young Italy 127, 185
Young Ottomans 231–32
Young Turk Revolution: and failure of constitutionalism 239; and influence of 273; and modernization 236, 239; and Ottomanism 235–36, 239; and purge of the state 237–38. *Also see* Committee of Union and Progress (CUP)
Ypsilantis, Alexandros 128
Yuan Shikai 284

Zasulich, Vera 183, 220
Zemstvo (zemstva) 217, 218, 225, 245
Zimmermann, Arthur 241